McGraw-Hill Reading

# Wonders

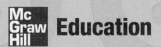 **Education**

*Bothell, WA • Chicago, IL • Columbus, OH • New York, NY*

 TextEvaluator.

**Cover and Title Pages:** Nathan Love

# www.mheonline.com/readingwonders

C

The **McGraw·Hill** Companies

 **Education**

# McGraw-Hill Reading Wonders

## CCSS Reading/Language Arts Program

### Program Authors

**Dr. Diane August**
Managing Director,
American Institutes for Research
Washington, D.C.

**Dr. Donald Bear**
Iowa State University
Ames, Iowa

**Dr. Janice A. Dole**
University of Utah
Salt Lake City, Utah

**Dr. Jana Echevarria**
California State University, Long Beach
Long Beach, California

**Dr. Douglas Fisher**
San Diego State University
San Diego, California

**Dr. David J. Francis**
University of Houston
Houston, Texas

**Dr. Vicki Gibson**
Educational Consultant
Gibson Hasbrouck and Associates
Wellesley, Massachusetts

**Dr. Jan Hasbrouck**
Educational Consultant
and Researcher
J.H. Consulting
Vancouver, Washington
Gibson Hasbrouck and Associates
Wellesley, Massachusetts

**Margaret Kilgo**
Educational Consultant
Kilgo Consulting, Inc.
Austin, Texas

**Dr. Jay McTighe**
Educational Consultant
Jay McTighe and Associates
Columbia, Maryland

**Dr. Scott G. Paris**
Vice President, Research
Educational Testing Service
Princeton, New Jersey

**Dr. Timothy Shanahan**
University of Illinois at Chicago
Chicago, Illinois

**Dr. Josefina V. Tinajero**
University of Texas at El Paso
El Paso, Texas

 Education

Bothell, WA • Chicago, IL • Columbus, OH • New York, NY

# PROGRAM AUTHORS

### Dr. Diane August

National Institutes of Child Health and Human Development, Washington, D.C.

Principal Investigator, National Institutes of Child Health and Human Development Program Project Grant focused on the Acquisition of Literacy in Spanish-speaking ELLs

### Dr. Donald R. Bear

University of Nevada, Reno

Director, E.L. Cord Foundation Center for Learning and Literacy
Professor, College of Education

Author of *Words Their Way: Word Study for Phonics, Vocabulary, and Spelling Instruction* and *Words Their Way with Struggling Readers*

### Dr. Janice A. Dole

University of Utah

Professor, University of Utah
Director, Utah Center for Reading and Literacy
Content Facilitator, National Assessment of Educational Progress (NAEP)
CCSS Consultant to Literacy Coaches, Salt Lake City School District, Utah

### Dr. Jana Echevarria

California State University, Long Beach

Author of *Making Content Comprehensible for English Learners: The SIOP Model*

Principal Researcher, Center for Research on the Educational Achievement and Teaching of English Language Learners

### Dr. Douglas Fisher

San Diego State University

Co-Director, Center for the Advancement of Reading, California State University

Author of *Language Arts Workshop: Purposeful Reading and Writing Instruction* and *Reading for Information in Elementary School*

### Dr. David J. Francis

University of Houston

Director of the Center for Research on Educational Achievement and Teaching of English Language Learners (CREATE)

### Dr. Vicki Gibson

Educational Consultant
Gibson Hasbrouck and Associates

Author of *Differentiated Instruction: Grouping for Success, Differentiated Instruction: Guidelines for Implementation,* and *Managing Behaviors to Support Differentiated Instruction*

### Dr. Jan Hasbrouck

J.H. Consulting
Gibson Hasbrouck and Associates

Developed Oral Reading Fluency Norms for Grades 1–8

Author of *The Reading Coach: A How-to Manual for Success* and *Educators as Physicians: Using RTI Assessments for Effective Decision-Making*

### Margaret Kilgo

Educational Consultant
Kilgo Consulting, Inc., Austin, TX

(Echevarria) Deborah Attoinese Photography; (Fisher) Photography by Monet; (Gibson) Courtesy Vicki Gibson; (Hasbrouck, Shanahan, Tinajero) McGraw-Hill Companies/Ken Karp, photographer; Kilgo (Courtesy Margaret Kilgo); (Bumgardner) Courtesy sixcentsphotography; (Walker-Dalhouse) Dan Johnson, Marquette University; (others) McGraw-Hill Companies.

**Dr. Scott G. Paris**

Educational Testing Service,
Vice President, Research

Professor, Nanyang Technological
University, Singapore, 2008–2011

Professor of Education and Psychology,
University of Michigan, 1978–2008

**Dr. Timothy Shanahan**

University of Illinois at Chicago

Distinguished Professor, Urban Education

Director, UIC Center for Literacy

Chair, Department of Curriculum &
Instruction

Member, English Language Arts Work
Team and Writer of the Common Core
State Standards

President, International Reading
Association, 2006

**Dr. Josefina V. Tinajero**

University of Texas at El Paso

Dean of College of Education

President of TABE

Board of Directors for the American
Association of Colleges for Teacher
Education (AACTE)

Governing Board of the National Network
for Educational Renewal (NNER)

# Consulting Authors

**Kathy R. Bumgardner**

National Literacy Consultant

Strategies Unlimited, Inc.
Gastonia, NC

**Jay McTighe**

Jay McTighe and Associates

Author of *The Understanding by Design
Guide to Creating High Quality Units* with
G. Wiggins; *Schooling by Design: Mission,
Action, Achievement* with G. Wiggins;
and *Differentiated Instruction and
Understanding By Design* with C. Tomlinson

**Dr. Doris Walker-Dalhouse**

Marquette University

Associate Professor, Department
of Educational Policy & Leadership

Author of articles on multicultural
literature, struggling readers, and
reading instruction in urban schools

**Dinah Zike**

Educational Consultant

Dinah-Might Activities, Inc.
San Antonio, TX

# Program Reviewers

**Kelly Aeppli-Campbell**
Escambia County School District
Pensacola, FL

**Marjorie J. Archer**
Broward County Public Schools
Davie, FL

**Whitney Augustine**
Brevard Public Schools
Melbourne, FL

**Antonio C. Campbell**
Washington County School District
Saint George, UT

**Helen Dunne**
Gilbert Public School District
Gilbert, AZ

**David P. Frydman**
Clark County School District
Las Vegas, NV

**Fran Gregory**
Metropolitan Nashville Public Schools
Nashville, TN

**Veronica Allen Hunt**
Clark County School District
Las Vegas, NV

**Michele Jacobs**
Dee-Mack CUSD #701
Mackinaw, IL

**LaVita Johnson Spears**
Broward County Public Schools
Pembroke Pines, FL

**Randall B. Kincaid**
Sevier County Schools
Sevierville, TN

**Matt Melamed**
Community Consolidated School
District 46
Grayslake, IL

**Angela L. Reese,**
Bay District Schools
Panama City, FL

**Eddie Thompson**
Fairfield City School District
Fairfield Township, OH

**Patricia Vasseur Sosa**
Miami-Dade County Public Schools
Miami, FL

**Dr. Elizabeth Watson**
Hazelwood School District
Hazelwood, MO

# TEACHING WITH

McGraw-Hill Reading
**Wonders**

## INTRODUCE

**Weekly Concept**
Grade Appropriate
Topics, including Science
and Social Studies

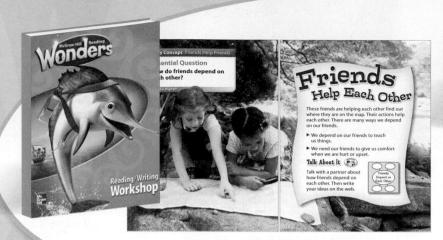

- **Videos**
- **Photographs**
- **Interactive Graphic Organizers**

**Reading/Writing Workshop**

## TEACH

**Close Reading**
Short Complex Texts

**Minilessons**
Comprehension
Strategies and Skills
Genre
Vocabulary Strategies
Writing Traits

**Grammar Handbook**

- **Visual Glossary**
- **Interactive Minilessons**
- **Interactive Graphic Organizers**

**Reading/Writing Workshop**

## APPLY

**Close Reading**
Anchor Texts
Extended Complex Texts
Application of
Strategies and Skills

- **eBooks**
- **Interactive Texts**
- **Listening Library**
- **English/Spanish Summaries**

**Literature Anthology**

#  Master the Common Core State Standards!

## DIFFERENTIATE

- eBooks
- Interactive Texts
- Leveled Reader Search
- Listening Library
- Interactive Activities

**Leveled Readers**

**Leveled Readers**
Small Group Instruction
with Differentiated Texts

## INTEGRATE

- Online Research
- Writer's Workspace
- Interactive Group Projects

**Collection of Texts**

**Research and Inquiry**
Short and Sustained Research Projects

**Text Connections**
Reading Across Texts

**Write About Reading**
Analytical Writing

## ASSESS

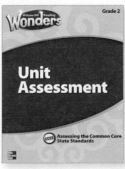

- Online Assessment
- Test Generator
- Reports

Weekly
Assessment

Unit
Assessment

Benchmark
Assessment

**Weekly Assessment**

**Unit Assessment**

**Benchmark Assessment**

# PROGRAM COMPONENTS

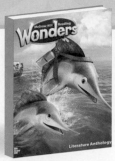

**Reading/Writing Workshop**

**Literature Anthology**

**Interactive Read-Aloud Cards**

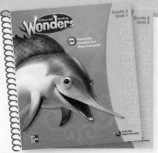

**Teacher Editions**

**Leveled Readers**

**Classroom Library Tradebooks**

**Your Turn Practice Book**

ball

**High-Frequency Word Cards**

**Visual Vocabulary Cards**

**Leveled Workstation Activity Cards**

## CCSS Assessing the Common Core State Standards

**Sound-Spelling Cards**

**Decodable Readers**

**Photo Cards**

**Response Board**

**Weekly Assessment**

**Unit Assessment**

**Benchmark Assessment**

---

 **Go Digital**

### For the Teacher

### For the Students

 **Plan**
Customizable Lesson Plans

 **Assess**
Online Assessments Reports and Scoring

 **Professional Development**
Lesson and CCSS Videos

 **Teach**
Classroom Presentation Tools Instructional Lessons

 **Collaborate**
Online Class Conversations Interactive Group Projects

**Additional Online Resources**
Leveled Practice
Grammar Practice
Phonics/Spelling
ELL Activities
Genre Study
Reader's Theater
Tier 2 Intervention
Retelling Cards
Word Building Cards

 **Manage and Assign**
Student Grouping and Assignments

 **School to Home**
Digital Open House Activities and Messages

**My To Do List**
Assignments
Assessment

**Words to Know**
Build Vocabulary

**Read**
eBooks
Interactive Texts

**Play**
Interactive Games

**Write**
Interactive Writing

**School to Home**
Activities for Home
Messages from the Teacher
Class Wall of Student Work

# UNIT 2 CONTENTS

## Unit Planning

## Weekly Lessons

## Writing Process

## Genre Writing: Informative

## Model Lesson

## Extended Complex Text

### Classroom Library

### Program Information

(l to r) Vincent Grafhorst/Foto Natura/Minden Pictures; Mircea Catusanu; Art Wolfe/The Image Bank/Getty Images; Frank Krahmer/Photographer's Choice RF/Getty Images; David Deas/DK Stock/Corbis

# UNIT OVERVIEW

**Text Complexity Range for Grades 2–3**

| Lexile | |
|---|---|
| 420 | 820 |

*TextEvaluator*™

| | |
|---|---|
| 2 | 35 |

| **Week 1** | **Week 2** | **Week 3** |
|---|---|---|

## READING

| **ANIMALS AND NATURE** | **ANIMALS IN STORIES** | **ANIMAL HABITATS** |
|---|---|---|

**ESSENTIAL QUESTION**
*How do animals survive?*

**ESSENTIAL QUESTION**
*What can animals in stories teach us?*

**ESSENTIAL QUESTION**
*What are features of different animal habitats?*

### Week 1

**Build Background**

**CCSS Oral Vocabulary**
L.2.5a *capture, chorus, croak, reason, visitor*

**CCSS Word Work**
RF.1.2 Phonemic Awareness: Phoneme Addition, Phoneme Substitution, Phoneme Blending
RF.2.3 Phonics/Spelling: Short *o*, Long *o*: *o_e*
L.2.4b Structural Analysis: Infectional Endings *-ed, -ing*
RF.1.3g High-Frequency Words: *because, cold, family, friends, have, know, off, picture, school, took*

**CCSS Vocabulary**
L.2.6 *adapt, climate, eager, freedom, fresh, sense, shadows, silence*
Prefixes

**CCSS Comprehension**
RL.2.3 Strategy: Make, Confirm, Revise Predictions
Skill: Character, Setting, Plot
Genre: Realistic Fiction

**CCSS Fluency**
RF.2.4b Phrasing

### Week 2

**Build Background**

**CCSS Oral Vocabulary**
L.2.5a *affection, crave, frustrated, nourishment, seek*

**CCSS Word Work**
RF.1.2 Phonemic Awareness: Phoneme Deletion, Phoneme Segmentation, Phoneme Blending
RF.2.3 Phonics/Spelling: Short *u*, Long *u*: *u_e*
L.2.4b Structural Analysis: CVC*e* Syllables
RF.1.3g High-Frequency Words: *change, cheer, fall, five, look, open, should, their, won, yes*

**CCSS Vocabulary**
L.2.6 *believe, delicious, feast, fond, lessons, remarkable, snatch, stories*
Suffixes

**CCSS Comprehension**
RL.2.3 Strategy: Make, Confirm, Revise Predictions
Skill: Character, Setting, Plot
Genre: Fable

**CCSS Fluency**
RF.2.4b Expression

### Week 3

**Build Background**

**CCSS Oral Vocabulary**
L.2.5a *defend, encounter, located, positive, react*

**CCSS Word Work**
RF.1.2 Phonemic Awareness: Phoneme Segmentation, Phoneme Substitution, Phoneme Blending
RF.2.3 Phonics/Spelling: Soft *c* and *g*; /j/ *dge, ge, lge, nge, rge*
L.2.4b Structural Analysis: Prefixes *re-, un-, dis-*
RF.1.3g High-Frequency Words: *almost, buy, food, out, pull, saw, sky, straight, under, wash*

**CCSS Vocabulary**
L.2.6 *buried, escape, habitat, journey, nature, peeks, restless, spies*
Suffixes

**CCSS Comprehension**
RL.2.3 Strategy: Make, Confirm, Revise Predictions
Skill: Main Topic and Key Details
Genre: Informational Text: Narrative Nonfiction

**CCSS Fluency**
RF.2.4b Phrasing

## LANGUAGE ARTS

### Week 1

**CCSS Writing**
W.2.3 Trait: Ideas

**CCSS Grammar**
L.2.1 Nouns
L.2.2 Mechanics: Commas in a Series

### Week 2

**CCSS Writing**
W.2.3 Trait: Ideas

**CCSS Grammar**
L.2.1 Singular and Plural Nouns
L.2.2 Mechanics: Commas in a Series

### Week 3

**CCSS Writing**
W.2.3 Trait: Organization

**CCSS Grammar**
L.2.1 Kinds of Nouns
L.2.2 Mechanics: Capital Letters

 **Writing Process** **Genre Writing: Informative** How-To Text T480–T485

# UNIT 2

**Review and Assess**

| Week 4 | Week 5 | Week 6 |
|---|---|---|

## BABY ANIMALS

### ESSENTIAL QUESTION
*How are offspring like their parents?*

**Build Background**

**CCSS Oral Vocabulary**
L.2.5a *guide, leader, protect, provide, separate*

**CCSS Word Work**
RF.1.2 Phonemic Awareness:
Identify and Generate Rhyme, Phoneme Segmentation, Phoneme Blending

RF.2.3 Phonics/Spelling:
Consonant Digraphs *ch, -tch, sh, ph, th, ng, wh*

L.2.4b Structural Analysis:
Suffixes *-ful, -less*

RF.1.3g High-Frequency Words:
*baby, early, eight, isn't, learn, seven, start, these, try, walk*

**CCSS Vocabulary**
L.2.6 *adult, alive, covered, fur, giant, groom, mammal, offspring*

Multiple-Meaning Words

**CCSS Comprehension**
RI.2.2 Strategy: Reread

Skill: Main Topic and Key Details

Genre: Informational Text: Expository Text

**CCSS Fluency**
RF.2.4b Pronunciation

## ANIMALS IN POEMS

### ESSENTIAL QUESTION
*What do we love about animals?*

**Build Background**

**CCSS Oral Vocabulary**
L.2.5a *alarm, howling, knobby, munch, problem*

**CCSS Word Work**
RF.1.2 Phonemic Awareness:
Identify and Generate Rhymes, Phoneme Substitution, Phoneme Blending

RF.2.3 Phonics/Spelling:
3-Letter Blends: *scr, spr, str, thr, spl, shr*

L.2.4a Structural Analysis:
Compound Words

RF.1.3g High-Frequency Words:
*bird, far, field, flower, grow, leaves, light, orange, ready, until*

**CCSS Vocabulary**
L.2.6 *behave, express, feathers, flapping*

Multiple-Meaning Words

**CCSS Comprehension**
RI.2.5 Strategy: Reread

Skill: Key Details

Genre: Poetry

**CCSS Fluency**
RF.2.4b Phrasing

## Week 6

**CCSS Reader's Theater**
RF.2.4b Focus on Vocabulary

Fluency: Intonation, Phrasing, Accuracy

**CCSS Reading Digitally**
SL.2.2 Notetaking

Evaluate Sources

Navigating Links

**CCSS Research and Inquiry**
W.2.8 Gathering Information From Multiple Sources

Unit Projects

Presentation of Ideas

**Unit 2 Assessment**

**Unit Assessment Book**
pages 27–53

**Fluency Assessment Book**
pages 72–81

---

**CCSS Writing**
W.2.3 Trait: Linking Words

**CCSS Grammar**
L.2.1 Plural Nouns

L.2.2 Mechanics: Abbreviations

**CCSS Writing**
W.2.3 Trait: Word Choice

**CCSS Grammar**
L.2.1 Possessive Nouns

L.2.2 Mechanics: Apostrophes

**CCSS Writing**
W.2.2 Publishing Celebrations

Portfolio Choice

**Writing Process**

**Genre Writing: Informative** How-To Directions T486–T491

# UNIT OPENER
## ANIMAL DISCOVERIES

**Reading/Writing Workshop**

### Unit 2 Animal Discoveries

**The Big Idea**
How do animals play a part in the world around us?

**Animals Are Amazing**

Kittens mew and dogs play catch,
Ducks and hens lay eggs to hatch.
Animals are amazing!

Bees make honey, lambs give wool,
Horses gallop, oxen pull.

Big game lions prowl and roar,
Turtles crawl and eagles soar.

Animals at work and play,
All around me, night and day.
Animals are amazing!

**by Winifred Califano**

**READING/WRITING WORKSHOP, pp. 96–97**

## The Big Idea *How do animals play a part in the world around us?*

### Talk About It

Have children read the Big Idea aloud. Ask children to tell about an animal that they have interacted with or learned about. Children may list events such as playing with a pet, visiting a farm or zoo, or watching a television program about wildlife.

Ask: *How can animals help people in everyday life?* Have children discuss in partners or in groups, then share their ideas with the class. Let children know that they will discuss the Big Idea throughout the unit. Each week they will talk, read, and write about an Essential Question related to the Big Idea.

### Read the Poem: "Animals Are Amazing"

Read aloud "Animals Are Amazing." Ask children questions to explore the theme.

→ What do animals do in the first stanza?

→ Why are large and small animals in the poem?

→ What could you add to this poem?

**Rhyme Scheme** A poem's rhyme scheme can be shown by letters that stand for the end sound of each line. Model identifying the rhyme scheme in "Animals Are Amazing." (aabccddeeb)

**Onomatopoeia** Explain that an onomatopoeic word is pronounced the way an action sounds. Point out the words *mew* and *roar*. These are like sounds made by cats and lions. Invite children to suggest other words that relate to animal sounds. (*buzz, woof*)

# RESEARCH AND INQUIRY

**Weekly Projects** Each week students will produce a project related to the Essential Question. They will then develop one of these projects more fully for the Unit Research Project. Through their research, children will focus their attention on:

→ selecting and gathering information from multiple sources.

→ organizing information into alphabetical order.

**Shared Research Board** You may wish to develop a Shared Research board. Children can post questions, ideas, and information that they research about the unit theme. Children can post photographs, stories, or hyperlinks they gather as they do their research. They can also post notes with questions they have as they read the text.

---

### WEEKLY PROJECTS

Children work in pairs or small groups.

**Week 1** Animal Discoveries, T56

**Week 2** Animals in Stories, T148

**Week 3** Animal Homes, T240

**Week 4** Baby Animals, T332

**Week 5** Animals in Poems, T422

### WEEK 6 UNIT PROJECT

Children work in small groups to complete and present one of the following projects.

→ Compare and Contrast Animals

→ Review of Two Fables

→ Shared Habitat Posters

→ Life Cycle Booklet

→ Animal Poems

---

  **COLLABORATE**
**Post children's questions and monitor children's online discussions. Create a Shared Research Board.**

*Go Digital!* www.connected.mcgraw-hill.com

---

# WRITING

 **Write about Reading** As children read and reread for close reading of text each week, they will take notes, cite evidence to support their ideas, write summaries of text, or develop character sketches.

## Writing Every Day: Focus on Writing Traits

Each week, children will focus on a writing trait. After analyzing an expert and student model, children will draft and revise shorter writing entries in their writer's notebook applying the trait to their writing.

## Writing Process: Focus on Informative/ Explanatory Writing

Over the course of the unit, children will develop one or two longer informative/explanatory texts. Children will work through the various stages of the writing process, allowing them time to continue revising their writing, conferencing with peers and teacher.

---

### WEEKLY WRITING TRAITS

**Week 1** Ideas, T22

**Week 2** Ideas, T114

**Week 3** Organization, T206

**Week 4** Linking Words, T298

**Week 5** Word Choice, T388

### GENRE WRITING: INFORMATIVE TEXT

Choose one or complete both 2–3 week writing process lessons over the course of the unit.

How-To Text, T480–T485

How-To Directions, T486–T491

---

  **WRITER'S WORKSPACE**
**Ask children to work through their genre writing using the online tools for support.**

# WEEKLY OVERVIEW

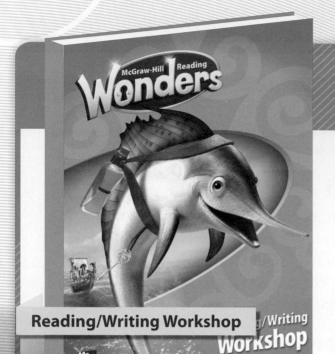

Reading/Writing Workshop

## TEACH AND MODEL

CCSS Shared Read | Genre · Realistic Fiction

### A Visit to the Desert

**Essential Question**
How do animals survive?
Read about how animals survive in a desert climate.

Tim was looking forward to this vacation. Then his parents told him the family would be visiting Grandma in Nevada. Tim was unhappy. He wanted to be with his friends this summer.

"Grandma is **eager** to see you," Mom said. "She can't wait to take you on a desert hike."

102

103

## ✔ Vocabulary

adapt

climate

eager

freedom

fresh

sense

shadows

silence

##  Close Reading of Complex Text

**Shared Read** "A Visit to the Desert," 102–107

**Genre** Realistic Fiction

**Lexile** 490L

**ETS** *TextEvaluator™* 36

## Minilessons

## ✔ Tested Skills CCSS

✔ **Comprehension Strategy** .............. Make Predictions, T32–T33

✔ **Comprehension Skill** .................. Character, Setting, Plot, T34–T35

✔ **Genre** ............................................ Realistic Fiction, T44–T45

✔ **Vocabulary Strategy** .................. Prefixes, T46–T47

✔ **Writing Traits** .............................. Ideas, T22–T23

✔ **Grammar** ...................................... Nouns, T24–T25

 **Go** Digital

http://connected.mcgraw-hill.com

# APPLY WITH CLOSE READING

## Complex Text

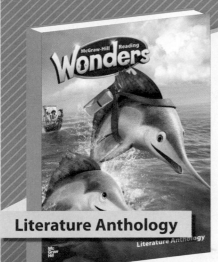

**Literature Anthology**

PAIRED READ

*Sled Dogs Run*, 110–129
**Genre** Realistic Fiction
**Lexile** 480L
ETS *TextEvaluator* 25

"Cold Dog, Hot Fox," 132–135
**Genre** Expository Text
**Lexile** 510L
ETS *TextEvaluator* 4

## Differentiated Text

**Leveled Readers**   *Including Paired Reads*

APPROACHING
**Lexile** 220
ETS *TextEvaluator* 4

ON LEVEL
**Lexile** 440
ETS *TextEvaluator* 13

BEYOND
**Lexile** 600
ETS *TextEvaluator* 23

ELL
**Lexile** 380
ETS *TextEvaluator* 5

## Extended Complex Text

*Nate the Great on the Owl Express*
**Genre** Fiction
**Lexile** 280L
ETS *TextEvaluator* 16

*Cam Jansen: The Mystery at the Monkey House #10*
**Genre** Fiction
**Lexile** 530L
ETS *TextEvaluator* 9

**Classroom Library**

Classroom Library lessons available online.

# TEACH AND MANAGE

## How You Teach

### INTRODUCE

**Weekly Concept**
Animals and Nature

**Reading/Writing Workshop
98–99**

 **Go Digital**

 Interactive Whiteboard

### TEACH

**Close Reading**
"A Visit to the Desert"

**Minilessons**
Make Predictions, Character, Setting, Plot, Realistic Fiction, Prefixes, Writing Traits

**Reading/Writing Workshop
102–107**

 Interactive Whiteboard

### APPLY

**Close Reading**
*Sled Dogs Run
Cold Dog, Hot Fox*

**Student Anthology
110–135**

 Mobile

## How Students Practice

### Weekly contract

**PDF Online**

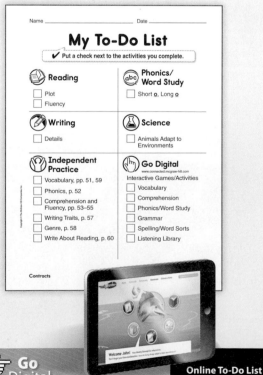

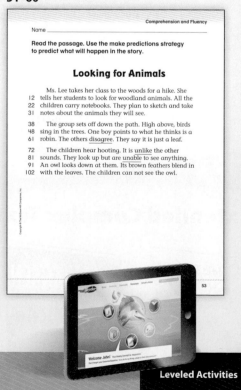 **Go Digital**

Online To-Do List

### Leveled practice and online activities

**Your Turn Practice Book
51–60**

Online Activities

**Leveled Readers**

Leveled Activities

Writer's Workspace

## DIFFERENTIATE

**SMALL GROUP INSTRUCTION**

**Leveled Readers**

**Mobile**

## INTEGRATE

**Research and Inquiry**
List Facts, T56–57

**Text Connections**
Compare How Animals Survive, T58

**Write About Reading**
Write an Analysis, T59

*Analytical Writing*

**Online Research and Writing**

## ASSESS

**Weekly Assessment
61–72**

**Online Assessment**

---

# Leveled workstation cards

More Activities on back

### ② Details, Details

**WRITING**

- Talk about a character in a story or book you like. Write a list of words that describe how the character looks, acts, and talks.

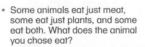

- Make up a new character

### ⑥ Go Fish

**PHONICS/W**

Do you have the word *box*: b-o-x?

Box: b-o-x. No. Go fish!

- Prepare a deck of cards by making two cards for each spelling word.

- Each player draws five cards.

- To play, you ask a player

### ⑥ Food for Animals

**SCIENCE**

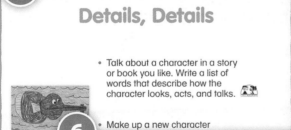

- Pick a wild animal you like. Draw its picture.

- Some animals eat just meat, some eat just plants, and some eat both. What does the animal you chose eat?

- Write a sentence that explains how the animal you chose gets its food.

**You need** 15
> paper
> pencil, crayons, or markers

### ⑤ What's the Plot?

**READING**

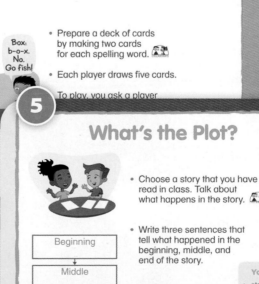

- Choose a story that you have read in class. Talk about what happens in the story.

| Beginning |
| Middle |
| End |

- Write three sentences that tell what happened in the beginning, middle, and end of the story.

- Then, write a sentence that tells the main idea of the story.

**You need** 20
> story
> pencil
> paper

# DEVELOPING READERS AND WRITERS

## Write to Sources and Research

Character, Setting, Plot, T34–T35, T47L

Key Details, T38

Note Taking, T47A, T53A

Author's Purpose, T47K

Make Connections: Essential Question, T47L, T53B, T58

Research and Inquiry, T56–T57

Analyze to Inform/Explain, T59

Comparing Texts, T65, T75, T79, T85

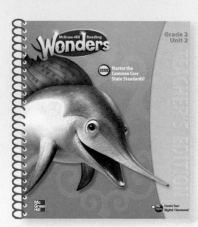

**Teacher's Edition**

**Literature Anthology**

Character, Setting, Plot, 131

**Interactive Whiteboard**

**Leveled Readers**
Comparing Texts
Character, Setting, Plot

**Your Turn Practice Book**

Character, Setting, Plot, 53–55
Genre, 58
Write About Reading, 60

**Narrative Text**
How-to Text, T480–T485

**Conferencing Routines**
Teacher Conferences, T482
Peer Conferences, T483

**Interactive Whiteboard**

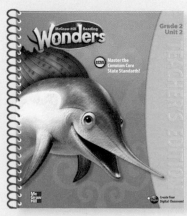

**Teacher's Edition**

**Leveled Workstation Card**
How-To, Card 23

**Writer's Workspace**
Informational Text: How-to Text
Writing Process
Multimedia Presentations

## Writing Traits • Write Every Day

**Writing Trait: Ideas**
Descriptive Details, T22–T23

**Conferencing Routines**
Teacher Conferences, T54
Peer Conferences, T55

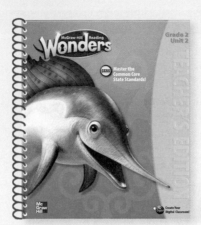

**Teacher's Edition**

Ideas: Descriptive
Details, 112–113

**Reading/Writing Workshop**

**Interactive
Whiteboard**

Ideas:
Descriptive
Details,
Card 2

**Leveled Workstation Card**

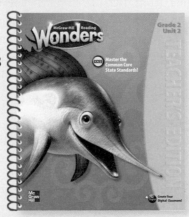

Ideas: Descriptive
Details, 57

**Your Turn Practice Book**

## Grammar and Spelling

**Grammar**
Nouns, T24, T37, T49, T55, T63

**Spelling**
Short *o* and Long *o*, T14, T30,
T41, T52, T61

**Interactive
Whiteboard**

**Teacher's Edition**

Nouns

Short and Long *o*
Word Sorts

**Online Spelling and Grammar Games**

# SUGGESTED LESSON PLAN

| ✔ TESTED SKILLS CCSS | DAY 1 | DAY 2 |
|---|---|---|
| **READING** | | |

### Whole Group

**Teach, Model, and Apply**

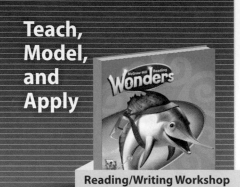

Reading/Writing Workshop

**DAY 1**

**Build Background** Animals and Nature, T8–T9

**Oral Vocabulary Words** *capture, chorus, croak, reason, visitor;* T10

**Listening Comprehension** Strategy: Make, Confirm, Revise Predictions; T11

**Interactive Read-Aloud Cards** "Swamp Life," T11

**Word Work**
Phonemic Awareness: Phoneme Addition, T12
Phonics/Spelling: Introduce Short *o,* Long *o: o_e;* T12–T14
High-Frequency Words: *because, cold, family, friends, have, know, off, picture, school, took;* T15

✔ **Vocabulary** Words in Context: *adapt, climate, eager, freedom, fresh, sense, shadows, silence;* T16–T17

**Close Reading of Complex Text** "A Visit to the Desert," 102–107

**Practice** *Your Turn* 51–52

**DAY 2**

**Oral Language** Animals and Nature, T26

**Review Oral Vocabulary Words,** T26

**Listening Comprehension** Strategy: Make, Confirm, Revise Predictions; T27

**Interactive Read-Aloud Cards** "Swamp Life," T27

**Word Work**
Phonemic Awareness: Phoneme Substitution, T28
Phonics/Spelling: Words with Short *o,* Long *o: o_e,* T28–T30
Structural Analysis: Inflectional Endings *-ed, -ing;* T29
High-Frequency Words, T30

**Vocabulary** Expand Vocabulary, T31

✔ **Comprehension**
• Strategy: Make, Confirm, Revise Predictions; T32–T33
• Skill: Character, Setting, Plot; T34–T35

**Practice** *Your Turn* 52–57

---

**DIFFERENTIATED INSTRUCTION** Choose across the week to meet your student's needs.

### Small Group

**Approaching Level**

**DAY 1**

**Leveled Reader** *Hippos at the Zoo,* T64–T65

**Phonemic Awareness** Phoneme Addition, T66 **TIER 2**

**Phonics** Connect *o* to /o/ and *o_e* to /ō/, T68 **TIER 2**

**High-Frequency Words** Review Words, T71 **TIER 2**

**Vocabulary** Review Words, T71

**DAY 2**

**Leveled Reader** *Hippos at the Zoo,* T64–T65

**Phonemic Awareness** Phoneme Substitution, T67

**Phonics** Blend with Short *o,* Long *o: o_e,* T68 **TIER 2**

**Comprehension** Identify Plot Events, T72 **TIER 2**

---

**On Level**

**DAY 1**

**Leveled Reader** *Where Are They Going?,* T74–T75

**Phonics** Build with Short *o,* Long *o (o_e),* T76

**DAY 2**

**Leveled Reader** *Where Are They Going?,* T74–T75

**Comprehension** Review Character, Setting, Plot; T77

---

**Beyond Level**

**DAY 1**

**Leveled Reader** *An Arctic Life for Us,* T78–T79

**Vocabulary** Review Domain-Specific Words, T80

**DAY 2**

**Leveled Reader** *An Arctic Life for Us,* T78–T79

**Comprehension** Review Character, Setting, Plot; T81

---

**English Language Learners**

**DAY 1**

**Shared Read** "A Visit to the Desert," T82–T83

**Phonemic Awareness** Phoneme Addition, T66

**Phonics** Connect *o* to /o/ and *o_e* to /ō/, T68

**Vocabulary** Preteach Vocabulary, T86

**DAY 2**

**Leveled Reader** *Where Are They Going?,* T84–T85

**Phonemic Awareness** Phoneme Substitution, T67

**Phonics** Blend with Short *o,* Long *o: o_e,* T68

**Vocabulary** Review Vocabulary, T86

**Writing** Writing Trait: Ideas, T88

---

**LANGUAGE ARTS** Writing Process: How-To T480–T485    Use with Weeks 1–3

### Whole Group

**Writing**

**Grammar**

**DAY 1**

✔ **Readers to Writers**
• Writing Trait: Ideas, T22–T23
• Writing Entry: Prewrite and Draft, T22

**Grammar**
• Nouns, T24
• Mechanics: Commas in a Series, T25

**DAY 2**

✔ **Readers to Writers**
• Writing Trait: Ideas, T36
• Writing Entry: Revise, T36

**Grammar**
• Nouns, T37
• Mechanics: Commas in a Series, T37

| **DAY 3** | **DAY 4** | **DAY 5** Review and Assess |
|---|---|---|

**READING**

**Interactive Read-Aloud Cards** "Swamp Life," T38

**Review Oral Vocabulary Words,** T38

**Comprehension** Maintain Skill: Key Details: Use Illustrations, T39

**Word Work**
Phonemic Awareness: Phoneme Blending, T40
Phonics/Spelling: Words with Short *o*, Long *o*: *o_e*, T40–T41
Structural Analysis: Inflectional Endings *-ed, -ing*; T41

**Fluency** Phrasing, T42

**Vocabulary** Reinforce Vocabulary, T43

✔**Genre** Realistic Fiction, T44–T45

✔**Vocabulary Strategy** Prefixes, T46–T47

**Close Reading** *Sled Dogs Run,* 110–130  *Analytical Writing*

**Practice** *Your Turn* 58–59

---

**Oral Language** Animals and Nature, T50

**Word Work**
Phonemic Awareness: Phoneme Substitution, T51
Phonics/Spelling: Words with Short *o*, Long *o*: *o_e*, T51–T52
Structural Analysis: Inflectional Endings *-ed, -ing*; T51
High-Frequency Words, T52

**Fluency** Phrasing, T53

**Vocabulary Strategy** Review: Root Words, T53

**Close Reading** "Cold Dog, Hot Fox," 132–135  *Analytical Writing*

**Integrate Ideas** Research and Inquiry, T56–T57 *Analytical Writing*

**Practice** *Your Turn* 53–55

---

**Integrate Ideas** *Analytical Writing*
• Text Connections, T58
• Write About Reading, T59
• Research and Inquiry, T59

**Word Work**
Phonemic Awareness: Phoneme Blending, T60
Phonics/Spelling: Words with Short *o*, Long *o*: *o_e*, T60–T61
Structural Analysis: Inflectional Endings *-ed, -ing*; T60
High-Frequency Words, T61

**Vocabulary** Review Words, T61

**Practice** *Your Turn* 60

**DIFFERENTIATED INSTRUCTION**

**Leveled Reader** *Hippos at the Zoo,* T64–T65

**Phonemic Awareness** Phoneme Blending, T66 **2**

**Phonics** Build with Short *o*, Long *o*: *o_e*, T69

**Structural Analysis** Review Inflectional Endings *-ed, -ing*; T70 **2**

**Comprehension** Review Character, Setting, Plot; T73

---

**Leveled Reader** Paired Read: "Hippos," T65 *Analytical Writing*

**Phonemic Awareness** Phoneme Substitution, T67

**Phonics** Blend with Short *o*, Long *o*: *o_e*, T69

**Structural Analysis** Reteach Inflectional Endings *-ed, -ing*; T70

**Comprehension** Read for Fluency, T72 **2**

---

**Leveled Reader** Literature Circle, T65

**Phonemic Awareness** Phoneme Blending, T66 **2**

**Phonics** Blend with Short *o*, Long *o*: *o_e*, T69

**Comprehension** Self-Selected Reading, T73

---

**Leveled Reader** *Where Are They Going?,* T74–T75

**Vocabulary** Review Words, T76

---

**Leveled Reader** Paired Read: "A Whale's Journey," T75 *Analytical Writing*

---

**Leveled Reader** Literature Circle, T75

**Comprehension** Self-Selected Reading, T77

---

**Leveled Reader** *An Arctic Life for Us,* T78–T79

**Vocabulary**
• Prefixes, T80
• Shades of Meaning, T80

*Gifted and Talented*

---

**Leveled Reader** Paired Read: "What Is a Ptarmigan?," T79 *Analytical Writing*

---

**Leveled Reader** Literature Circle, T79

**Comprehension**
• Self-Selected Reading, T81
• Independent Study: Animal Survival, T81

*Gifted and Talented*

---

**Leveled Reader** *Where Are They Going?,* T84–T85

**Phonemic Awareness** Phoneme Blending, T66

**Phonics** Build with Short *o*, Long *o*: *o_e*, T68

**Structural Analysis** Review Inflectional Endings *-ed, -ing*; T70

**Vocabulary Strategy** Prefixes, T87

**Grammar** Nouns, T89

---

**Leveled Reader** Paired Read: "A Whale's Journey," T85 *Analytical Writing*

**Phonemic Awareness** Phoneme Substitution, T67

**Phonics** Blend with Short *o*, Long *o*: *o_e*, T69

**Structural Analysis** Reteach Inflectional Endings *-ed, -ing*; T70

**Vocabulary** Additional Vocabulary, T87

---

**Leveled Reader** Literature Circle, T85

**Phonemic Awareness** Phoneme Blending, T66

**Phonics** Blend with Short *o*, Long *o*: *o_e*, T69

**Spelling** Words with Short *o*, Long *o*: *o_e*, T88

**LANGUAGE ARTS**

✔**Readers to Writers**
• Writing Trait: Ideas, T48
• Writing Entry: Prewrite and Draft, T48

**Grammar**
• Nouns, T49
• Mechanics: Commas in a Series, T49

---

✔**Readers to Writers**
• Writing Trait: Ideas, T54
• Writing Entry: Revise, T54

**Grammar**
• Nouns, T55
• Mechanics: Commas in a Series, T55

---

✔**Readers to Writers**
• Writing Trait: Ideas, T62
• Writing Entry: Share and Reflect, T62

**Grammar**
• Nouns, T63
• Mechanics: Commas in a Series, T63

# DIFFERENTIATE TO ACCELERATE

 **Scaffold to** **A**ccess **C**omplex **T**ext

**IF** ▶ the text complexity of a particular selection is too difficult for children

**THEN** ▶ use the Access Complex Text prompts to scaffold instruction.

Qualitative / Quantitative
**Reader and Task**
**TEXT COMPLEXITY**

| | Reading/Writing Workshop | Literature Anthology | Leveled Readers | Classroom Library |
|---|---|---|---|---|
| |  | 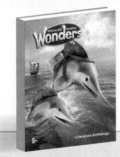 |  |  |

## Quantitative

**Reading/Writing Workshop**

*"A Visit to the Desert"*
**Lexile** 490
*TextEvaluator*™ 36

**Literature Anthology**

*Sled Dogs Run*
**Lexile** 480
*TextEvaluator*™ 25

*"Cold Dog, Hot Fox"*
**Lexile** 510
*TextEvaluator*™ 4

**Leveled Readers**

**Approaching Level**
**Lexile** 220
*TextEvaluator*™ 4

**Beyond Level**
**Lexile** 600
*TextEvaluator*™ 23

**On Level**
**Lexile** 440
*TextEvaluator*™ 13

**ELL**
**Lexile** 380
*TextEvaluator*™ 5

**Classroom Library**

*Nate the Great on the Owl Express*
**Lexile** 280
*TextEvaluator*™ 16

*Cam Jansen: The Mystery at the Monkey House #10*
**Lexile** 530
*TextEvaluator*™ 9

## Qualitative

**What Makes the Text Complex?**

• **Purpose** Facts, T19
• **Connection of Ideas** Inferences, T45

 *See Scaffolded Instruction in Teacher's Edition T19 and T45.*

**What Makes the Text Complex?**

• **Organization** Sequence, T47B, T47D, T47D
• **Specific Vocabulary** Domain-Specific Vocabulary, T47B, T47E
• **Prior Knowledge** Climates, T53B

 *See Scaffolded Instruction in Teacher's Edition T47B, T47D, T47E, T47H, T53B.*

**What Makes the Text Complex?**

• **Specific Vocabulary**
• **Sentence Structure**
• **Connection of Ideas**
• **Genre**

 *See Level Up lessons online for Leveled Readers.*

**What Makes the Text Complex?**

• **Genre**
• **Specific Vocabulary**
• **Prior Knowledge**
• **Sentence Structure**
• **Organization**
• **Purpose**
• **Connection of Ideas**

 *See Scaffolded Instruction in Teacher's Edition T496–T497.*

## Reader and Task

The Introduce the Concept lesson on pages T8–T9 will help determine the reader's knowledge and engagement in the weekly concept. See pages T18–T21, T32–T35, T44–T47, and T56–T59 for questions and tasks for this text.

The Introduce the Concept lesson on pages T8–T9 will help determine the reader's knowledge and engagement in the weekly concept. See pages T47A–T47L, T53A–T53B, and T56–T59 for questions and tasks for this text.

The Introduce the Concept lesson on pages T8–T9 will help determine the reader's knowledge and engagement in the weekly concept. See pages T64–T65, T74–T75, T78–T79, T84–T85, and T56–T59 for questions and tasks for this text.

The Introduce the Concept lesson on pages T8–T9 will help determine the reader's knowledge and engagement in the weekly concept. See pages T496–T497 for questions and tasks for this text.

## Monitor and *Differentiate*

| IF | If you need to differentiate instruction |
|---|---|
| THEN | use the Quick Check to assess children's needs and select the appropriate small group instruction focus. |

###  Quick Check

**Comprehension Strategy** Make Predictions, T33

**Comprehension Skills** Character, Setting, Plot, T35

**Genre** Realistic Fiction, T45

**Vocabulary Strategy** Prefixes, T47

**Phonics/Fluency** Short *o*, Long *o*, Phrasing, T41, T53

If No → | Approaching Level | Reteach T64–T73 |
|---|---|
| ELL | Develop T82–T89 |

If Yes → | On Level | Review T74–T77 |
|---|---|
| Beyond Level | Extend T78–T81 |

## Level Up with Leveled Readers

| IF | children can read their leveled text fluently and answer comprehension questions |
|---|---|
| THEN | assign the next level up to accelerate children reading with more complex text. |

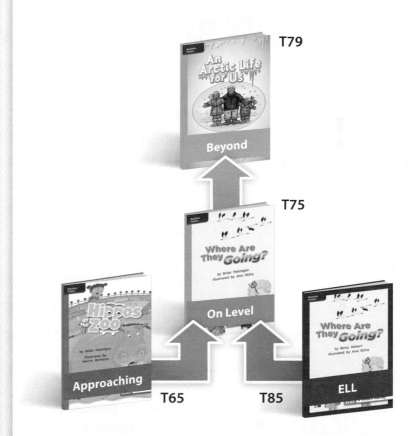

## ENGLISH LANGUAGE LEARNERS
### SCAFFOLD

| IF | ELL students need additional support. | THEN | scaffold instruction using the small group suggestions. |

| Reading/Writing Workshop "A Visit to the Desert," T82–T83 | Leveled Reader *Where Are They Going?*, T84–T85 "A Whale's Journey," T85 | Additional Vocabulary T87 adapt · desert burrows · homesick climate · migrate | Prefixes T87 | Writing Ideas, T88 | Spelling Words with short *o*, long *o*, T88 | Grammar Nouns, T89 |
|---|---|---|---|---|---|---|

**Note:** Include ELL Students in all small groups based on their needs.

## Materials

**Reading/Writing Workshop**

adapt

**Visual Vocabulary Cards**

| adapt | fresh |
|-------|-------|
| climate | sense |
| eager | shadows |
| freedom | silence |

a b c

**Word-Building Cards**

**Interactive-Read-Aloud Cards**

I predicted _____ because...

**Think Aloud Clouds**

because

**High-Frequency Word Cards**

octopus

**Sound-Spelling Cards**

---

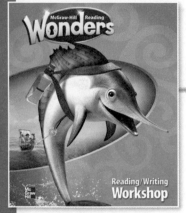

**Reading/Writing Workshop**

### OBJECTIVES

 Follow agreed-upon rules for discussions (e.g., gaining the floor in respectful ways, listening to others with care, speaking one at a time about the topics and texts under discussion). **SL.2.1a**

Build background knowledge.

### ACADEMIC LANGUAGE

*adapt, climate*
cognate: *adaptar*

---

## → Introduce the Concept

**MINILESSON**
**5 Mins**

## Build Background

### ESSENTIAL QUESTION

*How do animals survive?*

Have children read the Essential Question on page 98 of the **Reading/Writing Workshop**. Explain that *adapt* means to change or to adjust to something.

Discuss the photo of the meerkats with children. Point out the characteristics that help the meerkats survive in a hot, dry climate. Explain that *climate* is what the weather is like in a place.

→ Meerkats live underground in order to stay cool.

→ Meerkats have thin fur that does not trap their body heat.

→ Meerkats go out in the cool morning hours to look for food.

### Talk About It

**COLLABORATE**

**Ask:** *How do meerkats survive in a hot, dry **climate**? What do they do that helps them **adapt** to the heat?* Have children discuss in pairs or groups.

→ Use the Concept Web to model generating ideas about animal adaptations. Add children's words and phrases to the web.

### Collaborative Conversations

**Take Turns Talking** As children engage in partner, small-group, and whole-group discussions, encourage them to

→ wait for a person to finish before they speak.

→ quietly raise their hand when they want to speak.

→ ask others to share their ideas and opinions.

---

## Go Digital

**Animals and Nature**

**Video**

**Graphic Organizer**

peered

**Visual Glossary**

---

**Weekly Concept** Animals and Nature

**Essential Question**

How do animals survive?

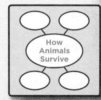 Go Digital!

# Animal Survival

Meerkats live in hot, dry places. Here are some ways they adapt to the heat.

▶ They live in underground burrows.

▶ They have thin fur.

▶ They search for food in the early morning hours when it is cool.

## Talk About It

Talk with a partner about how animals survive in hot climates. Write your ideas on the web.

How Animals Survive

98

99

Vincent Grafhorst/Foto Natura/Minden Pictures

**READING/WRITING WORKSHOP, pp. 98–99**

## ELL ENGLISH LANGUAGE LEARNERS SCAFFOLD

| Beginning | Intermediate | Advanced/High |
|---|---|---|
| **Use Visuals** Have children point to the parts of the photo and repeat after you. Point to the meerkats: *These are meerkats.* Point to the burrow: *They live in a burrow under the ground.* Point to the meerkats' fur: *They have thin fur. Their home and their fur helps them adapt to the hot climate.* | **Describe** Have children describe the meerkats. Ask: *Why do meerkats live under the ground? How does their thin fur help them adapt to the hot climate?* Encourage children to use the concept words as they respond. Restate children's responses in order to develop their oral language proficiency. | **Demonstrate Understanding** Ask children to explain how meerkats survive in a hot climate. Use prompts such as: *When do meerkats hunt for food? Why is that time a good time for them to hunt? What other things help meerkats survive in the heat?* Elicit more details to support children's answers. |

**GRAPHIC ORGANIZER**

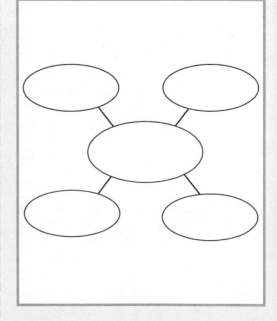

INTRODUCE THE CONCEPT **T9**

→ # Build the Concept

**MINILESSON 5 Mins**

# Oral Language

## OBJECTIVES

Ask and answer questions about what a speaker says in order to clarify comprehension, gather additional information, or deepen understanding of a topic or issue.
**SL.2.3**

- Develop oral language.
- Discuss the Essential Question.

## ACADEMIC LANGUAGE

*prediction, confirm, revise*

**ESSENTIAL QUESTION**

Remind children that this week you'll be talking and reading about how animals adapt to survive in their environment.

## Oral Vocabulary Words

Use the **Define/Example/Ask** routine to introduce the Oral Vocabulary words below. Prompt children to use the words as they discuss animals and how they survive.

### Oral Vocabulary Routine

**Define:** If you **capture** something, you use force to get or catch it.

**Example:** We tried to capture to the other team's flag.

**Ask:** What is something you have tried to capture? What did you do to capture it?

**Define:** A **chorus** is a group that sings or dances together.

**Example:** I am going to sing in the chorus at school.

**Ask:** Why might it be fun to sing in a chorus?

**Define:** A **croak** is a low sound.

**Example:** My voice croaked when I had a sore throat.

**Ask:** A frog makes a croaking sound. What else sounds like a frog's croak?

**Define:** The **reason** something happens is why it happens. The reason you do something is why you do it.

**Example:** The bump in the sidewalk was the reason I tripped.

**Ask:** Name something you like to do. What is the reason you like doing that thing?

**Define:** A **visitor** goes to a place to stay for a little while.

**Example:** We had a visitor stay at our house for three days.

**Ask:** Have you ever had a visitor? What did you do together?

## Go Digital

**Swamp Life**

**Make, Confirm, Revise Predictions**

# Listening Comprehension

**10 Mins**
MINILESSON

## Interactive Read Aloud

### Read "Swamp Life"

Tell children that you will read be reading a fictional story about a second grade class that visits a swamp. Display the Interactive Read-Aloud Cards.

#### Strategy: Make, Confirm, Revise Predictions

**Interactive Read-Aloud Cards**

**1** **Model** Tell children that as they read, they can make predictions about what will happen next or what they will learn about. Then they can continue reading to find out if their prediction was correct. They can revise, or change, any predictions that do not match what they read.

**Think Aloud** A prediction is an informed guess about what will happen or what you will learn about in a story. To make a prediction, you can use both the words and the pictures in a story. Today, as we read "Swamp Life," think about what may happen or what you may learn. As we read, confirm, or check, your predictions to see if they're correct.

**2** **Apply** As you read, use the Think Aloud Cloud to model applying the strategy. After each card, have children make a prediction and then confirm whether the prediction is correct. Point out that checking predictions can help children make sure that they understand the story.

**Think Aloud** On the first card, I read that Danny heard buzzing, humming, swishing, clicking, croaking, and chirping. I predict that on the next card, I will find out that frogs, birds, and insects were making some of those sounds. I'll read on to check my prediction.

### Make Connections

COLLABORATE

After reading, have children share what they learned about how animals survive. Then have them discuss the predictions they made and how making, checking, and revising those predictions helped them understand the story.

#### ENGLISH LANGUAGE LEARNERS

**Seek Clarification** Some children may be confused by unfamiliar words or phrases. Encourage them to always seek clarification when they encounter a word or phrase that does not make sense to them. For example, *I don't understand this. Can you give me an example?*

**WHOLE GROUP**
# DAY 1

 # Word Work

## Phonemic Awareness

**MINILESSON 5 Mins**

### OBJECTIVES

**CCSS** Know and apply grade-level phonics and word analysis skills in decoding words. **RF.2.3**

**CCSS** Distinguish long and short vowels when reading regularly spelled one-syllable words. **RF.2.3a**

Add phonemes to existing words to form new words.

### ACADEMIC LANGUAGE
*blend, sound*

### Phoneme Addition

**1 Model** Have children listen as you say *ox* and then add /b/ to the beginning to get *box. Listen carefully to this word:* ox. *Now I'll add /b/ at the beginning to make a new word:* box. *I can make a new word by adding a sound at the beginning.*

Continue modeling with /m/ *ask,* /s/ *top,* /p/ *age.*

**2 Guided Practice/Practice** Have children practice making new words by adding beginning sounds. Use the following examples. Do the first one together. *I will say* ate. *Then I will add /l/ at the beginning. The new word is* late.

| | |
|---|---|
| /l/ ate | /g/ oat |
| /b/ lock | /s/ take |
| /w/ in | /h/ old |

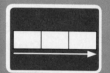

**Phonemic Awareness**

**Phonics**

## Phonics

**MINILESSON 10 Mins**

### Introduce Short *o*; Long *o*: *o_e*

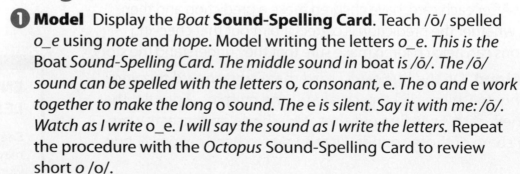

**Sound-Spelling Card**

**1 Model** Display the *Boat* **Sound-Spelling Card**. Teach /ō/ spelled *o_e* using *note* and *hope*. Model writing the letters *o_e. This is the* Boat *Sound-Spelling Card. The middle sound in* boat *is /ō/. The /ō/ sound can be spelled with the letters o, consonant, e. The o and e work together to make the long o sound. The e is silent. Say it with me: /ō/. Watch as I write* o_e. *I will say the sound as I write the letters.* Repeat the procedure with the *Octopus* Sound-Spelling Card to review short *o* /o/.

**2 Guided Practice/Practice** Have children practice connecting the letters *o_e* to the sound /ō/ through writing. *Now do it with me. Say /ō/ as I write the letters* o_e. *This time write the letters* o_e *five times as you say the /ō/ sound.* Repeat the procedure for short *o*.

# Blend Words with Short *o*; Long *o*

**❶ Model** Display **Word-Building Cards** *n, o, t*. Model how to blend the sounds. *This is the letter* n. *It stands for /n/. This is the letter* o. *It stands for /o/. This is the letter* t. *It stands for /t/. Listen as I blend these sounds together: /nooot/. Say it with me:* not. *Add an* e *to the end of the word. Point to the* e. *This is the letter* e. *It is silent; the* o *and* e *together make the long* o *sound /ō/. Listen as I blend all three sounds: /nōōōt/,* note. *Say it with me.*

Continue by modeling the words *joke, cop, cope, hop, hope, robe*, and *hose*.

**❷ Guided Practice/Practice** Display the Day 1 Phonics Practice Activity. Read each word in the first row, blending the sounds, for example, /nnnōōōz/. The word is *nose*. Have children blend each word with you. Prompt children to read the connected text, sounding out the decodable words.

| | | | | | |
|---|---|---|---|---|---|
| nose | robe | pop | not | job | pole |
| globe | rock | joke | drove | drop | broke |
| hop | cone | top | clock | mop | vote |
| bit | bite | pin | pine | rip | ripe |

There is a hole in the box.

I got on the bus and rode home.

She put the pot on the stove.

Also online

**Phonics Practice**

### Corrective Feedback

**Sound Error** Model the sound that children missed, then have them repeat the sound. Say: *My turn.* Tap under the letter and say: *Sound? /ō/ What's the sound?* Return to the beginning of the word Say: *Let's start over.* Blend the word with children again.

## ENGLISH LANGUAGE LEARNERS

**Phonemic Awareness: Minimal Contrasts** Focus on articulation. Say /o/ and note your mouth position. Have children repeat. Use the articulation photos. Repeat for /ō/. Have children say both sounds and notice the differences. Continue with *not/note, rob/robe, hop/hope*.

**Phonics: Variations in Language** In some languages such as Spanish, Cantonese, Vietnamese, Hmong, and Korean, the sound transfer for /o/ is approximate. Emphasize /o/, and show correct mouth position. Speakers of Cantonese, Vietnamese, and Hmong may also need support learning the /ō/ sound. Emphasize /ō/, and show correct mouth position. Practice with Approaching Level phonics lessons.

→ # Word Work

**5 Mins** MINILESSON

## Spelling

### Words with Short *o* and Long *o*

**Dictation** Use the spelling dictation routine to help children transfer their growing knowledge of sound-spellings to writing. Follow the Dictation Routine.

**Pretest** After dictation, pronounce each spelling word. Read the sentence and pronounce the word again. Ask children to say each word softly, stretching the sounds, before writing it. After the pretest, display the spelling words and write each word as you say the letter names. Have children check their words.

| | |
|---|---|
| **box** | You can pack the books in this **box**. |
| **fox** | The **fox** runs through the woods. |
| **dog** | Will you take the **dog** for a walk? |
| **lock** | I use a key to **lock** the door. |
| **pot** | We make soup in a big **pot**. |
| **cone** | She ordered a vanilla ice cream **cone**. |
| **home** | My **home** is near the park. |
| **nose** | You breathe through your **nose**. |
| **poke** | Why did you **poke** my arm? |
| **rope** | We tie the boat to the dock with a **rope**. |
| **side** | Set the bag on the **side** of the desk. |
| **line** | We got in **line** at the shop. |
| **have** | Do you **have** a pet? |
| **off** | Take **off** your hat. |
| **took** | I **took** my dog to the vet. |

For Approaching Level and Beyond Level children, refer to the Differentiated Spelling Lists for modified word lists.

### OBJECTIVES

**CCSS** Know and apply grade-level phonics and word analysis skills in decoding words. **RF.2.3**

**CCSS** Distinguish long and short vowels when reading regularly spelled one-syllable words. **RF.2.3a**

**CCSS** Recognize and read grade-appropriate irregularly spelled words. **RF.2.3f**

### ACADEMIC LANGUAGE
*blend, spelling*

**ELL**

### ENGLISH LANGUAGE LEARNERS

**Spelling** Review the meanings of these words by using pictures, pantomime, or gestures when possible. Have children repeat or act out the definition as they repeat the word.

# Go Digital

**Spelling Word Routine**

| they | together |
|------|----------|
| how | eat |

**High-Frequency Word Routine**

# High-Frequency Words

*because, cold, family, friends, have, know, off, picture, school, took*

**1 Model** Display the **High-Frequency Word Cards** for *because, cold, family, friends, have, know, off, picture, school,* and *took*. Use the **Read/Spell/Write** routine to teach each word.

→ **Read** Point to and say the word *because*. *This is the word* because. *Say it with me:* because. *I was late because I missed the bus.*

→ **Spell** *The word* because *is spelled b-e-c-a-u-s-e. Spell it with me.*

→ **Write** *Let's write the word in the air as we say each letter:* b-e-c-a-u-s-e.

→ Follow the same steps to introduce *friends, have, picture, school, off, know, cold, family,* and *took*.

→ As children spell each word with you, point out the irregularities in sound/spellings, such as the /a/ sound in the word *have* that ends with silent *e*.

 → Have partners create sentences using each word.

**2 Guided Reading** Have children read the sentences. Prompt them to identify the high-frequency words in connected text and to blend the decodable words.

1. I drink water **because** I am hot.
2. Jake and Bill are my **friends**.
3. We **have** blue socks.
4. Did you see this **picture** of my dog?
5. Pam likes to go to **school**.
6. The pen fell **off** the desk.
7. I **know** how to kick the ball into the net.
8. My nose is **cold**.
9. Do you have a big **family**?
10. She **took** the test.

**Monitor and Differentiate**

 **Quick Check**

Can children read and decode words with short *o* and long *o*? Can children recognize and read high-frequency words?

**Small Group Instruction**

If No → Approaching Reteach pp. T66-T71
ELL Develop pp. T82-T89
If Yes → On Level Review pp. T76-T77
Beyond Level Extend pp. T80-T81

# Vocabulary

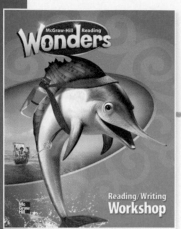

**Reading/Writing
Workshop**

## OBJECTIVES

**CCSS** Demonstrate understanding of word relationships and nuances in word meanings. **L.2.5**

**CCSS** Identify real-life connections between words and their use (e.g., describe foods that are *spicy* or *juicy*). **L.2.5a**

**CCSS** Determine the meaning of words and phrases in a text relevant to a *grade 2 topic or subject area.* **RI.2.4**

## ACADEMIC LANGUAGE

• *adapt, climate*
• cognate: *adaptar*

---

### MINILESSON 10 Mins

## Words in Context

### Model the Routine

Introduce each vocabulary word using the Vocabulary Routine found on the Visual Vocabulary Cards.

**Visual Vocabulary Cards**

Vocabu...
Define:
Example...
Ask:

#### Vocabulary Routine

**Define:** When something has to **adapt** to a new place, it must adjust to it.

**Example:** The polar bear's thick fur coat helps it adapt to the icy water.

**Ask:** How do you adapt to cold weather?

## Definitions

→ **climate** The **climate** of a place is the weather that it usually has.

→ **eager** When you are **eager** to do something, you want to do it very much.

→ **freedom** If you have **freedom**, you can do what you want and go where you want.

→ **fresh** When something is **fresh**, it is new or not spoiled.

→ **sense** **Sense** means a feeling you have about something.

→ **shadows** **Shadows** are dark shapes that are made when something is in front of a light.

→ **silence** If there is **silence**, it is still and quiet.

## Talk About It

 Have partners look at each picture and discuss the definition of each word. Then ask children to choose three words and write questions for their partner to answer.

**Go Digital**

**peered**

**Visual Glossary**

## CCSS Words to Know

# Vocabulary

**Use the picture and sentence to learn each word.**

**adapt** The polar bear's thick fur coat helps it **adapt** to the icy water.

*How do you adapt to cold weather?*

**climate** Tom lives in a hot and sunny **climate**.

*What is the climate like where you live?*

**eager** Mindy is **eager** to see her grandmother.

*What is something that you are eager to do?*

**freedom** Deer have the **freedom** to move about the open land.

*What animals are free to roam about the forest?*

**fresh** The baker made **fresh** bread every day.

*What word means the opposite of fresh?*

**sense** I felt a **sense** of pride when I won the race.

*When do you feel a sense of pride?*

**shadows** We made animal **shadows** on the wall.

*What shadows can you make?*

**silence** The baby needed **silence** to fall asleep.

*What word means the same as silence?*

### Your Turn
COLLABORATE

Pick three words. Write three questions for your partner to answer.

*Go Digital! Use the online visual glossary*

100

101

**READING/WRITING WORKSHOP, pp. 100–101**

## ENGLISH LANGUAGE LEARNERS
### ELL SCAFFOLD

| Beginning | Intermediate | Advanced/High |
|---|---|---|
| **Use Visuals** *Let's look at the picture for* adapt. *The water is very cold. The polar bear grows thick fur to stay warm.* Explain that when you *adapt*, you change to get ready for something. Ask: *How do you adapt to cold weather?* Restate children's responses in order to develop their oral language proficiency. | **Describe** Have children describe the polar bear in the picture. Ask: *How does the polar bear adapt to the cold water?* Repeat correct answers slowly and clearly to the class. Ask partners to tell each other how they adapt to cold weather. | **Discuss** Have partners work together to state the definition of *adapt* in their own words and then use the word in an oral sentence. Correct the meaning of children's responses as needed. |

### ON-LEVEL PRACTICE BOOK p. 51

| adapt | climate | eager | freedom |
|---|---|---|---|
| fresh | sense | shadows | silence |

**Use what you know about the words in the sentences to choose the word that makes sense in each blank. Then write the word on the line.**

1. My sister is excited and _____eager_____ to learn about polar bears.

2. The quiet _____silence_____ ended when birds began to chirp.

3. Desert animals must _____adapt_____ to hot, dry weather.

4. The air feels cool in the dark _____shadows_____ under the trees.

5. The eagle has the _____freedom_____ to fly where it wants.

6. A rainforest has a warm, wet _____climate_____.

7. The air outside felt _____fresh_____ and clean.

8. A wild animal will run away if it feels a _____sense_____ of danger.

| APPROACHING p. 51 | BEYOND p. 51 | ELL p. 51 |
|---|---|---|

# Comprehension

CLOSE READING

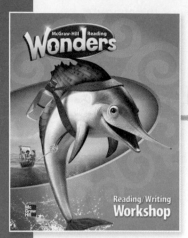

## Wonders

Reading/Writing
Workshop

**Reading/Writing
Workshop**

### OBJECTIVES

 Read with sufficient
accuracy and
fluency to support
comprehension.
**RF.2.4**

 Read on-level text
with purpose and
understanding.
**RF.2.4a**

Identify meanings
of words used in
context.

 **Shared Read**

**MINILESSON 10 Mins**

**Lexile** 490     *TextEvaluator*. 36

## Connect to Concept

### Animals and Nature

Explain to children that "A Visit to the Desert" will tell them about how
desert animals survive the hot, dry climate.

After reading the selection, have partners discuss what they learned
about how animals survive in a desert climate.

### Use Vocabulary Words in Context

| adapt | climate | eager | fresh |
| freedom | sense | shadows | silence |

The highlighted words in the text are vocabulary words children have
learned. As you read them, discuss the words' meanings.

## Close Reading

**Reread page 103:** Tell children you are going to take a closer look at
page 103. Reread the page together. Ask: *What is Tim's problem?* Model
how to cite evidence to answer the question.

*Tim is not happy about going to Nevada to visit Grandma. He would rather
spend time with his friends.*

Explain that the author states the problem of the story right away so
readers can look for the solution as they read.

*We want to find out what happens when Tim goes to Nevada.*

Point out that since the story is about Tim going somewhere, the
setting will be important. Model how to use text evidence to identify
and visualize the setting.

*The second sentence says that Tim and his family are going to Nevada. The
last sentence also tells me that the Grandma wants to take Tim on a desert
hike. So, I think that the story will take place in Nevada in the desert. I can
use the illustration and what I know about the desert to imagine what it
will be like. It will be hot and dry. There will be cacti and rocks. There will be
lizards and other animals.*

**Go
Digital**

**A Visit to the
Desert**

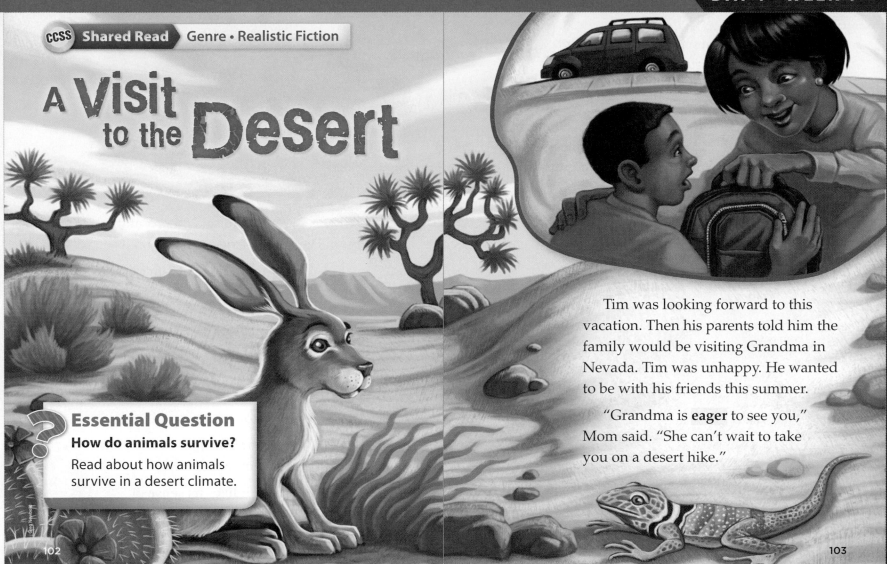

CCSS **Shared Read** Genre • Realistic Fiction

# A Visit to the Desert

**Essential Question**

**How do animals survive?**

Read about how animals survive in a desert climate.

102

Tim was looking forward to this vacation. Then his parents told him the family would be visiting Grandma in Nevada. Tim was unhappy. He wanted to be with his friends this summer.

"Grandma is **eager** to see you," Mom said. "She can't wait to take you on a desert hike."

103

**READING/WRITING WORKSHOP, pp. 102–103**

# ACT Access Complex Text

▶ **Purpose**

The genre of "A Visit to the Desert" is realistic fiction, but the author has also included facts about animals' survival. Guide children to understand that sometimes an author has more than one purpose in writing a text.

→ Point out that the author tells a story. However, the question on page 102 also gives us a clue that the author will include facts about desert animals' characteristics and behaviors to help readers learn how animals survive in a desert climate. Children should look for this information as they read.

The next morning Grandma met them at the airport. Then they drove to the desert. As they hiked, Grandma explained that animals enjoy the open desert space. It gives them the **freedom** to move from place to place. Tim learned that the animals find ways to **adapt** to the hot desert weather. He wondered if he could get used to the desert **climate**.

"Wow," Tim said, "Look at that! The turtle carries its home on its back!"

Grandma smiled at Tim's excitement. "Actually," she said. "That is a desert tortoise. It looks for the shade made by the **shadows** of rocks. That's how it cools off. He burrows underground to get away from the heat." The tortoise disappeared into its burrow. Tim leaned over the hole. He could not hear a sound.

"I'll bet it likes the **silence** of its burrow," Tim whispered.

"I think it likes its **sense** of safety too," Grandma added.

104

105

**READING/WRITING WORKSHOP,** pp. 104–105

# Shared Read  *CLOSE READING*

## Close Reading

**Reread page 104:** Tell children that you are going to take a closer look at page 104. Say: *as Grandma and Tim hike, Grandma tells Tim about the desert. What two things does Tim learn about desert animals?* Model how to cite evidence to answer the question.

*The author explains that animals enjoy the open desert space because it gives them freedom to move around. The author also tells us that animals find ways to adapt to the hot desert weather.*

## Make Connections

**ESSENTIAL QUESTION**
Encourage children to go back into the text for evidence as they discuss the ways the desert tortoise survives in the heat.

"That's the same feeling I get at home," Tim sighed. Just then a large rabbit hopped by. Grandma explained that the jack rabbit's large ears help it stay cool.

"These animals are so unlike the animals at home!" Tim said. He had forgotten about the desert heat.

"Some animals stay cool by sleeping during the day. Then they hunt at night," said Grandma. A Great Horned Owl hooted above them. Grandma said, "It will soon be time for the owl to hunt."

"Which means it's time for us to head back," Dad added.

"Aw, this vacation is going by too fast," Tim said. They asked Tim about the heat. "What heat?" Tim asked. "I feel as **fresh** and cool as a new flower. I've adapted!" Everyone laughed.

**Make Connections**

How does the desert tortoise survive in the heat? ESSENTIAL QUESTION

Think of another animal you know. How does it survive in its climate? TEXT TO SELF

106
107

**READING/WRITING WORKSHOP, pp. 106–107**

# Continue Close Reading

Use the following lessons for focused rereadings.

→ Make, Confirm, Revise Predictions, T32–T33

→ Character, Setting, Plot, T34–T35

→ Genre and Text Features, T44–T45

→ Prefixes, T46–T47

## ELL

### ENGLISH LANGUAGE LEARNERS

**Develop** Help children understand the concept of animals adapting to the hot desert climate. Say: *The climate, or weather, in the desert is hot, or very warm. To survive, desert animals have to find ways to stay cool. These are ways that the animals adapt to the enviornment.*

Point to the tortoise on page 104 and help children to complete these sentence frames: *How does the tortoise adapt to the hot desert weather? The tortoise _____.* Repeat with the jack rabbit and great horned owl.

→ # Language Arts

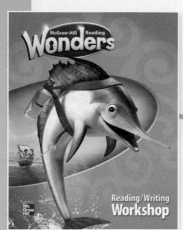

**Reading/Writing Workshop**

McGraw-Hill Reading

**Wonders**

Reading/Writing
**Workshop**

## OBJECTIVES

**CCSS** Write narratives in which they recount a well-elaborated event or short sequence of events, include details to describe actions, thoughts, and feelings, use temporal words to signal event order, and provide a sense of closure. **W.2.3**

**CCSS** With guidance and support from adults and peers, focus on a topic and strengthen writing as needed by revising and editing. **W.2.5**

## ACADEMIC LANGUAGE
*character, descriptive details, setting*

## Writing Traits: Ideas

**MINILESSON 10 Mins**

### Discuss the Expert Model

**Explain** Explain that writers use descriptive details to bring a story to life. These details also help readers better understand a story's setting and characters. Descriptive details:

→ create a clear picture of the setting in the readers' minds.

→ tell about the actions, thoughts, feelings, and responses of characters.

→ include sensory words that tell how things look, sound, taste, feel, or smell.

 Read aloud the expert model from "A Visit to the Desert." Ask **COLLABORATE** children to listen for descriptive details that tell about the characters' feelings and about the actions of the desert tortoise. Have children work in pairs to identify descriptive details.

### Discuss the Student Model

Remind children that descriptive details help readers understand a story's setting and characters. Read aloud the student draft of a realistic fiction story. As children follow along, have them pay attention to the descriptive details the writer added to her draft.

 Invite partners to talk about the draft and the descriptive details Ellie **COLLABORATE** added. Ask them to suggest other places in the story where Ellie could add more descriptive details.

### WRITING ENTRY: DESCRIPTIVE DETAILS

❶ **Prewrite** Provide children with the prompt below:

*Pick an animal. Think about where it lives. Write a story about a character seeing this animal for the first time. Be sure to use descriptive details.*

❷ **Draft** Have children choose a topic and make notes. Tell them to use their notes to write a draft. Remind children to use descriptive details as they write.

## Go Digital

**Present the Lesson**

**Writing**

CCSS **Writing Traits** Ideas

# Readers to...

# Writers

**Editing Marks**
∧ Add
∘y Take out.
⊙ Add a period.

**Grammar Handbook**
**Nouns**
See page 477.

Writers share their ideas by including details to describe actions, thoughts, and feelings. Reread the passage from "A Visit to the Desert."

Ellie wrote a realistic fiction story. Read Ellie's revision.

**Ideas**
Identify two descriptive **details**. How do these details help explain the **ideas**?

**Expert Model**

Grandma smiled at Tim's excitement. "Actually," she said. "That is a desert tortoise. It looks for shade made by the **shadows** of rocks. That is how it cools off. He burrows underground to get away from the heat."

**Student Model**

A Camel at the Zoo

at the zoo
Rosa is on a field trip.∧⊙
is eager
She ~~wants~~∧ to see the camel.
huge, brown
She sees the∧camel with
a large hump on its back⊙∧
Rosa is happy to see this
desert animal.

**Your Turn** COLLABORATE

☑ Identify the details Ellie used.
☑ Identify the nouns.
☑ Tell how the revisions improved her writing.

*Go Digital!*
*Write online in Writer's Workspace*

**READING/WRITING WORKSHOP, pp. 112–113**

## ENGLISH LANGUAGE LEARNERS
### BEGINNING

| Beginning | Intermediate | Advanced/High |
|---|---|---|
| **Complete Sentences** Provide model sentences based on the prompt: *The animal is a ____. It lives in ____.* Help children complete the sentence frames, using descriptive details. Ask *yes/no* questions such as, *Is your animal big? small? wild? Does it live in a tree? a park?* | **Add Words** Ask children to write three sentences based on the prompt: to name the animal, to tell where it lives, and to tell how the character reacts. Help them add a descriptive detail to each sentence. Ask *either/or* questions about details based on the animal, its home, and the character's actions, thoughts, or feelings. For example, *Does the character feel ____ or ____?* | **Write** Ask children to respond to the prompt. Remind them to include details that tell about the animal; the animal's home; and how the character acts, thinks, and feels upon seeing the animal. |

**Genre Writing**

**Writing: Informative/ Explanatory Text**
For full writing process lesson and rubrics, see:

→ How-to, pp. T480–T485

→ How-to, pp. T486•T461

**Language Arts**

## MINILESSON 10 Mins Grammar

### OBJECTIVES

**CCSS** Demonstrate command of the conventions of standard English grammar and usage when writing or speaking. **L.2.1**

**CCSS** Demonstrate command of the conventions of standard English capitalization, punctuation, and spelling when writing. **L.2.2**

• Identify nouns in sentences.

### ACADEMIC LANGUAGE

*comma, noun, series*

### Nouns

❶ **Explain/Model** Explain that a **noun** is a word that names a person, place, or thing. Display the following sentences:

The boy walks in the desert.

His mother sits on a rock.

Model identifying the noun that names a person in the first sentence. (boy) Then model identifying the noun that names a place in the first sentence. (desert)

**Think Aloud** *I read the first sentence and look for nouns. I see* boy *and* desert. *Which noun names a person? The word* boy *names a person. Which noun names a place? The word* desert *names a place.*

Repeat with the second sentence.

❷ **Guided Practice/Practice** Display the sentences below and read them aloud. Have partners identify the nouns in the sentence. Then have them tell whether the noun names a person, place, or thing.

One girl sees a turtle. (girl, person; turtle, thing)

Her friend sees a snake. (friend, person; snake, thing)

### Talk About It

**Using Nouns** Have small groups work together to make a list of nouns that name people, places, or things. Tell children to take turns choosing a noun from the list and using it in an oral sentence.

Go
Digital

I see a fish.

**Grammar**

## Mechanics: Commas in a Series

**1 Explain/Model** Tell children that commas are used to separate three or more words in a series. Explain that the word *and* or *or* comes before the last word in a series. Display the sentences below and read them aloud:

> The boy packs a map, sunscreen, and water for his desert trip.
>
> He hopes to see a rabbit, a turtle, a snake, or a bird.

Guide children to name the words in the series in each sentence. Have them point out the commas between the words. Have them also point out the word *and* or *or* before the last word in the series.

**2 Guided Practice/Practice** Display the sentences below and read them aloud:

> David saw a tortoise, a rabbit, and an owl on his vacation.
>
> Carol will pack a sweater, a jacket, or a scarf for her trip.

Have partners name the words in the series in each sentence. Have them tell where to put commas to separate the words.

---

**GRAMMAR PRACTICE BOOK** p. 26

Grammar: **Nouns**

Name _____

- A **noun** is a word that names something.
- Some nouns name people.
  Our <u>teacher</u> has a cat.

**A.** Circle the nouns that name people in each sentence.

1. The (boy) walks his dog.
2. His (mother) holds the leash.
3. My (sister) saw an owl.
4. The (family) visits the park.
5. A (farmer) cares for his horse.
6. A (baby) smiles at the cat.

**B.** Write two sentences about people. Circle each noun that names a person.

7. Answers will vary. _____

_____

8. _____

_____

26    Practice • Grade 2 • Unit 2 • Week 1

---

# Daily Wrap Up

→ Discuss the Essential Question and encourage children to discuss using the new concept and oral vocabulary words. Ask: *What animals did you learn about today? How do they survive in their environment?*

→ Prompt children to share what skills they learned. How might they use those skills?

## Materials

**Reading/Writing Workshop**

**Visual Vocabulary Cards**

adapt        fresh
climate      sense
eager        shadows
freedom      silence

**Word-Building Cards**

**Interactive Read-Aloud Cards**

box

**Spelling Word Cards**

because

**High-Frequency Word Cards**

octopus

**Sound-Spelling Cards**

→ # Build the Concept

### MINILESSON
### 5 Mins

# Oral Language

## OBJECTIVES

**CCSS** Recount or describe key ideas or details from a text read aloud or information presented orally or through other media. **SL.2.2**

• Develop oral language.
• Discuss the Essential Question.
• Retell story events.

## ACADEMIC LANGUAGE

*prediction, confirm, revise*

### ESSENTIAL QUESTION

**COLLABORATE**

Remind children that this week you are talking and reading about how animals survive. Remind them of the snakes, turtles, and other animals that hide in winter in "Swamp Life" and the desert tortoise, jack rabbit, and Great Horned Owl in "A Visit to the Desert." Guide children to talk about the Essential Question using information from what they have read and talked about on Day 1.

## Review Oral Vocabulary

Review the oral vocabulary words *capture, chorus, croak, reason,* and *visitor* using the **Define/Example/Ask** routine. Encourage children to discuss animals and how they survive when coming up with examples for each word.

## Go Digital

**Swamp Life**

**Retell Routine**

# Comprehension

MINILESSON
**5** Mins

## Interactive Read Aloud

### Reread "Swamp Life"

Tell children that you will reread "Swamp Life." Display the Interactive Read-Aloud Cards.

#### Strategy: Make, Confirm, Revise Predictions

Remind children that as they read, they should confirm and revise their predictions. Say: *As we reread "Swamp Life," think about the predictions you made yesterday. For example, when I read about the noises Danny heard, I predicted that frogs, birds, and insects were making some of those noises. I confirmed that those predictions were correct.*

**Interactive Read-Aloud Cards**

Read aloud "Swamp Life." Pause to model using the strategy. Prompt children to make predictions and to confirm and revise them as they read.

#### Model Retelling

Pause to retell parts of the selection. Say: *I can tell the story in my own words. "Swamp Life" is about a class that visits a swamp. When they get there, the ranger tells them to listen. At first, Danny doesn't hear anything. Then he hears noises that might be animals.*

Explain that when children retell a selection, they should tell the important events and details in the correct order.

#### Retell the Selection

After reading, guide children to retell the entire selection. Remind them to tell the important events and details in the correct order. You may wish to let children use the pictures on the Interactive Read-Aloud Cards to help them retell the selection.

### ENGLISH LANGUAGE LEARNERS

**Retell** Guide children to retell by using a question for each card. For example: *In the beginning of the story, what does Ranger Rachel tell the children to do? What are some of the animals that the children hear?* Provide sentence starters for children to complete orally. *Ranger Rachel tells the children to _____. The children hear _____.*

→ # Word Work

## Phonemic Awareness

**5 Mins** MINILESSON

### OBJECTIVES

**CCSS** Know and apply grade-level phonics and word analysis skills in decoding words. **RF.2.3**

**CCSS** Distinguish long and short vowels when reading regularly spelled one-syllable words. **RF.2.3a**

Substitute phonemes to form new words.

### ACADEMIC LANGUAGE
*blend, substitute*

## Phoneme Substitution

❶ **Model** Show children that changing the first sound in a word can sometimes form a new word. *Listen for the first sound in the word* got: */g/. I'll change the /g/ in* got *to /h/, and make a new word. The new word is* hot, */h/ /ot/,* hot.

Continue modeling with *lock/sock, top/mop, bone/cone.*

❷ **Guided Practice/Practice** Have children practice substituting phonemes. Do the first one with them. *The word is* fox. *I'll change the first sound /f/ to /b/. The new word is* box.

Have children substitute the first phoneme to form new words.

Change /h/ in *hose* to /r/.　　Change /r/ in *rope* to /h/.

Change /t/ in *take* to /b/.　　Change /p/ in *poke* to /j/.

Change /d/ in *dot* to /n/.　　Change /f/ in *fun* to /s/

## Phonics

**5 Mins** MINILESSON

### Review Short *o*; Long *o*

❶ **Model** Display the *Boat* **Sound-Spelling Card**. Review the sound /ō/ spelled *o_e* using the words *robe* and *doze*. Repeat with the *Octopus* Sound-Spelling Card. Review the sound /o/ spelled *o* using the words *job* and *pop*.

❷ **Guided Practice/Practice** Have children practice connecting the letters and sounds. Point to each Sound-Spelling Card. *What is the letter? What sound does it stand for?*

## Go Digital

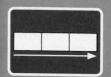

**Phonemic Awareness**

**Phonics**

**Structural Analysis**

## Blend Words with Short *o*, Long *o*

**1 Model** Display Word-Building Cards *n, o, t, e*. Model how to generate and blend the sounds to say the word. *This is the letter* n. *It stands for /n/. This is the letter* o. *It stands for /ō/. This is the letter* t. *It stands for /t/. The letter* e *is silent. Listen as I blend these sounds together: /nnnōōōt/. Let's read the word:* note.

Continue by modeling the words *drop, clock, smoke, drove,* and *globe*. Point out the silent *e* in the long vowel words.

**2 Guided Practice/Practice** Repeat the routine with children with *block, cone, not, hope, stone, flop, top, rode*.

## Build Words with Short *o*, Long *o*

**1 Model** Display Word-Building Cards *c, o, d, e*. Blend: /k/ /ō/ /d/, *code*.

→ Replace *c* with *r* and repeat with *rode*.

→ Change *d* to *p* and repeat with *rope*.

**2 Guided Practice/Practice** Continue with *rose, nose, note, not, hot, hop, hope, home*.

<sup>MINILESSON</sup> **5 Mins**

# Structural Analysis

## Inflectional Endings *-ed, -ing*

**1 Model** Write and read aloud *drop/dropped* and *drop/dropping*. Point out that you doubled the letter *p* before adding *-ed* and *-ing*. Explain that adding *-ed* to a verb makes the word tell about something that has already happened. Adding *-ing* makes the word tell about something that is happening now. Repeat with *hope/hoped* and *hope/hoping*, explaining that the final *e* in this word is dropped before the endings are added.

Say *dropped* and have children listen for the /t/ sound at the end of the word. Say *closed* and have children listen for the /d/ sound at the end of the word. Say *spotted* and have children listen for the /ed/ sound at the end of the word. Write each word and point out that the letters *-ed* at the end of a word can stand for /t/, /d/, or /ed/.

**2 Practice/Apply** Write the following words on the board: *poke, pose, nod, sob, pop, vote*. Have children write each word two times, adding the ending *-ed* and the ending *-ing*. Check their spelling before asking them to read their word lists aloud.

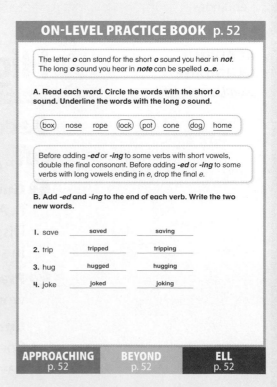

**ON-LEVEL PRACTICE BOOK** p. 52

The letter *o* can stand for the short *o* sound you hear in *not*. The long *o* sound you hear in *note* can be spelled *o_e*.

**A. Read each word. Circle the words with the short *o* sound. Underline the words with the long *o* sound.**

(box)   nose   rope   (lock)   (pot)   cone   (dog)   home

Before adding *-ed* or *-ing* to some verbs with short vowels, double the final consonant. Before adding *-ed* or *-ing* to some verbs with long vowels ending in *e*, drop the final *e*.

**B. Add *-ed* and *-ing* to the end of each verb. Write the two new words.**

| 1. save | saved | saving |
| 2. trip | tripped | tripping |
| 3. hug | hugged | hugging |
| 4. joke | joked | joking |

| APPROACHING p. 52 | BEYOND p. 52 | ELL p. 52 |

# → Word Work

## Spelling

**MINILESSON 5 Mins**

### OBJECTIVES

**CCSS** Know and apply grade-level phonics and word analysis skills in decoding words. **RF.2.3**

**CCSS** Distinguish long and short vowels when reading regularly spelled one-syllable words. **RF.2.3a**

**CCSS** Recognize and read grade-appropriate irregularly spelled words. **RF.2.3f**

- Use vocabulary words in context.
- Expand vocabulary by adding inflectional endings.

### ACADEMIC LANGUAGE
*plural, word sort*

### Word Sort with Short *o* and Long *o*

❶ **Model**  Display the Spelling Word Cards from the Teacher's Resource Book, one at a time. Have children read each word, listening for the vowel sound.

Use cards for *pot* and *home* to create a two-column chart. Say each word and pronounce the sounds: /p/ /o/ /t/; /h/ /ō/ /m/. Say each word again and ask children to chorally spell each word.

❷ **Guided Practice/Practice**  Have children place each Spelling Word in the column with the words containing the same vowel sound (short *o*, long *o*). When completed, have children chorally read the words in each column. Then call out a word. Have a child find the word card and point to it as the class chorally spells the word.

❸ **Build Fluency: Word Automaticity**  Have children chorally read words to build fluency. Conclude by asking children to orally generate additional short *o* and long *o* words. Write the words in the correct columns. Accept any long *o* word, but only list words with the CVC*e* pattern. Read the words together.

**MINILESSON 5 Mins**

## High-Frequency Words

*because, cold, family, friends, have, know, off, picture, school, took*

❶ **Guided Practice**  Say each word and have children Read/Spell/Write it. Ask children to picture the word, and write it the way they see it. Display the word for children to self-correct. Point out irregularities in sound/spellings, such as /k/ spelled *ch* in *school*.

❷ **Practice**  Add this week's high-frequency words to the cumulative word bank. Have partners create sentences using the words.

**Cumulative Review**  Review last week's words using the Read/Spell/Write routine. Repeat the above routine, mixing the words and having children chorally say each one.

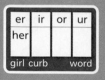

### Go Digital

**Spelling Word Sort**

**High-Frequency Word Routine**

**peered**

**Visual Glossary**

# Vocabulary

MINILESSON
**5** Mins

## Expand Vocabulary

Have children use the **Visual Vocabulary Cards** to review this week's vocabulary words: *adapt, climate, eager, freedom, fresh, sense, shadows, silence.*

**1 Explain** Tell children that words have different forms. Help them generate different forms of this week's words by adding the inflectional endings *-s, -ed,* or *-ing.* Review that s can be added to the end of a word to make it plural. The ending *-ed* can be added to the end of a word to make it tell about the past. The ending *-ing* can be added to a word to make it tell about something that is happening now.

**2 Model** Write the word *sense* on the board. Point out that the word means one sense. Then add s to the end to show the plural form. Discuss with children how the ending changes the meaning of the word.

Have children share aloud sentences using *sense* and *senses.*

**3 Guided Practice** Have children work in pairs to add the inflectional ending *-s* to *silence* and *freedom,* and deleting the ending *-s* from *shadows.* Then have them add the endings *-ed* and *-ing* to the word *adapt.* Ask them to share sentences using the different forms of the words.

## ENGLISH LANGUAGE LEARNERS

**More Practice** Practice spelling by helping children generate more words with short *o* and long *o* patterns. Provide clues: *It is something you wear on your foot. It rhymes with* lock. (sock) *It is a kind of flower. It rhymes with* nose. (rose) Write each word and have children practice reading it. Correct their pronunciation, if needed.

## Monitor and *Differentiate*

✓ **Quick Check**

Can children read and spell words with short *o* spelled *o* and long *o* spelled *o_e?*
Can children read high-frequency words?

⬇

### Small Group Instruction

| If No → | **Approaching** | Reteach pp. T66-T71 |
| | **ELL** | Develop pp. T82-T89 |
| If Yes → | **On Level** | Review pp. T76-T77 |
| | **Beyond Level** | Extend pp. T80-T81 |

# Comprehension Strategy

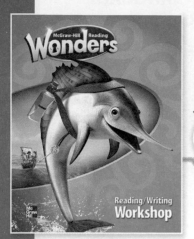

**Reading/Writing Workshop**

**OBJECTIVES**

**CCSS** Analyze how and why individuals, events, and ideas develop and interact over the course of a text. **R.CCR.3**

Make predictions about stories and read on to confirm or revise predictions.

**ACADEMIC LANGUAGE**
*prediction, confirm, revise*

# Make, Confirm, Revise Predictions

MINILESSON **10** Mins

## ❶ Explain

Tell children that when they read a story, they can make a prediction, or a guess, about what happens next. This will help them set a purpose, or decide what to look for, when reading. Explain that after children make their prediction, they can continue reading to check it.

→ To make prediction, children can use story clues in the text and illustrations.

→ Children may confirm that their prediction matches what happens in the story. They can continue to make predictions as they read.

→ Children may find that what happens in the story is different from their prediction. Then they can revise, or change, their prediction. Understanding how what happens is different from their predictions can help children to better understand a story.

## ❷ Model Close Reading: Text Evidence

Reread pages 104–105 of "A Visit to the Desert." Model how making and confirming a prediction can help children decide what to look for when reading and how it can help them understand a selection. Have children cite text evidence on page 104 that supports the prediction. Then have them cite additional text evidence on page 105 that confirms the prediction.

## ❸ Guided Practice

Have partners discuss the predictions that they made when reading the story, pointing out the details in the text on which they based their predictions. Partners should also discuss whether they confirmed or revised their predictions.

**Go Digital**

**A Visit to the Desert**

**Present the Lesson**

**Comprehension Strategy**

# Make Predictions

Use what you already know and what you read in the story to help you predict, or guess, what might happen next.

 **Find Text Evidence**

*After reading page 104 of "A Visit to the Desert," I predicted that Tim would enjoy his visit to the desert. I kept reading to confirm my prediction.*

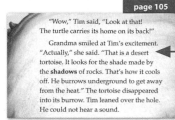

> page 105
>
> "Wow," Tim said, "Look at that! The turtle carries its home on its back!"
>
> Grandma smiled at Tim's excitement. "Actually," she said. "That is a desert tortoise. It looks for the shade made by the **shadows** of rocks. That's how it cools off. He **burrows** underground to get away from the heat." The tortoise disappeared into its burrow. Tim leaned over the hole. He could not hear a sound.

[On page 105, I read that Tim was excited to learn about different desert animals. I confirmed my prediction.

**Your Turn** COLLABORATE

Reread page 105. What did you predict would happen next? Look for clues in the text to decide if your prediction was correct.

Greg Newbold

108

**READING/WRITING WORKSHOP, p. 108**

 **ENGLISH LANGUAGE LEARNERS**
**ELL SCAFFOLD**

| Beginning | Intermediate | Advanced/High |
|---|---|---|
| Help children reread the first two paragraphs of "A Visit to the Desert" on page 105. Point out difficult words or phrases such as *excitement, cools off, burrows underground*. Define them for children. Help them replace the words with words they know. | Have children reread the first two paragraphs on page 105. Ask: *How does the desert tortoise get underground?* (It burrows.) *What is the name of the tortoise's home?* (burrow) Point out that *burrow* can be an action or a place (a hole in the ground). Then discuss how Tim feels about the desert now. Have children discuss whether Tim's feelings match their predictions. | Have children reread the first two paragraphs on page 105. Ask: *Why is it important to understand that* burrow *has different meanings?* Have partners discuss the question and tell the two meanings of the word as used on the page. Clarify responses as needed. Then have partners discuss what Tim learns and feels about the desert and tell if it matches their predictions. |

**ON-LEVEL PRACTICE BOOK** pp. 53–55

Read the passage. Use the make predictions strategy to predict what will happen in the story.

**Looking for Animals**

    Ms. Lee takes her class to the woods for a hike. She
12 tells her students to look for woodland animals. All the
22 children carry notebooks. They plan to sketch and take
31 notes about the animals they will see.

38     The group sets off down the path. High above, birds
48 sing in the trees. One boy points to what he thinks is a
61 robin. The others <u>disagree</u>. They say it is just a leaf.

72     The children hear hooting. It is <u>unlike</u> the other
81 sounds. They look up but are <u>unable</u> to see anything.
91 An owl looks down at them. Its brown feathers blend in
102 with the leaves. The children can not see the owl.

| APPROACHING pp. 53–55 | BEYOND pp. 53–55 | ELL pp. 53–55 |
|---|---|---|

## Monitor and *Differentiate*

 **Quick Check**

Do children make predictions about the story? Do they base their predictions on the text and what they know? Do they confirm or revise their predictions?

### Small Group Instruction

If No → **Approaching** Reteach pp. T64–T65

**ELL** Develop pp. T82–T83

If Yes → **On Level** Review pp. T74–T75

**Beyond Level** Extend pp. T78–T79

# Comprehension Skill  CLOSE READING

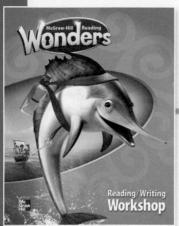

**Reading/Writing Workshop**

---

### OBJECTIVES

**CCSS** Describe how characters in a story respond to major events and challenges. **RL.2.3**

**CCSS** Describe the overall structure of a story, including describing how the beginning introduces the story and the ending concludes the action. **RL.2.5**

---

### ACADEMIC LANGUAGE
*character, setting, plot*

---

### SKILLS TRACE

**Character, Setting, Plot**

**INTRODUCE** Unit 1 Week 2

**REVIEW** Unit 1 Week 3; Unit 2 Week 1

**ASSESS** Units 1, 2

## MINILESSON 10 Mins — Character, Setting, Plot

### ❶ Explain

Tell children that stories have different elements. A character is a person or animal in a story. The setting is where and when the story takes place. The plot is the key events that happen in the story.

→ To identify the plot, children need to think about the key events that happen in the beginning, middle, and end of the story.

→ Children can look for details in both the text and the illustrations to determine the key events and the plot of the story.

### ❷ Model Close Reading: Text Evidence

Reread page 103 of "A Visit to the Desert." Point out that in the beginning of the story, we learn about the characters and the setting. We also learn about how the main character feels. Discuss how this information is included in the graphic organizer.

*Analytical Writing* **Write About Reading: Summary** Model for children how to begin a summary of the plot using details from the text and illustrations. For example: *In the beginning of the story, Tim finds out that he has to go to Nevada for his vacation. This makes Tim unhappy. In the middle, Tim goes to Nevada. He is excited to learn about desert animals.*

### ❸ Guided Practice of Close Reading

 Have partners work together to complete the graphic organizer. Tell them to go back to the story and find the key events that happen in the middle and at the end. Discuss each section as children complete the graphic organizer.

*Analytical Writing* **Write About Reading: Summary** Have children work in pairs to write a few sentences that summarize the plot of "A Visit to the Desert." Remind them to include information about the events in beginning, middle, and end of the story, and how Tim feels during those parts of the story. Invite pairs to share their summaries with the class.

## Go Digital

**A Visit to the Desert**

**Present the Lesson**

**Graphic Organizer**

Comprehension Skill CCSS

# Plot

The plot is the events that happen in the beginning, middle and end of the story.

 **Find Text Evidence**

*When I read "A Visit to the Desert," I think about the plot, or what happens in the story.*

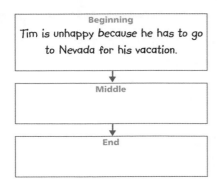

| Beginning |
| :---: |
| Tim is unhappy *because* he has to go to Nevada for his vacation. |

↓

| Middle |
| :---: |
| |

↓

| End |
| :---: |
| |

### Your Turn

Continue reading the story. Finish writing the plot in the graphic organizer.

*Go Digital!*
*Use the interactive graphic organizer*

109

**READING/WRITING WORKSHOP, p. 109**

---

**ON-LEVEL PRACTICE BOOK** pp. 53–55

A. Reread the passage and answer the questions.

1. What happened at the beginning of the story?

   Ms. Lee and her class went for a hike in the woods.

2. What happened in the middle of the story?

   The children looked for animals, but they didn't see any because the
   animals blended into the woods.

3. What happened at the end of the story?

   The hike was over and the class went back to the bus.

B. Work with a partner. Read the passage aloud. Pay attention to where you pause as you read. Stop after one minute. Fill out the chart.

| | Words Read | − | Number of Errors | = | Words Correct Score |
| :--- | :---: | :---: | :---: | :---: | :---: |
| First Read | | − | | = | |
| Second Read | | − | | = | |

| APPROACHING pp. 53–55 | BEYOND pp. 53–55 | ELL pp. 53–55 |

---

## ENGLISH LANGUAGE LEARNERS SCAFFOLD

| Beginning | Intermediate | Advanced/High |
| :--- | :--- | :--- |
| Reread page 103 in "A Visit to the Desert." Have children identify and discuss the key event in the beginning of the story. Ask: *At the beginning of the story, what does Tim find out? Is Tim unhappy because he has to go to Nevada or because it is time for vacation?* Allow children ample time to respond. | Reread page 103 in "A Visit to the Desert." Ask: *Who is the story about? How does Tim feel? Why does he feel that way?* Then have partners describe what happens at the beginning of the story. *At the beginning, ____.* Restate children's responses in order to develop their oral language proficiency. | Have children state what happened at the beginning of the story, using their own words. Ask them to explain to a partner how they figured out how Tim felt and why. Model correct pronunciation as needed. |

---

## Monitor and *Differentiate*

✓ **Quick Check**

Do children include the key story events in each section of the graphic organizer?

⬇

### Small Group Instruction

If No → **Approaching** Reteach pp. T72-T73

**ELL** Develop pp. T82-T85

If Yes → **On Level** Review pp. T76-T77

**Beyond Level** Extend pp. T80-T81

## → Language Arts

### MINILESSON 5 Mins

# Writing Traits: Ideas

**OBJECTIVES**

**CCSS** Write narratives in which they recount a well-elaborated event or short sequence of events, include details to describe actions, thoughts, and feelings, use temporal words to signal event order, and provide a sense of closure. **W.2.3**

❶ **Explain** Remind children that writers include descriptive details to tell about the setting and to tell about the characters' actions, thoughts, and feelings. Writers look for places where they can add details to bring the story to life.

❷ **Model** Read aloud the model from Your Turn page 57. Then think aloud to model revising to add descriptive details.

Meg and Tom go to the beach. They swim in the water. Meg sees birds flying in the sky. Tom finds shells on the beach. Then they see a crab near the water!

**Think Aloud** There is not enough information about the setting. I can add some descriptive words to tell more about it. I will revise the first sentence to say: *Meg and Tom go to the ocean beach on a hot, sunny day.* The descriptive details tell the kind of beach and the kind of day it is.

❸ **Guided Practice** Invite partners to continue adding descriptive details to the draft to tell more about the setting and characters. Use the prompts on Your Turn page 57 as a guide.

**Writing Model**

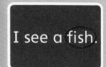

**Writing**

### Conferencing Routines

**Teacher Conference**

**STEP 1** Talk about the strengths of the writing.

**STEP 2** Focus on the target trait.

**STEP 3** Make concrete suggestions for revisions.

**Peer Conferences**

Provide these questions to guide peers as they review a partner's draft.

☑ Which details describe the setting?

☑ Which details describe actions, thoughts, or feelings?

☑ Where can descriptive details be added?

**I see a fish.**

**Grammar**

### 📝 WRITING ENTRY: PRECISE WORDS

❶ **Revise** Have children review their writing from Day 1. Ask them to revise their responses by adding descriptive details to tell more about the setting or characters.

Use the **Conferencing** Routines to help children revise. Circulate among children and stop briefly to talk with individuals. Provide opportunities for partners to work together using the **Peer Conferences** routine.

❷ **Edit** Ask children to review the rules on Grammar Handbook page 477 and check that they have used nouns correctly. Have children check for correct punctuation and errors in grammar and spelling. Have them use a dictionary to check their spelling.

**MINILESSON 5 Mins**

# Grammar

## Nouns

**1 Review** Remind children that a noun is a word that names a person, place, or thing. Read the following sentence aloud and guide children to identify the nouns.

> The man hikes up the mountain. (man, mountain)

**2 Guided Practice** Display the following sentences and read them aloud. Help children to identify the nouns.

> My grandmother enjoyed her vacation in the mountains.
> (grandmother, vacation, mountains)
>
> The guide talked about the snakes. (guide, snakes)

**3 Practice** Have partners read the following sentences. Have them identify the nouns.

> The teacher reads a book about animals.
> (teacher, book, animals)
>
> One student asks a question. (student, question)

## Mechanics: Commas in a Series

**1 Review** Remind children that commas are used to separate three or more words in a series. The word *and* or *or* comes before the last word in the series.

**2 Practice** Display the following sentences and read them aloud. Call on volunteers to write commas in the correct places.

> There are fish, turtles, and frogs in the pond.
>
> We can take a trip to the ocean, mountains, or desert.

---

**ON-LEVEL PRACTICE BOOK** p. 57

**A.** Read the draft model. Use the questions that follow the draft to help you add descriptive details.

> **Draft Model**
>
> Meg and Tom go to the beach. They swim in the water. Meg sees birds flying in the sky. Tom finds shells on the beach. Then they see a crab near the water!

1. What kind of beach is this? What kind of day is it?

2. What details can tell more about the birds, shells, and crab that Meg and Tom see?

3. What details might tell how Meg and Tom feel about their day at the beach?

**B.** Now revise the draft by adding descriptive details that help readers learn more about the setting and characters.

Answers will vary but should include descriptive details about the beach

setting, actions, and feelings of the characters.

| APPROACHING p. 57 | BEYOND p. 57 | ELL p. 57 |
| --- | --- | --- |

---

# Daily Wrap Up

→ Discuss the Essential Question and encourage children to use the oral vocabulary words.

→ Prompt children to review and discuss the skills they used today. How do those skills help them?

## Materials

**Reading/Writing Workshop**

**Literature Anthology "Sled Dogs Run"**

adapt

**Visual Vocabulary Cards**

| adapt | fresh |
| climate | sense |
| eager | shadows |
| freedom | silence |

**Interactive Read-Aloud Cards**

a  b  c

**Word-Building Cards**

because

**High-Frequency Word Cards**

box

**Spelling Word Cards**

Oo
octopus
o

**Sound-Spelling Cards**

# → Build the Concept

## MINILESSON 5 Mins — Interactive Read Aloud

## Go Digital

**Swamp Life**

**A Visit to the Desert**

### OBJECTIVES

**CCSS** Ask and answer such questions as *who, what, where, when, why,* and *how* to demonstrate understanding of key details in a text. **RL.2.1**

**CCSS** Use information gained from the illustrations and words in a print or digital text to demonstrate understanding of its characters, setting, or plot. **RL.2.7**

### ACADEMIC LANGUAGE

*illustration, key detail*

**ESSENTIAL QUESTION**

Remind children that this week they are talking and reading about how animals survive in their environments. Remind them of beavers in "Swamp Life" and the desert tortoise, jack rabbit, and Great Horned Owl in "A Visit to the Desert." Guide children to discuss the question using information from what they have read and discussed throughout the week.

### Review Oral Vocabulary

Review the oral vocabulary words *capture, chorus, croak, reason,* and *visitor* using the **Define/Example/Ask** routine. Encourage children to discuss animals and how they survive when coming up with examples for each word.

### Reread "Swamp Life"

Tell children that you will reread "Swamp Life." Pause as you read to model making, confirming, and revising predictions to better understand the selection. Prompt children to look at the illustrations and the text to find key details that can help them make, confirm, and revise predictions.

**Interactive Read-Aloud Cards**

### Analytical Writing — Write About Reading

Have children choose an animal from "Swamp Life" and write a few key details that tell about how that animal survives.

# Comprehension

## Key Details

**Use Visuals** Have partners use the illustrations on pages 102–107 to describe the things Tim sees when he visits the desert.

Remind children that this week they have been thinking about characters, settings, and especially the plot of a story, or the events that happen in beginning, middle, and end of a story. Remind them that one way to understand the plot is to identify key details, a skill they have used in previous weeks. Use the Shared Read, "A Visit to the Desert," to review this skill.

❶ **Explain** Review the definitions of the terms *key detail* and *illustration*.

→ A key detail is an important bit of information that helps readers understand more about the story. Children can use both the text and the illustrations to identify key details.

→ An illustration is a picture in a story.

❷ **Model** Display page 103 of "A Visit to the Desert." *I read that Tim and his family are going to visit Grandma in Nevada. What will it be like there? In the pictures, the setting looks like a dry place that might be a desert. I see a cactus and a lizard, which are animals that are in a desert. The illustration helps me predict that the setting of the story will be a desert.*

❸ **Guided Practice** Display "A Visit to the Desert." Prompt children to identify key details by using the illustrations and the text.

→ Have children look at all the illustrations in the selection. Ask: *How would you describe the desert environment?*

→ pages 104–105: Ask: *What does a desert tortoise look like? Is it big or small? Do you think Tim is having a good time? What other details do you notice in the illustrations?*

→ page 106: Ask: *What key details does the text give you about the jack rabbit ? What key details do you learn about the Great Horned Owl?*

→ Encourage children to use key details to confirm the predictions they made as they read the story.

 # Word Work

### Quick Review
**Build Fluency: Sound-Spellings**
Display the **Word-Building Cards** *o_e, o, i_e, i, a_e, a, sl, dr, sk, sp, st, tr, pr, pl.* Have children say each sound. For fluency in connected text see the Decodable Reader lesson in Small Group.

## Phonemic Awareness

### OBJECTIVES

**CCSS** Know and apply grade-level phonics and word analysis skills in decoding words. **RF.2.3**

**CCSS** Distinguish long and short vowels when reading regularly spelled one-syllable words. **RF.2.3a**

**CCSS** Demonstrate command of the conventions of standard English capitalization, punctuation, and spelling when writing. **L.2.2**

**CCSS** Generalize learned spelling patterns when writing words (e.g., cage → badge; boy → boil). **L.2.2d**

Blend phonemes to form words.

### ACADEMIC LANGUAGE
*blend, word sort*

### Phoneme Blending

❶ **Model** Show children how to orally blend phonemes. *Listen as I say the three sounds: The first sound is /m/. The second sound is /ō/. The third sound is /p/. Now I'll blend the sounds together to say the word, /mmmōōōp/,* mope. *The word is* mope.

❷ **Guided Practice/Practice** Have children practice blending phonemes. Do the first one together.

| | | |
|---|---|---|
| lone | got | top |
| log | hope | pose |
| rock | hose | knock |

## Phonics

### Blend Words with Short *o* and Long *o*

❶ **Model** Display **Word-Building Cards** *d, o, z, e.* Model how to blend the sounds. *This is the letter* d. *It stands for /d/. This is the letter* o. *It stands for /ō/. This is the letter* z. *It stands for /z/. This is the letter* e; *it is silent. The* o *and* e *work as a team to make the long* o *sound. Listen as I blend all three sounds: /dōōōzzz/. The word is* doze.

Continue by modeling the words *joke, hot, froze,* and *mop.* Point out the silent *e* in the long vowel words.

❷ **Guided Practice/Practice** Repeat the routine with *block, stop, mom, plop, stone, spoke, pond, broke, frog, froze.*

### Go Digital

**Phonemic Awareness**

**Phonics**

**Structural Analysis**

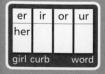
**Spelling Word Sort**

# Structural Analysis

## Inflectional Endings *-ed, -ing*

**1 Model** Write the words *hop/hopped* and *hop/hopping*. Point out that you doubled the letter *p* before adding the *-ed* ending and the *-ing* ending. Explain that adding *-ed* to a verb makes the word tell about something that has already happened. Adding *-ing* to a verb makes the word tell about something that is happening now. Repeat with the words *poke/poked* and *poke/poking*, explaining that the final *e* in this word is dropped before the endings are added.

Write the words *rocked, posed,* and *nodded.* As you read each word, point out the different sounds of the *-ed* ending: *rocked* (/t/), *posed* (/d/), *nodded* (/ed/).

**2 Practice/Apply** Help children blend the words *mop, mopping, mopped; stop, stopping, stopped; close, closed, closing;* and *joke, joked, joking.* Remind them that the letters *-ed* at the end of a word can stand for /t/ as in *mopped,* /d/ as in *closed,* and /ed/ as in *nodded.*

# Spelling

## Word Sort with Short *o* and Long *o*

**1 Model** Write the categories *Short o* and *Long o* on index cards. Place the cards in a pocket chart. Remind children of the short *o* sound, /o/, and the long *o* sound, /ō/.

Hold up the Spelling Word Card *dog.* Say and spell it. Pronounce each sound clearly: /d/ /o/ /g/. Blend the sounds, stretching the vowel sound to emphasize it: /dooog/. Place the Spelling Word Card below the *Short o* card in the pocket chart. Point out that *dog* has the short *o* vowel sound.

Repeat the process with the Spelling Word Card *home,* placing it in the Long *o* column.

**2 Guided Practice/Practice** Display the remaining Spelling Word Cards. Read and spell the words with children. Together, decide in which column to sort each word.

Conclude by asking children to orally generate additional short *o* and long *o* words. Write the additional words on the board. Underline the *o_e* spelling pattern in the long *o* words. Point out that long *o* words can have different spelling patterns.

---

**PHONICS/SPELLING PRACTICE BOOK** p. 28

| box | fox | dog | lock | pot |
| cone | home | nose | poke | rope |

**A. Word Sort**
Look at the spelling words in the box. Match each word to a vowel sound. Write the words on the lines.

| Long *o* | | Short *o* | |
|---|---|---|---|
| 1. cone | | 6. box | |
| 2. home | | 7. fox | |
| 3. nose | | 8. dog | |
| 4. poke | | 9. lock | |
| 5. rope | | 10. pot | |

**B. Compare Words**
Draw a line through the letter that does not belong. Write the correct word on the line.

| 11. poté ___ pot | 16. boxé ___ box |
| 12. hoḍme ___ home | 17. foxᵗ ___ fox |
| 13. pokke ___ poke | 18. nowse ___ nose |
| 14. dogg ___ dog | 19. locké ___ lock |
| 15. roḍpe ___ rope | 20. conṭe ___ cone |

**Monitor and *Differentiate***

**✓ Quick Check**

Can children blend words with short *o* and long *o*?

**Small Group Instruction**

If No → **Approaching** Reteach pp. T66-T71

**ELL** Develop pp. T82-T89

If Yes → **On Level** Review pp. T76-T77

**Beyond Level** Extend pp. T80-T81

 **Fluency**

### Quick Review

**High-Frequency Words:** Read, Spell, and Write to review this week's high-frequency words *because, friends, have, picture, school, off, know, cold, family, took.*

MINILESSON
**5 Mins**

## Phrasing

## OBJECTIVES

**CCSS** Demonstrate understanding of word relationships and nuances in word meanings. **L.2.5**

**CCSS** Identify real-life connections between words and their use (e.g., describe foods that are *spicy* or *juicy*). **L.2.5a**

**CCSS** Read with sufficient accuracy and fluency to support comprehension. **RF.2.4**

**CCSS** Read on-level text orally with accuracy, appropriate rate, and expression on successive readings. **RF.2.4b**

---

## ACADEMIC LANGUAGE
*phrasing, title*

**1 Explain** Explain that good readers read with correct phrasing. That means they group words together in phrases as they read. Tell children that they should pay attention to punctuation, such as commas and periods, to help them know how to group words together. This will make their reading sound smooth and natural.

**2 Model** Model prosody by reading page 103 of "A Visit to the Desert" aloud. Model how to read the page with appropriate phrasing and expression. Point out the places where you pause for punctuation and for groups of words that belong together in phrases. Model reading at an appropriate rate and with accuracy.

**3 Guided Practice** Have children read the text on page 104 to a partner. Observe their ability to read with appropriate phrasing and offer feedback as needed.

### Fluency Practice FLUENCY

Children can practice fluency using Practice Book passages.

**Go Digital**

peered

**Visual Glossary**

# → Vocabulary

**MINILESSON**
**5 Mins**

# Reinforce Vocabulary

**❶ Guided Practice**  Use the **Visual Vocabulary Cards** to review this week's and last week's vocabulary words: *eager, sense, silence, shadows, freedom, fresh, adapt, climate, customers, choose, check, tools, spend, chores, cost, jobs*. Work together with children to generate a new context sentence for each word.

**❷ Practice**  Have children work with a partner to orally complete each sentence stem using this week's and last week's vocabulary words.

1. There were two _____ in the store. (customers)

2. Tim will _____ whether to go to the pool or the park. (choose)

3. He will _____ the map to make sure he knows where to go. (check)

4. Kendra and her uncle use _____ to build a table. (tools)

5. Bill will _____ his money on a gift for his mom. (spend)

6. My _____ are folding the laundry and feeding the dog. (chores)

7. The girl felt a _____ of happiness when she helped her friend. (sense)

8. Jess gives his rabbit the _____ to run in the fenced yard. (freedom)

9. Our teacher asks for _____ when we take a test in class. (silence)

10. We filled the bowl with _____ fruit. (fresh)

11. Our class is _____ to go on a field trip. (eager)

12. We saw the _____ of the trees on the ground. (shadows)

13. It can be hard for wild animals to _____ to living in a house. (adapt)

14. Tropical plants grow in a warmer _____. (climate)

15. People work in different types of _____. (jobs)

16. How much does this book _____ ? (cost)

# Genre: Literature

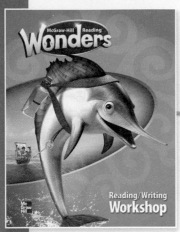

**Reading/Writing Workshop**

**OBJECTIVES**

**CCSS** Use information gained from the illustrations and words in print or digital text to demonstrate understanding of its characters, setting, or plot. **RL.2.7**

Recognize the features of realistic fiction.

**ACADEMIC LANGUAGE**
*realistic fiction, dialogue, illustrations*

**MINILESSON 10 Mins**

## Realistic Fiction

### ❶ Explain

Share with children the following key characteristics of **realistic fiction**.

→ Realistic fiction is an invented story that could happen in real life. The characters, setting, and story events are all believable.

→ In realistic fiction, the way characters act, think, and feel seems true to life. The dialogue, or what the people say, sounds real.

### ❷ Model Close Reading: Text Evidence

Model using the text on page 104 to decide if "A Visit to the Desert" is realistic fiction. Ask: *What events happen on page 104? Could these events happen in real life?* Then model using the illustration of "A Visit to the Desert."

**Illustrations** Point out the illustration. Remind children that illustrations show what is happening in the story and often carry key details. Ask: *How does the picture help you figure out that this story is realistic fiction?* Children should recognize that the picture shows a real place (the desert), a real animal (the tortoise), and an activity that could happen in real life (hiking).

### ❸ Guided Practice of Close Reading

**COLLABORATE**

Have children work with partners to find two other examples that show this story is realistic fiction. Encourage them to look at the text for the examples. Then have children share what they found with the class.

**Go Digital**

**Present the Lesson**

## Realistic Fiction

The story "A Visit to the Desert" is realistic fiction. **Realistic fiction**:
- is a story that could happen in real life.
- has characters that could be real people.

 **Find Text Evidence**

*I can tell from the text that "A Visit to the Desert" is realistic fiction. Tim acts like a real person. He wonders if he can get used to the heat.*

**page 104**

The next morning Grandma met them at the airport. Then they drove to the desert. As they hiked, Grandma explained that animals enjoy the open desert space. It gives them the **freedom** to move from place to place. Tim learned that the animals find ways to **adapt** to the hot desert weather. He wondered if he could get used to the desert **climate**.

**Use Illustrations**

The illustrations show me that Tim and his family are visiting a desert. I know that could happen in real life.

**Your Turn** COLLABORATE

Give two examples of how you know this story is realistic fiction.

110

**READING/WRITING WORKSHOP, p. 110**

### A C T Access Complex Text

▶ **Connections of Ideas**

Children may need support making inferences about characters and related ideas in the text.

→ *Is Tim still unhappy at the end of the story? Why does he change his mind about the desert?* (No. He has become interested in the desert and its animals.) *How do you know?* (On page 105, Tim is excited by seeing the desert tortoise. On page 106 he is so interested in the animals that he forgets about the desert heat.)

→ *At the end of the story, how is Tim like the desert animals he has seen?* (Tim's comments at the end of page 107 show that he has adapted to the desert climate as the animals have.)

---

**ON-LEVEL PRACTICE BOOK** p. 58

**Surviving the Winter**

In the summer, Jerry saw a family of chipmunks in his yard. What would they do in the cold winter? Jerry looked up chipmunk habits and learned they would hibernate all winter.

**Answer the questions about the text.**

1. How do you know this text is realistic fiction?

   It is a story that could happen in real life. The character Jerry could be a real person.

2. How does Jerry find out information about chipmunk habits?

   He looks up the information on the computer.

3. How does Jerry know the chipmunks will survive the cold winter?

   He learns that chipmunks hibernate in the winter.

| APPROACHING p. 58 | BEYOND p. 58 | ELL p. 58 |

---

## Monitor and Differentiate

✔ **Quick Check**

Are children able to identify two examples from "A Visit to the Desert" that show that the story is realistic fiction?

### Small Group Instruction

If No → **Approaching** Reteach pp. T64-T65

**ELL** Develop pp. T82-T85

If Yes → **On Level** Review pp. T74-T75

**Beyond Level** Extend pp. T78-T79

→ # Vocabulary Strategy

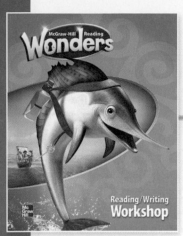

**Reading/Writing Workshop**

---

### OBJECTIVE

**CCSS** Determine or clarify the meaning of unknown and multiple-meaning words and phrases based on *grade 2 reading and content*, choosing flexibly from an array of strategies. **L.2.4**

**CCSS** Determine the meaning of the new word formed when a known prefix is added to a known word (e.g., *happy/ unhappy, tell/retell*). **L.2.4b**

---

### ACADEMIC LANGUAGE
*prefix, root word*

---

**MINILESSON**
**10** Mins

## Prefixes

### ❶ Explain

Remind children that they can often figure out the meaning of an unknown word by looking at its **word parts**. Tell children that a prefix is a word part that can be added to the beginning of a root word to make a new word. The prefix changes the meaning of the root word.

→ The prefix *re-* means "again." For example, if we *reread* something, it means we read it again.

→ The prefix *un-* means "not." If a door is *unlocked,* it means that door is not locked.

→ The prefix *dis-* means "opposite of" or "not." If you *dislike* carrots, that means you do not like carrots.

→ To learn the meaning of an unfamiliar word that has a prefix, children can separate the word into root word and a prefix. If children know the meaning of the prefix and the root word, they can find the meaning of the word.

### ❷ Model Close Reading: Text Evidence

Model using the prefix in *unhappy* to figure out the meaning of the word as shown on page 111.

### ❸ Guided Practice of Close Reading

Have children work with partners to figure out the meanings of *disappeared* and *unlike*. Remind children to identify the prefix and the root word and then use what they know about each prefix to define the entire word. Encourage children to think about whether or not the word meaning they have found makes sense in the sentence where the word is used.

**Go Digital**

**Present the Lesson**

---

### SKILLS TRACE

**Prefixes**

**INTRODUCE** Unit 2 Week 1

**REVIEW** Unit 2 Week 2; Unit 3 Week 5; Unit 4 Week 1

**ASSESS** Units 2, 3

Vocabulary Strategy CCSS

# Prefixes

A prefix is a word part at the beginning of a word. You can separate a prefix, such as *un-* or *dis-,* from the root word.

 **Find Text Evidence**

*I'm not sure what the word* unhappy *means. I know that* happy *means to feel good about something. The prefix* un- *means* not. *I think the word means* not happy.

Tim was unhappy.

 **Your Turn**

Use prefixes to figure out the meanings of the following words in "A Visit to the Desert."
**unlike,** page 106
**disappeared,** *page 105*

111

**READING/WRITING WORKSHOP, p. 111**

---

**ON-LEVEL PRACTICE BOOK** p. 59

To figure out a new word, look for a **prefix**, or word part at the beginning of the word.
The prefix **re-** means "again."
The prefix **un-** means "not."
The prefix **dis-** means "opposite of."

**Read each sentence. Underline the word that has a prefix. Then write the word and its meaning.**

1. The others <u>disagree</u>.

   disagree- the opposite of agree

2. They look up but are <u>unable</u> to see anything.

   unable- not able

3. Its brown coat makes it seem to <u>disappear</u> into the woods.

   disappear- the opposite of appear

4. The deer slips away <u>unseen</u>.

   unseen- not seen

5. The class <u>retraces</u> their steps back to the bus.

   retraces- traces again

| APPROACHING p. 59 | BEYOND p. 59 | ELL p. 59 |
|---|---|---|

---

## ENGLISH LANGUAGE LEARNERS

**ELL SCAFFOLD**

| **Beginning** | **Intermediate** | **Advanced/High** |
|---|---|---|
| Point out the words *disappeared* and *unlike* on pages 105 and 106. Demonstrate the meaning of each word using classroom objects. Help children use the words to complete sentence frames: *The pen ____ behind my back. A pen is ____ a book.* Then relate word meanings to prefixes and root words. | Point out the words *disappeared* and *unlike* and define them for children. Have children talk with a partner about the meaning of each prefix, *dis-* and *un-*, and the meanings of the root words. Allow children ample time to respond. | Point out the words *disappeared* and *unlike*. Ask partners to define each word and use it in a sentence to demonstrate their understanding of the words' meanings. Have them discusss how they used prefixes and root words to find word meanings. Correct children's responses as needed. |

---

## Monitor and *Differentiate*

 **Quick Check**

Can children identify and use prefixes and root words to determine the meanings of *disappeared* and *unlike*?

## Small Group Instruction

If No → **Approaching** Reteach pp. T64–T73

   **ELL** Develop pp. T86–T87

If Yes → **On Level** Review pp. T76–T77

   **Beyond Level** Extend pp. T80–T81

# Sled Dogs Run

*By* JONATHAN LONDON
*Illustrated by* JON VAN ZYLE

**Essential Question**
**How do animals survive?**
Read about sled dogs that live in a very cold environment.

*Go Digital!*

**❶** They were born in the spring: fat, tumbling puppy balls full of **fresh** puppy smell and puppy life. **❷**

**LITERATURE ANTHOLOGY, pp. 110–111**

**Wonders**
Literature Anthology

**Literature Anthology**

# Develop Comprehension

CLOSE READING

**Lexile** 480
*TextEvaluator™* 25

## Read Literature Anthology

### Before You Read
### Review Genre: Realistic Fiction
Review with children the key characteristics of realistic fiction:

→ Tells a story that could happen in real life.

→ Includes characters that act, feel, and think like real people.

**Preview and Predict** Have children look at the illustrations in the story. *What do you think this story will be about? What might you learn about sled dogs? Let's read to find out.*

**ESSENTIAL QUESTION**
Read the Essential Question: As children read, they should think about the characteristics of sled dogs.

*Analytical Writing* **Note Taking: Graphic Organizer**
As children read the selection, guide them to fill in **Your Turn Practice Book page 56.**

**❶ Strategy: Make, Confirm, Revise Predictions**

**Teacher Think Aloud** The title is *Sled Dogs Run*. The picture shows puppies. I know they will become adult dogs. I can predict that they will pull a sled. As I read, I'll check my prediction and revise it if I need to.

There was Skookum and Hawk and Bamboo.
Here in Alaska, in the Far North, *Skookum* means "smart."
"See how Hawk and Bamboo chase him but can't
catch him," says Papa. "He will be the leader."

112

113

**LITERATURE ANTHOLOGY, pp. 112–113**

## ❷ Skill: Character, Setting, Plot

What happens at the beginning of the story?
(The puppies are born in the spring. Let's add
a sentence to our Plot Chart to tell about the key
event at the beginning of the story.

| Beginning |
|---|
| The puppies are born in the spring. |

↓

| Middle |
|---|

↓

| End |
|---|

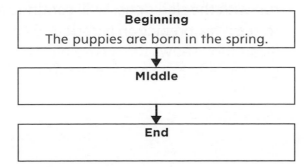

**A**ccess **C**omplex **T**ext

▶ **What Makes This Text Complex?**

**Organization** The beginning of the story
spans the four seasons. Then time slows
down to describe the events of just one day.
Identifying transition words is important to
understanding the passage of time.

**Specific Vocabulary** Some of the
vocabulary is particular to dog sledding.
Children may need help defining vocabulary.

Now, in summer, the training begins.
Sled dogs run. That's what they live for.
To run. To run and pull.

First, they wear a harness, to get used to it.
Then they pull a small log, bouncing and skidding
behind them.

114

**3** In the fall, they pull a cart for the
first time.
Papa runs behind me. I call out:
"Skookum! Hawk! Bamboo! Good dogs!"
For now, they run with older dogs.
I can't wait till the first snow.

> **STOP AND CHECK**
>
> **Make Predictions** What do you
> think will happen at the first
> snow? Use the Make Predictions
> strategy to help you.

115

**LITERATURE ANTHOLOGY, pp. 114–115**

---

**3** **Skill: Character, Setting, Plot**

Who is the main character in the story? How do
you know? What other characters have we read
about? What is the setting?

**STOP AND CHECK**

**Make, Confirm, Revise Predictions** What do
you think will happen at the first snow? Use the
Make Predictions strategy to help you. (Possible
response: I think that the girl will get to go on a
run with the sled dogs. I will continue reading
to see if my prediction is correct. Evidence: The
illustration shows the girl training with the pups.
She says she can't wait till the first snow.)

In the winter, the snow comes.
White on white, as soft as owl's feathers.
I lie down in the softness and make a snow angel,
but my dogs are **eager** to run.

116

**4 5** And by February, they are ready to pull as a team—
with me as musher. My first solo run! Mama heats
up a sloppy stew. The dogs must eat fast before it freezes.

Mama gives me a hug. "You will love the
quiet," she says, "and the oneness with nature."
"You will love the speed," Papa says, "and the
**sense** of **freedom**."

117

**LITERATURE ANTHOLOGY,** pp. 116–117

**4 Reread**

**Teacher Think Aloud** I'll stop here and make sure
I understand what I have read so far. The girl and her
father have been practicing with the sled dogs, but
now she is going on a run by herself. I'm not sure
why. I'll go back and reread page 117 to find out.
Now I understand. I can paraphrase: it is winter and
the sled dogs are ready to pull the sled with the girl.

**5 Strategy: Make Predictions**

Remember that you made a prediction at the
beginning of the story. Check your prediction to
see if it was correct. If not, you can change your
prediction based on what you have learned.

**A C T Access Complex Text**

**▶ Organization**

Prompt children to understand the
organization of the story. Have children
identify the season in which the
story begins:
spring. Explain that they can look for words
and picture clues to understand when the
story events take place. Continue with pages
114 (summer) and 115 (fall), helping children
understand that whole seasons are passing.
On page 116, ask what season it is. (winter)
Guide children to understand that from this
point on the story events occur on one day.

LITERATURE ANTHOLOGY **T47D**

When I come with the harnesses,
the dogs go crazy.
They run in circles,
howling and crying and yipping with joy.

Hitched to the gang line,
they are raring to go.
Mama says, "Be back by dark!"
In the North, in the winter, dark comes early.
Papa says "Trust the dogs.
They will know the way!"

118

6

I pull the snow hook and shout, "Hike!"
The sled feels like it's leaving the ground.
7 *Whoosh!* We're off—the dogs straining,
tugging, running out before me, huffing puffs
of breath.

We are racing cloud shadows.
We are racing a snowy owl.
We are racing the wind.

119

**LITERATURE ANTHOLOGY, pp. 118–119**

## A C T  Access Complex Text

### ▶ Specific Vocabulary

Prompt children to understand that some of
the vocabulary is directly related to the topic
of the story, dog sledding.

→ Have children reread the first sentence on
page 118. Ask them to use context clues
and the illustration to give a definition
of the word *harnesses*. Use the same
procedure for *gang line* (page 118), *snow
hook, Hike* (page 119), and other words in
the story specific to dog sledding.

### 6 Maintain: Key Details

Remember that we can get details about a
story by looking at the illustrations. Look at the
illustrations on pages 118 and 119 and explain
how the girl and the dogs feel about going on the
run. (They feel happy and excited.)

### 7 Author's Craft: Onomatopoeia

Read the first paragraph on page 119 and find
the word *Whoosh*. Sometimes authors use words
that sound like their meaning to make the writing
lively. How does the word *Whoosh* help you feel
hear and feel the movement of the sled over the
snow?

**8** We spook a snowshoe hare
and fly after it.
The sled whips.
The runners *shusshh*.
The collars and snaps jingle.
Hare disappears into white.
**9**

120    121

**LITERATURE ANTHOLOGY, pp. 120–121**

---

**8** ## Skill: Character, Setting, Plot

What happens in the middle of the story? Turn to a partner. Together, tell in your own words what has happened in the middle of the story. (The girl and the sled dogs go off on a solo run.) Now let's summarize the key events in one sentence and add it to the Middle box on our Plot Chart.

| **Beginning** |
| --- |
| The puppies are born in the spring. |

↓

| **Middle** |
| --- |
| The girl and the sled dogs go off on a solo run. |

**9** ## Prefixes

Here's the word *disappears*. If we didn't know its meaning, we could look for word parts we know. The word *disappear* has the prefix *dis-* and the root word *appear*. What does *appear* mean? What does the prefix *dis-* mean? Now tell what *disappear* means. (to come into sight; not; to go out of sight)

The dogs smell moose
and go after it.
Moose stops and turns around—
fire in her eyes.
With one kick, a moose can cave in a rib
cage. That's what Papa says.

I yell "Haw!" and my dogs swerve left,
away from the moose.
I yell "Gee!" and my dogs swerve right,
their keen noses scenting the trail.

122

123

**LITERATURE ANTHOLOGY, pp. 122–123**

# Develop Comprehension
CLOSE READING

## ⑩ Skill: Character, Setting, Plot

Turn to a partner and discuss what happens when the girl and the dogs see the moose. (The dogs want to go after the moose, but the girl steers them away from it.)

## ⑪ Maintain Skill: Key Details

Look at the illustration on pages 122 and 123. What details in the illustration help you understand that the moose might be a danger to the girl and the dogs? (Possible response: The moose is very big and looks strong and powerful.)

## ⑫ Genre: Realistic Fiction

Illustrations show what is happening in the story and often carry key details. How do the text and illustration on pages 122 and 123 help you figure out that this story is realistic fiction?

I hear a howl.
Is it the howl of wolves?
The hair stands up on my dogs' necks.

No, it is the howling wind blowing the snow sideways.
I hang on to the sled handle for dear life.
The storm is a hungry wolf, eating up the light. **13**
Just as we hit a frozen lake we are blinded.
We are lost.

**STOP AND CHECK**

**Ask and Answer Questions** What does the girl mean when she says that they are "blinded"? Go back to the text to find the answer.

124    125

**LITERATURE ANTHOLOGY, p. 124–125**

## **13 Author's Craft: Metaphor**

Sometimes authors compare two unlike things that are alike in one or more ways. Read page 125. How does the author compare a wolf and the storm? (They both howl.)

**STOP AND CHECK**

**Ask and Answer Questions** What does the girl mean when she says that they are "blinded"? (The girl means that the snow is falling so hard she can't see. The illustration shows heavy snow and the girl squinting. The text says that the snow is blowing sideways and the storm is "eating up the light.")

## **A C T Access Complex Text**

### ▶ **Organization**

Prompt children to understand the organization of the story.

→ Explain that the author includes a problem and solution in this story.

→ *What problem do the girl and sled dogs have?* (They are lost.) Tell children to read on and look for the solution to the problem.

But I remember what Papa says:
"Trust the dogs.
They will know the way!"
The dogs are my eyes.

Through the snow-blind world we drive.
All I hear is the howl of the wind—
and the boom of the lake ice shifting.
"Skookum! Hawk! Bamboo! Take me home!"

126

Suddenly the wind dies to a whisper, **14**
and the air clears, like a clean window.
"Whoa!" I call. We come to a stop.
"Good dogs! Good team!"
The sun is down and the full moon is rising,
tipping its golden light.

When my dogs stop panting,
there's a **silence**
as quiet as owl's breath.

127

**LITERATURE ANTHOLOGY, pp. 126–127**

# Develop Comprehension

CLOSE READING

**14 Strategy: Make, Confirm, Revise Predictions**

**Teacher Think Aloud** We predicted that the girl would run her sled dogs in the first snow. I've confirmed my prediction. We've read that the girl and the sled dogs are lost. What prediction can you make about what might happen next?

**Student Think Aloud** On page 127 I read that the moon came up, and there is golden light. I think that since the girl and the dogs can see where they're going, they'll find their way home. I'll keep reading to check my prediction.

**Skill: Character, Setting, Plot**

What key event happens at the end of the story? (The girl and the sled dogs find their way home after the storm.) Let's add it to our Plot Chart.

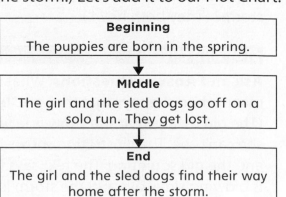

| **Beginning** |
|---|
| The puppies are born in the spring. |

| **Middle** |
|---|
| The girl and the sled dogs go off on a solo run. They get lost. |

| **End** |
|---|
| The girl and the sled dogs find their way home after the storm. |

Then I see, beyond the long blue **shadows** of the spruce: lights.
Our cabin in the woods!
Home.
And we become a part of the night and the moon and the snow and the trees and we run.

"Skookum! Hawk! Bamboo! Hike!"

We run to keep up with our hearts.

129

**LITERATURE ANTHOLOGY,** pp. 128–129

## Return to Predictions and Purposes

Review children's predictions. Ask them if their predictions matched what happened in the selection. Guide them to use the evidence in the text to confirm whether or not their predictions were on target. Discuss what children learned about how sled dogs survive by reading the selection. Did they learn what they wanted to by reading the selection?

## CONNECT TO CONTENT
### ANIMAL SURVIVAL

Remind children that this week they have been learning about how animals survive in different environments. Have partners make a list of the features and behaviors that help the sled dogs survive in the extreme cold. Ask them to explain how each entry in their list keeps the sled dogs alive in the cold climate.

## About the Author and Illustrator

**Jonathan London** and his sons love to go to "wild, snowy places." Jonathan started writing by making up stories for his children. Many of his stories are about nature and wild animals.

**Jon van Zyle** is the official artist of the Iditarod Sled Dog Race. This famous race goes 1,049 miles through the Alaskan wilderness each winter. Jon owns twenty Siberian huskies!

### Author's Purpose

Jonathan uses words like *softness* and *yipping with joy* in the story. These words describe things. How do they help you visualize what you are reading?

130

## Respond to Reading

### Summarize

Use important details about the characters, setting, and plot to summarize the story. Information from your Plot chart may help you.

| Beginning |
| Middle |
| End |

### Text Evidence

1. How do you know that *Sled Dogs Run* is realistic fiction? **GENRE**

2. How do you know that the story takes place where the weather is very cold during the winter? Include three important details in your answer. **CHARACTER, SETTING, PLOT**

3. Use what you know about prefixes to figure out the meaning of the word *disappears* on page 121 of the story. **PREFIXES**

4. Write about why the girl has to trust the dogs in the storm. Use details from the story to help you. **WRITE ABOUT READING**

### Make Connections

**?** How do animals survive in extreme environments? **ESSENTIAL QUESTION**

What can you learn from *Sled Dogs Run* about trust? **TEXT TO WORLD**

131

**LITERATURE ANTHOLOGY, pp. 130–131**

# Meet the Author and Illustrator

## Jonathan London and Jon van Zyle

Read aloud page 130 with children. *Why do you think Jonathan London decided to write about sled dogs in Alaska?*

## Author's Purpose

Have children find some favorite descriptive words they read in the selection. Ask them to draw a picture of what they visualized and use the words to write a caption about the picture in their Response Journals. Then prompt children to write another caption using their own descriptive words.

## AUTHOR'S CRAFT

### Word Choice: Imagery

Explain that authors use words to help create dramatic and exciting images for the reader. Discuss what imagery adds to the writing.

→ Authors use imagery to help readers visualize what things look like. Example: *The sun is down and the full moon is rising, tipping its golden light.* (p. 127)

→ Have children find other examples of imagery, such as ... *there's a silence as quiet as owl's breath.* (p. 127)

# Respond to Reading

## Summarize

Guide children through steps to summarize.

→ First, think about the most important events that happen at the beginning of the story.

→ Then think about the events that happen next. What does the girl do? Include only the main events, not every detail.

→ Write down the next main event. What does the girl do next?

→ Finally, tell about what happens at the end of the story.

## Text Evidence

Guide children to use text evidence to answer the Text Evidence questions on page 131. Model answering the questions as needed.

**1. Genre** This question asks how we know that the selection is realistic fiction. The characters in the story, a girl and her sled dogs, could exist in real life. The events could happen in real life.

**2. Character, Setting, Plot** We need to look at what the author tells us in the text. The author includes many details that tell you how cold it is. Three examples that tell us that this story takes place where it's very cold are that the dogs have to eat their food quickly before it freezes, the girl makes snow angels, and the lake is frozen.

**3. Prefixes** We know that *dis-* is a prefix at the beginning of the word *appears*. *Appears* means "comes into sight." Prefixes change the meaning of a word. The prefix *dis-* means "not" or "the opposite of." So, *disappears* means "not in sight" or "goes out of sight."

 **4. Write About Reading** This question asks why the girl has to trust the dogs in the storm. It asks children to use evidence from the text in their writing. For example: The girl feels lost, and I can tell from the illustrations that she can't see. But she tells the dogs to take her home and they do.

## Make Connections

### ESSENTIAL QUESTION

Have partners list ways that animals survive in extreme environments. Ask them to give examples of other animals they know, and to describe the extreme environment in which each lives.

**Text-to-World** Have children explain what they can learn about trust from reading *Sled Dogs Run.*

## ENGLISH LANGUAGE LEARNERS

**Retell** Help children by looking at each page of the selection and providing a prompt, such as: *What is the girl doing on this page? What are the dogs doing?* Point to and identify the girl and the dogs. Provide sentence starters to help children retell the selection, such as *The girl is ____. The dogs are ____.*

→ # Language Arts

## MINILESSON
**5 Mins**

# Writing Traits: Ideas

## OBJECTIVES

## Discuss Descriptive Details

**Review** Guide children to recall that writers can include descriptive details to tell about a story's setting and to describe the characters' actions, thoughts, and feelings.

**Share** Ask for a volunteer to share his or her revised writing from Day 2. Have the class listen for the descriptive details they hear in the volunteer's writing. Discuss with children how the details explain the ideas in the story. Invite the volunteer to point out his or her favorite descriptive details and tell why he or she chose to use them.

### OBJECTIVES

**CCSS** Write narratives in which they recount a well-elaborated event or short sequence of events, include details to describe actions, thoughts, and feelings, use temporal words to signal event order, and provide a sense of closure. **W.2.3**

**CCSS** With guidance and support from adults and peers, focus on a topic and strengthen writing as needed by revising and editing. **W.2.5**

### ACADEMIC LANGUAGE
*commas, descriptive details, nouns, series*

### WRITING ENTRY: DESCRIPTIVE DETAILS

**1 Prewrite** Ask children to choose a new topic for writing by searching their Writer's Notebook for ideas for a realistic fiction story. Or, provide a prompt such as the following one: *Write a story about an animal that seems to have lost its way home. Use descriptive details to tell about the setting and the characters.*

**2 Draft** Once children have chosen their topics, ask them to generate a list of descriptive details about the setting and characters in their story. Encourage children to refer to their lists as they write their drafts.

**Present the Lesson**

**Writing**

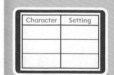

**Graphic Organizer**

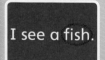

I see a fish.

**Grammar**

# Grammar

**5 Mins** MINILESSON

## Nouns

**Review** Remind children that a noun is a word that names a person, place, or thing.

**Practice** Display the sample sentences below. Ask children to identify the nouns in the first sentence. Continue in the same way with the remaining sentences.

My <u>father</u> reads a <u>book</u> about <u>animals</u>.

The <u>girl</u> draws a <u>picture</u> of a <u>lizard</u>.

A <u>neighbor</u> feeds the <u>birds</u>.

## Mechanics: Commas in a Series

**Review** Remind children that commas are used to separate three or more words in a series. The word *and* or *or* comes before the last word in the series.

**Practice** Ask children to rewrite the following sentences with the correct punctuation.

Kim sees lions zebras and camels at the zoo.

(Kim sees lions, zebras, and camels at the zoo.)

Rico wants a dog cat or rabbit.

(Rico wants a dog, cat, or rabbit.)

## Talk About It

**Guess My Noun** Have children in small groups write nouns on slips of paper and fold the papers. One at a time, have a child choose a paper, read the word silently, and then give clues to the group to guess the noun. Continue until all the nouns have been named.

### ENGLISH LANGUAGE LEARNERS

**Nouns** Show children a picture of a boy and then of a girl. Holding up one picture at a time and pointing to it, ask: "Who is this?" (a girl, a boy) Review that a noun is a word that can name a person. Display the following sentences:

The girl is happy.
The boy is sad.

Read the first sentence aloud as children follow along. Ask them to listen again to the sentence and raise their hand when they hear the word that names a person. (girl) Repeat with the second sentence. (boy)

# Daily Wrap Up

→ Review the Essential Question and encourage children to discuss using the oral vocabulary words.

→ Prompt children to review and discuss the skills they used today. Help them give examples of how they used each skill.

## Materials

Word-Building
Cards

a b c

because

High-Frequency
Word Cards

Literature Anthology
"Cold Dog, Hot Fox"

box

Spelling Word
Cards

Dinah Zike's
**FOLDABLES**

→ # Extend the Concept

### MINILESSON 5 Mins

# Oral Language

**OBJECTIVES**

CCSS Participate in collaborative conversations with diverse partners about *grade 2 topics and texts* with peers and adults in small and larger groups. **SL.2.1**

CCSS Recount or describe key ideas or details from a text read aloud or information presented orally or through other media. **SL.2.2**

CCSS Distinguish long and short vowels when reading regularly spelled one-syllable words. **RF.2.3a**

Substitute phonemes to form new words.

**ACADEMIC LANGUAGE**
*blend, substitute*

**ESSENTIAL QUESTION**

Remind children that this week they have been learning about how animals adapt to survive in different environments. Guide children to discuss the question using information from what they have read and discussed throughout the week.

Use the **Define/Example/Ask** routine to review the oral vocabulary words *visitor, croak, reason, capture,* and *chorus.* Prompt children to use the words as they discuss animals surviving in different environments. Then use the Define/Example/Ask routine to review last week's Oral Vocabulary Words *exchange, members, treasure, homework,* and *lucky.*

Phonemic
Awareness

m a
n t p

Phonics

I __ the jar.
fill | fills | filling

Structural
Analysis

# Word Work

 ## Phonemic Awareness

### Phoneme Substitution

**❶ Model** *I'm going to say a word and then change the first sound to make a new word. Here's the word:* coat. *Listen as I change /k/ to /n/, and make a new word. The new word is* note.

**❷ Guided Practice/Practice** Have children substitute the first phoneme to form new words. Do the first one together.

Change /f/ in *phone* to /k/.  Change /s/ in *sock* to /n/

Change /m/ in *mop* to /t/.  Change /l/ in *load* to /r/.

 # Phonics

## Build Words with Short *o* and Long *o*

**Review** Remind children that the short *o* sound /o/ can be represented by the letter *o*. Display the **Word-Building Cards** *h, o, p* and model how to blend the sounds to read the word *hop*. Repeat for the long *o* sound /ō/, blending the word *hope*.

Continue by changing one letter at a time with *mope, rope, rode, rod, nod, cod, code.*

 # Structural Analysis

## Inflectional Endings *-ed, -ing*

**Review** Write the words *stop/stopped/stopping* and *vote/voted/voting* and read them with children. Review the doubling of the final consonant *p* in *stop* before adding the endings and dropping the final *e* in *vote* before adding the endings. Remind children that when *-ed* is added to some verbs, the ending sound of the new word can be /t/, /d/, or /ed/.

**Practice** Write the following words: *hop, joke, trot, close.* Have partners work together to add the *-ed* and *-ing* ending to each word and write the words. Tell them to write sentences with two of the new words.

### Quick Review

**Build Fluency: Sound-Spellings** Display the **Word-Building Cards:** *o_e, o, i_e, i, a_e, a, sl, dr, sk, sp, st, tr, pr, pl.* Have children say each sound. Repeat, and vary the pace. For fluency in connected text, see the Decodable reader Lesson in Small Group.

 ### Monitor and *Differentiate*

 ### ✔ Quick Check

Can children read and decode words with short *o* spelled *o* and long *o* spelled *o_e*?

⬇

### Small Group Instruction

If No → | Approaching | Reteach pp. T66-T71

| ELL | Develop pp. T82-T89

If Yes → | On Level | Review pp. T76-T77

| Beyond Level | Extend pp. T80-T81

(→) # Word Work

## Spelling
*MINILESSON 5 Mins*

### Word Sort with Short *o* and Long *o*

**Review** Provide pairs of children with copies of the Spelling Word Cards. Have children place the cards face up on a table. One partner starts by giving a clue about a spelling word. When the other partner guesses the word, he or she should say it and spell it. Partners take turns giving clues until all the words have been named.

**Practice** Have partners work together to sort the words by vowel sound. After the words have been sorted, have children read the words in each group to confirm placement.

## High-Frequency Words
*MINILESSON 5 Mins*

### *because, friends, have, picture, school, off, know, cold, family, took*

**Review** Display **High-Frequency Word Cards** for *because, friends, have, picture, school, off, know, cold, family,* and *took.* Have children Read/Spell/Write each word.

→ Point to a word and call on a child to use it in a sentence.

→ Review last week's words using the same procedure.

**Spelling Word Sort**

**High-Frequency Word Routine**

## Go Digital

---

### OBJECTIVES

**CCSS** Read with sufficient accuracy and fluency to support comprehension. **RF.2.4**

**CCSS** Read on-level text orally with accuracy, appropriate rate, and expression on successive readings. **RF.2.4b**

**CCSS** Determine or clarify the meaning of unknown and multiple-meaning words and phrases based on *grade 2 reading and content,* choosing flexibly from an array of strategies. **L.2.4**

**CCSS** Determine the meaning of the new word formed when a known prefix is added to a known word (e.g., *happy/ unhappy, tell/retell*). **L.2.4b**

---

### ACADEMIC LANGUAGE
*phrasing, prefix, word sort*

# Fluency/Vocabulary Strategy

## Phrasing

**Review** Remind children that good readers read with correct phrasing. That means they group words together in phrases as they read. Tell children that they should pay attention to punctuation, such as commas and periods, to help them know how to group words together. This will make their reading sound smooth and natural.

**Guided Practice/Practice** Have children read a passage from the Shared Read aloud to a partner. Remind them to pause for punctuation and groups of words that belong together in phrases. Observe their ability to read with appropriate phrasing and offer feedback as needed.

### Fluency Practice

Children can practice fluency using Practice Book passages.

## Root Words

❶ **Explain/Model** Recall that to find the meaning of a root word, children can break the word into parts.

→ If the word has a prefix, such as *un-* or *dis-*, split the root from the prefix.

→ If the word has a suffix, *-ed*, *-es*, or *-ing*, split the root from the suffix.

Write and say *unhappy* and *jumping*. Model how to separate the root word from the prefix/suffix to understand the meaning of the root word.

❷ **Guided Practice** Write the words *unkind*, *disobey*, *boxes* and *packed*. Have partners figure out each word's root, and the word's meaning, by splitting the word into parts. Ask them to use each word in a sentence.

## Monitor and *Differentiate*

 **Quick Check**

**Can children read fluently with appropriate phrasing?**

### Small Group Instruction

If No → **Approaching** Reteach pp. T64-T73

**ELL** Develop pp. T82-T89

If Yes → **On Level** Review pp. T74-T77

**Beyond Level** Extend pp. T78-T81

CCSS **Genre** · Expository Text

**Compare Texts**
Read about one animal that lives in extreme cold and one that lives in extreme heat.

# Cold Dog, Hot Fox

There is a very cold place in Asia. It is called Siberia. The **climate** there is harsh. In winter, the temperature is far below freezing. The wind is strong. Few animals can live there because of the weather conditions.

## Siberian Husky

The Siberian husky is a kind of dog. It has body parts that help it **adapt** to very cold places. When the wind and snow blow, the dog squints its eyes. Even with its eyes almost closed it can still see.

A husky's fur has two parts. The bottom part is very short hair. The top part is long hair. The longer hair keeps water off the dog's body. It works like a warm raincoat.

The dog's tail is bushy. A husky can wrap its tail around its face when it goes to sleep. Its tail keeps its face warm.

If you look at the bottom of a husky's paw, you see thick black pads and fur. The paws help the dog stay warm.

The Siberian husky looks like other dogs. But it has special features that help it live in cold places.

**①** **Parts of a Husky**

Tail is furry.

Eyes have a special shape.

Ears have fur.

Fur is thick.

Paws have fur.

133

**LITERATURE ANTHOLOGY, pp. 132–133**

**Literature Anthology**

# Develop Comprehension

CLOSE READING

Lexile 510
*TextEvaluator™* 4

## Compare Texts   *Analytical Writing*

Review with children that in *Sled Dogs Run*, the sled dogs had physical features and behavior that helped them survive in extreme cold. Now they will read an informational text selection about other animals that survive in extreme climates. Tell children that as they read, they should think about how the animals in these selections are like the sled dogs in *Sled Dogs Run*. Have them **take notes.**

## ① Ask and Answer Questions

Look at the diagram at the bottom of page 133. What is the title of this diagram? (Parts of a Husky) Name two facts that the diagram labels help you learn about the Siberian husky. (Possible response: The husky's eyes have a special shape. The husky has a furry tail.)

## ② Ask and Answer Questions

Read the first paragraph on page 134. Use clues from the text to predict what you will read about in this section. (Possible response: The text will tell us about animals that can survive in the Sahara Desert.)

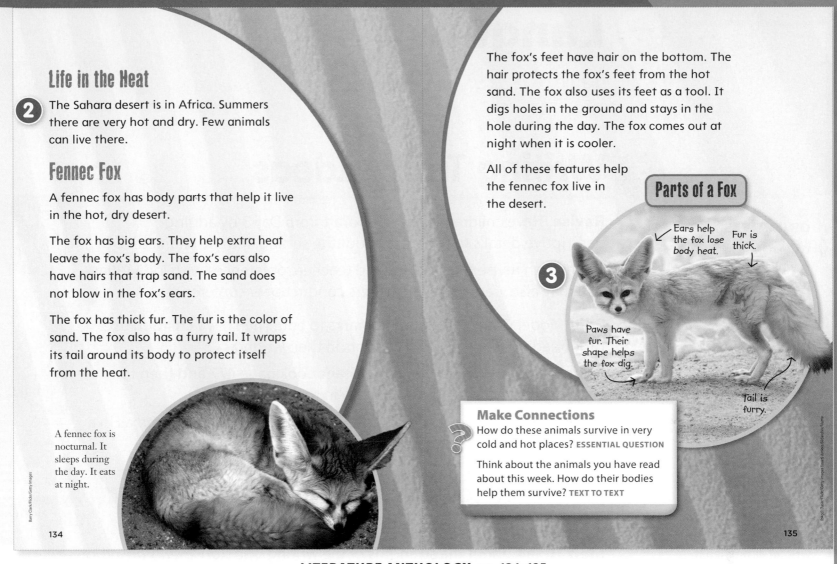

### Life in the Heat

**2** The Sahara desert is in Africa. Summers there are very hot and dry. Few animals can live there.

### Fennec Fox

A fennec fox has body parts that help it live in the hot, dry desert.

The fox has big ears. They help extra heat leave the fox's body. The fox's ears also have hairs that trap sand. The sand does not blow in the fox's ears.

The fox has thick fur. The fur is the color of sand. The fox also has a furry tail. It wraps its tail around its body to protect itself from the heat.

A fennec fox is nocturnal. It sleeps during the day. It eats at night.

134

The fox's feet have hair on the bottom. The hair protects the fox's feet from the hot sand. The fox also uses its feet as a tool. It digs holes in the ground and stays in the hole during the day. The fox comes out at night when it is cooler.

All of these features help the fennec fox live in the desert.

**Parts of a Fox**

**3**

Ears help the fox lose body heat.

Fur is thick.

Paws have fur. Their shape helps the fox dig.

Tail is furry.

**Make Connections**

How do these animals survive in very cold and hot places? ESSENTIAL QUESTION

Think about the animals you have read about this week. How do their bodies help them survive? TEXT TO TEXT

135

**LITERATURE ANTHOLOGY, pp. 134–135**

---

### ❸ Ask and Answer Questions

Let's look at the photograph of the fennec fox on page 134. What information can you learn by looking at the photograph? (You can learn what a fennec fox looks like, including the color of its fur and the shape of its body.) What information does the caption tell you that is in not included in the rest of the text? (A fennec fox is nocturnal. It sleeps during the day; it eats at night.)

### Make Connections
*Analytical Writing*

 Have partners make connections between the Siberian husky and fennec fox in "Cold Dog, Hot Fox" and the sled dogs in *Sled Dogs Run*.

### A C T  Access Complex Text

▶ **Prior Knowledge**

Tell children that this selection will cover a topic or topics they may not have any experience with—climates in Asia and Africa. They will read details about climates and animals that may be new to them. Encourage them to take notes and reread and ask questions when necessary.

**Language Arts**

 **Go Digital**

# Writing Traits: Ideas

## OBJECTIVES

CCSS Write narratives in which they recount a well-elaborated event or short sequence of events, include details to describe actions, thoughts, and feelings, use temporal words to signal event order, and provide a sense of closure. **W.2.3**

CCSS With guidance and support from adults and peers, focus on a topic and strengthen writing as needed by revising and editing. **W.2.5**

CCSS Demonstrate command of the conventions of standard English capitalization, punctuation, and spelling when writing. **L.2.2**

## ACADEMIC LANGUAGE

*commas, descriptive details, draft, revise*

**Revise** Have children revise their draft from Day 3 by adding descriptive details to tell more about the setting and the characters.

As children revise their drafts, hold teacher conferences with individuals. You may also want to have partners conduct peer conferences.

**Edit** Model using proofreading marks to edit. Then have children use proofreading marks to correct errors in their writing.

Invite children to review Grammar Handbook page 477 and then to check that they used nouns properly in their writing.

Encourage children to proofread for other errors, including commas in a series. Have children use a dictionary to check their spelling.

## Conference Routines

### Teacher Conference

**Step 1:** Talk about the strengths of the writing. *The story events are all in order, from beginning to end.*

**Step 2:** Focus on the target trait. *This descriptive detail helps me understand how the character feels.*

**Step 3:** Make concrete suggestions for revisions, such as those below, and then meet again to review progress.

## Suggested Revisions

**Focus on a Sentence** Read the draft and target one sentence for revision. *Add descriptive details to this sentence to tell how the character _____.*

**Focus on a Section** Underline a section that needs revision. Provide specific suggestions. *I'm not sure where the story takes place. Add some descriptive details to tell more about the setting.*

**Focus on a Revision Strategy** Underline a section of the writing and ask children to use a specific revision strategy, such as rearranging. *You have included all the parts of your story, but if you move this sentence to the beginning, you will help the reader understand why things happen.*

**Writing**

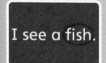

━ Make a capital letter.

∧ Add.

✐ Take out.

**Proofreader's Marks**

I see a fish.

**Grammar**

## Peer Conference

Provide these questions to guide peers as they review a partner's draft.

→ Do details describe the setting?

→ Do details describe actions, thoughts, and feelings?

→ Do details help explain the ideas in the story?

→ Where can descriptive details be added?

MINILESSON
**5** Mins

# Grammar

## Nouns

**Review** Recall with children that a noun is a word that names a person, place, or thing.

Display the following sentences. Identify the nouns in each.

The girl watches an owl in the desert. (girl, owl, desert)

Her sister sees a robin. (sister, robin)

**Practice** Write the following nouns on index cards: *teacher, beach, snail, girl, mountains, bluebird, boy, bear, desert, snake.* Have children choose a card and write a sentence containing the noun. Invite them to read their sentences to the class.

## Mechanics: Commas in a Series

**Review** Remind children that commas are used to separate three or more words in a series. The word *and* or *or* comes before the last word in the series.

**Practice** Display the following sentences and read them with children. Call on volunteers to write commas in the correct places.

The bird eats seeds, bugs, and worms.

I will draw a picture of a parrot, robin, or bluebird.

### Talk About It

COLLABORATE

**Series in a Sentence** Have pairs write two sentences, each with a series of three kinds of animals. For example: *I saw deer, bears, and raccoons in the mountains*. Have them read the sentences aloud, pausing slightly after each comma.

# Daily Wrap Up

→ Review the Essential Question and encourage children to discuss it using the oral vocabulary words.

→ Prompt children to discuss the skills they practiced and learned today. Guide them to talk about examples of how they used each skill.

**Go** Digital

www.connected.mcgraw-hill.com
RESOURCES
Research and Inquiry

→ **Wrap Up the Week**
# Integrate Ideas

## RESEARCH AND INQUIRY

**Animal Discoveries**

### OBJECTIVES

**CCSS** Participate in collaborative conversations with diverse partners *about grade 2 topics and texts* with peers and adults in small and larger groups. **SL.2.1**

**CCSS** Participate in shared research and writing projects. **W.2.7**

## Create a Fact Sheet

COLLABORATE

Tell children that they will work in groups to complete a research project about animals that live in cold and hot environments. Review the steps in the research process.

**STEP 1** ### Choose a Topic

Assign some groups to research animals that live in a cold environment and other groups to research animals that live in a hot environment. Guide groups to select one animal each to research for the project. It can be an animal they read about this week or another animal.

**STEP 2** ### Find Resources

Discuss how to use the selections, reference materials, and online sources. Have children use the Research Process Checklist online. Point out that their notes can help them answer "how do you know" questions.

**STEP 3** ### Keep Track of Ideas

Have children make a Layered Book Foldable® to keep track of ideas and facts from different sources. Model recording the names of the sources. Children can share information on the Shared Research Board.

Polar Bear
thick layer of fur
thick layer of fat
furs on soles of feet
small ears
den in snow

Dinah Zike's
**FOLDABLES**

### Collaborative Conversations

**Add New Ideas** As children engage in partner, small group, and whole group discussions, encourage them to:

→ stay on topic.

→ build on the ideas of others.

→ connect their personal experiences to the conversation.

**Polar Bears**

**Fact 1:** They have thick fur.

**Fact 2:** They use their fat for insulation.

**Fact 3:** They dig a den in the snow.

**Fact 4:** They have small ears to keep from losing heat.

**Fact 5:** They have fur on the soles of their feet to keep warm.

## STEM

**STEP 4** **Create the Project: Fact Sheet**

Tell children that they will create a fact sheet that includes five interesting facts about their animal and how it survives in its environment. Explain the characteristics of a fact sheet.

→ **Information** The purpose of a fact sheet is to familiarize the reader with a topic. In this project, all the facts should relate to the chosen animal and its environment.

→ **Text** A fact sheet does not give extensive information. Each fact should be delivered in one sentence that gets right to the point.

→ **Illustrations** A fact sheet often has illustrations that support or go beyond the text. The illustrations may be labeled.

Have groups work together to create the fact sheet about their animal.

→ Guide children to create drawings or use photographs that show characteristics of the animal and that show the animal in its natural environment.

→ Prompt children to include descriptive words in their sentences to make the facts interesting and fun to read.

## ELL ENGLISH LANGUAGE LEARNERS SCAFFOLD

| Beginning | Intermediate | Advanced |
|---|---|---|
| **Use Sentence Frames** Use sentence frames to help children identify the topic and facts on their fact sheet. *For example: Our fact sheet is about _____. Our animal lives in a _____ environment. Our animal has _____.* | **Discuss** Guide children to choose the most important facts about their animal. Ask: *What kind of environment does it live in? What does the animal need to survive? How has it adapted to its environment?* | **Generate Information** Prompt children to use their research to generate facts about how their animal survives in its environment. Encourage them to think about the most important facts to include on their poster. |

## Materials

**Reading/Writing Workshop**

**Literature Anthology Sled Dogs Run**

**Dinah Zike's Foldables®**

**Word-Building Cards**

**High-Frequency Word Cards**

**Spelling Word Cards**

# → Integrate Ideas

# TEXT CONNECTIONS  *Analytical Writing*

**Connect to Essential Question**

### OBJECTIVES

 Use information gained from the illustrations and words in a print or digital text to demonstrate understanding of its characters, setting, or plot. **RL.2.7**

• Develop answers to the essential question.

• Make text connections to the world.

### ACADEMIC LANGUAGE

*compare, opinion, present*

## Text to Text

**Cite Evidence** Remind children that they have been reading about how animals survive in their climates. Tell them that now they will compare these texts. Model comparing text using "A Visit to the Desert," **Reading/Writing Workshop** pages 102–107, and *Sled Dogs Run*, **Literature Anthology** pages 110–129. Use an Accordion Foldable® to record comparisons.

**Think Aloud** "A Visit to the Desert" and *Sled Dogs Run* are both about how animals survive in their climates. In "A Visit to the Desert," the animals have different ways to stay cool in the hot, dry climate. In *Sled Dogs Run,* the dogs' thick fur helps them stay warm in the cold climate.

 **Complete the Organizer** Have children use an Accordion Foldable® to record comparisons. Guide children to discuss and write about the animals in the selections and how they survive in their climates.

**Present Information** Ask groups to present their information to the class. Have children compare information given by different groups.

**Dinah Zike's FOLDABLES**

## Text to Self

**Discuss** Have children discuss what an animal needs to survive in their climate. Ask, *How can an animal adapt to live in our climate?*

## Text to World

**Discuss** Have children discuss what they have learned about animals surviving in different climates. Ask, *What can you learn from animals about how to live in different climates?*

# WRITE ABOUT READING  *Analytical Writing*

 **OBJECTIVES**

**CCSS** Draw evidence from literary or informational texts to support analysis, reflection, and research. **W.4.9**

## Write an Analysis

**Cite Evidence** Explain to children that as a group they will write about one of the selections that they read this week.

Tell children that using the evidence in the text, they will think about how the author uses details to support the genre of the story.

Review the Character, Setting, and Plot chart you completed for "A Visit to the Desert." Guide children to analyze the text evidence by asking *how* questions about the story.

→ How do the details of the story make this a realistic fiction story?

Work with children to compete the sentence frames using information from "A Visit to the Desert."

> I know this selection is realistic fiction because the author wrote about _____.
>
> I also know it is realistic fiction because the characters _____.
>
> The author included details, such as _____, that support the genre of the story.

Then have children select another text they have read this week and use the sentence frames to write about how the author supported the genre of the story.

**Present Your Ideas** Ask partners to share their paragraphs and discuss how the evidence they found supports their ideas.

# RESEARCH AND INQUIRY

 **OBJECTIVES**

**CCSS** Participate in shared research and writing projects. **W.2.7**

## Wrap Up the Project

Guide partners to share the information about the animals that they researched and to point out the details from their illustrated fact sheets. Prior to the presentations, preview the Presenting and Listening checklists online with children.

**STEM**

→ # Word Work

### Quick Review

**Build Fluency: Sound-Spellings**
Display the **Word-Building Cards** *o_e, o, i_e, i, a_e, a, sl, dr, sk, sp, st, tr, pr, pl.* Have children say each sound. Repeat, and vary the pace.

## Phonemic Awareness
*MINILESSON 5 Mins*

### OBJECTIVES

**CCSS** Distinguish long and short vowels when reading regularly spelled one-syllable words. **RF.2.3a**

**CCSS** Know and apply grade-level phonics and word analysis skills in decoding words. **RF.2.3**

**CCSS** Demonstrate command of the conventions of standard English capitalization, punctuation, and spelling when writing. **L.2.2**

**CCSS** Generalize learned spelling patterns when writing words (e.g., cage → badge; boy → boil). **L.2.2d**

**CCSS** Recognize and read grade-appropriate irregularly spelled words. **RF.2.3f**

Blend phonemes to form words.

### ACADEMIC LANGUAGE
*blend, word sort*

### Phoneme Blending

**Review** Guide children to blend phonemes to form words. *Listen as I say a group of sounds. Blend the sounds together to say the word.*

/j/ /o/ /b/ (job)          /f/ /ō/ /n/ (phone)          /b/ /ō/ /n/ (bone)

/k/ /r/ /o/ /p/ (crop)     /d/ /r/ /ō/ /v/ (drove)      /g/ /l/ /ō/ /b/ (globe)

## Phonics
*MINILESSON 5 Mins*

### Blend and Build Words with Short *o* and Long *o*

**Review** Have children read and say the words *vote, note, not,* and *hot*. Then have them follow the word building routine with Word-Building Cards to build *lot, pot, pop, hop, hope, cope, scope*.

**Word Automaticity** Help children practice word automaticity. Display decodable words and point to each word as children chorally read it. Test how many words children can read in one minute. Model blending words children miss.

## Structural Analysis
*MINILESSON 5 Mins*

### Inflectional Endings *-ed, -ing*

**Review** Review the rules for doubling the final consonant or dropping the final *e* before adding the endings *-ed* and *-ing*. Then have children practice writing words with *-ed* and *-ing*, such as *hopped, dozed, spotted, hopping, dozing,* and *spotting*.

## Go Digital

**Phonemic Awareness**

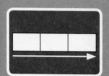

**Phonics**

**Structural Analysis**

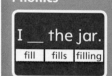

**Spelling Word Sort**

**High-Frequency Word Routine**

**peered**

**Visual Glossary**

# Spelling

## Word Sort with Short *o* and Long *o*

**Review** Have children use the **Spelling Word Cards** to sort the weekly words by vowel sound. Point out the two vowel sounds: short *o* /o/ and long *o* /ō/.

**Assess** Assess children on their ability to spell words with short *o* and long *o*. Say each word and provide a sentence so that children can hear the words used in a correct context. Then allow them time to write the words. In order to challenge children, you may wish to provide an additional word in each category in order to assess whether they understand the concept.

# High-Frequency Words

*because, cold, family, friends, have, know, off, picture, school, took*

**Review** Display **High-Frequency Word Cards** for *because, cold, family, friends, have, know, off, picture, school, took*. Have children Read/ Spell/Write each word. Have them write a sentence with each word.

# Vocabulary

**Review** Display **Visual Vocabulary Word Cards** *adapt, climate, eager, freedom, fresh, sense, silence, shadows*. Have children review each word using the Define/Example/Ask Routine on the back of each card.

## Monitor and *Differentiate*

### ✓ Quick Check

Can children read and decode words with short *o* and long *o*?

Can children recognize and read high-frequency words?

### Small Group Instruction

| If No → | Approaching | Reteach pp. T66–T71 |
|---|---|---|
| | ELL | Develop pp. T82–T89 |
| If Yes → | On Level | Review pp. T76–T77 |
| | Beyond Level | Extend pp. T80–T81 |

→ # Language Arts

MINILESSON
**5** Mins

# Writing Traits: Ideas

## Share and Reflect

**Discuss**  Discuss with the class what they have learned about including descriptive details to improve their writing. Guide them to recall that writers use descriptive details to explain ideas about the setting and characters.

**Present**  Invite volunteers to choose a writing entry from the week to share with the class. Compare the volunteer's draft with his or her revised text, and encourage the group to identify descriptive details the volunteer included. Have children discuss the writing by focusing on how descriptive details helped them picture the setting and understand the characters' actions, feelings, and thoughts.

**Reflect**  Have children use their Writer's Notebook to reflect on their progress as writers. Invite them to consider the following prompts as they write:

*How did descriptive details improve your writing this week?*

*What did you do well in your writing?*

*What would you like to do to make your writing better?*

**Publish**  After children finish presenting their stories, discuss how the class will publish a collection of their stories on a class blog or Website. Have children add titles and illustrations to their stories. Guide them to use digital tools to publish their stories and illustrations. Allow children to make decisions regarding the organization of their stories.

**Writing**

**Checklists**

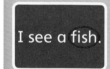

I see a fish.

**Grammar**

### OBJECTIVES

 **CCSS**  Write narratives in which they recount a well-elaborated event or short sequence of events, include details to describe actions, thoughts, and feelings, use temporal words to signal event order, and provide a sense of closure.  **W.2.3**

 **CCSS**  Demonstrate command of the conventions of standard English grammar and usage when writing or speaking.  **L.2.1**

**CCSS**  Demonstrate command of the conventions of standard English capitalization, punctuation, and spelling when writing.  **L.2.2**

### ACADEMIC LANGUAGE
*descriptive details, present, nouns, commas, series*

# Grammar

## Nouns

**Review** Ask children to tell what a noun is. (A noun names a person, place, or thing.) Ask them to provide some examples of nouns. Have them tell whether the nouns name people, places, or things.

**Practice** Display the following nouns: *child, lake, beach, shells*. Have children work in pairs to write each noun in a sentence. Ask pairs to read aloud their sentences to the class.

## Mechanics: Commas in a Series

**Review** Remind children that when there are three or more words in a series, commas are used to separate the words. The word *and* or *or* comes before the last word in the series.

**Practice** Write the following series of words. Have children choose one series and write the words in a sentence, using commas correctly.

> red yellow blue
>
> park school store
>
> horse cow goat

## Reteach

If children have difficulty identifying nouns in sentences or using commas in a series, review the use of each. Provide opportunities for children to practice the skills in small groups, with a partner, or independently.

### Talk About It

**List of Nouns** Have children work in pairs to write a list of three nouns. The first should name a person, the second a place, and the third a thing. Give an example, such as *guide* (person), *desert* (place), *cactus* (thing). After partners have completed their list, have them take turns reading a noun and using it in an oral sentence.

# Wrap Up the Week

→ Review the Essential Question and encourage children to discuss using the oral vocabulary words.

→ Review the comprehension strategy and the comprehension skill.

→ Review short o spelled *o* and long *o* spelled *o_e*.

→ Review the features of a realistic fiction story.

# → Approaching Level

**Lexile** 220
*TextEvaluator*™ 4

## OBJECTIVES

 Describe how characters in a story respond to major events and challenges. **RL.2.3**

 Describe the overall structure of a story, including describing how the beginning introduces the story and the ending concludes the action. **RL.2.5**

## MATERIALS

Leveled Reader
*Hippos at the Zoo*

## Leveled Reader:
### *Hippos at the Zoo*

### Before Reading

#### Preview and Predict

Have children turn to the title page. Read the title and author name and have children repeat. Preview the selection's illustrations. Prompt children to predict what the selection might be about.

#### Review Genre: Realistic Fiction

Have children recall that realistic fiction is a made-up story that could happen in real life. The characters, setting, and events are all believable.

##### ESSENTIAL QUESTION

Remind children of the Essential Question: How do animals survive? Set a purpose for reading: *Let's read to find out how hippos live at the zoo.*

Remind children that as they read a selection, they can ask questions about what they do not understand or want to know more about.

### During Reading

#### Guided Comprehension

As children whisper read *Hippos at the Zoo*, monitor and provide guidance, correcting blending and modeling the key strategies and skills.

#### Strategy: Make, Confirm, and Revise Predictions

Remind children that as they read, they can make predictions about what will happen next. Model making and confirming predictions on pages 5 and 6. *Val sees a pool of water where the hippos live. I predict that Val will see a hippo in the water. I'll check my prediction as I read page 6 to see if it's correct.*

#### Skill: Character, Setting, Plot

Remind children that a character is a person or animal in a story, the setting tells where and when the story takes place, and the plot is the events that happen at the beginning, middle, and end of the story. As you read, ask: *What key events happen in this part of the story?* Display a Beginning, Middle, and End graphic organizer for children to copy.

**Go Digital**

**Leveled Readers**

**Graphic Organizer**

**Retelling Cards**

Model recording children's answers in the Beginning, Middle, and End boxes of the chart. Have children record the answers in their charts.

**Think Aloud** In the story, the first thing Val and her mom do is go to the zoo. This happens at the beginning of the story. Let's add this event to the Beginning box in our Beginning, Middle, and End chart.

Lead children to record key events at the middle and end of the story.

## After Reading

### Respond to Reading

Have children complete Respond to Reading on page 16 after reading.

### Retell

Have children take turns retelling the selection, using the retelling cards as a guide. Help children make a personal connection by asking: *Have you seen animals at a zoo? What did you learn about them?*

### Model Fluency

Read the sentences one at a time. Have children chorally repeat. Point out how you pause for punctuation.

### Apply

Have children practice reading with partners. Provide feedback as needed.

## PAIRED READ ...

### "Hippos"

### Make Connections: Write About It · *Analytical Writing*

Before reading, ask children to note that the genre of this text is expository text. Then discuss the Compare Texts statement. After reading, ask children to make connections between "Hippos" and "Hippos at the Zoo."

**Leveled Reader**

### *Analytical Writing*

#### COMPARE TEXTS

→ Have children use text evidence to compare the expository text to the realistic fiction story.

---

## Literature Circles

Lead children in conducting a literature circle using the Thinkmark questions to guide the discussion. You may wish to discuss what children have learned about hippos from both selections in the leveled reader.

## Level Up

Level-up lessons available online.

**IF** children read the `Approaching Level` fluently and answered the questions

**THEN** pair them with children who have proficiently read the `On Level` and have approaching children

• echo-read the `On Level` main selection.

• use self-stick notes to mark one detail they would like to discuss in each section.

## A C T Access Complex Text

The `On Level` challenges children by including more **specific vocabulary** and **complex sentence structures**.

# → Approaching Level

## Phonemic Awareness

### PHONEME BLENDING

**TIER 2**

**OBJECTIVES**

Blend phonemes to form words.

 **I Do** Explain to children that they will be blending sounds to form words. *Listen as I say three sounds: /j/ /ōōō/ /k/. Say the sounds with me: /j/ /ōōō/ /k/. I'm going to blend the sounds together: /jōōōk/, joke. We blended the word joke.*

 **We Do** *Listen as I say three sounds: /hhh/ /ōōō/ /mmm/. Repeat the sounds: /hhh/ /ōōō/ /mmm/. Let's blend the sounds: /hhh/ /ōōō/ /mmm/, home. We made one word: home.*

Repeat this routine with the following words:

pop     cone     got     pole     hole     job     bone     woke

 **You Do** *It's your turn. I want you to blend the sounds I say together to form a word.*

crop     broke     lone     smoke     rode     mom     fog     stone

**Repeat** the blending routine with additional short and long *o* words.

### PHONEME ADDITION

**TIER 2**

**OBJECTIVES**

 **CCSS** Know and apply grade-level phonics and word analysis skills in decoding words. **RF.2.3**

**CCSS** Distinguish long and short vowels when reading regularly spelled one-syllable words. **RF.2.3a**

Add phonemes to existing words to form new words.

 **I Do** Explain to children that they will be adding phonemes. *Listen as I say a word: ox, /ooo/ /ks/. Now listen as I add the sound /f/ to the beginning of ox: /fff/ /ooo/ /ks/, fox. When I add /f/ to ox, the new word is fox.*

 **We Do** *Listen as I say a word: cope. Say the word with me: /k/ /ōōō/ /p/. Let's add the sound /s/ to the beginning of cope. What is the new word? The new word is scope. When we add /s/ to the beginning of cope, we make the word scope.*

 **You Do** *It's your turn. Add the sound to the beginning of the word to form a new word.*

/s/ poke     /p/ rose     /b/ ox     /t/ rot     /f/ lop     /s/ tone

**Repeat** the addition routine with additional short and long *o* words.

You may wish to review Phonemic Awareness with **ELL** using this section.

# PHONEME SUBSTITUTION

## OBJECTIVES

**CCSS** Know and apply grade-level phonics and word analysis skills in decoding words. **RF.2.3**

**CCSS** Distinguish long and short vowels when reading regularly spelled one-syllable words. **RF.2.3a**

Substitute phonemes to form new words.

**I Do** Explain to children that they will be substituting phonemes. *When you substitute, you replace something with something else. When you substitute a phoneme, you are replacing one sound with another sound.*

*Listen as I say a word:* cot, /k/ /ooo/ /t/. *The first sound in* cot *is* /k/. *Now I'll change the* /k/ *in* cot *to* /p/ *and make a new word:* /pooot/, pot. *The new word is* pot.

*Listen for the first sound in the word I say:* tone. *The first sound in* tone *is* /t/. *Now listen as I change the* /t/ *in* tone *to* /k/: /kōōōnnn/, cone. *The new word is* cone.

**We Do** *Listen as I say a word:* bone. *Say the word with me:* /b/ /ōōō/ /nnn/. *Let's change the first sound in* bone *to* /zzz/. *The new word is* zone. *We changed the* /b/ *in* bone *to* /z/ *and made the word* zone.

*Let's try another one. Listen to the first sound in this word:* rock. *Say the word with me:* /roook/. *Let's change* /r/ *to* /l/. *The new word is* lock.

Repeat this routine by substituting the initial phoneme in the following words:

hog, log    nod, cod    rope, hope    pole, mole    home, dome    job, rob

**You Do** *It's your turn. Change the first sound in each word to form a new word.*

Change /f/ in *phone* to /b/.          Change /n/ in *nose* to /p/.

Change /s/ in *sock* to /r/.          Change /v/ in *vote* to /n/.

Change /d/ in *dot* to /g/.          Change /p/ in *poke* to /w/.

## ELL ENGLISH LANGUAGE LEARNERS

For the **ELLs** who need **phonics, decoding,** and **fluency** practice, use scaffolding methods as necessary to ensure children understand the meaning of the words. Refer to the Language Transfers Handbook for phonics elements that may not transfer in children's native languages.

# → Approaching Level

## Phonics

### CONNECT *o* TO /o/ AND *o_e* TO /ō/

**OBJECTIVES**

 **CCSS** Know and apply grade-level phonics and word analysis skills in decoding words. **RF.2.3**

 **CCSS** Distinguish long and short vowels when reading regularly spelled one-syllable words. **RF.2.3a**

 **I Do** Display the Word-Building Card *o*. Say: *This is lowercase* o. *I am going to trace the letter* o *while I say the /ooo/ sound that the letter* o *stands for. The letter* o *can also stand for the /ō/ sound. Now say /ōōō/ with me.* Trace the letter *o* while saying each sound five times.

 **We Do** Have children trace the lowercase *o* on the Word-Building Cards with their finger while saying /ooo/. Trace the letter *o* five times and say /ooo/ with children. Repeat with long *o* spelled *o_e*.

 **You Do** Have children connect the letters *o_e* to the sound /ō/. Write the letters *o_e* as you say /ō/. Have children write *o_e* while saying /ō/ five to ten times. Repeat the process with /o/.

**Repeat,** connecting the letter *o* to /o/ and the letters *o_e* to /ō/ through tracing and writing the letters *oo* throughout the week.

**Sound/Spellings Fluency** Display the Word-Building Cards: *o_e, o, i_e, i, a_e, a, sl, dr, sk, sp, st, tr, pr, pl.* Have children chorally say each sound. Repeat and vary the pace.

### BLEND WORDS WITH SHORT *o*, LONG *o*

**OBJECTIVES**

**CCSS** Know and apply grade-level phonics and word analysis skills in decoding words. **RF.2.3**

**CCSS** Distinguish long and short vowels when reading regularly spelled one-syllable words. **RF.2.3a**

 **I Do** Display Word-Building Cards r, o, p, e. *This is the letter* r. *It stands for /r/. This is the letter* o. *It stands for /ō/ in this word. This is the letter* p. *It stands for /p/. The letter* e *is silent. I'll blend these sounds together: /rrrōōōp/, rope. Repeat for short* o *with fog.*

 **We Do** Guide children to blend the sounds and read: *stop, stone, job, broke, hot, home.*

 **You Do** Have children blend and decode: *mom, pop, tone, spoke, got, jog, bone.*

**Repeat,** blending additional words with short and long *o*.

You may wish to review Phonics with **ELL** using this section.

# BUILD WORDS WITH SHORT *o*, LONG *o*

**OBJECTIVES**

Distinguish long and short vowels when reading regularly spelled one-syllable words. **RF.2.3a**

**I Do** Display Word-Building Cards *r, o, d*. *These are the letters* r, o, *and* d. *They stand for* /r/, /o/, *and* /d/. *I will blend* /r/, /o/, *and* /d/ *together:* /rod/, rod. *The word is* rod. *Repeat for the long* o *sound, blending* rode.

**We Do** Make the word *hop* using Word-Building Cards. *Let's blend:* /h/ /o/ /p/, /hop/, hop. *I will add an* e *to the end of* hop. *The* e *is silent, and now the* o *stands for the* /ō/ *sound. Let's blend and read the new word:* /h/ /ō/ /p/, /hōp/, hope.

**You Do** Have children build the words: *lost, cot, pot, tot, tote, ton, tone, cone, bone.*

**Decodable Reader** Introduce the Decodable Reader selection. Point to the title. Have children sound out each word. Discuss the title and illustrations.

**First Read** Turn to page 2. Have children point to each word, sounding out decodable words and saying the high-frequency words quickly. Children should chorally read the story the first time through.

# BLEND WORDS WITH SHORT *o*, LONG *o*

**OBJECTIVES**

Distinguish long and short vowels when reading regularly spelled one-syllable words. **RF.2.3a**

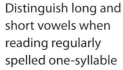

**I Do** Display Word-Building Cards *j, o, k, e*. *This is the letter* j. *It stands for* /j/. *This is the letter* o. *It stands for* /ō/. *This is the letter* k. *It stands for* /k/. *This is the letter* e. *It is silent. Listen as I blend all three sounds:* /jōōk/, joke. *The word is* joke.

**We Do** Blend and read the words *crop, poke, hot, job, hole* with children.

**You Do** Display the following words: *cod, fox, lot, not, drove, home, spoke, rode.* Have children blend and read the words.

**Decodable Reader** Have children reread the Decodable Reader selection.

**Check Comprehension** As children read, monitor their comprehension. Ask: *Why is the girl scared at first? What happens when the girl starts school in Nome?*

# BLEND WORDS WITH SHORT *o* /o/, LONG *o* /ō/

**Fluency in Connected Text**

Have children review the **Decodable Reader** selection. Identify short and long *o* words and blend words. Have children reread the selection on their own or with a partner.

# → Approaching Level

## Structural Analysis

### REVIEW INFLECTIONAL ENDINGS -*ed*, -*ing*

**OBJECTIVES**

 Know and apply grade-level phonics and word analysis skills in decoding words. **RF.2.3**

Read words with the inflectional endings -*ed*, -*ing*.

 **I Do** Write *jogged* and *jogging*. Read the words. Say: *I look at the words* jogged *and* jogging *and I see a word I know*, jog. Point out that the consonant *g* is doubled. *The* -ed *ending tells me that something has already happened. The* -ing *ending tells me that something is happening now. I'm going to use* jogged *and* jogging. *Mia jogged home yesterday. Dave is jogging right now.*

 **We Do** Write *voted* and *voting*. Say: *Look at* voted *and* voting. *Is there a word we know? Yes,* vote. Point out that the final *e* in *vote* was dropped before the endings were added. *Let's use* voted *and* voting *in sentences.*

 **You Do** Have children work with partners. Provide several words with -*ed* and -*ing* endings. Partners determine the root word and write sentences.

**Repeat** Have children create sentences using words with -*ed* and -*ing*.

### RETEACH INFLECTIONAL ENDINGS -*ed*, -*ing*

**OBJECTIVES**

 Know and apply grade-level phonics and word analysis skills in decoding words. **RF.2.3**

Read words with the inflectional endings -*ed*, -*ing*.

 **I Do** Write *hopped* and *hopping*. Read the words, pointing out the doubled consonant *p*. Say: *The* -ed *ending tells us that something has already happened. If I* hopped, *I did it before now. The* -ing *ending tells us that something is happening now. If I am* hopping, *I am doing it now.*

 **We Do** Write *vote*. *Let's add* -ed *and* -ing. Write *voted* and *voting*. *Say* voted: /vōted/. Point out that the final *e* drops when the endings -*ed* and -*ing* are added to words ending with silent *e*. Have the group come up with sentences for *voted* and *voting*.

 **You Do** Have children add -*ed* and -*ing* to verbs. Guide children to repeat the words as needed. *Now it's your turn. Add* -ed *and* -ing *to each word, then say each word and use each word in a sentence.*

pop     code     close     dot     pose

**Repeat** Have children add inflectional endings -*ed* and -*ing* to words.

# High-Frequency Words/Vocabulary

TIER 2

## REVIEW HIGH-FREQUENCY WORDS

**OBJECTIVES**

(CCSS) Read with sufficient accuracy and fluency to support comprehension. **RF.2.4**

Review high-frequency words.

**I Do** Use Word Cards 51–60. Display one word at a time, following the routine:

Display the word. Read the word. Then spell the word.

**We Do** Ask children to state the word and spell the word with you. Model using the word in a sentence and have children repeat after you.

**You Do** Display the word. Ask children to say the word and then spell it. When completed, quickly flip through the word card set as children chorally read the words. Provide opportunities for children to use the words in speaking and writing. For example, provide sentence starters, such as *I thought I saw _____*. Ask children to write each word in their Writer's Notebook.

## REVIEW VOCABULARY WORDS

**OBJECTIVES**

 Use words and phrases acquired through conversations, reading and being read to, and responding to texts, including using adjectives and adverbs to describe (e.g., *When other kids are happy that makes me happy*). **L.2.6**

**I Do** Display each Visual Vocabulary Card and state the word. Explain how the photograph illustrates the word. State the example sentence and repeat the word.

**We Do** Point to the word on the card and read the word with children. Ask them to repeat the word. Engage children in structured partner talk about the image as prompted on the back of the vocabulary card.

**You Do** Display each visual in random order, hiding the word. Have children match the definitions and context sentences of the words to the visuals displayed. Then ask children to complete Approaching Level Practice Book page 51.

# → Approaching Level

## Comprehension

### READ FOR FLUENCY

**OBJECTIVES**

 Read with sufficient accuracy and fluency to support comprehension. **RF.2.4**

 Read on-level text with purpose and understanding. **RF.2.4a**

**I Do** Read the first paragraph of the Practice Book selection. Model using correct phrasing and pausing for punctuation.

**We Do** Read the second paragraph and have children repeat each sentence after you. Point out how you grouped words into phrases and used punctuation to help group words together.

**You Do** Have children read the rest of the selection aloud. Remind them to use correct phrasing and pause for punctuation in order to group words together correctly.

### IDENTIFY PLOT EVENTS

**OBJECTIVES**

 Describe how characters in a story respond to major events and challenges. **RL.2.3**

 Describe the overall structure of a story, including describing how the beginning introduces the story and the ending concludes the action. **RL.2.5**

Identify events in a story's plot.

**I Do** Remind children that a fiction story has characters, settings, and events. *Characters are people or animals in the story. The setting is where and when the story takes place. The events are what happens. Identifying important events can help you understand the story.*

**We Do** Read the first page of the Practice Book selection aloud. Pause to identify the main events. *On these pages of the story, the teacher and the children are on a hike in the woods, looking for woodland animals. They hear a robin and an owl, but they don't see them. These are events.*

**You Do** Guide children to read the rest of the Practice Book selection. As they read, prompt them to identify important events.

## REVIEW CHARACTER, SETTING, PLOT

**OBJECTIVES**

 Describe how characters in a story respond to major events and challenges. **RL.2.3**

 Describe the overall structure of a story, including describing how the beginning introduces the story and the ending concludes the action. **RL.2.5**

**I Do** Remind children that fiction is a story about made-up characters and events. Explain that the characters in a story are the people or animals that do things in the story. The setting is where and when the story takes place. The plot is the action or events that take place at the beginning, middle, and end of the story.

**We Do** Read the first page of the Practice Book selection together. As you read, pause to point out the events on each page. Help children decide which are the main events. *We read that the teacher and her class are on a hike in the woods, looking for woodland animals. They hear a robin and an owl, but they don't see the animals. These are the events at the beginning of the story.*

**You Do** *Let's record the events from the beginning of the story in our Beginning, Middle, and End chart.* Record the events. Then have children continue reading the story. As they read, have them complete the chart.

## SELF-SELECTED READING

**OBJECTIVES**

 Read with sufficient accuracy and fluency to support comprehension. **RF.2.4**

 Read on-level text with purpose and understanding. **RF.2.4a**

Apply the strategy and skill to reread text.

### Read Independently

Have children pick a fiction selection that they have read for sustained silent reading. Remind them that:

→ fiction is a made-up story with characters, a setting, and a plot.

→ the plot is made up of the main events that happen at the beginning, middle, and end of a story.

→ they can make, confirm, and revise predictions about the story.

### Read Purposefully

Have children record the main events of the story on their Beginning, Middle, and End chart. After reading, guide children to participate in a group discussion about the selection they read. Guide children to:

→ share the information they recorded on their chart.

→ tell about the story's characters and the setting.

→ describe the predictions they made and revised and whether their predictions were correct.

# On Level

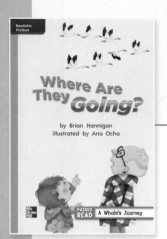

**Lexile** 440
*TextEvaluator™* 13

### OBJECTIVES

 Describe how characters in a story respond to major events and challenges. **RL.2.3**

 Describe the overall structure of a story, including describing how the beginning introduces the story and the ending concludes the action. **RL.2.5**

### MATERIALS

Leveled Reader
*Where Are They Going?*

## Leveled Reader:
## *Where Are They Going?*

### Before Reading

#### Preview and Predict

Have children turn to the title page. Read the title and author name and have children repeat. Preview the story's illustrations. Prompt children to predict what the story might be about.

#### Review Genre: Realistic Fiction

Have children recall that realistic fiction is a made-up story that could happen in real life.

#### ESSENTIAL QUESTION

Remind children of the Essential Question: How do animals survive? Set a purpose for reading: *Let's read to find out how snow geese survive.*

Remind children that as they read a selection, they can ask questions about what they do not understand or want to know more about.

### During Reading

#### Close Reading

**Note taking**  Ask students to use their graphic organizer while they read.

**Pages 2–4**  *Explain to a partner what is happening in the beginning of this story.* (Emma is from the city, visiting her grandparents in the country. She misses the city noise and is homesick. Then she hears snow geese honking.) *What do you predict will happen after Emma hears the snow geese?* (She will want to find out more about them.) *Why did you make this prediction?* (Emma wanted to know about the noise and big V shape. This shows she is curious and wants to know about things.)

**Pages 5–8**  *Paraphrase the events in Chapter 2.* (Grandpa explains facts about the snow geese to Emma. Emma sees more geese and is even more curious. She and Grandpa go inside to do research.) *What does the prefix re- mean on page 5?* (again)

**Go**
**Digital**

**Leveled Readers**

**Graphic Organizer**

**Retelling Cards**

**Pages 9–13** *What do you predict will happen in Chapter 3?* (Emma will learn more interesting facts about snow geese.)

**Pages 14–15** *What words does the author use to show how Emma feels on page 15?* (eager; sleepily) *What happens in the end of the story?* (Learning about snow geese helped Emma enjoy her visit to the country. She plans to make a poster about the birds.)

## After Reading

### Respond to Reading

Have children complete Respond to Reading on page 16 after reading.

### Retell

Have children take turns retelling the selection using the retelling cards as a guide. Help children make a personal connection by asking: *Have you ever been in a new place and felt homesick? Did your feelings change after you were there for awhile?*

### Model Fluency

Read the sentences, one at a time. Have children chorally repeat. Point out how you pause for punctuation and groups of words that belong together in phrases.

**Apply** Have partners practice repeated readings. Provide feedback.

## PAIRED READ ...

### "A Whale's Journey"

**Make Connections:**
**Write About It** *Analytical Writing*

Before reading, point out that this text is expository text. Then discuss the Compare Texts statement. After reading, have children make connections between "A Whale's Journey" and *Where Are They Going?*

**Leveled Reader**

## *Analytical Writing*

### COMPARE TEXTS

→ Have children use text evidence to compare the expository text to the realistic fiction story.

### Literature Circles

Lead children in conducting a literature circle using the Thinkmark questions to guide the discussion. You may wish to discuss ways animals survive in cold weather from both selections in the leveled reader.

## Level Up

Level-up lessons available online.

**IF** children read the On Level fluently and answered the questions

**THEN** pair them with children who have proficiently read the Beyond Level and have on-level children

• partner-read the Beyond Level main selection.

• Identify a part of the plot they would like to learn more about.

### A C T Access Complex Text

The Beyond Level challenges children by including more **specific vocabulary** and **complex sentence structures.**

# On Level

## Phonics

### BUILD WORDS WITH SHORT *o*, LONG *o*

**OBJECTIVES**

 Know and apply grade-level phonics and word analysis skills in decoding words. **RF.2.3**

 Distinguish long and short vowels when reading regularly spelled one-syllable words. **RF.2.3a**

**MATERIALS**
Word-Building Cards

 Display **Word-Building Cards** n, o, t. *This is the letter* n. *It stands for /n/. This is the letter* o. *It stands for /o/. This is the letter* t. *It stands for /t/. Listen as I blend these sounds together: /not/, not. The word is* not.

 *Now, let's do one together. Make the word* not *using Word-Building Cards. Place the letter* e *at the end of* not. *This will change the vowel sound in the word. Let's blend: /n/ /ō/ /t/, /nōt/, note. Now there is a new word,* note.

*Change the letter* n *to* v. *I am going to change the letter* n *in* note *to the letter* v. *Let's blend and read the new word: /v/ /ō/ /t/, /vōt/, vote. The new word is* vote.

 Have children build and blend the words: *tot, tote, pot, pop, hop, hope, mop, mope, mole, pole, stole.*

**Fluency in Connected Text** Have children read this week's Decodable Reader selection, *At Home in Nome.*

## Vocabulary

### REVIEW WORDS

**OBJECTIVES**

 Use words and phrases acquired through conversations, reading and being read to, and responding to texts, including using adjectives and adverbs to describe (e.g., *When other kids are happy that makes me happy*). **L.2.6**

 Use the **Visual Vocabulary Cards** to review each vocabulary word. Point to each word, read it aloud, and have children chorally repeat it.

 Guide children to use the **Define/Example/Ask** routine for a few vocabulary words using their **Response Boards**. Ask sample questions to help children respond and explain their answers.

 Have children work with a partner to do the Define/Example/Ask routine for the remaining vocabulary words. Then have children write sentences about this week's stories. Each sentence must contain at least one vocabulary word.

# Comprehension

## REVIEW CHARACTER, SETTING, PLOT

**OBJECTIVES**

 Describe how characters in a story respond to major events and challenges. **RL.2.3**

 Describe the overall structure of a story, including describing how the beginning introduces the story and the ending concludes the action. **RL.2.5**

 **I Do** Remind children that fiction has characters, a setting, and a plot. Explain that a story's characters are the people or animals in the story. The setting is where and when the story takes place. The plot is made up of the main events that happen in the story. *When we read fiction, we can look for the main events in the plot. This helps us understand what happens at the beginning, middle, and end of the story.*

 **We Do** Read the first page of the Practice Book selection aloud. Pause to point out information about the characters, setting, and plot. Help children identify the main events. *We read that the teacher and her class are on a hike in the woods, looking for woodland animals. They hear a robin and an owl, but they do not see the animals. These are the events at the beginning of the story.*

 **You Do** Guide children to read the rest of the selection. Remind them to identify the events from the middle and end of the story as they read.

## SELF-SELECTED READING

**OBJECTIVES**

 Read with sufficient accuracy and fluency to support comprehension. **RF.2.4**

 Read on-level text with purpose and understanding. **RF.2.4a**

 Describe the overall structure of a story, including describing how the beginning introduces the story and the ending concludes the action. **RL.2.5**

Apply the strategy and skill to reread text.

### Read Independently

Have children pick a fiction selection that they have read for sustained silent reading. Remind them to:

→ identify the events that occur at the beginning, middle, and end of the story's plot.

→ make, confirm, and revise predictions based on what they have read and seen in illustrations.

### Read Purposefully

Have children record the main events of the story on their Beginning, Middle, and End chart. After reading, guide partners to:

→ share the events they recorded on their Beginning, Middle, and End chart.

→ identify the story's characters and setting.

→ describe the predictions they made, how they revised their predictions, and whether their predictions were correct.

# → Beyond Level

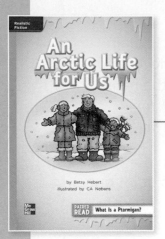

**Lexile** 600
*TextEvaluator™* 23

## OBJECTIVES

 Read with sufficient accuracy and fluency to support comprehension. **RF.2.4**

 Read on-level text with purpose and understanding. **RF.2.4a**

 Read on-level text orally with accuracy, appropriate rate, and expression on successive readings. **RF.2.4b**

## MATERIALS

Leveled Reader
*An Arctic Life for Us*

## Leveled Reader:
## *An Arctic Life for Us*

### Before Reading

#### Preview and Predict

Read the title and author name. Have children preview the title page and the illustrations. Ask: *What do you think this book will be about?*

#### Review Genre: Realistic Fiction

Have children recall that realistic fiction is a made-up story with believable characters, setting, and events. Prompt children to identify characteristics of realistic fiction. Tell them to look for these as they read the leveled reader.

#### ESSENTIAL QUESTION

Remind children of the Essential Question: *How do animals survive?* Have children set a purpose for reading by saying: *What do you want to find out about how animals survive in the Arctic?*

### During Reading

#### Close Reading

**Note taking** Ask students to use their graphic organizer while they read.

**Pages 2–5** *Explain to a partner how the beginning introduces the story.* (In the beginning, I learn about the main character, Marcos, and that he has a problem being very hot. To solve his problem, he and Mom go to the library. Marcos enjoys reading about the cool Arctic.)

**Pages 6–9** *What prediction can you make after reading the title of Chapter 2?* (Marcos will have an idea about living in the Arctic.) Why did you make this prediction? (Marcos has been reading a lot about how cool the Arctic is and he has been feeling so hot.)

*How does the illustration on page 6 give more information about the plot?* (The illustration shows a speech balloon for Marcos. He says he wants his family to live in the Arctic.)

**Go
Digital**

**Leveled
Readers**

**Graphic
Organizer**

**Pages 10–13** *How does the title of Chapter 3 help you make a prediction?* (The title gives me a clue that someone won't agree with Marcos's idea. I predict Mom won't want to move to the Arctic) *What word has a prefix on page 13?* (reread) *What does the prefix mean?* (again)

**Pages 14–15** *What words on page 13 help you know how a seal and Marcos's pajamas feel?* (slippery; fuzzy) *How does the author use a sound word to help you hear what is happening in the story on page 14?* (The text says that Marcos hit the floor with a thud.)

## After Reading

### Respond to Reading

Have children complete the Respond to Reading questions on page 16.

### Retell

Have children take turns retelling the selection. Help children make a personal connection by writing about a time when they were very hot. Say: *Write about a time when you were hot. What did you do to become more comfortable? What else can people do to cool off?*

## PAIRED READ ...

**Leveled Reader**

## "What Is a Ptarmigan?"

### Make Connections: Write About It ✏ *Analytical Writing*

Before reading, have children preview the title page and identify the genre. Discuss the Compare Texts statement. After reading, have partners discuss what they learned from "What Is a Ptarmigan?" and *An Arctic Life for Us*. Ask children to make connections by comparing and contrasting how animals adapt in each selection. Prompt children to discuss what they learned about how animals survive in the Arctic.

## *Analytical Writing*

### COMPARE TEXTS

→ Have children use text evidence to compare the expository text to the realistic fiction story.

## Literature Circles

Lead children in conducting a literature circle using the Thinkmark questions to guide the discussion. You may wish to discuss how animals survive in the Arctic from both selections in the leveled reader.

## Gifted and Talented

**SYNTHESIZE** Challenge students to describe the different ways that animals and people adapt to the very cold Arctic climate. Children should make a list of the different features that help animals survive. Then they should consider why few humans live in the Arctic region.

**EXTEND** Have them use facts they learned from the week or do additional research.

# Beyond Level

## Vocabulary

### REVIEW DOMAIN-SPECIFIC WORDS

**OBJECTIVES**

 Use words and phrases acquired through conversations, reading and being read to, and responding to texts, including using adjectives and adverbs to describe (e.g., *When other kids are happy that makes me happy*). **L.2.6**

 Use the Visual Vocabulary Cards to review the meaning of the words *adapt* and *climate*. Write science-related sentences on the board using these words.

Write the words *scorcher* and *camouflage* on the board and discuss the meanings with children. Then help children write sentences using these words.

 Have children work in pairs to review the meanings of the words *cost* and *jobs*. Then have partners write sentences using the words.

### PREFIXES

**OBJECTIVES**

 Determine or clarify the meaning of unknown and multiple-meaning words and phrases based on *grade 2 reading and content*, choosing flexibly from an array of strategies. **L.2.4**

 Use sentence-level context as a clue to the meaning of a word or phrase. **L.2.4a**

 Read aloud the first page of the Comprehension and Fluency passage on Beyond Level Practice Book pages 53–54.

**Think Aloud** When I read this page, I'm not sure what the word *unfamiliar* means. I know that *familiar* means "known." The prefix *un* means "not." I see that the word means "not known."

Help children figure out the meaning of *unlike*.

 Have pairs of children read the rest of the passage. Ask them to separate the word from its prefix to determine the meaning of the following words: *disappear, unseen, uneven, unnoticed, retraces, unlocks,* and *unsuccessful*.

**Gifted and Talented** **Shades of Meaning** Using their definition of *unlocks*, have partners write an explanation of the difference between *unlocks* and *opens*. Encourage them to quick-sketch to depict the two words.

# Comprehension

## REVIEW CHARACTER, SETTING, PLOT

**OBJECTIVES**

 Describe how characters in a story respond to major events and challenges. **RL.2.3**

 Describe the overall structure of a story, including describing how the beginning introduces the story and the ending concludes the action. **RL.2.5**

 **Model** Remind children that stories have characters, settings, and plots. Explain that the plot is made up of the events that take place in a story. Point out that the plot has a structure that includes a beginning, middle, and end. The beginning introduces the events of the story, while the end concludes it.

Have children read the first page of the Comprehension and Fluency passage of Beyond Level Practice Book pages 53–54. Ask open-ended questions to facilitate discussion, such as *How does this page introduce the story? What events occur at the beginning?* Children should support their responses with examples from the text.

 **Apply** Have children identify key events from each part of the story as they independently fill in a Beginning, Middle, and End graphic organizer. Then have partners use their work to describe how the events at the end of the story conclude the action.

## SELF-SELECTED READING

**OBJECTIVES**

Describe how characters in a story respond to major events and challenges. **RL.2.3**

Describe the overall structure of a story, including describing how the beginning introduces the story and the ending concludes the action. **RL.2.5**

Reread difficult sections in a text to increase understanding.

### Read Independently

Have children choose a fiction book for sustained silent reading.

→ As children read, have them fill in a Beginning, Middle, and End graphic organizer.

→ Remind them to reread difficult sections of the text.

### Read Purposefully

Encourage children to keep a reading journal. Ask them to read different books in order to learn about a variety of subjects.

→ Children can write summaries of the books in their journals.

→ Ask children to share their reactions to the books with classmates.

 **Independent Study** Challenge children to discuss how their books relate to the weekly theme of animal survival. Have children compare the way animals adapt in hot and cold climates. How do these adaptations help the animals survive?

# English Language Learners

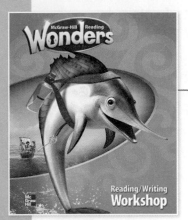

**Reading/Writing Workshop**

---

**ACADEMIC LANGUAGE**
*character, plot, setting, make predictions*

---

## Shared Read:
## *A Visit to the Desert*

### Before Reading

**Build Background**

Read the Essential Question: *How do animals survive?*

→ Explain the meaning of the Essential Question: *Survive means "stay alive." Animals survive in very hot and very cold climates.*

→ **Model an answer:** *In a very hot climate, animals need help to survive, or stay alive. A turtle digs a hole underground to stay cool. This helps it survive.*

→ Ask children a question that ties the Essential Question to their own background knowledge: *Think of an animal you know. What helps it survive in its climate?* Call on several pairs.

### During Reading

**Interactive Question Response**

→ Ask questions after each paragraph to help children understand the meaning of the text.

→ Reinforce the meanings of key vocabulary, providing meanings embedded in the questions.

→ Ask children questions that require them to use key vocabulary.

→ Reinforce strategies and skills of the week by modeling.

**Go**
**Digital**

**A Visit to the Desert**

**Graphic Organizer**

## A Visit to the Desert

### Page 102

Point to the title. *Listen as I read the title of the selection.* Point to each word as you read it. *What is the title?* (A Visit to the Desert)

Point to the illustration of the desert. *This is the desert. Say* desert *with me:* desert. *A desert is a hot, dry place. There is not much rain in a desert.* Point to the jack rabbit. *This jack rabbit lives in the desert. Let's read the story to find out how this animal and other animals survive in this hot, dry place.*

### Page 103

After reading this page with children, point out that a *hike* is a long walk. *Where does Grandma want to take Tim?* (on a desert hike)

**Explain and Model the Strategy**  Reread page 103 to help children understand the events at the beginning of the story. *We can make predictions, or guesses, about what will happen next in the story. What do you think Tim will do next? Will Tim have a good time when he visits his grandma? Will he like hiking in the desert? As we read, we can see if our predictions are correct. Then we can change our predictions as we read more of the story.*

*What do you predict will happen next?* (Accept reasonable responses.)

### Page 104

Read aloud the page with children. Point out that *adapt* means *get used to.*

*Why do the animals like the desert?* (They like the open space.) *What did Tim learn about the animals?* (They find ways to adapt to the hot desert weather.) *Do you think Tim will adapt to the desert climate?* (Accept reasonable responses.)

**Explain and Model the Phonics Skill**  Reread the second sentence. *Listen carefully. Raise your hand when you hear a word that has the /ō/ sound.* (drove) *Let's practice saying this word together: drove.*

### Page 105

*Let's read the first paragraph together:* "Wow," Tim said, "Look at that! The turtle carries its home on its back!" *Find the picture of the turtle on page 104. The turtle has a hard shell on its back. It is called a desert tortoise.*

*Let's read the rest of the page together. The turtle looks for shade. Now let's read the sentence that tells how the turtle stays cool:* He burrows underground to get away from the heat. *Let's pretend we are turtles and burrow, or dig a hole, into the ground.* Demonstrate burrowing with your hands and arms.

*Why does the turtle burrow into the ground?* (to get cool)

### Page 106

*Let's read this page together. How does the jack rabbit stay cool?* (Its large ears help it to stay cool.) Explain that they allow the blood in the ears to cool before it reenters the body. *How do other animals stay cool in the desert?* (They sleep during the day and hunt at night.)

*Find the sentence in the second paragraph that tells us Tim is adapting to the desert heat.* (He had forgotten about the desert heat.)

### After Reading

**Make Connections**

→ Review the Essential Question.

# → English Language Learners

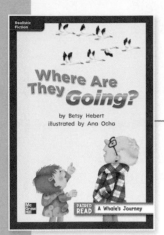

**Lexile** 380
*TextEvaluator™* 5

## OBJECTIVES

Describe the overall structure of a story, including describing how the beginning introduces the story and the ending concludes the action. **RL.2.5**

## MATERIALS

Leveled Reader
*Where are They Going?*

## Leveled Reader:
## *Where Are They Going?*

**Go Digital**

**Leveled Readers**

**Graphic Organizer**

**Retelling Cards**

### Before Reading

#### Preview

Read the title. Ask: *What is the title? Say it again.* Repeat with the author's name. Preview the selection's illustrations. Have children describe the images. Use simple language to tell about each page. Follow with questions, such as *Who is the girl with? What does she see in the sky?*

#### ESSENTIAL QUESTION

Remind children of the Essential Question. Say: *Let's read to find out how snow geese survive.* Encourage children to seek clarification when they encounter a confusing word or phrase.

### During Reading

#### Interactive Question Response

**Pages 2–3** *Look at the picture on page 2. How do you think the girl feels? Let's reread the sentence that tells how she feels:* She looked unhappy.

*Let's read page 3 to find out why Emma is unhappy. Emma is homesick. Homesick means you are sad about being away from home. Tell your partner why Emma is unhappy.* (She misses the city and her parents.)

**Pages 4–5** *Emma hears honking. Cars honk. So do some birds. Let's make a honking sound like birds. The birds fly together. They are a flock. Where are the birds going?* (They are flying south.) *Tell your partner why they are going south.* (They need to find a warm place to stay in the winter.)

**Pages 6–7** *What does Emma see on page 7? Tell your partner.*

**Pages 8–9** *What does Emma want to find out about?* (snow geese)

**Pages 10–11** *Talk with your partner about places where Emma will look for facts about snow geese. Emma's grandma gives Emma a book about birds. What topic does Emma look for in the index?* (snow goose) *Look at how* goose *is spelled.* Goose *means one bird. If there are two or more birds, they are called* geese. *Find the words* goose *and* geese.

**Pages 12–13** *What does Emma learn about snow geese? Tell your partner two facts.*

*Pages 14–15 Look at the picture on page 14. How does Emma feel now? Let's read page 15. Tell your partner how Emma changed in the story. How did she feel at the beginning? How does she feel now? Why?*

## After Reading

### Respond to Reading

Have partners answer the questions. Pair children with peers of varying language abilities.

### Retell

Model retelling using the Retelling Card prompts. Then guide children to retell the selection to a partner.

### Fluency: Phrasing

Read the sentences in the book, one at a time. Help children echo-read the pages with appropriate phrasing. Point out how you pause for punctuation and groups of words that belong together in phrases.

### Apply

Have children practice reading with a partner. Pair children with peers of varying language abilities. Provide provide feedback as needed.

## PAIRED READ ...

## "A Whale's Journey"

### Make Connections:
### Write About It ✏ *Analytical Writing*

Before reading, tell children that this text is expository text. Then discuss the Compare Texts statement. After reading, ask children to make connections between what they learned from "A Whale's Journey" and *Where Are They Going?* Prompt children by providing sentence frames: *Snow geese travel from cold places to _____. Humpback whales also go from cold places to _____.*

### ✏ *Analytical Writing*

#### COMPARE TEXTS

→ Have children use text evidence to compare the expository text to the realistic fiction story.

**Leveled Reader**

## Literature Circles

Lead children in conducting a literature circle using the Thinkmark questions to guide the discussion. You may wish to discuss what children learned about what animals do in cold weather from both selections in the leveled reader.

## Level Up

Level-up lessons available online.

**IF** children read the **ELL Level** fluently and answered the questions

**THEN** pair them with children who have proficiently read the **On Level** and have children

- echo-read the **On Level** main selection with their partners.

- list difficult words and phrases and discuss them with their partners.

### A C T **A**ccess **C**omplex **T**ext

The **On Level** challenges children by including more **specific vocabulary** and **complex sentence structures**.

# English Language Learners
## Vocabulary

### PRETEACH VOCABULARY

**OBJECTIVES**
Use words and phrases acquired through conversations, reading and being read to, and responding to texts, including using adjectives and adverbs to describe (e.g., *When other kids are happy that makes me happy*).
**L.2.6**

**LANGUAGE OBJECTIVE**
Use vocabulary words

**I Do** Preteach vocabulary from "A Visit to the Desert," following the Vocabulary Routine found on the Visual Vocabulary Cards for words *eager, freedom, fresh, sense, shadows, silence, adapt,* and *climate*.

**We Do** After completing the Vocabulary Routine for each word, point to the word on the Visual Vocabulary Card and read the word with children. Ask children to repeat the word.

**You Do** Have children work with a partner to complete sentences for two or more words. Then have each pair read the sentences aloud.

| Beginning | Intermediate | Advanced/High |
|---|---|---|
| Use sentence frames, such as *A polar bear can adapt to a cold _____.* | Help children write one sentence and one question. | Challenge children to write one sentence and one question for each word. |

### REVIEW VOCABULARY

**OBJECTIVES**
Use words and phrases acquired through conversations, reading and being read to, and responding to texts, including using adjectives and adverbs to describe (e.g., *When other kids are happy that makes me happy*).
**L.2.6**

**I Do** Review the previous week's vocabulary words. The words can be reviewed over a few days. Read each word pointing to the word on the Visual Vocabulary Card. Have children repeat after you. Then follow the Vocabulary Routine on the back of each card.

**We Do** Ask children to guess the word you describe. Provide clues, such as synonyms or antonyms. Have children name the word and define or use it in a sentence.

**You Do** Have children work with a partner to provide clues for the words and to guess the words.

| Beginning | Intermediate | Advanced/High |
|---|---|---|
| Help children list clue words and read them aloud. | Help children write clues as sentences. | Ask children to use synonyms or antonyms in their clues. |

## PREFIXES

**OBJECTIVES**

CCSS Determine or clarify the meaning of unknown and multiple-meaning words and phrases based on *grade 2 reading and content*, choosing flexibly from an array of strategies. **L.2.4**

CCSS Use sentence-level context as a clue to the meaning of a word or phrase. **L.2.4a**

**LANGUAGE OBJECTIVE**

Use prefixes.

**I Do** Read aloud the second paragraph of "A Visit to the Desert" on page 105 while children follow along. Summarize the paragraph. Point to the word *disappear.* Explain that sometimes we can separate the root word from a prefix to understand the word's meaning.

**Think Aloud** When I read this paragraph, I'm not sure what the word *disappeared* means. I know that *appeared* means "came into sight." The prefix *dis-* makes the new word mean the opposite of the original word. So, *disappeared* means "went out of sight." I'll try reading this phrase in the sentence to see if it makes sense.

**We Do** Have children point to the word *unlike* on page 106. Help children separate the prefix from the root word to determine its meaning.

**You Do** In pairs, have children separate the prefix from the root word and then write a definition for *unhappy* on page 103.

| Beginning | Intermediate | Advanced/High |
|---|---|---|
| Help children locate the word and define the prefix and root word. | Ask children to locate the word and define the prefix and root word. | Ask children to explain how they defined the word. |

## ADDITIONAL VOCABULARY

**OBJECTIVE**

CCSS Use knowledge of language and its conventions when writing, speaking, reading, or listening. **L.2.3**

CCSS Compare formal and informal uses of English. **L.2.3a**

**I Do** List academic language and concept words from "A Visit to the Desert": *desert, burrows, adapt, climate;* and "Where Are They Going?": *migrate, homesick.* Define each word for children: *A desert is a very dry place.*

**We Do** Model using the words for children in a sentence: *The desert is hot during the day and cold at night. Take water with you if you are going to hike in the desert.* Then provide sentence frames and complete them with children.

**You Do** Have pairs make up their own sentences and share them with the class to complete them.

| Beginning | Intermediate | Advanced/High |
|---|---|---|
| Help children copy the sentence frames correctly and complete them. | Provide sentence starters for children, if necessary. | Have children define the words they used. |

# English Language Learners
## Writing/Spelling

### WRITING TRAIT: IDEAS

 **OBJECTIVES**

Write narratives in which they recount a well-elaborated event or short sequence of events, include details to describe actions, thoughts, and feelings, use temporal words to signal event order, and provide a sense of closure. **W.2.3**

**LANGUAGE OBJECTIVE**

Include descriptive details.

 **I Do** Explain that writers use descriptive details. Write and read the sentences: *The owl lives in a tree./The owl lives high up in a hollow tree in the big, cool forest.* Help children compare the sentences.

 **We Do** Read the second sentence on page 106 of *A Visit to the Desert.* Ask children to name the words that tell about the rabbit's size and how it moves. (large, hopped) Explain that the writer used descriptive details to help readers picture the rabbit.

 **You Do** Have children write a sentence describing an animal Tim saw in the desert. Remind children to include descriptive details.

| Beginning | Intermediate | Advanced/High |
|---|---|---|
| Help children choose an animal and write a sentence. Provide a sentence frame. | Ask children to describe how an animal survives. Give sentence frames to complete. | Elicit details from children about how an animal survives. *Is it cold or hot where this animal lives?* |

### WORDS WITH SHORT *o*; LONG *o*: o_e

 **OBJECTIVES**

Know and apply grade level phonics and word analysis skills in decoding words. **RF.2.3**

**LANGUAGE OBJECTIVE**

Spell words with short and long *o*.

 **I Do** Read aloud the Spelling Words on page T14. Segment the word into sounds and attach a spelling to each sound. Point out the short *o* spelling. Read aloud, segment, and spell the remaining words, and have children repeat.

 **We Do** Read the first sentence from the Dictation Routine on page T14 aloud. Then, read the short *o* word slowly and ask children to repeat. Have them write the word. Repeat the process for the remaining sentences.

 **You Do** Display the words. Have children work with a partner to check their spelling lists. Have children correct misspelled words on their list.

| Beginning | Intermediate | Advanced/High |
|---|---|---|
| Help children copy the words with correct spelling and say the word. | After children have corrected their words, have pairs quiz each other. | Have children think of other words that have the short or long o sound. |

# Grammar

## NOUNS

**OBJECTIVES**

**CCSS** Demonstrate command of the conventions of standard English grammar and usage when writing or speaking. **L.2.1**

**CCSS** Demonstrate command of the conventions of standard English capitalization, punctuation, and spelling when writing. **L.2.2**

---

**LANGUAGE OBJECTIVE**

Recognize nouns name people, places, or things.

**ELL Language Transfers**

Stress to Spanish speakers that English nouns are not masculine or feminine and nouns do not change their ending to reflect gender. Provide an example, such as the word *friend*. The word *friend can stand for a boy or a girl in English.*

---

**I Do** Review that a noun names a person, place, or thing. Write the following sentence on the board: *The girl sees a bear at the zoo.* Read the sentence. Underline the nouns *girl, bear, zoo.* Say: *The words* girl, bear, *and* zoo *are nouns.*

**We Do** Write the following sentence frames on the board. Have children read the sentences and identify the noun in each. Have them say: *The noun is ____. It names a ____.* (person, place, thing)

*The rabbit hops in the desert.*
*The boy sees a bird.*
*A bear can climb a tree.*

**You Do** Write the following sentence frames on the board.

Emma sees ____.    Tim visits ____.

Pair children and have them complete each sentence frame by providing details from this week's readings. Circulate, listen in, and take note of each child's language use and proficiency.

| Beginning | Intermediate | Advanced/High |
|---|---|---|
| Describe the illustrations in *A Visit to the Desert*. Ask: *What do you see?* Model a response by providing a sentence frame: I see a ____. Help children identify the nouns in the sentence. | Ask children to describe the same illustrations and then identify the nouns they used in their descriptions. Encourage children to use complete sentences. | Ask children to describe the illustrations and name the nouns they included. Prompt children to identify whether each noun names a person, place, or thing. |

# PROGRESS MONITORING

## Weekly Assessment

| ✔**COMPREHENSION:** Character, Setting, Plot **RL.2.5** | ✔**VOCABULARY:** Prefixes **L.2.4b** | ✔**WRITING:** Writing About Text **RL.2.5** |
| --- | --- | --- |

### Assessment Includes

→ Pencil-and-Paper administration

→ Online administration

→ Approaching-Level Weekly Assessment also available

**Fluency Goal** **41 to 61 words correct per minute (WCPM)**

**Accuracy Rate Goal** 95% or higher

Administer oral reading fluency assessments using the following schedule:

→ **Weeks 1, 3, 5** Provide Approaching-Level children at least three oral reading fluency assessments during the unit.

→ **Weeks 2 and 4** Provide On-Level children at least two oral reading fluency assessments during the unit.

→ **Week 6** If necessary, provide Beyond-Level children an oral reading fluency assessment at this time.

**Also Available: Selection Tests online PDFs**

*Go Digital!* http://connected.mcgraw-hill.com

# Using Assessment Results

| TESTED SKILLS | If ... | Then ... |
|---|---|---|
| **COMPREHENSION** | Children answer 0–6 multiple-choice items correctly ... | ... assign Lessons 136–137 on Characters, Setting, and Plot from the ***Tier 2 Comprehension Intervention online PDFs.*** |
| **VOCABULARY** | Children answer 0–6 multiple-choice items correctly ... | ... assign Lessons 100–101 on Prefixes from the ***Tier 2 Vocabulary Intervention online PDFs.*** |
| **WRITING** | Children score less than "3" on the Constructed response ... | ... assign Lessons 136–137 and/or Write About Reading Lessons from Section 13 of the ***Tier 2 Comprehension Intervention online PDFs***. |
|  | Children have a WCPM score of 36–40 ... | ... assign a lesson from Section 1, 9, or 10 of the ***Tier 2 Fluency Intervention online PDFs.*** |
| | Children have a WCPM score of 0–35 ... | ... assign a lesson from Sections 2–8 of the ***Tier 2 Fluency Intervention online PDFs.*** |

## Response to Intervention

Use the appropriate sections of the ***Placement and Diagnostic Assessment*** as well as students' assessment results to designate students requiring:

**TIER 2** **Intervention Online PDFs**

**TIER 3** **WonderWorks Intervention Program**

# WEEKLY OVERVIEW

**Reading/Writing Workshop**

Mc Graw Hill

# TEACH *AND* MODEL

CCSS Shared Read   Genre · Fable

## The Boy Who Cried **Wolf**

Long ago a shepherd boy sat on a hilltop watching the village sheep. He was not **fond** of his job. He didn't like it one bit. He would have liked something wonderful to happen, but nothing **remarkable** ever did.

The shepherd boy watched the clouds move softly by to stay busy. He saw horses, dogs, and dragons in the sky. He made up **stories** with these things as characters.

**? Essential Question**
What can animals in stories teach us?
Read to find out what a shepherd boy learns.

118       119

---

## ✔ Vocabulary

believe

delicious

feast

fond

lessons

remarkable

snatch

stories

 **Close Reading of Complex Text**

**Shared Read** "The Boy Who Cried Wolf," 118–123

**Genre** Fable

**Lexile** 460L

 *TextEvaluator™* 4

## Minilessons     ✔ Tested Skills

✔ **Comprehension Strategy** .............. Make Predictions, T124–T125

✔ **Comprehension Skill** .............. Plot: Problem and Solution, T126–T127

✔ **Genre** .............. Fable, T136–T137

✔ **Vocabulary Strategy** .............. Suffixes, T138–T139

✔ **Writing Traits** .............. Ideas, T114–T115

✔ **Grammar** .............. Singular and Plural Nouns, T116–T117

☞ **Go** Digital

http://connected.mcgraw-hill.com

# WEEK 2

# APPLY WITH CLOSE READING

## Complex Text

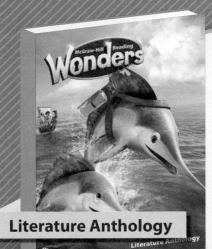

**Literature Anthology**

**PAIRED READ**

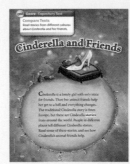

*Wolf! Wolf!*, 136–157
**Genre** Fable
**Lexile** 580L
**ETS** *TextEvaluator* 18

"Cinderella and Friends," 160–163
**Genre** Expository Text
**Lexile** 520L
**ETS** *TextEvaluator* 15

## Differentiated Text

**Leveled Readers** *Including Paired Reads*

| APPROACHING | ON LEVEL | BEYOND | ELL |
|---|---|---|---|
| **Lexile** 200 | **Lexile** 440 | **Lexile** 590 | **Lexile** 320 |
| **ETS** *TextEvaluator* 7 | **ETS** *TextEvaluator* 5 | **ETS** *TextEvaluator* 15 | **ETS** *TextEvaluator* 5 |

## Extended Complex Text

*Nate the Great on the Owl Express*
**Genre** Fiction
**Lexile** 280L
**ETS** *TextEvaluator* 16

*Cam Jansen: The Mystery at the Monkey House #10*
**Genre** Fiction
**Lexile** 530L
**ETS** *TextEvaluator* 9

**Classroom Library**

Classroom Library lessons available online.

# TEACH AND MANAGE

## How You Teach

### INTRODUCE

**Weekly Concept**
Animals in Stories

**Reading/Writing Workshop**
114–115

### TEACH

**Close Reading**
"The Boy Who Cried Wolf"

**Minilessons**
Make, Confirm and Revise Predictions, Character, Setting, Plot, Fable, Suffixes, Writing Traits

**Reading/Writing Workshop**
118–123

### APPLY

**Close Reading**
*Wolf! Wolf!*
*Cinderella and Friends*

**Student Anthology**
136–163

👉 **Go** Digital

Interactive Whiteboard

Interactive Whiteboard

Mobile

## How Students Practice

### Weekly contract

**PDF Online**

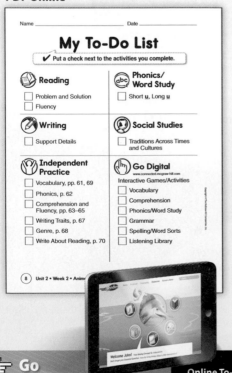

### Leveled practice and online activities

**Your Turn Practice Book**
**61–70**

**Leveled Readers**

👉 **Go** Digital

Online To-Do List

Leveled Activities

Writer's Workspace

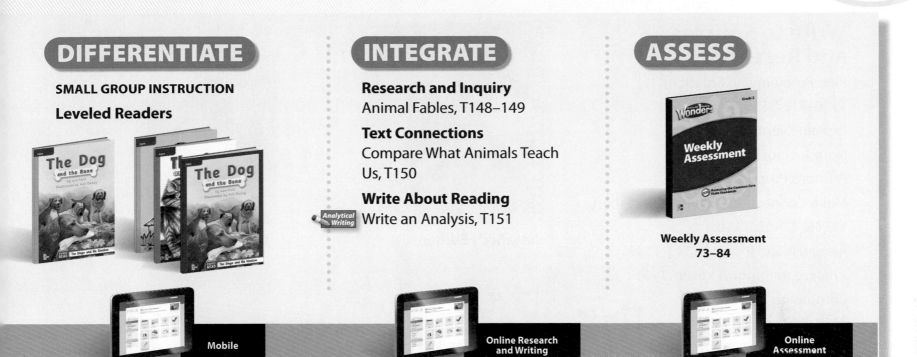

## DIFFERENTIATE

**SMALL GROUP INSTRUCTION**

**Leveled Readers**

Mobile

## INTEGRATE

**Research and Inquiry**
Animal Fables, T148–149

**Text Connections**
Compare What Animals Teach
Us, T150

**Write About Reading**
*Analytical Writing*
Write an Analysis, T151

Online Research
and Writing

## ASSESS

**Weekly Assessment
73–84**

Online
Assessment

## Leveled workstation cards

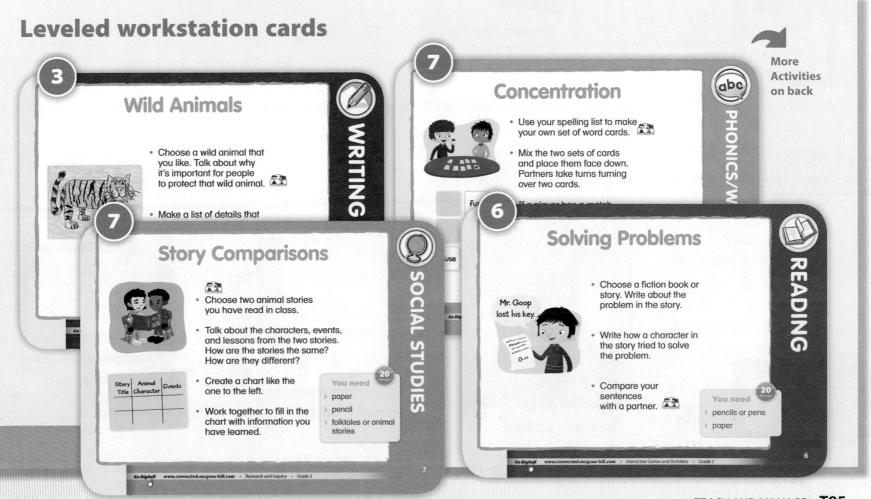

**3**

### Wild Animals

WRITING

- Choose a wild animal that you like. Talk about why it's important for people to protect that wild animal.

- Make a list of details that

**7**

### Concentration

PHONICS/W

- Use your spelling list to make your own set of word cards.

- Mix the two sets of cards and place them face down. Partners take turns turning over two cards.

**7**

### Story Comparisons

SOCIAL STUDIES

- Choose two animal stories you have read in class.

- Talk about the characters, events, and lessons from the two stories. How are the stories the same? How are they different?

- Create a chart like the one to the left.

| Story Title | Animal Character | Events |
|---|---|---|
| | | |

- Work together to fill in the chart with information you have learned.

**You need**
20 Minutes
> paper
> pencil
> folktales or animal stories

*Go Digital!* www.connected.mcgraw-hill.com • Research and Inquiry • Grade 2

7

**6**

### Solving Problems

READING

Mr. Goop lost his key.

- Choose a fiction book or story. Write about the problem in the story.

- Write how a character in the story tried to solve the problem.

- Compare your sentences with a partner.

**You need**
20 Minutes
> pencils or pens
> paper

*Go Digital!* www.connected.mcgraw-hill.com • Interactive Games and Activities • Grade 2

6

More
Activities
on back

# DEVELOPING READERS AND WRITERS

## Write About Reading • Analytical Writing

### Write to Sources and Research

Plot: Problem and Solution, T126–T127, T139N

Explain Events, T130

Note Taking, T139A, T145A

Author's Purpose, T139L

Make Connections: Essential Question, T139N, T145B, T150

Research and Inquiry, T148–T149

Analyze to Inform/Explain, T151

Comparing Texts, T157, T167, T171, T177

**Teacher's Edition**

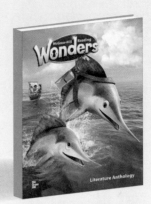

Plot: Problem and Solution, 159

**Literature Anthology**

**Interactive Whiteboard**

**Leveled Readers**
Comparing Texts
Plot: Problem and Solution

Plot: Problem and Solution, 63–65
Genre, 68
Write About Reading, 70

**Your Turn Practice Book**

## Writing Process • Genre Writing

**Narrative Text**
How-to Text, T480–T485

**Conferencing Routines**
Teacher Conferences, T482
Peer Conferences, T483

**Interactive Whiteboard**

**Teacher's Edition**

**Leveled Workstation Card**
How-To, Card 23

**Writer's Workspace**
Informational Text: How-to Text
Writing Process
Multimedia Presentations

## Writing Traits • Write Every Day

**Writing Trait: Ideas**
Supporting Details, T114–T115

**Conferencing Routines**
Teacher Conferences, T146
Peer Conferences, T147

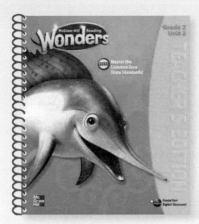

**Teacher's Edition**

Ideas: Supporting Details, 128–129

**Reading/Writing Workshop**

**Interactive Whiteboard**

### Wild Animals

- Choose a wild animal that you like. Talk about why it's important for people to protect that wild animal.
- Make a list of details that support your main idea.
- Use your details to write a paragraph.

Ideas: Supporting Details, Card 3

**Leveled Workstation Card**

Ideas: Supporting Details, 67

**Your Turn Practice Book**

## Grammar and Spelling

**Grammar**
Singular and Plural Nouns,
T116, T129, T141, T147, T155

**Spelling**
Short *u* and Long *u*, T106,
T122, T133, T144, T153

**Interactive Whiteboard**

**Teacher's Edition**

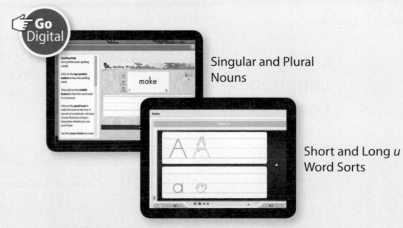

Singular and Plural Nouns

Short and Long *u* Word Sorts

**Online Spelling and Grammar Games**

# SUGGESTED LESSON PLAN

| | DAY 1 | DAY 2 |
|---|---|---|

## READING

### Whole Group

**Teach, Model, and Apply**

Reading/Writing Workshop
Workshop

**DAY 1**

**Build Background** Animals in Stories, T100–T101

**Oral Vocabulary Words** *affection, crave, frustrated, nourishment, seek;* T102

**Listening Comprehension** Strategy: Make, Confirm, Revise Predictions; T103

**Interactive Read-Aloud Cards** "The Fox and the Crane," T103

**Word Work**
Phonemic Awareness: Phoneme Deletion, T104
Phonics/Spelling: Introduce Long *u: u_e*, T104–T105
High-Frequency Words: *change, cheer, fall, five, look, open, should, their, won, yes;* T106

✔ **Vocabulary** Words in Context: *believe, delicious, feast, fond, lessons, remarkable, snatch, stories;* T108–T109

**Close Reading of Complex Text** "The Boy Who Cried Wolf," 118–123

**Practice** *Your Turn* 61–62

**DAY 2**

**Oral Language** Animals in Stories, T118

**Review Oral Vocabulary Words,** T118

**Listening Comprehension** Strategy: Make, Confirm, Revise Predictions; T119

**Interactive Read-Aloud Cards** "The Fox and the Crane," T119

**Word Work**
Phonemic Awareness: Phoneme Segmentation, T120
Phonics/Spelling: Words with Short *u,* Long *u: u_e,* T120–T122
Structural Analysis: CVC*e* Syllables, T121
High-Frequency Words, T122

**Vocabulary** Expand Vocabulary, T123

✔ **Comprehension**
• Strategy: Make Predictions, T124–T125
• Skill: Plot: Problem and Solution, T126–T127

**Practice** *Your Turn* 62–67

## DIFFERENTIATED INSTRUCTION   Choose across the week to meet your student's needs.

### Small Group

**Approaching Level**

The Cat and the Mice

**DAY 1**

**Leveled Reader** *The Cat and the Mice,* T156–T157

**Phonemic Awareness** Phoneme Deletion, T159

**Phonics** Connect *u* to /u/ and *u_e* to /ū/, T160

**High-Frequency Words** Review Words, T163

**Vocabulary** Review Words, T163

**DAY 2**

**Leveled Reader** *The Cat and the Mice,* T156–T157

**Phonemic Awareness** Phoneme Segmentation, T158

**Phonics** Blend with Short *u,* Long *u: u_e,* T160

**Comprehension** Identify the Plot, T164

---

**On Level**

The Dog and the Bone

**DAY 1**

**Leveled Reader** *The Dog and the Bone,* T166–T167

**Phonics** Build Words with Short and Long *u,* T168

**DAY 2**

**Leveled Reader** *The Dog and the Bone,* T166–T167

**Comprehension** Review Character, Setting, Plot: Problem and Solution; T169

---

**Beyond Level**

Spider and the Honey Tree

**DAY 1**

**Leveled Reader** *The Spider and the Honey Tree,* T170–T171

**Vocabulary** Review Domain-Specific Words, T172

**DAY 2**

**Leveled Reader** *The Spider and the Honey Tree,* T170–T171

**Comprehension** Review Plot: Problem and Solution; T173

---

**English Language Learners**

The Dog and the Bone

**DAY 1**

**Shared Read** "The Boy Who Cried Wolf," T174–T175

**Phonemic Awareness** Phoneme Deletion, T159

**Phonics** Connect *u* to /u/ and *u_e* to /ū/, T160

**Vocabulary** Preteach Vocabulary, T178

**DAY 2**

**Leveled Reader** *The Dog and the Bone,* T176–T177

**Phonemic Awareness** Phoneme Segmentation, T158

**Phonics** Blend with Short *u,* Long *u: u_e,* T160

**Vocabulary** Review Vocabulary, T178

**Writing** Writing Trait: Ideas, T180

## LANGUAGE ARTS   Writing Process: How-To T480–T485 | Use with Weeks 1–3

### Whole Group

**Writing**

**Grammar**

**DAY 1**

✔ **Readers to Writers**
• Writing Trait: Ideas, T114–T115
• Writing Entry: Prewrite and Draft, T114

**Grammar**
• Singular and Plural Nouns, T116
• Mechanics: Commas in a Series, T117

**DAY 2**

✔ **Readers to Writers**
• Writing Trait: Ideas, T128
• Writing Entry: Revise, T128

**Grammar**
• Singular and Plural Nouns, T129
• Mechanics: Commas in a Series, T129

## DAY 3

## DAY 4

## DAY 5 Review and Assess

### READING

**DAY 3**

**Interactive Read-Aloud Cards** "The Fox and the Crane," T130

**Review Oral Vocabulary Words,** T130

**Comprehension** Maintain Skill: Key Details: Use Illustrations, T131

**Word Work**
Phonemic Awareness: Phoneme Blending, T132
Phonics/Spelling: Words with Short *u*, Long *u*: *u_e*, T132–T133
Structural Analysis: CVC*e* Syllables, T133

**Fluency** Expression, T134

**Vocabulary** Reinforce Vocabulary, T135

✔**Genre** Fable, T136–T137

✔**Vocabulary Strategy** Suffixes, T138–T139

**Close Reading** *Wolf! Wolf!*, 136–158 ● *Analytical Writing*

*Literature Anthology*

**Practice** *Your Turn* 68–69

**DAY 4**

**Oral Language** Animals in Stories, T142

**Word Work**
Phonemic Awareness: Phoneme Segmentation, 143
Phonics/Spelling: Words with Short *u*, Long *u*: *u_e*, T143–T144
Structural Analysis: CVC*e* Syllables, T143
High-Frequency Words, T144

**Fluency** Expression, T145

**Vocabulary Strategy** Review: Prefixes, T145

**Close Reading** "Cinderella and Friends," 160–163 ● *Analytical Writing*

**Integrate Idea** Research and Inquiry, T148–T149 ● *Analytical Writing*

**Practice** *Your Turn* 63–65

**DAY 5 Review and Assess**

**Integrate Ideas** ● *Analytical Writing*
• Text Connections, T150
• Write About Reading, T151
• Research and Inquiry, T151

**Word Work**
Phonemic Awareness: Phoneme Segmentation, T152
Phonics/Spelling: Words with Short *u*, Long *u*: *u_e*, T152–T153
Structural Analysis: CVC*e* Syllables, T152
High-Frequency Words, T153

**Vocabulary** Review Words, T153

**Practice** *Your Turn* 70

### DIFFERENTIATED INSTRUCTION

**Leveled Reader** *The Cat and the Mice*, T156–T157
**Phonemic Awareness** Phoneme Blending, T158 TIER 2
**Phonics** Build with Short *u*, Long *u*: *u_e*, T161 TIER 2
**Structural Analysis** Review CVC*e* Syllables, T162 TIER 2
**Comprehension** Review Plot: Problem and Solution; T165

**Leveled Reader** Paired Read: "Beware of Tiger!" T157 ● *Analytical Writing*
**Phonemic Awareness** Phoneme Segmentation, T158 TIER 2
**Phonics** Blend with Short *u*, Long *u*: *u_e*, T161
**Structural Analysis** Reteach CVC*e* Syllables, T162
**Comprehension** Read for Fluency, T164 TIER 2

**Leveled Reader** Literature Circle, T157
**Phonemic Awareness** Phoneme Segmentation, T158 TIER 2
**Phonics** Blend with Short *u*, Long *u*: *u_e*, T161
**Comprehension** Self-Selected Reading, T165

**Leveled Reader** *The Dog and the Bone*, T166–T167
**Vocabulary** Review Words, T168

**Leveled Reader** Paired Read: "The Dingo and His Shadow," T167 ● *Analytical Writing*

**Leveled Reader** Literature Circle, T167
**Comprehension** Self-Selected Reading, T169

**Leveled Reader** *The Spider and the Honey Tree*, T170–T171
**Vocabulary**
• Suffixes, T172
• Shades of Meaning, T172
*Gifted and Talented*

**Leveled Reader** Paired Read: "The Girl and the Spider," T171 ● *Analytical Writing*

**Leveled Reader** Literature Circle, T171
**Comprehension**
• Self-Selected Reading, T173
• Independent Study: Animals in Stories, T173
*Gifted and Talented*

**Leveled Reader** *The Dog and the Bone*, T176–T177
**Phonemic Awareness** Phoneme Blending, T158
**Phonics** Build with Short *u*, Long *u*: *u_e*, T161
**Structural Analysis** Review CVC*e* Syllables, T162
**Vocabulary Strategy** Suffixes, T179
**Grammar** Singular and Plural Nouns, T181

**Leveled Reader** Paired Read: "The Dingo and His Shadow," T177 ● *Analytical Writing*
**Phonemic Awareness** Phoneme Segmentation, T158
**Phonics** Blend with Short *u*, Long *u*: *u_e*, T161
**Structural Analysis** Reteach CVC*e* Syllables, T162
**Vocabulary** Additional Vocabulary, T179

**Leveled Reader** Literature Circle, T177
**Phonemic Awareness** Phoneme Segmentation, T158
**Phonics** Blend with Short *u*, Long *u*: *u_e*, T161
**Spelling** Words with Short and Long *u*, T180

### LANGUAGE ARTS

✔**Readers to Writers**
• Writing Trait: Ideas, T140
• Writing Entry: Prewrite and Draft, T140

**Grammar**
• Singular and Plural Nouns, T141
• Mechanics: Commas in a Series, T141

✔**Readers to Writers**
• Writing Trait: Ideas, T146
• Writing Entry: Revise, T146

**Grammar**
• Singular and Plural Nouns, T147
• Mechanics: Commas in a Series, T147

✔**Readers to Writers**
• Writing Trait: Ideas, T154
• Writing Entry: Share and Reflect, T154

**Grammar**
• Singular and Plural Nouns, T155
• Mechanics: Commas in a Series, T155

# DIFFERENTIATE TO ACCELERATE

## A C T Scaffold to Access Complex Text

**IF** → the text complexity of a particular selection is too difficult for children

**THEN** → use the Access Complex Text prompts to scaffold instruction.

Qualitative  Quantitative

**Reader and Task**

**TEXT COMPLEXITY**

|  | Reading/Writing Workshop | Literature Anthology | Leveled Readers | | Classroom Library |
|---|---|---|---|---|---|

### Quantitative

**Reading/Writing Workshop**

"The Boy Who Cried Wolf"

Lexile 460
*TextEvaluator*™ 4

**Literature Anthology**

*Wolf! Wolf!*
Lexile 580
*TextEvaluator*™ 18

"Cinderella and Friends"
Lexile 520
*TextEvaluator*™ 15

**Leveled Readers**

**Approaching Level**
Lexile 200
*TextEvaluator*™ 7

**Beyond Level**
Lexile 590
*TextEvaluator*™ 15

**On Level**
Lexile 440
*TextEvaluator*™ 5

**ELL**
Lexile 320
*TextEvaluator*™ 5

**Classroom Library**

*Nate the Great and the Owl Express*
   Lexile 280
   *TextEvaluator*™ 16

*Cam Jansen: The Mystery at the Monkey House #10*
   Lexile 530
   *TextEvaluator*™ 9

### Qualitative

**What Makes the Text Complex?**

- **Connections of Ideas** Using Strategies, T111
- **Organization** Problems and Solutions, T127

**A C T** *See Scaffolded Instruction in Teacher's Edition T111 and T127.*

**What Makes the Text Complex?**

- **Genre** Fable, T139B
- **Specific Vocabulary** Domain-Specific Vocabulary, T139B, T139E, T139J
- **Organization** Text Summaries, T145B

**A C T** *See Scaffolded Instruction in Teacher's Edition T139B, T139E, T139J, T145B.*

**What Makes the Text Complex?**

- **Specific Vocabulary**
- **Sentence Structure**
- **Connection of Ideas**
- **Genre**

**A C T** *See Level Up lessons online for Leveled Readers.*

**What Makes the Text Complex?**

- **Genre**
- **Specific Vocabulary**
- **Prior Knowledge**
- **Sentence Structure**
- **Organization**
- **Purpose**
- **Connection of Ideas**

**A C T** *See Scaffolded Instruction in Teacher's Edition T496–T497.*

### Reader and Task

The Introduce the Concept lesson on pages T100–T101 will help determine the reader's knowledge and engagement in the weekly concept. See pages T110–T113, T124–T127, T136–T139, and T148–T151 for questions and tasks for this text.

The Introduce the Concept lesson on pages T100–T101 will help determine the reader's knowledge and engagement in the weekly concept. See pages T139A–T139N, T145A–T145B, and T148–T151 for questions and tasks for this text.

The Introduce the Concept lesson on pages T100–T101 will help determine the reader's knowledge and engagement in the weekly concept. See pages T156–T157, T166–T167, T170–T171, T176–T177, and T148–T151 for questions and tasks for this text.

The Introduce the Concept lesson on pages T100–T101 will help determine the reader's knowledge and engagement in the weekly concept. See pages T496–T497 for questions and tasks for this text.

***Go Digital!*** http://connected.mcgraw-hill.com

## Monitor and *Differentiate*

**IF** If you need to differentiate instruction

**THEN** use the Quick Check to assess children's needs and select the appropriate small group instruction focus.

### ✓ Quick Check

**Comprehension Strategy** Make Predictions, T125

**Comprehension Skills** Problem and Solution, T127

**Genre** Fable, T137

**Vocabulary Strategy** Suffixes, T139

**Phonics/Fluency** Short *u*, long *u*; Expression, T133, T145

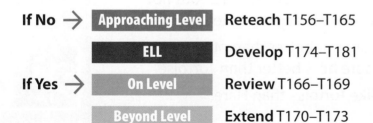

If No → **Approaching Level** Reteach T156–T165

**ELL** Develop T174–T181

If Yes → **On Level** Review T166–T169

**Beyond Level** Extend T170–T173

## Level Up with Leveled Readers

**IF** children can read their leveled text fluently and answer comprehension questions

**THEN** assign the next level up to accelerate children reading with more complex text.

T171 — Beyond

T167 — On Level

T157 — Approaching

T177 — ELL

## ENGLISH LANGUAGE LEARNERS SCAFFOLD

**IF** ELL students need additional support. **THEN** scaffold instruction using the small group suggestions.

| Reading/Writing Workshop "The Boy Who Cried Wolf," T174–T175 | Leveled Reader *The Dog and the Bone,* T176–T177 "The Dingo and His Shadow," T177 | Additional Vocabulary T179 characters lessons decided moral greed stories | Suffixes T179 | Writing Ideas, T180 | Spelling Words with short *u*, long *u*, T180 | Grammar Singular and Plural Nouns, T181 |

**Note: Include ELL Students in all small groups based on their needs.**

## Materials

**Reading/Writing Workshop**

believe

**Visual Vocabulary Cards**

believe      lessons
delicious    remarkable
feast        snatch
fond         stories

a  b  c

**Word-Building Cards**

**Interactive Read-Aloud Cards**

I predicted because...

**Think Aloud Clouds**

change

**High-Frequency Word Cards**

Uu
u
umbrella

**Sound-Spelling Cards**

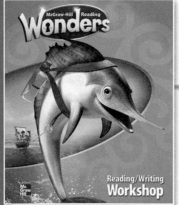

**Reading/Writing Workshop**

### OBJECTIVES

**CCSS** Participate in collaborative conversations with diverse partners about *grade 2 topics and texts* with peers and adults in small and larger groups. **SL.2.1**

**CCSS** Build on others' talk in conversations by linking their comments to the remarks of others. **SL.2.1b**

Build background knowledge.

### ACADEMIC LANGUAGE

• *lessons, stories*
• cognates: *lecciones, historias*

→ # Introduce the Concept

**MINILESSON**
**5 Mins**

# Build Background

### ESSENTIAL QUESTION

*What can animals in stories teach us?*

Read the Essential Question on page 114 of the **Reading/Writing Workshop**. Explain that there are animal **stories**, or made-up tales, that teach us **lessons** about how we should behave.

With children, discuss the illustration of the Tortoise and the Hare. Focus on the lesson learned in the story.

→ The story of the tortoise and the hare teaches a lesson about not giving up. The tortoise wins because of his slow and steady pace.

→ This story also teaches us that we are not better than other people. Hare loses the race because he is sure he is better than Tortoise.

→ The story reminds us to be more like Tortoise than Hare.

## Talk About It

**COLLABORATE**

**Ask:** *What are some animal **stories** you know? What **lessons** do they teach? What does each animal story help you learn about yourself and others?* Have children discuss in pairs or groups.

Model using the Concept Web to talk about the lessons learned from animal stories. Add children's responses.

### Collaborative Conversations

**Add New Ideas** As children engage in partner, small-group, and whole-class discussions, encourage them to:

→ stay focused on the topic of discussion.

→ build on the ideas of others.

→ connect their personal experiences to the topic discussed.

# Go Digital

**Animals in Stories**

**Video**

**Graphic Organizer**

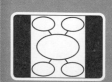
peered

**Visual Glossary**

**Weekly Concept** Animals in Stories

**Essential Question**
**What can animals in stories teach us?**

Go Digital!

FINISH

114

# Animal Lessons

Do you know the story of the Tortoise and the Hare? The Hare is ahead in a race with a slow Tortoise so he decides to take a nap. Then Tortoise ends up winning the race!

▶ Animals in stories teach us lessons.

▶ Animals in stories help us learn about each other.

**Talk About It**

Talk with a partner about the lessons we learn from animals in stories. Write the lessons on the word web.

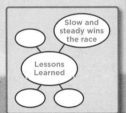

Slow and steady wins the race

Lessons Learned

115

**READING/WRITING WORKSHOP, pp. 114–115**

**ELL** **ENGLISH LANGUAGE LEARNERS**
**SCAFFOLD**

| Beginning | Intermediate | Advanced/High |
|---|---|---|
| **Use Visuals** Point to the hare. *This is a hare. It looks like a rabbit.* Point to the tortoise. *This is a tortoise.* Gesture and say: *They have a race. Hare takes a rest, so slow Tortoise wins. This story teaches us a lesson: Don't give up.* Have children restate the lesson in their own words. | **Explain** Lead children to summarize the animal story and the lesson, using concept words. *Who has a race? What happens when Hare takes a rest? What lesson do you learn from Tortoise?* Repeat children's responses, correcting grammar and pronunciation. | **Discuss** Have children discuss a familiar animal story and its lesson. Ask questions to help them elaborate. *What is the story about? What lesson does it teach?* Elicit details to support children's responses. |

**GRAPHIC ORGANIZER**

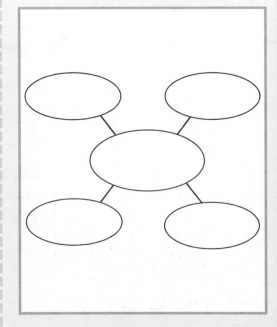

→ # Build the Concept

##  Oral Language
*MINILESSON 5 Mins*

---

### OBJECTIVES

 **CCSS** Ask and answer questions about what a speaker says in order to clarify comprehension, gather additional information, or deepen understanding of a topic or issue. **SL.2.3**

• Develop oral language.
• Discuss the Essential Question.

### ACADEMIC LANGUAGE
*fable, predictions, confirm, revise*

---

**ESSENTIAL QUESTION**

Remind children that this week you'll be talking and reading about lessons that animals in stories can teach us.

### Oral Vocabulary Words

Use the Define/Example/Ask routine to introduce the Oral Vocabulary words below. Prompt children to use the words as they discuss animal fables.

---

#### Oral Vocabulary Routine

**Define:** When you have an **affection** for someone or something, you like that person or thing a lot.

**Example:** Naomi's baby sister showed her affection by hugging Naomi's leg.

**Ask:** How do you show affection?

**Define:** When you **crave** something, you want it very much.

**Example:** When I get thirsty, I crave a glass of ice-cold water.

**Ask:** What do you crave when you're thirsty or hungry?

**Define:** People who are **frustrated** are discouraged because they are having a hard time doing something.

**Example:** I get frustrated when I have trouble untying a knot.

**Ask:** What makes you feel frustrated?

**Define:** **Nourishment** is what you get from healthful foods.

**Example:** Fruits and vegetables give a lot of nourishment.

**Ask:** What foods do you get nourishment from?

**Define:** **Seek** means to look for.

**Example:** The bear seeks a den to spend the winter in.

**Ask:** What do you seek when you go to the grocery store?

---

## Go Digital

**The Fox and the Crane**

**Make, Confirm, Revise Predictions**

# Listening Comprehension

 **MINILESSON 10 Mins**

## Interactive Read Aloud

### Read "The Fox and the Crane"

Tell children that you will read an animal story about a fox and a crane. The story is a fable. A fable is a made-up story that teaches a lesson. Display the Interactive Read-Aloud Cards.

**Interactive Read Aloud Cards**

### Strategy: Make, Confirm, Revise Predictions

**1 Model** Remind children that they can use what they read in a story to help them predict, or guess, what might happen next. Making predictions helps readers decide what to look for when reading. As they read, they can confirm or revise their predictions.

**Think Aloud** Remember, a prediction is an informed guess about what will happen in a story. To make a prediction, you can use both the words and the pictures in a story. Today, as we read "The Fox and the Crane," think about what may happen. Then read on to find out if your predictions are correct.

**2 Apply** As you read, use the Think Aloud Cloud to model applying the strategy. Have children make a prediction and then confirm whether the prediction is correct.

**Think Aloud** Remember that you should check, or confirm, your predictions as you read. You may need to change, or revise, them. We read that Fox invited Crane to dinner and tricked Crane. Then we read that Crane invited Fox to dinner. I predict that Crane will trick Fox. I'll read to check whether my prediction is correct.

### Make Connections

 After reading, have children share the lesson they learned from the animals in the fable. Then have them discuss the predictions they made and whether they were correct or had to be revised.

 **ELL**

**ENGLISH LANGUAGE LEARNERS**

**Seek Clarification** Some children may be confused by unfamiliar words. Encourage children to always seek clarification when they encounter a word or phrase that does not make sense to them. For example, *I don't understand the phrase* long and narrow necks. *Can you show me?*

→ # Word Work

## Quick Review

**Build Fluency: Sound Spellings**
Display the **Word-Building Cards:** *o_e, o, i_e, i, a_e, a, sl, dr, sk, sp, st, tr, pr, pl*. Have children say each sound.

**MINILESSON 5 Mins**

# Phonemic Awareness

**OBJECTIVES**

**CCSS** Know and apply grade-level phonics and word analysis skills in decoding words. **RF.2.3**

**CCSS** Distinguish long and short vowels when reading regularly spelled one-syllable words. **RF.2.3a**

- Delete phonemes in a word.
- Apply phonics when decoding words with short and long *u*.

## Phoneme Deletion

**1 Model** Show children that deleting the first sound in a word can sometimes form a new word. *Listen for the first sound in the word* trust: */t/. Now listen as I say the word and then take away the first sound:* trust, rust. *When I took away the first sound, /t/, I made a new word,* rust. *What is* trust *without the /t/?* Trust *without the /t/ is* rust.

Continue modeling phoneme deletion with the following word sets.

cluck/luck        fuse/use        spot/pot

**2 Guided Practice/Practice** Have children practice deleting phonemes. Do the first one together. *Listen for the sounds in each word. Take away the first sound and say the new word. Let's do the first one together. The word is* stuck, */s/ /t/ /u/ /k/. The first sound in* stuck *is /s/. What is* stuck *without the /s/?* Stuck *without the /s/ is /t/ /u/ /k/,* tuck.

Have children delete the first phoneme to create new words.

crust        plot        muse        flight        brain        send        clump

**Go Digital**

**Phonemic Awareness**

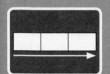

**Phonics**

### SKILLS TRACE

**Short *u* and Long *u***

**INTRODUCE** Unit 2 Week 2 Day 1

**REVIEW** Unit 2 Week 2 Day 2, Day 3, Day 4, Day 5

**ASSESS** Unit 2

**MINILESSON 10 Mins**

# Phonics

**Sound-Spelling Card**

## Introduce Long *u*: u_e

**1 Model** Display the *Cube* **Sound Spelling Card**.
Teach /ū/ spelled u_e using *cube* and *mule*. Model writing the letters u_e. *This is the* Cube *Sound-Spelling Card. The middle sound in* cube *is /ū/. The /ū/ sound can be spelled with the letters* u, consonant, e. *The* u *and* e *work together to make the long u sound. The* e *is silent. Say it with me: /ū/. Watch as I write* u_e. *I will say the sound as I write the letters.*

Repeat with the *Umbrella* Sound-Spelling Card to review short u /u/.

**2 Guided Practice/Practice** Have children practice connecting the letters u_e to the sound /ū/ through writing. *Now do it with me. Say /ū/ as I write the letters* u_e. *This time write the letters* u_e *five times as you say the /ū/ sound.* Repeat the procedure for short *u*.

# Blend Words with Short *u* and Long *u*

**1 Model** Display **Word-Building Cards** *f, u, m, e*. Model how to blend the sounds. This is the letter *f*. It stands for /f/. This is the letter *u*. It stands for /ū/. This is the letter *m*. It stands for /m/. *This is the letter e. It is silent; the* u *and* e *together make the long* u *sound /ū/. Listen as I blend all three sounds: /fffūūūmmm/,* fume. *Say it with me.*

Continue modeling the words *tub, cut, cute,* and *mute*.

**2 Guided Practice/Practice** Display the Day 1 **Phonics Practice Activity**. Read each word in the first row, blending the sounds, for example: */ruuun/. The word is* run. Have children blend each word with you. Prompt children to read the connected text, sounding out the decodable words.

| | | | | | |
|---|---|---|---|---|---|
| run | use | cube | up | gum | jump |
| cute | rub | us | fume | mule | plus |
| mute | hut | puff | plump | fuse | stub |
| flake | tone | mole | time | ride | late |

Gus will use a cup.

The little dog is cute.

Russ will run a race in June.

**Phonics Practice**

Also online

## Corrective Feedback

**Sound Error** Model the sound children missed, then have them repeat the sound. Say: *My turn.* Tap under the letter and say: *Sound? /u/ (/ū/). What's the sound?* Return to the beginning of the word. Say: *Let's start over.* Blend the word with children again.

## ENGLISH LANGUAGE LEARNERS SCAFFOLD

**Phonemic Awareness: Minimal Contrasts** Focus on articulation. Say /u/ and note your mouth position. Have children repeat. Use the articulation photos. Repeat for /ū/. Have children say both sounds and note the differences. Continue with *cub/cube, cut/cute, tub/tube*.

**Phonics: Variations in Language** In some native languages, including Spanish, Cantonese and Korean, there is no direct transfer for /ū/. They may also pronounce the silent *e* at the end of some long *u* words. Practice pronouncing *tube, June,* and *cube*.

### ON-LEVEL PRACTICE BOOK p. 62

The letter *u* can stand for the short *u* sound you hear in **cut**. The long *u* sound you hear in **cute** can be spelled *u_e*.

**A. Choose the word from the box that names each picture. Write it on the line.**

| mule | tub | cub | cube |
|---|---|---|---|

1. cub    2. mule

3. cube    4. tub

Vowel consonant *e* syllables often have the long sound of the vowel.

**B. Divide each word into syllables. Write each syllable.**

5. pancake    pan    cake

6. excuse    ex    cuse

| APPROACHING p. 62 | BEYOND p. 62 | ELL p. 62 |
|---|---|---|

→ # Word Work

## 5 Mins Spelling

### Words with Short *u* and Long *u*

**Dictation** Use the spelling dictation routine to help children transfer their growing knowledge of sound-spellings to writing. Follow the Dictation Routine.

**Pretest** After dictation, pronounce each spelling word. Read the sentence and pronounce the word again. Ask children to say each word softly, stretching the sounds, before writing it. After the pretest, display the spelling words and write each word as you say the letter names. Have children check their words.

**Go Digital**

**Spelling Word Routine**

**High-Frequency Word Routine**

| | |
|---|---|
| **mule** | A **mule** is a strong animal. |
| **fuse** | If you **fuse** two things, you put them together. |
| **plum** | A **plum** is a fruit I love to eat. |
| **use** | We will **use** crayons today. |
| **dug** | The dog **dug** a hole in the yard. |
| **cub** | The bear **cub** went into the den. |
| **hum** | I like to **hum** songs. |
| **huge** | The mountain is **huge**! |
| **must** | I **must** be home at 5:00. |
| **fun** | We had a lot of **fun** at the party. |
| **rope** | I used a **rope** to pull the cart. |
| **nose** | I cover my mouth and **nose** when I sneeze. |
| **look** | **Look** at the bird in the tree! |
| **yes** | The answer to the question is **yes**. |
| **their** | The dogs ate all of **their** food. |

For Approaching Level and Beyond Level children, refer to the Differentiated Spelling Lists for modified word lists.

**OBJECTIVES**

CCSS Demonstrate command of the conventions of standard English capitalization, punctuation, and spelling when writing. **L.2.2**

CCSS Generalize learned spelling patterns when writing words. (e.g., cage → badge; boy → boil). **L.2.2d**

CCSS Know and apply grade-level phonics and word analysis skills in decoding words. **RF.2.3**

CCSS Recognize and read grade-appropriate irregularly spelled words. **RF.2.3f**

Spell words with short *u* and long *u*.

**ENGLISH LANGUAGE LEARNERS**

**Understand Meaning** Review the meaning of spelling words by using pictures, pantomime, or gestures when possible. Have children repeat or act out the definition as they repeat and spell the word.

# High-Frequency Words

*change, cheer, fall, five, look, open, should, their, won, yes*

**❶ Model** Display the **High-Frequency Word Cards**, *change, cheer, fall, five, look, open, should, their, won,* and *yes*. Use the Read/Spell/Write routine to teach each word.

→ **Read** Point to and say the word *won. This is the word* won. *Say it with me:* won. *She won the game.*

→ **Spell** *The word* won *is spelled w-o-n. Spell it with me.*

→ **Write** *Let's write the word in the air as we say each letter:* w-o-n.

→ Follow the same steps to introduce *yes, change, fall, five, look, open, should, their,* and *cheer*.

→ As children spell each word with you, point out the irregularities in sound/spellings, such as the /u/ sound spelled *o* in the word *won*.

→ Have partners create sentences using each word.

**❷ Guided Reading** Have children read the sentences. Prompt them to identify the high-frequency words in connected text and to blend the decodable words.

1. Mike **won** the race!
2. **Yes**, we rode bikes to school.
3. Abe had to **change** the bus he rides.
4. She could **fall** on the ice.
5. There are **five** kids in the family.
6. **Look** at the huge kite!
7. The school is now **open**.
8. He **should** swim in June.
9. Dale and Brad have **their** notes.
10. I will **cheer** at the game.

## Monitor and *Differentiate*

**Quick Check**

Can children read and decode words with short and long *u*?

Can children recognize and read high-frequency words?

### Small Group Instruction

| If No → | Approaching | Reteach pp. T158–T163 |
| | ELL | Develop pp. T174–T181 |
| If Yes → | On Level | Review pp. T168–T169 |
| | Beyond Level | Extend pp. T172–T173 |

→ # Vocabulary

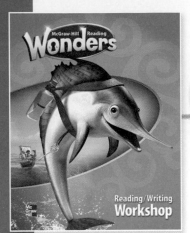

**Reading/Writing Workshop**

### OBJECTIVES

**CCSS** Demonstrate understanding of word relationships and nuances in word meanings. **L.2.5**

**CCSS** Identify real-life connections between words and their use (e.g. describe foods that are *spicy* or *juicy*). **L.2.5a**

**CCSS** Determine the meaning of words and phrases in a text relevant to a grade 2 topic or subject area. **RI.2.4**

### ACADEMIC LANGUAGE

• *lessons*

• *stories*

---

MINILESSON **10** Mins

## Words in Context

### Model the Routine

Introduce each vocabulary word using the Vocabulary Routine found on the **Visual Vocabulary Cards**.

**Visual Vocabulary Cards**

Vocabu...
Define:
Example
Ask:

**Vocabulary Routine**

**Define:** If you **believe** something, you think this is true.

**Example:** I believe it is going to rain today.

**Ask:** What is something you believe will happen today?

## Definitions

→ **delicious**    The dogs ate all of their food. When food is **delicious**, it tastes very good.

→ **feast**    If you **feast**, you eat a large or fancy meal.

→ **fond**    When you are **fond** of something, you like it a lot.

→ **lessons**    **Lessons** are things you can learn ideas or rules from.

→ **remarkable**    If something is **remarkable**, it is wonderful or outstanding.

→ **snatch**    If you **snatch** something, you grab it quickly.

→ **stories**    When you tell **stories**, you tell made-up tales.

### Talk About It

COLLABORATE

Have children work with a partner and look at each picture and discuss the meaning of each word. Then ask children to choose three words and write questions for their partner to answer.

---

**Go** Digital

**peered**

**Visual Glossary**

---

## CCSS Words to Know

# Vocabulary

Use the picture and sentence to learn each word.

**believe** I **believe** it is going to rain today.

What is something you believe will happen today?

**delicious** We ate the **delicious** pizza.

Describe something that tastes delicious.

**feast** Our family sat at the dinner table and started to **feast**.

When might you feast?

**fond** Rob is very **fond** of his puppy.

What is something that you are fond of?

**lessons** I learned a lot from the teacher's **lessons**.

What lessons do you learn at school?

**remarkable** I saw a **remarkable** rainbow in the sky.

Describe something that is remarkable.

**snatch** My dog can **snatch** a flying disc out of the air.

Show how you would snatch something off your desk.

**stories** Our dad reads us **stories** before bedtime.

What are some stories you like?

### Your Turn COLLABORATE

Pick three words. Write three questions for your partner to answer.

*Go Digital! Use the online visual glossary*

116

117

**READING/WRITING WORKSHOP, pp. 116–117**

## ELL ENGLISH LANGUAGE LEARNERS SCAFFOLD

### Beginning

**Use Visuals** *Let's look at the picture for the word* believe. Point to the child's raincoat and outstretched arm in the rain. Ask: *What do you think the weather will be like where the child is? Yes, I think it will rain. I believe it will rain.* Have children repeat the sentence.

### Intermediate

**Explain** Help children use the vocabulary words as they discuss the word meanings. Ask: *What do you believe will happen when the class bell rings?* Ask them to turn to a partner and talk about things they believe will happen at school today.

### Advanced/High

**Discuss** Display the picture for *believe* and read the sentence. Then ask: *What do you believe the weather will be like today?* Have children discuss other things they believe will happen today.

### ON-LEVEL PRACTICE BOOK p. 61

| believe | delicious | feast | fond |
|---------|-----------|-------|------|
| lessons | remarkable | snatch | stories |

**Read the story. Choose words from the box to complete the sentences. Then write the answers on the lines.**

There are some ___stories___ that teach

___lessons___. This is one of those tales. Lion was

very ___fond___ of cherries. He said, "I

___believe___ that cherries are the best food!"

When Lion heard that Hippo had lots of

___delicious___ food, he went over to take a look.

Seeing all of Hippos's food made him want to

___feast___. On the table was a bowl of the biggest

cherries he had ever seen. "That's ___remarkable___!"

thought Lion. He made a plan to ___snatch___ the

cherries. Then he ran home with them. At home, Lion

bit into a cherry. They were wax! The cherries had not

been worth taking after all.

| APPROACHING p. 61 | BEYOND p. 61 | ELL p. 61 |
|---|---|---|

VOCABULARY **T109**

# Comprehension

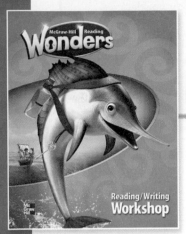

McGraw-Hill Reading
# Wonders

Reading/Writing
**Workshop**

**Reading/Writing
Workshop**

### OBJECTIVES

**CCSS** Read with sufficient accuracy and fluency to support comprehension. **RF.2.4**

**CCSS** Read on-level text with purpose and understanding. **RF.2.4a**

Identify meanings of words used in context.

### ACADEMIC LANGUAGE

*character, fable*

## Shared Read

**Lexile** 460    *TextEvaluator*™ 4

## Connect to Concept

### Animals in Stories

Explain to children that "The Boy Who Cried Wolf" is a fable about a boy who learns a lesson.

After reading each page, have partners discuss what they think the story's lesson may be.

### Use Vocabulary Words in Context

| | | | |
|---|---|---|---|
| believes | delicious | feast | fond |
| lessons | remarkable | snatch | stories |

The highlighted words in the text are vocabulary words that children have learned. As you read, have them discuss the words' meanings.

## Close Reading

**Reread Paragraph 1:** Tell children that you are going to take a closer look at the beginning of the story. Reread the first paragraph of page 119 together. Lead children to make observations and inferences about the main character and his motivation. Ask: *What is the boy's job? Look at the picture. How do you think the boy feels when he is doing his job?* Model how to cite text evidence to answer the questions.

*The story says that the boy's job is to watch all the sheep that belong to the villagers. In the picture he looks bored. The text says the boy doesn't like his job and that he would have liked something wonderful to happen. This also makes it sound like the boy is bored.*

**Reread Paragraph 2:** Reread the second paragraph of page 119 together. Help children connect the boy's actions and motivation to the inferences they have already made. Ask: *What does the boy do while he sits on the hilltop? Why do you think he does this?* Model how to use text evidence and your own experience to answer the questions.

*He watches the clouds and makes up stories. I think he does this because he is bored. I think he also likes to imagine things.*

## Go
## Digital

**The Boy Who Cried Wolf**

**Shared Read** Genre • Fable

# The Boy Who Cried Wolf

**Essential Question**

**What can animals in stories teach us?**

Read to find out what a shepherd boy learns.

118

Long ago a shepherd boy sat on a hilltop watching the village sheep. He was not **fond** of his job. He didn't like it one bit. He would have liked something wonderful to happen, but nothing **remarkable** ever did.

The shepherd boy watched the clouds move softly by to stay busy. He saw horses, dogs, and dragons in the sky. He made up **stories** with these things as characters.

119

**READING/WRITING WORKSHOP, pp. 118–119**

## A C T  **A**ccess **C**omplex **T**ext

▶ **Connections of Ideas**

Children may need help in making inferences about the boy's motivation and actions, and connecting them to story events.

→ Review the final paragraph on page 119 and the first paragraph on page 120. Say: *On the top of page 120, it says that boy had a better idea. What is the idea? What idea is it better than?* (Crying wolf is the better idea. The other is telling stories.) *Why does the boy do these things?* (He does them because he is bored.)

→ Help children connect the boy's actions on pages 120 and 121 with the villager's actions on page 122. Have children discuss why the villagers don't come when there is a real wolf.

Then one day he had a better idea! He took a deep breath and cried out, "Wolf! Wolf! The wolf is chasing the sheep!"

The villagers ran up the hill to help the boy. When they got there, they saw no harmful wolf. The boy laughed. "Shepherd boy! Don't cry 'wolf!' unless there really is a wolf!" said the villagers. They went back down the hill.

That afternoon the boy again cried out, "Wolf! Wolf! The wolf is chasing the sheep!"

The villagers ran to help the boy again. They saw no wolf. The villagers were angry. "Don't cry 'wolf!' when there is NO WOLF!" they said. The shepherd boy just smiled. The villagers went quickly down the hill again.

120

121

**READING/WRITING WORKSHOP,** pp. 120–121

# Shared Read  *CLOSE READING*

## Close Reading

**Reread page 120:** Tell children that you are going to take a closer look at page 120. Together, read the page. Ask questions to help children make inferences about the main character and what happens: *Why do the villagers run up the hill? Look at the illustration. How does the boy look? In the second paragraph, why does the boy laugh?*

Model using text evidence to answer the questions. *The text says that boy cried "wolf" and the villagers rushed up to help him. The boy has a smile. I think he laughs because he thinks it is funny he has tricked them by crying "wolf" when there is no wolf.*

## Make Connections

**ESSENTIAL QUESTION**

Encourage children to go back into the text for evidence and talk about what the shepherd boy learned. Then ask them to explain the lesson they learned from this animal story.

That afternoon the boy saw a REAL wolf. He did not want the wolf to grab any of the sheep! The boy thought the wolf would **snatch** one of them for a **delicious**, tasty meal. A sheep would be a big **feast** for a wolf. He quickly jumped to his feet and cried, "WOLF! WOLF!" The villagers thought he was tricking them again, so they did not come.

That night the shepherd boy did not return with their sheep. The villagers found the boy weeping real tears. "There really was a wolf here!" he said. "The flock ran away! When I cried out, 'Wolf! Wolf!' no one came. Why didn't you come?"

A kind man talked to the boy as they walked slowly back to the village. "In the morning, we'll help you look for the sheep," he said. "You have just learned one of life's important **lessons**. This is something you need to know. Nobody **believes** a person who tells lies. It is always better to tell the truth!"

### Make Connections

What did you learn after reading this animal story? ESSENTIAL QUESTION

Tell how you are similar or different from the shepherd boy. TEXT TO SELF

122

123

Peter Francis

**READING/WRITING WORKSHOP, pp. 122–123**

# Continue Close Reading

Use the following lesson for focused rereadings.

→ Make, Confirm, Revise Predictions, T124–T125

→ Plot: Problem and Solution, T126–T127

→ Genre and Story Structure, T136–T137

→ Suffixes, T138–T139

## ELL ENGLISH LANGUAGE LEARNERS SCAFFOLD

**Idioms** Explain that "to cry wolf" is a common idiom that comes from this story. It means to tell people there is a danger or an emergency when there is none. Help children understand the origin of this idiom. Have them look at pagees 120–121. Say: *The boy cries wolf. Cry can mean "say loudly" or "call for help."* Look at page 120. When the boy cries "wolf," is there really a wolf? (no) On page 121, when the boy cries "wolf," is there really a wolf? (no) Repeat for pages 122–123. Then ask: *What problem happens when the boy cries "wolf "this time?* (The villagers do not come because they think the boy is saying something untrue.)

→ # Language Arts

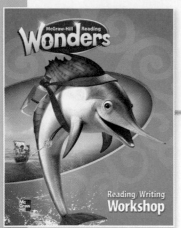

**Reading/Writing Workshop**

### OBJECTIVES

**CCSS** Write narratives in which they recount a well-elaborated event or short sequence of events, include details to describe actions, thoughts, and feelings. **W.2.3**

**CCSS** With guidance and support from adults and peers, focus on a topic and strengthen writing as needed by revising and editing. **W.2.5**

**CCSS** Demonstrate command of the conventions of standard English capitalization, punctuation, and spelling when writing. **L.2.2**

### ACADEMIC LANGUAGE
*ideas, supporting details*

 **MINILESSON 10 Mins** # Writing Traits: Ideas

## Discuss the Expert Model

**Explain** Explain that good writers use supporting details to explain their ideas. Supporting details:

→ give information about important events.

→ give words the characters say.

→ give information about how characters feel.

 Read aloud the expert model from "The Boy Who Cried Wolf." Ask children to listen for details that help them understand how the villagers feel when they realize the boy tricked them again. Have children talk with partners to identify these details.

## Discuss the Student Model

Remind children that details help readers understand the writer's ideas. Read aloud the student draft of the beginning of the fable. As children follow along, have them focus on the supporting details the writer included in her draft.

 Invite partners to talk about the draft and the supporting details Lisa used. Ask them to suggest places where Lisa could add or change details.

---

**WRITING ENTRY: SUPPORTING DETAILS**

**1 Prewrite** Provide children with the prompt below:

*Rewrite the beginning of the fable "The Boy Who Cried Wolf." Be sure to use supporting details to help readers understand your ideas.*

**2 Draft** Have children choose a topic and use their notes to write a draft. Suggest that children think about how the boy might have done something differently, such as written a letter to a friend. Remind children to include supporting details as they write.

**Go Digital**

**Present the Lesson**

**Writing**

CCSS **Writing Traits** Ideas

# Readers to...

Writers explain their **ideas** by using supporting details. Reread the passage from "The Boy Who Cried Wolf."

## Ideas
What **details** does the writer use to help you understand how the villagers feel?

**Expert Model**

The Villagers ran to help the boy again. They saw no wolf. The villagers were angry. "Don't cry 'wolf!' when there is NO WOLF!" they said. The shepherd boy just smiled. The villagers went quickly down the hill again.

# Writers

Lisa rewrote the beginning of the fable. Read Lisa's revision.

**Student Model**

The Boy Who Cried Wolf

the shepherd boy was bored.
He was so bored he fell asleep.
He dreamed a wolf came. He
was very scared. He woke
woke up and he screamed
"Wolf! There's a wolf running
this way!" The villager<sup>s</sup>
came running up the hill.

## Editing Marks
∧ Add
⊙ Add a period.
✐ Take out.
≡ Make a capital letter.

**Grammar Handbook**
**Plural Nouns**
See page 479.

## Your Turn COLLABORATE
☑ Identify the important details Lisa used.
☑ Identify a plural noun.
☑ Tell how the revisions improved her writing.

*Go Digital!*
*Write online in Writer's Workspace*

128

129

**READING/WRITING WORKSHOP, pp. 128–129**

## ELL ENGLISH LANGUAGE LEARNERS SCAFFOLD

### Beginning
**Write Sentences** Provide model sentences based on the prompt:

*The shepherd boy was _____. First, he _____. Then he _____. Last, he _____.*

Help children complete the sentence frames with important supporting details.

### Intermediate
**Identify Details** Lead children to write three sentences based on the prompt. Help them identify a main idea and three supporting details to include. Provide sentence frames and revise for meaning, as needed. Guide children in brainstorming the main idea and details.

### Advanced/High
**Respond** Ask children to respond to the prompt. Remind them to use supporting details that explain their ideas.

## Genre Writing

**Expository Text**
For full writing process lessons and rubrics, see:

→ How-to, pages T480–T485

→ How-to, pages T486–T491

→ # Language Arts

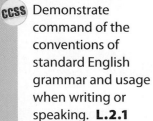 **MINILESSON 10 Mins** ## Grammar

## OBJECTIVES

**CCSS** Demonstrate command of the conventions of standard English grammar and usage when writing or speaking. **L.2.1**

**CCSS** Demonstrate command of the conventions of standard English grammar and usage when writing or speaking. **L.2.2**

## ACADEMIC LANGUAGE
*singular noun, plural noun, comma*

## Singular and Plural Nouns

**1 Explain/Model** Explain that some nouns name one person, place, or thing. These are singular nouns. Some nouns name more than one person, place, or thing. These nouns are called plural nouns. Tell children that you can usually make a noun plural by adding –s. Display the following sentence:

> The dogs trick the cat.

Model identifying the singular and plural nouns in the sentence. (dogs, plural; cat, singular)

**Think Aloud** Which words name a person, animal, place, or thing? The words *dogs* and *cat* name animals. The word *dogs* ends in -s. There is more than one dog. *Dogs* is a plural noun. *Cat* does not end in -s. There is only one cat. *Cat* is a singular noun.

Model adding -s to *cat* to form a plural noun. Discuss how adding -s changes the meaning of the sentence.

**2 Guided Practice** Display the sentences below and read them aloud. Have children identify the nouns and tell if they are singular or plural.

> The fox gave rocks to the crane. (fox–singular; rocks–plural; crane–singular)

> The boys yelled at the wolf. (boys–plural; wolf–singular)

**Practice** Display the sentence below and read it aloud. Have partners rewrite the sentence, changing the singular noun to a plural noun and the plural noun to a singular noun. Have them discuss the change in meaning of the sentence.

> The girls ran after the cat. (The girl ran after the cats.)

## Talk About It

 **Find Nouns** Display the following nouns: *lizard, lions, rabbits, snake, pet, animals, frogs, turtle.* Have partners record the nouns in a two-column chart labeled "singular nouns" and "plural nouns" and take turns using the nouns in sentences.

# Mechanics: Commas in a Series

**1 Explain/Model** Tell children that commas are used to separate three or more words in a series. Explain that the word *and* or *or* comes before the last word in a series. Display the sentences below and read them aloud:

*Fairy tales, folktales, and fables can have animal characters.*

*We may read about foxes, birds, or fish.*

Guide children to name the words in the series in each sentence. Have them point out the commas between the words.

**2 Guided Practice/Practice** Display the sentence below and read it aloud. Have partners tell where to add the commas.

*We know stories about a fox, a crane, a tortoise, and a hare.*

**GRAMMAR PRACTICE BOOK** p. 31

- A **singular noun** names one person, place, or thing.
- A **plural noun** names more than one person, place, or thing.
- Add *–s* to make the plural of most nouns.

  I see one <u>bird</u>.

  Tom sees two <u>birds</u>.

**A. Make the underlined noun plural. Write it on the line provided.**

1. Fox saw some <u>grape</u> in a tree. _____ grapes

2. Fox took a few <u>step</u> to reach them. _____ steps

3. The rabbit had many <u>friend</u>. _____ friends

4. A farmer found some golden <u>egg</u>. _____ eggs

# Daily Wrap Up

→ Discuss the Essential Question and encourage children to discuss using the new concept and oral vocabulary words. Ask: *What lessons did you learn from the animal stories today? What might happen if you tried to trick a friend?*

→ Prompt children to share what skills they learned. How might they use those skills?

## Materials

Reading/Writing Workshop

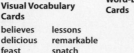
believes

**Visual Vocabulary Cards**

believes    lessons
delicious    remarkable
feast    snatch
fond    stories

a  b  c

**Word-Building Cards**

**Interactive Read Aloud Cards**

change

**High-Frequency Word Cards**

mule

**Spelling Word Cards**

Uu
u

umbrella

**Sound-Spelling Cards**

→ # Build the Concept

**MINILESSON**
**5 Mins**

# Oral Language

## OBJECTIVES

 Participate in collaborative conversations with diverse partners about grade 2 topics and texts with peers and adults in small and larger groups. **SL.2.1**

 Recount or describe key ideas or details from a text read aloud or information presented orally or through other media. **SL.2.2**

- Develop oral language.
- Discuss the Essential Question.
- Retell story events.

## ACADEMIC LANGUAGE

*fable, predictions, confirm, revise*

### ESSENTIAL QUESTION

**COLLABORATE**

Remind children that this week you are talking and reading about animals in fables. Remind them of the lesson they learned about in "The Fox and the Crane" and "The Boy Who Cried Wolf." Guide children to talk about the Essential Question using information from what they have read and talked about on Day 1.

### Review Oral Vocabulary

Review the oral vocabulary words *affection, crave, frustrated, nourishment,* and *seek* using the Define/Example/Ask routine. Encourage children to discuss animals in fables when coming up with examples for the word.

## Go Digital

**The Fox and the Crane**

**Retell Routine**

# Listening Comprehension

MINILESSON
5 Mins

## Interactive Read Aloud

### Reread "The Fox and the Crane"

Tell children that you will reread "The Fox and the Crane." Display the Interactive Read Aloud Cards.

### Strategy: Make, Confirm, Revise Predictions

Remind children that as they read they should confirm and revise their predictions. *As we reread "The Fox and the Crane," think about the predictions you made yesterday. I remember that I predicted Crane would trick Fox. I confirmed the prediction. Crane tricked Fox.*

**Interactive Read Aloud Cards**

Read aloud "The Fox and the Crane." Pause to model using the strategy. Prompt children to review the predictions they made yesterday. Guide them to point out story events that helped them to confirm or revise their predictions.

### Model Retelling

Pause to retell parts of the selection. *I can put the information from the text and the illustrations in my own words. So far, I have read that Fox and Crane were best friends, but that changed when Fox tricked Crane. Fox asked Crane to dinner. Fox served soup in a shallow bowls that Crane could not eat from. Crane asked Fox to come have dinner at her house.*

Remind children that when they retell a selection, they should tell the important events and details in the correct order.

### Retell the Selection

After reading, guide children to retell the entire selection. Remind them to tell the important events and details in the correct order. You may wish to let children use the pictures on the Interactive Read Aloud Cards to help them retell the selection.

 **Word Work**

**Quick Review**

**Build Fluency: Sound-Spellings** Display the **Word-Building Cards:** *u_e, u, o_e, o, i_e, i, a_e, a, sl, dr, sk, sp, st, tr, pr, pl.* Have children say each sound. Repeat, and vary the pace.

### MINILESSON 5 Mins

# Phonemic Awareness

**OBJECTIVES**

**CCSS** Know and apply grade-level phonics and word analysis skills in decoding words. **RF.2.3**

**CCSS** Distinguish long and short vowels when reading regularly spelled one-syllable words. **RF.2.3a**

• Segment phonemes to form new words.

• Blend and build words with short *u* spelled *u* and long *u* spelled *u_e.*

**ACADEMIC LANGUAGE**
*segment, phoneme, blend*

## Phoneme Segmentation

**1 Model** Show children that you can say each sound in a word. Say: *I am going to say a word. The word is* mud. *How many sounds are in the word* mud? */m/ /u/ /d/. I will place one counter on the ResponseBoard for each sound I hear in the word* mud. *Watch. /mmm/* (Place counter in the first box.) */uuu/* (Place counter in the second box.) */d/* (Place counter in the third box.) *The word* mud *has three sounds: /m/ /u/ /d/.*

Continue modeling phoneme segmentation with the following words.

cub    sun    mule    flute

**2 Guided Practice/Practice** Have children practice segmenting phonemes. Do the first one together. Listen carefully as I *say a word:* up. *Say it with me: /uuup/. How many sounds are in the word* up? *Let's place one counter on the ResponseBoard for each sound: /uuu/* (Place counter in the first box.) */p/* (Place counter in the second box.) *The word* up *has two sounds: /u/ /p/,* up.

Have children segment the following words into phonemes.

duck    cute    club    hug    muse

### MINILESSON 5 Mins

# Phonics

## Review Short u and Long *u*: u_e

**1 Model** Display the *Cube* **Sound Spelling Card** for /ū/ spelled *u_e* . Then review the short *u* sound using the *Umbrella* **Sound Spelling Card**. Use minimal contrast pairs to show how the vowel team *u_e* forms the long *u* sound.

**2 Guided Practice/Practice** Have children practice connecting the spelling and sound through writing. Point to the *Cube* Sound Spelling Card and say: *Write the spelling* u_e *five times as you say the /ū/ sound. Repeat with /u/,* u.

**Go Digital**

**Phonemic Awareness**

**Phonics**

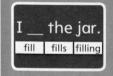

**Structural Analysis**

# Blend with Short *u* and Long *u* (*u_e*)

**1 Model** Display Word-Building Cards *c, u, t*. Model how to generate and blend the sounds to say the word. *This is the letter* c. *It stands for /k/. This is the letter* u. *It stands for /u/. This is the letter* t. *It stands for /t/. Listen as I blend all three sounds: /kut/. Say it with me:* cut. *Now place the letter* e *at the end of* cut. *The letter* e *does not stand for a sound when it is added to the end of a word. The letters* u *and* e *act as a team. Together they stand for /ū/, the long* u *sound. Listen as I blend these three sounds: /kūūt/,* cute. *Now you say it.*

→ Continue to model blending with: *fume*.

**2 Guided Practice/Practice** Repeat the routine with children with *cub/cube, us/use, mutt/mute.*

# Build Words with Short *u* and Long *u*

**1 Model** Display the Word-Building Cards *u, p*. Blend /u/ /p/ /up/, *up*.

→ Add *c* to *up* and repeat with *cup*.

→ Change *p* to *t* and repeat with *cut*.

→ Add *e* to *cut* and repeat with *cute*.

**2 Guided Practice/Practice** Continue with *cub, cube; tub, tube; us, use; plum, plume*. Guide children to build and blend each word.

---

MINILESSON
5 Mins

# Structural Analysis

## CVC*e* Syllables

**1 Model** Tell children that some words can be divided into syllables. Explain that every syllable in a word has one vowel sound. Write the word *inside* and read it aloud. Draw a vertical line between the *n* and the *s*. Point out that the last syllable ends in vowel, consonant, final *e*. Have children read each syllable with you. Explain that this is called a Final *e* syllable. *Final* e *syllables usually have long vowel sounds, and the* e *is silent. When a word or syllable ends in* e, *often the vowel before it and the letter* e *form a vowel team. Both of these vowel letters must stay in the same syllable.* Continue modeling with *amuse*. Explain to children that they may need to approximate sounds when reading multisyllabic words.

**2 Practice/Apply** Write the following words on the board: *inside, reptile, cupcake, sunrise, ignite*. Have children underline the CVC*e* syllable, then read the entire word.

---

**ON-LEVEL PRACTICE BOOK** p. 62

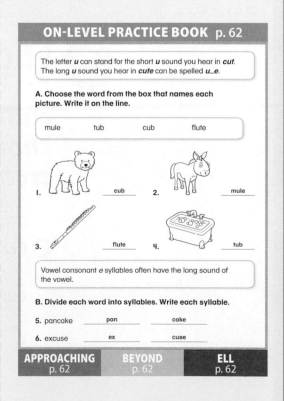

The letter *u* can stand for the short *u* sound you hear in *cut*. The long *u* sound you hear in *cute* can be spelled *u_e*.

**A. Choose the word from the box that names each picture. Write it on the line.**

| mule | tub | cub | flute |

1. cub    2. mule

3. flute    4. tub

Vowel consonant *e* syllables often have the long sound of the vowel.

**B. Divide each word into syllables. Write each syllable.**

5. pancake    pan    cake

6. excuse    ex    cuse

| APPROACHING p. 62 | BEYOND p. 62 | ELL p. 62 |

→ # Word Work

## MINILESSON 5 Mins

# Spelling

**OBJECTIVES**

**CCSS** Know and apply grade-level phonics and word analysis skills in decoding words. **RF.2.3**

**CCSS** Recognize and read grade-appropriate irregularly spelled words. **RF.2.3f**

**CCSS** Determine or clarify the meaning of unknown and multiple-meaning words and phrases based on *grade 2 reading and content*, choosing flexibly from an array of strategies. **L.2.4**

**CCSS** Use a known root word as a clue to the meaning of an unknown word with the same root (e.g., *addition, additional*). **L.2.4.c**

## Word Sort with Short *u* and Long *u*

❶ **Model** Display the Spelling Word Cards, one at a time. Have children read each word, listening for the short *u* and long *u* sound.

Use cards for *dug* and *mute* to make a two-column chart. Say each word and pronounce the sounds: /d/ /u/ /g/; /m/ /ū/ /t/. Say each word again. Ask children to chorally spell each word.

❷ **Guided Practice/Practice** Have children place each Spelling Word Card in the column with the same vowel sound. (short *u*: plum, dug, cub, hum, must, tub; long *u*: mule, fuse, use, huge)

When completed, have children chorally read the words in each column. Then call out a word. Have a child find the word card and point to it as the class chorally spells the word.

❸ **Build Fluency: Word Automaticity** Have children chorally read words to build fluency. Then conclude by asking children to generate additional words with short *u* and long *u* spelled *u_e*. List them in the correct columns.

## MINILESSON 5 Mins

# High-Frequency Words

*change, cheer, fall, five, look, open
should, their, won, yes*

❶ **Guided Practice** Say each word and have children Read/Spell/Write it. Ask children to picture the word, and write it the way they see it. Display the words for children to self-correct.

❷ **Practice** Add the week's High-Frequency words to the cumulative word bank. Have partners create sentences using the words.

**Cumulative Review** Review last week's words *because, cold, family, friends, have, know, off, picture, school, took* using the Read/Spell/Write routine. Repeat the above routine, mixing the words and having children say each one.

## Go Digital

**Spelling Word Sort**

**High-Frequency Word Routine**

**peered**

**Visual Glossary**

# → Vocabulary

**ENGLISH LANGUAGE LEARNERS**

**More Practice** Practice spelling by helping children generate more words with short *u* and long *u*, *u_e* patterns. Provide clues: *I drink from this. It rhymes with* pup. Write the word (*cup*) and have children practice reading it. Correct their pronunciation, if needed.

**MINILESSON**
**5 Mins**

## Expand Vocabulary

Have children use the Visual Vocabulary Cards to review this week's vocabulary words: *fond, believe, feast, remarkable, lessons, delicious, snatch, stories.*

**❶ Explain** Explain to children that words have different forms. Help children generate different forms of this week's words by adding, changing, or removing inflectional endings *-ed, -ing,* and *-s or -es.* Review the meaning of each ending.

**❷ Model** Draw a four-column T-chart on the board. Model how to add endings to the word *feast.* Write the vocabulary word *feast* in the first column. Then write *feasted, feasting,* and *feasts* in the next three columns. Read aloud the words with children.

Point out how the different endings change the meaning of *feast.* Discuss each form of the word and its meaning.

Have children share aloud sentences using *feast, feasted, feasting,* and *feasts.*

**❸ Guided Practice** Have children work in pairs to fill in charts for *lessons, stories, snatch* and *believe.* Then have children share sentences using the different forms of each word.

## Monitor and *Differentiate*

 **Quick Check**

Can children read and spell words with short *u* spelled *u* and long *u* spelled *u_e*?
Can children read high-frequency words?

⬇

**Small Group Instruction**

| | | |
|---|---|---|
| If No → | Approaching | Reteach pp. T158–T163 |
| | ELL | Develop pp. T174–T181 |
| If Yes → | On Level | Review pp. T168–T169 |
| | Beyond Level | Extend pp. T172–T173 |

# Comprehension Strategy

**CLOSE READING**

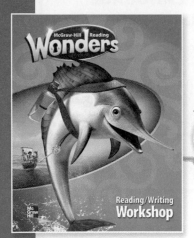

**Reading/Writing Workshop**

---

## OBJECTIVES

 Analyze how and why individuals, events, and ideas develop and interact over the course of a text.
**R.CCR.3**

 Read with sufficient accuracy and fluency to support comprehension.
**RF.2.4**

 Read on-level text with purpose and understanding.
**RF.2.4a**

---

Use text evidence to make, confirm, and revise predictions.

---

## ACADEMIC LANGUAGE
*predictions, confirm, revise*

**MINILESSON**
**10 Mins**

# Make, Confirm, Revise Predictions

### ① Explain

Remind children that a prediction is a reasonable guess about what might happen next in a story. As you read, it is important to confirm your predictions by reading on to find out whether or not the prediction was correct. Sometimes you need to revise, or change, a prediction based on an event in the story.

→ Good readers make predictions about what will happen next in a story. They base their predictions on the clues in the illustrations and on what they have read in the text.

→ Using the text to make, confirm, and revise predictions helps readers monitor their understanding. If a prediction is not confirmed, readers may need to reread to make sure they understand the story.

→ Confirming and revising predictions helps readers better understand characters and their actions.

### ② Model Close Reading: Text Evidence

Model how to make and confirm a prediction. Reread the last paragraph on page 120 of "The Boy Who Cried Wolf." Remind children of the prediction that the boy will repeat his actions and upset the villagers again. Ask: *Why might you predict that the boy will upset the villagers again?* Then have children reread page 121 and confirm the prediction.

### ③ Guided Practice of Close Reading

 Direct children to page 122 of "The Boy Who Cried Wolf." Have children work in pairs to talk about the predictions they made when the boy saw the wolf. Partners should reread the page to confirm or revise their predictions. Tell children to discuss other predictions they confirmed or revised.

**Go Digital**

**The Boy Who Cried Wolf**

**Present the Lesson**

**CCSS Comprehension Strategy**

# Make Predictions

Use what you read in the story to help you predict, or guess, what might happen next.

**Find Text Evidence**

*On page 120 of "The Boy Who Cried Wolf," I predicted that the boy will upset the villagers.*

---

**page 121**

That afternoon the boy again cried out, "Wolf! Wolf! The wolf is chasing the sheep!"

The villagers ran to help the boy again. They saw no wolf. The villagers were angry. "Don't cry 'wolf!' when there is NO WOLF!" they said. The shepherd boy just smiled. The villagers went quickly down the hill again.

*On page 121, I read that the villagers were angry with the boy. I confirmed my prediction.*

---

**Your Turn** COLLABORATE

When the boy saw the wolf, what did you predict would happen? Point to the place in the text that confirmed your prediction.

Peter Francis

124

**READING/WRITING WORKSHOP, p. 124**

---

**ON-LEVEL PRACTICE BOOK pp. 63–65**

Read the passage. Use the make predictions strategy to predict what will happen in the story.

### Fox Gets Help

One day, Fox was walking in the woods. High in a
11  tree, he saw a nice bunch of grapes. "Those will make a
23  <u>healthful</u> snack," Fox thought. He jumped up to get the
33  grapes.

34  Fox <u>nearly</u> reached the grapes, but he could not jump
44  high enough. He really wanted those grapes. So Fox
53  made a plan. He got a ladder and leaned it on the tree.
66  He should be able to reach the grapes <u>easily</u>.

| APPROACHING pp. 63–65 | BEYOND pp. 63–65 | ELL pp. 63–65 |
|---|---|---|

---

## Monitor and *Differentiate*

✓ **Quick Check**

Do children make predictions as they read? Do they base their predictions on the text and illustrations? Do they confirm or revise their predictions?

⬇

### Small Group Instruction

| | | |
|---|---|---|
| If No → | **Approaching** | Reteach pp. T156-T157 |
| | **ELL** | Develop pp. T174-T175 |
| If Yes → | **On Level** | Review pp. T166-T167 |
| | **Beyond Level** | Extend pp. T170-T171 |

---

## ELL ENGLISH LANGUAGE LEARNERS SCAFFOLD

| Beginning | Intermediate | Advanced/High |
|---|---|---|
| Help children reread the first paragraph on page 122 of "The Boy Who Cried Wolf." Explain unfamiliar words or phrases such as *feast* or *villagers*. Have children use their own words to describe what might happen to sheep and what sheep might do when a real wolf comes. Clarify children's responses as needed. | Have children reread the first two sentences of page 122. Say: *What did you predict the boy would do when he saw the wolf? What did you predict the villagers would do? Why?* Restate responses to develop children's oral language proficiency. Then have children explain how they confirmed or revised their predictions. | Have children reread the first two sentences of page 122 .Say: *What would you do if you were the boy? What would you do if you were one of the villagers? Why?* Then have partners discuss and explain the predictions they made in Your Turn, and cite text evidence to explain how they confirmed or revised their predictions. |

# Comprehension Skill

CLOSE READING

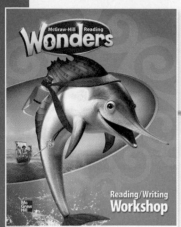
MINILESSON

**10** Mins

# Character, Setting, Plot: Problem and Solution

## ❶ Explain

Remind children that the plot is what happens in a story. Often, the plot includes a problem that the characters need to solve. The ending usually tells how the characters solved or tried to solve the problem.

→ To find the problem, readers should look at the beginning and decide what is wrong. What is the problem?

**Readers should identify the steps the characters take to solve the problem.**

→ To find the solution, readers should look to the end of the story and decide if and how the problem is solved.

## ❷ Model Close Reading: Text Evidence

Identify the problem at the beginning of "The Boy Who Cried Wolf." Model recording the problem on the graphic organizer.

 **Write About Reading: Plot Summary** Model for children how to use the notes from the graphic organizer and other text evidence to write a plot summary that describes important events. Tell children to think about what the shepherd boy says, does, and thinks to write their summary. Model by saying: *The shepherd boy has a problem. He is bored and does not like his job of watching the village sheep. The shepherd boy tries to solve his problem by crying wolf when there is no wolf. The villagers run to help the boy, but they are unhappy when they discover that he has lied.*

## ❸ Guided Practice of Close Reading

Have children work in pairs to identify steps the characters take to solve the problem and add them to the graphic organizer. Then have partners identify and record the solution. Discuss each section as children complete the graphic organizer.

 **Write About Reading: Plot Summary** Have partners complete the summary by using the following sentence frames: *First, the shepherd boy is bored so he _____. When the villagers come, they _____. Next, the shepherd boy _____. The villagers _____. Finally, the shepherd boy _____.* Select pairs to share their summaries with the class.

**OBJECTIVES**

**CCSS** Describe how characters in a story respond to major events and challenges. **RL.2.3**

**CCSS** Describe the overall structure of a story, including describing how the beginning introduces the story and the ending concludes the action. **RL.2.5**

**ACADEMIC LANGUAGE**
*plot, problem, solution*

### SKILLS TRACE

**Character, Setting, Plot: Problem and Solution**

**INTRODUCE** Unit 2 Week 2

**REVIEW** Unit 3 Week 2; Unit 5 Week 4

**ASSESS** Units 2, 5

## Go Digital

**The Boy Who Cried Wolf**

**Present the Lesson**

**Graphic Organizer**

## Comprehension Skill CCSS

# Problem and Solution

The plot is often about the problem in the story. The solution is how the characters solve the problem by the end of the story.

 **Find Text Evidence**

*In the beginning of "The Boy Who Cried Wolf," I read about the boy's problem of being bored.*

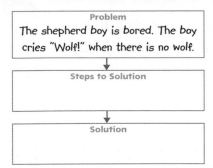

**Problem**

The shepherd boy is bored. The boy cries "Wolf!" when there is no wolf.

↓

**Steps to Solution**

↓

**Solution**

### Your Turn COLLABORATE

Finish rereading the story. Think about how the problem got solved. Fill in the boxes on the graphic organizer.

**Go Digital!**
*Use the interactive graphic organizer*

125

**READING/WRITING WORKSHOP, p. 125**

## A C T Access Complex Text

### ▶ Organization

Children may have difficulty identifying and relating problems and solutions. They may also become confused when a text has more than one problem.

→ When the boy cries wolf when there is no wolf, what problems does that create? (First, villagers run to help when there is no wolf. They stop believing the boy and do not come to help when there is a wolf. The boy loses the sheep.)

→ How does the ending solve the problems in the story? (The boy learns why it is important to tell the truth. A man tells the boy that the villagers will help him look for the sheep.)

---

**ON-LEVEL PRACTICE BOOK** pp. 63–65

A. Reread the passage and answer the questions.

1. What was the problem in the story?

   Fox wanted to get a bunch of grapes in a tree, but he couldn't reach them.

2. What steps did Fox take to solve the problem?

   He got a ladder so he could climb the tree. He accepted Turtle's help.

3. What was Fox's solution to the problem?

   Turtle held the ladder so Fox could climb the tree and get the grapes.

B. Work with a partner. Read the passage aloud. Pay attention to expression. Stop after one minute. Fill out the chart.

|  | Words Read | – | Number of Errors | = | Words Correct Score |
|---|---|---|---|---|---|
| First Read |  | – |  | = |  |
| Second Read |  | – |  | = |  |

| APPROACHING pp. 63–65 | BEYOND pp. 63–65 | ELL pp. 63–65 |
|---|---|---|

## Monitor and *Differentiate*

### ✓ Quick Check

As children complete the graphic organizer for each section, can they identify the steps to the solution? Can they identify the actual solution?

⬇

## Small Group Instruction

If No → **Approaching** Reteach pp. T164-T165

**ELL** Develop pp. T174-T177

If Yes → **On Level** Review pp. T168-T169

**Beyond Level** Extend pp. T172-T173

**Language Arts**

# Writing Traits: Ideas

**1 Explain** Remind children that writers use supporting details to help explain their ideas. Writers revise their writing by adding words and phrases to explain what characters do, what they think, and how they feel.

**2 Model** Read aloud the model from Your Turn page 67. Then think aloud to model revising to add important supporting details.

Every day a shepherd boy thought he saw a wolf. "Wolf!" he cried. The villagers came running. They felt sorry for the boy.

**Think Aloud** There are not enough supporting details to help me understand the writer's idea. I will add details. I can add a sentence to the beginning: The shepherd boy was afraid of wolves! Now readers can better understand the writer's idea.

**3 Guided Practice** Invite partners to continue adding details to the draft to make the ideas clearer. Use the prompts on Your Turn page 67 as a guide.

## WRITING ENTRY: SUPPORTING DETAILS

**1 Revise** Have children review their writing from Day 1. Ask them to revise their responses by adding supporting details to explain their ideas.

Use the Conferencing Routines to help children revise. Circulate among children and stop briefly to talk with individuals. Provide opportunities for partners to work together using the Peer Conferences routine.

**2 Edit** Ask children to review the rules on Grammar Handbook pages 478–479 and check their use of singular and plural nouns. Have children check that they have used commas in a series correctly. Have them use a dictionary to check their spelling.

## OBJECTIVES

CCSS With guidance and support from adults and peers, focus on a topic and strengthen writing as needed by revising and editing. **W.2.5**

CCSS Demonstrate command of the conventions of standard English capitalization, punctuation, and spelling when writing. **L.2.2**

## Conferencing Routines

**Teacher Conference**

**STEP 1** Talk about the strengths of the writing.
**STEP 2** Focus on the target trait.

**STEP 3** Make concrete suggestions for revisions.

**Peer Conferences**

Provide these questions to guide peers as they review a partner's draft.

- ☑ Which ideas is the writer trying to explain?

- ☑ Do supporting details make the writer's ideas clearer?

- ☑ Where do supporting details need to be added?

## Go Digital

**Writing Model**

**Writing**

I see a fish.

**Grammar**

# Grammar
**5 Mins**

## Singular and Plural Nouns

**1 Review** with children that some nouns name one person, place, or thing. These are singular nouns. Some nouns name more than one person, place, or thing. These nouns are plural nouns. Tell children that we can usually make a noun plural by adding -s. Read the following sentence aloud and guide children to identify the singular and plural nouns.

> The boys ran up the hill. (singular–hill; plural–boys)

Explain to children that not all plural nouns end in -s. Point out that we add -es to form the plural of singular nouns that end in -s, -ch, -sh, and -x. To form the plural of nouns ending in a consonant and y, we change y to i and then add -es.

**2 Guided Practice** Display the following words and read them aloud. Work with children to form the plural of each word.

ax (axes)  sock (socks)  box (boxes)  cube (cubes)

gas (gases)  peach (peaches)  dish (dishes)  baby (babies)

**3 Practice** Have partners form the plural of each word.

bus (buses)  hug (hugs)  flute (flutes)  fox (foxes)

lunch (lunches)  wish (wishes)  sky (skies)

## Mechanics: Commas in a Series

**1 Review** Remind children that commas are used to separate three or more words in a series. The word *and* or *or* comes before the last word in the series. Display the following sentence and read it aloud.

> We read about a pig, a duck, and a dog.

**2 Practice** Display the following sentences and read them aloud. Call on volunteers to write commas in the correct places.

> The fox, boy, and hare learned lessons.

> Will we read about a bird, wolf, or bear next?

---

**ON-LEVEL PRACTICE BOOK** p. 67

A. Read the draft model. Use the questions that follow the draft to help you add supporting details.

**Draft Model**

Every day a shepherd boy thought he saw a wolf. "Wolf!" he cried. The villagers came running. They felt sorry for the boy.

1. How does the shepherd boy feel?

2. What is he thinking about when he thinks he sees a wolf?

3. What details could explain more about the actions of the shepherd boy and the villagers?

B. Now revise the draft by adding supporting details that explain your ideas about how the shepherd boy and the villagers act, think, and feel.

Answers will vary but should include supporting details to explain the

characters' actions, thoughts, and feelings.

| APPROACHING | BEYOND | ELL |
|---|---|---|
| p. 67 | p. 67 | p. 67 |

---

# Daily Wrap Up

→ Discuss the Essential Question and encourage children to use the oral vocabulary words.

→ Prompt children to review and discuss the skills they used today. How do those skills help them?

## Materials

**Reading/Writing Workshop**

**Literature Anthology "Wolf, Wolf"**

believes

**Visual Vocabulary Cards**

believes    lessons
delicious    remarkable
feast    snatch
fond    stories

**Interactive Read Aloud Cards**

cub

**Spelling Word Cards**

change

**High-Frequency Word Cards**

a  b  c

**Word-Building Cards**

Uu

umbrella

**Sound-Spelling Cards**

## → Build the Concept

**MINILESSON**
**10 Mins**

# Interactive Read Aloud

## Go Digital

### OBJECTIVES

**CCSS** Ask and answer such questions as *who, what, where, when, why,* and *how* to demonstrate understanding of key details in a text. **RL.2.1**

**CCSS** Use information gained from the illustrations and words in a print or digital text to demonstrate understanding of character, setting, or plot. **RL.2.7**

**CCSS** Analyze how and why individuals, events, and ideas develop and interact over the course of a text. **R.CCR.3**

• Develop oral language.
• Discuss the Essential Question.

### ACADEMIC LANGUAGE
*key details, illustrations, character, setting, events*

### ESSENTIAL QUESTION

Remind children that this week they are talking and reading about lessons we learn from animals in stories. Remind them of the lesson that Fox learns in the "The Fox and the Crane" and of the lesson that the shepherd boy learns in "The Boy Who Cried Wolf." Guide children to discuss the Essential Question using information from what they have read and discussed throughout the week.

### Review Oral Vocabulary

Review the oral vocabulary words *affection, crave, frustrated, nourishment,* and *seek* using the Define/Example/Ask routine. Encourage children to discuss lessons in animal fables when coming up with examples for each word.

### Reread "The Fox and the Crane"

Tell children that you will reread "The Fox and the Crane." Pause as you read to review prior predictions and whether they were confirmed or revised. Prompt children to use the illustrations to identify key details.

**Interactive Read Aloud Cards**

**Analytical Writing** ### Write About Reading

Have children write about why Crane invites Fox to dinner and what happens.

**The Fox and the Crane**

**The Boy Who Cried Wolf**

# Comprehension

 ## Key Details Review

**❶ Explain** Remind children that this week they have been learning about problems and solutions to understand stories. Remind them that one way to understand problems and solutions, as well as characters and events, is to identify key details, a skill they have used in previous weeks.

Use the Shared Read, "The Boy Who Cried Wolf," to review this skill.

Review the definitions of the terms *key detail* and *illustration*:

→ A key detail is an important piece of of information that helps readers understand more about the story. Key details can be found in both the text and the illustrations.

→ An illustration is a picture in a story.

**❷ Model** Display pages 118–119 of "The Boy Who Cried Wolf." *In the illustration I see the boy and the sheep. This helps me know the key detail that the boy is in charge of the sheep. When I look at the boy's expression I see that he is bored. This is another key detail I need to know to understand the story. It may end up being a problem.*

**❸ Guided Practice** Reread "The Boy Who Cried Wolf" with children. Prompt children to answer questions about key details by using the illustrations.

→ Read page 120. Ask: *What is the boy's expression like when he is calling "Wolf!" Is he having fun?*

→ Read page 121. Say: *Look at the picture of the villagers. What does it show you about how they feel when the boy cries wolf? How do you know that it is a problem when the boy cries wolf?*

→ Reread pages 122–123. Ask: *What is happening in the illustration? Compare the boy's expression here to the picture on page 120. How does he change when the* real *wolf shows up?*

**ENGLISH LANGUAGE LEARNERS**

**Use Visuals** Have children use the illustrations to identify the key details in the story. For each page ask: *Who are the characters? What are they doing? How do they feel?*

 **Word Work**

**Quick Review**

**Build Fluency: Sound Spellings**
Display the **Word-Building Cards:** *u_e, u, o_e, o, i_e, i, a_e, a, sl, dr, sk, sp, st, tr, pr, pl.* Have children say each sound. For fluency in connected text, see the Decodable Reader Lesson in Small Group.

 **Phonemic Awareness**

### OBJECTIVES

**CCSS** Know and apply grade-level phonics and word analysis skills in decoding words. **RF.2.3**

**CCSS** Distinguish long and short vowels when reading regularly spelled one-syllable words. **RF.2.3a**

**CCSS** Demonstrate command of the conventions of standard English capitalization, punctuation, and spelling when writing. **L.2.2**

**CCSS** Generalize learned spelling patterns when writing words (e.g., cage → badge; boy → boil). **L.2.2d**

- Blend phonemes in a word.
- Identify letter-sound correspondence /u/ *u* and /ū/ *u_e*.
- Decode words with short and long *u* .
- Identify and read words with CVC*e* syllables.

### ACADEMIC LANGUAGE
*blend phoneme, syllable*

## Phoneme Blending

**1 Model** Place markers in the Response Board to represent sounds. Show children how to orally blend phonemes. *I'm going to put one marker in each box as I say each sound. Then I will blend the sounds to form a word.* Place a marker for each sound as you say: /f/ /ū/ /m/. *This word has three sounds:* /f/ /ū/ /m/. *Listen as I blend these sounds to form a word:* /fūūūmmm/, *fume. The word is* fume.

**2 Guided Practice/Practice** *Let's do some together. Using your own boards, place a marker for each sound you hear. I will say one sound at a time. Then we will blend the sounds to say the word.* Do the first three with children.

| | | |
|---|---|---|
| fuse | luck | plug |
| cube | drum | flute |
| mule | stuck | June |

 **Phonics**

## Blend Words with Short *u* and Long *u*

**1 Model** Display **Word-Building Cards** *m, u, s, e.* Model how to blend the sounds. Say: *This is the letter* m. *It stands for the sound* /m/. *This is the letter* u. *It stands for the sound* /ū/. *Listen as I blend these sounds together:* /mū/. *This is the letter* s. *It stands for* /z/. *This is the letter* e; *it is silent. The letters* u *and* e *work as a team to make the long u sound. Let's blend all three sounds together:* /mmmūūūzzz/. *The word is* muse.

Continue by modeling the words *mule, bug, tuck,* and *cute.*

**2 Guided Practice/Practice** Repeat the routine with *dug, cluck, stuff, hug, flute, prune, rule, fuse.*

### Go Digital

**Phonemic Awareness**

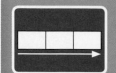

**Phonics**

**Structural Analysis**

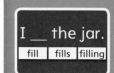

**Spelling Word Sort**

# Structural Analysis

## CVCe Syllables

**❶ Model** Say and write the word *amuse*. Point out the two syllables. Say: *Listen to the two syllables in this word:* a–muse. Clap the syllables as you say them.

→ Say: *The word* amuse *has two syllables or word parts. Each syllable in a word must have one vowel sound. Watch as I circle the vowels in this word.* (Circle the vowels *a* and *u, e*) *The second syllable is a CVCe syllable. It has the long* u *sound and the* e *is silent. These letters must stay in the same syllable. Say the syllables with me:* a–muse.

**❷ Guided Practice/Practice** Help children identify the CVCe syllable in the following words and read the words: *flagpole, refuse, unlike, invite.*

# Spelling

## Word Sort with Short *u* and Long *u*

**❶ Model** Make index cards for *u* and *u_e* and place them in columns in a pocket chart. Say each letter and pronounce each sound.

Hold up the *mule* **Spelling Word Card**. Say and spell it. Pronounce each sound clearly: /m/ /ū/ /l/. Blend the sounds: /mūūūl/. Repeat this step with *fuse*. Place both words below the *u_e* card. Read and spell each word together with children. Have children read each word and place it in the appropriate column. Point to the first column. Ask: *What do you notice about these spelling words?* (They have the /u/ sound spelled *u*.) Repeat with the second column.

**❷ Guided Practice/Practice** Have children spell each word with short *u*. Repeat the process with the long *u* words.

Display the review words *rope* and *nose*. Read and spell the words together with children. Point out that these spelling words do not contain the short or long *u* sound. They have the long *o* sound spelled *o_e*.

Conclude by asking children to orally generate other short and long *u* (*u_e*) words. Write the additional words on the board. Underline the common spelling patterns. If necessary, point out the differences and explain why they are unusual.

---

**PHONICS/SPELLING PRACTICE BOOK** p. 33

| mule | fuse | plum | use | dug |
| cub | hum | huge | must | fun |

**A. Word Sort**
Look at the spelling words in the box. Match each word to a vowel sound. Write the words on the lines.

| | Short *u* | | Long *u: u_e* |
|---|---|---|---|
| 1. | plum | 7. | mule |
| 2. | dug | 8. | fuse |
| 3. | cub | 9. | use |
| 4. | hum | 10. | huge |
| 5. | must | | |
| 6. | fun | | |

**B. Compare Words**
Look at each set of words. Circle the letters that are the same.

| | | | | | |
|---|---|---|---|---|---|
| 11. | mule | fuse | 14. | plum | dug |
| 12. | huge | use | 15. | cub | must |
| 13. | hum | fun | | | |

## Monitor and *Differentiate*

**✓ Quick Check**

Can children blend and spell words with short *u* and long *u*?

**Small Group Instruction**

If No → **Approaching** Reteach pp. T158–T163
**ELL** Develop pp. T174–T181
If Yes → **On Level** Review pp. T168–T169
**Beyond Level** Extend pp. T172–T173

# → Fluency

MINILESSON
**5** Mins

# Expression

### OBJECTIVES

CCSS Read with sufficient accuracy and fluency to support comprehension. **RF.2.4**

CCSS Read on-level text orally with accuracy, appropriate rate, and expression on successive readings. **RF.2.4b**

• Practice fluency.
• Use vocabulary words in context.

❶ **Explain** Remind children that an exclamation should be read with excitement and expression. Explain that this is part of reading with expression. When you read with expression, you can also show emotions by reading faster when a character is excited and slower when a character is sad. Good readers also raise the volume of their voice when they read an exclamation or a word that is emphasized.

❷ **Model** Model prosody by reading page 122 of the Shared Read ("The Boy Who Cried Wolf") aloud. Show children how to read at an appropriate rate and with accuracy. Model reading exclamatory sentences loudly to show excitement.

❸ **Guided Practice** Have children read the text on page 122 aloud to a partner. Make sure they pay attention to using the proper expression. Offer corrective feedback as necessary.

## Fluency Practice  FLUENCY

Children can practice fluency using the Practice Book passages.

**Go Digital**

**peered**

**Visual Glossary**

# → Vocabulary

MINILESSON
5 Mins

## Reinforce Vocabulary

**1 Guided Practice**  Use the Visual Vocabulary Cards to review this week's and last week's vocabulary words: *believe, delicious, feast, fond, lessons, remarkable, snatch, stories, adapt, climate, eager, freedom, fresh, sense, shadows, silence, stories*. Work together with children to generate a new context sentence for each word.

**2 Practice**  Have children work with a partner to complete each sentence stem orally using this week's and last week's vocabulary words.

**1.** It was _____ that the dog climbed the tree! (remarkable)

**2.** The children saw their _____ on the ground when the sun was up. (shadows)

**3.** Elise and I _____ cats make the best pets. (believe)

**4.** The air outdoors had a _____ smell. (fresh)

**5.** Emilio is very _____ of his new book. (fond)

**6.** Roberto is _____ to share his science experiment with the class. (eager)

**7.** There was _____ while the children read their books in class. (silence)

**8.** Yvette made a soup that tasted _____. (delicious)

**9.** There was lots of food at the _____! (feast)

**10.** At recess, you have the _____ to run and play. (freedom)

**11.** We watched the duck _____ the bread we threw. (snatch)

**12.** I have a _____ that it will rain soon. (sense)

**13.** Did you study your social studies _____? (lessons)

**14.** We live in a hot _____. (climate)

**15.** Many animals learn to _____ to their habitat. (adapt)

**16.** I read a lot of _____ about animals. (stories)

# Genre: Fiction

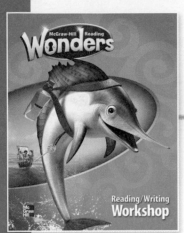

**Reading/Writing Workshop**

---

### OBJECTIVES

**CCSS** Recount stories, including fables and folktales from diverse cultures, and determine their central message, lesson, or moral. **RL.2.2**

**CCSS** Describe the overall structure of a story, including describing how the beginning introduces the story and the ending concludes the action. **RL.2.5**

Recognize the features of a fable.

---

### ACADEMIC LANGUAGE
*fable, beginning, middle, end*

---

## MINILESSON 10 Mins **Fable**

### ❶ Explain

Share with children the following key characteristics of a **fable**.

→ A fable is a made-up short story that teaches a lesson or moral and has a clear beginning, middle, and end.

→ A fable may have animal characters that speak and act like people.

### ❷ Model Close Reading: Text Evidence

Model identifying the genre of "The Boy Who Cried Wolf." *I can tell that this story is a fable. It is a made-up story. It has a clear beginning that tells about a problem. It has a middle in which the characters try to solve the problem. In the end, the character learns a lesson.*

**Story Structure** Elicit more details about the beginning and middle of the story. Have children review pages 119-120 Ask: *At the beginning of the story, what trick does the shepherd boy play on the villagers?* (He cries wolf when there is no wolf.) Review pages 121–122. *What happens in the middle of the story? How do the villagers try to teach the boy a lesson?* (First, they tell him not to cry wolf when there is no wolf. Then the villagers don't come when the boy cries wolf.)

### ❸ Guided Practice of Close Reading

Have children work with partners to tell what happens at the end of the story. Have them discuss the lesson the fable wants to teach readers. Then have them share their ideas with the rest of the class.

## Go Digital

**Present the Lesson**

CCSS Genre Literature

# Fable

"The Boy Who Cried Wolf" is a fable. A **fable**:
- is a made-up story that teaches a lesson.
- has a beginning, middle and end.

 **Find Text Evidence**

*I can use what I read to tell that "The Boy Who Cried Wolf" is a fable. It is a made-up story that has a beginning, middle, and end.*

page 119

Long ago a shepherd boy sat on a hilltop watching the village sheep. He was not **fond** of his job. He didn't like it one bit. He would have liked something wonderful to happen, but nothing **remarkable** ever did.

The shepherd boy watched the clouds move softly by to stay busy. He saw horses, dogs, and dragons in the sky. He made up **stories** with these things as characters.

119

**Story Structure**

In the **beginning** of the fable, the shepherd boy is bored and plays a trick on the villagers. In the **middle** of the story, the villagers try to teach the boy a lesson.

**Your Turn** COLLABORATE

Tell how the boy learns a lesson at the **end** of the story.

Peter Francis

126

**READING/WRITING WORKSHOP,** p. 126

---

**ON-LEVEL PRACTICE BOOK** p. 68

### The Fox and the Grapes

One day the fox saw a bunch of grapes high in a tree. He could not reach the grapes. The fox walked away. "Those grapes must be sour," he said. It is easy to dislike something you cannot get.

**Answer the questions about the text.**

1. How can you tell that this text is a fable?

   It is a made-up story that teaches a lesson. It has a beginning, middle, and end.

2. What happens at the beginning of the fable?

   The fox sees grapes in a tree.

3. What happens at the end of the fable?

   The fox says the grapes must be sour.

4. What lesson does the fable teach?

   Possible response: It's easy to dislike something you cannot get.

| APPROACHING p. 68 | BEYOND p. 68 | ELL p. 68 |
|---|---|---|

---

## Monitor and *Differentiate*

 **Quick Check**

Are children able to describe the lesson at the end of the fable?

### Small Group Instruction

If No → **Approaching** Reteach pp. T156–T157

**ELL** Develop pp. T174–T177

If Yes → **On Level** Review ppp. T166–T167

**Beyond Level** Extend pp. T170–T171

---

## ENGLISH LANGUAGE LEARNERS
### SCAFFOLD

**Beginning**

Help children identify the fable's lesson. Say: *At first, the boy cries wolf when there is no wolf. When a real wolf comes, why don't people help? What does this teach the boy about telling lies?* Point out the story's last two sentences.

**Intermediate**

Help children identify the fable's lesson. Ask: *What happens the first time the boy cries "wolf"? What do the villagers do? What happens when there is a real wolf? Why? What sentences tell you the lesson?* (the last two).

**Advanced/High**

Have children reread the final paragraph of the story. Ask: *What lies did the boy tell? What problems did these lies cause? What lesson does the boy learn as a result? What does this fable teach us?* Restate children's responses.

# Vocabulary Strategy

CLOSE READING

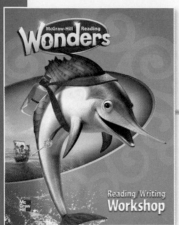

**Reading/Writing Workshop**

## OBJECTIVES

**CCSS** Determine or clarify the meaning of unknown and multiple-meaning words and phrases based on *grade 2 reading and content,* choosing flexibly from an array of strategies. **L.2.4**

**CCSS** Determine the meaning of the new word formed when a known prefix is added to a known word (e.g., *happy/unhappy, tell/ retell*). **L.2.4b**

## ACADEMIC LANGUAGE
- *suffix*
- Cognate: *sufijo*

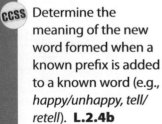

### SKILLS TRACE

**Suffixes**

**INTRODUCE** Unit 2 Week 2

**REVIEW** Unit 2 Week 3; Unit 4 Week 4; Unit 5, Weeks 1, 2

**ASSESS** Units 2 and 5

---

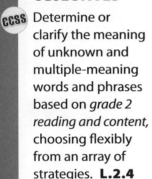
MINILESSON

**10** Mins

# Suffixes

## ❶ Explain

Remind children that they can often figure out the meaning of an unknown word by looking at its **word parts**. Tell children that a suffix is a word part that can be added to the end of a word to make a new word. The suffix changes the meaning of the root word.

→ The suffix *-ly* makes a word that describes an action. For example, if we talk *loudly*, this means we talk in a loud way.

→ The suffix *-ful* means "full of." If we say a picture is *colorful,* that means that the picture is full of color.

→ To learn the meaning of an unfamiliar word that has a suffix, children can separate the word into root word and suffix. If children know the meaning of the suffix and the root word, they may be able to understand the meaning of the word.

## ❷ Model Close Reading: Text Evidence

Model using root words and suffixes to figure out the meaning of *harmful* on page 120 of "The Boy Who Cried Wolf." Say: *I'm not sure what the word* harmful *means. I'll separate the word into parts. I see the word* harm *which means "hurt." I see the suffix* -ful, *which means "full of." I think* harmful *means "full of hurt." That makes sense. A wolf might hurt the sheep.*

## ❸ Guided Practice of Close Reading

Have children work in pairs to figure out the meanings of *wonderful* and *softly*. Encourage partners to separate the root word from the suffix. Remind children to identify the suffix and the root word and then use what they know about each suffix and root word to find the meaning of the entire word. Encourage children to think about whether or not the word meaning they have found makes sense in the sentence where the word is used.

# Go Digital

**Present the Lesson**

Vocabulary Strategy

# Suffixes

A suffix is a word part or syllable added to the end of a word. You can separate the root word from a suffix, such as *-ful* or *-ly*, to figure out what the word means.

 **Find Text Evidence**

*I'm not sure what the word* harmful *means. The root word is* harm, *which means "to hurt." The suffix is -ful which means "full of." I think the word* harmful *means "full of hurt."*

When they got there, they saw no harmful wolf.

**Your Turn**

 COLLABORATE

Use suffixes to figure out the meanings of these words in "The Boy Who Cried Wolf."
**wonderful,** *page 119*
**softly,** *page 119*

Peter Francis

127

**READING/WRITING WORKSHOP, p. 127**

---

## ENGLISH LANGUAGE LEARNERS SCAFFOLD

| Beginning | Intermediate | Advanced/High |
|---|---|---|
| Point out the words *wonderful* and *softly* on page 119. Help children separate the root word from the suffix. Define each word part for them. Lead children to put the meanings together to find the meaning of the whole word. Model correct pronunciation as needed. | Point out the words *wonderful* and *softly*. Have children separate the root word and the suffix. Review the suffixes and guide children to give the meaning of each word. Allow children ample time to respond. | Point out the words *wonderful* and *softly*, and ask children to define them. Have them explain how they used their knowledge of root words and suffixes to understand the meaning of the words. Repeat correct answers slowly and clearly to the class. |

---

**ON-LEVEL PRACTICE BOOK** p. 69

To figure out a new word, look for a **suffix**, or word part added to the end of the word.
The suffix *-ful* means "full of."
The suffix *-ly* means "in a way that is."

**Read each sentence. Underline the word that has a suffix. Then write the word and its meaning.**

1. "Those will make a healthful snack," Fox thought.

   healthful- full of health

2. He should be able to reach the grapes easily.

   easily- in a way that is easy

3. The wind began blowing strongly.

   strongly- in a way that is strong

4. Turtle had an idea that was helpful.

   helpful- full of help

5. When Fox was safely back on the ground, he shared the grapes with Turtle.

   safely- in a way that is safe

APPROACHING p. 69    BEYOND p. 69    ELL p. 69

---

## Monitor and *Differentiate*

 **Quick Check**

Are children able to identify and use suffixes to determine the meanings of *wonderful* and *softly*?

### Small Group Instruction

If No → **Approaching** Reteach pp. T156–T165

     **ELL** Develop pp. T178–T179

If Yes → **On Level** Review pp. T168–T169

     **Beyond Level** Extend pp. T172–T173

CCSS **Genre · Fable**

**1** The hungry old wolf was too slow to **snatch** birds and too stiff to chase rabbits, so he tried growing food in a small garden.

"Bah, weeds everywhere! There are so many I can't even find the vegetables." The old wolf growled, rubbing his empty stomach.

As he yanked dandelions from where his carrots should have been, his ears began to twitch.

**? Essential Question**
**What can animals in stories teach us?**
Read a different version of the story of the boy who cried wolf.

 Go Digital!

**LITERATURE ANTHOLOGY, pp. 136–137**

# Develop Comprehension

 CLOSE READING

Lexile 580
*TextEvaluator™* 18

**Literature Anthology**

## Read Literature Anthology

**Review Genre: Fable** Review the main characteristics of a fable:

→ Tells a made up story to teach a lesson

→ May have animal characters that speak and act like people

→ Has a beginning, middle, and end

**Preview and Predict** Read the title on page 136 and have children preview the illustrations. *What might this story be about? Let's find out.*

**ESSENTIAL QUESTION**

Read the Essential Question: *What can animals in stories teach us?* As children read, they should think about this fable's lesson.

**Story Words** Read and spell the words *morsel* and *scrumptious.* Tell children that a *morsel* is a tiny piece of food, or a crumb. Explain that something that is *scrumptious* is delicious.

**Analytical Writing** **Note Taking: Graphic Organizer**
As children read the selection, guide them to fill in **Your Turn Practice Book page 66.**

"WOLF! WOLF!"

The old wolf fumbled with his hearing aid.

*Who's calling me? I don't remember having any friends on this mountain.*

In fact, the old wolf didn't have any friends on any mountain.

"Maybe they have some food to share? A mere morsel would do," he said.

His bones creaked and his joints cracked as he slowly made his way toward the voice.

**2** After a tiring climb and two stubbed toes, the old wolf came to a clearing.

"What's this? A boy? With goats!" The old wolf drooled with excitement. "Surely he can spare *one* for a hungry wolf."

Before he could step into the meadow, a group of villagers came clambering up the hillside.

138

139

**LITERATURE ANTHOLOGY, pp. 138–139**

## **1 Skill: Problem and Solution**

What problem does the wolf have at the beginning of the story? (The wolf is hungry.) Let's add this information to the Problem box of our Problem and Solution Chart.

## **2 Strategy: Make Predictions**

**Teacher Think Aloud**  On pages 138 and 139, I read that the wolf hears someone calling his name. The wolf sees that it is a boy with goats who is calling his name. This reminds me of "The Boy Who Cried Wolf." I predict the villagers will be mad at the boy for crying, "Wolf!"

## **A C T Access Complex Text**

### ▶ **What Makes This Text Complex?**

**Specific Vocabulary**  Children may need help identifying words that are Chinese. Help children understand that the author included these words because the story is set in China.

**Genre**  Children may need help understanding that this is an alternate retelling of the fable, *The Boy Who Cried Wolf*. Explain that the original fable they read is told from the point of view of the people in the story. *Wolf! Wolf!* tells a similar story, but is different because it is told from the wolf's point of view.

③ The old wolf stayed hidden behind the bamboo as the villagers surrounded the boy.

"Where's the wolf?" a villager cried out, waving a stick.

"Did he take any goats?" another gasped.

"What wolf?" the boy giggled. "There is no wolf."

"We ran up this hill for *nothing*?" the eldest wheezed.

"Call us *only* if you see a wolf," scolded another. ④

140

141

**LITERATURE ANTHOLOGY,** pp. 140–141

# Develop Comprehension

CLOSE READING

## ③ Skill: Problem and Solution

We said that the wolf's problem is that he is hungry. What has he done so far to try to solve his problem? We can add that information to the Steps to Solution box.

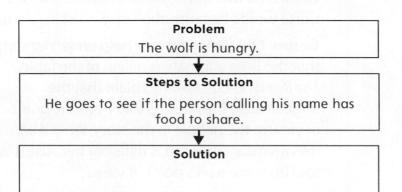

| **Problem** |
|---|
| The wolf is hungry. |

↓

| **Steps to Solution** |
|---|
| He goes to see if the person calling his name has food to share. |

↓

| **Solution** |
|---|
|  |

## ④ Strategy: Make Predictions

Remember, as you read, you should confirm or revise your predictions. We predicted the villagers would be mad at the boy for crying, "Wolf!" Was our prediction correct? How do you know? (Yes, the villagers scold the boy and tell him to only call, "Wolf!" if there really is a wolf.)

The old wolf wasn't **fond** of angry villagers, especially ones with sticks, so he limped down to a nearby stream.

"Kids. Humph! Always playing tricks on old folks and old wolves." He groaned as he soaked his tired feet.

Before long the boy's cry came again.

"WOLF! WOLF! The wolf is taking the goats!"

*Another wolf is taking those tasty goats?*

The old wolf couldn't stand the thought and quickly hobbled back to the meadow.

142

143

**LITERATURE ANTHOLOGY, pp. 142–143**

## ⑤ Maintain Skill: Character, Setting, Plot

What can we tell about how the wolf feels by looking at the illustration on pages 142 and 143? (He is tired and unhappy. His foot hurts.)

## ⑥ Author's Craft: Word Choice

The author uses the word *limped* to describe how the wolf walked in the first sentence on page 143. Why do you think the author used this word? (To help the reader understand that the wolf's feet hurt after climbing and stubbing his toes.) Turn to a partner. Reread page 143. Find another word the author uses to describe how the wolf walked. (hobbled)

The villagers were already there, huffing and puffing from running up the hill.

"Where is the wolf? Are the goats okay?" the villagers gasped.

"What wolf?" The boy laughed.

From behind a tree, the old wolf watched the villagers stagger back down the hill.

There's got to be a way to get one of those scrumptious goats from that trickster, he thought. Perhaps through a trick of my own.

**7**

**STOP AND CHECK**

**Make Predictions**
What do you think the Wolf's trick will be? Use the Make Predictions strategy to predict what will happen.

144

145

**LITERATURE ANTHOLOGY, pp. 144–145**

# Develop Comprehension

CLOSE READING

## A C T  Access Complex Text

### ▶ Specific Vocabulary

The author uses the phrases *mu shu goat* and *double-goat dumplings* on page 147. Guide them to understand that these are Chinese foods. The author includes them here because the story is set in China.

## 7 Reread

**Teacher Think Aloud** I realize that I don't understand why the wolf is thinking of a trick. Who is he going to trick and why? I will read this page slowly and look at the illustrations to find the answer. Now I understand. Like the villagers, the wolf has been tricked twice by the boy. He wants to trick the trickster and get a goat to eat!

**STOP AND CHECK**

**Make Predictions** What do you think the Wolf's trick will be? Use the Make Predictions strategy to predict what will happen. (I think that the Wolf will try to trick the boy into giving him a goat by pretending to be something other than a wolf.)

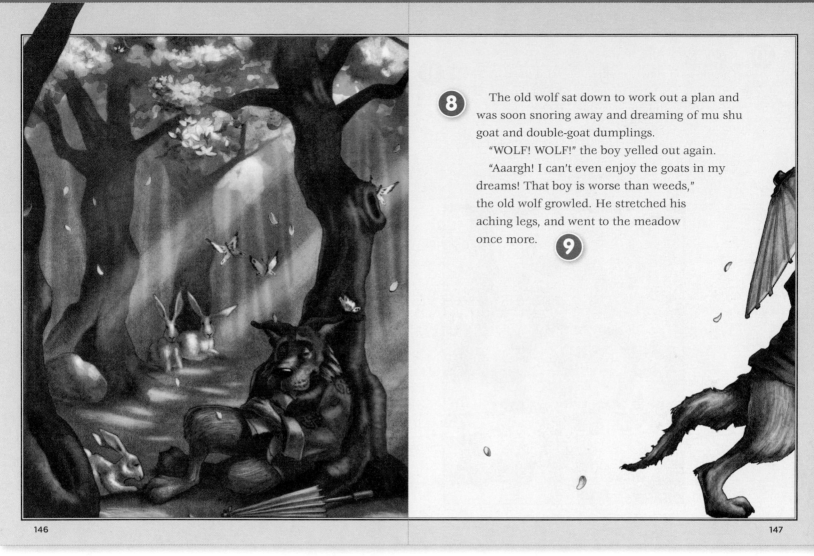

**8** The old wolf sat down to work out a plan and was soon snoring away and dreaming of mu shu goat and double-goat dumplings.

"WOLF! WOLF!" the boy yelled out again.

"Aaargh! I can't even enjoy the goats in my dreams! That boy is worse than weeds," the old wolf growled. He stretched his aching legs, and went to the meadow once more. **9**

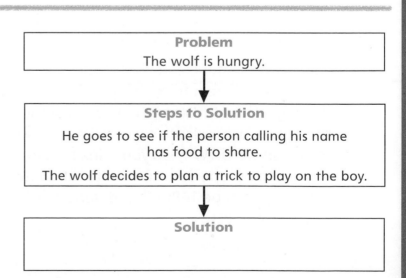

146 147

**LITERATURE ANTHOLOGY,** pp. 146–147

**8** **Maintain Skill: Character, Setting, Plot**

The setting of this story is in China. With a partner, find and discuss details in the text and the illustrations that give you information about the story's setting.

**9** **Skill: Problem and Solution**

Turn to a partner and discuss the next step the wolf takes to solve his hunger problem. (The Wolf plans to play a trick on the boy to get the goat.) Add it to the chart.

| Problem |
| --- |
| The wolf is hungry. |

↓

| Steps to Solution |
| --- |
| He goes to see if the person calling his name has food to share. |
| The wolf decides to plan a trick to play on the boy. |

↓

| Solution |
| --- |
|  |

**⑩** *Perfect. Not a villager in sight.*

The old wolf slowly crept out toward the boy. The goats swiftly scattered to the far edge of the meadow.

"Were you calling me over for lunch?" The old wolf grinned.

"WOLF! WOLF! There *is* a wolf!" the boy cried as he scrambled up a tree.

**⑪**

"Quit your yelling," said the wolf. Those villagers won't **believe** you, anyway."

"But this time it's true, they have to believe me. You're a *real* wolf, and you're going to take the goats."

The old wolf knew his legs were too tired to chase down goats. He carefully lowered himself onto a nearby rock and gazed up at the boy. His lips curled in a smile.

148                                                                                         149

**LITERATURE ANTHOLOGY, pp. 148–149**

# Develop Comprehension

CLOSE READING

## ⑩ Author's Craft: Text Features

Look at the sentences at the top of page 148. The text is different from the rest of the text on the page. The words are set in italics. Authors sometimes use italics to call special attention to certain words. Why do you think the author wanted to call special attention to the sentences at the top of page 148? (The sentences tell the wolf's thoughts.)

## ⑪ Suffixes

COLLABORATE

If you don't know the meaning of the word *slowly*, you can separate the word into its root and its suffix. What is the root and suffix? (root is *slow*; suffix is -*ly*) The suffix -*ly* tells how something looks, feels, acts, or moves. How does the wolf move? (slowly) With a partner, find another word on page 148 with the suffix -*ly*. Find a word on page 149 with two suffixes, -*ful* and -*ly*. Guide partners as they discuss the meaning of the words *swiftly* and *carefully*.

"The villagers are only going to believe you if you really are missing a goat. I can help you with that." He grinned.

"Just one goat?" The boy leaned forward on the branch.

"I'm a picky eater. That plump one looks about right. But you have to bring it to me, because if I go over there, I might change my mind and grab them all."

"Bring it to you?" the boy asked.

"On the other side of the mountain," the old wolf said, "you'll find a small garden. Just tie it to the fence post there." And he started home. ⓬

**STOP AND CHECK**

**Confirm Predictions**
Think about the prediction you made about Wolf's trick. Was it correct? How would you revise it?

150    151

**LITERATURE ANTHOLOGY,** pp. 150–151

⓬ **Reread**

**Teacher Think Aloud** I want to make sure I understand how the wolf plans to trick the boy. I reread more slowly. Then I can paraphrase this part of the story in my own words. The wolf tells the boy that the only way the villagers will believe his cry of, "Wolf!" is if one goat is really missing. So he tells the boy to bring a goat to his home. The wolf says if he goes to get the goat himself, he'll grab them all. Really, he knows his legs are too tired to catch a goat.

**STOP AND CHECK**

**Confirm Predictions** Think about the prediction you made about Wolf's trick. Was it correct? Go back to the text to revise your prediction. (My prediction was that the Wolf would pretend not to be a wolf. I will revise it so that the Wolf made a deal with the boy. Evidence: The wolf talks to the boy and tells him that the people will believe him again only if Wolf takes away a goat.)

The next morning the old wolf was overjoyed to see the plump goat nibbling away in his garden.

"Good fortune at last!" he said. "Today I'll **feast** like an old wolf should." He rubbed his paws together.

The wolf's mouth watered and his stomach grumbled as he crept up behind the goat. Suddenly he noticed something **remarkable**.

152     153

**LITERATURE ANTHOLOGY, pp. 152–153**

# Develop Comprehension

CLOSE READING

## 13 Skill: Problem and Solution

COLLABORATE

Turn to a partner and review what we have so far on the Problem and Solution Chart. Discuss the new steps the wolf has taken to solve his hunger problem. Then add them to the graphic organizer. (The wolf tells the boy to bring a goat to his garden.)

## 14 Skill: Problem and Solution

How is the goat helping to solve the wolf's problem of being hungry? It may not be the way the wolf had planned. (The goat is eating the weeds in the wolf's garden. The wolf's vegetables grow better when there are no weeds.)

154

**14** Everywhere he looked, there were ripe and juicy vegetables: baby bok choy, beautiful eggplant, ready-to-pick carrots, and even his favorite—onions. The old wolf couldn't believe his eyes.

Then he saw the goat happily eating the last few weeds. She saw him too, and froze in fear.

"You ate my weeds!" the old wolf said. "But why didn't you eat the vegetables?"

"Sorry, I'm a picky eater," she said. "Please don't eat me!" **15**

155

**LITERATURE ANTHOLOGY, pp. 154– 155**

**15 Strategy: Make Predictions**

**Teacher Think Aloud** I predicted earlier that the wolf would try to trick the boy, and he did. He got the boy to bring a goat to his house. I thought he would eat the goat, but now I'm not so sure. How could I revise my prediction?

**Student Think Aloud** The goat is eating the weeds in the wolf's garden. What the wolf really wanted at the beginning of the story was for the weeds to go away. The goat has helped to solve this problem. I predict that the wolf will keep the goat and let it eat the weeds. The wolf will eat the vegetables.

# A C T  Access Complex Text

▶ **Specific Vocabulary**

Page 155 contains a serial list of vegetables in the wolf's garden. Children may not be familiar with some of them. The named vegetables also provide additional opportunity to discuss the setting of China.

‡ Write the word *vegetables*. Explain that the wolf grows vegetables in a garden. Have children name the vegetables. Read aloud the first sentence on page 155. Identify each vegetable. Record the vegetables under the category name *vegetables*.

The wolf looked at the plump goat and then at all the juicy vegetables, and back at the goat again. He sighed.

"Don't be sorry! You did my work for me. What's one breakfast compared to **delicious** vegetables for the rest of my days?"

156

The wolf smiled as he untied the goat. "I could use a friend like you."

*Plus, double-goat dumplings are overrated, anyway!*

157

**LITERATURE ANTHOLOGY, pp. 156–157**

# Develop Comprehension

## Skill: Problem and Solution

*How does the wolf finally solve his problem?* Have children add their answer to the Problem and Solution Chart.

## Return to Predictions and Purposes

Review children's predictions. Ask children if their predictions about the selection were correct. Guide them to use evidence in the text to confirm whether or not their predictions turned out to be accurate. Discuss what lesson children learn by reading the animal fable. Did children learn what they wanted to by reading the selection?

| Problem |
| --- |
| The wolf is hungry. |

↓

| Steps to Solution |
| --- |
| He goes to see if the person calling his name has food to share. |
| The wolf decides to plan a trick to play on the boy. |
| The wolf tells the boy to bring a goat to his garden. |
| Goat eats all weeds in the wolf's garden. |

↓

| Solution |
| --- |
| The wolf decides to keep the goat so he will always have vegetables to eat. |

**About the Author and Illustrator**

John Rocco grew up in a small town in Rhode Island. He studied illustration at special art schools. He made illustrations for movies, theme parks, and museums. Now he makes children's books by writing stories and illustrating them. John and his family share a farmhouse with a family of mice, six bats, and some chipmunks.

**Author's Purpose**

Sometimes authors write to entertain their readers. Making characters say or do something surprising can be funny. What is something surprising the wolf says or does?

**LITERATURE ANTHOLOGY, p. 158**

# Meet the Author

## John Rocco

Read aloud page 158 with children. Ask them why John Rocco may have written and illustrated a story. *Why do you think he wrote about animals? Where can you find some of his illustrations?*

## Author's Purpose

Have children write one surprising thing the wolf says or does in their Response Journals. Use the sentence starters: *The wolf said _____. The wolf _____.* Remind children to use quotation marks around what the wolf says.

## AUTHOR'S CRAFT

### Author's Craft: Dialogue

Explain that authors often use dialogue, the words the characters say, to show how and what the characters think and feel.

→ Have children reread page 143. *What do you think the wolf is thinking and feeling when he says "Kids. Humph! Always playing tricks on old folks and old wolves."?*

→ Discuss how the dialogue helps their understanding of the characters and the story. Tell children they can use dialogue in their own writing.

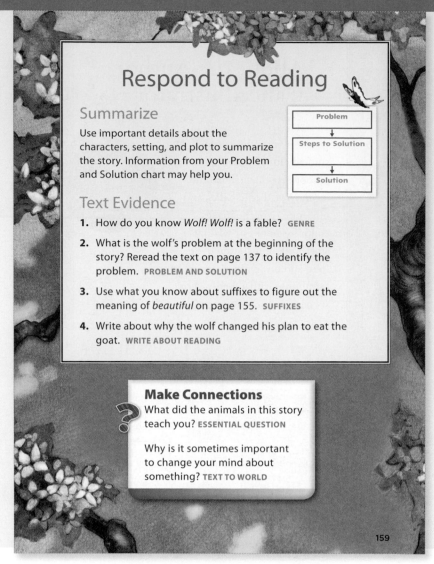

## Respond to Reading

### Summarize

Use important details about the characters, setting, and plot to summarize the story. Information from your Problem and Solution chart may help you.

| Problem |
|---|
| ↓ |
| Steps to Solution |
| ↓ |
| Solution |

### Text Evidence

1. How do you know *Wolf! Wolf!* is a fable? **GENRE**

2. What is the wolf's problem at the beginning of the story? Reread the text on page 137 to identify the problem. **PROBLEM AND SOLUTION**

3. Use what you know about suffixes to figure out the meaning of *beautiful* on page 155. **SUFFIXES**

4. Write about why the wolf changed his plan to eat the goat. **WRITE ABOUT READING**

**Make Connections**
What did the animals in this story teach you? **ESSENTIAL QUESTION**

Why is it sometimes important to change your mind about something? **TEXT TO WORLD**

159

**LITERATURE ANTHOLOGY,** p. 159

# Respond to Reading

## Summarize

Guide children through the steps to summarize.

→ First, select important details from the beginning of the story. These details will tell about the problem.

→ Next, select important details from the middle of the story. These details will tell how the wolf tried to solve his problem.

→ Then, select important details from the end of the story. These details will describe how the story ends and the problem is solved.

→ Use the events to state the summary.

# Text Evidence

Guide children to use text evidence to answer the Text Evidence questions on **Literature Anthology** p. 159. Model answering the question as needed.

1. **Genre** To answer this question, let's look back at the story. The story has animal characters that talk and act like people. The story teaches us lessons. All these are clues that "Wolf! Wolf!" is a fable.

2. **Plot: Problem and Solution** This question asks about the wolf's problem at the beginning of the story. To give the answer, we need to reread the text on page 137. The wolf is hungry. He is too old and slow to chase birds and rabbits. He tried growing food in a garden, but the garden has too many weeds. The wolf's problem is that his stomach is empty and that he is hungry.

3. **Suffixes:** This question asks about the meaning of a word with a suffix. Let's find the word *beautiful* on page 155. The suffix *-ful* is added to the root word *beauty*. The suffix *-ful* means "full of." So, *beautiful* means "full of beauty."

 4. **Write About Reading** This question asks about why the wolf changed his plan to eat the goat. The wolf was hungry, so at first he planned to eat the goat. He decides to keep her when she helps him weed his vegetable garden.

 # Make Connections

### ESSENTIAL QUESTION

Have partners list animal stories they have read and tell the lesson each taught. Tell them to include *Wolf! Wolf!* and other stories they have read or heard both in and outside of class.

**Text-to-World** Have children discuss times they have had to change their mind about something.

---

Language Arts

# Writing Traits: Ideas

## Discuss Supporting Details

**Review** Invite children to recall that writers use supporting details to help explain their ideas.

**Share** Ask for a volunteer to share his or her revised writing from Day 2. Encourage the class to point out supporting details they hear in the volunteer's writing. Invite the volunteer to point out the detail he or she thinks is the most important and what idea it helps to explain.

 **WRITING ENTRY: SUPPORTING DETAILS**

❶ **Prewrite** Ask children to choose a new topic for writing by searching their Writer's Notebook for ideas for a fable. Or, provide a prompt such as the following one: Write the beginning of a fable about a boy who tricks a wolf. Use supporting details to help readers understand your ideas.

❷ **Draft** Once children have chosen their topics, ask them to use a word web to generate details that tell about their characters' thoughts, feelings, and actions. Encourage children to refer to their webs as they write their drafts.

### OBJECTIVES

**CCSS** With guidance and support from adults and peers, focus on a topic and strengthen writing as needed by revising and editing. **W.2.5**

**CCSS** Demonstrate command of the conventions of standard English capitalization, punctuation, and spelling when writing. **L.2.2**

**CCSS** Demonstrate command of the conventions of standard English grammar and usage when writing or speaking. **L.2.1**

### ACADEMIC LANGUAGE

*ideas, supporting details, singular noun, plural noun*

**Go Digital**

**Present the Lesson**

**Writing**

**Graphic Organizer**

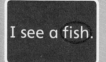

I see a fish.

**Grammar**

# Grammar

*MINILESSON 5 Mins*

## Singular and Plural Nouns

**Review** Remind children that a singular noun names one person, place, or thing. A plural noun names more than one person, place, or thing. Explain that we add -*s* to most singular nouns to make a plural noun. If a singular noun ends in -*s, -ch, -sh,* or -*x,* we add -*es* to make a plural noun. To form the plural of nouns ending in a consonant and *y,* we change *y* to *i* and add -*es.*

**Practice** Have partners form the plural of each word.

| | | | |
|---|---|---|---|
| gas (gases) | cub (cubs) | rule (rules) | lunch (lunches) |
| glass (glasses) | bunny (bunnies) | brush (brushes) | box (boxes) |

## Mechanics: Commas in a Series

**Review** Remind children that commas are used to separate three or more words in a series. The word *and* or *or* comes before the last word in the series. Review the following sentence with children.

Did the boy live in the mountains, village, or city?

**Practice** Ask children to rewrite the following sentences with the correct punctuation.

The wolf grows tomatoes, cabbage, and carrots in his garden.

Did the wolf trick the boy, sheep, or villagers?

## Talk About It

**Who Am I?** Have children work in small groups. A volunteer thinks of one of the characters he or she has read about in one of the animal stories this week. The other children ask questions, using singular and plural nouns to guess the character.

### ENGLISH LANGUAGE LEARNERS

**Singular and Plural Nouns**
Display the following sentences and pictures that illustrate them.

The wolf ate the vegetables.

The villagers didn't believe the boy.

Review with children that a singular noun names one person, place, or thing. A plural noun names more than one person, place, or thing. Read the first sentence aloud as students follow along. Say: *Name a noun in the sentence.* (wolf) *Is it singular or plural?* (singular) Have students identify *vegetables* as the other noun in the sentence. Follow the same procedure for the second sentence.

# Daily Wrap Up

→ Review the Essential Question and encourage children to discuss it using the oral vocabulary words.

→ Prompt children to review and discuss the skills they used today. Guide them to give examples of how they used each skill.

## Materials

Literature Anthology
"Wolf, Wolf"

Word-Building
Cards

Spelling Word
Cards

**change**

High-Frequency
Word Cards

**cub**

The Boy Who Cried Wolf    Wolf! Wolf!

Dinah Zike's
**FOLDABLES**

→ # Extend the Concept

MINILESSON
**5** Mins

# Oral Language

## OBJECTIVES

**CCSS** Participate in collaborative conversations with diverse partners about grade 2 topics and texts with peers and adults in small and larger groups. **SL.2.1**

**CCSS** Follow agreed-upon rules for discussions (e.g., gaining the floor in respectful ways, listening to others with care, speaking one at a time about the topics and texts under discussion). **SL.2.1.a**

**CCSS** Know and apply grade-level phonics and word analysis skills in decoding words. **RF.2.3**

• Segment phonemes.
• Read words with CVC*e* syllables.

## ACADEMIC LANGUAGE
*segment, syllables*

**ESSENTIAL QUESTION**

Remind children that this week they have been learning and reading about lessons they have learned from animal stories. Guide children to discuss the question using information from what they have read and discussed throughout the week.

Use the Define/Example/Ask routine to review the oral vocabulary words *affection, crave, frustrated, nourishment* and *seek*. Prompt children to use the words as they discuss animal stories.

Review last week's oral vocabulary words *capture, chorus, croak, reason*, and *visitor*.

**Go**
Digital

Phonemic
Awareness

| m | a |
|---|---|
| n | t | p |

Phonics

I __ the jar.
fill | fills | filling

Structural
Analysis

# Word Work

## Phonemic Awareness

### Phoneme Segmentation

**1 Model** *We are going to say the sounds in a word: use. How many sounds are in* use? /ū/ /z/. *Two sounds. There are two sounds in the word* use.

**2 Guided Practice/Practice** Have children segment the following words into phonemes. Do the first one together.

flute   snug   sub   rude   rule   fume

## Phonics

### Build Words with Short *u* /u/ and Long *u* /ū/

**Review** The short *u* sound /u/ can be represented by the letter *u*. The long *u* sound /ū/ can be spelled with the letters *u*, consonant, *e* (u_e). The *u* and *e* work together to make the long *u* sound. The *e* is silent. Use Word Building Cards to build words with /u/ and /ū/. Place the letters for *cub*. Let's blend the sounds and read the word. Let's add an *e* to the end of the word. That changes the /u/ sound to /ū/, *cube*.

Continue with *cut/cute; tub/tube; us/use*.

## Structural Analysis

### CVCe Syllables

**Review** Write the word *update* on the board. Have children clap out the number of syllables in the word: /up/ /dāt/. Remind children that a CVCe syllable includes the VCe pattern. *The vowel and the silent* e *must stay together in the same syllable.* Draw a vertical line between the *p* and *d*. Read the syllables, and have children repeat.

**Practice** Write the following words on the board: *awake, invite, classmate, explode*. Have children work in pairs to underline the CVCe syllable, then read the entire word.

### Quick Review

**Build Fluency: Sound Spellings:** Display the **Word-Building Cards:** *u_e, u, o_e, o, i_e, i, a_e, a, sl, dr, sk, sp, st, tr, pr, pl.* Have children say each sound. Repeat, and vary the pace. For fluency in connected text, see the Decodable Reader Lesson in Small Group.

## Monitor and *Differentiate*

### ✓ Quick Check

Can children read and spell words with short *u* spelled *u* and long *u* spelled u_e?

**Small Group Instruction**

If No → **Approaching**   Reteach pp. T158-T163

  **ELL**   Develop pp. T174-T181

If Yes → **On Level**   Review pp. T168-T169

  **Beyond Level**   Extend pp. T172-T173

→ # Word Work

### OBJECTIVES

**CCSS** Determine or clarify the meaning of unknown and multiple-meaning words and phrases based on grade 2 reading and content, choosing flexibly from an array of strategies. **L.2.4**

**CCSS** Determine the meaning of the new word formed when a known prefix is added to a known word (e.g., *happy/unhappy, tell/retell*). **L.2.4b**

**CCSS** Use a known root word as a clue to the meaning of an unknown word with the same root. (e.g. *addition, additional*). **L.2.4c**

**CCSS** Read with sufficient accuracy and fluency to support comprehension. **RF.2.4**

- Sort words with long *u* and short *u*.
- Review high-frequency words.
- Practice fluency.

---

## MINILESSON 5 Mins — Spelling

### Word Sort with Short *u* and Long *u*

**Review** Provide pairs of children with copies of the Spelling Word Cards. While one partner reads the words on at a time, the other partner should orally segment the word and then write the word. After reading all the words, partners should switch roles.

**Practice** Have children correct their own papers. Then have them sort the words by vowel sound.

## MINILESSON 5 Mins — High Frequency Words

*change, cheer, fall, five, look, open, should, their, won, yes*

**Review** Display High-Frequency Word Cards *change, cheer, fall, five, look, open, should, their, won, yes*. Have children Read/Write/Spell each word.

→ Point to a word and call on a child to use it in a sentence.

→ Review last week's words using the same procedure.

## Go Digital

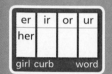

**Spelling Word Sort**

**High-Frequency Word Routine**

**Visual Glossary**

# Fluency/Vocabulary Strategy

**MINILESSON 10 Mins**

## Expression

**Review** Remind children that an exclamation should be read with excitement and expression. Explain that this is part of reading with expression. When you read with expression, you can also show emotions by reading faster when a character is excited and slower when a character is sad. Good readers also raise the volume of their voice when they read an exclamation or a word that is emphasized.

**Guided Practice/Practice** Have children read a passage from the Shared Read aloud to a partner. Remind them to pause for punctuation and to raise their voice at the end of questions. Make sure they pay attention to using proper expression. Offer corrective feedback as necessary.

### Fluency Practice

Children can practice fluency using the Practice Book passages.

**MINILESSON 5 Mins**

## Prefixes

❶ **Explain/Model** Remind children that adding a prefix to the beginning of a root word changes the meaning of the word.

→ The prefix -un means "not."

→ The prefix -dis means "not."

→ The prefix -re means "to do again."

Write and say *unripe*. Have children repeat it. Model how to use word parts to understand the meaning of *unripe*.

❷ **Guided Practice** Write the words *dislike, rename,* and *unwise* on the board. Have children work in pairs to figure out the meanings of these words. Ask them share their answers with the rest of the class.

## Monitor and *Differentiate*

### ✓ Quick Check

**Can children read fluently with good expression?**

⬇

### Small Group Instruction

| | | |
|---|---|---|
| If No → | Approaching | Reteach pp. T156–T165 |
| | ELL | Develop pp. T174–T181 |
| If Yes → | On Level | Review pp. T166–T169 |
| | Beyond Level | Extend pp. T170–T173 |

# Cinderella and Friends ①

Cinderella is a lonely girl with only mice for friends. Then her animal friends help her get to a ball and everything changes. The traditional Cinderella story is from Europe, but there are Cinderella **stories** from around the world. People in different places tell different Cinderella stories. Read some of these stories, and see how Cinderella's animal friends help.

## Yeh-Shen, A Chinese Cinderella

Yeh-Shen's only friend is a beautiful fish. One day her fish died. Yeh-Shen buried its bones. The fish bones were magical so Yeh-Shen made a wish. She wanted to go to the spring festival. The fish bones gave her a beautiful dress and golden slippers to wear. At the festival, Yeh-Shen lost one of the slippers. The king found the lost slipper. He said that he wanted to marry its owner. Many girls tried on the golden slipper. It only fit Yeh-Shen. She married the king, ② and they lived happily ever after.

161

**LITERATURE ANTHOLOGY, pp. 160–161**

# Develop Comprehension 🔍 CLOSE READING

Lexile 520
*TextEvaluator™* 15

## Read Literature Anthology

**Literature Anthology**

### Compare Texts *Analytical Writing*

Review with children that in the fable, *Wolf! Wolf!* a wolf helps to teach a boy a lesson about telling the truth. Explain that they will now compare and contrast Cinderella stories from four different cultures. Tell children that as they read, they should think about how *Wolf! Wolf!* and the Cinderella stories are alike and different. Have them **take notes.**

### ❶ Ask and Answer Questions

Look at the illustrations on pages 160–163. Now read the title: "Cinderella and Friends." What do you think these stories are about? What do you think the animals will do in these stories? (These are Cinderella stories from different cultures. The animals will help the main character in some way.)

### ❷ Ask and Answer Questions

What is special about Yeh-Shen's fish? How does the fish help her? (When the fish dies, its bones turn out to be magical. The bones give Yeh-Shen a dress and slippers to wear to the spring festival.)

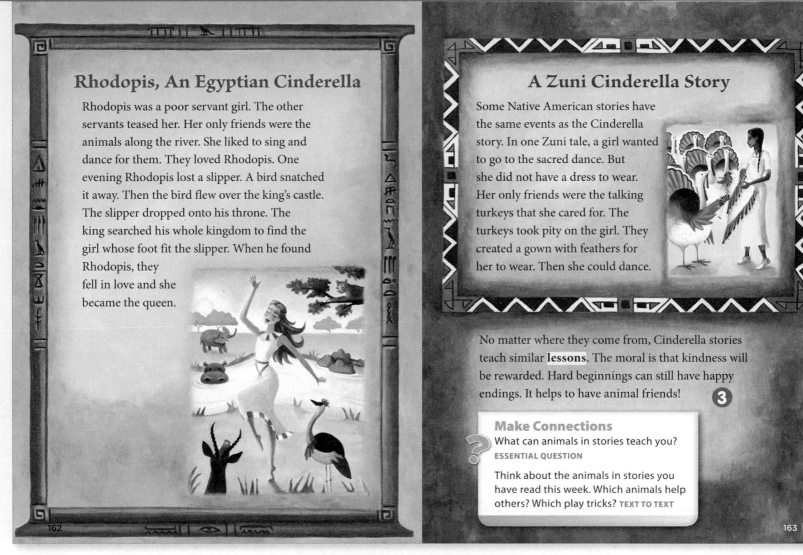

### Rhodopis, An Egyptian Cinderella

Rhodopis was a poor servant girl. The other servants teased her. Her only friends were the animals along the river. She liked to sing and dance for them. They loved Rhodopis. One evening Rhodopis lost a slipper. A bird snatched it away. Then the bird flew over the king's castle. The slipper dropped onto his throne. The king searched his whole kingdom to find the girl whose foot fit the slipper. When he found Rhodopis, they fell in love and she became the queen.

### A Zuni Cinderella Story

Some Native American stories have the same events as the Cinderella story. In one Zuni tale, a girl wanted to go to the sacred dance. But she did not have a dress to wear. Her only friends were the talking turkeys that she cared for. The turkeys took pity on the girl. They created a gown with feathers for her to wear. Then she could dance.

No matter where they come from, Cinderella stories teach similar **lessons**. The moral is that kindness will be rewarded. Hard beginnings can still have happy endings. It helps to have animal friends! ③

**Make Connections**
What can animals in stories teach you?
ESSENTIAL QUESTION

Think about the animals in stories you have read this week. Which animals help others? Which play tricks? TEXT TO TEXT

162     163

**LITERATURE ANTHOLOGY, pp. 162–163**

## ③ Ask and Answer Questions

How does the bird help Rhodopis? (It snatches her slipper and drops it onto the king's throne.) How do the talking turkeys help Cinderella? (They make a dress for her from their feathers for the sacred dance.) What do these four Cinderella stories teach us? (They teach us that kindness will be rewarded and that hard beginnings can have happy endings.)

## Make Connections • *Analytical Writing*

 Have partners make connections between animal helpers in "Cinderella and Friends" and *Wolf! Wolf!*

## A C T Access Complex Text

▶ **Organization**

Tell children they will read text summaries from different cultures about a familiar character—Cinderella. Point out that this selection is informational text asking children to answer questions and make connections about stories. Ask children to point out the features of this selection that show this is informational text.

# Language Arts

# Writing Traits: Ideas

**Revise** Have children revise their drafts from Day 3 by adding supporting details that help explain their idea.

As children revise their drafts, hold teacher conferences with individual children. You may also want to have partners conduct peer conferences.

**Edit** Model using proofreading marks to edit. Then have children use proofreading marks to correct errors in their writing.

Invite children to review Grammar Handbook and check for correct use of singular and plural nouns in their writing. Encourage children to proofread for other errors, including correct usage of commas in a series. Have children use a dictionary to check their spelling.

## Conference Routines

### Teacher Conference

**Step 1:** Talk about the strengths of the writing. *Your fable has a clear beginning. I understand the problem and what happens because of the problem.*

**Step 2:** Focus on the target trait. *You have a lot of supporting details that help explain how the characters feel.*

**Step 3:** Make concrete suggestions for revisions such as those below, and then meet again to review progress.

## Suggested Revisions

**Focus on a Sentence** Read the draft and target one sentence for revision. *Rewrite this sentence by adding a supporting detail to explain _____.*

**Focus on a Section** Underline a section that needs revision. Provide specific suggestions. *I would like to have a clearer idea of _____. Provide some supporting details so that readers know _____.*

**Focus on a Revision Strategy** Underline a section of the writing and ask children to use a specific revision strategy such as rearranging. *Your fable is easy to understand, but it could be even better if we changed the order of these sentences.*

## OBJECTIVES

**CCSS** With guidance and support from adults and peers, focus on a topic and strengthen writing as needed by revising and editing. **W.2.5**

**CCSS** Demonstrate command of the conventions of standard English grammar and usage when writing or speaking. **L.2.1**

**CCSS** Demonstrate command of the conventions of standard English capitalization, punctuation, and spelling when writing. **L.2.2**

**CCSS** With guidance and support from adults, use a variety of digital tools to produce and publish writing, including in collaboration with peers. **W.2.6**

## ACADEMIC LANGUAGE

*revise, conference, rearrange*

## Go Digital

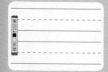

**Writing**

- Make a capital letter.
∧ Add.
↗ Take out.

**Proofreader's Marks**

I see a fish.

**Grammar**

## Peer Conference

Provide these questions to guide peers as they review a partner's draft.

→ Are there supporting details that tell about the characters?

→ Is the organization of the writing clear and easy to follow?

→ Where can more supporting details be added?

# Grammar

## Singular and Plural Nouns

**Review**  Remind children that a singular noun names one person, place, or thing. A plural noun names more than one person, place, or thing. We add -*s* to most singular nouns to make them plural. If a singular noun ends in -*s*, -*ch*, -*sh*, *or* -*x*, we add -*es* to make it plural. To form the plural of nouns ending in a consonant and *y*, we change *y* to *i* and then add -*es*.

**Practice**  Have partners form the plural of each noun.

horse (horses)     frog (frogs)     fox (foxes)     grape (grapes)
puppy (puppies)     bush (bushes)     lunch (lunches)

## Mechanics: Commas in a Series

**Review**  Remind children that commas are used to separate three or more words in a series. The word *and* or *or* comes before the last word in the series.

**Practice**  Display the following sentences and read them aloud. Have partners write commas in the correct places.

Did a fish, a bird, or a turkey help Cinderella?

I like animal stories, fables, and tales.

### Talk about It

**Matching Nouns!**  Prepare a game of Concentration. Select six nouns and write the singular and plural form of each on separate note cards: *fox, foxes, rule, rules, bus, buses, home, homes, cube, cubes, ax, axes*. For each word, draw or glue a simple picture on an index card. For example, draw one fox for *fox* and two for *foxes*. Small groups of children use the cards to play a game of Concentration: naming a picture, finding its match, and using the word correctly in a sentence.

# Daily Wrap Up

→ Review the Essential Question and encourage children to discuss it using the vocabulary words.

→ Prompt children to discuss the skills they practiced and learned today. Guide them to share examples of how they used each skill.

 **Go** Digital

**www.connected.mcgraw-hill.com**
RESOURCES
Research and Inquiry

→ ## Wrap Up the Week
# Integrate Ideas

## RESEARCH AND INQUIRY

**Animals in Stories**

### OBJECTIVES

 **CCSS** Participate in collaborative conversations with diverse partners about *grade 2 topics and texts* with peers and adults in small and larger groups. **SL.2.1**

 **CCSS** Ask and answer such questions as *who, what, where, when, why,* and *how* to demonstrate understanding of key details in a text. **RL.2.1**

- Build background knowledge.
- Research information using technology.

### ACADEMIC LANGUAGE
*topic, resources*

### Make a Chart

 Tell children that today they will do a research project with a group. They will select a fable and tell about the beginning, middle, and ending events and the lesson it teaches. Review the steps in the research process.

**STEP 1** ### Choose a Topic

Guide groups to review the selections from the week and the lessons they teach. Brainstorm a list of other animal fables and their lessons. Have children select one fable.

**STEP 2** ### Find Resources

Discuss how to use the selections, reference materials, and online sources. Have children use the Research Process Checklist online.

**STEP 3** ### Keep Track of Ideas

Have children make a Two Tab Foldable® to record ideas and facts from sources. Model recording the names of sources.

The Boy Who Cried Wolf    Wolf! Wolf!

**Dinah Zike's**
**FOLDABLES**

### Collaborative Conversations

**Add New Ideas** As children engage in partner, small group, and whole group discussions, review with them to:

→ stay on topic.

→ build on the ideas of others.

→ connect their personal experiences to the conversation.

**The Boy Who Cried Wolf.**

Beginning: The boy cries wolf, but there is no wolf.

Middle: A real wolf comes.

Ending: The boy cries wolf, but no one believes him.

Lesson: Always tell the truth.

**STEP 4** **Present the Project: Chart**

Tell children that they can make a chart about their fable. Explain the characteristics of a chart.

→ **Information** The purpose of a chart is to give information. In this project, the chart will give the title and the beginning, middle, and ending of the fable. It will also give the lesson.

→ **Image** A chart can have an engaging image related to the information.

→ **Text** A chart has text that gives information related to the image.

Have partners work together to create a chart about their fable.

→ Guide them to draw a picture about a character or scene from the fable.

→ Prompt children to write sentences that give the key events and the lesson they learned from the fable.

**ELL ENGLISH LANGUAGE LEARNERS SCAFFOLD**

| Beginning | Intermediate | Advanced/High |
|---|---|---|
| **Use Sentence Frames** Use sentence frames to help children identify the story structure for their fable. For example: *At the beginning _____. Next, _____. At the end, _____. The lesson is _____.* | **Discuss** Guide children to recall important details about the fable. Ask: *What happens at the beginning? in the middle? at the end? What is the lesson?* | **Describe** Prompt children to list details to summarize the beginning, middle, and end of their fable. Have them explain the lesson and why it is important. |

## Materials

**Reading/Writing Workshop**

**Literature Anthology**

**Word-Building Cards**

**Spelling-Word Cards**

**High-Frequency Word Cards**

Dinah Zike's **FOLDABLES**

**Dinah Zike's Foldables®**

# → Integrate Ideas

# TEXT CONNECTIONS *Analytical Writing*

**Connect to Essential Question**

### OBJECTIVES

 Ask and answer such questions as *who, what, where, when, why,* and *how* to demonstrate understanding of key details in a text. **RL.2.1**

 Recount stories, including fables and folktales from diverse cultures, and determine their central message, lesson, or moral. **RL.2.2**

 Compare and contrast two or more versions of the same story (e.g., Cinderella stories) by different authors or from different cultures. **RL.2.9**

Make text connections to the world.

## Text to Text

**Cite Evidence** Remind children that this week they have been reading animal fables. Tell them that now they will compare these texts. Model comparing text using "The Boy Who Cried Wolf," **Reading/Writing Workshop**, pages 118–123, and *Wolf! Wolf!*, **Literature Anthology**, pp. 136–157. Use a Two-Tab Foldable® to record comparisons.

**Think Aloud** "The Boy Who Cried Wolf" and *Wolf! Wolf!* are both fables about a shepherd boy who tricks villagers by calling, "Wolf!" when there is no wolf. "The Boy Who Cried Wolf" is the traditional story. It has been told for many years. *Wolf! Wolf!* is a new version.

 **Complete the Organizer** Have children use a Two-Tab Foldable® to record comparisons. Guide children to discuss and write about the characters in the selections and the lessons the characters learn.

**Present Information** Ask groups to present their information to the class.

## Text to Self

**Discuss** Have children discuss their favorite fable. Ask: *What did you learn from that fable?*

## Text to World

Have children discuss the fables they read this week. Ask: *Why is it important to have fables? How do fables help people get along?*

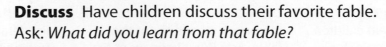

Dinah Zike's **FOLDABLES**

# WRITE ABOUT READING  *Analytical Writing*

**OBJECTIVES**

ccss Draw evidence from literary or informational texts to support analysis, reflection, and research. **W.4.9**

## Write an Analysis

**Cite Evidence** Explain to children that as a group they will write about one of the selections that they read this week.

Tell children that using the evidence in the text, they will analyze how two versions of the same story are the same and different.

Ask children what lessons the authors want readers to learn in "The Boy Who Cried Wolf" and another retelling of the story, such as *Wolf! Wolf!* Guide children to analyze the ways the stories are similar and different using *how* questions about the story.

→ How are the stories the same?

→ How are the stories different?

Work with children to complete the sentence frames using information from "The Boy Who Cried Wolf" and another version of the story.

> The stories are similar because _____.
>
> The stories are different because _____.
>
> Both authors wanted readers to learn _____.

Then have children select two versions of another story and use similar sentence frames to write about how the versions are the same and different.

**Present Your Ideas** Ask partners to share their paragraphs and discuss how the evidence they found supports their ideas.

# RESEARCH AND INQUIRY

**OBJECTIVES**

ccss Participate in shared research and writing projects. **W.2.7**

## Wrap Up the Project

Guide groups to present their projects. Prior to the presentations, review the Presenting and Listening checklists with children.

 → # Word Work

### Quick Review

**Build Fluency: Sound Spellings**
Display the **Word-Building Cards**: *u_e, u, o_e, o, i_e, i, a_e, a, sl, dr, sk, sp, st, tr, pr, pl*. Have children say each sound. Repeat, and vary the pace.

 MINILESSON **5** Mins

# Phonemic Awareness

## OBJECTIVES

**CCSS** Know and apply grade-level phonics and word analysis skills in decoding words. **RF.2.3**

**CCSS** Distinguish long and short vowels when reading regularly spelled one-syllable words. **RF.2.3a**

**CCSS** Recognize and read grade-appropriate irregularly spelled words. **RF.2.3f**

**CCSS** Demonstrate command of the conventions of standard English capitalization, punctuation, and spelling when writing. **L.2.2**

Segment phonemes in words.

## Phoneme Segmentation

**Review** Guide children to segment words into phonemes. *Listen as I say a word. Place one counter on the WorkBoard for each sound.* Use: *tube, mules, stuck, luck, cube, flute.*

 MINILESSON **5** Mins

# Phonics

## Blend Words with Short *u* and Long *u*

**Review** Have children read and say the words *prune, sum, fuzz, June,* and *cute.* Then have children follow the word building routine with Word-Building Cards to build *up, cup, cub, cube, cute, mute, muse, use, us, bus.*

**Word Automaticity** Help children practice word automaticity. Display decodable words and point to each word as children chorally read it. Test how many words children can read in one minute. Model blending words children miss.

 MINILESSON **5** Mins

# Structural Analysis

## CVCe Syllables

**①** **Review** Remind children of the definition of a CVCe, *or final e* syllable. (A CVCe syllable contains the vowel, consonant, silent *e* pattern.) Ask children to divide the following words into syllables: *amuse, alone, excuse, inside,* and *mistake.* Then have children identify the CVCe syllable in each word.

## Go Digital

**Phonemic Awareness**

**Phonics**

**Structural Analysis**

**Spelling Word Sort**

**High-Frequency Word Routine**

**Visual Glossary**

# Spelling

## Word Sort with Short *u* and Long *u*

**Review** Have children use the Spelling Word Cards to sort the weekly words by short *u* and long *u* words.

**Assess** Assess children on their abilities to spell words short *u* and long *u*. Say each word and provide a sentence so that children can hear the words used in a correct context. Then allow them to write down the words. In order to challenge children, you may wish to provide an additional word for both short *u* and long *u* in order to assess whether they understand the concept.

# High-Frequency Words

## *change, cheer, fall, five, look, open, should, their, won, yes*

**Review** Display High-Frequency Word Cards *change, cheer, fall, five, look, open, should, their, won, yes*. Have children Read/Spell/Write each word. Have children write a sentence with each word.

# Vocabulary Words

**Review** Display Visual Vocabulary Word Cards *believe, delicious, feast, fond, lessons, remarkable, snatch, stories*. Have children review each word using the Define/Example/Ask Routine on the back of each card.

---

**Monitor and Differentiate**

**✓ Quick Check**

Can children read and decode words with short *u* and long *u*? Can children read high-frequency words?

⬇

### Small Group Instruction

| | | |
|---|---|---|
| If No → | **Approaching** | Reteach pp. T158–T163 |
| | **ELL** | Develop pp. T174–T181 |
| If Yes → | **On Level** | Review pp. T168–T169 |
| | **Beyond Level** | Extend pp. T172–T173 |

→ # Language Arts

## MINILESSON
**5** Mins
# Writing Traits: Ideas

## Share and Reflect

**Discuss** Discuss with the class what they learned about supporting details to improve their writing. Guide them to recall that supporting details help writers explain their ideas.

**Present** Invite volunteers to choose a writing entry from the week to share with the class. Compare the volunteer's draft with his or her revised text, and encourage children to identify supporting details the volunteer added. Have children discuss the writing by focusing on how the details helped explain the ideas in the volunteer's fable.

**Reflect** Have children use their Writer's Notebook to reflect on their progress as writers. Invite them to consider the following prompts as they write:

How did adding supporting details improve your writing this week?

What part of your writing did you like best this week?

What part of your writing this week would you like to improve?

What other animal fables might you like to write about this week? Why?

**Publish** After children finish presenting their fables, discuss how the class will publish a collection of their stories on a class blog or Website. Have children add illustrations to their stories. Guide them to use digital tools to publish their stories and illustrations. Allow children to make decisions regarding the organization of their stories.

**Go Digital**

**Writing**

**Checklists**

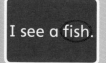

I see a fish.

**Grammar**

# Grammar

## Singular and Plural Nouns

**Review** Review with children the definition of singular and plural nouns. A singular noun names one person, place, or thing. A plural noun names more than one person, place, or thing. Also review the rules for making singular nouns plural. We form the plural of most singular nouns by adding -*s*. We form the plural of nouns ending in -*s*, -*ch*, -*sh*, and -*x* by adding -*es*. We form the plural of nouns ending in a consonant and *y* by changing the *y* to *i* and adding -*es*.

**Practice** Display the following singular nouns. Have partners form the plural of each singular noun.

| | | |
|---|---|---|
| city (cities) | brush (brushes) | inch (inches) |
| fox (foxes) | bus (buses) | dress (dresses) |

## Mechanics: Commas in a Series

**Review** Remind children that when there are three or more words in a series, commas are used to separate the words. The word *and* or *or* comes before the last word in the series.

**Practice** Display the following sentences. Have children tell where to add commas.

We saw horses, cows, and goats in the fields.

They grow carrots, peas, and tomatoes on their farm.

## Reteach

If children have difficulty identifying singular or plural nouns, forming plural nouns, or using a comma in a series, review the use of each. Provide opportunities for children to practice the skills in small groups, with a partner, or independently.

### Talk About It

**Nouns in Sentences** Have children work with a partner. Ask one partner to make a list of three plural nouns and then read them aloud. The other partner uses each noun in an original sentence. Then partners switch roles.

# Wrap Up the Week

→ Review the Essential Question and encourage children to discuss using the oral vocabulary words.

→ Review the comprehension strategy and skill.

→ Review short *u* and long *u* words.

→ Use the High-Frequency Word Cards to review the Words to Know.

→ Review the different purposes for writing fables.

→ # Approaching Level

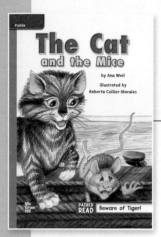

**Lexile** 200
*TextEvaluator™* 7

 ## OBJECTIVES

**CCSS** Describe how characters in a story respond to major events and challenges. **RL.2.3**

 **CCSS** Describe the overall structure of a story, including describing how the beginning introduces the story and the ending concludes the action. **RL.2.5**

## MATERIALS

Leveled Reader
*The Cat and the Mice*

## Leveled Reader:
## *The Cat and the Mice*

**Go Digital**

### Before Reading

#### Preview and Predict

Have children turn to the title page. Read the title and author name and have children repeat. Preview the selection's illustrations. Prompt children to predict what the selection might be about.

#### Review Genre: Fable

Have children recall that fables are made-up stories that teach a lesson or moral. The characters in many fables are talking animals.

**ESSENTIAL QUESTION**

Set a purpose for reading: *Let's read to find out what we can learn from the animals in this story.*

Remind children that as they read a selection, they can ask questions about what they do not understand or want to know more about.

### During Reading

#### Guided Comprehension

As children whisper read *The Cat and the Mice*, monitor and provide guidance, correcting blending and modeling the key strategies and skills.

#### Strategy: Make, Confirm, and Revise Predictions

Remind children that a prediction is a thoughtful guess about what might happen. Model predicting using pages 2 and 3. *Cats like mice and hunt them. The story says the mice did something remarkable. I predict the mice will stop the cat from hunting them. As I read, I'll check my prediction and change it if I need to.*

#### Skill: Character, Setting, Plot: Problem and Solution

Remind children that the plot is what happens in a story. Explain that the plot often tells about a problem at the beginning and a solution to the problem at the end. After reading, ask: *What is the problem at the beginning? What steps do the characters take to solve the problem?* Display a Problem/ Solution graphic organizer for children to copy.

**Leveled Readers**

**Graphic Organizer**

**Retelling Cards**

Model recording children's answers in the first two boxes of the chart. Have children record the answers in their own charts.

**Think Aloud** The beginning of the story tells about how cats like mice. They hunt and chase the mice all day. This is a problem for the mice. The mice are not safe. I can write this problem in the Problem box of my graphic organizer.

Guide children to identify the steps to the problem and the solution.

## After Reading

### Respond to Reading

Have children complete the Respond to Reading questions on page 16.

### Retell

Have children take turns retelling the selection. Help children make a personal connection by asking: *How would you feel if you were a mouse? What would you do to stay safe from the cat?*

### Model Fluency

Read the sentences one at a time. Have children chorally repeat. Point out to children how your voice goes up at the end of a question.

**Apply** Have children practice reading with partners. Provide feedback as needed.

## PAIRED READ ...

### "Beware of Tiger!"

#### Make Connections:
#### Write About It ✏ *Analytical Writing*

Before reading, ask children to note that the genre of this text is also a fable. It tells a story about a tiger. Then discuss the Compare Texts statement. After reading, ask children to make connections between what they read in "Beware of Tiger!" and *The Cat and the Mice.*

**Leveled Reader**

### FOCUS ON LITERARY ELEMENTS

Children can extend their understanding of the use of dialogue in stories by completing the activity on page 20.

## Literature Circles

Lead children in conducting a literature circle using the Thinkmark questions to guide the discussion. You may wish to discuss what children have learned from animals in stories from both selections in the leveled reader.

## Level Up

Level-up lessons available online.

**IF** children read the `Approaching Level` fluently and answered the questions

**THEN** pair them with children who have proficiently read the `On Level` and have approaching children

- echo-read the `On Level` main selection.

- use self-stick notes to mark one detail they would like to discuss in each section.

### A C T Access Complex Text

The `On Level` challenges children by including more **specific vocabulary** and **complex sentence structures.**

# → Approaching Level
## Phonemic Awareness

### PHONEME BLENDING

**OBJECTIVES**

Orally produce single-syllable words by blending sounds (phonemes), including consonant blends. **RF.1.2b**

Blend phonemes to form words.

 **I Do** Explain to children that they will be blending sounds to form words. *Listen as I say three sounds: /mmm/ /ūūū/ /lll/. Say the sounds with me: /m/ /ū/ /l/. Blend the sounds with me: /mūl/,* mule. *The word is* mule.

 **We Do** *Listen as I say three sounds: /hhh/ /uuu/ /g/. Repeat the sounds: /hhh/ /uuu/ /g/. Let's blend the sounds: /hhhuuug/,* hug. *We made one word:* hug. Repeat this routine with the following words:

pup    cube    jug    mute    huge    duck    run    muse

 **You Do** *It's your turn. I want you to blend the sounds I say to form words.*

cute    fume    duck    mud    use    fuse    duke    sun

**Repeat** the blending routine with additional words with short and long *u*.

### PHONEME SEGMENTATION

**OBJECTIVES**

Segment spoken single-syllable words into their complete sequence of individual sounds (phonemes). **RF.1.2d**

Segment words into phonemes.

 **I Do** Explain to children that they will be segmenting words into sounds today. *Listen as I say a word:* up. *I hear two sounds: /uuu/ and /p/. There are two sounds in the word* up: */uuu/ and /p/.*

 **We Do** *Let's do some together. I am going to say a word: /fume/. How many sounds do you hear? The sounds in* fume *are /f/, /ū/, and /m/.* Repeat this routine with the following words:

*up    huge    use    mute    must    stuck*

 **You Do** It's your turn. I'll say a word. Tell me how many sounds. Then tell me each sound you hear in the word.

*tube    hum    tune    stuff    mule    jug    spun    muse    cute    fuse*

You may wish to review Phonemic Awareness with **ELL** using this section.

# PHONEME DELETION

## OBJECTIVES

 Demonstrate understanding of spoken words, syllables, and sounds (phonemes). **RF.1.2**

Delete sounds in words to form new words.

 **I Do** Explain to children that they will be deleting phonemes. *When you delete, you subtract or take away. When you delete a phoneme, you are removing or taking away a sound.*

*Listen as I say a word:* cup, */kuuup/. I want to take away the /k/ sound from* cup. *That leaves /uuu/ and /p/.* Cup *without /k/ is* up.

*Now listen as I say the word /f/ /ūūū/ /z/. I want to take away the /f/ sound in* fuse. *That leaves /ūūū/ /zzz/. The new word is* use. Fuse *without /f/ is* use.

 **We Do** *Listen as I say a word:* pluck. *Say the word with me, /pllluuuk/. Let's take away /p/ from* pluck. *That leaves /lll/ /uuu/ /k/. Let's blend them. /llluuuk/,* luck. Pluck *without /p/ is* luck.

Repeat this routine with the following pairs of words:

*pup/up       smug/mug       slump/lump*

**You Do** *It's your turn. Take away the sound from one word to form a new word.*

| | |
|---|---|
| muse/use | stuck/tuck |
| fuse/use | stalk/talk |
| trust/rust | stub/tub |
| clump/lump | floss/loss |
| pink/ink | |

## ELL ENGLISH LANGUAGE LEARNERS

For the ELLs who need **phonics, decoding,** and **fluency** practice, use scaffolding methods as necessary to ensure children understand the meaning of the words. Refer to the Language Transfer Handbook for phonics elements that may not transfer in children' native languages.

# Approaching Level

## Phonics

### CONNECT *u* TO /u/ AND *u_e* TO /ū/

TIER 2

**OBJECTIVES**

 Know and apply grade-level phonics and word analysis skills in decoding words. **RF.2.3**

 Distinguish long and short vowels when reading regularly spelled one-syllable words. **RF.2.3a**

 **I Do** Display the Cube Sound-Spelling Card. Say: *The middle sound in* cube *is /ū/. The /ū/ sound can be spelled with the letters* u, consonant, e. *The* u *and* e *work together to make the long u sound. The* e *is silent. Say it with me: /ū/.* Model saying the sound as you write the letters. Repeat for /u/, *u* using the Umbrella Sound-Spelling Card.

 **We Do** *Now do it with me. Say /ū/ as I write the letters* u_e. *This time write the letters* u_e *five times as you say the /ū/ sound.* Repeat the process with /u/, *u*.

 **You Do** Have children connect the letters *u_e* to the sound /ū/. Write the letters *u_e* as you say /ū/. Have children write *u_e* while saying /ū/ five to ten times. Repeat the process with /u/.

**Repeat,** connecting the letter *u* to /u/ and the letters *u_e* to /ū/ through writing the letters throughout the week.

**Sound/Spellings Fluency** Display the letters *u_e, u, o_e, o, i_e, i, a_e, a, sl, dr, sk, sp, st, tr, pr, pl*. Have children chorally say each sound. Repeat and vary the pace.

### BLEND WORDS WITH SHORT *u*, LONG *u*

TIER 2

**OBJECTIVES**

 Know and apply grade-level phonics and word analysis skills in decoding words. **RF.2.3**

 Distinguish long and short vowels when reading regularly spelled one-syllable words. **RF.2.3a**

 **I Do** Display Word-Building Cards *f, u, m, e*. *This is the letter* f. *It stands for /f/. This is the letter* u. *It stands for /ū/ in this word. Let's say it together: /ū/. This is the letter* m. *It stands for /m/. The letter* e *is silent. I'll blend these sounds together: /fūūūm/,* fume. *The word is* fume. Repeat with *rug*.

 **We Do** Guide children to blend the sounds and read: *mute, mule, but, truck, must*.

 **You Do** Have children blend and decode: *cute, mud, run, sun, mute, use*.

**Repeat,** blending additional long *u* and short *u* words.

You may wish to review Phonics with **ELL** using this section.

# BUILD WORDS WITH SHORT *u*, LONG *u*

## OBJECTIVES

 **CCSS** Distinguish long and short vowels when reading regularly spelled one-syllable words. **RF.2.3a**

**I Do** Display Word-Building Cards n, u, t. *These are the letters* n, u, *and* t. *They stand for /n/, /u/, and /t/. I will blend /n/, /u/, and /t/ together:/nut/,* nut.

**We Do** Make the word *nut. Let's blend the new word: /k/ /uuu/ /t/, /kuuut/,* cut. *I am adding an* e *to the end of* cut. *The* e *is silent, and now the* u *stands for /ū/. Let's read the new word: /kūt/,* cute.

**You Do** Have children build the words: *cub, cube, run, sun, bun, bus, us, use, fuse, muse, mute.*

**Decodable Reader** Introduce the Decodable Reader selection, *Duke and Bud's Run.* Point to the book's title. Have children sound out each word. Discuss the cover.

**First Read** Turn to page 8. Have children point to each word, sounding out decodable words and saying the high-frequency words quickly. Children should chorally read the story the first time through.

# BLEND WORDS WITH SHORT *u*, LONG *u*

## OBJECTIVES

 **CCSS** Distinguish long and short vowels when reading regularly spelled one-syllable words. **RF.2.3a**

**I Do** Display Word-Building Cards u, s, e. Say: *This is the letter* u. *It stands for /ū/. This is the letter* s. *It stands for /z/. This is the letter* e. *It is silent. Listen as I blend these sounds: /ūūūz/,* use. *The word is* use.

**We Do** *Let's do some together.* Blend and read the words *muse, cup,* and *but* with children.

**You Do** Display the following words: *tub, cub, cube, cute.* Have children blend and read the words.

**Decodable Reader** Have children reread the Decodable Reader selection.

**Check Comprehension** As children read, monitor their comprehension. Ask the following: *Why does Bud stop during the race? Why does Duke win the race?*

# BLEND WORDS WITH SHORT *u*, LONG *u*

## Fluency in Connected Text

Have children review the Decodable Reader selection. Identify short and long *u* words and blend words as needed. Model rereading and using context to confirm or self-correct word recognition and understanding. Have children read the selection on their own or with a partner.

# Approaching Level
## Structural Analysis

## REVIEW CVCe SYLLABLES

 **TIER 2**

### OBJECTIVES

 Know and apply grade-level phonics and word analysis skills in decoding words. **RF.2.3**

 Distinguish long and short vowels when reading regularly spelled one-syllable words. **RF.2.3a**

Read syllables with the CVCe pattern.

**I Do** Review that a syllable is a word part with one vowel sound. Explain that a word can have one or more syllables. Write *mule* and read it aloud. Mule *has one vowel sound, so it has one syllable. Look how* mule *is spelled. There is a consonant* (m), *a vowel* (u), *a consonant* (l), *and an* e *on the end. When a syllable has this pattern, the vowel sound is usually long and the* e *is silent.*

**We Do** Write *game* and *kite. Let's read these words: /gāāāmmm/; /kīīt/. Now let's look at the spellings. What letter do these words end in? Yes,* e. *The* e *is silent.*

**You Do** Have children work with partners. Give them several words with CVC and CVCe syllables. Children can work together to underline the syllables with CVCe and then read each word.

**Repeat** Have children name other words that have the CVCe pattern.

## RETEACH CVCe SYLLABLES

### OBJECTIVES

 Know and apply grade-level phonics and word analysis skills in decoding words. **RF.2.3**

 Distinguish long and short vowels when reading regularly spelled one-syllable words. **RF.2.3a**

Read syllables with the CVCe pattern.

**I Do** Write *cub* and *cube. These words are* cub *and* cube. *Listen to the different vowel sounds: /kub/; /kūb/. Point to each letter in* cube. *When a word or syllable has this pattern, a consonant, a vowel, a consonant, and an* e, *the syllable usually has a long vowel sound and the* e *is silent.*

**We Do** Write *tadpole. Listen to the two syllables: tad-pole. Let's look at the spelling of the second syllable. It has a consonant, a vowel, a consonant, and an* e. *How do we say this syllable? That's right, /pōl/. The* o *stands for /ō/ and the* e *is silent. Repeat this routine with the following examples:* inside, reptile, resuse.

**You Do** Have children identify the syllables with CVCe and read the words aloud. Guide children to repeat the words as needed. *Now it's your turn. Find the syllables with a consonant, vowel, consonant, and silent* e. *Then read the words.*

flute    joke    cake    invite    sidekick    excuse

# High-Frequency Words/ Vocabulary

## REVIEW HIGH-FREQUENCY WORDS

**OBJECTIVES**

Read with sufficient accuracy and fluency to support comprehension. **RF.2.4**

Review high-frequency words.

 **I Do** Use Word Cards 61-70. Display one word at a time, following the routine:

Display the word. Read the word. Then spell the word.

 **We Do** Ask children to state the word and spell the word with you. Model using the word in a sentence and have children repeat after you.

**You Do** Display the word. Ask children to say the word and then spell it. When completed, quickly flip through the word card set as children chorally read the words. Provide opportunities for children to use the words in speaking and writing. For example, provide sentence starters, such as *I saw five _____.* Ask children to write each word in their Writer's Notebook.

## REVIEW VOCABULARY WORDS

**OBJECTIVES**

Use words and phrases acquired through conversations, reading and being read to, and responding to texts, including using adjectives and adverbs to describe (e.g., *When other kids are happy that makes me happy*). **L.2.6**

 **I Do** Display each Visual Vocabulary Card and state the word. Explain how the photograph illustrates the word. State the example sentence and repeat the word.

 **We Do** Point to the word on the card and read the word with children. Ask them to repeat the word. Engage children in structured partner talk about the image as prompted on the back of the vocabulary card.

 **You Do** Display each visual in random order, hiding the word. Have children match the definitions and context sentences of the words to the visuals displayed. Then ask children to complete Approaching Level Practice Book page 61.

# → Approaching Level

## Comprehension

### READ FOR FLUENCY

**OBJECTIVES**

 Read with sufficient accuracy and fluency to support comprehension. **RF.2.4**

**I Do** Read the first paragraph of the Practice Book selection. Model reading with and showing expression with different punctuation.

**We Do** Read the next paragraph and have children repeat each sentence after you. Point out how you used your voice to express the emotions in what you were reading. Then point out using punctuation to show expression.

**You Do** Have children read the rest of the selection aloud. Remind them to change their voice and pay attention to punctuation to show expression as they read.

### IDENTIFY THE PLOT

**OBJECTIVES**

 Describe how characters in a story respond to major events and challenges. **RL.2.3**

 Describe the overall structure of a story, including describing how the beginning introduces the story and the ending concludes the action. **RL.2.5**

Identify events in a story's plot.

**I Do** Remind children that they have been reading fiction. Explain that fiction stories have a plot. *The plot is the events that happen in the beginning, middle, and end story. The plot tells what the characters do and where they go.*

**We Do** Read the first page of the Practice Book selection aloud. Pause to identify *important events in the plot. At the beginning of the story, Fox wants to reach the grapes high up on the tree. Fox jumps, but he can't jump high enough. He gets a ladder.*

**You Do** Guide children to read the rest of the Practice Book selection. As they read, prompt them to identify the important events in the middle and end of the story.

## REVIEW CHARACTER, SETTING, PLOT: PROBLEM AND SOLUTION

**OBJECTIVES**

 Describe how characters in a story respond to major events and challenges. **RL.2.3**

 Describe the overall structure of a story, including describing how the beginning introduces the story and the ending concludes the action. **RL.2.5**

 **I Do** Remind children that fiction stories have a plot with a beginning, middle, and end. Often the beginning will describe a problem. The ending of the story will tell how the characters solved or tried to solve the problem.

 **We Do** Read the first page of the Practice Book selection together. Help children determine what the story's problem is. *We read that Fox wanted to reach the grapes high up in the tree.*

 **You Do** Stop reading after page 63 and say: *What do I know about the problem at the beginning of the story? What steps has Fox taken to solve the problem so far?* Record information about the problem on the graphic organizer. Continue having children add steps to the solution on their charts. Then guide them to record the solution.

## SELF-SELECTED READING

**OBJECTIVES**

 Read with sufficient accuracy and fluency to support comprehension **RF.2.4**

 Read on-level text with purpose and understanding. **RF.2.4a**

 Describe the overall structure of a story, including describing how the beginning introduces the story and the ending concludes the action. **RL.2.5**

Apply the strategy and skill to reread text.

### Read Independently

Have children pick a fable selection that they have read for sustained silent reading. Remind them that:

→ they should look for the lesson the fable teaches.

→ the story may describe a problem that the characters try to solve.

→ as they read, they can make, confirm, and revise predictions about the story.

### Read Purposefully

Have children record the problem, steps to the solution, and solution on their Problem/Solution Chart. After reading, guide children to participate in a group discussion about the selection they read. Guide children to:

→ share the information they recorded on their Problem/Solution Chart.

→ tell about the story's lesson and how the characters solved or tried to solve their problem.

→ describe the predictions they made, how they checked their predictions, and whether they revised them.

# → On Level

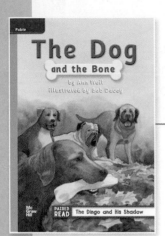

**Lexile** 440
*TextEvaluator™* 5

## OBJECTIVES

 Describe how characters in a story respond to major events and challenges. **RL.2.3**

 Describe the overall structure of a story, including describing how the beginning introduces the story and the ending concludes the action. **RL.2.5**

 Read with sufficient accuracy and fluency to support comprehension. **RF.2.4**

 Read on-level text orally with accuracy, appropriate rate, and expression on successive readings. **RF.2.4b**

## MATERIALS

Leveled Reader
*The Dog and the Bone*

## Leveled Reader:
## *The Dog and the Bone*

### Before Reading

#### Preview and Predict

Have children turn to the title page. Read the title and author name and have children repeat. Preview the selection's illustrations. Prompt children to predict what the selection might be about.

#### Review Genre: Fable

Have children recall that fables are a kind of fiction. They are made-up stories that teach a lesson or moral. The characters in fables are often talking animals.

#### ESSENTIAL QUESTION

Set a purpose for reading: *Let's read to find out what lesson the animals in this story can teach us.*

Remind children that as they read a selection, they can ask questions about what they do not understand or want to know more about.

### During Reading

#### Close Reading

**Note taking** Ask students to use their graphic organizer while they read.

**Pages 2–4** *Describe the beginning of the story to a partner. Then make a prediction about what will happen in Chapter 2.* (Possible response: Dog finds a big bone in some leaves and feels really lucky. I predict that he will fight with other dogs over his bone.)

**Pages 5–8** *Discuss your prediction with a partner. How do you know your prediction is correct? How would you revise it?* (Possible response: My prediction was partly correct, because the other dogs wanted his bone, but Dog avoided a fight by deciding to take his bone home to eat it. I would revise my prediction to say that Dog *might* fight with the other dogs.) *Why are the chapter titles printed on a bone?* (This design helps readers remember that the story is about a dog bone.) *What word has the suffix -y on page 8?* (chilly)

### Go Digital

**Leveled Readers**

**Graphic Organizer**

**Retelling Cards**

**Pages 9–11** *How does the bridge help Dog with his problem?* (Dog didn't want to swim in the chilly, deep brook, so he used the bridge to cross on foot.) *Why is the word* splash *printed in all capital letters?* (This lets readers know that it was a very loud splash.)

**Pages 12–15** *What is Dog's new problem? Why can't he solve it?* (He has to find a way to get the other, bigger bone in the brook. He can't solve it, because the other bone was only a reflection.)

## After Reading

### Respond to Reading

Have children complete the Respond to Reading on page 16 after reading.

### Retell

Have children take turns retelling the selection. Help children make a personal connection by asking: *Dog really cares about his bone and wants to protect it. Have you ever had something you wanted to protect or keep safe? What did you do?*

### Model Fluency

Read the sentences, one at a time. Have children chorally repeat. Point out to children how your voice goes up at the end of a question.

**Apply** Have partners practice repeated reading. Provide feedback.

## PAIRED READ ...

## "The Dingo and His Shadow"

### Make Connections: Write About It ✏ *Analytical Writing*

Before reading, ask children to note that the genre of this text is also a fable. Then discuss the Essential Question. After reading, ask children to make connections between what they read in "The Dingo and His Shadow" and *The Dog and the Bone*.

**Leveled Reader**

---

### FOCUS ON LITERARY ELEMENTS

Children can extend their understanding of the use of dialogue in stories by completing the activity on page 20.

---

## Literature Circles

Lead children in conducting a literature circle using the Thinkmark questions to guide the discussion. You may wish to discuss what lessons we can learn from the animals from both selections in the leveled reader.

## Level Up

*Level-up lessons available online.*

**IF** children read the On Level fluently and answered the questions

**THEN** pair them with children who have proficiently read the Beyond Level and have on-level children

• partner-read the Beyond Level main selection.

• Identify a part of the plot they would like to learn more about.

## A C T Access Complex Text

The Beyond Level challenges children by including more **specific vocabulary** and **complex sentence structures**.

# On Level

## Phonics

### BUILD WORDS WITH SHORT *u*, LONG *u*

**OBJECTIVES**

**CCSS** Know and apply grade-level phonics and word analysis skills in decoding words. **RF.2.3**

**CCSS** Distinguish long and short vowels when reading regularly spelled one-syllable words. **RF.2.3a**

**I Do** Display **Word-Building Cards** *c, u, t.* Say: *This is the letter* c. *It stands for /k/. This is the letter* u. *It stands for /u/. Listen as I blend these two sounds together: /kuuu/. This is the letter* t. *It stands for /t/. Now listen as I blend these three sounds together: /kuuut/,* cut. *The word is* cut.

**We Do** Say: *Now, let's do one together. Make the word* cut *using Word-Building Cards. Place the letter* e *at the end of* cut. *This will change the vowel sound in the word. Let's blend: /k/ /ūūū/ /t/, /kūūūt/,* cute. *The new word is* cute.

**You Do** Have children build and blend the words: *cube, fuse, must, husk, hunt, rust, run, huge, mule, muse.*

**Fluency in Connected Text** Have children read this week's Decodable Reader selection, *Duke and Bud's Run.*

## Vocabulary

### REVIEW WORDS

**OBJECTIVES**

**CCSS** Use words and phrases acquired through conversations, reading and being read to, and responding to texts, including using adjectives and adverbs to describe (e.g., *When other kids are happy that makes me happy*). **L.2.6**

Review Vocabulary Words.

**I Do** Use the **Visual Vocabulary Cards** to review each vocabulary word. Point to each word, read it aloud, and have children chorally repeat it.

**We Do** Guide children to use the **Define/Example/Ask** routine for a few vocabulary words using their **Response Boards**. Ask sample questions to help children respond and explain their answers.

**You Do** Have children work with a partner to do the Define/Example/Ask routine on their own for the remaining vocabulary words. Then have children write sentences about this week's stories. Each sentence must contain at least one vocabulary word.

# Comprehension

## REVIEW CHARACTER, SETTING, PLOT: PROBLEM AND SOLUTION

**OBJECTIVES**

 Describe how characters in a story respond to major events and challenges.
**RL.2.3**

 Describe the overall structure of a story, including describing how the beginning introduces the story and the ending concludes the action.
**RL.2.5**

 **I Do** Remind children that in many fiction stories, the beginning of the plot tells about a problem the characters have. The middle tells the steps the characters take to solve the problem. The end of the story tells the solution to the problem. *When we read fables, we can look for the problem at the beginning of the story. As we read, we can see how characters try to solve the problem and what the solution is.*

 **We Do** Read the first page of the Practice Book selection aloud. As you read, pause to discuss what is happening in the story. Help children identify the problem. *We read that Fox wanted to reach the grapes high up in the tree. This is the story's problem.*

**You Do** Guide children to read the rest of the Practice Book selection. Remind them to look for steps characters take to solve the problem. Then have them point out the solution to the problem.

## SELF-SELECTED READING

**OBJECTIVES**

 Read with sufficient accuracy and fluency to support comprehension.
**RF.2.4**

 Read on-level text with purpose and understanding.
**RF.2.4a**

 Describe the overall structure of a story, including describing how the beginning introduces the story and the ending concludes the action.
**RL.2.5**

### Read Independently

Have children pick a fable that they have read for sustained silent reading. Remind them to:

→ identify the story's problem, the steps characters take to solve the problem, and the solution.

→ make, confirm, and revise predictions based on what they have read and seen in illustrations.

### Read Purposefully

Have children record the problem, steps to solution, and solution on their Problem/Solution graphic organizer. After reading, guide partners to:

→ share what they recorded on their Problem/Solution graphic organizer.

→ tell what lesson or moral the story teaches.

→ describe the predictions they made, whether their predictions were correct, and how they revised their predictions.

# Beyond Level

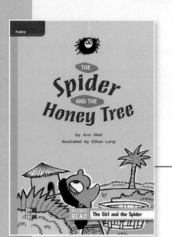

**Lexile** 590
*TextEvaluator.* 15

---

## OBJECTIVES

 Describe how characters in a story respond to major events and challenges. **RL.2.3**

 Describe the overall structure of a story, including describing how the beginning introduces the story and the ending concludes the action. **RL.2.5**

---

## MATERIALS

Leveled Reader
*The Spider and the Honey Tree*

## Leveled Reader:
# *The Spider and the Honey Tree*

### Before Reading

#### Preview and Predict

Read the title and author name. Have children preview the title page and the illustrations. Ask: *What do you think this book will be about?*

#### Review Genre: Fable

Have children recall that fables are fiction stories that often teach a lesson or have a moral. The characters can be animals that talk.

##### ESSENTIAL QUESTION

Remind children of the Essential Question: *What can animals in stories teach us?* Have children set a purpose for reading by asking: *What lesson can we learn from the spider in this story?*

Remind children that as they read a selection, they can ask questions about what they do not understand or want to know more about.

### During Reading

#### Close Reading

**Note taking** Ask students to use their graphic organizer while they read.

**Pages 2–3** *Describe page 2 to a partner. Then make a prediction about whether Spider can be trusted.* (Possible response: A girl can find the best things to eat, and a lazy Spider wants her to help him. I predict that Spider cannot be trusted.) *Why did you make that prediction?* (Possible response: The text says that Spider is too lazy to find food for himself.) *What word has the suffix -ly on page 3?* (politely) *How does the suffix add to the meaning of polite?* (It tells you that someone did something in a polite way.)

**Pages 4–7** *Discuss your prediction with a partner. How do you know your prediction is correct?* (Possible response: My prediction was correct because the text says that Spider was greedy and ate all the plums and bananas without saying thank you.) *What problem do you predict the girl will have now?* (Spider will trick her and eat all the honey.)

**Go**
**Digital**

**Leveled
Readers**

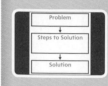

**Graphic
Organizer**

**Pages 8–11** *How did the girl solve her problem?* (She tricked Spider into eating so much he got stuck in the hole.) *What is Spider's problem now?* (He is trapped in the tree because he ate too much.) *What do you predict will happen next?* (The girl won't help Spider.)

**Pages 12–15** *What helped you make your prediction?* (This story is a fable, and fables always have morals that teach lessons. I knew Spider was going to learn a lesson.)

## After Reading

### Respond to Reading

Have children complete the Respond to Reading questions on page 16.

### Retell

Have children take turns retelling the selection. Help children make a personal connection by writing about another animal fable they know. Say: *Write about what happened in the fable. Who were the characters? What lesson did the characters learn?*

## PAIRED READ ...

**Leveled Reader**

### "The Girl and the Spider"

**Make Connections:
Write About It** *Analytical Writing*

Before reading "The Girl and the Spider," have children preview the title page and prompt them to identify the genre. Then discuss the Compare Texts statement. After reading, have children work with a partner to discuss what they read in "The Girl and the Spider" and "The Spider and the Honey Tree." Ask children to make connections by comparing and contrasting the characters in each selection. Prompt children to discuss what they learned from the animals in these fables.

### FOCUS ON LITERARY ELEMENTS

Children can extend their understanding of the use of dialogue in stories by completing the activity on page 20.

## Literature Circles

Lead children in conducting a literature circle using the Thinkmark questions to guide the discussion. You may wish to discuss what lessons children have learned from the animals in both fables in the leveled reader.

## Gifted and Talented

**SYNTHESIZE** Challenge students to describe the lessons they learned from the animals in the fables. Then have them read other fables. Ask them to compare the lessons and the animal characters in different fables. Children should write a brief summary of how the animals helped teach a lesson.

**EXTEND** Have them use fables they read during the week or read additional fables.

# Beyond Level

## Vocabulary

### REVIEW DOMAIN-SPECIFIC WORDS

**OBJECTIVES**

 Use words and phrases acquired through conversations, reading and being read to, and responding to texts, including using adjectives and adverbs to describe (e.g., *When other kids are happy that makes me happy*). **L.2.6**

 **Model** Use the Visual Vocabulary Cards to review the meaning of the words *stories* and *lessons*. Write sentences relating the week's Essential Question on the board using these words.

Write the words *believe* and *delicious* on the board and discuss the meanings with children. Then help children write sentences using these words.

 **Apply** Have children work in pairs to review the meanings of the words *adapt* and *climate*. Then have partners write sentences using the words.

### SUFFIXES

**OBJECTIVES**

 Determine or clarify the meaning of unknown and multiple-meaning words and phrases based on *grade 2 reading and content*, choosing flexibly from an array of strategies. **L.2.4**

 Use sentence-level context as a clue to the meaning of a word or phrase. **L.2.4a**

 **Model** Read aloud the first two paragraphs of the Comprehension and Fluency passage on Beyond Level Practice Book pages 63–64.

**Think Aloud** When I read these paragraphs, I'm not sure what the word *greedily* means. I can separate the root word from the suffix or ending. The root word is "greed," which means "a selfish desire of wanting more than what is needed." The suffix is *-ly*, which means "full of." I think this word means "full of greed."

With children, read the second paragraph. Help them figure out the meaning of *nearly*.

 **Apply** Have pairs of children read the rest of the passage. Ask them to use context clues to determine the meaning of the following words: *really* and *easily*.

 **Shades of Meaning** Using their definition of *nearly*, have partners write an explanation of the difference between *nearly* and *almost*. Encourage them to also use artwork to depict the two words.

# Comprehension

## REVIEW CHARACTER, SETTING, PLOT: PROBLEM AND SOLUTION

**OBJECTIVES**

 Describe how characters in a story respond to major events and challenges. **RL.2.3**

 Describe the overall structure of a story, including describing how the beginning introduces the story and the ending concludes the action. **RL.2.5**

 **Model** Remind children that the plot of many stories is organized around a problem and its solution. Explain that the problem is often explained through the actions of the characters at the beginning of the story. They can then look for the steps characters take to solve the problem and find the solution at the end of the story.

Have children read the beginning of the Comprehension and Fluency passage of Beyond Level Practice Book pages 63–64. Ask open-ended questions to facilitate discussion, such as *What happens at the beginning? What problem do the characters face?* Children should support their responses with examples from the text.

 **Apply** Have children identify steps the characters take to solve the problem as they independently fill in a Problem/Solution graphic organizer. Then have partners use their work to describe the solution reached at the end of the story.

## SELF-SELECTED READING

**OBJECTIVES**

 Describe how characters in a story respond to major events and challenges. **RL.2.3**

 Describe the overall structure of a story, including describing how the beginning introduces the story and the ending concludes the action. **RL.2.5**

### Read Independently

Have children choose a fiction book for sustained silent reading.

→ As children read, have them fill in a Problem/Solution graphic organizer.

→ Remind them to reread difficult sections of the text.

### Read Purposefully

Encourage children to keep a reading journal. Ask them to read different books in order to learn about a variety of subjects.

→ Children can write summaries of the books in their journals.

→ Ask children to share their reactions to the books with classmates.

 **Independent Study** Challenge children to discuss how their books relate to the weekly theme of lessons we can learn from animals in stories. Have children compare the animals and the lessons the stories teach.

# → English Language Learners

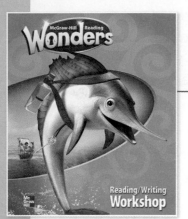

**Reading/Writing Workshop**

## OBJECTIVES

 Read with sufficient accuracy and fluency to support comprehension. **RF.2.4**

 Read on-level text with purpose and understanding. **RF.2.4a**

 Describe how characters in a story respond to major events and challenges. **RL.2.3**

 Describe the overall structure of a story, including describing how the beginning introduces the story and the ending concludes the action. **RL.2.5**

## ACADEMIC LANGUAGE

*plot, problem, solution, characters*

## Shared Read
### *The Boy Who Cried Wolf*

### Before Reading

#### Build Background

Read the Essential Question: *What can animal stories teach us?*

→ Explain the meaning of the Essential Question: *Often, animal stories teach us important lessons.*

→ **Model an answer:** *An example of an animal story is* The Tortoise and the Hare. (Show the picture of the tortoise and the hare on page 114. Point to each animal and say each animal's name.) *In the story, the tortoise and the hare have a race. The hare knows he is very fast, so he takes a nap during the race. The tortoise keeps on running—slowly but steadily—and wins the race. The animal story teaches us to keep trying.*

→ Ask children a question that ties the Essential Question to their own background knowledge: *Turn to a partner and talk about an animal story you know.* (Give some examples of fables as examples.) *What can you learn from the animal story?* Call on several pairs.

### During Reading

#### Interactive Question Response

→ Ask questions that help children understand the meaning of the text after each paragraph.

→ Reinforce the meanings of key vocabulary providing meanings embedded in the questions.

→ Ask children questions that require them to use key vocabulary.

→ Reinforce strategies and skills of the week by modeling.

**Go Digital**

**The Boy Who Cried Wolf**

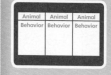

**Graphic Organizer**

## The Boy Who Cried Wolf

### Page 118

Point to the title. *Listen as I read the title of the selection.* Point to each word as you read it. *What is the title?* (The Boy Who Cried Wolf) Point to the sheep. *Say: These animals are sheep. Say sheep with me:* sheep. *The boy has a job. He watches the sheep and keeps them safe from harm, or danger. Let's read the story to find out why the boy cries, "Wolf!"*

### Page 119

Let's read the first sentence together. A shepherd is a person who watches sheep. He keeps the sheep safe.

Let's read the rest of the first paragraph. It tells how the shepherd boy feels about his job. How does the boy feel about his job? (He doesn't like it.)

Let's read the second paragraph. The boy has nothing to do, so he looks at the clouds. He thinks the clouds look like animals. He makes up stories about the animals.

**Explain and Model the Strategy** Reread the page to help children understand the problem at the beginning of the story. *We can predict, or guess, what will happen next in the story. The boy does not like his job. He doesn't like to watch the sheep.*

*What do you predict will happen next? What will the boy do?* (Accept reasonable responses.)

### Page 120

One day the boy has another idea. What does he do? There is no wolf, but he pretends, or makes believe, there is a wolf. He cries out, "Wolf! Wolf!"

Look at the word villagers. Villagers *are the people who live in a village.*

The villagers run up the hill. Why do they run up the hill? (They want to help the boy and save the sheep.) Why does the boy laugh? (There is no wolf.)

**Explain and Model the Phonics Skill** Read aloud the first sentence of paragraph 2. *Listen carefully. Raise your hand when you hear a word that has the /u/ sound.* (up) *Let's practice saying this word together: up.*

### Page 121

The boy calls out "Wolf! Wolf!" again. He says a wolf is chasing the sheep. Villagers come to help. They are angry because there is no wolf.

*Why do the villagers run up the hill?* (They want to help the boy and save the sheep.) *How do they feel?* (angry) *Why?* (There is no wolf. )

The boy sees a real wolf. What do you predict will happen? (Possible answer: He'll cry, "Wolf!" but the villagers won't come. They won't believe him.)

### Page 122

Now the boy really does see a wolf. The boy calls for help again. What happens this time? (No one comes to help.)

*Why don't the villagers come to help?* (They think it is another trick.)

The boy doesn't return to the village with the sheep. He is weeping. Weeping *means crying.*

### Page 123

Let's read the end of the story. It tells about an important lesson the boy learns.

*What lesson does the boy learn?* (It is better to always tell the truth.)

### After Reading

#### Make Connections

→ Review the Essential Question.

# English Language Learners

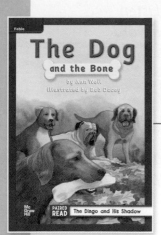

**Lexile** 320
*TextEvaluator™* 5

## OBJECTIVES

 Describe how characters in a story respond to major events and challenges. **RL.2.3**

 Describe the overall structure of a story, including describing how the beginning introduces the story and the ending concludes the action. **RL.2.5**

## MATERIALS

Leveled Reader
*The Dog and the Bone*

## Leveled Reader:
## *The Dog and the Bone*

**Go**
Digital

### Before Reading

**Preview**

Read the title. Ask: *What is the title? Say it again.* Repeat with the author's name. Preview the selection's illustrations. Have children describe the images. Use simple language to tell about each page. Follow with questions, such as *What animal is this? What does the dog have in its mouth?*

**ESSENTIAL QUESTION**

Remind children of the Essential Question. Say: *Let's read to find out what the animals in this story can teach us.* Encourage children to seek clarification when they encounter a confusing word or phrase.

### During Reading

**Interactive Question Response**

**Pages 2–3** Point to the illustration on pages 2 and 3. *Look at the dog. What is he doing? What do you think is in the pile of leaves? Let's reread the sentence that tells what the dog finds. Say the words with me:* It was a bone.

**Pages 4–5** *How does Dog feel about the bone? Why does he say is his lucky day?* (Dog is happy to find a huge bone.) *Dog sees some other dogs. Why are the other dogs watching Dog?* (They want the bone.)

**Pages 6–7** *What does Dog decide to do on page 6? How will Dog get home? Let's read the sentence on page 7 that tells us:* He decided to try a new way home. *Why does he want to find a shortcut?* (He is far from home. He wants to find a shorter way to get home.)

**Pages 8–9** *Dog comes to a brook. Point to the brook in the picture. Tell your partner what a brook is. How will Dog get across the brook? Tell your partner.* (He will walk across a log bridge.)

**Pages 10–11** *What does Dog see when he looks down? Why is Dog so interested in the other dog?* (It has a bigger bone than the one Dog has.) *Tell your partner what happens when Dog tries to snatch the bone.*

**Pages 12–13** *What does Dog see when he looks in the water? Why do you think the other dog lost his bone, too?* (Dog sees himself in the water, not another dog.)

**Leveled Readers**

**Graphic Organizer**

**Retelling Cards**

**Pages 14–15** *Look at the picture on page 14. How do you think Dog feels? Why?* (He feels sad. He lost his bone.) Read the moral on page 15. Help children understand the word *greed*. Ask: *What lesson does this story teach us? How does Dog's story teach us this lesson?*

### Literature Circles

Lead children in conducting a literature circle using the Thinkmark questions to guide the discussion. You may wish to discuss what lessons children learned from animal stories in both selections in the leveled reader.

## After Reading

### Respond to Reading

Have partners answer the questions. Pair children with peers of varying language abilities.

### Retell

Model retelling using the Retelling Card prompts. Then guide children to retell the selection to a partner.

### Fluency: Expression

Read the sentences in the book, one at a time. Help children echo-read the pages expressively and with appropriate expression. Remind them to read exclamations in a way that shows excitement.

**Apply**  Have children practice reading with a partner. Pair children with peers of varying language abilities. Provide feedback as needed.

### Level Up

Level-up lessons available online.

**IF** children read the **ELL Level** fluently and answered the questions

**THEN** pair them with children who have proficiently read the **On Level** and have children

- echo-read the **On Level** main selection with their partners.
- list difficult words and phrases and discuss them with their partners.

## PAIRED READ ...

### "The Dingo and His Shadow"

**Leveled Reader**

### Make Connections: Write About It  *Analytical Writing*

Before reading, tell children that this story is also a fable. Then discuss the Compare Texts statement. After reading, ask children to make connections between what they read in "The Dingo and His Shadow" and *The Dog and His Bone*. Prompt children by providing sentence frames: *Dog loses his bone because _____. Dingo loses the meat because _____.*

### ACT Access Complex Text

The **On Level** challenges children by including more **specific vocabulary** and **complex sentence structures.**

### FOCUS ON LITERARY ELEMENTS

Children can extend their understanding of the use of dialogue in stories by completing the activity on page 20.

# English Language Learners
## Vocabulary

### PRETEACH VOCABULARY

**OBJECTIVES**

**CCSS** Use words and phrases acquired through conversations, reading and being read to, and responding to texts, including using adjectives and adverbs to describe (e.g., *When other kids are happy that makes me happy*). **L.2.6**

Preteach vocabulary words.

 **I Do** Preteach vocabulary from "The Boy Who Cried Wolf," following the Vocabulary Routine found on the Visual Vocabulary Cards for words *believes, delicious, feast, fond, lessons, remarkable, snatch,* and *stories*.

 **We Do** After completing the Vocabulary Routine for each word, point to the word on the Visual Vocabulary Card and read the word with children. Ask children to repeat the word.

 **You Do** Have partners write vocabulary words correctly on small cards. Then have them taking turns selecting a word, pronouncing the word, and using it in an oral sentence.

| Beginning | Intermediate | Advanced/High |
|---|---|---|
| Help children write two or three words correctly and read them aloud. | Ask children to write the words, select two words, and write one sentence and one question. | Challenge children to write one sentence and one question for each word. |

### REVIEW VOCABULARY

**OBJECTIVES**

**CCSS** Demonstrate understanding of word relationships and nuances in word meanings. **L.2.5**

**CCSS** Determine the meaning of words and phrases in a text relevant to a *grade 2 topic or subject area*. **RI.2.4**

Review vocabulary words.

 **I Do** Review the previous week's vocabulary words. The words can be reviewed over a few days. Read each word aloud pointing to the word on the Visual Vocabulary Card. Have children repeat after you. Then follow the Vocabulary Routine on the back of each card.

 **We Do** Ask children to guess the word you describe. Provide clues, such as synonyms or antonyms. Have children name the word and define or use it in a sentence.

 **You Do** In pairs, have children make a list of clues for two or more words. Ask them to read them aloud for the class to guess the word and define or use it in a sentence.

| Beginning | Intermediate | Advanced/High |
|---|---|---|
| Help children list clue words and read them aloud. | Have children write clues as sentences. | Ask children to use synonyms or antonyms in their clues. |

# SUFFIXES

**CCSS**

**OBJECTIVES**

Determine or clarify the meaning of unknown and multiple-meaning words and phrases based on *grade 2 reading and content,* choosing flexibly from an array of strategies. **L.2.4**

 Use sentence-level context as a clue to the meaning of a word or phrase. **L.2.4a**

**LANGUAGE OBJECTIVE**

Use suffixes.

 **I Do** Read aloud the second paragraph of "The Boy Who Cried Wolf" on page 120, while children follow along. Summarize the paragraph. Point to the word *harmful.* Explain that sometimes we can separate the root word from its suffix to understand the word's meaning.

 **We Do** **Think Aloud** When I read this paragraph, I'm not sure what the word *harmful* means. I know that *harm* means hurt. The suffix *-ful* means full of. I see that the word is *harmful.* It means full of harm. I'll try reading this phrase in the sentence to see if it makes sense.

 **You Do** Have children point to the word *wonderful* on page 119. Help children separate the suffix from the root word to determine its meaning. Write the meaning on the board.

| Beginning | Intermediate | Advanced/High |
|---|---|---|
| Help children separate the root word and its suffix. | Help children explain the meaning of the word and its suffix. | Ask children to explain how they applied the skill. |

# ADDITIONAL VOCABULARY

**OBJECTIVES**

 Use knowledge of language and its conventions when writing, speaking, reading, or listening. **L.2.3**

 Compare formal and informal uses of English. **L.2.3a**

 Use academic language.

**LANGUAGE OBJECTIVE**

Use context clues.

 **I Do** List academic language and additional vocabulary from "The Boy Who Cried Wolf": *characters, lessons, stories;* and "The Dog and the Bone": *decided, greed, moral.* Define each word for children: *The* characters *are the people or animals in a story.*

 **We Do** Model using the words for children in a sentence: *The characters in this story are the boy, the villagers, and the kind man. The characters in that fable are animals that can talk.* Then provide sentence frames and complete them with children: *The characters in my favorite fable are _____.*

 **You Do** Have pairs use the illustrations in the fables to make up their own sentences with the words.

| Beginning | Intermediate | Advanced/High |
|---|---|---|
| Help children copy the sentence frames correctly and complete them. | Provide support to help children use the words in the activity. | Lead children to define the words they used. |

# English Language Learners
## Writing/Spelling

### WRITING TRAIT: IDEAS

**OBJECTIVES**

Write narratives in which they recount in a well-elaborated event or short sequence of events, include details to describe actions, thoughts, and feelings, use temporal words to signal event order, and provide a sense of closure. **W.2.3**

**LANGUAGE OBJECTIVE**

Use supporting details.

**I Do** Explain that writers explain their main ideas by including supporting details. Write and read the sentences: *The dog was sad. He lost his big, tasty bone.* Point out how the second sentence is a supporting detail.

**We Do** Read the first four sentences on page 122 of *The Boy Who Cried Wolf.* Say: *The boy does not want the wolf to grab any of the sheep. What supporting details does the writer include?*

**You Do** Have children write a sentence describing an animal they like from one of this week's stories. Have them write a second sentence that gives supporting details about the animal.

| Beginning | Intermediate | Advanced/High |
|---|---|---|
| Help children write a sentence about an animal they like. Provide sentence frames. | Have children write a sentence naming an animal they like. Then have them describe the animal. | Ask children what animal they like. Then elicit supporting details. |

### WORDS WITH SHORT *u*; LONG *u*: u_e

**OBJECTIVES**

Know and apply grade-level phonics and word analysis skills in decoding words. **RF.2.3**

**I Do** Read aloud the Spelling Words on T106. Segment the word *cub* into sounds and attach a spelling to each sound. Point out the short *u*. Read aloud, segment, and spell the remaining words. Have children repeat.

**We Do** Read the first sentence from the Dictation Routine on page T106 aloud. Then read the short *u* word slowly and ask children to repeat. Have them write the word. Repeat the process for the remaining sentences.

**You Do**  Display the words. Have children work with a partner to check their spelling lists. Have children correct misspelled words on their list.

| Beginning | Intermediate | Advanced/High |
|---|---|---|
| Help children copy the words with correct spelling and say the words. | After children have corrected their words, have pairs quiz each other. | Have children think of other words that have the short or long *u* sound. |

# Grammar

## SINGULAR AND PLURAL NOUNS

### OBJECTIVES

**CCSS** Demonstrate command of the conventions of standard English grammar and usage when writing or speaking. **L.2.1**

### LANGUAGE OBJECTIVE

Identify singular and plural nouns.

**ELL Language Transfers**

In languages such as Chinese, Hmong, Korean, and Vietnamese, there is no plural form for nouns. Adjectives are used to express a plural in these languages. Emphasize to speakers of these languages that most plural nouns in English are formed by adding an *-s* or *-es* ending.

**I Do**

Review that a singular noun names one person, place, or thing. A plural noun names more than one person, place, or thing. Write the following sentence on the board: *The foxes live in a den.* Read the sentence. Underline *foxes*. Say: *This is a plural noun. It tells about more than one fox.* Underline *den.* Say: *This is a singular noun. It tells about one place, a den.*

**We Do**

Write the following sentences on the board. Have children read the sentences and underline singular nouns and circle plural nouns. Have them say: *The singular nouns are _____. The plural nouns are _____.*

*Three dogs stared at the bone.*
*The bird feeds her babies tasty worms.*
*The boy thinks the clouds look like animals.*

**You Do**

Write the following sentence frames on the board.
*The dog finds _____. The boy sees _____.*

Pair children and have them complete each sentence frame by providing details from this week's readings. Circulate, listen in, and take note of each child's language use and proficiency.

| Beginning | Intermediate | Advanced/High |
|---|---|---|
| Describe the illustrations in *The Boy Who Cried Wolf.* Ask: *What do you see?* Model a response by providing a sentence frame: *I see _____.* Help children identify whether the nouns are singular or plural. | Ask children to describe the same illustrations and then identify whether the nouns they used were singular or plural. Encourage children to use complete sentences. | Ask children to look at the illustrations and name as many things as they see. Prompt children to sort the words into singular or plural nouns. |

# PROGRESS MONITORING

## Weekly Assessment

| ✔ **COMPREHENSION:** | ✔ **VOCABULARY:** | ✔ **WRITING:** |
|---|---|---|
| Problem and Solution **RL.2.3, RL.2.5** | Suffixes **L.2.4b** | Writing About Text **RL.2.3, RL.2.5** |

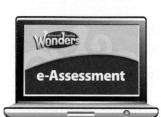

### Assessment Includes

→ Pencil-and-Paper administration

→ Online administration

→ Approaching Level Weekly Assessment also available

**Fluency Goal** 41 to 61 words correct per minute (WCPM)

**Accuracy Rate Goal** 95% or higher

Administer oral reading fluency assessments using the following schedule:

→ **Weeks 1, 3, 5** Provide Approaching Level children at least three oral reading fluency assessments during the unit.

→ **Weeks 2 and 4** Provide On Level children at least two oral reading fluency assessments during the unit.

→ **Week 6** If necessary, provide Beyond Level children an oral reading fluency assessment at this time.

**Also Available: Selection Tests online PDFs**

*Go Digital!* http://connected.mcgraw-hill.com

# Using Assessment Results

| TESTED SKILLS | If ... | Then ... |
|---|---|---|
| **COMPREHENSION** | Children answer 0–6 multiple-choice items correctly ... | ... assign Lessons 40–42 on Problem and Solution from the *Tier 2 Comprehension Intervention online PDFs.* |
| **VOCABULARY** | Children answer 0–6 multiple-choice items correctly ... | ... assign Lessons 105–106 on Suffixes from the *Tier 2 Vocabulary Intervention online PDFs.* |
| **WRITING** | Children score less than "3" on the Constructed response ... | ... assign Lessons 40–42 and/or Write About Reading Lessons from Section 13 of the *Tier 2 Comprehension Intervention online PDFs.* |
| **FLUENCY** | Children have a WCPM score of 36–40 ... | ... assign a lesson from Section 1, 9, or 10 of the *Tier 2 Fluency Intervention online PDFs.* |
| | Children have a WCPM score of 0–35 ... | ... assign a lesson from Sections 2–8 of the *Tier 2 Fluency Intervention online PDFs.* |

## Response to Intervention

Use the appropriate sections of the *Placement and Diagnostic Assessment* as well as students' assessment results to designate students requiring:

 **Intervention Online PDFs**

 **WonderWorks Intervention Program**

# WEEKLY OVERVIEW

# TEACH AND MODEL

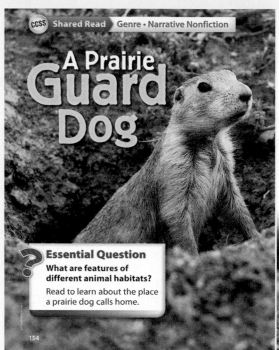

**CCSS Shared Read** | Genre • Narrative Nonfiction

## A Prairie Guard Dog

**? Essential Question**
What are features of different animal habitats?
Read to learn about the place a prairie dog calls home.

134

I am on a **journey**. My trip is to a prairie. It is in the outdoor world called **nature**. Many animals live in a prairie **habitat**. This place has what prairie dogs need to survive. A prairie has a lot of grasses but few trees. Without places to hide, a prairie can be dangerous for some animals.

**Good Morning!**

It is early in the morning. First, I see a prairie dog. I name him Pete. He **peeks** his head out of his **burrow** underground. He looks around. Then Pete calls loudly to his family, "Yip!" He lets them know it is safe to come out. Soon four prairie dogs come out.

Prairie dogs build underground burrows to keep themselves safe from predators.

135

## ✓ Vocabulary

buried

escape

habitat

journey

nature

peeks

restless

spies

## 🔍 Close Reading of Complex Text

**Shared Read** "A Prairie Guard Dog," 134–139

**Genre** Narrative Nonfiction

**Lexile** 490L

**ETS** *TextEvaluator*™ 26

## Minilessons

✓ **Tested Skills** CCSS

✓ **Comprehension Strategy** .................. Make Predictions, T216–T217

✓ **Comprehension Skill** ..................... Main Topic and Key Details, T218–T219

✓ **Genre** .......................................... Narrative Nonfiction, T228–T229

✓ **Vocabulary Strategy** ..................... Suffixes, T230–T231

✓ **Writing Traits** .............................. Organization, T206–T207

✓ **Grammar** ..................................... Kinds of Nouns, T208–T209

☞ **Go** Digital

http://connected.mcgraw-hill.com

ANIMAL DISCOVERIES
**Essential Question**
What are features of different
animal habitats?

WEEK 3

# APPLY WITH CLOSE READING

## Complex Text

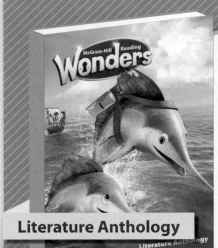

**Literature Anthology**

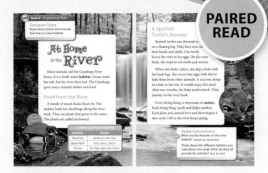

PAIRED READ

*Turtle, Turtle, Watch Out!*, 164–181
**Genre** Narrative Nonfiction
**Lexile** 520L
ETS *TextEvaluator* 13

"At Home in the River," 184–185
**Genre** Expository Text
**Lexile** 500L
ETS *TextEvaluator* 5

## Differentiated Text

**Leveled Readers** *Including Paired Reads*

APPROACHING
**Lexile** 310
ETS *TextEvaluator* 4

ON LEVEL
**Lexile** 460
ETS *TextEvaluator* 9

BEYOND
**Lexile** 630
ETS *TextEvaluator* 13

ELL
**Lexile** 410
ETS *TextEvaluator* 4

## Extended Complex Text

*Life in an Ocean*
**Genre** Nonfiction
**Lexile** 290L
ETS *TextEvaluator* 6

*Let's Look at Monarch Butterflies*
**Genre** Nonfiction
**Lexile** 510L
ETS *TextEvaluator* 6

**Classroom Library**

Classroom Library lessons available online.

# TEACH AND MANAGE

## How You Teach

### INTRODUCE

**Weekly Concept**
Animal Habitats

**Reading/Writing Workshop**
**130–131**

### TEACH

**Close Reading**
"A Prairie Guard Dog"

**Minilessons**
Make Predictions, Main Topic and Key Details, Narrative Nonfiction, Writing Traits

**Reading/Writing Workshop**
**134–139**

### APPLY

**Close Reading**
*Turtle, Turtle, Watch Out!*
*At Home in the River*

**Student Anthology**
**164–185**

 **Go Digital**

 Interactive Whiteboard

 Interactive Whiteboard

 Mobile

## How Students Practice

### Weekly contract

**PDF Online**

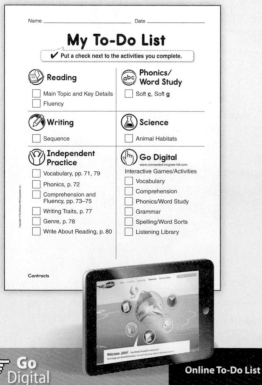

Name _____ Date _____

#### My To-Do List
✔ Put a check next to the activities you complete.

**📖 Reading**
☐ Main Topic and Key Details
☐ Fluency

**abc Phonics/ Word Study**
☐ Soft c, Soft g

**✏️ Writing**
☐ Sequence

**🔬 Science**
☐ Animal Habitats

**✋ Independent Practice**
☐ Vocabulary, pp. 71, 79
☐ Phonics, p. 72
☐ Comprehension and Fluency, pp. 73–75
☐ Writing Traits, p. 77
☐ Genre, p. 78
☐ Write About Reading, p. 80

**👆 Go Digital**
www.connected.mcgraw-hill.com
Interactive Games/Activities
☐ Vocabulary
☐ Comprehension
☐ Phonics/Word Study
☐ Grammar
☐ Spelling/Word Sorts
☐ Listening Library

Contracts

### Leveled practice and online activities

**Your Turn Practice Book**
**71–80**

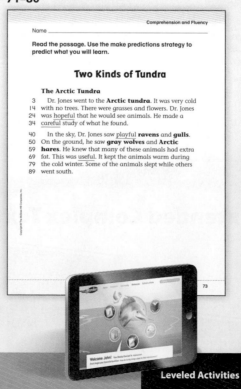

Name _____

Read the passage. Use the make predictions strategy to predict what you will learn.

#### Two Kinds of Tundra

**The Arctic Tundra**

3   Dr. Jones went to the **Arctic tundra**. It was very cold
14  with no trees. There were grasses and flowers. Dr. Jones
24  was hopeful that he would see animals. He made a
34  careful study of what he found.

40  In the sky, Dr. Jones saw playful **ravens** and **gulls**.
50  On the ground, he saw **gray wolves** and **Arctic**
59  **hares**. He knew that many of these animals had extra
69  fat. This was useful. It kept the animals warm during
79  the cold winter. Some of the animals slept while others
89  went south.

73

**Leveled Readers**

 **Go Digital**

Online To-Do List

Leveled Activities

Writer's Workspace

## DIFFERENTIATE

**SMALL GROUP INSTRUCTION**

**Leveled Readers**

**Mobile**

## INTEGRATE

**Research and Inquiry**
Habitat Cards, T240–241

**Text Connections**
Compare Habitats, T242

**Write About Reading**
*Analytical Writing* Write an Analysis, T243

**Online Research and Writing**

## ASSESS

**Weekly Assessment 85–96**

**Online Assessment**

---

## Leveled workstation cards

**More Activities on back**

### ⑦ Sequence — WRITING

- Think about a board game you like to play.

- Write four or five sentences that tell how to play the game. Say what happens first, next,

### ⑧ Guess My Word — PHONICS/W

Does it rhyme with *face?* Yes, it does!

- Write the words from the list.

- Take turns choosing a spelling word. Don't say the word.

- Your partner tries to guess the word by asking questions

trace
badg
spa
rang

### ⑧ Habitat Web — SOCIAL STUDIES

- A habitat is where things live. Choose a habitat you have learned about in class.

- Make your own habitat web like the one shown. Fill in the circles with details about your habitat.

Fish and Whales

Ocean

- Share your web with your partner. Talk about how your habitats are alike and different.

**You need**
> paper
> pencil

*Go Digital!* www.connected.mcgraw-hill.com • Research and Inquiry • Grade 2

### ⑦ The Main Idea — READING

- Choose an informational book you have read.

- Draw a picture that shows the main idea. Talk about your picture.

- Add details to your picture to show supporting details.

**You need**
> informational book
> pencil, crayons, or markers
> paper

*Go Digital!* www.connected.mcgraw-hill.com • Interactive Games and Activities • Grade 2

# DEVELOPING READERS AND WRITERS

### Write to Sources and Research

Main Topic and Key Details, T218–T219, T231L

Details, T222

Note Taking, T231A, T237A

Author's Purpose, T231J

Make Connections: Essential Question, T231L, T237B, T242

Research and Inquiry, T240–T241

Analyze to Inform/Explain, T243

Comparing Texts, T249, T259, T263, T269

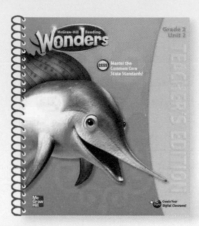

**Teacher's Edition**

**Literature Anthology**

Main Topic and Key Details, 183

**Go Digital**

**Interactive Whiteboard**

**Leveled Readers**
Comparing Texts
Main Topic and Key Details

**Your Turn Practice Book**

Main Topic and Key Details, 73–75
Genre, 78
Write About Reading, 80

---

**Narrative Text**
How-to Text, T480–T485

**Conferencing Routines**
Teacher Conferences, T482
Peer Conferences, T483

**Go Digital**

**Interactive Whiteboard**

**Teacher's Edition**

**Leveled Workstation Card**
How-To, Card 23

**Go Digital**

**Writer's Workspace**
Informational Text: How-to Text
Writing Process
Multimedia Presentations

## Writing Traits • Write Every Day

**Writing Trait: Organization**
Sequence, T206–T207

**Conferencing Routines**
Teacher Conferences, T238
Peer Conferences, T239

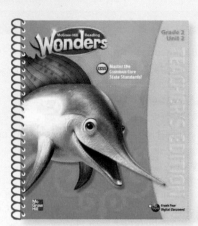

**Teacher's Edition**

**Reading/Writing Workshop**

Organization:
Sequence, 144–145

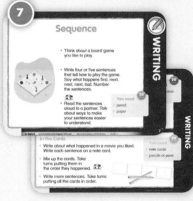

**Leveled Workstation Card**

Organization:
Sequence,
Card 7

**Interactive Whiteboard**

**Your Turn Practice Book**

Organization:
Sequence, 77

## Grammar and Spelling

**Grammar**
Kinds of Nouns, T208, T221, T233, T239, T247

**Spelling**
Soft *c* and *g*, T198, T214, T225, T236, T245

**Interactive Whiteboard**

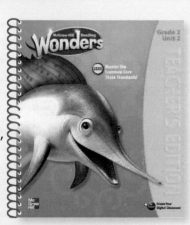

**Teacher's Edition**

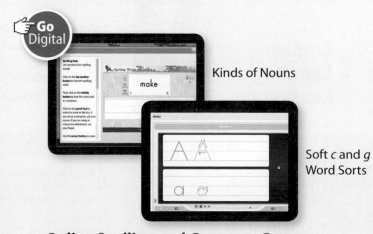

Kinds of Nouns

Soft *c* and *g*
Word Sorts

**Online Spelling and Grammar Games**

# SUGGESTED LESSON PLAN

| | DAY 1 | DAY 2 |
|---|---|---|

## READING

**Whole Group**

### Teach, Model, and Apply

Reading/Writing Workshop

**DAY 1**

**Build Background** Animal Habitats, T192–T193

**Oral Vocabulary Words** *defend, encounter, located, positive, react;* T194

**Listening Comprehension** Strategy: Make, Confirm, Revise Predictions; T195

**Interactive Read-Aloud Cards** "Explore a Coral Reef," T195

**Word Work**
Phonemic Awareness: Phoneme Segmentation, T196
Phonics/Spelling: Introduce Soft *c* and *g,* T196–T198
High-Frequency Words: *almost, buy, food, out, pull, saw, sky, straight, under, wash;* T199

✔**Vocabulary** Words in Context: *buried, escape, habitat, journey, nature, peeks, restless, spies;* T200–T201

**Close Reading of Complex Text** "A Prairie Guard Dog," 134–139

**Practice** *Your Turn* 71–72

**DAY 2**

**Oral Language** Animal Habitats, T210

**Review Oral Vocabulary Words,** T210

**Listening Comprehension** Strategy: Make, Confirm, Revise Predictions; T211

**Interactive Read-Aloud Cards** "Explore a Coral Reef," T211

**Word Work**
Phonemic Awareness: Phoneme Substitution, T212
Phonics/Spelling: Words with Soft *c* and *g,* T212–T214
Structural Analysis: Prefixes *re-, un-, dis-;* T213
High-Frequency Words, T214

**Vocabulary** Expand Vocabulary, T215

✔**Comprehension**
• Strategy: Make, Confirm, Revise Predictions; T216–T217
• Skill: Main Topic and Key Details, T218–T219

**Practice** *Your Turn* 72–77

## DIFFERENTIATED INSTRUCTION  Choose across the week to meet your student's needs.

**Small Group**

### Approaching Level

**Leveled Reader** *A Tree Full of Life,* T248–T249

**Phonemic Awareness** Phoneme Segmentation, T250 ②

**Phonics** Connect Soft *c* to /s/ and Soft *g* to /j/, T252 ②

**High-Frequency Words** Review Words, T255 ②

**Vocabulary** Review Words, T255

**Leveled Reader** *A Tree Full of Life,* T248–T249

**Phonemic Awareness** Phoneme Substitution, T251 ②

**Phonics** Blend Words with Soft *c* and *g,* T252 ②

**Comprehension** Identify the Topic, T256 ②

### On Level

**Leveled Reader** *A Tree Full of Life,* T258–T259

**Phonics** Build Words with Soft *c* and *g,* T260

**Leveled Reader** *A Tree Full of Life,* T258–T259

**Comprehension** Review Main Topic and Key Details, T261

### Beyond Level

**Leveled Reader** *A Tree Full of Life,* T262–T263

**Vocabulary** Review Domain-Specific Words, T264

**Leveled Reader** *A Tree Full of Life,* T262–T263

**Comprehension** Review Main Topic and Key Details, T265

### English Language Learners

**Shared Read** "A Prairie Guard Dog," T266–T267

**Phonemic Awareness** Phoneme Segmentation, T250

**Phonics** Connect Soft *c* to /s/ and Soft *g* to /j/, T252

**Vocabulary** Preteach Vocabulary, T270

**Leveled Reader** *A Tree Full of Life,* T268–T269

**Phonemic Awareness** Phoneme Substitution, T251

**Phonics** Blend Words with Soft *c* and *g,* T252

**Vocabulary** Review Vocabulary, T270

**Writing** Writing Trait: Organization, T272

## LANGUAGE ARTS    Writing Process: How-To T480–T485 | Use with Weeks 1–3

**Whole Group**

### Writing  Grammar

**DAY 1**

✔**Readers to Writers**
• Writing Trait: Organization, T206–T207
• Writing Entry: Prewrite and Draft, T206

**Grammar**
• Kinds of Nouns, T208
• Mechanics: Capital Letters, T209

**DAY 2**

✔**Readers to Writers**
• Writing Trait: Organization, T220
• Writing Entry: Revise, T220

**Grammar**
• Kinds of Nouns, T221
• Mechanics: Capital Letters, T221

| DAY 3 | DAY 4 | DAY 5 Review and Assess |
|---|---|---|

## READING

**Interactive Read-Aloud Cards** "Explore a Coral Reef," T222

**Review Oral Vocabulary Words,** T222

**Comprehension** Maintain Skill: Key Details: Use Illustrations and Photos, T223

**Word Work**
Phonemic Awareness: Phoneme Blending, T224
Phonics/Spelling: Words with Soft *c* and *g*, T224–T225
Structural Analysis: Prefixes, T225

**Fluency** Phrasing, T226

**Vocabulary** Reinforce Vocabulary, T227

✔ **Genre** Narrative Nonfiction, T228–T229

✔ **Vocabulary Strategy** Suffixes, T230–T231

**Close Reading** *Turtle, Turtle, Watch Out!,* 164–181 ● *Analytical Writing*

**Practice** *Your Turn* 78–79

Literature Anthology

**Oral Language** Animal Habitats, T234

**Word Work**
Phonemic Awareness: Phoneme Substitution, T235
Phonics/Spelling: Words with Soft *c* and *g*, T235–T236
Structural Analysis: Prefixes *re-, un-, dis-;* T235
High-Frequency Words, T236

**Fluency** Phrasing, T237

**Vocabulary Strategy** Review: Root Words, T237

**Close Reading** "At Home in the River," 184–185 ● *Analytical Writing*

**Integrate Ideas** Research and Inquiry, T240–T241 ● *Analytical Writing*

**Practice** *Your Turn* 73–75

**Integrate Ideas** ● *Analytical Writing*
• Text Connections, T242
• Write About Reading, T243
• Research and Inquiry, T243

**Word Work**
Phonemic Awareness: Phoneme Blending, T244
Phonics/Spelling: Words with Soft *c* and *g*, T244–T245
Structural Analysis: Prefixes *re-, un-, dis-;* T244
High-Frequency Words, T245

**Vocabulary** Review Words, T245

**Practice** *Your Turn* 80

## DIFFERENTIATED INSTRUCTION

**Leveled Reader** *A Tree Full of Life,* T248–T249
**Phonemic Awareness** Phoneme Blending, T250 ②
**Phonics** Build Words with Soft *c* and *g*, T253
**Structural Analysis** Review Prefixes; T254 ②
**Comprehension** Review Main Topic and Key Details, T257

**Leveled Reader** Paired Read: "Life in a Termite Mound," T249 ● *Analytical Writing*
**Phonemic Awareness** Phoneme Substitution, T251
**Phonics** Blend Words with Soft *c* and *g*, T253
**Structural Analysis** Reteach Prefixes; T254
**Comprehension** Read for Fluency, T256 ②

**Leveled Reader** Literature Circle, T249
**Phonemic Awareness** Phoneme Blending, T250 ②
**Phonics** Blend Words with Soft *c* and *g*, T253
**Comprehension** Self-Selected Reading, T257

**Leveled Reader** *A Tree Full of Life,* T258–T259
**Vocabulary** Review Words, T260

**Leveled Reader** Paired Read: "Life in a Termite Mound," T259 ● *Analytical Writing*

**Leveled Reader** Literature Circle, T259
**Comprehension** Self-Selected Reading, T261

**Leveled Reader** *A Tree Full of Life,* T262–T263
**Vocabulary**
• Suffixes, T264
• Shades of Meaning, T264

*Gifted and Talented*

**Leveled Reader** Paired Read: "Life in a Termite Mound," T263 ● *Analytical Writing*

**Leveled Reader** Literature Circle, T263
**Comprehension**
• Self-Selected Reading, T265
• Independent Study: Animal Habitats, T265

*Gifted and Talented*

**Leveled Reader** *A Tree Full of Life,* T268–T269
**Phonemic Awareness** Phoneme Blending, T250
**Phonics** Build Words with Soft *c* and *g*, T253
**Structural Analysis** Review Prefixes *re-, un-, dis-;* T254
**Vocabulary Strategy** Suffixes, T271
**Grammar** Kinds of Nouns, T273

**Leveled Reader** Paired Read: "Life in a Termite Mound," T269 ● *Analytical Writing*
**Phonemic Awareness** Phoneme Substitution, T251
**Phonics** Blend Words with Soft *c* and *g*, T253
**Structural Analysis** Reteach Prefixes *re-, un-, dis-;* T254
**Vocabulary** Additional Vocabulary, T271

**Leveled Reader** Literature Circle, T269
**Phonemic Awareness** Phoneme Blending, T250
**Phonics** Blend Words with Soft *c* and *g*, T253
**Spelling** Words with Soft *c* and *g*, T272

## LANGUAGE ARTS

✔ **Readers to Writers**
• Writing Trait: Organization, T232
• Writing Entry: Prewrite and Draft, T232

**Grammar**
• Kinds of Nouns, T233
• Mechanics: Capital Letters, T233

✔ **Readers to Writers**
• Writing Trait: Organization, T238
• Writing Entry: Revise, T238

**Grammar**
• Kinds of Nouns, T239
• Mechanics: Capital Letters, T239

✔ **Readers to Writers**
• Writing Trait: Organization, T246
• Writing Entry: Share and Reflect, T246

**Grammar**
• Kinds of Nouns, T247
• Mechanics: Capital Letters, T247

# DIFFERENTIATE TO ACCELERATE

 **Scaffold to** **A**ccess **C**omplex **T**ext

**Qualitative** · **Quantitative**
**Reader and Task**
**TEXT COMPLEXITY**

**IF** ▸ the text complexity of a particular selection is too difficult for children

**THEN** ▸ use the Access Complex Text prompts to scaffold instruction.

|  | **Reading/Writing Workshop** | **Literature Anthology** | **Leveled Readers** | **Classroom Library** |
|---|---|---|---|---|
| |  |  |  |  |

## Quantitative

**Reading/Writing Workshop**

"A Prairie Guard Dog"
**Lexile** 480
*TextEvaluator*™ 26

**Literature Anthology**

*Turtle, Turtle, Watch Out!*
**Lexile** 520
*TextEvaluator*™ 13

"At Home in the River"
**Lexile** 500
*TextEvaluator*™ 5

**Leveled Readers**

**Approaching Level**
**Lexile** 310
*TextEvaluator*™ 4

**Beyond Level**
**Lexile** 630
*TextEvaluator*™ 13

**On Level**
**Lexile** 460
*TextEvaluator*™ 9

**ELL**
**Lexile** 410
*TextEvaluator*™ 4

**Classroom Library**

*Life in an Ocean*
**Lexile** 290
*TextEvaluator*™ 6

*Let's Look at Monarch Butterflies*
**Lexile** 510
*TextEvaluator*™ 6

## Qualitative

**What Makes the Text Complex?**

- **Connections of Ideas** Synthesize, T203
- **Genre** Text Features T229

**A C T** *See Scaffolded Instruction in Teacher's Edition T203 and T229.*

**What Makes the Text Complex?**

- **Purpose** Inform, T231B
- **Connection of Ideas** Repetition, T231B; Inferences, T231H
- **Prior Knowledge** Animal Environments, T237B

**A C T** *See Scaffolded Instruction in Teacher's Edition T231B, T231H, T237B.*

**What Makes the Text Complex?**

- **Specific Vocabulary**
- **Prior Knowledge**
- **Sentence Structure**
- **Connection of Ideas**
- **Genre**

**A C T** *See Level Up lessons online for Leveled Readers.*

**What Makes the Text Complex?**

- **Genre**
- **Specific Vocabulary**
- **Prior Knowledge**
- **Sentence Structure**
- **Organization**
- **Purpose**
- **Connection of Ideas**

**A C T** *See Scaffolded Instruction in Teacher's Edition T496–T497.*

## Reader and Task

The Introduce the Concept lesson on pages T192–T193 will help determine the reader's knowledge and engagement in the weekly concept. See pages T202–T205, T216–T219, T228–T231, and T240–T243 for questions and tasks for this text.

The Introduce the Concept lesson on pages T192–T193 will help determine the reader's knowledge and engagement in the weekly concept. See pages T231A–T231L, T237A–T237B, and T240–T243 for questions and tasks for this text.

The Introduce the Concept lesson on pages T192–T193 will help determine the reader's knowledge and engagement in the weekly concept. See pages T248–T249, T258–T259, T262–T263, T268–T269, and T240–T243 for questions and tasks for this text.

The Introduce the Concept lesson on pages T192–T193 will help determine the reader's knowledge and engagement in the weekly concept. See pages T496–T497 for questions and tasks for this text.

*Go Digital!* http://connected.mcgraw-hill.com

## Monitor and *Differentiate*

**IF** If you need to differentiate instruction

**THEN** use the Quick Check to assess children's needs and select the appropriate small group instruction focus.

 **Quick Check**

**Comprehension Strategy** Make Predictions, T217
**Comprehension Skills** Main Topic and Key Details, T219
**Genre** Narrative Nonfiction, T229
**Vocabulary Strategy** Suffixes, T231
**Phonics/Fluency** Soft *c* and *g*, Phrasing, T225, T237

**If No →**

| Approaching Level | Reteach T248–T257 |
| ELL | Develop T266–T273 |

**If Yes →**

| On Level | Review T258–T261 |
| Beyond Level | Extend T262–T265 |

## Level Up with Leveled Readers

**IF** children can read their leveled text fluently and answer comprehension questions

**THEN** assign the next level up to accelerate children reading with more complex text.

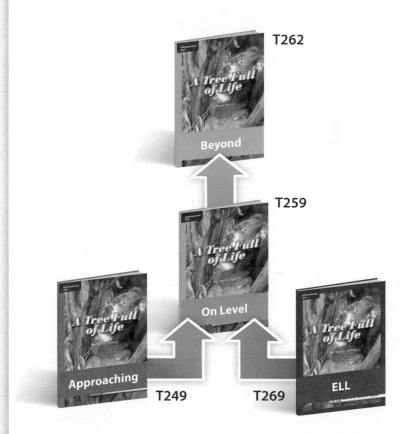

T262

T259

T249        T269

## ENGLISH LANGUAGE LEARNERS
### SCAFFOLD

**IF** ELL students need additional support.    **THEN** scaffold instruction using the small group suggestions.

| Reading/Writing Workshop "A Prairie Guard Dog," T266–T267 | Leveled Reader *A Tree Full of Life*, T268–T269 "Life in a Termite Mound," T269 | Additional Vocabulary T271 burrow    nature forest    pollen habitat    recognize healthy | Suffixes T271 | Writing Organization, T272 | Spelling Words with soft *c* and *g*, T272 | Grammar Kinds of Nouns, T273 |
|---|---|---|---|---|---|---|

**Note: Include ELL Students in all small groups based on their needs.**

## Materials

**Reading/Writing Workshop**

buried

**Visual Vocabulary Cards**

buried        nature
escape        peeks
habitat       restless
journey       spies

a b c

**Word-Building Cards**

**Interactive Read-Aloud Cards**

I predicted because...

**Think Aloud Clouds**

almost

**High-Frequency Word Cards**

Jj
j      dge
ge     gi—
       jump

**Sound-Spelling Cards**

---

## → Introduce the Concept

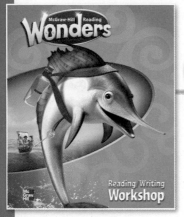

**Reading/Writing Workshop**

Build background knowledge.

**ACADEMIC LANGUAGE**
• habitat, nature
• cognate: hábitat, naturaleza

## ⏱ Build Background
MINILESSON 5 Mins

**ESSENTIAL QUESTION**
*What are features of different animal habitats?*

Read aloud the Essential Question on page 130 of the **Reading/Writing Workshop**. Explain that a *habitat* is the place where a plant or an animal lives. Animal habitats are in the outdoor world called *nature*.

Discuss the photograph of the owl with children. Focus on the features of its *habitat*, and how owls build their homes in *nature*.

→ An owl's feathers keep it safe. They are the color of the owl's habitat.

→ Most owls do not build their own nests. Some kinds of owls look for holes in trees to use for a home. Other owls use nests left by other kinds of birds.

## Talk About It

COLLABORATE

**Ask:** *What are the features of the owl's **habitat**? Why do animals live in forest **habitats**?* Have children discuss in pairs or groups.

Model using the Concept Web to generate words and phrases related to animal habitats. Add children's contributions.

### Collaborative Conversations

**Ask and Answer Questions** As children engage in partner, small-group, and whole-group discussions, encourage them to:

→ ask questions about ideas that are unclear.

→ wait a few seconds after asking a question to give others time to respond.

→ answer questions using sentences, not one-word responses.

---

**Go Digital**

**Animal Habitats**

**Video**

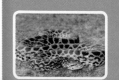
**Photos**

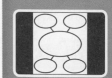
**Graphic Organizer**

peered
**Visual Glossary**

**Weekly Concept** Animal Habitats

## Essential Question

**What are features of different animal habitats?**

*Go Digital!*

# Animal Homes

Hi! I'm an owl. I live in a special place in nature. I live in a forest habitat. Here's why:

▶ My feathers are the same colors as the trees. This helps me hide from predators.

▶ I can live inside this hole. My babies will be safe.

**Talk About It**  COLLABORATE

Talk with a partner about why animals live in forest habitats. Write your ideas on the web.

Forest Habitat

130    131

**READING/WRITING WORKSHOP, pp. 130–131**

## ELL ENGLISH LANGUAGE LEARNERS
### SCAFFOLD

| Beginning | Intermediate | Advanced/High |
|---|---|---|
| **Use Visuals** Point to the owl. Say: *This is an owl.* Point to the tree. *Owls make their homes in trees.* Have children repeat after you. *The trees are part of an outdoor world, called nature. What are some other things you find in nature?* | **Describe** Have children describe the owl's home. Ask: *Where do owls make their home? What do owls use to make their homes?* Encourage children to use a concept word in their response. Clarify children's responses as needed. | **Discuss** Ask children to describe the features of an owl's habitat. Ask questions to help them expand their first response. *How do owls find homes? How does an owl's habitat help it stay safe?* Elicit details to support children's answers. |

**GRAPHIC ORGANIZER**

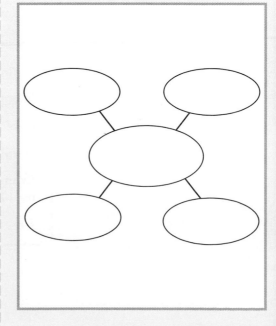

**Build the Concept**

**MINILESSON**
**5** Mins
# Oral Language

## OBJECTIVES

**CCSS** Ask and answer questions about what a speaker says in order to clarify comprehension, gather additional information, or deepen understanding of a topic or issue. **SL.2.3**

- Develop oral language.
- Discuss the Essential Question.

## ACADEMIC LANGUAGE
*predictions, confirm, revise*

### ESSENTIAL QUESTION
Remind children that this week you'll be talking and reading about animal habitats.

## Oral Vocabulary Words

Use the Define/Example/Ask routine to introduce the Oral Vocabulary words below. Prompt children to use the words as they discuss animal habitats.

### Oral Vocabulary Routine

**Define:** To **defend** means to protect from harm.

**Example:** A cat uses its claws to defend itself.

**Ask:** Why do animals need to defend themselves?

**Define:** **Encounter** means meet or see.

**Example:** Sometimes I encounter deer when I walk in the woods.

**Ask:** What other animals might you encounter in the woods? What might you encounter in the ocean?

**Define:** When you tell where something is **located**, you tell where it is found.

**Example:** Our school is located on Pine Street, next to the park.

**Ask:** Where is your house located?

**Define:** **Positive** means helpful and supportive.

**Example:** Our coach said positive things about the way we played today.

**Ask:** What positive steps can you take to clean up your classroom?

**Define:** When you **react**, you do something because something else happened.

**Example:** When I hit a home run, Mom reacts by jumping up and clapping her hands.

**Ask:** How do you react when something good happens to you?

## Go Digital

**Explore a Coral Reef**

**Make and Confirm Predictions**

# → Listening Comprehension

## Interactive Read Aloud

**MINILESSON 10 Mins**

### Read "Explore a Coral Reef"

Tell children that you will read a true story about an underwater habitat where plants and animals live. Display the Interactive Read Aloud cards.

**Interactive Read-Aloud Cards**

### Strategy: Make, Confirm, Revise Predictions

**❶ Model** Remind children that as they read they can make predictions about the text. This can help them decide what to look for when reading. It can also help them better understand the information.

**Think Aloud** You can use what you see in the photos and what you read in the text to make predictions about what you learn in this selection. Doing this can help you to better understand the selection. Today as we read "Exploring a Coral Reef," make predictions about coral reefs and what you will learn about them. As we read on, check whether your predictions are correct and revise them as needed.

**❷ Apply** As you read, use the Think Aloud Cloud to model applying the strategy. Have children make a prediction and then confirm whether the prediction is correct.

**Think Aloud** Remember you can make predictions as you read. When I looked at the photograph, I predicted that coral reefs were rocks with colorful plants growing out of them. I'll revise my prediction. I know now that coral reefs are actually made of tiny living creatures called coral polyps.

### Make Connections

**COLLABORATE** After reading, have children share what they learned about the features of coral reefs. Then have them discuss their predictions and how they confirmed or revised them.

**ENGLISH LANGUAGE LEARNERS**

**Synonyms and Circumlocution**
Remind children that they can ask for synonyms to help clarify words or expressions they do not understand. Ask: *What is another word for* encounter? (meet)

→ # Word Work

## Quick Review

**Build Fluency: Sound Spellings**
Display the **Word-Building Cards:** *u_ e, u, o_e, o, i_e, i, a_e, a, sl, dr, sk, sp, st, tr, pr, pl.* Have children say each sound.

# Phonemic Awareness

### OBJECTIVES

**CCSS** Know and apply grade-level phonics and word analysis skills in decoding words. **RF.2.3**

- Segment phonemes in words.
- Apply phonics when decoding words with soft *c* /s/ and *g* /j/.

## Phoneme Segmentation

**①** **Model** Introduce the sounds /s/ and /j/. *We are going to say the sounds in a word. Listen carefully as I say a word:* cage. *How many sounds do you hear in* cage? /k/, /ā/, /j/. *Three sounds. There are three sounds in the word* cage.

**②** **Guided Practice/Practice** Have the children segment the following words into phonemes. Do the first one with them.

| | | |
|---|---|---|
| place | age | race |
| ice | range | rice |

# Phonics

**Sound-Spelling Card**

### SKILLS TRACE

**Soft *c* and *g***

**INTRODUCE** Unit 2 Week 3 Day 1

**REVIEW** Unit 2 Week 3 Day 2, Day 3, Day 4

**ASSESS** Unit 2

## Introduce Soft *c* and *g*

**①** **Model** Display the *Jump* Sound-Spelling Card. Teach *g* /j/ using *page. This is the* Jump *Sound-Spelling Card. The sound is* /j/. *The* /j/ *sound can be spelled with the letter* g. *Say it with me* /j/. *This is the sound at the end of the word* page. Write the word *page* on the board. *Listen: /pāāāj/,* page. *I'll say* /j/ *as I underline the letter* g *in* page *several times.* Repeat with the *Sun* Sound-Spelling Card for *c* /s/, using *mice*.

Circle the *ce* in *mice* and the *ge* in *page*. Say: *When the letter* c *or* g *is followed by the vowel* e *or* i *it often makes the "soft* c *or* g" *sounds* /s/ *and* /j/. Point out that some common word endings with the /j/ sound are *dge* as in *edge*, *lge* as in *bulge*, and *nge* as in *fringe*.

**②** **Guided Practice/Practice** Have children practice connecting the letter *c* with the sound /s/ by writing it, pointing out that the letter *c* stands for the /s/ sound when it is followed by the letter *e* or *i*. *Now, do it with me, say* /s/ *as I write the letter* c. *This time, write the letter* c *five times as you say the* /s/ *sound.* Repeat with the letter *g* for /j/, pointing out that the letter *g* stands for /j/ when it is followed by *e* or *i*.

## Go Digital

**Phonemic Awareness**

**Phonics**

# Blend Words with Soft *c* and *g*

**① Model** Display Word Building Cards *g, e, m*. Model how to blend the sounds. *This is the letter* g. *It stands for /j/.* (Point out that the letter *g* stands for the sound /j/ because it is followed by the letter *e*.) *This is the letter* e. *It stands for /e/. This is the letter* m. *It stands for /m/. Listen as I blend these sounds together /jeeemmm/. Say it with me:* gem.

Continue by modeling these words: *age, cell, nice*

**② Guided Practice/Practice** Display the Day 1 Phonics Practice Activity. Read each word in the first row, blending the sounds, for example, /īsss/. The word is *ice*. Have children blend each word and prompt children to read the connected text, sounding the decodable words.

| | | | | |
|---|---|---|---|---|
| ice | ace | mice | slice | trace |
| range | cage | badge | bulge | stage |
| wage | place | ledge | dance | cent |
| use | huge | cup | mule | bus |

The mice ran in the cage.

We dance at a fast pace.

This space is huge!

`Also online`

**Phonics Practice**

### Corrective Feedback

**Sound Error** Model the sound the children missed, then have them repeat the sound. Say: *My turn. Tap the letter and say the sound. Sound /s/. What's the sound?* Return to the beginning of the word. Say: *Let's start over.* Blend the word with the children again.

## ENGLISH LANGUAGE LEARNERS SCAFFOLD

**Phonemic Awareness: Minimal Contrasts** Focus on articulation. Say the soft c /s/ and note your mouth position. Have children repeat. Use the articulation photos. Repeat for soft g /j/. Have children say both sounds, note the differences. Continue with *minimal contrasts ache/ace, rake/race, bug/ budge, leg/ledge, get/jet*.

**Phonics: Variations in Language** In some languages, including Spanish, Hmong, and Khmer, there is no direct transfer for /j/ as in *ledge*. Emphasize /j/ and show the correct mouth position. Then review words with /j/. Practice with the Approaching Level phonics page.

---

**ON-LEVEL PRACTICE BOOK** p. 72

The *c* in **cent** stands for the /s/ sound. It is soft *c*. The *g* in **germ** stands for the /j/ sound. It is soft *g*.

**A. Read each word in the box. Then write the words that belong in each list.**

| space | range | trace | cage | badge | ice |
|---|---|---|---|---|---|

| | Soft *g* | | Soft *c* |
|---|---|---|---|
| 1. | range | 4. | space |
| 2. | cage | 5. | trace |
| 3. | badge | 6. | ice |

A prefix is a word part added to the beginning of a word to make a new word.
• The prefix **re-** means "again."
• The prefixes **un-** and **dis-** mean "not" or "opposite of."

**B. Read each word. Write its meaning.**

1. dislike ___ not like ___    2. reuse ___ use again ___

3. unkind ___ not kind ___    4. redo ___ do again ___

| APPROACHING p. 72 | BEYOND p. 72 | ELL p. 72 |
|---|---|---|

# Word Work

**MINILESSON 5 Mins**

# Spelling

## Words with Soft *c* and *g*

**Dictation** Use the spelling dictation routine to help children transfer their growing knowledge of sound-spellings to writing. Follow the Dictation Routine.

**Pretest** After dictation, pronounce each spelling word. Read the sentence and pronounce the word again. Ask children to say each word softly, stretching the sounds, before writing it. After the pretest, display the spelling words and write each word as you say the letter names. Have children check their words.

| | |
|---|---|
| **place** | This is my favorite **place**. |
| **barge** | The logs were put on a **barge**. |
| **trace** | Can you **trace** this letter? |
| **ice** | Put this **ice** in your glass. |
| **bulge** | My bag is so full it has a **bulge**. |
| **badge** | The leaders have a red **badge**. |
| **space** | I want to fly in **space**. |
| **range** | Can you see it or is it out of **range**? |
| **mice** | We keep pet **mice** at my school. |
| **cage** | Anna's cat sleeps in a **cage**. |
| **mule** | We rode a **mule** on my aunt's farm. |
| **huge** | That boat is **huge**! |
| **out** | My big brother took the trash **out**. |
| **wash** | I helped my dad **wash** the car. |
| **saw** | We **saw** a bird outside the window. |

For Approaching Level and Beyond Level children, refer to the Differentiated Spelling Lists for modified word lists.

## OBJECTIVES

**CCSS** Demonstrate command of the conventions of standard English capitalization, punctuation, and spelling when writing. **L.2.2**

**CCSS** Generalize learned spelling patterns when writing words (e.g., cage → badge; boy → boil). **L.2.2d**

**CCSS** Know and apply grade-level phonics and word analysis skills in decoding words. **RF.2.3**

**CCSS** Recognize and read grade-appropriate irregularly spelled words. **RF.2.3f**

## Go Digital

**Spelling Word Routine**

| they | together |
|---|---|
| how | eat |

**High-Frequency Word Routine**

# High-Frequency Words

*almost, buy, food, out, pull, saw, sky, straight, under, wash*

**1** **Model** Display the **High-Frequency Word Cards** *almost, buy, food, out, pull, saw, sky, straight, under, wash.* Use the Read/Spell/Write routine to teach each word.

→ **Read** Point to and say the word *sky. This is the word* sky. *Say it with me:* sky. *The* sky *is blue.*

→ **Spell** *The word* sky *is spelled* s-k-y. *Spell it with me.*

→ **Write** *Let's write the word in the air as we say each letter:* s-k-y.

→ Follow the same steps to introduce *almost, buy, food, out, pull, saw, straight, under,* and *wash.*

→ As children spell each word with you, point out the irregularities in sound/spellings, such as the /ī/ sound spelled *uy* in the word *buy.*

→ Have partners create sentences using each word.

**2** **Guided Reading** Have the children read the sentences. Prompt them to identify the high-frequency words in connected text and to blend the decodable words.

1. It is **almost** time to go home.
2. Tom went to **buy** milk.
3. We got a lot of **food**.
4. Put **out** water for the dog.
5. Will Lee **pull** the sled?
6. We **saw** the sun set.
7. Make the line **straight**.
8. The bug ran **under** the rug.
9. **Wash** your hands.
10. The **sky** is blue.

## Monitor and Differentiate

**✓ Quick Check**

Can students read and decode words with soft *c* and *g*? Can students recognize and read high-frequency words?

### Small Group Instruction

| | | |
|---|---|---|
| If No → | **Approaching** | Reteach pp. T250-T255 |
| | **ELL** | Develop pp. T266-T273 |
| If Yes → | **On Level** | Review pp. T260-T261 |
| | **Beyond Level** | Extend pp. T264-T265 |

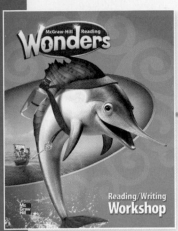

**Wonders**

Reading/Writing
**Workshop**

**Reading/Writing Workshop**

---

## OBJECTIVES

**CCSS** Demonstrate understanding of word relationships and nuances in word meanings. **L.2.5**

**CCSS** Identify real-life connections between words and their use (e.g., describe foods that are *spicy* or *juicy*). **L.2.5a**

**CCSS** Determine the meaning of words and phrases in a text relevant to a *grade 2 topic or subject area*. **RI.2.4**

---

## ACADEMIC LANGUAGE
*habitat, nature*

---

# → Vocabulary

High-Frequency Words

almost buy food out pull saw
enough under most

**MINILESSON**
**10 Mins**

## Words in Context

### Model the Routine

Introduce each vocabulary word using the Vocabulary Routine found on the Visual Vocabulary Cards.

**Visual Vocabulary Cards**

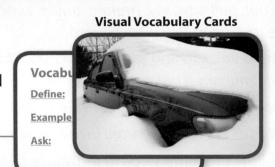

Vocabu...

Define:

Example

Ask:

> **Vocabulary Routine**
>
> **Define:** When something is **buried**, it is covered up or hidden.
>
> **Example:** The car was buried in the deep snow.
>
> **Ask:** What buried things have you found?

**Go**
# Digital

**peered**

**Visual Glossary**

## Definitions

→ **escape**  If you **escape** something, you get out of it or away from it.

→ **habitat**  A **habitat** is the place where an animal or plant usually lives or grows.

→ **journey**  A **journey** is a trip.

→ **nature**  **Nature** is all the things outdoors not made by people.

→ **peeks**  If a person **peeks**, they take a quick look.

→ **restless**  If you cannot stay still or quiet, then you are **restless**.

→ **spies**  If a person **spies** something, that person watches for something and sees it.

### Talk About It

**COLLABORATE**

Have children work with a partner and look at each picture and discuss the definition of each word. Then ask children to choose three words and write questions for their partner to answer.

# Vocabulary

Use the picture and sentence to learn each word.

**buried**

The car was **buried** in the deep snow.

*What buried things have you found?*

**escape**

The cat could **escape** through a hole in the fence.

*What are other ways an animal could escape from a backyard?*

**habitat**

Prairie dogs live in a desert **habitat**.

*What animals live in a forest habitat?*

**journey**

Maya and her family went on a **journey** in the woods.

*What is another word for journey?*

**nature**

We walk in the woods because we like to be in **nature**.

*What do you like about nature?*

**peeks**

While hiding, Kate **peeks** out from behind the tree.

*Show how a person peeks out from behind something.*

**restless**

The child became **restless** during the long car ride.

*When have you felt restless?*

**spies**

Carlos **spies** an eagle in the sky.

*What is a synonym for spies?*

## Your Turn

COLLABORATE

Pick three words. Write three questions for your partner to answer.

*Go Digital!  Use the online visual glossary*

132

133

**READING/WRITING WORKSHOP, pp. 132–133**

## ENGLISH LANGUAGE LEARNERS
### ELL SCAFFOLD

| Beginning | Intermediate | Advanced/High |
|---|---|---|
| **Use Visuals** Say *Let's look at the picture for the word* buried. Point to the picture of the car covered with snow. Guide children to understand that something that is buried is covered with snow, sand, or dirt. Ask: *What would you do to find the car in this picture? Have you ever found anything that was buried?* | **Describe** Have children describe the picture. Help them with pronunciation. Ask: *Have you ever seen a car buried in snow? Have you ever seen something buried in sand?* Ask them to turn to a partner and talk about their experiences. | **Discuss** Ask students to talk about the picture with a partner and write a definition. Then share the definition with the class. |

### ON-LEVEL PRACTICE BOOK p. 71

| buried | escape | habitat | journey |
| nature | peeks | restless | spies |

**A.** Read each clue below. Then find the vocabulary word on the right that matches the clue. Draw a line from the clue to the word.

1. the outdoor world
2. takes a quick look
3. the natural place where an animal lives
4. get away
5. cannot stay still
6. a long trip
7. covered up in the ground
8. watches and sees something

  a. habitat
  b. escape
  c. spies
  d. buried
  e. peeks
  f. nature
  g. journey
  h. restless

**B.** Choose one vocabulary word from the box above. Write the word in a sentence of your own.
Possible response provided.

9. The squirrels buried nuts for the winter.

| APPROACHING p. 71 | BEYOND p. 71 | ELL p. 71 |

# Comprehension

 CLOSE READING

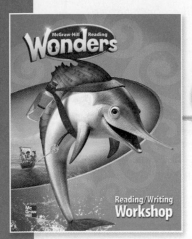

McGraw-Hill Reading
# Wonders

Reading/Writing
**Workshop**

**Reading/Writing
Workshop**

## OBJECTIVES

 **CCSS** Read with sufficient accuracy and fluency to support comprehension.
**RF.2.4**

 **CCSS** Read on-level text with purpose and understanding.
**RF.2.4a**

Identify meanings of words used in context.

 **Shared Read**          **Lexile** 480    *TextEvaluator* 26

## Connect to Concept

### Animal Habitats

Explain to children that "A Prairie Guard Dog" will tell them more about a prairie dog's home.

After reading each section, have partners discuss what they have learned about a prairie dog's habitat.

### Use Vocabulary Words in Context

| buried | escape | habitat | journey |
| nature | peeks | restless | spies |

The highlighted words in the text are the vocabulary words children have learned. As you read, have them discuss the words' meanings.

## Close Reading

**Reread the Introduction:** Tell children that you are going to take a closer look at page 135. Reread the first paragraph together. Ask: *Why can the prairie be dangerous for some animals? Why aren't there many places to hide?* Model how to cite text evidence to answer the questions.

*The author says that the prairie can be dangerous because animals don't have many places to hide. The author also says that a prairie is a grassy place without many trees. Without the trees, there aren't many hiding spots.*

**Reread "Good Morning!":** Model how to paraphrase the section "Good Morning!" Remind children that restating key details from the text in your own words helps you understand what you are reading.

*Pete is a prairie dog. In the morning, Pete checks to see if it is safe to come out of the burrow. Then he calls to his family to let them know that it is safe. Since Pete is guarding his family, and the title of the selection is "A Prairie Guard Dog," I think that Pete is a prairie guard dog.*

## Go
## Digital

**A Prairie
Guard Dog**

**CCSS** **Shared Read** **Genre • Narrative Nonfiction**

# A Prairie Guard Dog

**? Essential Question**

**What are features of different animal habitats?**

Read to learn about the place a prairie dog calls home.

134

I am on a **journey**. My trip is to a prairie. It is in the outdoor world called **nature**. Many animals live in a prairie **habitat**. This place has what prairie dogs need to survive. A prairie has a lot of grasses but few trees. Without places to hide, a prairie can be dangerous for some animals.

## Good Morning!

It is early in the morning. First, I see a prairie dog. I name him Pete. He **peeks** his head out of his **burrow** underground. He looks around. Then Pete calls loudly to his family, "Yip!" He lets them know it is safe to come out. Soon four prairie dogs come out.

Prairie dogs build underground burrows to keep themselves safe from predators.

135

**READING/WRITING WORKSHOP,** pp. 134–135

## A C T Access Complex Text

▶ **Connections of Ideas**

Children may need help in connecting the information in "Good Morning" to information about the prairie in the first paragraph.

→ *In "Good Morning," Pete makes sure that it is safe to come out of the burrow. Why might he do this? How does the first paragraph on the page support your answer?* (There might be danger outside of the burrow. The first paragraph says a prairie can be dangerous for some animals.)

→ *What other information does the page give that shows that prairie dogs may face danger?* (The caption tells us that there are predators that can harm prairie dogs.)

Pete is the guard and he is **restless**. He cannot rest because he is always looking around for danger. This allows the other prairie dogs to safely munch on grasses and seeds. They can also groom each other or work on their burrow.

*Yap! Yap!*

**Prairie dogs can make 11 different sounds to communicate with each other.**

136

### A Scare

Oh no! Pete **spies** a large badger! When he sees it, he gives a loud bark, "Yap! Yap!" His family recognizes the warning. Some hide in tall grasses, and some jump into the burrow. The badger runs at Pete, but the watchful guard is able to **escape** into the burrow. I am glad he is able to get away from danger.

After a few minutes, Pete peeks his head out again and he is back on the job.

**Badgers live on prairies and hunt prairie dogs.**

137

**READING/WRITING WORKSHOP, pp. 136–137**

# Shared Read · CLOSE READING

## Close Reading

**Reread page 136:** Tell children that you are going to take a closer look at page 136. Reread the page together. Ask: *Why can't Pete rest? What is he doing? How does Pete help his family?* Model how to use the text to answer the questions.
*The author tells us that Pete cannot rest because he is the guard. He looks for danger. This allows the other prairie dogs to be safe while they eat.*

## Make Connections

**ESSENTIAL QUESTION**
Encourage children to go back into the text for details of a prairie dog's habitat. Ask children to describe the pairie dog's habitat and how burrows help prairie dogs survive in that habitat.

## Break Time

The sun gets higher, and it is hot now. The prairie dogs slip into their deep burrow where it is cooler. Even Pete goes in. **Tunnels**, like hallways, lead to different areas. There is a sleeping room. There is a room used like a bathroom. The prairie dogs cover up roots and seeds in one room. Later, they eat the **buried** food there.

## Second Shift

I keep watching the burrow. Finally, the sun begins to set and a different prairie dog peeks its head out. I name him Gary. Pete must be off duty. "Yip," Gary calls. The other prairie dogs come back out.

The prairie dogs eat and play until the moon is high in the sky. Then they go to sleep in their burrows. I wonder if Pete will be back on duty. I will see in the morning.

| Prairie Dog Facts | |
|---|---|
| Size | 12 to 15 inches tall |
| Weight | 2 to 4 pounds |
| Habitat | short and medium grass desert prairies |
| Food | roots, seeds, leaves of plants, grasses |
| Shelter | underground burrows with many rooms |
| Predators | coyotes, bobcats, badgers, foxes, weasels |

### Make Connections

What are two features of a prairie dog's habitat?
**ESSENTIAL QUESTION**

What animal did the prairie dog remind you of?
**TEXT TO SELF**

138 139

**READING/WRITING WORKSHOP, pp. 138–139**

# Continue Close Reading

Use the following lesson for focused rereadings.

→ Make, Confirm, Revise Predictions, T216–T217

→ Main Topic and Key Details, T218–T219

→ Genre and Text Features, T228–T229

→ Suffixes, T230–T231

## ELL

### ENGLISH LANGUAGE LEARNERS

**Clarify** ELLs may be unfamiliar with vocabulary used to describe the work day and Pete's "job" as a prairie guard dog. Focus on the section "Second Shift" on page 139. Explain that a *shift* is a work period. Say: *Some jobs, such as guards or police, have three shifts each day. The workers in the first shift begin work in the morning. A second shift begins in the afternoon. A third shift works through the night.* Remind children that Pete is a guard dog. *Ask: Which shift does Pete have?* (the first shift) *Which prairie dog has the second shift?* (Gary)

Discuss other work-related vocabulary in this section. Point out the phrases *on duty* and *off duty*. Explain that when a guard is *on duty*, that means the guard is working. Ask: *What do you think* off duty *means?* (not working) *During the first shift, is Pete on duty or off duty?* (Pete is on duty.)

→ # Language Arts

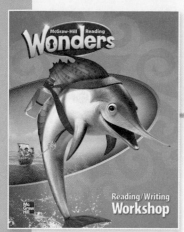

**Reading/Writing Workshop**

---

## OBJECTIVES

**CCSS** Write informative/explanatory texts in which they introduce a topic, use facts and definitions to develop points, and provide a concluding statement or section. **W.2.2**

**CCSS** Demonstrate command of the conventions of standard English capitalization, punctuation, and spelling when writing. **L.2.2**

---

## ACADEMIC LANGUAGE

*sequence words, common noun, proper noun*

---

**MINILESSON 10 Mins**

# Writing Traits: Organization

## Discuss the Expert Model

**Explain** Explain that good writers put their ideas in order. They use words such as *first, next,* and *then* to show the sequence, or order, of events in the text. Sequence:

→ helps readers understand the order of ideas and events in the text.

→ creates an order by using words, such as *first, next, then,* and *last.*

 Read aloud the expert model from "A Prairie Guard Dog." Ask children to listen for the sequence words that help them understand the order of events in the text. Have children talk with partners to identify these words.

## Discuss the Student Model

 Remind children that sequence words help the reader to understand how the story is organized. Read aloud the draft of Adam's nonfiction story. As children follow along, have them focus on how the model is organized. Have them identify the sequence words that Adam uses.

 Invite partners to talk about the draft and the sequence words the writer added. Ask them to suggest other sequence words that could be added to the text.

---

 **WRITING ENTRY: SEQUENCE**

**❶ Prewrite** Provide children with the prompt below:

*Write a story about an animal you've seen in a park or at the zoo. Explain what it was doing. Be sure to organize your ideas in a way that makes sense.*

**❷ Draft** Have children choose a topic and use their notes to write a draft. Remind children to use sequence words to show the order of their ideas.

---

 # Go Digital

**Present the Lesson**

**Writing**

**Editing Marks**

≡ Make a capital letter.

/ Make a small letter.

∧ Add

⟋ Take out.

**Grammar Handbook**
**Kinds of Nouns**
See page 477–478.

**CCSS Writing Traits › Organization**

# Readers to ...

# Writers

Writers use sequence to put their ideas in an order. Words, such as *first, next,* and *then* help readers understand the order of the ideas.

**Organization**
Identify the **sequence** words. How does this help the **organization** of the story?

**Expert Model**

### Good Morning!

It is early in the morning. First, I see a prairie dog. I name him Pete. He peeks his head out of his burrow underground. He looks around. Then Pete calls loudly to his family, "Yip!" He lets them know it is safe to come out. Soon four prairie dogs come out.

Jeff Foot/Getty Images

144

Adam wrote a nonfiction story about a seal. Read Adam's revision.

**Student Model**

### Sam Learns to Swim

At two weeks old, ~~sam~~ Seal has his first swimming lesson. His mother guides him into the water. ~~He is two weeks old.~~ At first He does not want to go in. He gets out and shakes his head. Then Mom guides him back in. He flaps his flippers. Finally, he is learning!

**Your Turn** COLLABORATE

☑ Point out the sequence words Adam used.
☑ Identify the proper nouns.
☑ Tell how revisions improved his writing.

*Go Digital!*
Write online in Writer's Workspace

145

**READING/WRITING WORKSHOP, pp. 144–145**

## ELL ENGLISH LANGUAGE LEARNERS SCAFFOLD

| Beginning | Intermediate | Advanced/High |
|---|---|---|
| **Write Sentences** Provide model sentences based on the prompt:<br><br>*I went to the zoo last summer. First, the giraffe _____. Then _____. Finally, it _____.*<br><br>Help children complete the sentence frames. | **Identify** Help children to order the events in their writing. Have children write two or three sentences describing what happened first, next, and finally in their story. Help them to identify sequence words to show the order of events. | **Respond** Ask children to respond to the prompt. Remind them to use sequence words to order the events in their writing. Provide model sentences and revise them as needed. |

📄 **Genre Writing**

**Expository Text**
For full writing process lesson and rubrics, see:

→ How To, pages T480–T485

→ How To, pages T486–T491

LANGUAGE ARTS **T207**

→ # Language Arts

 MINILESSON
**10** Mins
## Grammar

### Kinds of Nouns

**OBJECTIVES**

**CCSS** Demonstrate command of the conventions of standard English grammar and usage when writing or speaking. **L.2.1**

**CCSS** Demonstrate command of the conventions of standard English capitalization, punctuation, and spelling when writing. **L.2.2**

**CCSS** Capitalize holidays, product names, and geographic names. **L.2.2a**

❶ **Explain/Model** Explain that a common noun is a word that names any person, place, or thing. The words *girl, house,* and *flower* are common nouns. A proper noun names a particular person, place, or thing. The words *Sarah, California,* and *Scottish Terrier* are proper nouns. Tell children that a proper noun begins with a capital letter. Display the following sentences:

> Dr. Chavez studies animals that live in the forest.

> He travels to Oregon every winter.

Model identifying the proper noun in the first sentence.

**Think Aloud** Which word in the sentence names a particular person? *Dr. Chavez* names a particular person. The words *Dr. Chavez* make up a proper noun.

Repeat with the second sentence.

❷ **Guided Practice/Practice** Display the sentences below and read them aloud. Have partners identify the proper nouns in each sentence. Prompt children by asking, *What word names a particular person, place, or thing?*

> Jessica wrote a report on elephants. (Jessica)

> We saw Mrs. Brown at the zoo. (Mrs. Brown)

### Talk About It

 **Name the Proper Noun** Have pairs create sentences with proper nouns. Remind them that a proper noun begins with a capital letter. Have them read aloud their sentences to other pairs. Have the other pairs name the proper nouns in the sentences.

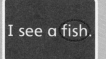

**Go**
Digital

I see a fish.

**Grammar**

# Mechanics: Capital Letters

**1 Explain/Model** Explain to children that a proper noun begins with a capital letter. The days of the week, months, and holidays are all proper nouns. They begin with a capital letter.

Also explain that an abbreviation is a short way of writing a word. An abbreviation begins with a capital letter and ends with a period. Days of the week and months of the year are often abbreviated. Titles that come before names are usually abbreviated.

Guide children to identify the proper nouns and abbreviations in the following sentences. Have children rewrite the sentences, beginning each proper noun with a capital letter. They should also begin each abbreviation with a capital letter and end it with a period.

> We went bird watching with mr seager.
>
> (We went bird watching with Mr. Seager.)
>
> dr adams takes care of sick animals.
>
> (Dr. Adams takes care of sick animals.)

**2 Guided Practice/Practice** Display the sentences below. Have children identify the proper nouns and abbreviations in the following sentences. Then have children rewrite the sentences, beginning each proper noun with a capital letter. They should also begin each abbreviation with a capital letter and end it with a period.

> My sister and I went to the cincinnati zoo with mrs mason.
>
> (My sister and I went to the Cincinnati Zoo with Mrs. Mason.)
>
> On friday, my dad will take my dog to see our vet dr. ricardo.
>
> (On Friday, my dad will take my dog to see our vet Dr. Ricardo.)

### GRAMMAR PRACTICE BOOK p. 36

- A **common noun** names any person, place, or thing.
- A **proper noun** names a special person, place, or thing.
- A proper noun begins with a capital letter.
  Polar bears live near the <u>Arctic Circle</u>.
  Bats sleep in caves all over the <u>United States</u>.

**A. Circle the proper nouns.**

1. Many frogs live on the banks of the (Mississippi River).
2. Beavers can be found in wetlands across (North America).
3. Prairie dogs live in the grasslands of (Montana).
4. Many different fish swim in the (Atlantic Ocean).
5. Some alligators live in the (Florida Everglades).

**B. List the common nouns in the sentences above.**

| frogs | prairie dogs |
|---|---|
| banks | grasslands |
| beavers | fish |
| wetlands | alligators |

# Daily Wrap Up

→ Discuss the Essential Question and encourage children to discuss using the new concept and oral vocabulary words. Ask: *What are the features of a prairie dog's habitat? How would you describe the animal's home?*

→ Prompt children to share what skills they learned. How might they use those skills?

## Materials

**Reading/Writing Workshop**

buried

**Visual Vocabulary Cards**

| | |
|---|---|
| buried | nature |
| escape | peeks |
| habitat | restless |
| journey | spies |

a b c

**Word-Building Cards**

**Interactive Read-Aloud Cards**

almost

**High-Frequency Word Cards**

badge

**Spelling Word Cards**

Jj

j dge
ge g—
jump

**Sound-Spelling Cards**

→ # Build the Concept

MINILESSON
**5 Mins**

# Oral Language

## OBJECTIVES

**CCSS** Recount or describe key ideas or details from a text read aloud or information presented orally or through other media. **SL.2.2**

- Develop oral language.
- Discuss the Essential Question.
- Retell story events.

## ACADEMIC LANGUAGE

*predictions, confirm, revise*

### ESSENTIAL QUESTION

**COLLABORATE** Remind children that this week you are talking and reading about animal habitats. Remind them of the animals that live in the coral reefs from "Explore a Coral Reef" and the habitat of the prairie dogs in "A Prairie Guard Dog." Guide children to talk about the Essential Question using information they have read and talked about on Day 1.

### Review Oral Vocabulary

Review the Oral Vocabulary words *defend, encounter, located, positive,* and *react* using the Define/Example/Ask routine. Encourage children to discuss animal habitats when coming up with examples for each word.

## Go Digital

**Explore a Coral Reef**

**Retell Routine**

# Listening Comprehension

MINILESSON
**10** Mins

## Interactive Read Aloud

### Reread "Explore a Coral Reef"

Tell children that you will reread "Explore a Coral Reef." Display the Interactive Read-Aloud Cards.

#### Comprehension Strategy: Make, Confirm, Revise Predictions

Remind children that as they read they should make, confirm, and revise predictions. Doing so can help

**Interactive Read-Aloud Cards**

them understand information. Say: *As we reread "Explore a Coral Reef," think about your predictions. When I saw the photo of the ocean food web, I predicted that I would find out what the animals near the coral reef eat. I thought they might eat each other and plants. I confirmed my prediction.*

Read aloud "Explore a Coral Reef." Pause to model using the strategy. Have children use the text to make, confirm, and revise predictions.

#### Model Retelling

Pause to retell parts of the selection. *I can put the information from the text and photos in my own words. I have read that coral reefs are underwater habitats. They are made of millions of tiny animals called coral polyps. Coral reefs are found in warm, shallow ocean waters.*

Point out that some informational texts contain a lot of information. Explain that when children retell this selection they may not be able to retell all the facts. Instead, they should try to pick out the important facts and details and tell them in the correct order.

#### Retell the Selection

After reading, guide children to retell the entire selection. Remind them to tell the important facts and details in the correct order. You may wish to let the children use the Interactive Read-Aloud Cards to help them retell the selection.

**ELL**

#### ENGLISH LANGUAGE LEARNERS

**Retell** Guide children to retell by using a question for each card. For example: *What are coral reefs made of? What is one animal that lives in a coral reef?* Then provide sentence frames for children to complete orally. *Coral reefs are made of ____. One animal that lives near a coral reef is ____.*

→  # Word Work

### Quick Review
**Build Fluency: Sound Spellings**
Display the **Word-Building Cards**: *o_e, o, u_e, u, i_e, i, a_e, a, c, g, dge, ge, lge, nge, rge*. Have children say each sound.

## OBJECTIVES

**CCSS** Know and apply grade-level phonics and word analysis skills in decoding words. **RF.2.3**

**CCSS** Decode words with common prefixes and suffixes. **RF.2.3d**

**CCSS** Determine or clarify the meaning of unknown and multiple-meaning words and phrases based on *grade 2 reading and content*, choosing flexibly from an array of strategies. **L.2.4**

**CCSS** Determine the meaning of the new word formed when a known prefix is added to a known word (e.g., *happy/unhappy, tell/retell*). **L.2.4b**

- Substitute phonemes to form new words.
- Build words with soft *c* and *g*.

## ACADEMIC LANGUGE

*substitute, build*

 **MINILESSON 5 Mins**

# Phonemic Awareness

## Phoneme Substitution

**❶ Model** Show children by substituting a sound in a word it forms a new word. Say: *Listen for the last sound in the word* age. *The sound is /j/. Now listen as I say the word and then change the last sound:* age, ace. *I changed the last sound /j/ to /s/ and made a new word,* ace.

Continue modeling phoneme substitution with the beginning sound in the following word sets.

face/mace        page/cage        nudge/budge

**❷ Guided Practice/Practice** Have children practice substituting phonemes. Do the first one together. *Listen for the sounds in each word. Substitute the first sound and say the new word. Let's do the first one together. The word is* lace. *The first sound in* lace *is /l/. Substitute the first sound /l/ with the /r/ sound. What is the new word? The new word is* race. Repeat with *dance/lance*.

Have children practice substituting phonemes to create new words.

bent/cent        mice/rice        dodge/lodge

 **MINILESSON 5 Mins**

# Phonics

## Review Soft *c* and *g*

**❶ Model** Display the *Jump* and *Sun* Sound-Spelling Cards. Review the soft c /s/ and g /j/ sounds using the words *ice* and *page*.

**❷ Guided Practice/Practice** Have the children practice connecting the letter *c* with the sound /s/, pointing out that the letter *c* stands for the /s/ sound when it is followed by the letter *e* or *i*. Repeat with *g* for /j/. Have the children practice connecting the letters and sounds. Point to the sound spelling cards. *What is this letter? What sound does this letter make when it is followed by the letter* e *or* i?

## Go Digital

▬ Make a capital letter.
∧ Add.
✐ Take out.

**Phonemic Awareness**

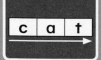
c a t

**Phonics**

I __ the jar.
| fill | fills | filling |

**Structural Analysis**

# Blend Words with Soft *c* and *g*

**❶ Model** Display Word-Building Cards *r, i, d, g, e* to form the word *ridge*. Model how to generate and blend the sounds to say the word. *This is the letter* r. *It stands for /r/. This is the letter* i. *It stands for /i/. These are the letters* d, g, e. *They stand for /j/. Listen as I blend these sounds together /rrriiij/. Say it with me:* ridge.

→ Continue by modeling the words: *stage, rice,* and *cage*.

**❷ Guided Practice/Practice** Repeat the routine with children with *cent, mice, gem, badge, slice*.

# Build Words with Soft *c* and *g*

**❶ Model** Display the Word-Building Cards *f, a, c, e*. Blend the word /f/ /ā/ /s/, *face*.

→ Replace *f* with *r* and with repeat with *race*.

→ Change *r* to *p* and repeat with *pace*.

**❷ Guided Practice/Practice** Continue with *page, rage, sage; space, trace, trance*. Guide children to build and blend each new word.

---

**MINILESSON**
**5 Mins**

# Structural Analysis

## Prefixes *re-, un-, dis-*

**❶ Model** Write and read aloud *make, remake, happy, unhappy, like,* and *dislike*. Underline the prefixes *re-, un-,* and *dis-*. Tell children that adding the prefix *re-, un-,* or *dis-* to the beginning of a word changes its meaning.

Explain that the prefix *re-* means "again." *Remake* means to make again. The prefixes *un-* and *dis-* both mean "not" or "opposite of." *Unhappy* means the opposite of happy, and *dislike* means not to like.

**❷ Guided Practice/Practice** Have children add the prefixes *re-, un-,* or *-dis* to the words as shown. Then have them use each new word in a sentence: *tell, send, trust, use, lace, place, pile, ripe* and *run*.

re-: run, use, send, tell      un-: ripe, pile, lace      dis-: trust, place

---

### ENGLISH LANGUAGE LEARNERS

**Phonics: Build Vocabulary**
Review the meanings of the example words that can be explained or demonstrated in a concrete way. For example, ask children to point to their face and a page of a book. Have children repeat the sentences *Look at my face. I turn the page.* Provide sentence starters such as: *Put some ____ in the glass. The lion is in the ____.* Correct grammar and pronunciation as needed.

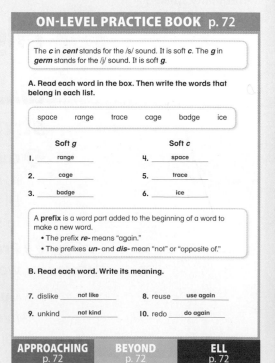

**ON-LEVEL PRACTICE BOOK** p. 72

The *c* in **cent** stands for the /s/ sound. It is soft *c*. The *g* in **germ** stands for the /j/ sound. It is soft *g*.

**A. Read each word in the box. Then write the words that belong in each list.**

| space | range | trace | cage | badge | ice |

| Soft *g* | | Soft *c* | |
|---|---|---|---|
| 1. range | | 4. space | |
| 2. cage | | 5. trace | |
| 3. badge | | 6. ice | |

A **prefix** is a word part added to the beginning of a word to make a new word.
• The prefix *re-* means "again."
• The prefixes *un-* and *dis-* mean "not" or "opposite of."

**B. Read each word. Write its meaning.**

| 7. dislike | not like | 8. reuse | use again |
| 9. unkind | not kind | 10. redo | do again |

| APPROACHING p. 72 | BEYOND p. 72 | ELL p. 72 |

WORD WORK **T213**

→  # Word Work

**Quick Review**

**High-Frequency Words:** Read, Spell and Write to review this week's high-frequency words: *almost, buy, food, out, pull, saw, sky, straight, under, wash.*

**MINILESSON 5 Mins**

## Spelling

**OBJECTIVES**

**CCSS** Demonstrate command of the conventions of standard English capitalization, punctuation, and spelling when writing. **L.2.2**

**CCSS** Generalize learned spelling patterns when writing words (e.g., cage → badge; boy → boil). **L.2.2d**

**CCSS** Know and apply grade-level phonics and word analysis skills in decoding words. **RF.2.3**

**CCSS** Recognize and read grade-appropriate irregularly spelled words. **RF.2.3f**

### Word Sort with Soft *c* and *g*

❶ **Model** Display the Spelling Word Cards from the Teacher's Resource Book, one at a time. Have children read each word, listening for soft *c* and *g*.

Use cards for *ice* and *cage* to create a two-column chart. Say each word and pronounce the sounds: /ī/ /s/; /k/ /ā/ /j/. Say each word again. Ask children to chorally spell each word.

❷ **Guided Practice/Practice** Have children place each spelling word in either the soft *c* or soft *g* column. When completed have children chorally read the words in each column. Then call out a word. Have a child find the word chart and point to it as the class chorally spells the word.

❸ **Build Fluency: Word Automaticity** Have the children read words to build fluency. Then conclude by asking children to orally generate additional words that have the soft *c* or soft *g* sound. List them in the correct columns and help children identify the soft *c* and *g* spellings.

**Go Digital**

| er | ir | or | ur |
|----|----|----|----|
| her | | | |
| girl curb | | word | |

**Spelling Word Sort**

| they | together |
|------|----------|
| how | eat |

**High-Frequency Word Routine**

**peered**

**Visual Glossary**

**MINILESSON 5 Mins**

# High-Frequency Words

## *almost, buy, food, out, pull, saw, sky, straight, under, wash*

❶ **Guided Practice** Say each word and have children Read/Spell/Write it. Ask children to picture the word, and write the way they see it. Display the word for children to self-correct. Point out irregularities in sound spellings, such as the long *i* sound in *buy*.

**COLLABORATE** ❷ **Practice** Add the week's high-frequency words to the cumulative word bank. Have partners create sentences using the words.

**Cumulative Review** Review last week's words *change, cheer, fall, five, look, open, should, their, won,* and *yes* using the Read/Spell/Write routine. Repeat the routine, mixing the words and having children say each one.

# Vocabulary

## Expand Vocabulary

**MINILESSON 5 Mins**

Have children use the Visual Vocabulary Cards to review this week's vocabulary words: *buried, escape, habitat, journey, nature, peeks, spies*.

**1 Explain** Explain to children that words have different forms. Help children generate different forms of this week's words by adding, changing, or removing inflectional endings *-ed*, *-ing*, and *-s* or *-es*. Review the meaning of each ending.

**2 Model** Draw a four-column T-chart on the board. Model how to add endings to the word *journey*. Write the vocabulary word *journey* in the first column. Then write *journeyed, journeying*, and *journeys* in the next three columns. Read aloud the words with children.

Point out how the different endings change the meaning of *journey*. Discuss each form of the word and its meaning.

Have children share aloud sentences using *journeyed, journeying*, and *journeys*.

**3 Guided Practice** Have children work in pairs to fill in charts for *habitat, peeks, escape, spies*, and *buried*. Then have children share sentences using different forms of the words.

### ENGLISH LANGUAGE LEARNERS

**More Practice** Practice spelling by helping children generate more words with soft *c* and *g*. Provide clues: It is frozen water. It rhymes with *mice*. Write the word and have children practice reading it. Correct their pronunciation, if needed.

## Monitor and *Differentiate*

 **Quick Check**

Can children read and spell words with soft *c* and *g*?
Can children read high-frequency words?

 **Small Group Instruction**

| | | |
|---|---|---|
| If No → | **Approaching** | Reteach pp. T250–T255 |
| | **ELL** | Develop pp. T266–T273 |
| If Yes → | **On Level** | Review pp. T260–T261 |
| | **Beyond Level** | Extend pp. T264–T265 |

# Comprehension Strategy

CLOSE READING

## MINILESSON 10 Mins

# Make, Confirm, Revise Predictions

### ❶ Explain

Remind children that a prediction is a reasonable guess about what might happen or what they might learn.

Readers base their predictions on what they have read in the text.

→ Readers can use pictures, headings, and key words, as well as the text, to make predictions.

→ Making predictions helps readers decide what to look for when reading.

→ If a prediction is not correct, it can be a sign that readers are confused. Readers can reread to find information they missed or misunderstood.

→ Readers revise their predictions to make sure they understand what they have read.

### ❷ Model Close Reading: Text Evidence

Model how to use text evidence to make predictions. Reread page 137 of "A Prairie Guard Dog." Say: *As I read page 137, I predicted that the badger would chase the prairie dog. What text evidence supports this prediction?* (When Pete sees the badger, he gives a warning cry. The caption on page 137 says that badgers hunt prairie dogs.) Continue by having children cite text evidence that confirms this prediction.

### ❸ Guided Practice of Close Reading

Have children work in pairs to talk about the predictions they made when they read page 138. Partners should reread the page to confirm or revise their predictions. Tell children to discuss other predictions they confirmed or revised.

**Go Digital**

**A Prairie Guard Dog**

**Present the Lesson**

**Comprehension Strategy**

# Make Predictions

Use what you already know and what you read in the selection to help you predict what you will learn about. As you read, you can confirm or revise your predictions.

 **Find Text Evidence**

*As I read page 137 of "A Prairie Guard Dog," I predicted that the badger will chase the prairie dog. I read on to see if my prediction was correct.*

page 137

**A Scare**

Oh no! Pete **spies** a large badger! When he sees it, he gives a loud bark, "Yap! Yap!" His family recognizes the warning. Some hide in tall grasses, and some jump into the burrow. The badger runs at Pete, but the watchful guard is able to **escape** into the burrow. I am glad he is able to get away from danger.

*On page 137, I read that the badger ran at Pete. My prediction was correct.*

**Your Turn** COLLABORATE

Reread page 138. What did you predict would happen next? Look for text clues to decide if your prediction was correct.

140

**READING/WRITING WORKSHOP, p. 140**

## ENGLISH LANGUAGE LEARNERS
### SCAFFOLD

| Beginning | Intermediate | Advanced/High |
|---|---|---|
| Help children reread the section "A Scare" on page 137. Point out difficult words or phrases such as *spies, badger, warning, burrow*, and *danger*. Use photos from the selection to help children understand words such as *badger* or *burrow*. Define and act out other word meanings. Help children replace words with words they know. | Have children reread the section "A Scare" on page 137. Ask, *How does a group of prairie dogs know when there is danger?* (The guard dog barks.) *What do prairie dogs do when the guard dog warns them of danger?* (They hide in tall grasses and burrows.) Clarify children's responses as needed. Then remind children to make and check predictions as they read. | Have children reread the section titled "A Scare" on page 137. Ask: *Why is the guard dog important to the other prairie dogs? Turn to a partner and explain.* Elicit more details to support children's answers. Remind children that making, confirming, and revising predictions can help them understand the selection. |

---

Read the passage. Use the make predictions strategy to predict what you will learn.

### Two Kinds of Tundra

**The Arctic Tundra**

3    Dr. Jones went to the **Arctic tundra**. It was very cold
14  with no trees. There were grasses and flowers. Dr. Jones
24  was hopeful that he would see animals. He made a
34  careful study of what he found.

40    In the sky, Dr. Jones saw playful **ravens** and **gulls**.
50  On the ground, he saw **gray wolves** and **Arctic**
59  **hares**. He knew that many of these animals had extra
69  fat. This was useful. It kept the animals warm during
79  the cold winter. Some of the animals slept while others
89  went south.

| APPROACHING pp. 73–75 | BEYOND pp. 73–75 | ELL pp. 73–75 · |
|---|---|---|

## Monitor and *Differentiate*

 **Quick Check**

**Do children make predictions as they read? Do they confirm and revise their predictions?**

### Small Group Instruction

| If No → | **Approaching** | Reteach pp. T248-T249 |
|---|---|---|
| | **ELL** | Develop pp. T266-T267 |
| If Yes → | **On Level** | Review pp. T258-T259 |
| | **Beyond Level** | Extend pp. T262-T263 |

# Comprehension Skill

CLOSE READING

MINILESSON **10** Mins

# Main Topic and Key Details

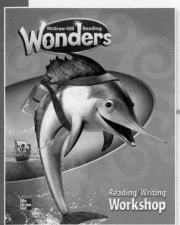

**Reading/Writing Workshop**

## OBJECTIVES

**CCSS** Ask and answer such questions as *who, what, where, when, why,* and *how* to demonstrate understanding of key details in a text. **RI 2.1**

**CCSS** Identify the main topic of a multi-paragraph text as well as the focus of specific paragraphs within the text. **RI.2.2**

## ACADEMIC LANGUAGE

*main topic, key details*

## ❶ Explain

Explain to children that the main topic is what the selection is mostly about. Key details are important facts and information that tell about the main topic.

## ❷ Model Close Reading: Text Evidence

Model identifying the main topic of "A Prairie Guard Dog." Then point out the key detail on the graphic organizer and lead children to see that it is a key detail because it gives an important fact about the main topic.

*Analytical Writing* **Write About Reading: Summary** Model for children how to use the notes from the graphic organizer and additional text evidence to write a summary of what they learned about how Pete keeps the other guard dogs safe. For example: *Pete watches for danger. He lets his family know when it is safe to come out. He also tells them when they should run away. He does this by making sounds such as "yip" and "yap."*

## ❸ Guided Practice of Close Reading

Have children work in pairs to complete the graphic organizer "A Prairie Guard Dog," going back into the text to find key details. Remind them that to identify key details, they should think about the main topic of the selection. Discuss each section as children complete the graphic organizer.

*Analytical Writing* **Write About Reading: Summary** Ask pairs to work together to write a summary of the section, "A Scare" on page 137. Encourage them to explain why the prairie dogs are scared, what Pete does, and how the prairie dogs stay safe.

## Go Digital

**A Prairie Guard Dog**

**Present the Lesson**

| Main Topic | | |
|---|---|---|
| Detail | Detail | Detail |

**Graphic Organizer**

## SKILLS TRACE

**Main Topic and Key Details**

**INTRODUCE** Unit 2 Week 3

**REVIEW** Unit 2 Week 4; Unit 3, Weeks 1, 3; Unit 4, Weeks 1, 2

**ASSESS** Unit 2

## Comprehension Skill CCSS

# Main Topic and Key Details

The main topic is what the selection is about. Key details give information about the main topic.

 **Find Text Evidence**

*As I read "A Prairie Guard Dog," I learn a lot about prairie dogs. This must be the main topic. On page 135, I learn a key detail about prairie dogs.*

| Main Topic |
|:---:|
| Prairie Dogs |

| Key Detail | Key Detail | Key Detail |
|---|---|---|
| A prairie dog acts as a guard. | | |

 **Your Turn**

Continue rereading the story. Fill in key details about the main topic on the graphic organizer.

*Go Digital!*
*Use the interactive graphic organizer*

141

**READING/WRITING WORKSHOP, p. 141**

 **ELL ENGLISH LANGUAGE LEARNERS SCAFFOLD**

### Beginning

Reread "Good Morning!" on pages 135 and 136. Ask after each sentence: *What is this sentence about?* Help children identify the main topic. *The main topic is what this section is mostly about. The main topic is ____.* (Pete's job guarding his family.) Repeat correct answers slowly to the class.

### Intermediate

Have children reread "Good Morning!" Ask: *What does Pete do in the morning? Why can't Pete rest??* Have partners describe the main topic of this section and key details. *The main topic is ____. The key details are ____.* Allow children ample time to respond.

### Advanced/High

Have children reread "Good Morning!"and list the main topic and key details. Then have them explain how they identified the main topic and key details to a partner. Encourage children to use the vocabulary words in their responses. Clarify children's answers as needed.

---

**ON-LEVEL PRACTICE BOOK** pp. 73–75

**A. Reread the passage and answer the questions.**

1. What is the main topic of the passage?

There are two kinds of tundra: Arctic and alpine.

2. What is a key detail about the Arctic tundra?

Possible response: The Arctic tundra has no trees, but it has grasses and flowers.

3. What is a key detail about the alpine tundra?

Possible response: Sheep and elk live in the alpine tundra.

**B. Work with a partner. Read the passage aloud. Pay attention to how you group words together as you read. Stop after one minute. Fill out the chart.**

| | Words Read | – | Number of Errors | = | Words Correct Score |
|---|---|---|---|---|---|
| First Read | | – | | = | |
| Second Read | | – | | = | |

| APPROACHING pp. 73–75 | BEYOND pp. 73–75 | ELL pp. 73–75 |
|---|---|---|

## Monitor and *Differentiate*

 **Quick Check**

As children complete the graphic organizer, do they determine the main topic? Do they list key details that are related to the main topic?

### Small Group Instruction

If No → **Approaching** Reteach pp. T256-T257

**ELL** Develop pp. T266-T269

If Yes → **On Level** Review pp. T260-T261

**Beyond Level** Extend pp. T264-T265

→ # Language Arts

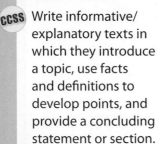
# Writing Traits: Organization

MINILESSON 5 Mins

**OBJECTIVES**

CCSS Write informative/ explanatory texts in which they introduce a topic, use facts and definitions to develop points, and provide a concluding statement or section. **W.2.2**

❶ **Explain** Remind children that writers use sequence to put their ideas in order. Sequence words such as *first, next, then,* and *last* help readers understand the order of ideas and events.

❷ **Model** Read aloud the model from Your Turn page 77. Then think aloud to model revising to put the ideas in a clear sequence.

I saw a white tiger when I visited the zoo last summer. It was a very hot day, and the white tiger was panting. He splashed around in a lake that surrounded his pen. Caretakers threw him giant ice cubes. He licked and ate the cubes that contained fruit. He moved to a shady area of his pen.

**Think Aloud** I don't have a clear picture in my mind of what happened first, next, *and so on.* I can add sequence words to show the order. I will revise the third sentence to say: *First, he splashed around in a lake that surrounded his pen.* Now readers know which event happened first.

❸ **Guided Practice** Invite partners to continue adding sequence words to the draft to make the writing easier to understand. Use the prompts on Your Turn page 77 as a guide.

## 📄 WRITING ENTRY: SEQUENCE

❶ **Revise** Have children review their writing from Day 1. Ask them to revise their responses by adding sequence words such as *first, next, then,* and *last* to help readers understand the order of ideas.

Use the Conferencing Routines to help children revise. Circulate among children and stop briefly to talk with individuals. Provide opportunities for partners to work together using the Peer Conferences routine.

❷ **Edit** Ask children to review the rules on Grammar Handbook pages 477–478 and check their use of nouns. Have children check for correct capitalization of proper nouns. Have children also check for errors in grammar, spelling, and punctuation.

## Conferencing Routines

**Teacher Conference**

**STEP 1** Talk about the strengths of the writing.
**STEP 2** Focus on the target trait.

**STEP 3** Make concrete suggestions for revisions.

**Peer Conferences**

Provide these questions to guide peers as they review a partner's draft.

☑ Is the writing clear and easy to understand?

☑ Which words show the order in which things happened?

☑ Where can other sequence words be added to make the writing clearer?

**Go Digital**

**Writing Model**

**Writing**

I see a fish.

**Grammar**

# Grammar

## Kinds of Nouns

**1** **Review** Remind children that a **common noun** names a person, place, or thing. A **proper noun** names a particular person, place, or thing. Remind children that a proper noun begins with a capital letter. Display the following sentence and guide children to identify the common and proper nouns.

Trina and her family will go to the zoo on the Fourth of July. (Trina—proper noun; family—common noun; zoo—common noun; Fourth of July—proper noun)

Tell children that a noun that names a group or collection of people, animals, or things is called a collective noun. Offer the following examples and explain: *flock (of birds), pack (of dogs or wolves), school (of fish)*. Point out that a school (of fish) is different from a school that children attend. The latter is a common noun.

**2** **Guided Practice/Practice** Display the following sentence, and have children sort the common, proper, and collective nouns.

Victor visited the aquarium in Newport and saw a huge school of fish. (Victor, Newport—proper nouns; aquarium, fish—common nouns; school—collective noun)

## Mechanics: Capital Letters

**1** **Review** Remind children that the names of the days of the week, the months of the year, and holidays all begin with a capital letter. Also review that an abbreviation is a shortened form of a word. An abbreviation begins with a capital letter and ends with a period. Remind children of the abbreviations for titles (*Mr., Mrs., Ms., Dr., Jr., Sr.*); addresses (*St., Ave., Rd.*); and the days of the week and the months of the year.

**2** **Practice** Write the following sentence on the board. Have pairs rewrite the sentence, beginning the proper nouns with a capital letter.

leah will go to the zoo on maple street on saturday. (Leah will go to the Zoo on Maple Street on Saturday.)

dr. radin helped the injured bird.

(Dr. Radin helped the injured bird.)

# Daily Wrap Up

→ Discuss the Essential Question and encourage children to use the oral vocabulary words.

→ Prompt children to review and discuss the skills they used today. How do those skills help them?

## Materials

**Reading/Writing Workshop**

**Literature Anthology "Turtle, Turtle, Watch Out!"**

**buried**

**Visual Vocabulary Cards**

buried    nature
escape    peeks
habitat   restless
journey   spies

**Interactive Read-Aloud Cards**

**a  b  c**

**Word-Building Cards**

**almost**

**High-Frequency Word Cards**

**badge**

**Spelling Word Cards**

**Sound-Spelling Cards**

→ # Build the Concept

MINILESSON
**5** Mins

# Interactive Read Aloud

## OBJECTIVES

CCSS Ask and answer such questions as *who, what, where, when, why,* and *how* to demonstrate understanding of key details in a text. **RI.2.1**

CCSS Use information gained from the illustrations and words in a print or digital text to demonstrate understanding of its character, setting, or plot. **RL.2.7**

- Develop oral language.
- Discuss the Essential Question.

## ACADEMIC LANGUAGE

*key details, illustrations*

**ESSENTIAL QUESTION**

Remind children that this week they are talking and reading about animal habitats. Remind them of the animal habitats in "Explore a Coral Reef" and "A Prairie Guard Dog." Guide children to discuss the Essential Question using information from what they have read and discussed throughout the week.

## Review Oral Vocabulary

Review the oral vocabulary words *defend, encounter, located, positive,* and *react* using the Define/Example/Ask routine. Encourage children to discuss animals and their habitats when coming up with examples for each word.

## Reread "Explore a Coral Reef"

Tell children that you will reread "Explore a Coral Reef." Pause as you read to model making, confirming, and revising predictions. Prompt children to describe the key details about the coral reef habitat and how the animals make it their home.

**Interactive Read-Aloud Cards**

 **Write About Reading**

Have children write a few sentences about the animals of the coral reef and how the features of that habitat help them survive. Remind children to include key details from the text.

**Go Digital**

**Explore a Coral Reef**

**A Prairie Guard Dog**

# Comprehension

**10 Mins**

## Key Details

**① Explain** Remind children that this week they have been learning about identifying the main topic and key details to understand a text. Remind them that they have also learned to use photos and illustrations to identify and understand key details. Use the Shared Read, "A Prairie Guard Dog," to review this skill.

Review the definitions of the terms *key detail* and *illustration*:

→ A key detail is an important bit of information that helps readers understand more about the story.

→ An illustration is a picture in a story.

**② Model** Read and display page 135 of "A Prairie Guard Dog." *The photo gives me key details about prairie dogs and where they live. For example, the photo helps me picture what the text means when it says, "A prairie has a lot of grasses but few trees." The photo helps me understand why there are few places to hide in the prairie. The photo also shows me what prairie dogs look like and that they live in underground burrows.*

**③ Guided Practice** Reread the rest of "A Prairie Guard Dog" with children. Prompt children to answer questions about key details by using the photos and illustrations.

→ Read and display page 136. Ask: *What does the prairie dog look like when it is looking around for danger? What else do you learn from the photo and the caption below it?*

→ Read and display page 137. Say: *Here is a picture of a badger, one of the prairie dog's predators. What do the photo and caption tell you about the badger?*

→ Read page 138 and display the illustration. Ask: *What does this illustration show? How does it help you to understand what the prairie dog's burrow is like?*

→ # Word Work

MINILESSON **5** Mins
## Phonemic Awareness

**OBJECTIVES**

CCSS Know and apply grade-level phonics and word analysis skills in decoding words. **RF.2.3**

CCSS Decode words with common prefixes and suffixes. **RF.2.3d**

CCSS Demonstrate command of the conventions of standard English capitalization, punctuation, and spelling when writing. **L.2.2**

CCSS Generalize learned spelling patterns when writing words (e.g., cage → badge; boy → boil). **L.2.2d**

Blend phonemes to form new words.

**ACADEMIC LANGUAGE**
*blend, prefix, root word*

### Phoneme Blending

❶ **Model** Place markers in the WorkBoard to represent sounds. Show children how to orally blend phonemes. *I'm going to put one marker in each box as I say each sound. Then I will blend the sounds to form a word.* Place a marker for each sound you say. */p/ /ā/ /j/.* This word has three sounds. */p/ /ā/ /j/.* Listen as I blend these sounds to form a word: */pāāāj/,* page. *The word is* page.

❷ **Guided Practice/Practice** *Let's do some together. Using your own boards, place a marker for each sound you hear. I will say one sound at a time. Then we will blend the sounds to say the word.* Do the first three with children.

| | | |
|---|---|---|
| cage | hinge | trace |
| rice | space | dodge |
| dance | place | wage |

MINILESSON **5** Mins
## Phonics

### Blend Words with Soft *c* and *g*

❶ **Model** Display the Word-Building Cards *r, a, n, g, e.* Review soft *g* using the word *range.* Model how to blend the sounds. Say: *Let's blend this word together. This is the letter* r. *It stands for the sound /r/. This is the letter* a. *It stands for the sound /ā/. This is the letter* n. *It stands for the /n/ sound. This is the letter* g *followed by a silent* e. *It makes the /j/ sound. Let's blend the sounds together: /rrrāāānnnj/. The word is* range.

Continue by modeling the words *huge, cage,* and *nice.*

❷ **Guided Practice/Practice** Repeat the routine with *badge, ace, edge,* and *ice.*

## Go Digital

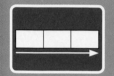

**Phonemic Awareness**

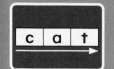

**Phonics**

**Structural Analysis**

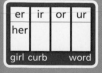

**Spelling Word Sort**

# Structural Analysis

## Prefixes

**❶ Model** Write *make, cut,* and *like* on the board. Blend the sounds in the words.

→ Add prefixes to the words to form *remake, uncut,* and *dislike.* Circle the prefix in each word. Say: *The word* remake *has the prefix* re- *and the root word* make. *The prefix* -re *means "again." * Remake *means to make again. The prefixes* un- *and* dis- *mean "not" or "the opposite of." * Point to and read the words *uncut* and *dislike.* Discuss the meaning of each word.

**❷ Guided Practice/Practice** Help children circle the prefix and underline the root in each of the following words *unlock, repack, distrust,* and *remix.* Guide them to blend the prefix with the root word to read the whole word. Have children discuss the meaning of each word.

# Spelling

## Soft *c* and *g*

**❶ Model** Make index cards for *ce* and *ge* and place them in columns in a pocket chart. Point out that the spelling *ce* has the soft *c* sound /s/, and the spelling *ge* has the soft *g* sound /j/.

Hold up the *trace* Spelling Word Card. Say and spell it. Pronounce each sound clearly: /t/ /r/ /ā/ /s/. Blend the sounds, emphasizing the soft *c* sound. Place it in the *ce* column in the pocket chart. Repeat with *cage,* emphasizing the soft *g* sound and placing it in the *ge* column.

**❷ Guided Practice/Practice** Read and spell each spelling word together with children. Have children identify the soft *c* or *g* sound and place the word in the correct column in the chart.

Conclude by asking children to orally generate additional words that rhyme with each word. Write the additional words on the board. Underline the common spelling patterns in the additional words. If necessary, point out the differences and explain why they are unusual.

---

**PHONICS/SPELLING PRACTICE BOOK** p. 38

| trace | place | badge | cage | space |
| ice | bulge | range | barge | mice |

**A. Word Sort**
Look at the spelling words in the box. Fill in the blanks below with spelling words that match each spelling pattern.

| Soft *c* spelled *ce* | | Soft *g* spelled *ge* | |
|---|---|---|---|
| 1. _trace_ | | 6. _badge_ | |
| 2. _place_ | | 7. _cage_ | |
| 3. _space_ | | 8. _bulge_ | |
| 4. _ice_ | | 9. _range_ | |
| 5. _mice_ | | 10. _barge_ | |

**B. Compare Words**
Look at each set of words. Circle the letters that are the same.

11. tra(ce)  mi(ce)
12. bul(ge)  ran(ge)
13. i(ce)  spa(ce)
14. ca(ge)  bul(ge)
15. spa(ce)  tra(ce)

## Monitor and *Differentiate*

## ✓ Quick Check

Can children blend and read words with soft *c* and *g*?

⬇

## Small Group Instruction

| If No → | **Approaching** | Reteach pp. T250–T255 |
| | **ELL** | Develop pp. T266–T273 |
| If Yes → | **On Level** | Review pp. T260–T261 |
| | **Beyond Level** | Extend pp. T264–T265 |

→ # Fluency

**MINILESSON 10 Mins**

# Phrasing

## OBJECTIVES

**CCSS** Demonstrate understanding of word relationships and nuances in word meanings. **L.2.5**

**CCSS** Identify real-life connections between words and their use (e.g., describe foods that are *spicy* or *juicy*). **L.2.5a**

**CCSS** Read with sufficient accuracy and fluency to support comprehension. **RF.2.4**

**CCSS** Read on-level text orally with accuracy, appropriate rate, and expression on successive readings. **RF.2.4.b**

• Practice fluency.

• Use vocabulary words in context.

❶ **Explain** Explain that part of reading with proper phrasing means grouping words together in a natural way as you read. Punctuation helps you to read with proper phrasing. Pause for a short time at a comma and for a longer time at a period, exclamation point, or question mark. Tell children that when you read with natural phrasing your voice pauses, rises, and falls as it does when you are speaking in your usual voice.

❷ **Model** Model prosody by reading the first paragraph on page 135 of the Shared Read ("A Prairie Guard Dog") aloud. Model grouping words together in phrases. Point out how you pause for a shorter time after a comma and for a longer time for punctuation at the end of each sentence. Model reading at an appropriate rate and with accuracy.

❸ **Guided Practice** Have children read the second paragraph on page 135 aloud to a partner. Make sure they pay attention to using the proper phrasing. Offer corrective feedback as necessary.

## Fluency Practice FLUENCY

Children can practice fluency using the Practice Book passages.

## Go Digital

peered

Visual Glossary

# → Vocabulary

## Reinforce Vocabulary

**MINILESSON 5 Mins**

**1 Guided Practice** Use the Visual Vocabulary Cards to review this week's and last week's vocabulary words: *buried, escape, habitat, journey, nature, peeks, restless, spies, believe, delicious, feast, fond, lessons, remarkable, snatch, stories*. Work together with children to generate a new context sentence for each word.

**2 Practice** Have children work with partners to orally complete each sentence stem using this week's and last week's vocabulary words.

1. It is a long _____ across the sea by boat. (journey)
2. Are you _____ of hiking, too? (fond)
3. Watch the bird _____ the fish from the pond! (snatch)
4. Daisy _____ at the clock to see the time. (peeks)
5. The actor felt _____ before the big show. (restless)
6. Bert _____ his cat hiding under the bed. (spies)
7. Will the dog _____ by digging under the fence? (escape)
8. My book was _____ under all the clothes on my bed. (buried)
9. I _____ it will be a hot day. (believe)
10. This cake tastes _____! (delicious)
11. I felt full after the big _____. (feast)
12. That huge pumpkin is _____! (remarkable)
13. I asked my mom if I could take piano _____. (lessons)
14. The polar bear lives in a cold _____. (habitat)
15. My grandfather tells us many _____. (stories)
16. There are many different types of plants in _____. (nature)

# Genre: Informational Text

CLOSE READING

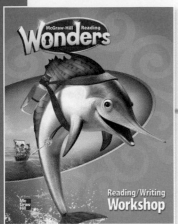

**Reading/Writing Workshop**

**OBJECTIVES**

CCSS Know and use various text features (e.g., captions, bold print, subheadings, glossaries, indexes, electronic menus, icons) to locate key facts or information in a text efficiently. **RI.2.5**

Recognize the features of narrative nonfiction.

**ACADEMIC LANGUAGE**
• *narrative nonfiction, headings, bold print*
• Cognate: *narrativa*

**MINILESSON**

**10 Mins**

# Narrative Nonfiction

## ❶ Explain

Share with children the following key characteristics of **narrative nonfiction**.

→ Narrative nonfiction tells about living things, people, or events.

→ Narrative nonfiction includes text features such as headings, bold print, photographs and captions, diagrams, maps, and timelines.

→ Narrative nonfiction is told by a narrator and follows a sequence.

## ❷ Model Close Reading: Text Evidence

Model identifying the genre of "A Prairie Guard Dog." *I can tell that this is informational text. It gives facts and information about a living thing, the prairie guard dog. A narrator, who is on a journey, tells the story. The text follows a sequence, or order, of events in the day of a life of Pete, the prairie guard dog.*

**Headings** Explain that headings tell what a section is mostly about. Point out the heading "Break Time" on page 138. Ask: *Why is "Break Time" a good heading for this section?* (The section describes the underground home where Pete and the other prairie dogs go to sleep and eat in the middle of the day.)

**Bold Print** Point out the word *tunnels*, which is in bold print on page 138. Explain that writers often use bold print to point out important ideas or key terms that will help readers understand the text. Ask: *Why do you think the writer put this word in bold print? How does understanding the word help you understand how and where prairie dogs live?*

## ❸ Guided Practice of Close Reading

Have children work with partners to find other examples of headings and bold print in "A Prairie Guard Dog" and discuss what they learned from these text features. Then have them share their ideas with the class.

**Go Digital**

**Present the Lesson**

**Genre** Informational Text

# Narrative Nonfiction

"A Prairie Guard Dog" is narrative nonfiction.
A **Narrative Nonfiction**:
- tells about living things, people, or events.
- is told by a narrator and follows a sequence.

 **Find Text Evidence**

*I can use what I read to tell that "A Prairie Guard Dog" is a narrative nonfiction. A narrator tells the story about what real prairie dogs do.*

**page 138**

**Break Time**

The sun gets higher, and it is hot now. The prairie dogs slip into their deep burrow where it is cooler. Even Pete goes in. **Tunnels**, like hallways, lead to different areas. There is a sleeping room. There is a room used like a bathroom. The prairie dogs cover up roots and seeds in one room. Later, they eat the **buried** food there.

**Text Features**

**Headings** Headings tell what a section of text is mostly about.

**Bold Print** These words are important to understanding the text.

**Your Turn** COLLABORATE

Identify text features on a different page. Tell what information you learned from these features.

142

**READING/WRITING WORKSHOP, p. 142**

## A C T Access Complex Text

▶ **Genre**

Some children may have an incomplete understanding of the text because they ignore or fail to connect text features with the rest of the selection. Have children look at the chart on page 139

→ *How does the chart help you understand why the prairie might be dangerous for prairie dogs?* (The chart lists five different predators that could harm prairie dogs. The chart also shows that prairie dogs are small.)

→ *What other information does the chart give that you did not get from the rest of the selection?* (Possible response: The chart tells you that prairie dogs eat leaves and roots.)

---

**ON-LEVEL PRACTICE BOOK** p. 78

### In the Cave

The scientist enters the cave. It is cold and dim. She spies **shrimp** and **cave beetles**. These animals never leave the cave. Then she sees a **snail**. It may leave the cave at times.

| Cave Animals | |
|---|---|
| Always live in caves: cave shrimp, cave beetle, and cave fish. | Sometimes live in caves: snail, spider, and worm. |

Answer the questions about the text.

1. How can you tell that this text is narrative nonfiction?
   It gives facts about animals in a cave. A narrator tells it in sequence.

2. What happens after the scientist sees shrimp and cave beetles?
   She sees a snail.

3. Why are the words **shrimp**, **cave beetles**, and **snail** in bold print?
   They are key vocabulary words that help readers understand the text.

4. What information can you get from the chart?

| APPROACHING p. 78 | BEYOND p. 78 | ELL p. 78 |
|---|---|---|

## Monitor and *Differentiate*

 **Quick Check**

Are children able to identify the text features in "A Prairie Guard Dog"? Can they tell what they learned from these text features?

### Small Group Instruction

If No → **Approaching** Reteach pp. T248-T249

**ELL** Develop pp. T266-T269

If Yes → **On Level** Review pp. T258-T259

**Beyond Level** Extend pp. T262-T263

# Vocabulary Strategy

CLOSE READING

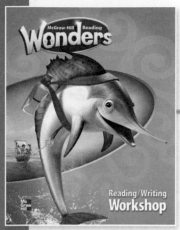

**Reading/Writing Workshop**

## OBJECTIVES

**CCSS** Determine or clarify the meaning of unknown and multiple-meaning words and phrases based on *grade 2 reading and content,* choosing flexibly from an array of strategies. **L.2.4**

**CCSS** Determine the meaning of the new word formed when a known prefix is added to a known word (e.g., *happy/unhappy, tell/ retell*). **L.2.4b**

## ACADEMIC LANGUAGE
- *suffix*
- Cognate: *sufijo*

### SKILLS TRACE

**Word Parts: Suffix**

**INTRODUCE** Unit 2, Week 2

**REVIEW** Unit 2 Week 3; Unit 4 Week 4; Unit 5, Weeks 1, 2

**ASSESS** Units 2, 5

## MINILESSON 10 Mins — Suffixes

### ❶ Explain

Tell children that they can often figure out the meaning of an unknown word by looking at **word parts**. Remind them that a suffix is a word part that can be added to the end of a root word to make a new word and that the suffix changes the meaning of the root word. Review the meanings of the suffixes *-ly* and *-ful*.

→ The suffix *-ly* makes a word that describes a way we do something. For example, if we talk *quietly*, this means we talk in a quiet way.

→ The suffix *-ful* means "full of." If we say that someone is *hopeful*, that means that they are full of hope.

→ If a word has a suffix, children can separate the root word from the suffix to determine the word's meaning.

### ❷ Model Close Reading: Text Evidence

Model using the suffix to figure out the meaning of *loudly* on page 135. Say: *I'm not sure what the word* loudly *means. The word* loud *means "full of noise." The suffix -ly means in a certain way. I think* loudly *means "in a noisy way." That word meaning makes sense in the orginal sentence. Pete would call in a noisy way so that the other prairie dogs would hear him.*

### ❸ Guided Practice of Close Reading

COLLABORATE

Have children work in pairs to figure out the meanings of *safely, watchful,* and *finally* in "A Prairie Guard Dog." Encourage partners to find the root words and suffixes in each word to help them figure out the meanings. Remind children to check whether or not the meaning they have found makes sense in the sentence in which the word was used.

## Go Digital

**Present the Lesson**

## Vocabulary Strategy CCSS

# Suffixes

A suffix is a word part or syllable added to the end of a word. You can separate the root word from a suffix, such as *-ful* or *-ly*, to figure out what the word means.

### Find Text Evidence

*I'm not sure what the word* loudly *means. The root word is* loud, *which means "full of noise." The suffix is* -ly *which means "in a certain way." I think the word* loudly *means "in a noisy way."*

Then, Pete calls loudly to his family, "Yip!"

### Your Turn

COLLABORATE

Use suffixes to figure out the meanings of these words in "A Prairie Guard Dog."
**safely,** *page 136*
**watchful,** *page 137*
**finally,** *page 139*

143

Corbis Flirt/Alamy

**READING/WRITING WORKSHOP, p. 143**

---

### ON-LEVEL PRACTICE BOOK p. 79

To figure out a new word, look for a **suffix,** or word part added to the end of the word.
The suffix *-ful* means "full of."
The suffix *-ly* means "in a way that is."

**A. Underline the word that has a suffix in each sentence. Then write the word and its meaning.**

1. Dr. Jones was hopeful that he would see animals.
   hopeful- full of hope

2. He made a careful study of what he found.
   careful- full of care

3. He was greatly interested in comparing the two places.
   greatly- in a way that is great, very

**B. Write a word that means the same as the group of words. Your new word will end in *-ful* or *-ly*.**

4. full of play
   playful

5. in way that is clear
   clearly

| APPROACHING p. 79 | BEYOND p. 79 | ELL p. 79 |
|---|---|---|

---

## ENGLISH LANGUAGE LEARNERS
### ELL SCAFFOLD

| Beginning | Intermediate | Advanced/High |
|---|---|---|
| Point out the words *safely* (page 136), *watchful* (page 137), and *finally* (page 139). Help children separate the root word from the suffix. Define each word part for them. Help children replace the words with words they know. | Point out the words *safely, watchful,* and *finally.* Review the suffixes and root words and guide children to give the meaning of each word. Point out cognates such as *finalmente* (finally) and ask children how they help them understand the words. Clarify children's responses as needed. | Point out the words *safely, watchful,* and *finally,* and ask children to define them. Have them explain how they used their knowledge of root words and suffixes to understand the meaning of the words. |

---

## Monitor and *Differentiate*

### ✓ Quick Check

Can children identify and use suffixes to determine the meanings of *safely, watchful,* and *finally*?

### Small Group Instruction

If No → **Approaching** Reteach pp. T248–T257
        **ELL** Develop pp. T270–T271
If Yes → **On Level** Review pp. T260–T261
        **Beyond Level** Extend pp. T264–T265

**CCSS Genre • Narrative Nonfiction**

# Turtle, Turtle, Watch Out!

By **April Pulley Sayre**

Illustrated by **Annie Patterson**

**? Essential Question**

**What are features of different animal habitats?**

Read about sea turtles that live in the ocean.

 **Go Digital!**

165

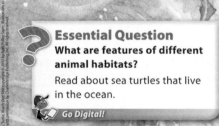

**Literature Anthology**

**LITERATURE ANTHOLOGY, pp. 164–165**

# Develop Comprehension

**CLOSE READING**

**Lexile** 520
*TextEvaluator* 13

## Read Literature Anthology

**Review Genre: Narrative Nonfiction** Review with children the main characteristics of nonfiction narrative:

→ tells about living things, people, or events.

→ is told by a narrator and follows a sequence.

→ has text features such as headings and bold print.

**Preview and Predict** Read the title and look at the illustration on pages 164 and 165. *What do you think this selection is going to be about? Why might Turtle have to watch out? Let's find out.*

**ESSENTIAL QUESTION**

Read aloud the Essential Question: What are the features of different animal habitats? Tell children that as they read, they should think about the many habitats where animals live.

**Story Words** Read and spell the words *raccoon* and *hatch*. Make sure that children are familiar with a raccoon. Tell children *to hatch* means "to break an egg and a baby animal is born." Many animal babies hatch out of an egg. Tell children they will read these words in the selection.

 **Analytical Writing** **Note Taking: Graphic Organizer**

As children read the selection, guide them to fill in **Your Turn Practice Book page 76.**

**1** Late one night, on a beach in Florida, a baby turtle's story begins. It could be a short story—or no story at all—if not for helping hands.

Turtle is only an egg now. Her mother's flippers cover her with sand.

Hungry raccoons watch. And when Mother Turtle crawls back to sea . . .

Furry feet scurry. Noses sniff. Paws dig.

## Turtle, Turtle, watch out!

Young hands, holding a flashlight, scare the bandits away.

166    167

**LITERATURE ANTHOLOGY,** pp. 166–167

## **1** Skill: Main Topic and Key Details

Often, the author lets us know the main topic at the beginning of the selection. Read the first paragraph. What do you think is the topic of this selection? (the life of a sea turtle) Let's write that in the Main Topic section of our graphic organizer.

| Main Topic The life of a sea turtle | | |
|---|---|---|
| Detail | Detail | Detail |
|  |  |  |

## A C T  Access Complex Text

▶ **What Makes This Text Complex?**

**Purpose of the Text**  The purpose of the selection is to provide information about how sea turtles survive in their habitat. Identifying key details will help the reader to understand a sea turtle habitat.

**Connections of Ideas**  Children may need help connecting ideas. Guide children to understand that the repeated sentence "Turtle, Turtle, watch out!" is used to indicate things that are a danger to the turtle.

They place wire mesh around the turtle nest to protect the **buried** eggs.

Morning comes. So does a car. It speeds toward the eggs.

## Turtle, Turtle, watch out!

The car stops. Hands have put up a painted sign. NO DRIVING ON THE BEACH, the sign says. The car leaves. The turtle nest is safe and undisturbed. Turtle sees none of this, inside her egg.

168

169

**LITERATURE ANTHOLOGY, pp. 168–169**

# Develop Comprehension

CLOSE READING

## 2 Reread

**Teacher Think Aloud** After reading pages 168 and 169, I'm not sure why the people are putting wire around the nest. I know that when I read I can get information from the text and the illustrations. I can paraphrase what I read to help me better understand what is happening. After rereading, looking at the illustrations, and putting what I read into my own words, I begin to understand that there are many dangers to the turtle nest and the people are trying to help protect it.

## 3 Strategy: Make Predictions

**Teacher Think Aloud** The clues in the text and illustrations tell me that there are many dangers to the turtle nest and that the people are trying to protect the buried eggs. I can make a prediction. I predict that the turtle nest will remain safe and the eggs will hatch. I will keep reading to confirm my prediction.

Two months later, Turtle begins to tear her leathery eggshell. She rips it open with a special tooth. She rocks and wiggles to escape. Then she rests, still half in her shell. Her yolk sac, attached to the bottom of her shell, shrinks as her body absorbs its energy.

A day later, nudging and pushing, she and the other hatchlings dig toward the surface. They scramble, then rest. Scramble, then rest. Their upward journey takes three whole days.

170

Finally, on a moonlit August night, Turtle **peeks** out of the sand. Other hatchlings below her are pushing her upward. All around her, the hatchlings dig out.

Pushing against the sand, Turtle crawls across the beach. Go to the light! That's all Turtle knows. At night the brightest light should be the horizon over the sea.

④

Tonight it is not. Turtle crawls toward the wrong light, shining from across the street.

## Turtle, Turtle, watch out!

**STOP AND CHECK**

**Make Predictions** Where do you think Turtle will crawl to? Make a prediction about what will happen.

171

**LITERATURE ANTHOLOGY,** pp. 170–171

## ④ Skill: Main Topic and Key Details

On these pages we read about an important detail in the life of the sea turtle. What happens? Let's add the first detail to our graphic organizer.

| Main Topic | | |
|---|---|---|
| The life of a sea turtle | | |
| **Detail** | **Detail** | **Detail** |
| The turtle hatches and crawls toward the light. | | |

**STOP AND CHECK**

**Make Predictions** Where do you think Turtle will crawl to? Make a prediction about what will happen. (Possible Answer: The illustration shows a light shining from the house. The text says Turtle is crawling towards the wrong light. I think Turtle will crawl toward the house and away from the water. )

**⑤** Small hands switch off the light. Turtle turns and crawls the other way. She scurries toward the ocean waves.

Step by step, she **journeys** down the beach. Animals gather: night herons, cats, and raccoons. They are hungry and are here to eat the hatchlings.

## Turtle, Turtle, watch out!

Quickly, Turtle scoots to the water. *Whoosh!* Water picks her up and carries her seaward, then pushes her back toward the beach. *Whoosh!* Waves tumble her tiny body, then carry her to sea again. She pushes her flippers. She can swim! She swims past hungry fish. Currents catch her and carry her far from shore.

172

173

**LITERATURE ANTHOLOGY, pp. 172–173**

# Develop Comprehension  CLOSE READING

 **CONNECT TO CONTENT**
**ANIMAL HABITATS**

A habitat is a place where plants and animals live. Animals can find the food, homes, and water they need to survive. There are many kinds of habitats. Different animals need different habitats to live. Above, children read about a sea turtle's habitat and how the sea turtle survives and uses its habitat to meet its basic needs.

**STEM**

**⑤ Strategy: Make Predictions**

**Teacher Think Aloud** I can confirm my earlier prediction that the baby sea turtle would hatch. We have read about a lot of dangers the sea turtle must face. What other dangers do you predict she will face now that she is living in the ocean?

**Student Think Aloud** I have already read about many creatures that want to eat her. I predict she will face more predators in the ocean, such as fish and birds. Other dangers might also be people, boats, and pollution.

For months, she drifts in patches of seaweed. She dines on tiny plants and animals. She grows. Currents carry her thousands of miles, circling an ocean wide, until one day she leaves the floating sargassum, a mass of algae. She begins to swim. Past islands. Past sailfish. Past humpback whales.

She reaches a coral reef, where she **spies** a tasty ❻ jellyfish. . . .

## Turtle, Turtle, watch out!

*Splash!* Quick hands dip down, grabbing the plastic bag. It looks like a jellyfish, but it is not. It could choke a turtle or clog its belly. ❼

174

175

**LITERATURE ANTHOLOGY,** pp. 174–175

## ❻ Suffixes

As you try to figure out the meaning of unknown words, one strategy is to use the root word and suffix to determine meaning. If you didn't know the meaning of the word *tasty* on page 174, look at the root word *taste* and the suffix *-y*, which means "having" or "full of" to figure it out. What is the meaning of the word *tasty*? (*Taste* also means *flavor*. The suffix *-y* means "having" or "full of." So *tasty* must mean "having good flavor." That makes sense in the sentence.)

## ❼ Skill: Main Topic and Key Details

COLLABORATE

Turn to a partner and discuss what key details you read on pages 174–175. Add them to your Main Topic and Key Details Chart.

| Main Topic | | |
|---|---|---|
| The life of a sea turtle | | |
| Detail | Detail | Detail |
| The turtle hatches and crawls toward the light. | The turtle drifts on the ocean currents, eats, and grows. | |

Turtle swims onward. She looks for other food. As she grows, her jaws crack open conchs, crabs, and clams. For twenty years this is her turtle life . . . until one day she feels **restless**.

It is time for her to travel, far and fast. She flaps her flippers like underwater wings. She swims and swims—past ships, sailing and sunken.

Three sharks see her.

176

## Turtle, Turtle, watch out! ⑨

**STOP AND CHECK**

**Make Predictions** What do you think will happen with the sharks? Make a prediction about what will happen.

177

**LITERATURE ANTHOLOGY, pp. 176–177**

# Develop Comprehension
 CLOSE READING

### ⑧ Maintain Skill: Key Details

Discuss with your partner how the illustration on pages 176 and 177 helps you to understand the kind of danger the turtle is in. (The illustration shows three sharks. It helps me to understand what the sharks look like and that the turtle is outnumbered.)

### ⑨ Author's Craft: Text Features

Author's often use large, boldface text to get readers to pay attention to important information. What do you think the writer wants you to know with the line, *Turtle, Turtle, watch out?*

**STOP AND CHECK**

**Make Predictions** What do you think will happen with the sharks? Make a prediction about what will happen. (The text says that three sharks see Turtle. But it also says that Turtle can swim fast and far. I think Turtle will swim fast and get away from the sharks.)

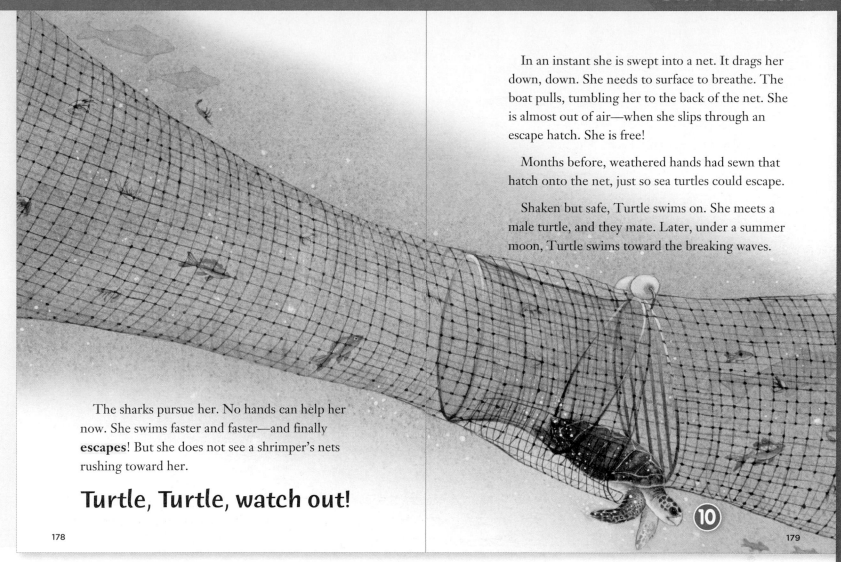

In an instant she is swept into a net. It drags her down, down. She needs to surface to breathe. The boat pulls, tumbling her to the back of the net. She is almost out of air—when she slips through an escape hatch. She is free!

Months before, weathered hands had sewn that hatch onto the net, just so sea turtles could escape.

Shaken but safe, Turtle swims on. She meets a male turtle, and they mate. Later, under a summer moon, Turtle swims toward the breaking waves.

The sharks pursue her. No hands can help her now. She swims faster and faster—and finally **escapes**! But she does not see a shrimper's nets rushing toward her.

## Turtle, Turtle, watch out!

178

179

⑩

**LITERATURE ANTHOLOGY, pp. 178–179**

---

### ⑩ Maintain Skill: Key Details

Turn to your partner and tell how the illustration on page 179 helps you to understand what an escape hatch is and how it helps the turtle. (The illustration shows the turtle swimming out of a large hole in the fishing net. The escape hatch is a space in the fishing net that is big enough for the turtle to swim out of so she can surface to breathe.)

### A C T Access Complex Text

▶ **Connections of Ideas**

Children may need help making connections to ideas that the author does not explicitly explain.

→ On page 178, guide children to understand that the net comes from a boat that is fishing for shrimp. The shrimp fishermen don't intend to catch the turtle.

→ On page 179, the author doesn't say who sewed the escape hatch into the net or why. Lead them to infer that the shrimp fishermen sewed the hatch so turtles and other large creatures could escape the net.

Thud! Her heavy body hits the hard shore. It is the same beach where she hatched. But now things are different: now she is a mother turtle, about to lay her eggs.

One day those eggs will hatch. The tiny turtles will begin their journeys, scrambling across the sand. And some will make it, with a little luck, and fast-moving flippers, and the help of many hands.

180

181

**LITERATURE ANTHOLOGY, pp. 180–181**

# Develop Comprehension

## Skill: Main Topic and Key Details

So far, we have identified the topic and key details about the turtle's life. What does the turtle do after 20 years of living in the ocean? Let's add that last key detail to our Main Topic and Key Details Chart.

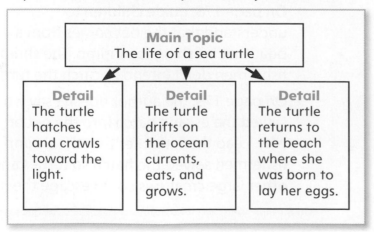

**Main Topic**
The life of a sea turtle

| **Detail** | **Detail** | **Detail** |
|---|---|---|
| The turtle hatches and crawls toward the light. | The turtle drifts on the ocean currents, eats, and grows. | The turtle returns to the beach where she was born to lay her eggs. |

## Return to Predictions and Purposes

Review children's predictions. Ask children if their predictions about the selection were correct. Guide them to use evidence in the text to confirm whether or not their predictions turned out to be accurate. Discuss what children learned about the features of the sea turtle's habitat by reading the selection. Did children learn what they wanted to by reading the selection?

**LITERATURE ANTHOLOGY, p. 182**

# Meet the Author and Illustrator

## April Pulley Sayre

Read aloud page 182. Ask them why they think April Pulley Sayre chose to write about sea turtles. *What other animals might she write about?*

## Annie Patterson

*Annie Patterson enjoys watching the ocean and animals where she lives. How do you think this might have helped her to illustrate this selection?*

## Author's Purpose

Have children write in their Response Journals about why the author repeated the sentence, "Turtle, Turtle, watch out!"

## AUTHOR'S CRAFT

### Repetition

Explain that authors use repetition to make readers notice something in the text that is important. Point out the sentence "Turtle, Turtle, watch out!" repeated throughout the text. Explain that it is used to emphasize that there are many dangers the turtle faces.

→ Flip through the text and have children identify the specific danger the turtle faces each time "Turtle, Turtle, watch out!" is repeated. Tell children that they can use repetition in their own writing.

**LITERATURE ANTHOLOGY, p. 183**

# Respond to Reading

## Summarize

Guide children through the steps to summarize.

→ First, tell the topic of the selection.

→ Next, select important details from each section of the text. Make sure to use only important details that relate to the main topic about events and dangers in the turtle's life as she grows up.

→ Use the details to state the summary in the correct order from beginning to end.

# Text Evidence

Guide children to use text evidence to answer the Text Evidence questions on **Literature Anthology**, page183. Model answering the question as needed.

1. **Genre**  To answer this question, let's look back at the selection. On each page, we read facts about living things, sea turtles. The story is told by a narrator and follows the sequence of the sea turtle's life. I know from those traits that this is a narrative nonfiction text.

2. **Main Topic and Key Details**  A turtle faces many dangers as it grows up. Some dangers are other animals. Some are things people do. Evidence I read that raccoons might eat the eggs before they hatch. Lights that humans use sometimes make hatchlings crawl the wrong way. Turtles can choke on plastic bags or get caught in fishing nets.

3. **Suffixes**  Suffixes are word parts added to the end of a word to change the word's meaning. To figure out the meaning of the word *restless*, I can separate the suffix from the root word. In the word *restless*, the root word is *rest*. The suffix -*less* means "without". The word *restless* must mean "without rest ".

 4. **Writing About Reading**  People do many different things to help turtles survive. The selection uses the word *hands* when telling about what people do. Evidence I read that hands hold flashlights to scare away raccoons, place mesh around the eggs, put up signs about not driving on the beach, and sew escape hatches into nets.

 # Make Connections

## ESSENTIAL QUESTION

Have partners list the features of the ocean habitat where turtles live. Ask: What food and shelter does the ocean provide?

**Text-to-World**  Have children discuss the ways that people have helped sea turtles survive. Point out that hands hold flashlights to scare away raccoons. Humans also put wire mesh around the eggs, pull a plastic bag from the ocean, and sew escape hatches into a net.

**Language Arts**

 MINILESSON 5 Mins

# Writing Traits: Organization

## Discuss Sequence

**Review** Remind children that writers use sequence words to help the reader understand the order of ideas and events in their writing.

**Share** Ask a volunteer to share his or her writing from Day 2. Encourage the class to point out the sequence words they hear in the volunteer's writing. Invite the volunteer to tell how he or she put the ideas in a clear order.

### WRITING ENTRY: SEQUENCE

❶ **Prewrite** Ask children to choose a new topic for writing by searching their writer's notebook for ideas for an expository text. Or, provide a prompt such as the following one:
*Write a nonfiction story about an animal you've seen in a park or at the zoo. Describe what it was doing. Be sure to organize your ideas in a way that makes sense.*

❷ **Draft** Once children have chosen their topics, ask them to use a chart to organize the sequence, or order, of the events and ideas in their story. Encourage children to use their charts as they write their draft.

### OBJECTIVES

**CCSS** Write informative/explanatory texts in which they introduce a topic, use facts and definitions to develop points, and provide a concluding statement or section. **W.2.2**

**CCSS** Demonstrate command of the conventions of standard English capitalization, punctuation, and spelling when writing. **L.2.2**

**CCSS** Capitalize holidays, product names, and geographic names. **L.2.2a**

## Go Digital

**Present the Lesson**

**Writing**

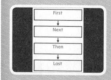

**Graphic Organizer**

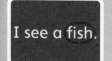

I see a fish.

**Grammar**

## Grammar

### Kinds of Nouns

**Review** Remind children that a common noun names a person, place, or thing. A proper noun names a specific person, place, or thing. A proper noun begins with a capital letter. Also review that a collective noun names a group of people or things. Point out that the names of many animal groups are collective nouns, such as *flock (of geese)*, *herd (of cattle)*, *litter (of puppies)*, and *pack (of wolves)*.

**Practice** Display the sample sentences. Invite partners to identify the common and proper nouns. Then have children write additional sentences with proper nouns.

> Yellowstone National Park is the habitat to many different animals. (Common: habitat, animals. Proper: Yellowstone National Park.)

> Do you know the habitat of the Peruvian Screech-Owl? (Common: habitat. Proper: Peruvian Screech-Owl.)

## Mechanics: Capital Letters

**Review** Remind children that the names of the days of the week, the months of the year, and holidays are proper nouns and begin with a capital letter. Offer several examples, such as *Tuesday, March, Martin Luther King, Jr. Day,* and *New Year's Day*. Also remind children that an abbreviation is a shortened way of writing a word. An abbreviation begins with a capital letter and ends with a period. Offer examples, such as *Mr., Mrs., Dr., Mon.,* and *Feb.*

**Practice** Have the children rewrite the following sentences using correct capitalization.

> mrs. murray took us on a nature hike on labor day.
> (Mrs. Murray, Labor Day)

> How big is an african elephant? (African)

### Talk About It

**Matching Game** Have the class generate a list of specific animal habitats, such as the *Atlantic Ocean, Rocky Mountains, Florida Everglades*. Then divide the class into two teams and have them give sentence clues for each animal habitat. Using the clues children give, have the two teams match the clues to the habitat. Provide help, as needed.

### ENGLISH LANGUAGE LEARNERS

**Kinds of Nouns** Hold up a picture of a girl. Point to the girl and ask: *Who is this?* (a girl) Identify *girl* as a common noun. Say: *A common noun names any person, place, or thing.* Then ask a female child: *What is your name?* Have the girl say her name. Indicate that the girl's name is a proper noun. Say: *A proper noun names a particular person, place, or thing.* Then display and read the following sentence and have children identify the proper nouns. Remind children that a proper noun always begins with a capital letter.

Dr. Torres studies whales that live in the Pacific Ocean.
(Dr. Torres, Pacific Ocean)

# Daily Wrap Up

→ Review the Essential Question and encourage children to discuss it using the oral vocabulary words.

→ Prompt children to review and discuss the skills they used today. Guide them to give examples of how they used each skill.

## Materials

**Literature Anthology**
**"At Home in the River"**

**a b c**

**Word-Building Cards**

almost

**High-Frequency Word Cards**

badge

**Spelling Word Cards**

Red Fox | lives in forest | sleeps in den | thick red fur | large ears

**Dinah Zike's**
**FOLDABLES®**

---

→ # Extend the Concept

**MINILESSON**
**5 Mins**

# Oral Language

### OBJECTIVES

**CCSS** Ask and answer such questions as *who, what, where, when, why,* and *how* to demonstrate understanding of key details in a text. **RL.2.1**

**CCSS** Know and apply grade-level phonics and word analysis skills in decoding words. **RF.2.3**

**CCSS** Decode words with common prefixes and suffixes. **RF.2.3d**

### ACADEMIC LANGUAGE
*prefix, root word*

### ESSENTIAL QUESTION

Remind children that this week they have been learning about animal habitats. Guide children to discuss the question using information from what they have read and discussed throughout the week.

Use the Define/Example/Ask routine to review the oral vocabulary words *located, encounter, defend, react,* and *positive*. Prompt children to use the words as they discuss how animals survive in their habitats. Then have children review last week's oral vocabulary words *affection, nourishment, crave, seek*, and *frustrated* using the Define/Example/Ask routine.

**Go**
**Digital**

**Phonemic Awareness**

**m a**
**n t p**

**Phonics**

I __ the jar.
fill | fills | filling

**Structural Analysis**

# Word Work

## Phonemic Awareness

### Phoneme Substitution

**1 Model** *Say: Listen as I say a word:* race. *Now listen as I change the first sound in* race /r/, *to* /f/. *The new word is* face.

**2 Guided Practice/Practice** Have children practice substituting phonemes. Do the first three with children.

| | | |
|---|---|---|
| mice/rice | page/cage | wage/rage |
| nudge/budge | pace/race | brace/trace |

## Phonics

### Build Words with Soft *c* and *g*

**Review** Remind children that soft *c* /s/ and *g* /j/ often occur when the letter *c* or *g* is followed by letter *e* or *i*.

Place the letters s, i, n, c, e. Let's blend the sounds together and read the word: /sssiiinnnsss/. Now, change the s to r. Blend the sounds and read the new word.

Use the Word Building Cards to build these words with soft *c* and *g*: *prince, price, rice, race, rage, wage, page, stage, age, ace, ice.*

## Structural Analysis

### Prefixes *re-, un-, dis-*

**1 Review** Write the words *rerun, untwist,* and *disclose.* Read them with children and underline the prefix in each word. Remind children how the prefixes *re-, un-,* and *dis-* are added to the beginning of a root word to change its meaning. Read each word again and discuss its meaning.

**2 Practice** Write the following words: *retest, displace, unsafe.* Have children work in pairs to identify the prefix in each word. Have them take turns using each word orally in a sentence.

### Quick Review

**Build Fluency: Sound Spellings** Display the **Word-Building Cards:** *o_e, o, u_e, u, i_e, i, a_ e, a, c, g, dge, ge, lge, nge, rge.* Have children say each sound. Repeat and vary the pace. For fluency in connected text, see the Decodable Reader Lesson in Small Group.

**Monitor and Differentiate**

**✓ Quick Check**

Can children read and decode words with soft *c* and *g*?

**Small Group Instruction**

| | | |
|---|---|---|
| **If No →** | **Approaching** | Reteach pp. T250-T255 |
| | **ELL** | Develop pp. T266-T273 |
| **If Yes →** | **On Level** | Review pp. T260-T261 |
| | **Beyond Level** | Extend pp. T264-T265 |

## → Word Work

**Quick Review**

**High-Frequency Words:** Read, Spell and Write to review this week's high-frequency words: *almost, buy, food, out, pull, saw, sky, straight, under, wash.*

**MINILESSON 5 Mins**

# Spelling

**OBJECTIVES**

**CCSS** Determine or clarify the meaning of unknown and multiple-meaning words and phrases based on *grade 2 reading and content,* choosing flexibly from an array of strategies. **L.2.4**

**CCSS** Use a known root word as a clue to the meaning of an unknown word with the same root. **L.2.4c**

**CCSS** Read with sufficient accuracy and fluency to support comprehension. **RF.2.4**

**CCSS** Read on-level text orally with accuracy, appropriate rate, and expression on successive readings. **RF.2.4b**

• Spell words with soft *c* and *g*.
• Practice fluency.

## Word Sort with Soft *c* and *g*

**Review** Provide pairs of children with copies of the Spelling Word Cards. While one partner reads the words one at a time, the other partner should orally segment the word and then write the word. After reading all the words, partners should switch roles.

**Practice** Have children correct their own papers. Then have them sort the words into soft *c* and soft *g* piles.

**MINILESSON 5 Mins**

# High-Frequency Words

*almost, buy, food, out, pull, saw, sky, straight, under, wash*

**Review** Display High Frequency Word Cards: *almost, buy, food, out, pull, saw, sky, straight, under, wash.* Have children Read/Write/Spell each word.

→ Point to a word and call on a child to use it in a sentence.

→ Review last week's words using the same procedure. *(won, yes, change, fall, five, look, open, should, their, cheer)*

**Go Digital**

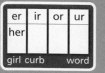

**Spelling Word Sort**

**High-Frequency Word Routine**

# Fluency/Vocabulary Strategy

## Phrasing

MINILESSON 5 Mins

**Review** Remind children that part of reading with proper phrasing means grouping words together in a natural way as you read. Punctuation helps you to read with proper phrasing. Pause for a short time at a comma and for a longer time at a period, exclamation point, or question mark. Tell children that when you read with natural phrasing your voice pauses, rises, and falls as it does when you are speaking in your usual voice.

**Practice** Have children read a passage from the Shared Read aloud to a partner. Remind them to pause for a shorter time after a comma and for a longer time for punctuation at the end of each sentence. Make sure they pay attention to using the proper phrasing. Offer corrective feedback as necessary.

### Fluency Practice

Children can practice fluency using the Practice Book passages.

## Root Words

MINILESSON 5 Mins

❶ **Explain/Model** Recall that to find the meaning of a word, children can break the word into parts. They can split the root word from its ending such as:

→ If the word has a prefix, such as *un-* or *dis-*, split the root from the prefix.

→ If the word has a suffix, *-ed*, *-es*, or *-ing*, split the root from the suffix.

Write and say *unlock* and *playing*. Model how to separate the root word from the prefix/suffix to understand the meaning of the root word.

❷ **Guided Practice** Write the words *dislike, unbend, buses, brushed,* and *picking*. Have partners figure out each word's root, and the word's meaning, by splitting the word into parts. Ask them to use each word in a sentence.

**Monitor and *Differentiate***

 **Quick Check**

Can children read fluently with natural phrasing?

⬇

**Small Group Instruction**

| | | |
|---|---|---|
| If No → | **Approaching** | Reteach pp. T248–T257 |
| | **ELL** | Develop pp. T266–T273 |
| If Yes → | **On Level** | Review pp. T258–T261 |
| | **Beyond Level** | Extend pp. T262–T265 |

# Develop Comprehension

CLOSE READING

**MINILESSON 5 Mins**

# Read Literature Anthology

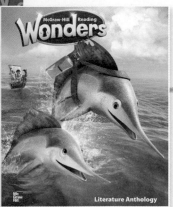

**Literature Anthology**

---

### OBJECTIVES

**CCSS** Ask and answer such questions as *who, what, when, where, why,* and *how* to demonstrate understanding of key details in a text. **RI.2.1**

**CCSS** Know and use various text features (e.g., captions, bold print, subheadings, glossaries, indexes, electronic menus, icons) to locate key facts or information in a text efficiently. **RI.2.5**

**CCSS** Compare and contrast the most important points presented by two texts on the same topic. **RI.2.9**

## Compare Texts *Analytical Writing*

Remind children that they read about a sea turtle's habitat in *Turtle, Turtle, Watch Out!* They will now read another expository text about animal habitats. Tell them that as they read they should think about how the features of the two habitats are alike and different. Have them **take notes.**

### ❶ Ask and Answer Questions

How is the Cuyahoga River habitat different from an ocean habitat? (The Cuyahoga is a fresh water habitat. An ocean is a salt water habitat.)

### ❷ Ask and Answer Questions

Look at the chart on page 184. What important details do we learn from it? (We learn about foods that animals on the Cuyahoga eat. )

### ❸ Ask and Answer Questions

What does the river bank provide for the spotted turtles? (The river bank provides food. It also provides a place for a mother spotted turtle to lay her eggs.

## AUTHOR'S CRAFT

### Vivid Verbs

Explain that authors want readers to picture what happens in expository text. One way they do that is by using vivid verbs.

→ Point out the author's use of the verb *floats* in the second paragraph. It vividly describes how the family of wood ducks moves.

→ Also point out the verb *sun* on page 185. Have children tell the meaning of the verb based on the context clues.

→ Have children suggest other vivid verbs in the text, and the pictures they visualize from those verbs.

## Go Digital

**At Home in the River**

**Genre • Expository Text**

**Compare Texts**
Read about plants and animals that live in a river habitat.

# At Home in the River

Many animals call the *Cuyahoga River* home. It is a fresh-water **habitat**. Ocean water has salt, but the river does not. The Cuyahoga gives many animals shelter and food. **1**

## Food from the River

A family of wood ducks floats by. The mother leads her ducklings along the river bank. They eat plants that grow in the water. The plants are called duckweed.

**Wood Duck**

**2**

| CUYAHOGA RIVER HABITAT | |
|---|---|
| **ANIMAL** | **FOOD** |
| Wood Duck | duckweed, seeds, fruit |
| Spotted Turtle | snails, worms, spiders |
| Raccoon | fish, frogs, eggs, mice, insects |

## A Spotted Turtle's Journey

Spotted turtles sun themselves on a floating log. They have dots on their heads and shells. One turtle leaves the river to lay eggs. On the river bank, she stops to eat snails and worms.

When she finds a place, she digs a hole with her back legs. She covers her eggs with dirt to hide them from other animals. A raccoon sleeps in a hole in the tree. It would enjoy this meal. After two months, the baby turtles hatch. They journey to the river bank. **3**

Every living thing is important in **nature**. Each living thing needs and helps another. Each plant and animal lives and then begins a new cycle. Life in the river keeps going.

**Spotted Turtle**

**Raccoon**

**Make Connections**
What are the features of this river habitat? ESSENTIAL QUESTION

Think about the different habitats you read about this week. What do they all provide for animals? TEXT TO TEXT

184 / 185

**LITERATURE ANTHOLOGY,** pp. 184–185

**Lexile** 500
*TextEvaluator*™ 5

# Make Connection  *Analytical Writing*

COLLABORATE Have partners make connections between the river habitat in "At Home in the River" and the ocean habitat in *Turtle, Turtle, Watch Out!*

## A C T Access Complex Text

### ▶ Prior Knowledge

Point out that the children will read about an environment that may be new to them and that they may not have experienced. Most informational text will contain text features like graphs and charts that will call out important information.

→ # Language Arts

# Writing Traits: Organization

**OBJECTIVES**

**CCSS** With guidance and support from adults and peers, focus on a topic and strengthen writing as needed by revising and editing. **W.2.5**

**CCSS** With guidance and support from adults, use a variety of digital tools to produce and publish writing, including in collaboration with peers. **W.2.6**

**CCSS** Demonstrate command of the conventions of standard English capitalization, punctuation, and spelling when writing. **L.2.2**

**CCSS** Capitalize holidays, product names, and geographic names. **L.2.2a**

**ACADEMIC LANGUAGE**

*revise, edit, conference, common noun, proper noun, collective noun, abbreviation*

**Revise** Have children revise their drafts from Day 3 by focusing on the sequence of ideas and events in their writing. As children revise their drafts, hold teacher conferences with individual children. You may also want to have partners conduct peer conferences.

**Edit** Model using proofreading marks to edit. Then have children use proofreading marks to correct errors in their writing.

Invite children to review Grammar Handbook pages 477–478 and check that they have used nouns correctly.

Encourage children to proofread for other errors, including capitalization of proper nouns and spelling.

## Conference Routines

### Teacher Conference

**Step 1:** Talk about the strengths of the writing. *The sequence, or order, of your ideas is very clear.*

**Step 2:** Focus on the target trait. *You tell your readers what happens first, next, and last.*

**Step 3:** Make concrete suggestions for revisions, such as those below and then meet again to review progress.

## Suggested Revisions

**Focus on a Sentence** Read the draft and target one sentence for revision. *Rewrite this sentence by adding a sequence word to show what happens _____.*

**Focus on a Section** Underline a section that needs revision. Provide specific suggestions. *I would like to have a clearer idea of _____. Add a sequence word here and here so that your readers can understand the order better.*

**Focus on a Revision Strategy** Underline a section of the writing and ask children to use a specific revision strategy, such as rearranging. *I can see you know your topic well; however, this paragraph could show that better if you rearranged sentences to make the order of your ideas clearer.*

**Go Digital**

**Writing**

Make a capital letter.
Add.
Take out.

**Proofreader's Marks**

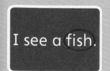
I see a fish.

**Grammar**

## Peer Conference

Provide these questions to guide peers as they review a partner's draft.

→ Which words show the sequence, or order, of the ideas or events?

→ Where can other sequence words be added to make the writing clearer?

# Grammar

MINILESSON
5 Mins

## Kinds of Nouns

**Review** Review common, proper, and collective nouns. Remind children that a noun names a person, place, or thing. A proper noun names a particular person, place, or thing. A collective noun names a group of people or things.

Display the following sentence on the board. Have children point out the common, proper, and collective nouns.

> A flock of birds flew over Washington Elementary School.
> (Collective: *flock*. Common: *birds*. Proper: *Washington Elementary School*.)

**Practice** Have partners use nouns to name a general kind of animal, a specific animal in that group, and a collective noun that can be used for that kind of animal. Example: *fish* (common), *Great White Shark* (proper), *school* of fish (collective).

## Mechanics: Capital Letters

**Review** Review with children that the names of the days of the week, the months of the year, and holidays are proper nouns. A proper noun begins with a capital letter. Also remind children that abbreviations begin with a capital letter and end with a period.

**Practice** Have children correct the capitalization in the following sentence:

> dr. charap traveled to the statue of liberty on the fourth of july. (Dr. Charap; Statue of Liberty; Fourth of July.)

## Talk About It

**In Your Own Words** Ask children to tell a partner about one selection this week they particularly enjoyed. The partner listens and writes down common and proper nouns he or she hears. Then partners switch roles.

# Daily Wrap Up

→ Review the Essential Question and encourage children to discuss it using the oral vocabulary words.

→ Prompt children to discuss the skills they practiced and learned today. Guide them to share examples of how they used each skill.

**Go** Digital

www.connected.mcgraw-hill.com
RESOURCES
Research and Inquiry

→ **Wrap Up the Week**
# Integrate Ideas

## RESEARCH AND INQUIRY

**Animal Homes**

### OBJECTIVES

 Participate in collaborative conversations about *grade 2 topics and texts* with peers and adults in small and larger groups. **SL.2.1**

 Participate in shared research and writing projects (e.g., read a number of books on a single topic to produce a report; record science observations). **W.2.7**

Build background knowledge.

## Make Animal and Habitat Cards

 Explain to children that they will work with a group to complete a short research project about an animal habitat. They will then use their research to make animal and habitat cards.

**STEP 1** **Choose a Topic**

Guide groups to think about their own experiences and the week's selections to choose a habitat.

**STEP 2** **Find Resources**

Discuss how to use the selections. Remind children that they can find more details about animal habitats in reference materials and online. Have children use the Research Process Checklist online.

**STEP 3** **Keep Track of Ideas**

Have children make an Accordion Foldable® to record ideas and facts from sources. Model recording the names of the sources.

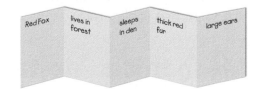

Dinah Zike's
**FOLDABLES**

### Collaborative Conversations

**Add New Ideas** As children engage in partner, small-group, and whole-group discussions, encourage them to:

→ stay on topic.

→ build on the ideas of others.

→ connect their personal experiences to the conversation.

**STEM**

**Red Fox**

A red fox lives
in a forest
habitat. It
sleeps in a den.
It is a good
hunter. It has
large ears and
thick, red fur.

STEP 4 **Create the Project: Animal and Habitat Cards**

Tell children that they will make animal and habitat cards. On one side of the card, they will draw or show a photograph of an animal. On the other side of the card, they will describe that animal and its habitat.

→ **Information** The purpose of the cards is to give information. In this project, the cards will give information about an animal and its habitat.

→ **Image** The cards show photographs or drawings of an animal on one side.

→ **Text** The cards give information about the animal and its habitat.

Have groups create the cards about their animals and their chosen habitat.

→ Guide them to draw animals or use photographs from magazines or other sources.

→ Prompt children to use precise words to describe the animals and their habitats.

**ELL ENGLISH LANGUAGE LEARNERS**
**SCAFFOLD**

| Beginning | Intermediate | Advanced |
|---|---|---|
| **Use Sentence Frames** Use sentence frames to help children tell about the animal and describe it. For example: *The animal is ____. It lives in a ____ habitat. It eats ____.* | **Discuss** Guide children to focus on the most important details about their animal habitat. Ask, *Where does this animal live? How does it hunt? Where does it sleep?* | **Describe** Prompt children to brainstorm lists of words that could describe the animal and its habitat. Encourage them to think about the most important details. |

## Materials

**Reading/Writing Workshop**

**Literature Anthology**

Word-Building Cards

almost
**High-Frequency Word Cards**

badge
**Spelling-Word Cards**

Grassland Habitat   Ocean Habitat
Dinah Zike's
**FOLDABLES**

# → Integrate Ideas

# TEXT CONNECTIONS *Analytical Writing*

## Connect to Essential Question

### OBJECTIVES

**CCSS** Compare and contrast the most important points presented by two texts on the same topic. **RI.2.9**

**CCSS** Write informative/ explanatory texts in which they introduce a topic, use facts and definitions to develop points, and provide a concluding statement or section. **W.2.2**

• Develop answers to the Essential Question.

• Make text connections to the world.

### ACADEMIC LANGUAGE
*text, present, compare analysis*

## Text to Text

**Cite Evidence** Remind children that this week they have been reading selections about animal habitats. Tell them that now they will compare these texts. Model comparing text using "A Prairie Guard Dog," **Reading/ Writing Workshop,** pages 134–139, and *Turtle, Turtle, Watch Out!*, **Literature Anthology,** pp. 164–181. Use a Shutter Foldable® to record comparisons.

**Think Aloud** *"A Prairie Guard Dog" and* Turtle, Turtle, Watch Out! *are both about how animals live in their habitats. In "A Prairie Guard Dog," Pete makes sure that his family is safe in their burrow. In* Turtle, Turtle, Watch Out!, *people help a baby sea turtle grow up and live safely in its habitats.*

**Complete the Organizer** Have children use a Shutter Foldable® to record comparisons. Guide children to discuss and write about the features of different animal habitats and ways animals adapt to them.

**Present Information** Ask groups to present their information to the class. Have children compare information given by the other groups.

Grassland Habitat   Ocean Habitat
Dinah Zike's
**FOLDABLES**

## Text to Self

**Discuss** Have children discuss what they have read this week about animal habitats. Ask: *How are some animal homes like your home?*

## Text to World

**Discuss** Have children discuss what they have learned about animal habitats this week. Ask: *What effect do people have on animal habitats?*

# WRITE ABOUT READING  *Analytical Writing*

## OBJECTIVES

**CCSS** Draw evidence from literary or informational texts to support analysis, reflection, and research. **W.4.9**

## Write an Analysis

**Cite Evidence** Explain to children that as a group they will write about one of the selections that they read this week.

Tell children that using the evidence in the text, they will think about how the author used key details to write about the main topic

Review the Main Topic and Details chart you completed for "A Prairie Guard Dog." Guide children to analyze the text evidence by asking *how* questions about the text

→ How does the author use key details to help explain the main topic?

Work with children to complete the sentence frames using information from "A Prairie Guard Dog."

> In _____, the author wrote about _____.
>
> The author used details _____ to support the main topic.
>
> The selection helped us understand _____.

Then have children select another text they have read this week and use the sentence frames to write about how the author used main topic and details.

**Present Your Ideas** Ask partners to share their paragraphs and discuss how the evidence they found supports their ideas.

# RESEARCH AND INQUIRY  SCIENCE

## OBJECTIVES

**CCSS** Participate in shared research and writing projects. **W.2.7**

## Wrap Up the Project

Guide partners to share information about the animal habitats they researched and to point out the details in their cards. Prior to the presentations, review the Presenting and Listening checklists online with children.

**STEM**

 → # Word Work

### Quick Review

**Build Fluency: Sound Spellings**
Display the **Word-Building Cards**
*o_e, o, u_e, u, i_e, i, a_e, a, c, g, dge, ge, lge, nge, rge.* Have children say each sound.

## Phonemic Awareness

 MINILESSON 5 Mins

### Phoneme Blending

**Review** Guide children to blend phonemes to form words. *Listen as I say a group of sounds. Then blend those sounds to form a word.*

/r/ /ā/ /s/ (race)        /s/ /p/ ī/ /s/ (spice)        /k/ /ā/ /j/ (cage)

/r/ /ā/ /n/ /j/ (range)        /b/ /a/ /j/ (badge)        /d/ /o/ /j/ (dodge)

## Phonics

 MINILESSON 5 Mins

### OBJECTIVES

**CCSS** Know and apply grade-level phonics and word analysis skills in decoding words. **RF.2.3**

**CCSS** Demonstrate command of the conventions of standard English capitalization, punctuation, and spelling when writing. **L.2.2**

**CCSS** Generalize learned spelling patterns when writing words (e.g., cage → badge; boy → boil). **L.2.2d**

---

• Spell words with soft *c* and *g*.
• Blend phonemes to form new words.

### Blend and Build Words with Soft *c* and *g*

**Review** Have children read and say the words *stage, face, rice, badge,* and *bulge.* Then have children follow the word building routine with Word-Building Cards to build *dance, range, mice, page, space, grace, since,* and *huge.*

**Word Automaticity** Help children practice word automaticity. Display decodable words and point to each word as children chorally read it. Test how many words children can read in one minute. Model blending words children miss.

## Structural Analysis

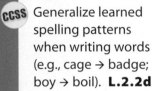 MINILESSON 5 Mins

### Prefixes *re-, un-, dis-*

**Review** Remind children of the meaning of prefixes *re-, un-,* and *dis-.* Have the children practice writing the following words, underlining the prefix, and reading them aloud to a partner: *retell, unpack, dislike, rerun, unhappy,* and *distrust.*

## Go Digital

**Phonemic Awareness**

**Phonics**

**Structural Analysis**

**Spelling Word Sort**

| they | together |
| how | eat |

**High-Frequency Word Routine**

peered

**Visual Glossary**

# Spelling

## Word Sort with Soft *c* and *g*

**Review** Have children use the Spelling Word Cards to sort the weekly words by soft *c* and *g* spellings.

**Assess** Assess children on their abilities to spell words with the soft *c* and *g* sound. Say each word and provide a sentence so that children can hear the words used in a correct context. Then allow them to write down the words. In order to challenge children, you may wish to provide an additional word for each initial or final blend in order to assess whether they understand the concept.

# High-Frequency Words

### *buy, under, wash, straight, almost, saw, food, out, pull, sky*

**Review** Display High-Frequency Word Cards *buy, under, wash, straight, almost, saw, food, out, pull, sky*. Have children Read/Spell/Write each word. Have children write a sentence with each word.

# Vocabulary

### *buried, journey, peeks, spies, escape, habitat, nature, restless*

**Review** Display Visual Vocabulary Word Cards *buried, journey, peeks, spies, escape, restless, habitat, nature*. Have children review each word using the Define/Example/Ask Routine on the back of each card.

---

## Monitor and *Differentiate*

 **Quick Check**

Can children read and decode words with the soft *c* and *g* sounds? Can children recognize and read high-frequency words?

⬇

### Small Group Instruction

If No → **Approaching** Reteach pp. T250–T255

**ELL** Develop pp. T266–T273

If Yes → **On Level** Review pp. T260–T261

**Beyond Level** Extend pp. T264–T265

→ # Language Arts

**MINILESSON 5 Mins**

# Writing Traits: Organization

## OBJECTIVES

**CCSS** With guidance and support from adults, use a variety of digital tools to produce and publish writing, including in collaboration with peers. **W.2.6**

**CCSS** Demonstrate command of standard English capitalization, punctuation, and spelling when writing. **L.2.2**

**CCSS** Capitalize holidays, product names, and geographic names. **L.2.2a**

## ACADEMIC LANGUAGE
*share, reflect, common noun, proper noun, collective noun, abbreviation*

## Share and Reflect

**Discuss** Discuss with the class what they learned about arranging their ideas in an order that makes sense to their readers. Guide them to recall that sequence words help make a writer's message clearer and more interesting to read.

**Present** Invite volunteers to choose a writing entry from the week to share with the class. Compare the volunteer's draft with his or her revised text, and encourage children to identify the sequence words the volunteer added. Have children discuss how the sequence and sequence words make the writing easier to follow.

**Reflect** Have children use their Writer's Notebook to reflect on their progress as writers. Invite them to consider the following prompts as they write:

*How did arranging your ideas in a sequence, or order, improve your writing this week?*

*What other topic for a narrative nonfiction would you like to write about this week?*

*What sequence words would you use? Why?*

**Publish** After children finish presenting their nonfiction stories, discuss how the class will publish a collection of their stories on a class blog or Website. Have children add titles and illustrations to their stories. Guide them to use digital tools to publish their stories and illustrations. Allow children to make decisions regarding the organization of their stories.

**Go Digital**

**Writing**

**Checklists**

I see a fish.

**Grammar**

# Grammar

## Kinds of Nouns

**Review** Ask: *What is a common noun?* (a word that names a person, place, or thing) *What is a proper noun?* (a word that names a particular person, place, or thing) *How do you begin a proper noun?* (with a capital letter) *What is a collective noun?* (a word that names a group of people, places, or things)

**Practice** Write the following sentence on the board. Have children identify the common nouns and proper nouns. Then have them use those nouns in sentences of their own.

> Our class saw a tiger at the Cleveland Zoo. (class—collective noun; tiger—common noun; Cleveland Zoo—proper noun)

## Mechanics: Capital Letters

**Review** Review with children that the names of the days of the week, months of the year, and holidays are proper nouns. A proper noun always begins with a capital letter. Also review that an abbreviation is a shortened form of a word. It begins with a capital letter and ends with a period.

**Practice** Write the following sentences on the board. Have children identify common nouns and proper nouns, and correctly capitalize any proper nouns.

> The san diego zoo is open on thanksgiving. (San Diego Zoo, Thanksgiving—proper nouns)

> Many buffalo live in yellowstone national park. (Yellowstone National Park—proper noun; buffalo—common noun)

## Reteach

If children have difficulty identifying kinds of nouns or using capital letters, review the use of each. Provide opportunities for children to practice the skills in small groups, with a partner, or independently.

## Talk About It

**Proper Nouns in Sentences** Have children work with a partner. Ask one partner to make a list of proper nouns and then read each one aloud. Have the partner use each proper noun in a sentence. Then ask partners to switch roles.

# Wrap Up the Week

→ Review the Essential Question and encourage children to discuss it using the oral vocabulary words.

→ Review the comprehension strategy and skill.

→ Review soft *c* and *g*.

→ Use the High-Frequency Word Cards to review the Words to Know.

→ Review the different purposes for writing expository text.

# Approaching Level

**Lexile** 310
*TextEvaluator™* 4

## OBJECTIVES

 Read with sufficient accuracy and fluency to support comprehension. **RF.2.4**

 Read on-level text with purpose and understanding. **RF.2.4a**

 Read on-level text orally with accuracy, appropriate rate, and expression on successive readings. **RF.2.4b**

## MATERIALS

Leveled Reader
*A Tree Full of Life*

## Leveled Reader:
## *A Tree Full of Life*

### Before Reading

#### Preview and Predict

Have children turn to the title page. Read the title and author name and have children repeat. Preview the selection's photos. Prompt children to predict what the selection might be about.

#### Review Genre: Narrative Nonfiction

Have children recall that nonfiction text is about real things. Narrative nonfiction tells about people, living things, or events. It is told by a narrator and gives information in a sequence, or order.

#### ESSENTIAL QUESTION

Remind children of the Essential Question: *What are the features of different animal habitats?* Set a purpose for reading: *Let's read to find out about animal habitats.*

Remind children that as they read a selection, they can ask questions about what they do not understand or want to know more about.

### During Reading

#### Guided Comprehension

As children whisper read *A Tree Full of Life*, monitor and provide guidance, correcting blending and modeling the key strategies and skills.

#### Strategy: Make, Confirm, and Revise Predictions

Remind children that they can make a prediction, or a thoughtful guess, as they read. They should revise their predictions as they read on. Say: *Making and revising predictions can help you understand a text.* Model predicting using page 2: *The text says the eucalyptus tree is home to animals. I predict I will learn what animals live in this tree.*

#### Skill: Main Topic and Key Details

Remind children that the main topic is what the selection is mostly about. The key details give information about the main topic. After reading, ask: *What is the main topic? What key details tell about it?*

**Go Digital**

**Leveled Readers**

**Graphic Organizer**

**Retelling Cards**

Display a Main Topic and Key Details graphic organizer for children to copy. Model recording children's answers in the top box. Have children record answers in their charts. Provide spelling support for *eucalyptus*.

**Think Aloud**  The selection tells me about a tree called the eucalyptus. Many things live in this tree. This is what the selection is mostly about, so I'll write this in the Main Topic box of the graphic organizer.

Guide children to identify key details about the main topic.

## After Reading

### Respond to Reading

Have children complete the Respond to Reading questions on page 16.

### Retell

Have children take turns retelling the selection. Help children make a personal connection by asking: *What other animals live in trees?*

### Model Fluency

Read the sentences one at a time. Have children chorally repeat. Point out to children how your voice goes up at the end of a question.

**Apply**  Have children practice reading with partners. Provide feedback.

## PAIRED READ ...

### "Life in a Termite Mound"

#### Make Connections:
#### Write About It • *Analytical Writing*

Before reading, ask children to note that the genre is expository text. It gives facts and details about the nests of termites. Then discuss the Compare Texts statement. After reading, ask children to make connections between "Life in a Termite Mound" and *A Tree Full of Life*.

**Leveled Reader**

**FOCUS ON SCIENCE**

Children can extend their knowledge of animal habitats by completing the science activity on page 20.

**STEM**

## Literature Circles

Lead children in conducting a literature circle using the Thinkmark questions to guide the discussion. You may wish to discuss what children have learned about animal homes from both selections in the leveled reader.

## Level Up

Level-up lessons available online.

**IF** children read the **Approaching Level** fluently and answered the questions

**THEN** pair them with children who have proficiently read the **On Level** and have approaching children

• echo-read the **On Level** main selection.

• use self-stick notes to mark one detail they would like to discuss in each section.

**A C T ccess omplex ext**

The **On Level** challenges children by including more **specific vocabulary** and **complex sentence structures.**

# → Approaching Level
## Phonemic Awareness

### PHONEME BLENDING

**OBJECTIVES**

 Demonstrate understanding of spoken words, syllables, and sounds (phonemes). **RF.1.2**

Blend phonemes to form words

 **I Do** Explain to children that they will be blending sounds to form words. *Listen as I say three sounds: /j/ /e/ /m/. Say the sounds with me: /j/ /e/ /m/. I'm going to blend the sounds together: /j/ /e/ /m/, /jem/, gem. The word is* gem.

 **We Do** *Listen as I say three sounds: /n/ /ī/ /s/. Repeat the sounds: /n/ /ī/ /s/. Let's blend the sounds: /nnn/ /īī/ /sss/, /nnnīīsss/,* nice. *We made one word:* nice. Repeat this routine with the following words:

cage    rice    edge    mice    ace    dodge    huge

 **You Do** *It's your turn. I want you to blend the sounds I say together to form a word.*

age   page   badge   ledge   race   cent   dance   fudge   cell

**Repeat** the blending routine with additional soft *c* and soft *g* words.

### PHONEME SEGMENTATION

**OBJECTIVES**

 Segment spoken single-syllable words into their complete sequence of individual sounds (phonemes). **RF.1.2d**

Segment words into separate phonemes

 **I Do** Explain to children that they will be segmenting words into sounds today. *Listen as I say a word:* ice. *I hear two sounds: /īī/ and /sss/. There are two sounds in the word* ice: */īī/ and /sss/. Repeat with the word* age.

 **We Do** *Let's do some together. I am going to say a word: /eeej/. How many sounds do you hear? The sounds in* edge *are /eee/ and /j/.* Repeat with the following words:

badge    hedge    huge    space    spice    cell

 **You Do** *I'll say a word. Tell me how many sounds you hear. Then say the sounds.*

race    lace    ace    wage    trace    piece

**Repeat** the segmentation routine with additional words with soft *c, g.*

You may wish to review Phonemic Awareness with **ELL** using this section.

# PHONEME SUBSTITUTION

**OBJECTIVES**

 Demonstrate understanding of spoken words, syllables, and sounds (phonemes). **RF.1.2**

Substitute phonemes to form new words

**I Do** Explain to children that they will be substituting phonemes. *When you substitute a phoneme, you are replacing one sound with another sound.*

*Listen as I say a word:* race, /rrrāāāsss/. *The first sound in* race *is* /r/. *Now I'll change the* /r/ *in* race *to* /p/ *and make a new word. The new word is* pace, /p/ /āāā/ /s/.

**We Do** *Listen as I say a word:* page. *Say the word with me:* /p/ /āāā/ /j/. *Let's change the first sound in* page *from* /p/ *to* /k/. *The new word is* cage. *We changed the* /p/ *in* page *to* /k/ *and made the word* cage.

*Let's try another one. Listen to the first sound in this word:* game. *Say the word with me:* /g/ /āāā/ /m/. *Let's change* /g/ *to* /k/. *The new word is* came.

Repeat this routine by substituting the initial phoneme in the following words:

ace, ice     cube, tube     gaze, maze     trace, grace     hedge, ledge     lodge, dodge

**You Do** *It's your turn. Change the first sound in each word to form a new word.*

Change /f/ in *face* to /l/.         Change /m/ in *mice* to /r/.
Change /r/ in *rage* to /w/.         Change /h/ in *hedge* to /l/.
Change /g/ in *gate* to /d/.         Change /c/ in *cave* to /g/.

---

## ELL ENGLISH LANGUAGE LEARNERS

For the ELLs who need **phonics, decoding,** and **fluency** practice, use scaffolding methods as necessary to ensure children understand the meaning of the words. Refer to the Language Transfer Handbook for phonics elements that may not transfer in children's native languages.

# → Approaching Level

## Phonics

### CONNECT SOFT *c* TO /s/ AND SOFT *g* TO /j/

**OBJECTIVES**

Know and apply grade-level phonics and word analysis skills in decoding words. **RF.2.3**

 **I Do**  Display the Word-Building Cards *d, g, e. These are the letters* d, g, e. *I am going to trace the letters while I say /j/, the sound that these letters stand for.* Trace the letters *d, g, e* while saying /j/ five times. Repeat with /s/ *c*. Point out that when *g* is followed by *e* or *i*, it usually stands for the /j/. Explain that when *c* is followed by *e* or *i*, it usually stands for the /s/ sound.

 **We Do**  *Now do it with me.* Have children trace the letters *dge* on the Word-Building Cards with their finger while saying /j/. Trace the letters five times and say /j/ with children. Repeat the process with *c*/s/ and *g*/j/.

 **You Do**  Have children connect the letters *dge* and *ge* to the sound /j/ and the letter *c* to the sound /s/ by tracing the letters while saying the sounds. Then have children write the letters while saying the sounds five to ten times.

**Repeat,** connecting the letters *dge* and *ge* to /j/ and the letter *c* to /s/ through tracing and writing the letters throughout the week.

**Sound/Spellings Fluency**  Display the Word-Building Cards: *o_e, o, u_e, u, i_e, i, a_e, a, c, g, dge, ge, lge, nge, rge.* Have children chorally say each sound.

### BLEND WORDS WITH SOFT *c* AND SOFT *g*

**OBJECTIVES**

Know and apply grade-level phonics and word analysis skills in decoding words. **RF.2.3**

Decode words with soft *c* and *g*

 **I Do**  Display Word-Building Cards *a, g, e. This is the letter* a. *It stands for /ā/. These are the letters* g *and* e. *When* g *is followed by* e *or* i, *it usually stands for /j/. Let's say it together: /j/. I'll blend these sounds together: /āāāj/, age.*

 **We Do**  Guide children to blend the sounds and read: *ice, face, edge, ridge, page, huge.*

 **You Do**  Have children blend and decode: *race, mice, lodge, badge, cage, hinge*

**Repeat,** blending additional words with soft *g* and soft *c*.

You may wish to review Phonics with **ELL** using this section.

## BUILD WORDS WITH SOFT *c* AND SOFT *g*

**OBJECTIVES**

Know and apply grade-level phonics and word analysis skills in decoding words. **RF.2.3**

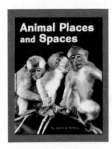

 **I Do**

Display Word-Building Cards *m, i, c, e*. These are the letters m, i, c, *and* e. *They stand for /m/, /ī/, and /s/. The e is silent. I will blend /m/, /ī/, and /s/ together: /mīs/,* mice. *The word is* mice. *Repeat with* age *and* hedge.

 **We Do**

*Let's do one together.* Make the word race. *Let's blend: /r/ /ā/ /s/, /rās/,* race. Change the letter r to f. *Let's blend the new word: /f/ /ā/ /s/, /fās/,* face.

**You Do**

Have children build the words: *ledge, lodge, dodge; cage, page, rage.*

**Decodable Reader**  Introduce the Decodable Reader selection, *Animal Places and Spaces*. Point to the title. Have children sound it out. Discuss the title and photos.

**First Read**  Turn to page 16. Have children point to each word, sounding out decodable words and saying the high-frequency words quickly. Children should chorally read the story the first time through.

## BLEND WORDS WITH SOFT *c* AND SOFT *g*

**OBJECTIVES**

Know and apply grade-level phonics and word analysis skills in decoding words. **RF.2.3**

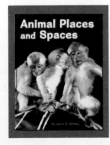

 **I Do**

Display Word-Building Cards *r, i, c, e*. This is the letter r. *It stands for /r/. This is the letter* i. *It stands for /ī/. These are the letters* ce. *When c is followed by e, it stands for /s/. The e is silent. Listen as I blend these sounds: /rīs/,* rice.

 **We Do**

*Let's do some together.* Blend and read the words: *hedge, wage, fringe, place.*

**You Do**

Display the following words: *page, wage, large, budge, slice, space, place, face*. Have children blend and read the words.

**Decodable Reader**  Have children reread the Decodable Reader selection.

**Check Comprehension**  As children read, monitor their comprehension. Ask the following: *Where do wolves live? What other animals make homes in that place?*

## BLEND WORDS WITH WITH SOFT *c* AND SOFT *g*

**Fluency in Connected Text**

Have children review the **Decodable Reader** selection. Identify words with soft *c* and soft *g* and blend as needed. Have children reread the selection on their own or with a partner.

# → Approaching Level

## Structural Analysis

### REVIEW PREFIXES *re-, un-, dis-*

**OBJECTIVES**

**CCSS** Know and apply grade-level phonics and word analysis skills in decoding words. **RF.2.3**

**CCSS** Decode words with common prefixes and suffixes. **RF.2.3d**

Read words with prefixes *re-, un-, dis-*.

 Review that a prefix is a word part added to the beginning of a word to change the word's meaning. Write *replace, unsafe, dislike*. Read the words aloud. Underline the prefixes. *The prefix* re- *means "to do again."* Replace *means "to place again." The prefixes* un- *and* dis- *mean "not" or "the opposite of."* Unsafe *means "not safe."* Dislike *means "not like."*

 Write *repack. Let's look at this word. Do you see a smaller word you know? Yes,* pack. *This word has the prefix* re-. *The prefix* re- *means "to do again," so* repack *means "pack again." Let's read the word together: /rēpak/,* repack.

 Give partners words with prefixes *re-, un-,* and *dis-*. Have children read each, identify prefixes, and explain the word's meaning.

**Repeat** Have children create sentences using words with prefixes.

### RETEACH PREFIXES *re-, un-, dis-*

**OBJECTIVES**

**CCSS** Know and apply grade-level phonics and word analysis skills in decoding words. **RF.2.3**

**CCSS** Decode words with common prefixes and suffixes. **RF.2.3d**

Read words with prefixes *re-, un-, dis-*.

 Write *well* and *unwell*. Read the words aloud. Then point out the prefix *un-* in *unwell. The letters* un *are a prefix. A prefix changes the meaning of a word. The prefix* un- *means "not" or "opposite of," so* unwell *means "not well."*

 Write *stack. Let's read this word together:* stack. *What does* stack *mean? Let's add the prefix* re- *to* stack. *What is the word? What does* it *mean?*

 Have children add prefixes to words. *Now it's your turn. Add these prefixes to the words. Say each new word and use it in a sentence.*

re: place, tell          un: bend, well          dis: use, place

**Repeat** Have children find examples of words with the prefixes *re-, un-,* and *dis-* and explain their meanings.

# High-Frequency Words/ Vocabulary

**TIER 2**

## REVIEW HIGH-FREQUENCY WORDS

**OBJECTIVES**

 Read with sufficient accuracy and fluency to support comprehension. **RF.2.4**

Review high-frequency words

 **I Do** Use Word Cards 71-80. Display one word at a time, following the routine:

Display the word. Read the word. Then spell the word.

 **We Do** Ask children to state the word and spell the word with you. Model using the word in a sentence and have children repeat after you.

**You Do** Display the word. Ask children to say the word and then spell it. When completed, quickly flip through the word card set as children chorally read the words. Provide opportunities for children to use the words in speaking and writing. For example, provide sentence starters, such as *I want to buy _____*. Ask children to write each word in their Writer's Notebook.

## REVIEW VOCABULARY WORDS

**OBJECTIVES**

Use words and phrases acquired through conversations, reading and being read to, and responding to texts, including using adjectives and adverbs to describe (e.g., *When other kids are happy that makes me happy*). **L.2.6**

 **I Do** Display each Visual Vocabulary Card and state the word. Explain how the photograph illustrates the word. State the example sentence and repeat the word.

 **We Do** Point to the word on the card and read the word with children. Ask them to repeat the word. Engage children in structured partner talk about the image as prompted on the back of the vocabulary card.

 **You Do** Display each visual in random order, hiding the word. Have children match the definitions and context sentences of the words to the visuals displayed. Then ask children to complete Approaching Level Practice Book page 71.

# → Approaching Level

## Comprehension

### READ FOR FLUENCY

**OBJECTIVES**

 Read with sufficient accuracy and fluency to support comprehension. **RF.2.4**

 Read on-level text with purpose and understanding. **RF.2.4a**

 **I Do** Read the first paragraph of the Practice Book selection. Model phrasing by grouping words together in a natural way and using punctuation to group words.

 **We Do** Read the next paragraph and have children repeat each sentence after you. Point out how you grouped words into phrases, paused for a short time at a comma, and paused for a longer time at the end of a sentence.

 **You Do** Have children read the rest of the selection aloud. Remind them to group words into natural phrases and use punctuation to help them group words together as they read.

### IDENTIFY THE TOPIC

**OBJECTIVES**

 Ask and answer such questions as *who, what, where, when, why,* and *how* to demonstrate understanding of key details in a text. **RI.2.1**

 Identify the main topic of a multi-paragraph text as well as the focus of specific paragraphs within the text. **RI.2.2**

 **I Do** Remind children that they have been reading narrative nonfiction. Explain that narrative nonfiction tells about a topic. Point out that as children read, they should look for key details. *Key details are important pieces of information. I look for key details in the text and the pictures.*

 **We Do** Read the first sentences of the Practice Book selection aloud. Pause to identify what children are reading about. *This sentence tells about how tundra is cold. The next sentence also tells about plants in the tundra.*

 **You Do** Guide children to read the rest of the Practice Book selection. After every couple of sentences, prompt them to identify key details in the text and in the photo.

## REVIEW MAIN TOPIC AND KEY DETAILS

**OBJECTIVES**

 Ask and answer such questions as *who, what, where, when, why,* and *how* to demonstrate understanding of key details in a text. **RI.2.1**

 Identify the main topic of a multi-paragraph text as well as the focus of specific paragraphs within the text. **RI.2.2**

 **I Do** Remind children that narrative nonfiction selections give information about a real person, place, thing, or event. Explain that children can identify the topic of these selections by figuring out what the selection is mainly about. They can look for clues in the text and photos or illustrations.

 **We Do** Read both pages of the Practice Book selection together. Pause to identify the topic. Then point out key details about the topic. *The first page tells about Arctic tundra. The next page tells about Alpine tundra. I think the main topic is the two types of tundra. Now I will look for key details that tell me more about the topic. We read that both types of tundra have similar plants.*

 **You Do** Stop reading on page 74 and say: *What key detail did we just read about the topic?* Record the topic and the key detail in a Main Topic and Key Details chart. Continue having children add details.

## SELF-SELECTED READING

**OBJECTIVES**

 Ask and answer such questions as *who, what, where, when, why,* and *how* to demonstrate understanding of key details in a text. **RI.2.1**

Identify the main topic of a multi-paragraph text as well as the focus of specific paragraphs within the text. **RI.2.2**

Apply the strategy and skill to reread text.

### Read Independently

Have children pick a nonfiction text selection that they have read for sustained silent reading. Remind them to:

→ look for the main topic in the text and photos.

→ look for key details that provide facts and information about the topic.

→ make, confirm, and revise predictions about the selections before and during reading.

### Read Purposefully

Have children record the main topic and key details in their Main Topic and Key Details chart. After reading, guide children to participate in a group discussion about the selection they read. Guide children to:

→ share the information they recorded in their Main Topic and Key Details chart.

→ tell what interesting facts and information they learned from the selections.

→ describe the predictions they made, how they checked their predictions, and whether they revised them.

# → On Level

## Leveled Reader:
### *A Tree Full of Life*

**Lexile** 460
*TextEvaluator™* 9

### OBJECTIVES

 Read with sufficient accuracy and fluency to support comprehension. **RF.2.4**

 Read on-level text with purpose and understanding. **RF.2.4a**

 Read on-level text orally with accuracy, appropriate rate, and expression on successive readings. **RF.2.4b**

### MATERIALS

Leveled Reader
*A Tree Full of Life*

### Before Reading

#### Preview and Predict

Have children turn to the title page. Read the title and author name and have children repeat. Preview the selection's photos. Prompt children to predict what the selection might be about.

#### Review Genre: Narrative Nonfiction

Have children recall that narrative nonfiction is informational text. It tells about real people, things, or events. It uses text features, such as photos, captions, and maps to give information. It tells information in sequence.

#### ESSENTIAL QUESTION

Remind children of the Essential Question: *What are the features of different animal habitats?* Set a purpose for reading: *Let's read to find out how this tree provides a habitat for animals.* Remind children that as they read, they can ask questions about what they do not understand or want to know more about.

### During Reading

#### Close Reading

**Note taking** Ask students to use their graphic organizer while they read.

**Pages 2–3** *Turn to a partner and discuss what you see in the map. Make a prediction about what you will read.* (Possible response: I see a map of Australia on page 2. I predict that we will read about trees in Australia.) *How do you know what the green parts are on the map?* (I look at the map key and see that the green parts are eucalyptus forests.)

**Pages 4–8** *What is the main topic on pages 4–6?* (how eucalyptus trees help koala bears) *What key details do you learn about this topic?* (Eucalyptus trees give koala bears food, shelter, water, and protection.) *What is the green box for on page 7?* (The green box is a text box for a caption. It tells me about the termites in the photo.)

### Go Digital

**Leveled Readers**

**Graphic Organizer**

**Retelling Cards**

**Pages 9–12** *What prediction can you make after reading the chapter title?* (I predict this chapter will be about homes for animals in eucalyptus trees.) *What helps you confirm your prediction?* (I read about kookaburras, sugar gliders, and possums that make homes in eucalyptus trees.) *What word has the suffix –ly on page 9?* (quickly)

**Pages 13–14** *What is the main topic on these pages?* (Plants and animals work together to keep eucalyptus trees full of life.)

## After Reading

### Respond to Reading

Have children complete Respond to Reading on page 15.

### Retell

Have children take turns retelling the selection. Help children make a personal connection by asking: *What other animal do you know that lives in a tree? Why is the tree a good place for the animal to live and find food?*

### Model Fluency

Read the sentences, one at a time. Have children chorally repeat. Point out to children how your voice goes up at the end of a question.

**Apply** Have partners practice repeated reading. Provide feedback.

## PAIRED READ ...

### "Life in a Termite Mound"

### Make Connections: Write About It ● *Analytical Writing*

Before reading, ask children to note that "Life in a Termite Mound" is expository text. Then discuss the Compare Texts statement. After reading, ask children to make connections between in "Life in a Termite Mound" and *A Tree Full of Life*.

**Leveled Reader**

 **FOCUS ON SCIENCE**

Children can extend their knowledge of the different features of animal habitats by completing the science activity on page 20. **STEM**

## Literature Circles

Lead children in conducting a literature circle using the Thinkmark questions to guide the discussion. You may wish to discuss what children have learned about animal habitats from both selections in the leveled reader.

## Level Up

Level-up lessons available online.

**IF** children read the On Level fluently and answered the questions,

**THEN** pair them with children who have proficiently read the Beyond Level and have on-level children

• partner-read the Beyond Level main selection.

• Identify a part of the selection they would like to learn more about.

### A C T Access Complex Text

The Beyond Level challenges children by including more **specific vocabulary** and **complex sentence structures.**

# On Level

## Phonics

### BUILD WORDS WITH SOFT *c* AND SOFT *g*

**OBJECTIVES**

Know and apply grade-level phonics and word analysis skills in decoding words. **RF.2.3**

- Build and decode words with soft *c* and *g*.
- Read for fluency.

 **I Do**

Display **Word-Building Cards** *p, a, c, e.* Say: *This is the letter* p. *It stands for* /p/. *This is the letter* a. *It stands for* /ā/. *This is the letter* c. *It stands for* /s/. Point out that *c* stands for the /s/ sound when it's followed by *e* or *i*. Explain that the *e* is silent. Say: *Listen as I blend the three sounds together:* /pās/, pace. *The word is* pace. *Repeat for* /j/ *spelled* ge *and* dge, *with* budge *and* huge.

 **We Do**

*Let's do one together. Make the word* pace *using Word-Building Cards. Place the letter* s *at the beginning of* pace. *Let's blend:* /s/ /pās/, /spās/, space. *The new word is* space. *I am going to change the letter* a *in* space *to the letter* i. *Let's blend and read the new word:* /spīs/, spice. *The new word is* spice.

 **You Do**

Have children build and blend *rice, price; budge, fudge; wage, stage.*

**Fluency in Connected Text** Have children read this week's Decodable Reader selection, *Animal Places and Spaces.*

## Vocabulary

### REVIEW WORDS

**OBJECTIVES**

Use words and phrases acquired through conversations, reading and being read to, and responding to texts, including using adjectives and adverbs to describe (e.g., *When other kids are happy that makes me happy*). **L.2.6**

 **I Do**

Use the **Visual Vocabulary Cards** to review each vocabulary word. Point to each word, read it aloud, and have children chorally repeat it.

 **We Do**

Guide children to use the **Define/Example/Ask** routine for a few Vocabulary words using their **Response Boards**. Ask sample questions to help students respond and explain their answers.

 **You Do**

Have children work with a partner to do the Define/Example/Ask routine on their own for the remaining vocabulary words. Then have children write sentences about this week's selections. Each sentence must contain at least one vocabulary word.

# Comprehension

## REVIEW MAIN TOPIC AND KEY DETAILS

**OBJECTIVES**

Ask and answer questions such as *who, what, where, when, why,* and *how* to demonstrate understanding of key details in a text. **RI.2.1**

Identify the main topic of a multi-paragraph text as well as the focus of specific paragraphs within the text. **RI.2.2**

 **I Do** Remind children that when they read informational text they can look for the topic and the key details about the topic. *When we read informational text, we can look for the topic, or what the selection is mostly about. Then we can look for key details about the topic in the words and the photos. The key details give information about the main topic.*

 **We Do** Read the first pages of the Practice Book selection aloud. As you read, pause to identify the topic. *We read about two types of tundra. This is the topic of the selection. What key details tell more about this topic?*

**You Do** Guide children to read the rest of the Practice Book selection. Remind them to look for more key details that give information about the main topic.

## SELF-SELECTED READING

**OBJECTIVES**

Ask and answer questions such as *who, what, where, when, why,* and *how* to demonstrate understanding of key details in a text. **RI.2.1**

Identify the main topic of a multi-paragraph text as well as the focus of specific paragraphs within the text. **RI.2.2**

Apply the strategy and skill to reread text.

### Read Independently

Have children pick a nonfiction text that they have read for sustained silent reading. Remind them to:

→ find the main topic and look for key details that give information about it.

→ make predictions about what they think they will read and learn, then confirm and revise their predictions.

### Read Purposefully

Have children record the main topic and key details in their Main Topic and Key Details chart. After reading, guide partners to:

→ share the information they recorded in their Main Topic and Key Details chart.

→ tell what interesting facts and information they learned from reading the selections.

→ share the predictions they made and explain how they checked and revised them.

# → Beyond Level

**Lexile** 630
*TextEvaluator™* 13

## OBJECTIVES

 Read with sufficient accuracy and fluency to support comprehension. **RF.2.4**

 Read on-level text with purpose and understanding. **RF.2.4a**

 Read on-level text orally with accuracy, appropriate rate, and expression on successive readings. **RF.2.4b**

## MATERIALS

Leveled Reader
*A Tree Full of Life*

## Leveled Reader:
## *A Tree Full of Life*

### Before Reading

#### Preview and Predict

Read the title and author name. Have children preview the title page and the photos. Ask: *What do you think this book will be about?*

#### Review Genre: Narrative Nonfiction

Have children recall that narrative nonfiction gives facts about real people, places, or things. Prompt children to name key characteristics of informational text. Tell them to look for these as they read.

#### ESSENTIAL QUESTION

Remind children of the Essential Question: *What are features of different animal habitats?* Have children set a purpose for reading by asking: *What do you want to learn about how this tree is a habitat for animals?*

### During Reading

#### Close Reading

**Note taking** Ask students to use their graphic organizer while they read.

**Pages 2–3** *Turn to a partner and discuss what you see in the illustrations. Make a prediction about what you will read.* (Possible response: I see a map of Australia on page 2. I predict that we will read about trees in Australia. I see a eucalyptus tree on page 3. I predict we will read about these kinds of trees.) *How do you use a map key?* (The green symbol stands for eucalyptus forests. I look at the green parts of the map to see where eucalyptus forests are in Australia.)

**Pages 4–8** *What prediction can you make about the main topic on pages 4–6?* (I predict I will read how eucalyptus trees help koala bears.) *What key details do you learn about this topic?* (Eucalyptus trees give koala bears food, shelter, water, and protection.) *Why is there text in a green box on page 7?* (This text box is for a caption. It tells me about the termites in the photo.)

**Go
Digital**

**Leveled
Readers**

**Graphic
Organizer**

**Pages 9–12** *What prediction can you make from the chapter title?* (This chapter will be about animal homes in eucalyptus trees.) *What word has the suffix –ful on page 9?* (wonderful) *How does the suffix change the root word?* (It tells me that something is full of wonder.)

**Pages 13–14** *What is the main topic on these pages?* (Plants and animals work together to keep eucalyptus trees full of life.) *What are some key details on page 14?* (The mistletoe plant eats the sap of the eucalyptus tree, and mistletoe birds eat the fruit of this plant.)

### After Reading

### Respond to Reading

Have children complete the Respond to Reading questions on page 15.

### Retell

Have children take turns retelling what they learned from the selection. Have children make a personal connection by writing about another animal habitat they know. Say: *Write about another animal habitat. What animals live there? Why is it a good place for them to live?*

## PAIRED READ ...

**Leveled Reader**

## "Life in a Termite Mound"

### Make Connections: Write About It *Analytical Writing*

Before reading, have children preview the title page and identify the genre. Then discuss the Compare Texts statement. After reading, have partners discuss what they read in "Life in a Termite Mound" and *A Tree Full of Life*. Ask children to make connections by comparing and contrasting the animal habitats in each selection. Prompt children to discuss what they learned about the features of animal habitats.

### FOCUS ON SCIENCE

Children can extend their knowledge of the different features of animal habitats by completing the science activity on page 20.  **STEM**

## Literature Circles

Lead children in conducting a literature circle using the Thinkmark questions to guide the discussion. You may wish to discuss what children have learned about animal habitats from both selections in the leveled reader.

## Gifted and Talented

**SYNTHESIZE** Challenge students to describe what might happen if eucalyptus trees disappeared from Australia. Children should make a prediction and write about how this might affect the animals and plants that depend on the eucalyptus trees.

**EXTEND** Have them use facts they learned from the week or do additional research to find out which living things would be most affected.

# Beyond Level

## Vocabulary

### REVIEW DOMAIN-SPECIFIC WORDS

**OBJECTIVES**
Use words and phrases acquired through conversations, reading and being read to, and responding to texts, including using adjectives and adverbs to describe (e.g., *When other kids are happy that makes me happy*). **L.2.6**

 **Model**   Use the Visual Vocabulary Cards to review the meaning of the words *habitat* and *nature*. Write science-related sentences on the board using the words.

Write the words *raccoons* and *hatch* on the board and discuss the meanings with children. Then help children write sentences using the words.

 **Apply**   Have children work in pairs to review the meanings of the words *journey* and *features*. Then have partners write sentences using the words.

### SUFFIXES

**OBJECTIVES**
Determine or clarify the meaning of unknown and multiple-meaning words and phrases based on *grade 2 reading and content*, choosing flexibly from an array of strategies. **L.2.4**

Use sentence-level context as a clue to the meaning of a word or phrase. **L.2.4a**

 **Model**   Read aloud the first two paragraphs of the Comprehension and Fluency passage on Beyond Level Practice Book pages 73–74.

**Think Aloud**   When I read these paragraphs, I see the word *extremely*. I'm not sure what this word means. I'll separate the root word from the ending. The root word is *extreme*, which means "very great or severe." The suffix is *-ly*, which means "in this way." I think the word *extremely* means "in a great way."

With children, read the second paragraph. Help them figure out the meaning of *playful*.

 **Apply**   Have pairs of children read the rest of the passage. Ask them to use context clues to determine the meaning of the following words: *careful, useful,* and *seriously*.

 **Shades of Meaning** Using their definition of *playful*, have partners write an explanation of the difference between *playfully* and *carefully*. Encourage them to also use artwork to depict the two words.

# Comprehension

## REVIEW MAIN TOPIC AND KEY DETAILS

**OBJECTIVES**

 Ask and answer such questions as *who, what, where, when, why,* and *how* to demonstrate understanding of key details in a text. **RI.2.1**

 Identify the main topic of a multi-paragraph text as well as the focus of specific paragraphs within the text. **RI.2.2**

 **Model** Remind children that the main topic of a passage is what the passage is mostly about and what the author is writing about. Explain that key details give information about the main topic. Point out that each paragraph has its own topic that is part of the main focus of the passage.

Have children read the first paragraph of the Comprehension and Fluency passage of Beyond Level Practice Book pages 73–74. Ask open-ended questions to facilitate discussion, such as *What is this paragraph mostly about? What key details give us information about the main topic?* Children should support their responses with examples and details from the text.

**Apply** Have children identify the main topic and the key details in the rest of the passage. Have them independently record this information in a Main Topic and Key Details chart. Then have partners use their work to summarize the whole passage.

## SELF-SELECTED READING

**OBJECTIVES**

 Ask and answer such questions as *who, what, where, when, why,* and *how* to demonstrate understanding of key details in a text. **RI.2.1**

 Identify the main topic of a multi-paragraph text as well as the focus of specific paragraphs within the text. **RI.2.2**

### Read Independently

Have children choose an informational book for sustained silent reading.

→ As children read, have them fill in a Main Topic and Key Details chart.

→ Remind them to reread difficult sections of the text.

### Read Purposefully

Encourage children to keep a reading journal. Ask them to read different books in order to learn about a variety of subjects.

→ Children can write summaries of the books in their journals.

→ Ask children to share their reactions to the books with classmates.

 **Independent Study** Challenge children to discuss how their books relate to the weekly theme of animal habits. What features of the habitats are most important to the animals that live there.

# English Language Learners

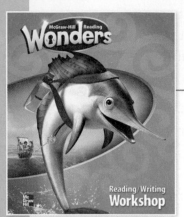

**Reading/Writing Workshop**

---

**OBJECTIVES**

 Read with sufficient accuracy and fluency to support comprehension. **RF.2.4**

 Read on-level text with purpose and understanding. **RF.2.4a**

 Ask and answer such questions as *who, what, where, when, why,* and *how* to demonstrate understanding of key details in a text. **RI.2.1**

 Identify the main topic of a multiparagraph text as well as the focus of specific paragraphs within the text. **RI.2.2**

---

**ACADEMIC LANGUAGE**

*reread, main topic, key details, make predictions*

## Shared Read
## *A Prairie Guard Dog*

### Before Reading

#### Build Background

Read the Essential Question: *What are features of different animal habitats?*

→ Explain the meaning of the Essential Question: *An animal habitat is a place where animals live. The features of a habitat include the climate, the animals and plants, and the land. What are the features of a desert habit?*

→ **Model an answer:** *Some animals, such as jack rabbits, live in the desert. The desert has a hot, dry climate. The desert does not have many plants.*

→ Ask children a question that ties the Essential Question to their own background knowledge: *Turn to a partner and tell about an animal you know about. Where does the animal live? What is its habitat, or what is it like where this animal lives?* Call on several pairs.

### During Reading

#### Interactive Question-Response

→ Ask questions that help children understand the meaning of the text after each paragraph.

→ Reinforce the meanings of key vocabulary providing meanings embedded in the questions.

→ Ask children questions that require them to use key vocabulary.

→ Reinforce strategies and skills of the week by modeling.

---

**Go Digital**

**A Prairie Guard Dog**

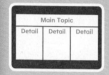

**Graphic Organizer**

---

## "A Prairie Guard Dog"

### Page 134

Point to the title. *Listen as I read the title of the selection.* Point to each word as you read it. *What is the title?* (A Prairie Guard Dog)

*This selection is about an animal called a prairie dog. Say the name with me: prairie dog. A prairie dog is not really a dog. It is a small furry animal. Find the prairie dog in the picture.*

*What does a prairie dog look like?* (It is brown and covered with fur. )

### Page 135

*Look at the picture. I see prairie dogs. I see three prairie dogs. Where are the prairie dogs?* (in the ground)

*Look for the caption. The caption is the sentence next to the picture. The caption tells more about the picture. Let's read the caption together:* Prairie dogs build underground burrows to keep themselves safe from predators. *Where are the burrows?* (underground)

*Why do prairie dogs build underground burrows?* (to keep themselves safe)

*Let's read the first paragraph together. The prairie dog lives in prairie habitat. A habitat is the place animals live. A prairie has a lot of grass but not many trees. What does a prairie have?* (grass)

**Explain and Model the Phonics Skill** Repeat the last sentence of the first paragraph. *Look at the word* places. *Say the word with me:* places. *What sound does the letter c stand for in places? Yes, /s/. Now look at* dangerous. *Say the word with me:* dangerous. *Listen for the /j/ sound in* dangerous. *What letter stands for /j/ in* dangerous? *Yes,* g.

### Pages 136–137

*A prairie dog named Pete is the guard. He watches for danger. Pete cannot rest, because he is always looking around. Let's look for the word that tells us Pete cannot rest.* (restless) *The word is* restless. *The suffix –less means without, so restless means without rest.*

*The caption on page 137 tells us about the picture. The picture shows a badger. Badgers live on prairies, too. Badgers hunt prairie dogs. Prairie dogs are food for badgers.*

**Explain and Model the Strategy** Reread the first three sentences on page 137 to help children predict what might happen next. *We can predict, or guess, what will happen next. We will use what we already know. We can also use the text. We know that badgers hunt prairie dogs. Now Pete sees a badger. He must be scared! He gives a bark.*

 *What do you predict will happen next?*

### Page 138

Reread the text. *The burrow has many rooms. The prairie dogs do different things in the rooms. Find the diagram. It shows what the burrow looks like.*

*What kind of rooms does the burrow have?* (sleeping room, bathroom, a room for food)

### Page 139

*Let's pretend we are prairie dogs. What does a prairie dog look like? Use the photo and the chart on page 139 to help you describe a prairie dog. Now let's peek our head out of our burrow and look at the sky. Give a bark like a prairie dog, "Yap, yap."*

### After Reading

**Make Connections**

→ Review the Essential Question.

# → English Language Learners

**Lexile** 410
*TextEvaluator™* 4

## OBJECTIVES

 Ask and answer such questions as *who, what, where, when, why,* and *how* to demonstrate understanding of key details in a text. **RI.2.1**

 Identify the main topic of a multi-paragraph text as well as the focus of specific paragraphs within the text. **RI.2.2**

 Read with sufficient accuracy and fluency to support comprehension. **RF.2.4**

---

## ACADEMIC LANGUAGE

*reread, retell*

## Leveled Reader:
## *A Tree Full of Life*

### Before Reading

#### Preview

Read the title. Ask: *What is the title? Say it again.* Repeat with the author's name. Preview the selection's photos. Have children describe the images. Use simple language to tell about each page. Follow with questions, such as *Is this tree big or small? What is this animal doing?*

#### ESSENTIAL QUESTION

Remind children of the Essential Question. Say: *Let's read to find out about a tree that is a home to animals.* Encourage children to seek clarification when they encounter a confusing word or phrase.

### During Reading

#### Interactive Question Response

**Pages 2–3** Point to the map on page 2. *What place is on the map? Let's read the caption:* Australia has many eucalyptus forests. *What is the place?* (Australia) *Listen as I say the name of a kind of tree:* eucalyptus. *Say it with me:* eucalyptus. *What is a eucalyptus tree like? Tell your partner.*

**Pages 4–5** *A koala bear, or koala, is an animal. What does a koala do in the eucalyptus tree?* (It eats the leaves and it sleeps there.)

**Pages 6–7** *Koalas eat the leaves on a eucalyptus tree. What part of the tree do termites eat? Let's read the sentence that tells us:* They eat its bark.

**Pages 8–9** *Now look at page 9. The picture shows a bird called the* kookaburra. *What sound does it make? Let's make the sound together: ha!*

**Pages 10–11** *What other animal lives in holes in the eucalyptus tree? Find the label on the picture on page 10 to help you answer. Now look at page 11.*

**Pages 12–13** *Where does the wombat find its food?* (on the ground) *What tree parts do fruit bats eat? Let's read the sentence that tells us:* They eat its pollen and fruit.

**Page 14** *Let's read what else lives in a eucalyptus tree. Say it with me.* Even plants live in this eucalyptus tree! *Read the last sentence. Tell your partner why the author says the eucalyptus tree is full of life.*

**Go Digital**

**Leveled Readers**

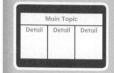

**Graphic Organizer**

**Retelling Cards**

## After Reading

### Respond to Reading

Have partners answer the questions. Pair children with peers of varying language abilities.

### Retell

Model retelling using the Retelling Card prompts. Then guide children to retell the selection to a partner.

### Fluency: Intonation

Read the sentences in the book, one at a time. Help children echo-read the pages expressively and with appropriate intonation. Remind them to read exclamations in a way that shows excitement.

**Apply** Have children practice reading with a partner. Pair children with peers of varying language abilities. Provide feedback as needed.

## PAIRED READ ...

## "Life in a Termite Mound"

### Make Connections: Write About It ✏ *Analytical Writing*

**Leveled Reader**

Before reading, tell children that this text is also informational text. Then discuss the Compare Texts statement.

After reading, ask children to make connections between what they read in "Life in a Termite Mound" and *A Tree Full of Life*. Prompt children by providing sentence frames: A termite mound is a home to one kind of animal. A eucalyptus tree is a home. Many animals live there.

 **FOCUS ON SCIENCE**

Children can extend their knowledge of the different features of animal habitats by completing the science activity on page 20. **STEM**

## Literature Circles

Lead children in conducting a literature circle using the Thinkmark questions to guide the discussion. You may wish to discuss what children have learned about the features of different animal habitats from both selections in the leveled reader.

## Level Up

**Level-up lessons available online.**

**IF** children read the **ELL Level** fluently and answered the questions

**THEN** pair them with children who have proficiently read the **On Level** and have children

• echo-read the **On Level** main selection with their partners.

• list difficult words and phrases and discuss them with their partners.

## A C T Access Complex Text

The **On Level** challenges children by including more **specific vocabulary** and **complex sentence structures.**

# English Language Learners
## Vocabulary

## PRETEACH VOCABULARY

**OBJECTIVES**

 **CCSS** Use words and phrases acquired through conversations, reading and being read to, and responding to texts, including using adjectives and adverbs to describe (e.g., *When other kids are happy that makes me happy*). **L.2.6**

**LANGUAGE OBJECTIVE**

Use vocabulary words.

**I Do** Preteach vocabulary from "A Prairie Guard Dog," following the Vocabulary Routine found on the Visual Vocabulary Cards for words *buried, escape, habitat, journey, nature, peeks, restless,* and *spies.*

**We Do** After completing the Vocabulary Routine, point to the word on the Visual Vocabulary Card and read it with children. Ask them to repeat it.

**You Do** Have children work with a partner to write the words. Then have a child select a card and give clues about the meaning for the partner to guess.

| Beginning | Intermediate | Advanced/High |
|---|---|---|
| Help children write the sentences correctly and give clues about the word. | Ask children to write one sentence and one question about the word they select. | Challenge partners to take turns saying clues for for each word. |

## REVIEW VOCABULARY

**OBJECTIVES**

**CCSS** Use words and phrases acquired through conversations, reading and being read to, and responding to texts, including using adjectives and adverbs to describe (e.g., *When other kids are happy that makes me happy*). **L.2.6**

**LANGUAGE OBJECTIVE**

Use vocabulary words.

**I Do** Review the previous week's vocabulary words over a few days. Read each word aloud pointing to the word on the Visual Vocabulary Card. Have children repeat after you. Then follow the Vocabulary Routine on the back.

**We Do** Ask children to guess the word you describe. Provide clues, such as synonyms or antonyms. Have children name the word and define or use it in a sentence.

**You Do** In pairs, have children make a list of clues for two or more words. Ask them to read them aloud for the class to guess the word.

| Beginning | Intermediate | Advanced/High |
|---|---|---|
| Help children list clue words and read them. | Have children write clues as sentences. | Ask children to use synonyms or antonyms in their clues. |

## SUFFIXES

### OBJECTIVES

 **CCSS** Determine or clarify the meaning of unknown and multiple-meaning words and phrases based on *grade 2 reading and content*, choosing flexibly from an array of strategies. **L.2.4**

**CCSS** Use sentence-level context as a clue to the meaning of a word or phrase. **L.2.4a**

### LANGUAGE OBJECTIVE

Use suffixes.

**I Do** Read aloud the first two paragraphs of "A Prairie Guard Dog" on page 135, while children follow along. Summarize the paragraphs. Point to the word *loudly*. Explain that sometime we can separate the root word from its suffix to understand the word's meaning. Then we can try reading the word in the sentence to see if it makes sense.

**Think Aloud** When I read this paragraph, I'm not sure what the word *loudly* means. I know that *loud* means "noisy." The suffix *-ly* means "in this way." I see that the word is *loudly*. It means "in a noisy way." I'll try reading this word in the sentence to see if it makes sense.

**We Do** Have children point to the word *restless* on page 136. Help children separate the suffix from the root word to determine its meaning. Write the meaning on the board.

**You Do** In pairs, have children write a definition for *watchful* on page 137, using the root word and suffix to determine its meaning.

| Beginning | Intermediate | Advanced/High |
|---|---|---|
| Help children complete the activity. | Help children complete the activity. | Ask children to explain how they applied the skill. |

## ADDITIONAL VOCABULARY

### OBJECTIVES

**CCSS** Use knowledge of language and its conventions when writing, speaking, reading, or listening. **L.2.3**

**CCSS** Compare formal and informal uses of English. **L.2.3a**

### LANGUAGE OBJECTIVE

Use academic and concept words

**I Do** List academic language and additional vocabulary from "A Prairie Guard Dog": *recognize, habitat, burrow, nature*; and *A Tree Full of Life: forest, healthy, pollen*. Define each word for children: When you recognize something, you know it.

**We Do** Model using the words for children in a sentence: *The prairie dogs recognize Pete's cries. The baby birds recognize their own mother.* Then provide sentence frames and complete them with children: *I recognized the girl because ____.*

**You Do** Have pairs make up their own sentences. Have the class complete them.

| Beginning | Intermediate | Advanced/High |
|---|---|---|
| Help children complete the activity. | Provide support to help children use the words in the activity. | Ask children to define the words. |

# English Language Learners
## Writing/Spelling

## WRITING TRAIT: ORGANIZATION

**OBJECTIVES**

 With guidance and support from adults, use a variety of digital tools to produce and publish writing, including in collaboration with peers. **W.2.5**

 Demonstration command of the conventions of standard English grammar and usage when writing or speaking. **L.2.1**

 **I Do** Explain that writers use words such as *first, next, then,* and *last* to show the order of what happens. Write and read the sentences: *First, the bird finds a tasty worm. Next, it flies back to the nest. Then, it feeds the worm to hungry babies.* Help children find the words that show the order of events.

 **We Do** Read the first two sentences of paragraph 2 on page 139 of *A Prairie Guard Dog.* Ask children to name what happens first and next. Repeat the exercise having children identify the sequence word (Then) that helps organize the events.

**You Do** Have children write two sentences about animals, using sequence words.

| Beginning | Intermediate | Advanced/High |
|---|---|---|
| Help children name an animal. Ask them to tell what the animal does. Provide sentence frames to copy and complete. | Ask children to describe things the animal does. Repeat their responses. Give sentence frames for children to complete. | Ask children to tell things the animal does. Elicit responses with questions. *What does it do first? Then what does it do?* |

## WORDS WITH SOFT *c* and *g*

**OBJECTIVES**

 Demonstrate command of the conventions of standard English grammar and usage when writing or speaking. **L.2.1**

**LANGUAGE OBJECTIVE**

Spell words with soft *c* and *g*

 **I Do** Read aloud the Spelling Words on page T198. Segment the word *place* into sounds and attach a spelling to each sound. Point out that the letters *ce* stand for /s/ in *place*. Read aloud, segment, and spell the remaining words and have children repeat. Point out the soft *c* and soft *g* spellings.

 **We Do** Read the first sentence from the Dictation Routine on page T198. Then, read the soft *c* word slowly and ask children to repeat. Have them write the word. Repeat the process for remaining sentences with soft *c* and *g* words.

 **You Do** Display the words. Have partners check and correct their spelling lists.

| Beginning | Intermediate | Advanced/High |
|---|---|---|
| Help children copy the words with correct spelling and say the word. | After children have corrected their words, have pairs quiz each other. | Challenge children to think of other words that have the soft *c* or *g* sound. |

# Grammar

## KINDS OF NOUNS

**OBJECTIVES**

 Demonstrate command of the conventions of standard English grammar and usage when writing or speaking. **L.2.1**

 Use collective nouns (e.g., *group*). **L.2.1a**

Demonstrate command of the conventions of standard English capitalization, punctuation, and spelling when writing. **L.2.2**

 Capitalize holidays, product names, and geographic names. **L.2.2a**

**LANGUAGE OBJECTIVE**

Recognize common, proper, and collective nouns.

**ELL Language Transfers**

Spanish rules for capitalization of proper nouns differ from those in English. For example, the names of days and months are not capitalized in Spanish. Words such as *river, mountain,* and *lake* are also not capitalized in Spanish when naming a geographical feature. Provide extra practice to help Spanish speakers with capitalizing proper nouns.

---

**I Do**

Review that nouns name people, places, or things.

→ Common nouns name any person, place, or thing, such as *boy, country,* or *day.*

→ Proper nouns name a particular person, place, or thing, such as *Jim, Australia,* and *Monday.* They begin with a capital letter.

→ Collective nouns name a group of people, animals, or things, such as *group, class, family, team, flock.* Collective nouns are not capitalized.

**We Do**

Write the sentences on the board. Have children read the sentences and underline nouns. Have them say: *The common nouns are _____. The proper nouns are _____. The collective nouns are _____.*

*Our class made pictures of turkeys for Thanksgiving.*
*A flock of birds eats corn from the field near Grantville.*
*Amy will fly on a plane from Florida to Mexico.*

**You Do**

Write the following sentence frames on the board.

*My favorite day of the week is _____.      Our school is in _____.*
*This week our class read about _____.*

Pair children and have them complete each sentence frame. Circulate, listen in, and take note of each child's language use and proficiency.

| Beginning | Intermediate | Advanced/High |
|---|---|---|
| Describe the photos in *A Prairie Guard Dog.* Ask: *What do you see?* Model a response by providing a sentence frame: *I see _____.* Help children identify common, proper, and collective nouns. | Ask children to describe the same photos and then identify the nouns they used. Have children identify common, proper, and collective nouns. Encourage children to use complete sentences. | Ask children to look at the photos and name as many things as they see. Prompt children to sort the words into lists of common and proper nouns. Have them point out any collective nouns. |

# PROGRESS MONITORING

## Weekly Assessment

| ✓**COMPREHENSION:** Main Topic and Key Details **RI.2.1, RI.2.2** | ✓**VOCABULARY:** Suffixes **L.2.4b** | ✓**WRITING:** Writing About Text **RI.2.1, RI.2.2** |

### Assessment Includes

→ Pencil-and-Paper administration

→ Online administration

→ Approaching Level Weekly Assessment also available

**Fluency Goal** 41 to 61 words correct per minute (WCPM)

**Accuracy Rate Goal** 95% or higher

Administer oral reading fluency assessments using the following schedule:

→ **Weeks 1, 3, 5** Provide Approaching Level children at least three oral reading fluency assessments during the unit.

→ **Weeks 2 and 4** Provide On Level children at least two oral reading fluency assessments during the unit.

→ **Week 6** If necessary, provide Beyond Level children an oral reading fluency assessment at this time.

**Also Available: Selection Tests online PDFs**

**Go Digital!** http://connected.mcgraw-hill.com

# Using Assessment Results

| TESTED SKILLS | If ... | Then ... |
|---|---|---|
| **COMPREHENSION** | Children answer 0–6 multiple-choice items correctly ... | ... assign Lessons 85–87 on Main Idea and Details from the **_Tier 2 Comprehension Intervention online PDFs._** |
| **VOCABULARY** | Children answer 0–6 multiple-choice items correctly ... | ... assign Lessons 105–106 on Suffixes from the **_Tier 2 Vocabulary Intervention online PDFs._** |
| **WRITING** | Children score less than "3" on the Constructed response ... | ... assign Lessons 85–87 and/or Write About Reading Lessons from Section 13 of the **_Tier 2 Comprehension Intervention online PDFs._** |
|  | Children have a WCPM score of 36–40 ... | ... assign a lesson from Section 1, 9, or 10 of the **_Tier 2 Fluency Intervention online PDFs._** |
| | Children have a WCPM score of 0–35 ... | ... assign a lesson from Sections 2–8 of the **_Tier 2 Fluency Intervention online PDFs._** |

## Response to Intervention

Use the appropriate sections of the **_Placement and Diagnostic Assessment_** as well as students' assessment results to designate students requiring:

 **Intervention Online PDFs**

**WonderWorks Intervention Program**

**Text Complexity Range for Grades 2–3**

Lexile

420 — *TextEvaluator™* — 820

2 — 35

Reading **Wonders**

**Reading/Writing Workshop**

McGraw Hill

# TEACH AND MODEL

CCSS **Shared Read** ▸ Genre • Expository Text

## Eagles and Eaglets

Bald eagles are birds. The baby birds, or **offspring** are called eaglets. Let's read about how eaglets are like their parents.

### It's Nesting Time

All birds lay eggs. Bald eagles build their nests in the tops of trees so the eggs will be safe. Their nests are built of sticks and grass. They add on to their nests each year. They can become huge! These **giant** nests can be as large as nine feet across. That's bigger than your bed!

The mother eagle lays from one to three eggs. She sits on her eggs until they hatch. Then both parents watch over the nest.

**Essential Question**
How are offspring like their parents?
Read to learn how young bald eagles are like their parents.

## ✔ Vocabulary

adult
alive
covered
fur
giant
groom
mammal
offspring

 **Close Reading of Complex Text**

**Shared Read** "Eagles and Eaglets," 150–155

**Genre** Expository Text

**Lexile** 490L

ETS *TextEvaluator™* 4

## Minilessons

✔ **Tested Skills** CCSS

✔ **Comprehension Strategy** ............... Reread, T308-T309

✔ **Comprehension Skill** ............... Main Topic and Key Details, T310–T311

✔ **Genre** ............... Expository Text, T320–T321

✔ **Vocabulary Strategy** ............... Multiple-Meaning Words, T322–T323

✔ **Writing Traits** ............... Word Choice, T298–T299

✔ **Grammar** ............... Plural Nouns, T300–T301

  **Go** Digital

http://connected.mcgraw-hill.com

ANIMAL DISCOVERIES
**Essential Question**
How are offspring like their
parents?

WEEK 4 →

# APPLY *WITH* **CLOSE READING**

## Complex Text

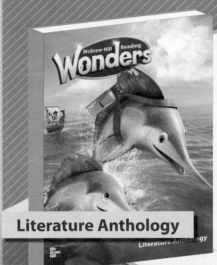

**Literature Anthology**

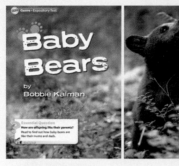

*Baby Bears*, 186–201
**Genre** Expository Text
**Lexile** 590L
(ETS) *TextEvaluator* 4

**PAIRED READ**

*"From Caterpillar to Butterfly,"* 204–205
**Genre** Expository Text
**Lexile** 560L
(ETS) *TextEvaluator* 7

## Differentiated Text

**Leveled Readers** *Including Paired Reads*

APPROACHING
**Lexile** 320
(ETS) *TextEvaluator* 4

ON LEVEL
**Lexile** 490
(ETS) *TextEvaluator* 4

BEYOND
**Lexile** 600
(ETS) *TextEvaluator* 5

ELL
**Lexile** 390
(ETS) *TextEvaluator* 4

## Extended Complex Text

*Life in an Ocean*
**Genre** Nonfiction
**Lexile** 290L
(ETS) *TextEvaluator* 6

*Let's Look at Monarch Butterflies*
**Genre** Nonfiction
**Lexile** 510L
(ETS) *TextEvaluator* 6

**Classroom Library**

Classroom Library lessons available online.

# TEACH AND MANAGE

## How You Teach

### INTRODUCE

**Weekly Concept**
Baby Animals

**Reading/Writing Workshop**
146–147

**Go Digital**

Interactive Whiteboard

### TEACH

**Close Reading**
"Eagles and Eaglets"

**Minilessons**
Reread, Main Topic and Key Details, Expository Text, Multiple-Meaning Words, Writing Traits

**Reading/Writing Workshop**
150–155

Interactive Whiteboard

### APPLY

**Close Reading**
*Baby Bears*
*From Caterpillar to Butterfly*

**Student Anthology**
186–205

Mobile

## How Students Practice

### Weekly contract

**PDF Online**

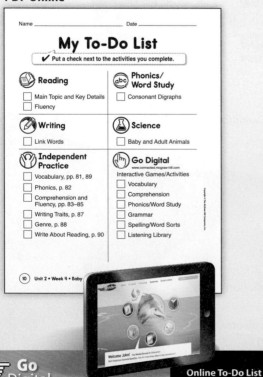

**Go Digital**

Online To-Do List

### Leveled practice and online activities

**Your Turn Practice Book**
81–90

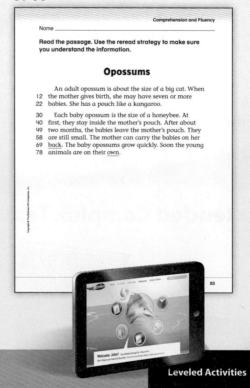

Leveled Activities

**Leveled Readers**

Writer's Workspace

## DIFFERENTIATE

**SMALL GROUP INSTRUCTION**

**Leveled Readers**

**Mobile**

## INTEGRATE

**Research and Inquiry**
Animal Comparison, T332–T333

**Text Connections**
Compare Animal Families, T334

**Write About Reading**
*Analytical Writing* Write an Analysis, T335

**Online Research and Writing**

## ASSESS

Wonders

**Weekly Assessment**

**Weekly Assessment**
**97–108**

**Online Assessment**

# Leveled workstation cards

**More Activities on back**

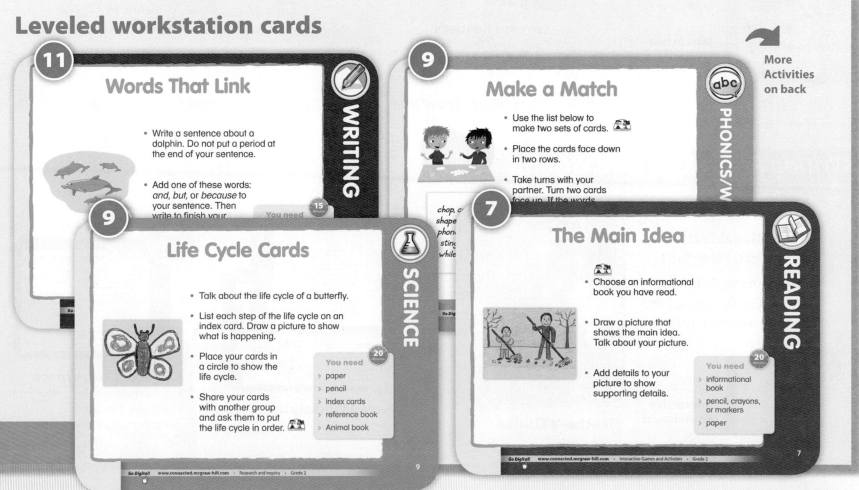

**11**

## Words That Link

- Write a sentence about a dolphin. Do not put a period at the end of your sentence.

- Add one of these words: *and, but,* or *because* to your sentence. Then write to finish your

**15** Minutes

**You need**

**WRITING**

**9**

## Make a Match

- Use the list below to make two sets of cards.

- Place the cards face down in two rows.

- Take turns with your partner. Turn two cards face up. If the words

chop, c
shape
phon
sting
while

**PHONICS/W**

**9**

## Life Cycle Cards

- Talk about the life cycle of a butterfly.

- List each step of the life cycle on an index card. Draw a picture to show what is happening.

- Place your cards in a circle to show the life cycle.

- Share your cards with another group and ask them to put the life cycle in order.

**20** Minutes

**You need**
> paper
> pencil
> index cards
> reference book
> Animal book

**SCIENCE**

**7**

## The Main Idea

- Choose an informational book you have read.

- Draw a picture that shows the main idea. Talk about your picture.

- Add details to your picture to show supporting details.

**20** Minutes

**You need**
> informational book
> pencil, crayons, or markers
> paper

**READING**

# DEVELOPING READERS AND WRITERS

### Write to Sources and Research

Main Topic and Key Details, T310–T311, T314, T323J

Note Taking, T323A, T329A

Author's Purpose, T323I

Make Connections: Essential Question, T323J, T329B, T334

Research and Inquiry, T332–T333

Analyze to Inform/Explain, T335

Comparing Texts, T341, T351, T355, T361

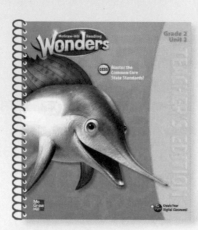

**Teacher's Edition**

Main Topic and Key Details, 203

**Literature Anthology**

**Interactive Whiteboard**

**Leveled Readers**
Comparing Texts
Main Topic and Key Details

Main Topic and Key Details, 83–85
Genre, 88
Write About Reading, 90

**Your Turn Practice Book**

**Informational Text**
How-to Text, T486–T491

**Conferencing Routines**
Teacher Conferences, T488
Peer Conferences, T489

**Interactive Whiteboard**

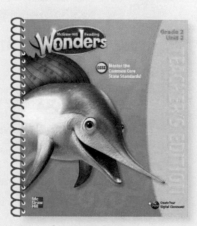

**Teacher's Edition**

**Leveled Workstation Card**
How-To, Card 23

**Writer's Workspace**
Informational Text: How-to Text
Writing Process
Multimedia Presentations

## Writing Traits • Write Every Day

**Writing Trait: Word Choice**
Linking Words, T298–T299

**Conferencing Routines**
Teacher Conferences, T330
Peer Conferences, T331

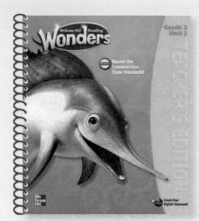

**Teacher's Edition**

Word Choice: Linking
Words, 160–161

**Reading/Writing Workshop**

**Interactive
Whiteboard**

Word Choice:
Linking Words,
Card 11

**Leveled Workstation Card**

Word Choice: Linking
Words, 87

**Your Turn Practice Book**

## Grammar and Spelling

**Grammar**
Plural Nouns, T300, T313,
T325, T331, T339

**Spelling**
Consonant Digraphs, T290,
T306, T317, T328, T337

**Interactive
Whiteboard**

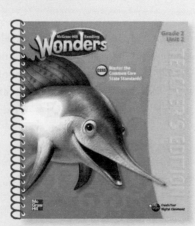

**Teacher's Edition**

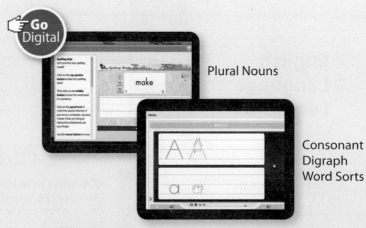

Plural Nouns

Consonant
Digraph
Word Sorts

**Online Spelling and Grammar Games**

# SUGGESTED LESSON PLAN

✓ **TESTED SKILLS** CCSS

| | **DAY 1** | **DAY 2** |
|---|---|---|

## READING

### Whole Group — Teach, Model, and Apply

**Reading/Writing Workshop**

**DAY 1**

**Build Background** Baby Animals, T284–T285
**Oral Vocabulary Words** *guide, leader, protect, provide, separate;* T286
**Listening Comprehension** Strategy: Reread, T287
**Interactive Read-Aloud Cards** "Wild Animal Families," T287
**Word Work**
Phonemic Awareness: Identify and Generate Rhyme, T288
Phonics/Spelling: Introduce Consonant Digraphs, T288–T290
High-Frequency Words: *baby, early, eight, isn't, learn, seven, start, these, try, walk;* T291
✓**Vocabulary** Words in Context: *adult, alive, covered, fur, giant, groom, mammal, offspring;* T292–T293
**Close Reading of Complex Text** "Eagles and Eaglets," 150–155
**Practice** *Your Turn* 81–82

**DAY 2**

**Oral Language** Baby Animals, T302
**Review Oral Vocabulary Words,** T302
**Listening Comprehension** Strategy: Reread, T303
**Interactive Read-Aloud Cards** "Wild Animal Families," T303
**Word Work**
Phonemic Awareness: Phoneme Segmentation, T304
Phonics/Spelling: Words with Consonant Digraphs, T304–T306
Structural Analysis: Suffixes *-ful, -less;* T305
High-Frequency Words, T306
**Vocabulary** Expand Vocabulary, T307
✓**Comprehension**
• Strategy: Reread, T308–T309
• Skill: Main Topic and Key Details, T310–T311
**Practice** *Your Turn* 82–87

## DIFFERENTIATED INSTRUCTION  Choose across the week to meet your student's needs.

### Small Group

#### Approaching Level

**DAY 1**

**Leveled Reader** *Animal Families,* T340–T341
**Phonemic Awareness** Identify and Generate Rhyme, T342 ②
**Phonics** Connect to Consonant Digraphs, T344 ②
**High-Frequency Words** Review Words, T347 ②
**Vocabulary** Review Words, T347

**DAY 2**

**Leveled Reader** *Animal Families,* T340–341
**Phonemic Awareness** Phoneme Segmentation, T343
**Phonics** Blend Words with Consonant Digraphs, T344 ②
**Comprehension** Identify Main Topic, T348 ②

#### On Level

**DAY 1**

**Leveled Reader** *Animal Families,* T350–T351
**Phonics** Blend Words with Consonant Digraphs, T352

**DAY 2**

**Leveled Reader** *Animal Families,* T350–T351
**Comprehension** Review Main Topic and Key Details, T353

#### Beyond Level

**DAY 1**

**Leveled Reader** *Animal Families,* T354–T355
**Vocabulary** Review Domain-Specific Words, T356

**DAY 2**

**Leveled Reader** *Animal Families,* T354–T355
**Comprehension** Review Main Topic and Key Details, T357

#### English Language Learners

**DAY 1**

**Shared Read** "Eagles and Eaglets," T358–T359
**Phonemic Awareness** Identify and Generate Rhyme, T342
**Phonics** Connect to Consonant Digraphs, T344
**Vocabulary** Preteach Vocabulary, T362

**DAY 2**

**Leveled Reader** *Animal Families,* T360–T361
**Phonemic Awareness** Phoneme Segmentation, T343
**Phonics** Blend Words with Consonant Digraphs, T344
**Vocabulary** Review Vocabulary, T362
**Writing** Writing Trait: Word Choice, T364

## LANGUAGE ARTS  Writing Process: How-To T486–T491                    Use with Weeks 4–6

### Whole Group — Writing / Grammar

**DAY 1**

✓**Readers to Writers**
• Writing Trait: Word Choice, T298–T299
• Writing Entry: Prewrite and Draft, T298
**Grammar**
• Plural Nouns, T300
• Mechanics: Abbreviations, T301

**DAY 2**

✓**Readers to Writers**
• Writing Trait: Word Choice, T312
• Writing Entry: Revise, T312
**Grammar**
• Plural Nouns, T313
• Mechanics: Abbreviations, T313

| DAY 3 | DAY 4 | DAY 5 Review and Assess |
|---|---|---|

**READING**

**DAY 3**

**Interactive Read-Aloud Cards** "Wild Animal Families," T314

**Review Oral Vocabulary Words,** T314

**Comprehension** Maintain Skill: Key Details: Use Photos, T315

**Word Work**
Phonemic Awareness: Phoneme Blending, T316
Phonics/Spelling: Words with Consonant Digraphs, T316–T317
Structural Analysis: Suffixes -ful, -less; T317

**Fluency** Pronunciation, T318

**Vocabulary** Reinforce Vocabulary, T319

✓ **Genre** Expository Text, T320–T321

✓ **Vocabulary Strategy** Multiple-Meaning Words, T322–T323

**Close Reading** Baby Bears, 186–201 • Analytical Writing

**Practice** Your Turn 88–89

Literature Anthology

**DAY 4**

**Oral Language** Baby Animals, T326

**Word Work**
Phonemic Awareness: Phoneme Segmentation, T327
Phonics/Spelling: Words with Consonant Digraphs, T327–T328
Structural Analysis: Suffixes -ful, -less; T327
High-Frequency Words, T328

**Fluency** Pronunciation, T329

**Vocabulary Strategy** Review: Inflectional Endings, T329

**Close Reading** "From Caterpillar to Butterfly," 204–205 • Analytical Writing

**Integrate Ideas** Research and Inquiry, T332–T333 • Analytical Writing

**Practice** Your Turn 83–85

**DAY 5 Review and Assess**

**Integrate Ideas** • Analytical Writing
• Text Connections, T334
• Write About Reading, T335
• Research and Inquiry, T335

**Word Work**
Phonemic Awareness: Phoneme Blending, T336
Phonics/Spelling: Words with Consonant Digraphs, T336–T337
Structural Analysis: Suffixes -ful, -less; T336
High-Frequency Words, T337

**Vocabulary** Review Words, T337

**Practice** Your Turn 90

**DIFFERENTIATED INSTRUCTION**

**Leveled Reader** Animal Families, T340–341
**Phonemic Awareness** Phoneme Blending, T342 ②
**Phonics** Build Words with Consonant Digraphs, T345
**Structural Analysis** Review Suffixes -ful, -less; T346 ②
**Comprehension** Review Main Topic and Key Details, T349

**Leveled Reader** Paired Read: "Tadpoles into Frogs," T341 • Analytical Writing
**Phonemic Awareness** Phoneme Segmentation, T343
**Phonics** Blend Words with Consonant Digraphs, T345
**Structural Analysis** Reteach Suffixes -ful, -less; T346
**Comprehension** Read for Fluency, T348 ②

**Leveled Reader** Literature Circle, T341
**Phonemic Awareness** Phoneme Blending, T342 ②
**Phonics** Blend Words with Consonant Digraphs, T345
**Comprehension** Self-Selected Reading, T349

**Leveled Reader** Animal Families, T350–T351
**Vocabulary** Review Words, T352

**Leveled Reader** Paired Read: "Tadpoles into Frogs," T351 • Analytical Writing

**Leveled Reader** Literature Circle, T351
**Comprehension** Self-Selected Reading, T353

**Leveled Reader** Animal Families, T354–T355
**Vocabulary**
• Multiple-Meaning Words, T356
• Shades of Meaning, T356
Gifted and Talented

**Leveled Reader** Paired Read: "Tadpoles into Frogs," T355 • Analytical Writing

**Leveled Reader** Literature Circle, T355
**Comprehension**
• Self-Selected Reading, T357
• Independent Study: Adult and Baby Animals, T357
Gifted and Talented

**Leveled Reader** Animal Families, T360–T361
**Phonemic Awareness** Phoneme Blending, T342
**Phonics** Build Words with Consonant Digraphs, T345
**Structural Analysis** Review Suffixes -ful, -less; T346
**Vocabulary** Multiple-Meaning Words, T363
**Grammar** More Plural Nouns, T365

**Leveled Reader** Paired Read: "Tadpoles into Frogs," T361 • Analytical Writing
**Phonemic Awareness** Phoneme Segmentation, T343
**Phonics** Blend Words with Consonant Digraphs, T345
**Structural Analysis** Reteach Suffixes -ful, -less; T346
**Vocabulary** Additional Vocabulary, T363

**Leveled Reader** Literature Circle, T361
**Phonemic Awareness** Phoneme Blending, T342
**Phonics** Blend Words with Consonant Digraphs, T345
**Spelling** Words with Consonant Digraphs, T364

**LANGUAGE ARTS**

✓ **Readers to Writers**
• Writing Trait: Word Choice, T324
• Writing Entry: Prewrite and Draft, T324

**Grammar**
• Plural Nouns, T325
• Mechanics: Abbreviations, T325

✓ **Readers to Writers**
• Writing Trait: Word Choice, T330
• Writing Entry: Revise, T330

**Grammar**
• Plural Nouns, T331
• Mechanics: Abbreviations, T331

✓ **Readers to Writers**
• Writing Trait: Word Choice, T338
• Writing Entry: Share and Reflect, T338

**Grammar**
• Plural Nouns, T339
• Mechanics: Abbreviations, T339

# DIFFERENTIATE TO ACCELERATE

## A C T  Scaffold to Access Complex Text

**IF** the text complexity of a particular selection is too difficult for children

**THEN** use the Access Complex Text prompts to scaffold instruction.

Qualitative / Quantitative
**Reader and Task**
**TEXT COMPLEXITY**

| | Reading/Writing Workshop | Literature Anthology | Leveled Readers | Classroom Library |
|---|---|---|---|---|
| |  |  | 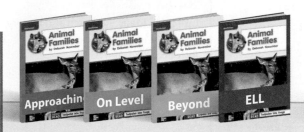 |  |

## Quantitative

**Reading/Writing Workshop**

"Eagles and Eaglets"
**Lexile** 520
*TextEvaluator™* 4

**Literature Anthology**

*Baby Bears*
**Lexile** 590
*TextEvaluator™* 4

"From Caterpillar to Butterfly"
**Lexile** 560
*TextEvaluator™* 7

**Leveled Readers**

**Approaching Level**
**Lexile** 320
*TextEvaluator™* 4

**Beyond Level**
**Lexile** 600
*TextEvaluator™* 5

**On Level**
**Lexile** 490
*TextEvaluator™* 4

**ELL**
**Lexile** 390
*TextEvaluator™* 4

**Classroom Library**

*Life in an Ocean*
**Lexile** 290
*TextEvaluator™* 6

*Let's Look at Monarch Butterflies*
**Lexile** 510
*TextEvaluator™* 6

## Qualitative

**What Makes the Text Complex?**
- **Genre** Expository Text, T295
- **Sentence Structure** Complex Ideas, T309

A C T *See Scaffolded Instruction in Teacher's Edition T295 and T309.*

**What Makes the Text Complex?**
- **Lack of Prior Knowledge** Bears, T323B
- **Specific Vocabulary** Domain-Specific Vocabulary, T323B
- **Genre** Text Features, T323B
- **Organization** Flow Chart, T329B

A C T *See Scaffolded Instruction in Teacher's Edition T323B, T329B.*

**What Makes the Text Complex?**
- **Specific Vocabulary**
- **Prior Knowledge**
- **Sentence Structure**
- **Connection of Ideas**
- **Genre**

A C T *See Level Up lessons online for Leveled Readers.*

**What Makes the Text Complex?**
- **Genre**
- **Specific Vocabulary**
- **Prior Knowledge**
- **Sentence Structure**
- **Organization**
- **Purpose**
- **Connection of Ideas**

A C T *See Scaffolded Instruction in Teacher's Edition T496–T497.*

## Reader and Task

The Introduce the Concept lesson on pages T284–T285 will help determine the reader's knowledge and engagement in the weekly concept. See pages T294–T297, T308–T311, T320–T323, and T332–T335 for questions and tasks for this text.

The Introduce the Concept lesson on pages T284–T285 will help determine the reader's knowledge and engagement in the weekly concept. See pages T323A–T323J, T329A–T329B, and T332–T335 for questions and tasks for this text.

The Introduce the Concept lesson on pages T284–T285 will help determine the reader's knowledge and engagement in the weekly concept. See pages T340–T341, T350–T351, T354–T355, T360–T361, and T332–T335 for questions and tasks for this text.

The Introduce the Concept lesson on pages T284–T285 will help determine the reader's knowledge and engagement in the weekly concept. See pages T496–T497 for questions and tasks for this text.

## Monitor and *Differentiate*

**IF** If you need to differentiate instruction

**THEN** use the Quick Check to assess children's needs and select the appropriate small group instruction focus.

 **Quick Check**

**Comprehension Strategy** Reread, T309

**Comprehension Skills** Main Topic and Key Details, T311

**Genre** Expository Text, T321

**Vocabulary Strategy** Multiple-Meaning Words, T323

**Phonics/Fluency** Consonant Digraphs, Pronunciation, T316, T329

**If No →**

| Approaching Level | Reteach T340–T349 |
| ELL | Develop T358–T365 |

**If Yes →**

| On Level | Review T350–T353 |
| Beyond Level | Extend T354–T357 |

## Level Up with Leveled Readers

**IF** children can read their leveled text fluently and answer comprehension questions

**THEN** assign the next level up to accelerate children reading with more complex text.

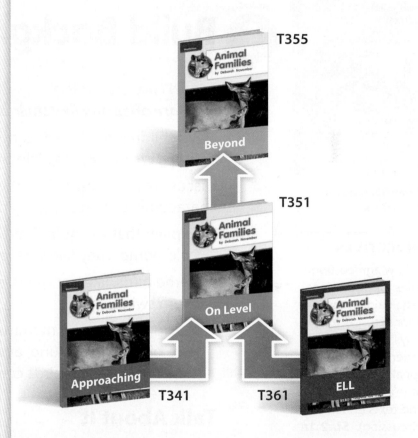

T355

T351

**IF** ELL students need additional support. **THEN** scaffold instruction using the small group suggestions.

| Reading/Writing Workshop | Leveled Reader | Additional Vocabulary T363 | | Multiple-Meaning Words T363 | Writing | Spelling | Grammar |
|---|---|---|---|---|---|---|---|
| "Eagles and Eaglets," T358–T359 | *Animal Families,* T360–T361 "Tadpoles into Frogs," T361 | enemies hatches human mammal | offspring protects soar young | | Word Choice, T364 | Consonant Digraphs, T364 | More Plural Nouns, T365 |

**Note:** Include ELL Students in all small groups based on their needs.

## Materials

 **Reading/Writing Workshop**

 **Visual Vocabulary Cards**

adult
alive
covered
fur

giant
groom
mammal
offspring

 **Word-Building Cards**

 **Interactive Read-Aloud Cards**

 **Think Aloud Clouds**

**High-Frequency Word Cards**

**Sound-Spelling Cards**

→ # Introduce the Concept

**MINILESSON** **5 Mins**

## Build Background

### ESSENTIAL QUESTION
*How are offspring like their parents?*

Have children read the Essential Question on page 146 of the **Reading/Writing Workshop**. Explain that *offspring* is another word for *children*.

Discuss the photograph of the penguins with children. Focus on the characteristics that the baby penguin and his mother share.

→ Explain that penguins have layers of fat to keep them warm in their cold home. They live where it is cold all year long.

→ Some birds, like penguins, cannot fly. They use their flippers to help them swim.

→ Compare birds and mammals. Explain that mammals have hair or fur, give birth to live young, and feed their young milk. Prompt children to tell where baby birds come from. (eggs)

## Talk About It

**COLLABORATE** **Ask:** *How is the larger bird different from the smaller one? How are the two birds the same?* Have children discuss in pairs or groups.

Model using the graphic organizer to generate words that can describe how the two penguins in the picture are alike and different.

### Collaborative Conversations

**Take Turns Talking** As children engage in partner, small-group, and whole-class discussions, encourage them to:

→ wait for a person to finish before they speak.

→ quietly raise their hand when they want to speak.

→ ask others to share their ideas and opinions.

## Go Digital

**Baby Animals**

**Video**

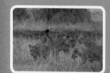
**Photos**

**Graphic Organizer**

peered

**Visual Glossary**

**READING/WRITING WORKSHOP,** pp. 146–147

### Weekly Concept Baby Animals

**Essential Question**
How are offspring like their parents?

Go Digital!

# Animal
## Babies and Parents

This baby penguin and his mother look different but they are the same in many ways.

► They both have layers of fat to keep warm.

► They are both birds, not mammals.

► They both use their flippers to swim.

### Talk About It

Talk with a partner about how baby penguins are the same as and different from their parents. Write your ideas on the chart.

| Same | Different |
|------|-----------|
|      |           |

## ENGLISH LANGUAGE LEARNERS SCAFFOLD

| Beginning | Intermediate | Advanced/High |
|-----------|--------------|---------------|
| **Use Visuals** Point to the penguins. Say: *These are penguins. One of these is a baby penguin. The other is its mother. Which one is the baby? How is the baby penguin different from its mother?* Model correct pronunciation as needed. | **Describe** Have children describe the penguins. Ask: *What color are the penguins? How are their sizes different?* Remind children that *offspring* means "children." Ask: *How do animals take care of their offspring?* Elicit more details to support children's answers. | **Discuss** Ask: *How are the adult penguin and its baby alike? How are they different?* Expand the topic by having children discuss what an adult penguin might be able to do that its offspring cannot. Clarify children's responses as needed by providing vocabulary. |

**GRAPHIC ORGANIZER**

| | |
|---|---|
| | |

INTRODUCE THE CONCEPT **T285**

# → Build the Concept

MINILESSON
**5**
Mins

# Oral Language

## OBJECTIVES

**CCSS** Ask and answer questions about what a speaker says in order to clarify comprehension, gather additional information, or deepen understanding of a topic or issue. **SL.2.3**

- Develop oral language.
- Discuss the Essential Question.

## ACADEMIC LANGUAGE

*informational text, reread*

### ESSENTIAL QUESTION

COLLABORATE

Remind children that this week you'll be talking and reading about ways that baby animals are like their parents.

## Oral Vocabulary Words

Use the Define/Example/Ask routine to introduce the Oral Vocabulary words below. Prompt children to use the words as they discuss animal offspring and their parents.

### Oral Vocabulary Routine

**Define:** To **guide** is to lead or show someone how to do something.

**Example:** My dad guides us on our hike through the woods.

**Ask:** Who guides you in school?

**Define:** The **leader** is the one who is in charge of a group.

**Example:** Our teacher is the leader of our class.

**Ask:** Why is being a good leader important?

**Define:** If you **protect** something, you keep it safe.

**Example:** A helmet protects your head when you ride a bike.

**Ask:** What do you use to protect yourself in a car?

**Define:** To **provide** means to give someone what they need.

**Example:** The art teacher provides paper, paints, and brushes for the students.

**Ask:** What does a library provide for you?

**Define:** To **separate** is to divide people or things, or keep them apart.

**Example:** The coach separated the players into two teams.

**Ask:** What should you do if you become separated from your parents in a public place?

**Wild Animal Families**

When I read _____, I had to reread...

**Reread**

# Listening Comprehension

**MINILESSON 10 Mins**

## Interactive Read Aloud

### Read "Wild Animal Families"

Tell children that you will be reading an informational text that contains facts about how wild animals care for their babies. Display the Interactive Read-Aloud Cards.

**Interactive Read-Aloud Cards**

### Strategy: Reread

❶ **Model** Explain to children as they read, they can stop at any time to reread something that they are unsure about. This will help them better understand the information in the selection.

**Think Aloud** As we read "Wild Animal Families," we may come across new words or sentences that contain information that is unfamiliar or hard to understand. I will reread these parts to help you better understand and remember the text.

❷ **Apply** As you read, use the Think Aloud Cloud to model applying the strategy. Then reread the first card to clarify information about baby wolves.

**Think Aloud** Remember that you can reread parts of the text that you would like to understand better. After I read about the baby wolves, I didn't understand when the babies were able to do certain things, such as join the pack or hunt. I'll reread to find out this information about baby wolves.

### Make Connections

**COLLABORATE**

After reading, have children share what they learned about how wild animals care for their babies and how baby animals are different from their parents. Then have partners discuss parts of the text that were new or unfamiliar. Reread these sections of text to help children clarify the information.

**ENGLISH LANGUAGE LEARNERS**

**Synonyms and Circumlocution** Remind children that they can ask for synonyms to clarify words or expressions they do not understand. Ask: *The text says the father wolf stands guard outside. What is another word for* stands guard? (*Stands guard* means "watches for danger." The father *watches for danger*. He protects the wolf pups, or keeps them safe from harm.)

 → # Word Work

### ⏱ 5 Mins MINILESSON
## Phonological Awareness

**OBJECTIVES**

CCSS Know and apply grade-level phonics and word analysis skills in decoding words. **RF.2.3**

• Identify and generate rhyming words.

• Apply phonics when decoding words with consonant digraphs.

### Identify and Generate Rhyme

❶ **Model** Model how to identify and then generate rhyme. *I am going to say two words:* lunch, bunch. *The words* lunch *and* bunch *rhyme because they both end in the same sounds,* /unch/. *Now I will say other words that rhyme with* lunch *and* bunch. *Listen:* /kr/ /unch/, crunch. *The word* crunch *ends in the same sound as* lunch *and* bunch. *Crunch rhymes with* lunch *and* bunch.

❷ **Guided Practice/Practice** *Listen to these word pairs. If the words rhyme, repeat the words. If the words do not rhyme, remain silent.*

shop/hop        math/bath        chip/chin      ring/sung

catch/batch    such/touch      rush/crush    king/sing

*Listen as I say the words again. Let's think of other words that rhyme with each rhyming pair.*

**SKILLS TRACE**

**Consonant Digraphs**

**INTRODUCE** Unit 2 Week 4 Day 1

**REVIEW** Unit 2 Week 4 Day 2, Day 3, Day 4, Day 5

**ASSESS** Unit 2

### ⏱ 10 Mins MINILESSON
## Phonics

**Sound-Spelling Card**

### Introduce Consonant Digraphs

❶ **Model** Display the *Cheese* Sound-Spelling Card. Teach /ch/ spelled *ch* and *tch* using *chin* and *itch*. Model writing the letters *ch*. *This is the* Cheese *Sound-Spelling Card. The sound is* /ch/. *Together the letters* c *and* h *stand for* /ch/. *Say it with me:* /ch/. *This is the sound at the beginning of the word* cheese. *Listen:* /chēz/, cheese. *I'll say* /ch/ *as I write the letters* ch *several times. Continue with* /ch/ tch. Repeat routine for *sh, ph, th, ng,* and *wh* using the *Shell, Whale, Sing, Thumb,* and *Fire* Sound-Spelling Cards.

❷ **Guided Practice/Practice** Have children practice connecting the consonant digraph *ch* to the sound /ch/ by writing it. Point out that the letters work together to make one sound. *Now do it with me, say* /ch/ *as you write the letters* ch. *This time, write the letters* ch *five times as you say* /ch/. Continue with tch. Repeat with *sh, th, wh, ng, ph.*

# Blend Words with Consonant Digraphs
## *ch, tch, sh, ph, th, ng, wh*

**❶ Model** Display Word-Building Cards *c, h, i, n*. Model how to generate and blend the sounds to say the word. *This is the letter* c. *This is the letter* h. *Together the letters* c *and* h *stand for /ch/. This is the letter* i. *It stands for /i/. This is the letter* n. *It stands for /n/. Listen as I blend these sounds together: /chiiinnn/. Say it with me:* chin.

Continue by modeling the words *fetch, phone, shop, whip,* and *sing.*

**❷ Guided Practice/Practice** Display the Day 1 Phonics Practice Activity. Read each word in the first row, for example, /chip/. *The word is* chip.

| | | | | | |
|---|---|---|---|---|---|
| chip | witch | shape | phone | thin | sing |
| when | chop | hatch | ship | graph | thing |
| ring | whisk | chat | match | mash | king |
| gem | cell | space | badge | stage | change |

I watch him catch the fish.

We sing for the king.

The phone will ring.

**Also online**

**Phonics Practice**

### Corrective Feedback

**Sound Error** Model the sound that children missed, then have them repeat the sound. Say: *My turn. Tap under the letter and say: Sound? /ch/. What's the sound?* Return to the beginning of the word. Say: *Let's start over.* Blend the words with children again.

**ON-LEVEL PRACTICE BOOK** p. 82

A consonant digraph is two consonants together that stand for only one sound.

**A. Say each picture name. Read the words and circle the word with the same beginning sound. Write the word.**

1. ⓒhop    sting    ____chop____

2. pitch    ⓦhile    ____while____

A suffix is a word part added to the end of a word to make a new word.
- The suffix *-ful* means "full of."
- The suffix *-less* means "without."

**B. Read each word. Write its meaning.**

3. helpless    ____without help____

4. careful    ____full of care____

| **APPROACHING** p. 82 | **BEYOND** p. 82 | **ELL** p. 82 |
|---|---|---|

WORD WORK **T289**

→ # Word Work

**Quick Review**

**High-Frequency Words:** Read, Spell, and Write to review last week's high-frequency words: *buy, under, wash, straight, almost, saw, food, out, pull, sky.*

 **MINILESSON 5 Mins**

## Spelling

### Words with Consonant Digraphs *ch, tch, sh, ph, th, ng, wh*

**Dictation** Use the spelling dictation routine to help children transfer their growing knowledge of sound-spellings to writing. Follow the Dictation Routine.

**Pretest** After dictation, pronounce each spelling word. Read the sentence and pronounce the word again. Ask children to say each word softly, stretching the sounds, before writing it. After the pretest, display the spelling words and write each word as you say the letter names. Have children check their words.

| | |
|---|---|
| **chop** | **Chop** the fruit before it goes in the salad. |
| **catch** | I can **catch** the ball. |
| **shape** | The table is in the **shape** of a square. |
| **trash** | Dave will throw out the **trash** today. |
| **phone** | I just got a **phone** call. |
| **that** | **That** is a very funny joke. |
| **sting** | The bee did not **sting** us. |
| **thin** | The book was **thin** and easy to read. |
| **bring** | I will **bring** food to the park. |
| **while** | You can dance **while** I sing. |
| **place** | I put my favorite book in a safe **place**. |
| **badge** | I will wear my winner's **badge** to school. |
| **seven** | The movie begins at **seven**. |
| **isn't** | The computer **isn't** turned on. |
| **early** | I have to wake up **early** for school. |

For Approaching Level and Beyond Level children, refer to the Differentiated Spelling Lists for modified word lists.

### OBJECTIVES

 **CCSS** Demonstrate command of the conventions of standard English capitalization, punctuation, and spelling when writing. **L.2.2**

**CCSS** Generalize learned spelling patterns when writing words (e.g., cage → badge; boy → boil). **L.2.2d**

Spell words with consonant digraphs *ch, tch, sh, ph, th, ng, wh.*

### ENGLISH LANGUAGE LEARNERS

**Spelling** Practice spelling by helping children generate more words with consonant digraphs *ch, tch, sh, ph, th, ng,* and *wh.* Write an example and have children circle the consonant digraph. Then have them think of another word on their own that uses that same digraph.

**Go Digital**

**Spelling Word Routine**

| they | together |
|---|---|
| how | eat |

**High-Frequency Word Routine**

# High-Frequency Words

## these, start, walk, seven, eight, learn, try, isn't, baby, early

**1 Model** Display the High-Frequency Word Cards *these, start, walk, seven, eight, learn, try, isn't, baby,* and *early.* Use the Read/Spell/Write routine to teach each word.

→ **Read** Point to and say the word *these. This is the word* these. *Say it with me:* these. *I like* these *crayons.*

→ **Spell** *The word* these *is spelled* t-h-e-s-e. *Spell it with me.*

→ **Write** *Let's write the word in the air as we say each letter:* t-h-e-s-e.

→ Follow the same steps to introduce *start, walk, seven, eight, learn, try, isn't, baby,* and *early.*

→ Have partners write sentences using each word.

**2 Guided Reading** Have children read the sentences. Prompt them to identify the high-frequency words in connected text and to blend the decodable words.

1. **These** are my best pants.
2. **Start** the next game now.
3. We can **walk** to school.
4. I have **seven** pens.
5. He picks up **eight** rocks.
6. We **learn** to play ball.
7. **Try** to run in the race.
8. This **isn't** my bag.
9. The **baby** is cute.
10. The game starts **early**.

## Monitor and *Differentiate*

 **Quick Check**

Can children read and decode words with consonant digraphs? Can children recognize and read high-frequency words?

### Small Group Instruction

| | | |
|---|---|---|
| If No → | Approaching | Reteach pp. T342-T347 |
| | ELL | Develop pp. T358-T365 |
| If Yes → | On Level | Review pp. T352-T353 |
| | Beyond Level | Extend pp. T356-T357 |

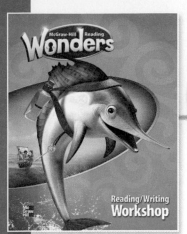

**Reading/Writing Workshop**

## OBJECTIVES

**CCSS** Demonstrate understanding of word relationships and nuances in word meanings. **L.2.5**

**CCSS** Identify real-life connections between words and their use (e.g., describe foods that are *spicy* or *juicy*). **L.2.5a**

**CCSS** Determine the meaning of words and phrases in a text relevant to a *grade 2 topic or subject area*. **RI.2.4**

## ACADEMIC LANGUAGE
• *mammal, offspring*
• cognate: *mamífero*

**MINILESSON**
**10** Mins

## Words in Context

### Model the Routine

Introduce each vocabulary word using the Vocabulary Routine found on the Visual Vocabulary Cards.

**Visual Vocabulary Cards**

**Vocabulary Routine**

**Define:** An **adult** is a person or animal that is fully-grown.

**Example:** My father is an **adult**.

**Ask:** What is the opposite of an adult?

Vocab

Define:

Example

Ask:

## Definitions

→ **alive**     If something is **alive**, it is living.

→ **covered**     If something is **covered**, there is something all over it.

→ **fur**     **Fur** is thick animal hair.

→ **giant**     Something that is **giant** is very large.

→ **groom**     When animals **groom** each other, they clean each other.

→ **mammal**     A **mammal** is any warm-blooded animal that feeds milk to its babies.
           **Cognate:** *mamífero*

→ **offspring**     **Offspring** are the children or young of people or animals.

### Talk About It

**COLLABORATE**

Have children work with a partner and preview each picture and definition they will find in their reading. Then have children choose three vocabulary words and write three questions for their partner to answer.

## CCSS Words to Know

# Vocabulary

**Use the picture and sentence to learn each word.**

**adult** — My father is an **adult**.

*What is the opposite of an adult?*

**alive** — I water the flowers to keep them **alive**.

*How can you tell that a plant is alive?*

**covered** — Polar bears are **covered** with thick, white fur.

*What are birds covered with?*

**fur** — My kitten has **fur** that is soft and fluffy.

*What are some other animals that have fur?*

**giant** — That **giant** tree is taller than my house.

*Tell about the most giant thing you have ever seen.*

**groom** — I use a brush to **groom** my horse each day.

*What is another word for groom?*

**mammal** — A **mammal** has fur or hair and breathes air.

*Describe a mammal you know about.*

**offspring** — At the zoo, we saw a mother rabbit and two **offspring**.

*What is the name for the offspring of a dog?*

### Your Turn COLLABORATE

Pick three words. Write three questions for your partner to answer.

*Go Digital! Use the online visual glossary*

148

149

**READING/WRITING WORKSHOP, pp. 148–149**

## ELL ENGLISH LANGUAGE LEARNERS SCAFFOLD

### Beginning

**Use Visuals** *Let's look at the picture for the word alive. Point to the picture of the flowers. These flowers are alive. They are living. Point to other pictures here that show something alive. Then say: Where are people? Where are plants? Where are animals? These things are all alive.*

### Intermediate

**Describe** Have children describe the picture. Help them with pronunciation. Ask: *What is the boy doing in the picture? What do you need to stay alive?* Ask them to turn to a partner and name other things they know about that are alive.

### Advanced/High

**Discuss** Ask children to talk about the picture with a partner and discuss how they know the flowers are alive. Have them talk about what the boy in the picture is doing to keep the flower alive.

### ON-LEVEL PRACTICE BOOK p. 81

| adult | alive | covered | fur |
| giant | groom | mammal | offspring |

**Choose the word that makes sense in each blank. Then write the word on the line.**

1. A baby chick is _____covered_____ with soft feathers.

2. Some _____offspring_____ look a lot like their parents.

3. Whales are _____giant_____ sea animals.

4. A cat will _____groom_____ itself to stay clean.

5. A horse is a _____mammal_____ because it feeds its babies milk.

6. A fox's _____fur_____ coat helps to keep it warm.

7. Some baby animals need to be cared for by an _____adult_____.

8. Animals need food and water to stay _____alive_____.

| APPROACHING p. 81 | BEYOND p. 81 | ELL p. 81 |

# Comprehension

CLOSE READING

 **MINILESSON 10 Mins** ## Shared Read

**Lexile** 520    *TextEvaluator™* 4

**OBJECTIVES**

 **CCSS** Read with sufficient accuracy and fluency to support comprehension. **RF.2.4**

**CCSS** Read on-level text with purpose and understanding. **RF.2.4a**

Identify meanings of words used in context.

## Connect to Concept

### Baby Animals

Explain to children that "Eagles and Eaglets" will tell them more about how baby animals, or offspring, are like their parents.

After reading each section, have partners discuss what they have learned about eagles and eaglets and the ways eaglets are like or different from their parents.

### Use Vocabulary Words in Context

| | | | |
|---|---|---|---|
| adult | alive | covered | fur |
| giant | groom | mammal | offspring |

The highlighted words in the text are the vocabulary words children have learned. As you read, have them discuss the words' meanings.

## Close Reading

**Reread the Introduction:** Tell children you are going to take a closer look at the beginning of "Eagles and Eaglets." Reread the first paragraph together. Ask: *What facts does this paragraph give? What will "Eagles and Eaglets" be about?* Model how to cite text evidence to answer the questions and to use the answers to set a purpose for reading.

*The author tells us that bald eagles are birds and that their babies are called eaglets. The last sentence tells us we will read about how eaglets are like their parents. So as I read, I will look for information about eaglets and how they are like or different from their parents.*

**Reread "It's Nesting Time":** Tell children that you are going to take a closer look at "It's Nesting Time." Together, reread the first paragraph in this section. Ask: *What is this paragraph mostly about? What does this paragraph have to do with eaglets?* Model how to cite text evidence to answer the questions.

*The paragraph is mostly about eagles' nests. It says that bald eagles build their nests in the tops of trees so the eggs will be safe. I know that eaglets come from eggs. This paragraph tells me about how nests keep eaglets safe.*

# Go Digital

**Eagles and Eaglets**

# Eagles and Eaglets

**? Essential Question**

**How are offspring like their parents?**

Read to learn how young bald eagles are like their parents.

Bald eagles are birds. The baby birds, or **offspring** are called eaglets. Let's read about how eaglets are like their parents.

## It's Nesting Time

All birds lay eggs. Bald eagles build their nests in the tops of trees so the eggs will be safe. Their nests are built of sticks and grass. They add on to their nests each year. They can become huge! These **giant** nests can be as large as nine feet across. That's bigger than your bed!

The mother eagle lays from one to three eggs. She sits on her eggs until they hatch. Then both parents watch over the nest.

150    151

**READING/WRITING WORKSHOP, pp. 150–151**

## A C T Access Complex Text

**▶ Genre**

The expository text "Eagles and Eaglets" includes text features that help readers locate and understand information in the text.

→ Read the heading "It's Nesting Time" on page 151. Explain that headings tell what each section of this text is about. The details in this section tell about nests and nesting.

→ Point out the diagram on page 153. Have children read the labels and relate them to the text in "Eaglets Grow Up."

→ Remind children that captions can give important information. Point out the caption on page 154. Discuss how the photo and caption help children understand how an eagle soars.

### Proud Parents

At first the eaglets are helpless. They cannot walk. They need their parents for food. They also cannot see well. Birds are not **mammals**. They do not have milk to feed their young. They hunt for food. Eaglets also need their parents for safety.

### Eaglets Grow Up

Bald eagles use their sharp eyes to hunt. They use their strong wings to fly fast. They also use their claws and beak to catch fish. Young eaglets must learn all these things. Then they can live on their own.

The eagles must bring food to the eaglets.

152

Unlike mammals, birds have feathers, not **fur**. An eaglet is born **covered** with soft gray down. It cannot fly until it grows dark feathers like its parents. The eaglet stays near the nest until its wings grow strong. That takes about five months.

**Bald Eagle**

powerful eyes

hooked yellow beak

dark feathers on body and wings

white tail feathers

long claws

Frank Leung/Getty Images

153

**READING/WRITING WORKSHOP, pp. 152–153**

# Shared Read · CLOSE READING

## Close Reading

**Reread "Proud Parents":** Tell children that you are going to take a closer look at the section, "Proud Parents," which focuses on how eaglets need their parents. Ask: *What two things must eagle parents do for their babies? Why?* Model how to cite evidence to answer the questions. *The text says eaglets need their parents for food and protection. This is because eaglets are helpless when they are born. Eaglets cannot walk or see.* Continue by asking: *What do eagle parents do to get food for their babies? Why can't they give their babies milk?* Use text evidence to restate and elaborate upon children's answers.

*The text says that eagles hunt for food. They can't give milk to eaglets because they are not mammals. Only mammals can give milk.*

## Make Connections

### ESSENTIAL QUESTION

Remind children to go back to the text for evidence as they talk about how eaglets and their parents are similar to and different from each other. Ask them to describe how these differences help them understand why eaglets need their parents in order to survive.

An eaglet becomes an **adult** when it has learned to do all the things its parents do. This takes about five years. Bald eagles can stay **alive** for up to thirty years.

When the bald eagle soars, the feathers on its huge wings spread out like fingers.

Ken Canning/Getty Images

154

## Bald Eagles Soar

Once it learns to fly, the bald eagle can soar for hours. The bald eagle must take good care of its feathers. It uses its beak to **groom** itself. It must keep its feathers clean. Can you believe this powerful eagle began life as a helpless baby?

### Make Connections

How is the eaglet like its parents? How is it different? ESSENTIAL QUESTION

Compare how your parents and eagle parents take care of their young. TEXT TO SELF

155

**READING/WRITING WORKSHOP, pp. 154–155**

## Continue Close Reading

Use the following lessons for focused rereadings.

→ Reread, T308–T309

→ Main Topic and Key Details, T310–T311

→ Genre and Text Features, T320–T321

→ Multiple-Meaning Words, T322–T323

## ELL

### ENGLISH LANGUAGE LEARNERS

**Develop** Help ELLs develop content area vocabulary and information. Have them point to and read aloud the word *eagles* in the title on page 150, then point to an eagle in the photograph. Repeat for *eaglets*. Say: *What are some ways an eaglet is different from an eagle?* Record children's answers.

Continue by pointing out the word *hatch* in the second paragraph of "It's Nesting Time" on page 151. Say: *The mother eagle sits on her eggs until they* hatch. Point out that in the photo on page 151, there are no eggs, but there are eaglets. *What do you think* hatch *means?*

→ # Language Arts

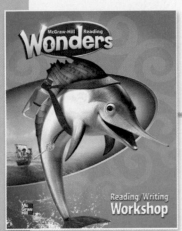

**Reading/Writing Workshop**

McGraw-Hill Reading
**Wonders**

Reading/Writing
**Workshop**

### OBJECTIVES

**CCSS** Write informative/ explanatory texts in which they introduce a topic, use facts and definitions to develop points, and provide a concluding statement or section. **W.2.2**

**CCSS** With guidance and support from adults and peers, focus on a topic and strengthen writing as needed by revising and editing. **W.2.5**

### ACADEMIC LANGUAGE
*linking words, story ideas*

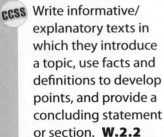

**MINILESSON**
**10 Mins**

# Writing Traits: Word Choice

## Discuss the Expert Model

**Explain** Explain that good writers use linking words to show how ideas are related. Explain that:

→ the words *and, another,* and *also* show how two thoughts are related.

→ the words *but* or *however* show how two thoughts are different.

→ the words *for instance* or *for example* show examples of ideas.

→ the words *because, therefore,* and *since* show relationships between ideas.

**COLLABORATE** Read aloud the expert model from "Eagles and Eaglets." Ask children to listen for linking words that help them understand how ideas are related. Have children talk with partners to identify these linking words. (*so, and*)

## Discuss the Student Model

Remind children that linking words help readers understand the writer's ideas. Read aloud the student draft. As children follow along, have them focus on the linking words the writer included in his draft. (*and, soon*)

**COLLABORATE** Invite partners to talk about the draft and the linking words Robert used. Ask them to suggest places where Robert could have used more linking words to show how ideas are related.

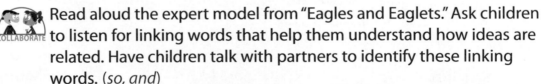

📝 **WRITING ENTRY: LINKING WORDS**

❶ **Prewrite** Provide children with the prompt below:

*Write an expository text about a baby animal and its parents. Be sure to use linking words.*

❷ **Draft** Have children choose a topic and use their notes to write a draft. Remind children to use linking words as they write.

## Go Digital

**Present the Lesson**

**Writing**

## CCSS Writing Traits — Word Choice

# Readers to...

Writers choose linking words to show how ideas in a story are related. Some linking words are *and, so,* and *also*. Reread the section from "Eagles and Eaglets" below.

**Word Choice**
Identify two **linking words.** How do these words help you understand the selection?

**Expert Model**

### It's Nesting Time

All birds lay eggs. Bald eagles build their nests in the tops of trees so the eggs will be safe. Their nests are built of sticks and grass. They add on to their nests each year. They can become huge! These **giant** nests can be as large as nine feet across. That's bigger than your bed!

Louis Gagnon/naturepl.com

160

# Writers

Robert wrote an expository text. Read Robert's revision.

**Editing Marks**
☰ Make a capital letter.
∧ Add
✄ Take out.
(SP) Check spelling.

**Grammar Handbook**
**Plural Nouns**
See page 479.

**Student Model**

fawns
A mother deer's baby is
            fawn         (SP) mammals
called a baby. Deer are mamals.
          ∧
The mother gives milk to the
fawn and keeps it hidden. Later,
the fawn follows the mother and
looks for plants. Soon the young
deer can be on
its own.

### Your Turn

☑ Identify the linking words Robert used.
☑ Identify a plural noun.
☑ Tell how revisions improved his writing.

*Go Digital!*
Write online in Writer's Workspace

161

**READING/WRITING WORKSHOP, pp. 160–161**

## ELL ENGLISH LANGUAGE LEARNERS SCAFFOLD

### Beginning

**Write Sentences**
Provide model sentences based on the prompt:

*A baby _____ is called a _____. The baby is like its parent because _____. The baby is not like its parent because _____.*

Help children complete the sentence frames.

### Intermediate

**Linking Ideas** Ask children to write down some of their ideas based on the prompt. Help them identify places where they can link ideas together with linking words. Help them to identify which linking words they can use and how they help to link the ideas.

### Advanced/High

**Respond** Ask children to respond to the prompt. Remind them to use linking words that help to identify how different ideas are connected. When they are finished, have them underline the linking words in their writing.

## Genre Writing

**Writing: Expository Text**
For full writing process lessons and rubrics, see:

→ How-to, pages T480–T485

→ How-to, pages T486–T491

**Language Arts**

 MINILESSON **10** Mins

# Grammar

**OBJECTIVES**

**CCSS** Demonstrate command of the conventions of standard English grammar and usage when writing or speaking. **L.2.1**

**CCSS** Form and use frequently occurring irregular plural nouns (e.g., *feet, children, teeth, mice, fish*). **L.2.1b**

**ACADEMIC LANGUAGE**
*plural nouns, abbreviations*

## More Plural Nouns

**❶ Explain/Model** Explain that a **singular noun** names one person, place, or thing. A **plural noun** names more than one person, place, or thing. Display the following sentences:

Jake walked the dog.        Jake walked the two dogs.

Model identifying which sentence has a plural noun.

**Think Aloud** The first sentence uses the word *dog*. That means just one dog. In the second sentence, an *-s* is added to the end of *dog*, making it *dogs*. When *-s* or *-es* is added to the end of a noun, it makes the word mean more than one. The word *dogs* is a plural noun. It means more than one dog. We can also use context clues to help us know whether a noun is singular or plural.

Repeat the exercise with additional sentences. Then explain that for some nouns, to make the plural form of the singular noun, the spelling of the word changes. Display the following list of singular and plural nouns.

*foot/feet        tooth/teeth    man/men        mouse/mice*

*woman/women        child/children        person/people*

**❷ Guided Practice/Practice** Display the following sentences and ask children to change the underlined singular noun to a plural noun. Remind them that they can refer to the list displayed earlier to see how each of the nouns changes to become plural.

Look at the baby <u>mouse</u>! (mice)

The <u>child</u> played with the puppies. (children)

The birds were afraid of the <u>person</u>. (people)

## Talk About It

 **Create Your Own Sentence** Ask partners to choose a singular/plural pair of nouns from the list displayed earlier. Have one child create a sentence with the singular noun and the other child create a sentence with the plural noun. Have them listen to each other's sentence for correct grammar and sense.

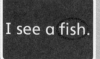

**Go Digital**

I see a fish.

**Grammar**

# Mechanics: Abbreviations

**❶ Explain/Model** Explain to children that an abbreviation is a shortened way of writing a word. An abbreviation begins with a capital letter and ends with a period. Give examples of common words that are often abbreviated, such as Doctor (Dr.), Mister (Mr.), Street (St.), Avenue (Ave.). Point out that the names of the days of the week and months of the year have abbreviations also.

Guide children to identify abbreviations and their meaning in the following street address.

> Mr. Alan Gonzales (Mister)
>
> 150 Green St. (Street)

Write the days of the week on the board. One at a time, read the first three days aloud and write the correct abbreviation. Then have volunteers come to the board to try to write the abbreviations for the remaining days. Provide guidance, as necessary.

| | | |
|---|---|---|
| Monday (Mon.) | Thursday (Thurs.) | Saturday (Sat.) |
| Tuesday (Tues.) | Friday (Fri.) | Sunday (Sun.) |
| Wednesday (Wed.) | | |

Follow the same procedure for the months of the year.

**❷ Guided Practice/Practice** Display the following abbreviations. Have children write each abbreviation correctly.

| | | |
|---|---|---|
| jan (Jan.) | apr (Apr.) | aug (Aug.) |
| mon (Mon.) | fri (Fri.) | sat (Sat.) |
| mr (Mr.) | mrs (Mrs.) | dr (Dr.) |
| st (St.) | rd (Rd.) | ave (Ave.) |

**GRAMMAR PRACTICE BOOK** p. 41

- A **plural noun** names more than one person, place, or thing.
- Most nouns add **-s** or **-es** to make their plural form.
- Some nouns change their spelling to make their plural form.

| | | |
|---|---|---|
| foot → feet | child → children | woman → women |
| tooth → teeth | man → men | mouse → mice |

**A. Complete each sentence with the nouns in ( ). Write the nouns in their plural forms.**

1. Three ____children____ took a hike in the woods. (child)
2. Two ____women____ led the hike. (woman)
3. Ten ____men____ were in the group. (man)
4. The hike hurt their ____feet____. (foot)
5. They found two baby ____mice____! (mouse)

**B. Write a sentence using the plural form of the noun in ( ).**

6. (tooth)

____Answers will vary.____

7. (child)

# Daily Wrap Up

→ Review the Essential Question and encourage children to discuss using the new concept and oral vocabulary words. Ask: *What did we learn today about the ways baby animals are like their parents? How are they different from their parents?*

→ Prompt children to share what skills they learned. How might they use those skills?

## Materials

**Reading/Writing Workshop**

adult

**Visual Vocabulary Cards**

| adult | giant |
| alive | groom |
| covered | mammal |
| fur | offspring |

baby

**High-Frequency Word Cards**

a b c

**Word-Building Cards**

**Interactive Read-Aloud Cards**

bring

**Spelling Word Cards**

ch
fch
cheese

**Sound-Spelling Cards**

→ # Build the Concept

MINILESSON
**5** Mins

# Oral Language

## OBJECTIVES

CCSS Recount or describe key ideas or details from a text read aloud or information presented orally or through other media. **SL.2.2**

• Develop oral language.
• Discuss the Essential Question.
• Retell story events.

## ACADEMIC LANGUAGE
*reread*

### ESSENTIAL QUESTION

Remind children that this week you are talking and reading about wild animal families. Remind them about the parents and offspring they read about in "Wild Animal Families" and "Eagles and Eaglets." Guide children to talk about the Essential Question using information from what they have read and talked about on Day 1.

## Review Oral Vocabulary

Review the oral vocabulary words *guide, leader, protect, provide,* and *separate* using the Define/Example/Ask routine. Encourage children to discuss how animal babies are alike or different from their parents when coming up with examples for each word.

# Go Digital

**Wild Animal Families**

**Retell Routine**

# Listening Comprehension

MINILESSON
**5** Mins

## Interactive Read Aloud

### Reread "Wild Animal Families"

Tell children that you will reread "Wild Animal Families." Display the Interactive Read Aloud Cards.

### Strategy: Reread

Remind children that as they read they can stop at any time to reread something that is unclear to them. This will help them to better understand the facts in the text.

**Interactive Read-Aloud Cards**

*As we reread "Wild Animal Families," think about information that was new or hard to understand. For example, I did not remember how long the father emperor penguin stands with the egg, and what he does at that time. Rereading will help me better understand and remember this information.*

Read aloud "Wild Animal Families." Pause to model using the strategy. Prompt children to tell you when you should reread. Remind them that they should reread when they are reading on their own.

### Model Retelling

Pause to retell parts of the selection. *I can put information from the text and the photos in my own words. So far, I have read that wolf families work together to care for their pups. At first, the pups are very tiny. They cannot see or hear. By the time they are six months old, they begin to hunt with the pack.*

Explain that when children retell a selection, they should tell the important facts and details in the correct order.

### Retell the Selection

After reading, guide children to retell the entire selection. Remind them to tell the important facts and details in correct order. You may wish to let children use the pictures on the Interactive Read-Aloud Cards to help them retell the selection.

**ELL**

### ENGLISH LANGUAGE LEARNERS

**Retell** Guide children to retell by using a question prompt for each card, such as *What do the wolf pups eat? Who cares for the emperor penguin chick after it hatches? How do the elephants protect the baby if there is danger? Who is the leader of a gorilla family?* Use sentence frames, such as *At first, the wolf pups drink ____.* (milk) *Later, they eat ____.* (meat) *The ____ cares for the penguin chick.* (mother) *When there is danger, the elephants ____.* (stand together and hide the baby) *The leader of the gorilla family is called a ____.* (silverback)

 # Word Work

**Quick Review**

**Build Fluency: Sound-Spellings**
Display the **Word-Building Cards:** *ch, th, sh, wh, tch, ph, ng, o_e, o, u_e, u, i_e, i, a_e, a, c, g, dge, ge, lge, nge, rge.* Have children say each sound.

## Phonemic Awareness

**5 Mins** MINILESSON

**OBJECTIVE**

**CCSS** Know and apply grade-level phonics and word analysis skills in decoding words. **RF.2.3**

**CCSS** Decode words with common prefixes and suffixes. **RF.2.3d**

• Use phoneme segmentation.

• Apply phonics when decoding words with consonant digraphs.

**ACADEMIC LANGUAGE**
*blend, stretch*

### Phoneme Segmentation

❶ **Model** Show children how to segment words. *I am going to say the sounds in the word* shake. *Listen /sh/ /ā/ /k/. The first sound is /sh/. The second sound is /ā/. The last sound is /k/. I'll place a marker in a box for each sound I hear. This word has three sounds: /sh/ /ā/ /k/. Say the word with me:* shake.

Continue to model segmenting with the following words.

check     think     phone     when     sing

❷ **Guided Practice/Practice** Have children practice segmenting words. Do the first few together. *Now it's your turn. I will say a word. Place one marker in each box to stand for each sound.*

ring     match     shop     math     fish     chance     graph

bench     shell     catch     whip     thing     while     wing

## Phonics

**5 Mins** MINILESSON

### Review Consonant Digraphs *ch, tch, sh, ph, th, ng, wh*

❶ Display the *Cheese* Sound-Spelling Card. Review the sound /ch/ spelled *ch* and *tch* using *chase* and *catch*.

Repeat the routine for *sh, ph, th, ng,* and *wh* using the *Shell, Fire, Thumb, Sing,* and *Whale* Sound-Spelling Cards and the words *shop, phone, thin, ring,* and *white.*

❷ **Guided Practice/Practice** Have children practice connecting the letters and sounds. Point to the Sound-Spelling Card. *What are the letters? What sound do they stand for?*

**Go Digital**

**Phonemic Awareness**

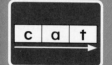

**Phonics**

**Structural Analysis**

# Blend Words with Consonant Digraphs

**❶ Model** Display Word-Building Cards *c, a, t, c, h.* Model how to blend the sounds to say the word. *This is the letter* c. *It stands for* /k/. *This is the letter* a. *It stands for* /a/. *These are the letters* t, c, h. *Together these letters stand for the sound* /ch/. *Listen as I blend these three sounds together:* /kaaach/. *Say it with me:* catch.

→ Continue by modeling the words *fresh, think, phone, wing,* and *whim.*

**❷ Guided Practice/Practice** Repeat the routine with children with *match, math, ring, shock, graph, which.*

# Build Words with Consonant Digraphs

**❶ Model** Display the Word-Building Cards *c, h, i, p.* Blend /ch/ /i/ /p/, /chiiip/, *chip.*

→ Replace *i* with *o* and repeat with *chop.*

→ Change *ch* to *sh* and repeat with *shop.*

**❷ Guided Practice/Practice** Continue with *ship, shin, chin, thin, then, when; clang, clash, cash, catch, match, math.* Guide children to build and blend each word.

## ENGLISH LANGUAGE LEARNERS

**Phonics: Build Vocabulary**
Review the meanings of example words that can be explained or demonstrated in a concrete way. For example, ask children to model the actions for *catching, talking on the phone,* and *singing.* Say: "*I can catch a ball. I can talk on a phone. I can sing.*" Have children repeat the words. Provide sentence starters such as *I can _____* for children to complete. Correct grammar and pronunciation as needed.

---

**MINILESSON 5 Mins**

# Structural Analysis

## Suffixes *-ful, -less*

**❶ Model** Write and read aloud the words *wish* and *wishful.* Underline *-ful* in *wishful.* Tell children that *-ful* is a word part called a *suffix.* A suffix is added to the end of a word to change the meaning of the word. Explain that the suffix *-ful* means *full of.*

Say *wish* and *wishful* again and point out that the suffix makes a one-syllable word into a two-syllable word. Then repeat the routine with the words *shape* and *shapeless.* Explain that the suffix *less* means *without.* Ask children what the word *shapeless* means. Ask them how many syllables the word *shapeless* has. (two)

**❷ Guided Practice/Practice** Write the words *thank* and *hope* on the board two times each. Have children add a *-ful and -less* suffix to each of the words to form the words *thankful, thankless, hopeful,* and *hopeless.* Ask children to use each word in a sentence.

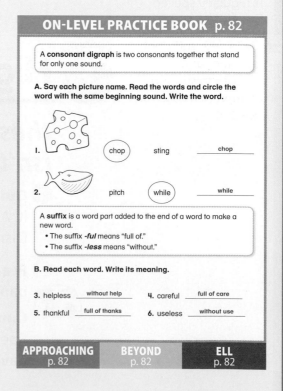

**ON-LEVEL PRACTICE BOOK** p. 82

A **consonant digraph** is two consonants together that stand for only one sound.

**A.** Say each picture name. Read the words and circle the word with the same beginning sound. Write the word.

1. (chop) sting ___chop___

2. pitch (while) ___while___

A **suffix** is a word part added to the end of a word to make a new word.
• The suffix *-ful* means "full of."
• The suffix *-less* means "without."

**B.** Read each word. Write its meaning.

3. helpless ___without help___   4. careful ___full of care___

5. thankful ___full of thanks___   6. useless ___without use___

| APPROACHING p. 82 | BEYOND p. 82 | ELL p. 82 |
| --- | --- | --- |

→  # Word Work

 **MINILESSON 5 Mins**

## Spelling

**OBJECTIVES**

**CCSS** Demonstrate command of the conventions of standard English capitalization, punctuation, and spelling when writing. **L.2.2**

**CCSS** Generalize learned spelling patterns when writing words (e.g., cage → badge; boy → boil). **L.2.2d**

**CCSS** Know and apply grade-level phonics and word analysis skills in decoding words. **RF.2.3**

**CCSS** Recognize and read grade-appropriate irregularly spelled words. **RF.2.3f**

**CCSS** Read with sufficient accuracy and fluency to support comprehension. **RF.2.4**

### Word Sort with *ch, tch, sh, ph, th, ng, wh*

❶ **Model** Display the Spelling Word Cards from the Teacher's Resource Book, one at a time. Have children read each word, listening for the consonant digraph for each word.

Use Word Building Cards to build the consonant digraphs: *sh, ch, tch, wh, th, ph,* and *ng.* Make a chart in which each column represents one of the consonant digraphs. Say each sound and have children chorally repeat each sound after you.

❷ **Guided Practice/Practice** Have children place each Spelling Word Card in the column that shows its correct consonant digraph. When completed, have children chorally read the words in each column. Then call out a word. Have a child find the word card and point to it as the class chorally spells the word.

❸ **Build Fluency: Word Automaticity** Have children chorally read the spelling words to build fluency. Then conclude by asking children to orally generate additional words that have the same consonant digraphs as the spelling words. List them in the correct columns of the chart.

 **MINILESSON 5 Mins**

## High-Frequency Words

*these, start, walk, seven, eight, learn, try, isn't, baby, early*

❶ **Guided Practice** Say each word and have children Read/Spell/Write it. Ask children to picture the word, and write it in the way they see it. Display word for children to self-correct.

❷ **Practice** Add the High-Frequency words to the cumulative word bank. Have partners create sentences using the words.

**COLLABORATE**

**Cumulative Review** Review last week's words using the Read/ Spell/Write routine. Repeat the above routine, mixing the words and having children say each one.

**Go Digital**

**Spelling Word Sort**

**High-Frequency Word Routine**

**peered**

**Visual Glossary**

# Vocabulary

## Expand Vocabulary

Have children use the Visual Vocabulary Cards to review this week's vocabulary words: *adult, alive, covered, fur, giant, groom, mammal, offspring.*

**1 Explain** Explain to children that words have different forms. Help children generate different forms of this week's words by adding suffixes such as *-s, -ed, -ing*. Review the meaning of each ending.

**2 Model** Write the numbers 1 through 4 on the board and explain that you will write the word *groom* in four different forms. By the number 1, write *groom*. Ask children how they can add different endings to fill in answers for numbers 2, 3, and 4. As you write *grooms, groomed,* and *grooming*, emphasize the suffix and circle it as you write it down.

Point out how the different endings change the meaning of *groom*. Discuss how each form of the word has a different meaning.

Have children share aloud sentences using *groom, grooms, groomed,* and *grooming*.

**3 Guided Practice** Have children work in pairs to fill in chart with a different form or forms of the words *mammal, adult, giant,* and *covered*. Have children share sentences using the different forms of the word.

---

**ELL**

### ENGLISH LANGUAGE LEARNERS

**More Practice** Review spelling by helping children generate words with consonant digraphs. Provide clues: *It is someone who rules a country. He is married to a queen.* (king) Write the word and have children practice reading it. Correct their pronunciation, if needed.

---

## Monitor and *Differentiate*

 **Quick Check**

**Can children read and decode words with consonant digraphs? Can children recognize and read high-frequency words?**

### Small Group Instruction

| | | |
|---|---|---|
| If No → | **Approaching** | Reteach pp. T342-T347 |
| | **ELL** | Develop pp. T358-T365 |
| If Yes → | **On Level** | Review pp. T352-T353 |
| | **Beyond Level** | Extend pp. T356-T357 |

# Comprehension Strategy

CLOSE READING

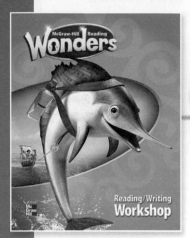

**Reading/Writing Workshop**

### MINILESSON
**10 Mins**

## Reread

### ❶ Explain

Explain that when they read an informational text, children may come across unfamiliar information and detailed explanations. Remind children that they can reread difficult sections of text to increase their understanding.

→ Children should reread something that they do not understand.

→ When they find unclear or difficult text, children can stop and reread that section. They may need to reread it more than once before they understand it.

→ Often, children may find that rereading will improve their understanding of informational texts.

Point out that rereading will also help children remember key facts and ideas.

### ❷ Model Close Reading: Text Evidence

Model how rereading can help you understand why eaglets are helpless. Reread "Proud Parents" on page 152. After pointing out that eaglets cannot walk and so they need their parents for food, have children find other examples of how eaglets are helpless. (They cannot see well. They need their parents for safety.)

### ❸ Guided Practice of Close Reading

COLLABORATE

Have children work in pairs to explain why eagles are not able to fly when they are born. Direct them to reread the section "Eaglets Grow Up" on page 152. Partners can reread that section to find their answers. Have partners discuss other sections of "Eagles and Eaglets" that they might want to reread.

**Go Digital**

**Eagles and Eaglets**

**Present the Lesson**

## CCSS Comprehension Strategy

# Reread

As you read, you may come across new words or information you don't understand. You can reread to help you understand the text.

### 🔍 Find Text Evidence

*On page 152 of "Eagles and Eaglets," the text tells how birds are helpless. I will go back and reread to understand how they are helpless.*

---

**page 152**

**Proud Parents**

At first the eaglets are helpless. They cannot walk. They need their parents for food. They also cannot see well. Birds are not **mammals**. They do not have milk to feed their young. They hunt for food. Eaglets also need their parents for safety.

**Eaglets Grow Up**

Bald eagles use their sharp eyes to hunt. They use their strong wings to fly fast.

---

[ *I read that eaglets cannot walk so they need their parents to get them food.* This explains how they are helpless.

---

### Your Turn COLLABORATE

Why are eagles not able to fly when they are born? Reread page 153 to help you answer the question.

156

Accent Alaska.com/Alamy

**READING/WRITING WORKSHOP, p. 156**

---

### A C T Access Complex Text

#### ▶ Sentence Structures

Children may need support in understanding sentences that have complex structures or that contain more than one idea.

→ Reread the first sentence on page 153. *Ask: What two things does the sentence compare? What did you learn about birds and mammals?* (Birds have feathers. Mammals have fur.)

→ Reread the second and third sentences on page 153. Focus on the third sentence: "It cannot fly…" Ask: *What cannot fly?* (the eaglet) *When can it fly?* (It can fly when it grows dark feathers.) Use similar questioning to help children understand the fourth sentence in the paragraph.

---

**ON-LEVEL PRACTICE BOOK** pp. 83–85

Read the passage. Use the reread strategy to make sure you understand the information.

### Opossums

An adult opossum is about the size of a big cat. When the mother gives birth, she may have seven or more babies. She has a <u>pouch</u>, like a kangaroo.

Each baby opossum is the size of a honeybee. At first, they stay inside the mother's pouch. After about two months, the babies leave the mother's pouch. They are still small. The mother can carry the babies on her <u>back</u>. The baby opossums grow quickly. Soon the young animals are on their <u>own</u>.

| **APPROACHING** pp. 83–85 | **BEYOND** pp. 83–85 | **ELL** pp. 83–85 |
|---|---|---|

---

## Monitor and *Differentiate*

### ✓ Quick Check

Do children reread informational text that they do not understand? Do they reread it more than once if necessary?

⬇

### Small Group Instruction

| | | |
|---|---|---|
| If No → | **Approaching** | Reteach pp. T340–T341 |
| | **ELL** | Develop pp. T358–T359 |
| If Yes → | **On Level** | Review pp. T350–T351 |
| | **Beyond Level** | Extend pp. T354–T355 |

# Comprehension Skill

CLOSE READING

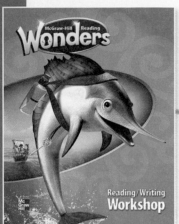

**Reading/Writing Workshop**

## OBJECTIVES

**CCSS** Identify the main topic of a multiparagraph text as well as the focus of specific paragraphs within the text. **RI.2.2**

**CCSS** Ask and answer such questions as *who, what, where, when, why,* and *how* to demonstrate understanding of key details in a text. **RI.2.1**

Identify key details.

## ACADEMIC LANGUAGE
*main topic, key details*

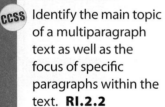

### SKILLS TRACE

**Main Topic and Key Details**

**INTRODUCE** Unit 2 Week 3

**REVIEW** Unit 2 Week 4; Unit 3 Weeks 1, 3

**ASSESS** Unit 2

---

**MINILESSON 10 Mins**

# Main Topic and Key Details

## ❶ Explain

Remind children that the main topic is what the text is mostly about. The key details are the important facts and information that tell about the main topic.

→ To find the main topic, children can ask themselves what a text is mainly about.

→ They can find key details by looking for important information about the main topic.

## ❷ Model Close Reading: Text Evidence

Model using pages 151 and 152 to identify the main topic of "Eagles and Eaglets." Then use the key detail on the graphic organizer to model identifying key details. Reinforce the concept by having children explaining why this is a key detail and by finding another key detail on the pages.

*Analytical Writing* **Write About Reading: Sentences** Model for children how to use key details from the graphic organizer to write a few sentences about how baby eagles are different from their parents. Provide a sample sentence such as: *The baby eaglet is different from its parents because it cannot fly.*

## ❸ Guided Practice of Close Reading

Have children work in pairs to complete the graphic organizer for "Eagles and Eaglets," going back into the text to find key details. Discuss the key details in each section as children complete the graphic organizer.

*Analytical Writing* **Write About Reading: Sentences** Ask pairs to work together to write sentences about how eaglets are different from their parents. Provide sentence frames such as the following: *The baby eaglet is different from its parents because it cannot _____. Another difference is that the baby eaglet has _____ and its parents have _____.* Select pairs of children to share their sentences with the class.

## Go Digital

**Eagles and Eaglets**

**Present the Lesson**

**Graphic Organizer**

Comprehension Skill CCSS

# Main Topic and Key Details

The main topic is what the selection is about. Key details give information about the main topic.

 **Find Text Evidence**

*As I read page 151 I learn a lot about eagles. This must be the main topic. I also read details about eagles.*

| Main Topic |  |  |
|---|---|---|
| Eagles |  |  |
| **Key Detail** | **Key Detail** | **Key Detail** |
| Eagles build nests and lay eggs. |  |  |

**Your Turn** COLLABORATE

Continue reading the story. Fill in the graphic organizer with more key details that tell about the topic.

*Go Digital!*
*Use the interactive graphic organizer*

157

**READING/WRITING WORKSHOP, p. 157**

---

A. Reread the passage and answer the questions.

I. What is the main topic of the passage?

The main topic is about opossums and their babies.

2. What is a key detail about an adult opossum?

Possible response: An adult opossum is about the size of a big cat.

3. What is a key detail about a baby opossum?

Possible response: A baby opossum is the size of a honeybee.

B. Work with a partner. Read the passage aloud. Pay attention to pronunciation. Stop after one minute. Fill out the chart.

|  | Words Read | – | Number of Errors | = | Words Correct Score |
|---|---|---|---|---|---|
| First Read |  | – |  | = |  |
| Second Read |  | – |  | = |  |

| APPROACHING pp. 83–85 | BEYOND pp. 83–85 | ELL pp. 83–85 |
|---|---|---|

---

## ELL ENGLISH LANGUAGE LEARNERS SCAFFOLD

| **Beginning** | **Intermediate** | **Advanced/High** |
|---|---|---|
| Reread the section "It's Nesting Time" on page 151. Help children complete this sentence frame: *The main topic is ____.* (eagle nests) As you read, ask after each sentence: *Is this a key detail? What does it tell about eagle nests?* Clarify children's responses. | Reread "It's Nesting Time." Ask: *What is the main topic of this section?* (eagle nests) *What are the nests made of? How big are they?* Have children complete this sentence frame. *One key detail about this topic is ____.* Correct children's responses as needed. | Have partners tell each other the main topic and key details of the section "It's Nesting Time." Guide them to explain their responses by asking: *Why is that a key detail? Show me where in the text you found that detail.* Allow children ample time to respond. |

---

## Monitor and *Differentiate*

 **Quick Check**

As children complete the graphic organizer, do they find key details that tell about the main topic?

### Small Group Instruction

If No → **Approaching** Reteach pp. T348-T349

**ELL** Develop pp. T358-T361

If Yes → **On Level** Review pp. T352-T353

**Beyond Level** Extend pp. T356-T357

**Language Arts**

## MINILESSON 5 Mins
## Writing Traits: Word Choice

**OBJECTIVES**

CCSS Write informative/ explanatory texts in which they introduce a topic, use facts and definitions to develop points, and provide a concluding statement or section. **W.2.2**

CCSS With guidance and support from adults and peers, focus on a topic and strengthen writing as needed by revising and editing. **W.2.5**

**1 Explain** Remind children that writers use linking words to help connect ideas clearly. Writers revise their writing by using words such as *and* and *also* to show how ideas are alike. They use words such as *but* or *however* to show how ideas are different.

**2 Model** Read aloud the model from Your Turn page 87. Then think aloud to model revising to add linking words.

A puppy is the name for a baby dog. A puppy is much smaller than its parent. It is the same shape as its parent. It has fur like its parent. It cannot do many things for itself.

**Think Aloud** The model makes sense, but it would read in a clearer way if the ideas were connected. I can use linking words to tell how some ideas are alike and how some ideas are different. I can rewrite the third and fourth sentences so that they are one. Listen: It is the same shape as its parent, and it has fur like its parent. Now readers are sure that these are both ways that the puppy is like its parent.

**3 Guided Practice** Invite partners to continue adding and replacing words in the draft to connect more ideas with linking words. Use the prompts on the Your Turn page 87 as a guide.

### Conferencing Routines

**Teacher Conference**

**STEP 1** Talk about the strengths of the writing.

**STEP 2** Focus on the target trait.

**STEP 3** Make concrete suggestions for revisions.

**Peer Conferences**

Provide these questions to guide peers as they review a partner's draft.

☑ Does the writing clearly connect ideas?

☑ Can I tell how ideas are alike and different?

☑ Where can the writing use more linking words?

📝 **WRITING ENTRY: LINKING WORDS**

**1 Revise** Have children review their writing from Day 1. Ask them to revise their responses by adding a linking word to show how ideas are connected. They may also write a better linking word than the one they used in their first draft.

Use the Conferencing Routines to help children revise. Circulate among children and stop briefly to talk with individuals. Provide opportunities for partners to work together using the Peer Conferences routine.

**2 Edit** Ask children to review the rules on Grammar Handbook page 479 and check that they have used plural nouns correctly. Have children also check for correct use of abbreviations and for errors in grammar, spelling, and punctuation.

**Go**
# Digital

**Writing Model**

**Writing**

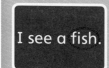

I see a fish.

**Grammar**

**MINILESSON 5 Mins**

# Grammar

## More Plural Nouns

**❶ Review** Remind children that a plural noun names more than one person, place, or thing. Review that we add *-s* or *-es* to form the plural of many singular nouns. Point out that some singular nouns change their spelling to form the plural. Offer examples, such as *foot/feet* and *man/men*. Explain to children that there are also singular nouns that do not change their spelling to form the plural, such as *fish/fish,* and *sheep/sheep*.

Read the following sentence aloud and guide children to identify the nouns and to tell whether they are singular or plural.

The mouse had two baby mice. (mouse—singular; mice—plural)

**❷ Guided Practice** Display the following sentence and read it aloud.

We saw a group of five deer in the field.

Point out that in this sentence the word *deer* is a plural noun. We know from the rest of the sentence that there are five deer in the field, not just one. Invite children to replace the word *deer* in the sentence with other plural nouns.

**❸ Practice** Have partners add plural nouns to the following sentences and share their sentences with the class. Remind them to pay attention to the correct form of the plural noun.

The offpsring of dogs are called _____.

We saw three _____ on the farm.

## Mechanics: Abbreviations

**❶ Review** Remind children that an abbreviation is a shortened way of writing a word. An abbreviation begins with a capital letter and ends with a period.

**❷ Practice** Write the following street address on the board. Invite volunteers to write the abbreviations of the underlined words.

<u>Mister</u> Alan Lee (Mr.)

110 West <u>Avenue</u> (Ave.)

Then write the following days of the week and months of the year on the board. Invite volunteers to abbreviate them.

February (Feb.) March (Mar.) Monday(Mon.) Thursday (Thurs.)

---

**ON-LEVEL PRACTICE BOOK** p. 87

**A. Read the draft model. Use the questions that follow the draft to help you add linking words.**

> **Draft Model**
> A puppy is the name for a baby dog. A puppy is much smaller than its parent. It is the same shape as its parent. It has fur like its parent. It cannot do many things for itself.

1. What are some ways you can connect the ideas in the draft?

2. How is a puppy different from its parent?

3. How is a puppy the same as its parent?

**B. Now revise the draft by adding and replacing words to connect ideas with linking words, such as *and, so, also, but,* or *however*.**

Answers will vary but should demonstrate the use of linking words to

connect ideas.

| APPROACHING p. 87 | BEYOND p. 87 | ELL p. 87 |
|---|---|---|

---

# Daily Wrap Up

→ Discuss the Essential Question and encourage children to use the oral vocabulary words.

→ Prompt children to review and discuss the skills they used today. How do those skills help them?

LANGUAGE ARTS **T313**

## Materials

**Reading/Writing Workshop**

**Literature Anthology "Baby Bears"**

adult
**Visual Vocabulary Cards**
adult      giant
alive      groom
covered    mammal
fur        offspring

**Interactive Read-Aloud Cards**

a b c
**Word-Building Cards**

baby
**High-Frequency Word Cards**

chop
**Spelling Word Cards**

ch
tch
cheese
**Sound-Spelling Cards**

→ # Build the Concept

MINILESSON
**5 Mins**

# Interactive Read Aloud

### OBJECTIVES

**CCSS** Ask and answer such questions as *who, what, where, when, why,* and *how* to demonstrate understanding of key details in a text. **RI.2.1**

• Develop oral language.
• Discuss the Essential Question.

### ACADEMIC LANGUAGE

*reread, main topic, key details*

**ESSENTIAL QUESTION**

Remind children that this week they are talking and reading about how baby animals are like and unlike their parents, and how animals care for their offspring. Remind them of the wild animal babies in "Wild Animal Families," and the bald eagles and their offspring in "Eagles and Eaglets." Guide children to discuss the Essential Question using information from what they have read and discussed throughout the week.

## Review Oral Vocabulary

Review the oral vocabulary words *guide, leader, protect, provide,* and *separate* using the Define/Example/Ask routine. Encourage children to discuss how animal offspring are like their parents when coming up with examples for each word.

## Reread "Wild Animal Families"

Tell children that you will reread "Wild Animal Families." Pause occasionally to model rereading to help children make sure they understand the text. Prompt children to identify and describe the main topic and key details of the text.

**Interactive Read-Aloud Cards**

**Analytical Writing** ## Write About Reading

Have children choose one animal from the selection and write about how that animal cares for its offspring. Remind them to include key details in their descriptions.

**Go Digital**

**Wild Animal Families**

**Eagles and Eaglets**

# Comprehension

## Key Details

❶ **Explain** Remind children that this week and last week they have been learning to identify the main topic and key details of a text. Remind them that in past weeks they have learned how to use photos and illustrations to identify key details. Use the Shared Read, "Eagles and Eaglets," to review this skill.

→ The main topic is what the selection is mostly about.

→ Key details help explain or tell more about the main topic.

→ Children can look for key details in the text, photos, or illustrations.

❷ **Model** Display pages 152–153 of "Eagles and Eaglets." Remind children can use photos to identify key details and to help them understand key details in the text. *I can look at the section called "Eaglets Grow Up" to find key details. The author describes the eagle's sharp eyes, strong wings, claws, and beak needed for hunting. I can see these details in the photo on page 153. Now I can clearly see and better understand the information the author is describing. These details about help me understand why eagles are able to hunt and catch fish.*

❸ **Guided Practice** Reread pages 152–153 of "Eagles and Eaglets" with children. Pause as you read to model finding key details using the photographs and text. Prompt children to use the key details to tell more about the main topic of this selection. Guide them to refer to the photos and reread the text to find key details.

→ Help children describe how an eaglet is the same and different than its parents. Begin by having children use the photos of eagles and eaglets to compare to identify similarities and differences.

→ Prompt children to locate additional key details by asking text-based questions, such as *In what ways do the parents help the eaglets? How long does it take for the eaglet's wings to grow strong?*

**ELL**

## ENGLISH LANGUAGE LEARNERS

**Use Visuals** Have children use the photos on pages 150–153 to help them describe how eaglets are the same and different than their parents. Ask: *Are the eaglets and eagles both birds? What size is the eaglet compared to its parents? Do the eaglets have feathers?*

→ # Word Work

## Quick Review

**Build Fluency: Sound-Spellings** Display the **Word-Building Cards:** *ch, th, sh, wh, tch, ph, ng, o_e, o, u_e, u, i_e, i, a_e, a, c, g, dge, ge, lge, nge, rge.* Have children say each sound. For fluency in connected text, see the Decodable reader Lesson in Small Group.

## MINILESSON 5 Mins — Phonemic Awareness

### Phoneme Blending

## Go Digital

**OBJECTIVES**

**CCSS** Know and apply grade-level phonics and word analysis skills in decoding words. **RF.2.3**

**CCSS** Decode words with common prefixes and suffixes. **RF.2.3d**

**CCSS** Demonstrate command of the conventions of standard English capitalization, punctuation, and spelling when writing. **L.2.2**

**CCSS** Generalize learned spelling patterns when writing words (e.g., cage → badge; boy → boil). **L.2.2d**

- Blend phonemes to form words.
- Apply phonics when decoding words with consonant digraphs.
- Identify and read words with the suffixes *-ful* and *-less.*

❶ **Model** Place markers in the WorkBoard to represent sounds. Show children how to orally blend phonemes. *I'm going to put one marker in each box as I say each sound. Then I will blend the sounds to form a word.* Place a marker for each sound as you say /b/ /a/ /ch/. *This word has three sounds. /b/ /a/ /ch/. Listen as I blend these sounds to form a word: /bach/,* batch. *The word is* batch.

❷ **Guided Practice/Practice** *Let's do some together. Using your own boards, place a marker for each sound you hear. Listen as I say one sound at a time. Then let's blend the sounds to say each word.* Do the first three with children.

| | | |
|---|---|---|
| shape | phone | path |
| sing | what | chip |
| match | wish | whip |

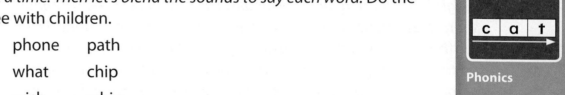

## MINILESSON 5 Mins — Phonics

### Blend Words with Consonant Digraphs
### *ch, tch, sh, ph, th, ng, wh*

❶ **Model** Display Word-Building Cards *h, u, n, g.* Model how to blend the sounds. *This is the letter* h. *It stands for /h/. This is the letter* u. *It stands for /u/. The letters* n *and* g *go together to make a single sound, /ng/. Let's blend all three sounds: /huuung/. The word is* hung.

Continue by modeling the words *catch, thing, king, when.*

❷ **Guided Practice/Practice** Repeat the routine with *batch, path, sing, mash, phone, graph, when, whisk, branch, them.*

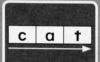

**Phonemic Awareness**

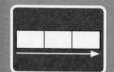

**Phonics**

**Structural Analysis**

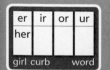

**Spelling Word Sort**

# Structural Analysis

## Suffixes -*ful*, -*less*

**1 Model** Say the words *home* and *homeless*. Ask children to listen closely to hear what is different about each word. Point out that the second word has a suffix -*less* at the end of it. The suffix means "without" and it turns the one-syllable word *home* into a two-syllable word.

→  Write the words *home* and *homeless*. Underline the letters -*less* at the end of *homeless*. Tell children that suffixes change the meaning of the words they are added to. Explain that -*ful* is another suffix that changes the meaning of the word it is attached to.

**2 Practice/Apply** Help children blend the words *shame, shameful, shape, shapeless, hope, hopeless, hopeful, wish, wishful*.

# Spelling

## Words with *ch, tch, sh, ph, th, ng, wh*

**1 Model** Make index cards for *ch, sh*, and *wh* and form three columns in a pocket chart, one for each consonant digraph. Blend the sounds with children and reinforce that they make one sound when they are pronounced in a word.

Hold up the *chop* **Spelling Word Card**. Say and spell it. Pronounce each sound clearly: /ch/ /o/ /p/. Blend the sounds. Then place the word in the correct pocket chart. Repeat this step with *shape* and emphasize the /sh/ digraph. Then repeat with *while* and place it in the correct pocket chart.

**2 Guided Practice/Practice** Have children spell each word. Repeat the process by making pocket charts for the *tch, ph, th*, and *ng* words.

Display the words, *catch, trash, phone, that, sting, thin,* and *bring* in a separate column. Read and spell the words together with children. Point out that these spelling words all contain consonant digraphs.

Conclude by asking children to orally generate additional words that rhyme with each word on the list. Write the additional words on the board. Underline the common spelling pattern in each additional word. If necessary, point out the differences and explain why they are unusual.

---

**PHONICS/SPELLING PRACTICE BOOK** p. 43

| chop | catch | shape | trash | phone |
|------|-------|-------|-------|-------|
| that | sting | thin | bring | while |

**A. Word Sort**
Look at the spelling words in the box. Fill in the blanks below with spelling words that match each consonant digraph.

| | ng | | tch | | ph | | wh |
|--|----|--|-----|--|----|--|----|
| 1. | sting | 3. | catch | 4. | phone | 5. | while |
| 2. | bring | | | | | | |

| | sh | | th | | ch |
|--|----|--|----|--|----|
| 6. | shape | 8. | that | 10. | chop |
| 7. | trash | 9. | thin | | |

**B. Compare Words**
Draw a line through the letter that does not belong. Write the correct word on the line.

| | | |
|--|--|--|
| 11. catᶳch | catch | 16. whiᵧle ___ while |
| 12. traᶳsh | trash | 17. briᵧng ___ bring |
| 13. pᶠhone | phone | 18. thᵢin ___ thin |
| 14. stingᵧ | sting | 19. sᶜhape ___ shape |
| 15. thaᵈt | that | 20. ᶠchop ___ chop |

**Monitor and Differentiate**

✓ **Quick Check**

Can children blend words with consonant digraphs?

↓

**Small Group Instruction**

| If No → | **Approaching** | Reteach pp. T342–T347 |
| | **ELL** | Develop pp. T358–T365 |
| If Yes → | **On Level** | Review pp. T352–T353 |
| | **Beyond Level** | Extend pp. T356–T357 |

 **Fluency**

### Quick Review

**High-Frequency Words:** Read, Spell, and Write to review this week's high-frequency words: *these, start, walk, seven, eight, learn, try, isn't, baby, early.*

**MINILESSON**
**10 Mins**

# Pronunciation

**OBJECTIVES**

CCSS Read with sufficient accuracy and fluency to support comprehension. **RF.2.4**

CCSS Use context to confirm or self-correct word recognition and understanding, rereading as necessary. **RF.2.4c**

- Recognize and read high-frequency words.
- Apply grade-level phonics in decoding words in connected text.
- Practice fluency.
- Use vocabulary words in context.

**1 Explain** Tell children that part of reading with the correct pronunciation is taking your time to spell out difficult words before trying to read them fluently in a sentence. Tell children that it helps to preview a selection before reading it aloud to locate any words that they may be unfamiliar with. They can sound out the word and pronounce it correctly before reading it aloud as part of their fluency.

**2 Model** Model prosody by reading page 155 of the Shared Read aloud. Model identifying a more difficult word to pronounce, such as *soar* or *feathers* and practice blending the letters before incorporating it in the whole fluency read-aloud. In addition, model rereading and using context clues to confirm or self-correct word recognition and understanding.

**3 Guided Practice** Have children read the passage aloud to a partner. Make sure they preview the passage to look for words they may have trouble pronouncing before they read the whole passage aloud. Offer feedback as needed.

## Fluency Practice

Children can practice fluency using Practice Book pages.

**Go Digital**

**peered**

**Visual Glossary**

# Vocabulary

## Reinforce Vocabulary

**1 Guided Practice** Use the Visual Vocabulary Cards to review last week's words (*buried, journey, peeks, spies, escape, restless, habitat, nature*) and this week's vocabulary words (*groom, alive, adult, covered, fur, giant, mammal, offspring*). Work together with children to generate a new context sentence for each word.

**2 Practice** Have children work with a partner to orally complete each sentence stem using this week's and last week's vocabulary words.

1. The dog dug a hole in the yard and _____ the stick in it. (buried)

2. I know it will be a long _____ across the country. (journey)

3. Sara wins hide and seek because she _____ to see where you hide. (peeks)

4. The wolf _____ on the other animals in the forest. (spies)

5. The rabbit tried to _____ the storm by running away. (escape)

6. I feel _____ after sitting in school all day. (restless)

7. The animals _____ each other so they look neat and clean. (groom)

8. The flowers are not living, but the grass is still _____. (alive)

9. The puppy is a baby, but its mother is an _____. (adult)

10. The snow _____ the street in just a few minutes. (covered)

11. The bear stays warm because it has thick _____. (fur)

12. We are going to have a _____ party with everyone from school. (giant)

13. A lion is a _____. (mammal)

14. Fish live in a water _____ . (habitat)

15. The mother bear protects her _____. (offspring)

16. I go hiking with my family to spend time looking at _____. (nature)

# Genre: Informational Text

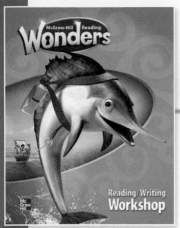

**Reading/Writing Workshop**

## ACADEMIC LANGUAGE

• *expository text, diagram, labels*

• cognates: *expositivo, diagrama*

 **10 Mins** MINILESSON

## Expository Text

### ❶ Explain

Share with children the following key characteristics of **expository text**.

→ Expository text gives important facts about a topic. Topics may include a real person, a real event, a real place, or a real thing.

→ Expository text may include text features such as photos, captions, headings, and diagrams with labels. However, a text may still be expository even if it does not have these features.

### ❷ Model Close Reading: Text Evidence

Model identifying the genre of "Eagles and Eaglets." Then discuss the text features on page 153.

**Diagrams** Point out the diagram of the bald eagle. Explain that diagrams help give a picture of what something is, what features something has, or how something works.

**Labels** Point out that there are five labels around the diagram of the eagle. Each of them points out and describes a different feature of the eagle.

### ❸ Guided Practice of Close Reading

 Have children work with partners to discuss and write about what they learned about bald eagles by looking at the diagram and reading the labels on page 153. Have them share their ideas with the class.

**Go Digital**

**Present the Lesson**

CCSS **Genre** Informational Text

# Expository Text

The selection "Eagles and Eaglets" is an expository text. An **Expository text**:
- gives facts about a topic.
- can have text features.

 **Find Text Evidence**

*I know that "Eagles and Eaglets" is an expository text because it gives facts about eagles. It also has text features that help me learn about eagles.*

**page 153**

Unlike mammals, birds have feathers, not fur. An eaglet is born covered with soft gray down. It cannot fly until it grows dark feathers like its parents. The eaglet stays near the nest until its wings grow strong. That takes about five months.

Bald Eagle — powerful eyes — dark feathers on body and wings — hooked yellow beak — white tail feathers — long claws

**Text Features**

A **diagram** is a picture that shows information.

The **labels** explain the parts of the diagram.

 **Your Turn** COLLABORATE

Tell what information you learned from looking at the diagram and reading the labels.

158

**READING/WRITING WORKSHOP, p. 158**

---

**Leopards and Their Cubs**

Leopard cubs are born with their eyes closed. Their fur is longer and thicker than their parents. It is grayer, too. The cub's spots are not easy to see.

**Leopard**

long tail — yellow eyes — whiskers — claws — black spots

**Answer the questions about the text.**

1. How do you know this is an expository text?

   It gives facts about leopards and their cubs. It has a diagram with labels.

2. What information can you learn from looking at the diagram?

   what the leopard cub looks like

3. What information can you learn by reading the labels?

   the names of parts of the leopard

| APPROACHING p. 88 | BEYOND p. 88 | ELL p. 88 |
|---|---|---|

---

## Monitor and *Differentiate*

✓ **Quick Check**

Are children able to understand the diagram and the labels? Can they identify information they learned from the diagram and the labels?

### Small Group Instruction

If No → **Approaching**  Reteach pp. T340–T341

   **ELL**  Develop pp. T358–T361

If Yes → **On Level**  Review pp. T350–T351

   **Beyond Level**  Extend pp. T354–T355

---

ELL **ENGLISH LANGUAGE LEARNERS SCAFFOLD**

| **Beginning** | **Intermediate** | **Advanced/High** |
|---|---|---|
| Focus on the diagram of the bald eagle on page 153 of "Eagles and Eaglets." Have children repeat after you as you read each caption. Have children point out unfamiliar words. Help children use the diagram to understand these words and each caption as a whole. | Help children read each caption on the diagram on page 153. Point out the caption *powerful eyes*. Ask: *What does* powerful *mean? How do powerful eyes help an eagle?* Clarify children's responses as needed. Have children point to the text on page 152 that gives the answer. | Have partners reread pages 152 and 153 together. Have them discuss each feature on the diagram on page 153 and use text evidence from page 152 to talk about any ways in which each feature helps the eagle. Allow children ample time to respond. |

# Vocabulary Strategy

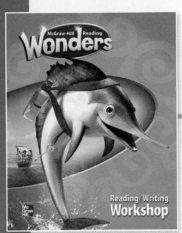
**MINILESSON**
**10 Mins**

# Multiple-Meaning Words

## 1 Explain

Explain to children that some words have more than one meaning. For example, *rattled* can mean "made short, sharp sounds" or "made someone upset."

→ To find out which meaning a multiple-meaning word has in a sentence, children should read the whole sentence and look for **context clues**. Children can also look at nearby sentences.

## 2 Model Close Reading: Text Evidence

Model reading the entire sentence on page 151 to find the correct meaning of the multiple-meaning word *add*. Have children confirm that the meaning makes sense in the sentence.

## 3 Guided Practice of Close Reading

Have children work in pairs to figure out the correct meanings of *watch* and *fly* as they are used in "Eagles and Eaglets." Encourage partners to go back to the text to read the whole sentence to determine which meaning of the word is being used.

# Go Digital

**Present the Lesson**

---

## OBJECTIVES

**CCSS** Determine or clarify the meaning of unknown and multiple-meaning words and phrases based on *grade 2 reading and content*, choosing flexibly from an array of strategies. **L.2.4**

**CCSS** Use sentence-level context as a clue to a meaning of a word or phrase. **L.2.4a**

---

## ACADEMIC LANGUAGE

*multiple-meaning words, context clues*

---

### SKILLS TRACE

**Multiple-Meaning Words**

**INTRODUCE** Unit 2 Week 4

**REVIEW** Unit 2 Week 5; Unit 4 Weeks 3, 5; Unit 5 Week 5

**ASSESS** Units 2, 5

---

## Vocabulary Strategy CCSS

# Multiple-Meaning Words

Multiple-meaning words have more than one meaning. Use the other words in a sentence to figure out which meaning is being used.

🔍 **Find Text Evidence**

*I'm not sure what the word* add *means. This word could mean "to put on something extra," or it could mean "to put numbers together." Since the eagles are making a nest, I think the first meaning makes sense in this sentence.*

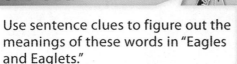

They add on to their nests each year.

### Your Turn COLLABORATE

Use sentence clues to figure out the meanings of these words in "Eagles and Eaglets."
**watch,** *page 151*
**fly,** *page 152*

159

**READING/WRITING WORKSHOP, p. 159**

**ON-LEVEL PRACTICE BOOK** p. 89

| across | borrow | countryside | idea |
| insists | lonely | solution | villages |

**Choose the word that makes sense in each blank. Then write the word on the line.**

1. The road passes through many small towns and ___villages___.
2. We saw a sheep farm in the ___countryside___.
3. She felt ___lonely___ when everyone left the house.
4. May I please ___borrow___ your pencil?
5. The boy has a good ___idea___ for his art project.
6. They use the bridge to get ___across___ the stream.
7. I know the ___solution___ to this math problem.
8. The teacher ___insists___ that students do their best.

| **APPROACHING** p. 89 | **BEYOND** p. 89 | **ELL** p. 89 |

## Monitor and Differentiate

✓ **Quick Check**

**Can children identify which meaning of** *watch* **and** *fly* **is being used in the sentences in "Eagles and Eaglets?"**

⬇

### Small Group Instruction

If No → **Approaching** Reteach pp. T340-T349
**ELL** Develop pp. T362-T363
If Yes → **On Level** Review pp. T352-T353
**Beyond Level** Extend pp. T356-T357

## ELL ENGLISH LANGUAGE LEARNERS SCAFFOLD

**Beginning**

Help children find the words *watch* on page 151 and *fly* on page 152. Read the sentence where each word appears. Then use questioning to help children determine the meaning of each worrd. Ask: *Do you think the author meant a watch that you wear on your wrist? Do you think the author meant "to look"?*

**Intermediate**

Have children find the words *watch* on page 151 and *fly* on page 152. Ask them to talk with a partner about the different meanings of each multiple-meaning word and have them decide together which meaning is correct in the sentence where it appears.

**Advanced/High**

Have children find the words *watch* and *fly* in the selection "Eagles and Eaglets." Ask them to explain the multiple-meanings of each word and then explain which meaning is correct in the sentence where it appears. Encourage them to give their own explanation of why they chose that particular meaning.

**Genre · Expository Text**

# Baby Bears

by
Bobbie Kalman

 **Essential Question**
**How are offspring like their parents?**
Read to find out how baby bears are like their moms and dads.

*Go Digital!*

187

**LITERATURE ANTHOLOGY, pp. 186–187**

**Wonders**
Literature Anthology

**Literature Anthology**

# Develop Comprehension

**CLOSE READING**

**Lexile** 590
*TextEvaluator* 4

## Read Literature Anthology

**Review Genre: Informational Text** Review with children the key characteristics of expository nonfiction:

→ Provides facts and details about real people, places, events, or things.

→ Presents information about a topic.

→ Uses information that people have collected and studied.

**Preview and Predict** Read the title on page 186 and ask children to look at the photo. *What do you think this selection will be about? Let's find out.*

**ESSENTIAL QUESTION**

Read the Essential Question: How are offspring like their parents? As children read, tell them to think about how animal babies are like their moms and dads.

**Story Words** Read and spell the words *nurse, watch, hard,* and *litters.* Tell children that they will read these words in the selection. Ask them what they know about any of these words before you begin reading.

 *Analytical Writing* **Note Taking: Graphic Organizer**
As children read the selection, guide them to fill in **Your Turn Practice Book page 86.**

① **What is a bear?**

Bears are animals called mammals. Mammals have hair or fur on their bodies. Bears are covered with fur. Mammals are born. You were born, too. You are a mammal.

Baby bears are called cubs. Cubs are born with their eyes shut. Their eyes open when they are about six weeks old. This brown bear cub was just born. It has very little fur.

188

These polar bear cubs are nursing.

Mammal mothers make milk inside their bodies. Mammal babies nurse from their mothers. To nurse is to drink mother's milk. ②

189

**LITERATURE ANTHOLOGY,** pp. 188–189

① **Strategy: Reread**

**Teacher Think Aloud** Page 188 tells me what a mammal is. But it seemed like a lot of information to remember when I first read it. I would like to reread that section. When I reread I can tell that mammals have hair or fur and they are born. A bear is a mammal, and so am I. Rereading helps me understand the text better.

② **Skill: Main Topic and Key Details**

Based on the title and information you have read so far, what is the main topic of this selection? (bears and baby bears) What is one key detail you have read about the topic?

**A C T Access Complex Text**

▶ **What Makes This Text Complex?**

**Lack of Prior Knowledge** Some facts may be brand new to children. Provide background or clarification of facts as needed.

**Specific Vocabulary** Some vocabulary in this informational text may be brand new to children. Provide definitions of specific words as needed.

**Genre** This text uses text features such as headings, photos, and captions. Make sure children understand these text features and that the information in them is important.

③
## Kinds of bears

There are eight kinds of bears. The bears shown on this page are an American black bear, a brown bear, and a polar bear. These bears all live in North America.

American black bears can be different colors. What color is this black bear?

There are different kinds of brown bears. These grizzly bears are one kind of brown bear.

Polar bears have white fur. They live in a cold place called the Arctic.

People who study bears once thought that **giant** pandas were raccoons. Now people think that these animals are bears. There are not many giant pandas left in the world. Giant pandas live in China.

**STOP AND CHECK**

Reread  What animal did people used to think giant pandas were? Reread to check your understanding.

190

④

191

**LITERATURE ANTHOLOGY, pp. 190–191**

# Develop Comprehension
CLOSE READING

## ③ Strategy: Reread

Remember that rereading helps you to understand a text. If there is something that you do not understand about bears when you read the text the first time, you should stop and read the part of the text that you did not understand. For example, I am not sure I understand the difference between the bears shown on page 190. If I reread, I can get a better understanding. An American black bear is shown, and so are a brown bear and a polar bear. Sometimes I just need to slow down and look again.

## ④ Summarize

**Teacher Think Aloud**  I know that when I read nonfiction text, there can be a lot of information in the text and in the photos and captions. To make sure I understand all the information on page 190, I can summarize what I have read.

**STOP AND CHECK**

**Reread**  What animal did people used to think giant pandas were? (People used to think giant pandas were raccoons. Now they think they are bears.)

## Bear bodies

Bears have four legs. They can walk on all four legs or on their two back legs. They have five toes with claws on each foot. Claws are curved nails.

**5** This grizzly bear cub has brown fur covering its body.

Bears can smell, hear, and see very well.

Bears use their claws to climb and dig.

192

## Bear coats

Bears have two kinds of fur. Some of their fur is short, and some is long. Their short fur keeps them warm. Their long fur keeps water away from their skin.

Polar bears have thick white fur.

**6**

Pandas have black-and-white fur.

193

**LITERATURE ANTHOLOGY, pp. 192–193**

### 5 Skill: Main Topic and Key Details

Look at your graphic organizer. Recall that we already identified that the main topic of this selection is "Bears and Baby Bears." One detail we learned is that bears are mammals and baby bears are called cubs. What is another detail we read about bears? Let's add it to our chart.

### 6 Maintain Skill: Key Details

How do the photos and captions on page 193 help you to understand what is the same and different about polar bears and panda bears? (Both have fur, but the polar bear's fur is white, while the panda's fur is black and white.)

| Main Topic Bears and Baby Bears | | |
|---|---|---|
| **Detail** Bears are mammals. Baby bears are called cubs. | **Detail** | **Detail** |

## Bear families

A bear family is made up of a mother bear and her cubs. Most mother bears have litters of cubs. A litter is two or more babies that are born at the same time. This mother grizzly bear has three cubs.

194

This mother bear is teaching her cubs how to climb a tree. Mothers also teach cubs how to **groom** their fur and stay clean.

Cubs stay with their mothers until they are two to three years old. They watch their mothers to learn how to live on their own. Mother bears teach their cubs where to find food and how to stay safe.

195

**LITERATURE ANTHOLOGY, pp. 194–195**

# Develop Comprehension

CLOSE READING

## ❼ Strategy: Reread

**Teacher Think Aloud** After I read pages 194 and 195, I am not sure I remembered everything I read about bear families. I will read page 194 to remind myself about what I read. This will help me to remember details and understand the whole passage more.

**Student Think Aloud** When I went back to read page 194, I came across the word litters. I kept rereading so I could remember more about what this meant. I found out by rereading that a litter is two or more babies that are born at the same time. Sometimes I have to reread text to help me understand and remember what I have read.

## ❽ Skill: Main Topic and Key Details

COLLABORATE

Turn to a partner and discuss some key details you have read about so far on pages 194 and 195. Add the information to the chart.

| Main Topic Bears and Baby Bears | | |
|---|---|---|
| **Detail** | **Detail** | **Detail** |
| Bears are mammals. Baby bears are called cubs. | Cubs stay with their mother until they are 2 to 3 years old. | |

## What do bears eat? ⑨

Most bears are omnivores. Omnivores are animals that eat both plants and animals. Bears eat honey, berries, leaves, and eggs. They also eat insects, fish, and other animals. Polar bears are carnivores. Carnivores eat mainly other animals. Pandas are herbivores. Herbivores eat mainly plants.

Pandas eat plants called bamboo.

196

## Bear habitats

Bears live in different places. The natural place where a bear lives is called its habitat. Many bears live in forests. Forests are habitats with many trees. Some bears live on mountains. Pandas live in forests that grow high on mountains. Bamboo grows in these forests.

Black bears live in North American forests.

**STOP AND CHECK**

**Make Predictions** What do you think this bear will find to eat? Use the Make Predictions strategy to help you.

197

**LITERATURE ANTHOLOGY, pp. 196–197**

---

## ⑨ Multiple-Meaning Words

Find the word *leaves* on page 196. This is a multiple-meaning word. Do you think it means "something from a tree" or "to go away from somewhere" on this page? Remember, you can read the whole sentence to help you figure out which meaning the author meant. (something from a tree)

**STOP AND CHECK**

**Make Predictions** What do you think this bear will find to eat? (Possible response: The text says bears live in forests, so I predict this bear will eat things it finds in the forest such as plants, berries, nuts, and small animals.)

## CONNECT TO CONTENT
### LIFE CYCLES

A life cycle tells how an animal starts life, grows to become an adult, has young, and dies. Mammals give birth to live babies. When mammals are born, they need their mothers to live. On page 195, children read about cubs watching their mothers to learn how to live on their own.

**STEM**

## Winter sleep

Some bears live in places that have cold winters. It is hard for the bears to find food when it is cold. To stay **alive**, they sleep through most of the winter. During the summer and fall, the bears eat a lot of food. They store the food as fat on their bodies. The bears live off the fat during the winter.

These grizzly bears are eating a lot of salmon. They are getting ready for winter.

198

Mother bears that live in cold places have their cubs in winter. Before the cubs are born, the mother builds a home called a den. The den is a warm and safe place for the bears to live. Many bears make their dens by digging holes in hills or under tree roots. Some bears use caves or holes in logs for their dens. After the cubs are born, the mother goes to sleep. The cubs nurse while their mother sleeps. ⑩ ⑪

Some polar bears make tunnels in the snow to use as dens.

199

**LITERATURE ANTHOLOGY,** pp. 198–199

# Develop Comprehension
*CLOSE READING*

⑩ **Skill: Main Topic and Key Details**

What key detail did you learn about how bears and baby bears spend the winter? Let's add it to our Main Topic and Key Details Chart.

| Main Topic Bears and Baby Bears | | |
|---|---|---|
| **Detail** | **Detail** | **Detail** |
| Bears are mammals. Baby bears are called cubs. | Cubs stay with their mother until they are 2 to 3 years old. | Many bears store fat and sleep in dens through the winter. |

⑪ **Author's Craft: Details and Facts**

Authors of nonfiction text try to give details and facts in a clear way. Look at the word *den* in the second sentence on page 199. The author introduces the word *den* by telling us that it is a home. Reread page 199. Work with a partner to find three more facts about *dens*.

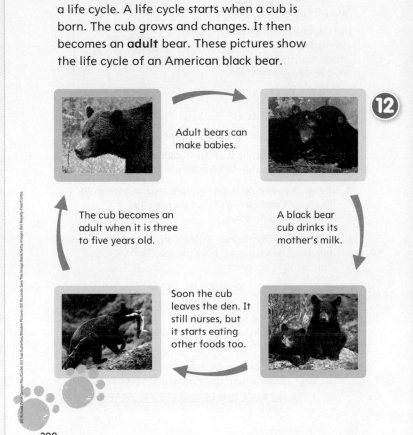

## Cubs grow up

Each bear goes through a set of changes called a life cycle. A life cycle starts when a cub is born. The cub grows and changes. It then becomes an **adult** bear. These pictures show the life cycle of an American black bear.

Adult bears can make babies. ⑫

The cub becomes an adult when it is three to five years old.

A black bear cub drinks its mother's milk.

Soon the cub leaves the den. It still nurses, but it starts eating other foods too.

200

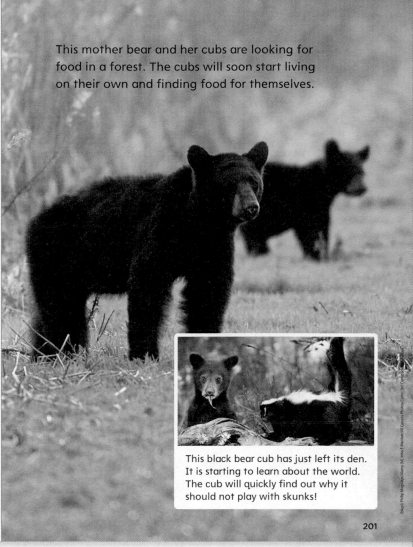

This mother bear and her cubs are looking for food in a forest. The cubs will soon start living on their own and finding food for themselves.

This black bear cub has just left its den. It is starting to learn about the world. The cub will quickly find out why it should not play with skunks!

201

**LITERATURE ANTHOLOGY, pp. 200–201**

## ⑫ Strategy: Reread

**Student Think Aloud** The diagram of the bear life cycle looks important. It gives information about how baby bears grow. I can reread it carefully and look at the pictures. When I reread it, I learn more information about the bear's life cycle. I can paraphrase what I read. Cubs are born, drink their mother's milk, and grow up when they are 3 to 5 years old. Then they can have cubs of their own and the life cycle starts over again.

## Skill: Main Topic and Key Details

Look back through the selection with a partner. Make sure you've added all the important key details about the main topic "bears and baby bears" to your graphic organizer.

## Return to Predictions and Purposes

Ask children if their predictions about the selection were correct. Guide them to use evidence in the text to confirm whether or not their predictions turned out to be accurate. Discuss what children learned about offspring and their parents. Did children learn what they wanted to by reading the selection?

## About the Author

**Bobbie Kalman** has written books about almost every kind of animal. Once she spent months in Hawaii swimming with dolphins and whales so she could write about them. *Baby Bears* is Bobbie's first book about baby animals. She loves writing about how they learn, grow, and change.

### Author's Purpose

Authors often use headings in expository text. What are some of the headings in *Baby Bears*? How do these headings help you understand the information?

202

## Respond to Reading

### Summarize

Use important details to summarize the selection. Information from your Main Topic and Key Details chart may help you.

| Main Topic | | |
|---|---|---|
| Detail | Detail | Detail |

### Text Evidence

1. How do you know *Baby Bears* is expository text? GENRE

2. What is a bear family like? Use details in the selection to support your answer. MAIN TOPIC AND KEY DETAILS

3. Use what you know about multiple-meaning words to figure out the meaning of *store* on page 198. MULTIPLE-MEANING WORDS

4. Write about how all kinds of bears are the same and different. Use key details from the selection to help you. WRITE ABOUT READING

**Make Connections**

How do baby bears learn from their mothers? ESSENTIAL QUESTION

What can people learn about babies and parents from studying bears? TEXT TO WORLD

203

**LITERATURE ANTHOLOGY, pp. 202–203**

# Meet the Author

## Bobbie Kalman

Read aloud page 202 with children. Ask them why they think Bobbie Kalman wrote about baby bears. *What kind of research do you think she had to do?* (Possible answer: She probably researched the bears online and then studied them in nature.)

## Author's Purpose

Have children think about how the headings in the text helped them to understand the information. Have them answer the following prompt in their Response Journals. *The headings helped me _____.*

## AUTHOR'S CRAFT

### Photos and Diagrams

Explain that an author of nonfiction text chooses photos and diagrams to show information and create interest for the reader.

→ Point out how the author used photos and text in the diagram to show and tell about each stage of the bear's life cycle. (p. 200)

→ Ask children to find their favorite photograph. Have them tell why they think it is interesting and what they learned from it.

# Respond to Reading

## Summarize

Guide children through steps to summarize.

→ First, select important details from each section of text.

→ Decide what the details of each section have in common and decide on the main idea of the selection.

→ Use the main idea to state the summary.

## Text Evidence

Guide children to use text evidence to answer the Text Evidence questions on Literature Anthology page 203. Model answering the questions as needed.

1. **Genre**  To answer this question, let's look back at the text. It presents facts about real living things. It gives information about different kinds of baby bears and how they grow up.

2. **Main Topic and Key Details**  To answer this question we need to go back to the text and look for the heading that says "Bear Families." A bear family is a mother and her litter of cubs. The cubs stay with their mother until they are two or three years old. The mother teaches the cubs how to find food and how to stay safe.

3. **Multiple-Meaning Words**  *Store* can be a noun that means "a place to buy things" or a verb that means "to save." Here it means "to save."

**Analytical Writing** 4. **Write About Reading**  Bears are the same in some ways, but they are different in other ways. We read in the text that all bears have four legs, two kinds of fur, and five toes with curved claws. They can walk on two or four legs. They are born in litters and live with their mothers. Bears are different colors, live in different places, and eat different foods.

**Analytical Writing**
## Make Connections

**ESSENTIAL QUESTION**

Have partners list two examples of ways baby bears are like their parents. Have them give examples from the text and discuss the examples as a class. (Possible response: Baby bears are covered with fur and sleep in dens.)

**Text-to-World**  Have children discuss different ways people can learn about babies and parents from studying bears.

### ENGLISH LANGUAGE LEARNERS

**Retell**  Help children by looking at each page of the selection and asking a prompt, such as: *What do you see here? What is the bear doing?* Use the pictures to retell or summarize the selections. Provide sentence starters to help children retell the selection, such as: *Now the bear is _____.*

→ # Language Arts

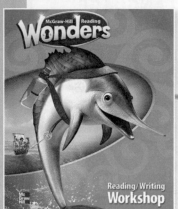

**Reading/Writing Workshop**

### OBJECTIVES

**CCSS** Write informative/explanatory texts in which they introduce a topic, use facts and definitions to develop points, and provide a concluding statement or section. **W.2.2**

**CCSS** With guidance and support from adults and peers, focus on a topic and strengthen writing as needed by revising and editing. **W.2.5**

**CCSS** Demonstrate command of the conventions of standard English grammar and usage when writing or speaking. **L.2.1**

**MINILESSON**
**5 Mins**

# Writing Traits: Word Choice

## Discuss Linking Words

**Review** Invite children to recall that writers use linking words to connect ideas.

**Share** Ask for a volunteer to share his or her revised writing from Day 2. Encourage the class to point out linking words they hear in the volunteer's writing. Invite the volunteer to point out the most useful linking word and tell why it was needed in the text.

### WRITING ENTRY: LINKING WORDS

**1 Prewrite** Ask children to choose a new topic for writing by searching their Writer's Notebook for ideas for an expository text. Or, provide a prompt such as the following one: Choose a baby animal. Write about ways it looks different from its parents.

If children choose to write about how a baby animal looks different from its parents, have them choose an animal they know about. They can use their own knowledge to write facts about the animal.

**2 Draft** Once children have chosen their topics, ask them to use a flow chart to show how ideas in their writing connect. Have them write linking words between the boxes of the flow chart.

## Go Digital

**Present the Lesson**

**Writing**

**Graphic Organizer**

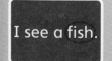

**Grammar**

# Grammar

**5 Mins**

## More Plural Nouns

**Review** Remind children that a plural noun names more than one person, place, or thing. Review that we add -s or -es to form the plural of many singular nouns. Point out that some singular nouns change their spelling to form the plural. Offer examples, such as *mouse/mice* and *woman/women*. Also point out that that some singular nouns do not change their spelling to form the plural. Offer examples, such as *fish/fish* and *deer/deer*.

**Practice** Display the following sentences. Invite partners to identify the nouns and to tell whether they are singular or plural.

We saw a deer on the road. (deer–singular; road–singular)

The man caught two fish at the lake. (man–singular; fish–plural; lake–singular)

Two mice ran into the forest. (mice–plural; forest–singular)

## Mechanics: Abbreviations

**Review** Remind children that many words, such as *street, doctor, mister,* days of the week, and months of the year have abbreviations. Abbreviations are shortened words that begin with a capital letter and end with a period.

**Practice** Have children write abbreviations for the following words.

Monday (Mon.)    November (Nov.)    Avenue (Ave.)

Doctor (Dr.)    August (Aug.)

Street (St.)    Saturday (Sat.)

Then have children complete the following sentence frame with the correctly abbreviated street address:

*Our school is at* _____.

## Talk About It

**Abbreviation Game** Ask children to write their own sentence that includes words that can be abbreviated. Then ask them to switch papers with a partner. Have their partner find the words that can be abbreviated, write the abbreviations, and read them aloud.

## ENGLISH LANGUAGE LEARNERS

**Plural Nouns** Write the word *frogs.* Say: *These are two frogs.* Have children repeat as you point to the picture and the word. Review with children that *frogs* is a plural noun. Point out that a plural noun names more than one person, place, or thing. Follow the same procedure for a picture of two mice and two fish. Point out that some singular nouns change their spelling to form the plural. Share the example *mouse/mice.* Other nouns do not change their spelling to form the plural. Share the example *fish/fish.*

# Daily Wrap Up

→ Review the Essential Question and encourage children to discuss it using the oral vocabulary words.

→ Prompt children to review and discuss the skills they used today. Guide them to give examples of how they used each skill.

## Materials

Literature Anthology
"Baby Bears"

Word-Building Cards

Spelling Word Cards

High-Frequency Word Cards

Dinah Zike's
**FOLDABLES**

→ # Extend the Concept

MINILESSON
**5**
Mins

# Oral Language

### OBJECTIVES

**CCSS** Ask and answer such questions as *who, what, where, when, why,* and *how* to demonstrate understanding of key details in a text. **RI.2.1**

**CCSS** Know and apply grade-level phonics and word analysis skills in decoding words. **RF.2.3**

### ESSENTIAL QUESTION

Remind children that this week they have been learning about ways that offspring are like their parents. Guide children to discuss the question using information from what they have read and discussed.

Use the Define/Example/Ask routine to review the oral vocabulary words *provide, protect, guide, separate,* and *leader*. Prompt children to use the words as they talk about animals and their characteristics. Then review last week's oral vocabulary words *located, encounter, defend, react,* and *positive* using the Define/Example/Ask routine.

**Go Digital**

Phonemic Awareness

Phonics

Structural Analysis

# → Word Work

## Phonemic Awareness

### Phonemic Segmentation

**❶ Model** *We are going to say the sounds in a word. I am going to say a word. Then I will say the word sound by sound. Listen as I say the word* match. *How many sounds are in* match? /m/ /a/ /ch/. *Three sounds. There are three sounds in the word* match.

**❷ Guided Practice/Practice** Have children segment the following words in to phonemes. Do the first three with children.

> ship    this    ring    whisk    catch    chip    graph

## Phonics

### Build Words with Consonant Digraphs

**Review** *Let's use Word Building Cards* s, h, o, t *to build a word with a consonant digraph. We can place the letters in the right order and blend the* s *and* h *together like this: /sh/. Now we can add the rest of the letter sounds: /o/ /t/. The letters blend to make the word* shot.

Continue with *chat, pitch, wash, phone, path, long, when.*

## Structural Analysis

### Suffixes *-ful, -less*

**Review** Write the words *shame, shameful,* and *shameless* on the board and read them with children. Remind children that when words endings such as *-ful* and *-less* are added to the end of a word, they change the meaning of the word. They also add an extra syllable to the end of a word. Remind children that the suffix *-ful* means "full of" and the suffix *-less* means "without."

**Practice** Write the following words: *help, grace, hope, end,* and *home.* Have children work in pairs to construct words that add the suffix *-ful* or *-less* to the end of the word. Then have them use each of the new words in a sentence.

### Quick Review

**Build Fluency: Sound-Spellings**

Display the **Word-Building Cards:** *ch, th, sh, wh, tch, ph, ng, o_e, o, u_e, u, i_e, i, a_e, a, c, g, dge, ge, lge, nge, rge.* Have children say each sound. For fluency in connected text, see the Decodable Reader lesson in Small Group.

**Monitor and Differentiate**

 **Quick Check**

Can children read and decode words with consonant digraphs?

⬇

**Small Group Instruction**

If No → **Approaching** Reteach pp. T342-T347
**ELL** Develop pp. T358-T365
If Yes → **On Level** Review pp. T352-T354
**Beyond Level** Extend pp. T356-T357

→ # Word Work

## Spelling
*MINILESSON · 5 Mins*

**OBJECTIVES**

CCSS Read with sufficient accuracy and fluency to support comprehension. **RF.2.4**

CCSS Know and apply grade-level phonics and word analysis skills in decoding words. **RF.2.3**

• Spell words with two-letter blends.
• Practice fluency.

### Word Sort with *ch, tch, sh, ph, th, ng, wh*

**Review** Provide pairs of children with copies of the Spelling Word Cards. While one partner reads the words one at a time, the other partner should orally segment the word and then write the word. After reading all of the words, partners should switch roles.

**Practice** Have children correct their own papers. Then have them sort the words by their consonant digraph. Have them include a pile for words with no consonant digraph at all.

## High Frequency Words
*MINILESSON · 5 Mins*

### *these, start, walk, seven, eight, learn, try, isn't, baby, early*

**Review** Display High-Frequency Word Cards: *these, start, walk, seven, eight, learn, try, isn't, baby, early.* Have children Read/Spell/Write each word.

→ Point to a word and call on a child to use it in a sentence.

→ Review last week's words using the same procedure.

**Go Digital**

| er | ir | or | ur |
|----|----|----|----|
| her | | | |

girl curb    word

**Spelling Word Sort**

| they | together |
|------|----------|
| how | eat |

**High-Frequency Word Routine**

# → Fluency/Vocabulary Strategy

**MINILESSON 5 Mins**

# Pronunciation

**Review** Remind children that part of reading with the correct pronunciation is taking your time to spell out difficult words before trying to read them fluently in a sentence. Tell children that it helps to preview a selection before reading it aloud to locate any words that they may be unfamiliar with. They can sound out the word and pronounce it correctly before reading it aloud as part of their fluency.

**Practice** Have children read a passage from the Shared Read aloud to a partner. Remind them to preview the passage to look for words they may have trouble pronouncing before they read the whole passage aloud. Offer feedback as needed.

## Fluency Practice

Children can practice fluency using Practice Book pages.

**MINILESSON 5 Mins**

# Inflectional Endings

❶ **Explain/Model** Explain to children that word parts that go at the end of a word will change the meaning of the word and sometimes add an extra syllable to the word. Write examples of word endings on the board, such as *-ing, -ed, -s,* or *-es.* Explain the following points to children.

→ The ending *-ed* is added to the end of a verb to show that the action took place in the past.

→ The ending *-ing* is added to the end of a verb to show that the action is taking place right now.

→ The endings *-s* and *-es* are added to the end of nouns to show more than one.

Write and say *talk, talking, talked,* and *talks* on the board. Ask children to circle each ending on the root word *talk.*

❷ **Guided Practice** Write the words *swims, singing,* and *jumped* on the board. Have children work in pairs to underline the root word and circle the ending. Have them tell what each word means.

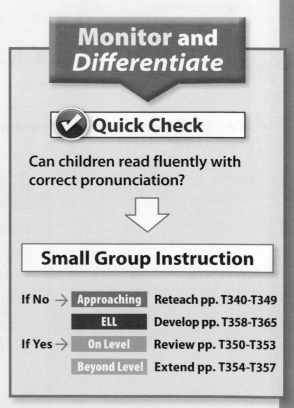

**Monitor and *Differentiate***

✔ **Quick Check**

Can children read fluently with correct pronunciation?

⬇

**Small Group Instruction**

| | | |
|---|---|---|
| If No → | **Approaching** | Reteach pp. T340–T349 |
| | **ELL** | Develop pp. T358–T365 |
| If Yes → | **On Level** | Review pp. T350–T353 |
| | **Beyond Level** | Extend pp. T354–T357 |

# Develop Comprehension

CLOSE READING

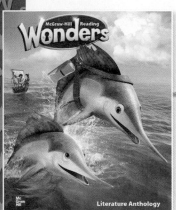

McGraw-Hill Reading
**Wonders**

Literature Anthology

**Literature Anthology**

MINILESSON
**5** Mins

## Read Literature Anthology

### Compare Texts
*Analytical Writing*

Review with children that in *Baby Bears*, they learned about mother bears and their cubs. Now they will read an expository text about butterflies and their offspring, caterpillars. Tell children that as they read they should think about how caterpillars are unlike bear cubs. Have them **take notes**.

### ❶ Ask and Answer Questions

Look at page 204. What is a caterpillar? (a baby butterfly) How do the text and the photo help you to understand that the caterpillar and butterfly are different? (The text tells the reader that they do not look alike. The photo shows how they are not alike.)

### ❷ Ask and Answer Questions

What is the title of the diagram on page 205? (Butterfly Life Cycle) What does a "butterfly life cycle" show? (It shows how a butterfly begins life, develops into a caterpillar, builds a chrysalis, and becomes a butterfly.)

### ❸ Ask and Answer Questions

Why is a chrysalis important in the butterfly's life cycle? (It is important because the caterpillar turns into a butterfly while it is inside the chrysalis.)

## AUTHOR'S CRAFT

### Text Features: Diagrams

→ Display diagram on p. 205. Explain that the title tells what the diagram is about. A photo and text explain each step in a butterfly's cycle.

→ Each step is numbered and includes arrows to show order of steps.

→ Have children talk through the cycle with a partner.

### OBJECTIVES

CCSS Ask and answer such questions as *who, what, where, when, why* and *how* to demonstrate understanding of key details in a text. **RI.2.1**

CCSS Explain how specific images (e.g., a diagram showing how a machine works) contribute to and clarify a text. **RI.2.7**

### ACADEMIC LANGUAGE
*diagram, labels, life cycle*

## Go Digital

**Eagles and Eaglets**

CCSS **Genre** • Expository Text

**Compare Texts**
Read about how baby caterpillars become butterflies.

**①**

# From Caterpillar to Butterfly

A butterfly is not a **mammal**. It does not have live babies or feed milk to its young. A butterfly is an insect. It lays eggs.

Look at the photo. Can you tell which is the parent and which is the **offspring**? Probably not! The parent is the butterfly, and its baby is the caterpillar. The parent and the offspring do not look alike right now. However, when the caterpillar is grown, it will look like its parent.

204

**②**  Butterfly Life Cycle

**1. Egg**
The adult butterfly lays an egg on a milkweed leaf.

**2. Larva**
After 3 or 4 days, a tiny caterpillar comes out of the egg. Caterpillars are a kind of larva. The caterpillar eats its shell for food.

**5. Adult**
Two weeks later, an adult butterfly comes out of the chrysalis. It will lay an egg on a leaf, and the cycle will continue.

**③**

**4. Chrysalis**
The caterpillar forms a shell around itself. The shell is called a chrysalis.

**3. Caterpillar**
For about two weeks, the caterpillar eats leaves and grows bigger.

**Make Connections**
How is a caterpillar like its parents?
**ESSENTIAL QUESTION**

How is a butterfly's offspring different from a bear cub? **TEXT TO TEXT**

205

**LITERATURE ANTHOLOGY,** pp. 204–205

Lexile 560
*TextEvaluator* 7

## Make Connections  *Analytical Writing*

**COLLABORATE** Have partners make connections between the caterpillar in "From Caterpillar to Butterfly" and the bear cubs in *Baby Bears*.

**A C T** **A**ccess **C**omplex **T**ext

▶ **Organization**

Tell children that informational text might present information in different ways. Authors do this to help us understand the text better. In this selection they will see information of a butterfly life cycle represented in a flow chart.

# → Language Arts

# Writing Traits: Word Choice

**Revise** Have children revise their draft from Day 3 by adding linking words or identifying places where ideas could be connected better. As children revise their drafts, hold teacher conferences with individual children. You may also want to have partners conduct peer conferences.

**Edit** Model using proofreading marks to edit. Then have children use proofreading marks to correct errors in their writing.

Invite children to review Grammar Handbook pages 477–480 and check that they have used plural nouns and possessive nouns correctly.

Encourage children to proofread for other errors, including punctuation, capitalization, and spelling.

## Conference Routines

### Teacher Conference

**Step 1:** Talk about the strengths of the writing. *I like how you used linking words to connect your ideas.*

**Step 2:** Focus on the target trait. *I understand how these two ideas go together because you used a linking word to connect them.*

**Step 3:** Make concrete suggestions for revisions, such as those below, and then meet again to review progress.

## Suggested Revisions

**Focus on a Sentence** Read the draft and target one sentence for revision. *These ideas are connected. They should have a linking word such as because to tell how _____ links with _____.*

**Focus on a Section** Underline a section that needs revision. Provide specific suggestions. *This section is about _____. It might help to show how these ideas link together. Try to rewrite these ideas in a new sentence with a linking word.*

**Focus on a Revision Strategy** Underline a section of the writing and ask children to use a specific revision strategy, such as deleting. *This section includes details that do not relate to the main topic. Delete those ideas so that the section only talks about the main topic.*

## OBJECTIVES

**CCSS** Write informative/explanatory texts in which they introduce a topic, use facts and definitions to develop points, and provide a concluding statement or section. **W.2.2**

**CCSS** With guidance and support from adults and peers, focus on a topic and strengthen writing as needed by revising and editing. **W.2.5**

**CCSS** With guidance and support from adults, use a variety of digital tools to produce and publish writing, including in collaboration with peers. **W.2.6**

**CCSS** Demonstrate command of the conventions of standard English grammar and usage when writing or speaking. **L.2.1**

## ACADEMIC LANGUAGE
*word choice, linking words, conference*

## Go Digital

**Writing**

⬛ Make a capital letter.

Λ Add.

↗ Take out.

**Proofreader's Marks**

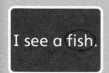

I see a fish.

**Grammar**

## Peer Conference

Provide these questions to guide peers as they review a partner's draft.

→ Is the writing clear and easy to understand?

→ Which ideas are related? Do linking words connect those ideas?

→ Where else can linking words be added?

# Grammar

### More Plural Nouns

**Review** Remind children that a plural noun names more than one person, place, or thing. Review that we add -s or -es to form the plural of many singular nouns. Point out that some singular nouns change their spelling to form the plural. Offer examples, such as *tooth/teeth* and *child/children*. Also point out that that some singular nouns do not change their spelling to form the plural. Offer examples, such as *sheep/sheep* and *fish/fish*.

**Practice** Display the following sentences. Invite partners to identify the nouns and to tell whether they are singular or plural.

> Five children were in the library. (children–plural; library–singular)
>
> Three mice are in the backyard. (mice–plural; backyard–singular)
>
> The man counted ten sheep. (man–singular; sheep–plural)

### Mechanics: Abbreviations

**Review** Review with children that an abbreviation is a shortened form of a word. It begins with a capital letter and ends with a period.

**Practice** Have children identify words that can be abbreviated in the following date and address and rewrite them correctly.

> Sunday, January 5, 2015 (Sun., Jan. 5, 2015)
>
> 15 Red Rock Drive (15 Red Rock Dr.)

### Talk About It

**Abbreviation Memory Game** On pairs of index cards, have partners write a word that can be abbreviated on one card and its abbreviated form on another card. When partners have a group of at least four pairs of cards, have them play a memory game where they match each word to its abbreviated form.

## Daily Wrap Up

→ Review the Essential Question and encourage children to discuss it using the vocabulary words.

→ Prompt children to discuss the skills they practiced and learned today. Guide them to share examples of how they used each skill.

**Go** Digital

**www.connected.mcgraw-hill.com**
RESOURCES
Research and Inquiry

→ **Wrap Up the Week**
# Integrate Ideas

## RESEARCH AND INQUIRY

Baby Animals

### OBJECTIVES

 Participate in collaborative conversations with diverse partners about *grade 2 topics and texts* with peers and adults in small and larger groups. **SL.2.1**

 Participate in shared research and writing projects (e.g., read a number of books on a single topic to produce a report; record science observations). **W.2.7**

### ACADEMIC LANGUAGE

*Venn diagram, organize, research, sources*

## Make a Venn Diagram

 Tell children that they will do a research project in a group to find out the differences between an animal baby and its parents. Review the steps of the research process.

**STEP 1 Choose a Topic**

Guide children to choose a baby animal and parent animal to research, such as a caterpillar and butterfly, a tadpole and frog, or other animals such as geese or ladybugs.

**STEP 2 Find Resources**

Discuss how to use the selections, reference materials, and online sources. Have children use the Research Process Checklist online.

**STEP 3 Keep Track of Ideas**

Have children make an Accordion Foldable® to record ideas and facts from sources. Model recording the names of the sources.

Dinah Zike's
**FOLDABLES**

### Collaborative Conversations

**Take Turns Talking** As children engage in partner, small group, and whole group discussions, encourage them to:

→ wait for a person to finish before they speak.

→ quietly raise their hand when they want to speak.

→ ask others to share their ideas and opinions.

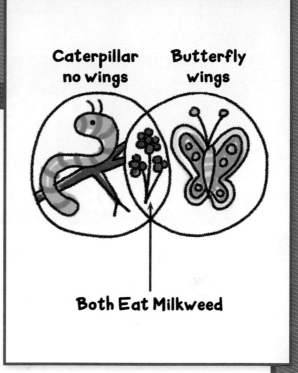

Caterpillar
no wings

Butterfly
wings

Both Eat Milkweed

## STEM

**STEP 4** **Create the Project: Venn Diagram**

Tell children that they can make a Venn diagram to tell how baby animals are alike and different from their parents. Explain the characteristics of a Venn diagram.

→ **Information** A Venn diagram tells how two things are alike and different. In this project, the Venn diagram will compare a baby animal and its parent.

→ **Compare** The place where the two circles overlap is where information goes about how two things are alike.

→ **Contrast** The place where the two circles are separate is where information goes about how two things are different from each other.

Have partners create a Venn diagram about the baby animal and parent animal that they have chosen.

→ Guide them to fill in the diagram correctly.

→ Prompt children to think of additional ideas to add to the Venn diagram.

### ELL ENGLISH LANGUAGE LEARNERS SCAFFOLD

| Beginning | Intermediate | Advanced |
|---|---|---|
| **Use Sentence Frames** Use sentence frames to help children communicate what is in their Venn diagram. For example: *This part tells how _____ and _____ are alike. It says _____.* | **Discuss** Guide children to narrow down their findings to the most important ideas. Ask: *What is the most important way that this baby and its parent are alike? How did you find this out?* | **Describe** Prompt children to describe the differences orally between the baby animal and parent animal that they chose. Have them point out sections of their Venn diagram that they are talking about as they go through their oral presentation. |

## Materials

**Reading/Writing Workshop**

**Literature Anthology**

**a  b  c**
**Word-Building Cards**

**bring**
**Spelling-Word Cards**

**baby**
**High-Frequency Word Cards**

**Dinah Zike's FOLDABLES**
**Dinah Zike's Foldables**

→ # Integrate Ideas

# TEXT CONNECTIONS  *Analytical Writing*

**Connect to Essential Question**

 **OBJECTIVES**

**CCSS** Ask and answer such questions as *who, what, where, when, why,* and *how* to demonstrate understanding of key details in a text. **RI.2.1**

 **CCSS** Demonstrate command of the conventions of standard English capitalization, punctuation, and spelling when writing. **L.2.2**

- Develop answers to the Essential Question.

- Make text connections to the world.

**ACADEMIC LANGUAGE**
*organize, compare, discuss*

## Text to Text

**Cite Evidence** Remind children that this week they have been reading selections about baby animals. Tell them that now they will compare these texts. Model comparing text using "Eagles and Eaglets," **Reading/Writing Workshop** pages 150–155, and *Baby Bears,* **Literature Anthology** pages 186–201. Use an Accordion Foldable® to record comparisons.

**Think Aloud** "Eagles and Eaglets" and *Baby Bears* are both about how baby animals are like their parents. Even though the selections are about different animals, we learn the same thing about each of them. We learn about how the babies grow to be like their parents.

 **Complete the Organizer** Have children use an Accordion Foldable® to record comparison of the two selections. Guide children to discuss and write about the way the animals grow to be like their parents.

How Babies grow | Need parents for food | Become stronger | Grow bigger
**Dinah Zike's FOLDABLES**

**Present Information** Ask groups to present their information to the class. Have children compare information given by different groups.

## Text to Self

**Discuss** Have children discuss animal babies that they have seen and talk about how the babies were like their parents. Ask: *How did the baby animal find its food and stay safe?*

## Text to World

Have children discuss what they have learned about baby animals this week. Ask: *How are baby animals like their parents?*

# WRITE ABOUT READING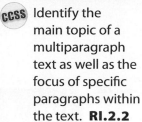

**OBJECTIVES**

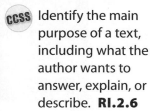 Identify the main topic of a multiparagraph text as well as the focus of specific paragraphs within the text. **RI.2.2**

Identify the main purpose of a text, including what the author wants to answer, explain, or describe. **RI.2.6**

Draw evidence from literary or informational texts to support analysis, reflection, and research. **W.4.9**

## Write an Analysis

**Cite Evidence** Explain to children that as a group they will write about one of the selections that they read this week.

Tell children that using the evidence in the text, they will give their opinion about how the author used details to support the main topic of the text.

Review the Main Topic and Details chart you completed for "Eagles and Eaglets." Guide children to analyze the text evidence by asking a *how* question about the text.

→ How does the author use key details to support the main topic of the text?

Work with children to complete the sentence frames using information from "Eagles and Eaglets."

> The author wrote this text to tell about _____.
>
> I think the most important details are _____ and _____.
>
> The most important text feature is _____.

Then have children select another text they have read this week and use the sentence frames to write about how the author used details to support the main topic of the text.

**Present Your Ideas** Ask partners to share their paragraphs and discuss how the evidence they found supports their ideas.

# RESEARCH AND INQUIRY

**OBJECTIVES**

 Participate in shared research and writing projects. **W.2.7**

## Wrap Up the Project

Guide partners to share the information about the animals that they researched and to point out how they are alike and different using their completed Venn diagrams. Prior to the presentations, preview the Presenting and Listening checklists online with children.

**STEM**

 → **Word Work**

 ## Phonemic Awareness

### Phoneme Blending

**OBJECTIVES**

**CCSS** Know and apply grade-level phonics and word analysis skills in decoding words. **RF.2.3**

**CCSS** Demonstrate command of the conventions of standard English capitalization, punctuation, and spelling when writing. **L.2.2**

**CCSS** Generalize learned spelling patterns when writing words (e.g., cage → badge; boy → boil). **L.2.2d**

Spell words with consonant digraphs.

**Review** Guide children to blend phonemes to form words. *Listen as I say a group of sounds. Then blend those sounds to form a word.*

/m/ /a/ /ch/    /k/ /a/ /ch/    /f/ /i/ /sh/    /f/ /ō/ /n/

/th/ /a/ /t/    /k/ /i/ /ng/    /hw/ /i/ /ch/    /sh/ /ā/ /p/

## Phonics

### Blend and Build Words with Consonant Digraphs *ch, tch, sh, ph, th, ng, wh*

**Review** Have children read and say the words *patch, chip, shop,* and *wing.* Then have children follow the word building routine with Word-Building Cards to build *phone, shone, shine, whine, while, whale, whack, shack, back, bath, bang, sang, sung, such,* and *much.*

**Word Automaticity** Help children practice word automaticity. Display decodable words and point to each word as children chorally read it. Test how many words children can read in one minute. Model blending words children miss.

 ## Structural Analysis

### Suffixes *-ful, -less*

**Review** Have children explain what the word endings *-ful* and *-less* mean. Then have children practice adding *-ful* to the words *help, skill,* and *respect.* Have them add the suffix *-less* to the words *bed, hat, rest,* and *age.*

**Go Digital**

**Phonemic Awareness**

**Phonics**

**Structural Analysis**

**Spelling Word Sort**

**High-Frequency Word Cards**

peered

**Visual Glossary**

# Spelling

## Word Sort with *ch, tch, sh, ph, th, ng, wh*

**Review** Have children use the Spelling Word Cards to sort the weekly words by their consonant digraphs. Remind children that not all words will have a consonant digraph.

**Assess** Assess children on their abilities to spell words with consonant digraphs *ch, tch, sh, ph, th, ng,* and *wh*. Say each word and provide a sentence so that children can hear the words in a correct context. Then allow them time to write down the words. In order to challenge children, you may wish to provide an additional word in each digraph group in order to assess whether they understand each category.

# High-Frequency Words

### *these, start, walk, seven, eight, learn, try, isn't baby, early*

**Review** Display High-Frequency Word Cards *these, start, walk, seven, eight, learn, try, isn't baby, early*. Have children Read/Spell/Write each word. Have children write a sentence with each word.

# Vocabulary Words

### *adult, alive, covered, fur, giant, groom, mammal, offspring*

**Review** Display Visual Vocabulary Word Cards *adult, alive, covered, fur, giant, groom, mammal, offspring*. Have children review each word using the Define/Example/Ask Routine on the back of each card.

**Monitor and Differentiate**

### ✓ Quick Check

**Can children read and decode words with consonant digraphs?**

**Can children recognize and read high-frequency words?**

⬇

### Small Group Instruction

| If No → | Approaching | Reteach pp. T342–T347 |
| | ELL | Develop pp. T358–T365 |
| If Yes → | On Level | Review pp. T352–T353 |
| | Beyond Level | Extend pp. T356–T357 |

→ # Language Arts

**MINILESSON**
**5 Mins**

## Writing Traits: Word Choice

### OBJECTIVES

**CCSS** With guidance and support from adults, use a variety of digital tools to produce and publish writing, including in collaboration with peers. **W.2.6**

**CCSS** Demonstrate command of the conventions of standard English grammar and usage when writing or speaking. **L.2.1**

**CCSS** Demonstrate command of the conventions of standard English capitalization, punctuation, and spelling when writing. **L.2.2**

___

### ACADEMIC LANGUAGE

*word choice, linking words, plural nouns, abbreviations*

### Share and Reflect

**Discuss** Discuss with the class what they learned about using linking words to improve their writing. Guide them to recall that linking words help connect ideas and make them clearer for the reader.

**Present** Invite volunteers to choose a writing entry from the week to share with the class. Compare the volunteer's draft with his or her revised text, and encourage children to identify linking words the volunteer added. Have children discuss the writing by focusing on how linking words helped connect important ideas in the text.

**Reflect** Have children use their Writer's Notebook to reflect on their progress as writers. Invite them to consider the following prompts as they write:

*How did linking words improve your writing this week?*

*How can you tell when you need to use linking words?*

*Which linking words tell how ideas are alike?*

*Which linking words tell how ideas are different?*

**Publish** After children finish presenting their expository texts, discuss how the class will publish them in a class magazine. Display magazines so children can see the use of titles and illustrations. Have children add titles and illustrations to their expository texts before you assemble them into a magazine. Guide them to use digital tools to put the magazine together. Display the magazine in your classroom library and allow children to read it independently.

### Go Digital

**Writing**

**Checklists**

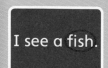

**Grammar**

# Grammar

## More Plural Nouns

**Review**  Remind children that a plural noun names more than one person, place, or thing. Review that we add *-s* or *-es* to form the plural of many singular nouns. Point out that some singular nouns change their spelling to form the plural. Offer examples, such as *foot/feet* and *man/men*. Also point out that that some singular nouns do not change their spelling to form the plural. Offer examples, such as *fish/fish* and *deer/deer*.

**Practice**  Display the following phrases. Invite partners to identify the noun in each phrase and to tell whether it is singular or plural Then have partners work together to write sentences using the phrases.

| | | | |
|---|---|---|---|
| one tooth | a man | one fish | a deer |
| many teeth | six men | two fish | several deer |

## Mechanics: Abbreviations

**Review**  Remind children that an abbreviation is a shortened way of writing a word. Remind them that an abbreviation begins with a capital letter and ends with a period, as in *Mrs., Dr., St.,* and *Ave.*

**Practice**  Have children write a name, address, or date that uses an abbreviation. Have them ask a partner to circle the abbreviation and say the word that the abbreviation stands for.

## Reteach

If children have difficulty identifying plural nouns review their use. Provide opportunities for children to practice the skill in small groups, with a partner, or independently.

### Talk About It

**Silly Sentences**  Have children orally tell a partner a silly sentence that uses at least one word that can be abbreviated. Have their partner identify the word and write its abbreviation.

# Wrap Up the Week

→ Review the Essential Question and encourage children to discuss using the oral vocabulary words.

→ Review the comprehension strategy and skill.

→ Review consonant digraphs *ch, tch, sh, ph, th, ng,* and *wh.*

→ Use the High-Frequency Word Cards to review the Words to Know.

→ Review the expository text writing genre and the specific text features of the genre.

# → Approaching Level

**Lexile** 320
*TextEvaluator™* 4

 **OBJECTIVES**
Read with sufficient accuracy and fluency to support comprehension. **RF.2.4**

 Ask and answer such questions as *who, what, where, when, why,* and *how* to demonstrate understanding of key details in a text. **RI.2.1**

 Identify the main topic of a multiparagraph text as well as the focus of specific paragraphs within the text. **RI.2.2**

**MATERIALS**
Leveled Reader
*Animal Families*

## Leveled Reader:
## *Animal Families*

### Before Reading

#### Preview and Predict

Have children turn to the title page. Read the title and author name and have children repeat. Preview the selection's photos. Prompt children to predict what the selection might be about.

#### Review Genre: Expository Text

Have children recall that expository text is about real people, places, or things. Expository text gives facts and information about a topic. It often has text features, such as diagrams, labels, photos, and captions.

**ESSENTIAL QUESTION**

Remind children of the Essential Question: *How are offspring like their parents?* Set a purpose for reading: *Let's read to find out what animal families are like.* Remind children that as they read, they can ask questions about what they do not understand or want to know more about.

### During Reading

#### Guided Comprehension

As children whisper read *Animal Families*, monitor and provide guidance, correcting blending and modeling the key strategies and skills.

#### Strategy: Reread

Remind children that when they read informational text they may see words they don't understand. Say: *Rereading can help you understand difficult parts. It can also help you find details.* Model using the strategy on page 3. Say: *I read that a deer is a mammal. To understand this part, I will reread. Now I understand what it means. Mammals do not usually grow from eggs.*

#### Skill: Main Topic and Key Details

Remind children that the main topic is what the selection is mostly about. The key details give information about the main topic. After reading, ask: *What is this selection mostly about?*

**Go Digital**

**Leveled Readers**

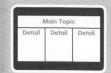
**Graphic Organizer**

**Retelling Cards**

Display a Main Topic and Key Details graphic organizer for children to copy. Model recording children's answer in the top box. Have children record the answer in their own charts.

**Think Aloud** The selection tells me about different kinds of animal families. This is what the selection is mostly about, so I'll write *animal families* in the Main Topic box. Then I will look for key details.

Guide children to identify key details about the main topic.

## After Reading

### Respond to Reading

Have children complete Respond to Reading on page 16 after reading.

### Retell

Have children take turns retelling the selection. Help children make a personal connection by asking: *What baby animals have you seen?*

### Model Fluency

Read the sentences one at a time. Have children chorally repeat. Point out to children how your voice goes up at the end of a question.

**Apply** Have children practice reading with partners. Provide feedback.

## PAIRED READ ...

### "Tadpoles into Frogs"

**Make Connections:
Write About It** ✏️ *Analytical Writing*

Before reading, ask children to note that the genre of this text is expository. It gives facts and information. Then discuss the Compare Texts statement. After reading, ask children to make connections between "Tadpoles into Frogs" and *Animal Families.*

**Leveled Reader**

 **FOCUS ON SCIENCE**

Children can extend their knowledge of how animal babies are like their parents by completing the science activity on page 20. **STEM**

## Literature Circles

Lead children in conducting a literature circle using the Thinkmark questions to guide the discussion. You may wish to discuss what children have learned about animal babies and their parents from both selections in the leveled reader.

## Level Up

Level-up lessons available online.

**IF** children read the **Approaching Level** fluently and answered the questions

**THEN** pair them with children who have proficiently read the **On Level** and have approaching children

• echo-read the **On Level** main selection.

• use self-stick notes to mark questions they have about a key detail in each section.

**A C T** **A**ccess **C**omplex **T**ext

The **On Level** challenges children by including more **specific vocabulary** and **complex sentence structures.**

# → Approaching Level
## Phonemic Awareness

### IDENTIFY AND GENERATE RHYME

**TIER 2**

**OBJECTIVES**

 Demonstrate understanding of spoken words, syllables, and sounds (phonemes). **RF.1.2**

Identify and generate rhyming words.

 **I Do**  Explain identifying and naming rhyming words. *Listen as I say two words:* catch, match. Catch *and* match *end with the same sound, /ach/. They rhyme.*

 **We Do**  *Listen as I say:* whip, ship. *When I say* whip *and* ship, *I hear the same sounds at the end.* Whip *and* ship *both end with /ip/. They rhyme. Now tell me if these words rhyme:* chip, chop. *No,* chip *and* chop *do not rhyme. They have different ending sounds, /ip/, /op/.* Have children repeat the rhyming words:

fling, sing    those, these    wash, wish    lunch, punch    mash, crash

 **You Do**  *It's your turn. Repeat the words if they rhyme. Tell me another word that rhymes with the rhyming words.*

cash, rash    pitch, patch    bang, sang    chin, thin    hush, crush

**Repeat** the rhyming routine with additional consonant digraph words.

### PHONEME BLENDING

**TIER 2**

**OBJECTIVES**

 Demonstrate understanding of spoken words, syllables, and sounds (phonemes). **RF.1.2**

Blend phonemes to form words.

 **I Do**  Explain blending sounds to form words. *Listen as I say three sounds: /b/ /aaa/ /th/. Say the sounds with me: /b/ /aaa/ /th/. Now I'm going to blend the sounds together: /b/ /aaa/ /th/, /baaath/,* bath. *We blended the word* bath.

 **We Do**  *Listen as I say three sounds: /rrr/ /iii/ /ng/. Repeat them: /rrr/ /iii/ /ng/. Let's blend them: /rrr/ /iii/ /ng/, /rrriiing/,* ring. *The word is* ring. Repeat this routine:

shot    chose    while    these    catch    phone    shine    king

 **You Do**  *It's your turn. I want you to blend the sounds I say together to form words.*

long    graph    match    chin    whale    cash    think    phone    think

**Repeat** the blending routine with additional consonant digraph words.

You may wish to review Phonemic Awareness with **ELL** using this section.

## PHONEME SEGMENTATION

**OBJECTIVES**

 Segment spoken single-syllable words into their complete sequence of individual sounds (phonemes). **RF.1.2d**

Segment phonemes in words.

 **I Do** Explain to children that they will be segmenting words into sounds today. *When you segment words, you break them into their sounds.*

*Listen as I say a word:* itch. *I hear two sounds: /iii/ and /ch/. There are two sounds in the word* itch: */iii/ and /ch/.*

*Listen as I say another word:* shop. *I hear three sounds: /sh/, /ooo/, and /p/ There are three sounds in the word* shop: */sh/, /ooo/, and /p/.*

**We Do** *Listen as I say this word: /thin/. Say it with me:* thin. *How many sounds do you hear? There are three sounds in* thin. *The sounds in* thin *are /th/, /iii/, and /nnn/.*

Repeat this routine with the following words:

catch   math   chill   phone   shine   sung   white

 **You Do** *It's your turn. I'll say a word. Tell me how many sounds you hear. Then tell me each sound you hear.*

pitch   both   whale   king   graph   chime   shell   rush

**Approaching Level**

# Phonics

TIER **2**

## CONNECT *ch* AND *tch* TO /ch/; *sh* TO /sh/; *ph* TO /f/; *th* TO /th/; *ng* TO /ng/; AND *wh* TO /hw/

 **OBJECTIVES**

Know and apply grade-level phonics and word analysis skills in decoding words. **RF.2.3**

 **I Do**

Display the Word-Building Cards *s, h*. These are the letters s *and* h. *I am going to trace the letters while I say /sh/, the sound that these letters stand for when they are together.* Trace the letters *sh* while saying /sh/ five times. Repeat with /ch/ *ch* and *tch*, /th/ *th*, /hw/ *wh*, /ng/ *ng*, and /f/ *ph*.

 **We Do**

*Now do it with me.* Have children trace the letters *sh* on the Word-Building Cards while saying /sh/. Trace the letters five times and say /sh/ with children. Repeat with /ch/ *ch*, *tch*; /th/ *th*; /hw/ *wh*; /ng/ *ng*; /f/ *ph*.

 **You Do**

Have children connect the letters *sh* to the sound /sh/, *ch* and *tch* to /ch/, *th* to /th/, *wh* to /hw/, *ng* to /ng/, and *ph* to /f/ by tracing the letters while saying the sounds. Then have children write the letters while saying the sounds five to ten times.

**Repeat,** connecting the consonant digraphs to the sounds through tracing and writing the letters throughout the week.

TIER **2**

## BLEND WORDS WITH CONSONANT DIGRAPHS

**OBJECTIVES**

Know and apply grade-level phonics and word analysis skills in decoding words. **RF.2.3**

Decode words with consonant digraphs.

 **I Do**

Display Word-Building Cards *c, h, i, p*. These are the letters c *and* h. *Together they stand for /ch/. Say it with me: /ch/. This is the letter* i. *It stands for /i/. This is the letter* p. *It stands for /p/. I'll blend these sounds together: /chiiip/,* **chip.** Repeat the procedure with *shop, pitch, thin, when, king, phone.*

 **We Do**

Guide children to blend and read: *ship, much, pitch, that, whale, long, graph*

 **You Do**

Have children blend: *dash, chat, stitch, with, when, bang, phone.*

**Repeat,** blending additional words with consonant digraphs.

You may wish to review Phonics with 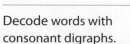 using this section.

## BUILD WORDS WITH CONSONANT DIGRAPHS

**OBJECTIVES**

 Know and apply grade-level phonics and word analysis skills in decoding words. **RF.2.3**

 **I Do** Display Word-Building Cards *i, t, c, h.* Say: *These are the letters* i, t, c, *and* h. *The letter* i *stands for /iii/, and the letters* tch *together stand for /ch/. I will blend /iii/ and /ch/ together: /iiich/,* itch. *The word is* itch.

 **We Do** *Make the word* itch *using Word-Building Cards. Place the letter* w *in front of it. Let's blend: /w/ /iiich/, /wiiich/,* witch.

**You Do** Have children build the words: *pitch, patch, path, math; when, then, thin.*

**Decodable Reader** Introduce the Decodable Reader selection, *Baby Watch*. Point to the title and have children sound it out. Discuss what the illustration shows.

**First Read** Turn to page 24. Have children point to each word, sounding out decodable words and saying the high-frequency words quickly. Children should chorally read the story the first time through.

## BLEND WORDS WITH CONSONANT DIGRAPHS

**OBJECTIVES**

Know and apply grade-level phonics and word analysis skills in decoding words. **RF.2.3**

 **I Do** Display Word-Building Cards *w, i, s, h.* Say: *This is the letter* w. *It stands for /w/. This is the letter* i. *It stands for /i/. These are the letters* s *and* h. *Together they stand for /sh/. Now listen as I blend these sounds: /wiiish/,* wish.

 **We Do** Say: *Let's do some together.* Blend and read the words: *think, phone, dash, such, catch, bring, while* with children.

 **You Do** Display the following words: *chimp, shut, which, think, phone, sang, much, batch, path, graph.* Have children blend and read the words.

**Decodable Reader** Have children reread the Decodable Reader selection.

**Check Comprehension** As children read, monitor their comprehension. Ask the following: *How does a mother cat chat with her baby?*

## DECODE WORDS WITH CONSONANT DIGRAPHS

**Fluency in Connected Text**

Have children review the **Decodable Reader** selection. Identify words with consonant digraphs and blend as needed. Have children reread the selection on their own or with a partner.

# → Approaching Level

## Structural Analysis

### REVIEW SUFFIXES *-ful, -less*

**OBJECTIVES**

 Know and apply grade-level phonics and word analysis skills in decoding words. **RF.2.3**

 Decode words with common prefixes and suffixes. **RF.2.3d**

Read words with suffixes *-ful, -less.*

**I Do** Review that a suffix is a word part added to the end of a word to change the word's meaning. Write *hopeful* and *hopeless*. Read the words. Underline the suffixes. *The suffix* -ful *means "full of."* Hopeful *means "full of hope." The suffix* -less *means "without."* Hopeless *means "without hope."*

**We Do** Write *careful. Let's look at this word. Do you see a smaller word you know? Yes,* care. *The word* careful *is made from the word* care *and the suffix* -ful. *The suffix* -ful *means "full of," so* careful *means "full of care."*

**You Do** Give partners several words with suffixes *-ful* and *-less*, such as *careless, wasteful,* and *endless*. Have children identify the suffix in each.

**Repeat** Have children create sentences using words with *-ful* and *-less*.

### RETEACH SUFFIXES *-ful, -less*

**OBJECTIVES**

 Know and apply grade-level phonics and word analysis skills in decoding words. **RF.2.3**

 Decode words with common prefixes and suffixes. **RF.2.3d**

Read words with suffixes *-ful, -less.*

**I Do** Write *use* and *useful*. Read the words aloud. Then point out the *-ful* in *useful. The letters* ful *are a suffix. A suffix changes the meaning of a word that it is added to. The suffix* -ful *means "full of" so* useful *means "full of use."*

**We Do** Write the word *rest*. Read the word: *rest*. Ask: *What does* rest *mean? Yes, it means "a break from work or activity." Let's add the suffix* -less *to* rest. *What is the word? Yes,* restless. *What does* restless *mean? It means "without rest."*

**You Do** Have children add suffixes to words. Say: *Now it's your turn. Add these suffixes to the words. Say each new word and use it in a sentence.*

-ful: thank, help, watch, joy          -less: thank, home, help, spot

**Repeat** Have children find examples of other words with the suffixes *-ful* and *-less* and explain their meanings.

# High-Frequency Words/ Vocabulary

**TIER 2**

## REVIEW HIGH-FREQUENCY WORDS

**OBJECTIVES**

**CCSS** Read with sufficient accuracy and fluency to support comprehension.
**RF.2.4**

Review high-frequency words.

 **I Do** Use Word Cards 81-90. Display one word at a time, following the routine:

Display the word. Read the word. Then spell the word.

 **We Do** Ask children to state the word and spell the word with you. Model using the word in a sentence, and have children repeat after you.

 **You Do** Display the word. Ask children to say the word then spell it. When completed, quickly flip through the word card set as children chorally read the words. Provide opportunities for children to use the words in speaking and writing. For example, provide sentence starters, such as *I want to learn about _____*. Ask children to write each word in their Writer's Notebook.

## REVIEW VOCABULARY WORDS

**OBJECTIVES**

**CCSS** Use words and phrases acquired through conversations, reading and being read to, and responding to texts, including using adjectives and adverbs to describe (e.g., *When other kids are happy that makes me happy*).
**L.2.6**

 **I Do** Display each Visual Vocabulary Card and state the word. Explain how the photograph illustrates the word. State the example sentence and repeat the word.

 **We Do** Point to the word on the card and read the word with children. Ask them to repeat the word. Engage children in structured partner talk about the image as prompted on the back of the vocabulary card.

 **You Do** Display each visual in random order, hiding the word. Have children match the definitions and context sentences of the words to the visuals displayed. Then ask children to complete Approaching Level Practice Book page 81.

# → Approaching Level

## Comprehension

### READ FOR FLUENCY

**OBJECTIVES**

**CCSS** Read with sufficient accuracy and fluency to support comprehension. **RF.2.4**

**CCSS** Read on-level text with purpose and understanding. **RF.2.4a**

**I Do** Explain to children that before they read a paragraph or section of text, they can scan it for difficult words. Model finding and pronouncing difficult words on the first page of the Practice Book passage. Then model reading the first page of the Practice Book selection with correct pronunciation.

**We Do** Preview the second page and locate words that are unfamiliar and might be difficult to pronounce. Then read the pages aloud and have children repeat each sentence after you. Point out how knowing how to pronounce words allowed you to read more fluently.

**You Do** Have children read the rest of the selection aloud. Remind them to preview the text for words that might be difficult to pronounce.

### IDENTIFY MAIN TOPIC

**OBJECTIVES**

**CCSS** Ask and answer questions such as *who, what, where, when, why,* and *how* to demonstrate understanding of key details in a text. **RI.2.1**

**CCSS** Identify the main topic of a multi-paragraph text as well as the focus of specific paragraphs within the text. **RI.2.2**

 **I Do** Remind children that they have been reading informational text. Tell them that when they read informational text, they should find the topic. *When we read informational text, we can look for the topic. The topic is what the text is mostly about. We can find the topic by reading the words and looking at photographs.*

 **We Do** Read the first paragraph of the Practice Book selection aloud. Pause to identify what children are reading about. *This sentence tells about how big opossums are. The next sentences tell about mother opossums. I can tell that the selection is mostly about opossums, so that is the topic.*

 **You Do** Guide children to read the rest of the Practice Book selection. As they read each page, prompt them to confirm the topic of the selection. Point out that there is a main topic for the selection and the paragraphs give details about the main topic.

## REVIEW MAIN TOPIC AND KEY DETAILS

**OBJECTIVES**

 Ask and answer such questions as *who, what, where, when, why,* and *how* to demonstrate understanding of key details in a text. **RI.2.1**

 Identify the main topic of a multi-paragraph text as well as the focus of specific paragraphs within the text. **RI.2.2**

 **I Do** Remind children that an informational text has a main topic. Explain that the main topic is what the text is mostly about. Point out that children can look at what the photos show and look for words and ideas that repeat in the text. These are clues about the main topic. Key details in the text give more information about the main topic.

 **We Do** Read the first few paragraphs of the Practice Book selection together. Pause to identify the topic. Then point out key details about the topic. *This sentence tells about baby opossums. The next sentence tells more about how mothers carry babies, so opossums are the main topic.*

 **You Do** Stop reading on page 84 and say: *What key detail did we just read about the topic?* Record the topic and the key detail in a Main Topic and Key Details chart. Continue having children add details.

## SELF-SELECTED READING

**OBJECTIVES**

 Ask and answer such questions as *who, what, where, when, why,* and *how* to demonstrate understanding of key details in a text. **RI.2.1**

Identify the main topic of a multi-paragraph text as well as the focus of specific paragraphs within the text. **RI.2.2**

Apply the strategy and skill to reread text.

### Read Independently

Have children pick a nonfiction text selection that they have read for sustained silent reading. Remind them to:

→ look for the main topic in the text and photos.

→ look for key details that provide facts and information about the topic.

→ reread to understand unfamiliar words or difficult text.

### Read Purposefully

Have children record the main topic and key details in their Main Topic and Key Details chart. After reading, guide children to participate in a group discussion about the selection they read. Guide children to:

→ share the information they recorded in their Main Topic and Key Details chart.

→ tell what interesting facts they learned from the selections.

→ share which parts they didn't understand and needed to reread.

# On Level

**Lexile** 490
*TextEvaluator™* 4

## OBJECTIVES

 Read with sufficient accuracy and fluency to support comprehension. **RF.2.4**

 Read on-level text with purpose and understanding. **RF.2.4a**

 Read on-level text orally with accuracy, appropriate rate, and expression on successive readings. **RF.2.4b**

## MATERIALS

Leveled Reader
*Animal Families*

## Leveled Reader:
## *Animal Families*

**Go Digital**

### Before Reading

#### Preview and Predict

Have children turn to the title page. Read the title and author name and have children repeat. Preview the selection's photos. Prompt children to predict what the selection might be about.

#### Review Genre: Expository Text

Have children recall that expository text gives information about real people, places, things, or events. It often includes text features that provide information, such as photos, captions, diagrams, labels, and maps.

#### ESSENTIAL QUESTION

Remind children of the Essential Question: *How are offpring like their parents?* Set a purpose for reading: *Let's read to find out about animal families.* Remind children that as they read, they can ask questions about what they do not understand or want to know more about.

### During Reading

#### Close Reading

**Note taking** Ask students to use their graphic organizer while they read.

**Pages 2–5** *Turn to a partner and discuss any difficult words or unfamiliar ideas. What part can you reread if you want to know how baby deer stay safe?* (I can reread page 3 to find out that mother deer hide babies in bushes, baby deer have no smell for enemies to find them, and baby deer have spots that help them hide.) *What word on page 3 also means "sees something"?* (spots)

**Pages 6–9** *What is the main topic of this chapter? What are some key details you learn about it?* (The main topic is: animals who carry babies in pouches. Some key details are: kangaroos carry baby joeys in pouches; koala babies live in their mother's pouch for five to seven months.)

**Leveled Readers**

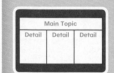
**Graphic Organizer**

**Retelling Cards**

**Pages 10–11** *What key detail do you learn about father penguins on page 10?* (The father penguin watches over the penguin egg for about 65 days, and keeps it warm near his feet.)

**Pages 12–14** *How will rereading page 13 help you understand what you read about the size of alligators on page 14?* (I can reread page 13 to remember that baby alligators are only six inches long. This will help me picture how big an alligator grows each year.)

## After Reading

### Respond to Reading

Have children complete Respond to Reading on page 15 after reading.

### Retell

Have children take turns retelling the selection. Help children make a personal connection by asking: *Think of another animal you know. How does it take care of its babies?*

### Model Fluency

Read the sentences, one at a time. Have children chorally repeat. Point out to children how your voice goes up at the end of a question.

**Apply** Have partners practice repeated reading. Provide feedback.

## PAIRED READ ...

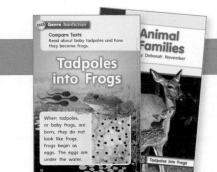

**Leveled Reader**

## "Tadpoles into Frogs"

### Make Connections:
### Write About It ● *Analytical Writing*

Before reading, ask children to note that "Tadpoles into Frogs" is expository. Then discuss the Compare Texts statement. After reading, ask children to make connections between what they learned in "Tadpoles into Frogs" and *Animal Families*.

 **FOCUS ON SCIENCE**

Children can extend their knowledge of how baby animals are like their parents by completing the science activity on page 20. **STEM**

---

## Literature Circles

Lead children in conducting a literature circle using the Thinkmark questions to guide the discussion. You may wish to discuss what children have learned about animal babies and their parents from both selections in the leveled reader.

## Level Up

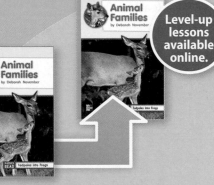

Level-up lessons available online.

**IF** children read the **On Level** fluently and answered the questions

**THEN** pair them with children who have proficiently read the **Beyond Level** and have on-level children

- partner-read the **Beyond Level** main selection.
- Identify a part of the selection they would like to learn more about.

### A C T Access Complex Text

The **Beyond Level** challenges children by including more **specific vocabulary** and **complex sentence structures**.

# On Level

## Phonics

### BLEND WORDS WITH CONSONANT DIGRAPHS

**OBJECTIVES**

 Know and apply grade-level phonics and word analysis skills in decoding words. **RF.2.3**

- Build and decode words with consonant digraphs.
- Read for fluency.

 **I Do**   Display **Word-Building Cards** *r, a, s, h.* Say: *This is the letter* r. *It stands for /r/. This is the letter* a. *It stands for /a/. These are the letters* s *and* h. *Together* s-h *stands for /sh/. Now listen as I blend these three sounds together: /rash/,* rash.

 **We Do**   *Now, let's do one together. Make the word* rash *using Word-Building Cards. Place the letter* c *at the beginning of* rash. *Let's blend: /k/ /rrraaash/, /kraaash/,* crash. *Now there is a new word,* crash. *Change the letter* a *to* u. *I am going to change the letter* a *in* crash *to the letter* u. *Let's blend and read the new word: /k/ /rrr/ /uuu/ /sh/,* crush. *The new word is* crush.

 **You Do**   Have children build and blend the words: *brush, brunch, lunch, punch, pinch, inch, itch, pitch, patch, path, bath, bang, sang.*

**Fluency in Connected Text**   Have children read this week's Decodable Reader selection, *Baby Watch.*

## Vocabulary

### REVIEW WORDS

**OBJECTIVES**

 Use words and phrases acquired through conversations, reading and being read to, and responding to texts, including using adjectives and adverbs to describe (e.g., *When other kids are happy that makes me happy*). **L.2.6**

**I Do**   Use the **Visual Vocabulary Cards** to review each vocabulary word. Point to each word, read it aloud, and have children chorally repeat it.

**We Do**   Guide children to use the **Define/Example/Ask** routine for a few Vocabulary words using their **Response Boards**. Ask sample questions to help students respond and explain their answers.

 **You Do**   Have children work with a partner to do the Define/Example/Ask routine on their own for the remaining vocabulary words. Then have children write sentences about this week's selections. Each sentence must contain at least one vocabulary word.

# Comprehension

## REVIEW MAIN TOPIC AND KEY DETAILS

**OBJECTIVES**

 Ask and answer such questions as *who, what, where, when, why,* and *how* to demonstrate understanding of key details in a text. **RI.2.1**

 Identify the main topic of a multi-paragraph text as well as the focus of specific paragraphs within the text. **RI.2.2**

 **I Do** Remind children that when they read informational text, they should identify the main topic and then look for key details about the topic. *When we read informational text, we can look for the topic, or what the selection is mostly about. Then we can look for key details that tell about the topic in the words and the photos.*

**We Do** Read the first paragraphs of the Practice Book selection aloud. As you read, pause to identify the main topic. *We read about opossums. This is the topic of the selection. What key details tell more about this topic?*

**You Do** Guide children to read the rest of the Practice Book selection. Remind them to look for more key details that give information about the main topic.

## SELF-SELECTED READING

**OBJECTIVES**

 Ask and answer such questions as *who, what, where, when, why,* and *how* to demonstrate understanding of key details in a text. **RI.2.1**

 Identify the main topic of a multi-paragraph text as well as the focus of specific paragraphs within the text. **RI.2.2**

Apply the strategy and skill to reread text.

### Read Independently

Have children pick a nonfiction text that they have read for sustained silent reading. Remind them to:

→ find the main topic and look for key details that give information about it.

→ reread parts that were difficult or that they did not understand.

### Read Purposefully

Have children record the main topic and key details in their Main Topic and Key Details chart. After reading, guide partners to:

→ share the information they recorded in their Main Topic and Key Details chart.

→ tell what interesting facts and information they learned from reading the selections.

→ tell which parts were difficult and where they reread for better understanding of the text.

# → Beyond Level

Lexile 600
*TextEvaluator*™ 5

## OBJECTIVES

 Read with sufficient accuracy and fluency to support comprehension. **RF.2.4**

 Ask and answer such questions as who, what, where, when, why, and how to demonstrate understanding of key details in a text. **RI.2.1**

 Identify the main topic of a multiparagraph text as well as the focus of specific paragraphs within the text. **RI.2.2**

## MATERIALS

Leveled Reader
*Animal Families*

# Leveled Reader:
## *Animal Families*

### Before Reading

#### Preview and Predict

Read the title and author name. Have children preview the title page and the photos. Ask: *What do you think this book will be about?*

#### Review Genre: Expository Text

Have children recall that expository text gives facts and information about real people, places, things, or events. Prompt children to name key characteristics of expository text. Tell them to look for these as they read the leveled reader.

#### ESSENTIAL QUESTION

Remind children of the Essential Question: *How are offspring like their parents?* Have children set a purpose for reading by asking: *What do you want to find out about animal parents and their babies?* Remind children that as they read a selection, they can ask questions about what they do not understand or want to know more about.

### During Reading

#### Close Reading

**Note taking** Ask students to use their graphic organizer while they read.

**Pages 2–5** *Turn to a partner and discuss any difficult words or unfamiliar ideas. What part can you reread if you want to remember which deer grow antlers?* (I can reread the text about bucks and the caption about does on page 4.) *What word on page 3 also means "parts of a plant"?* (leaves) *What does the word mean on this page?* (goes away)

**Pages 6–9** *What is the main topic of this chapter? What are some key details you learn about it?* (The main topic is: animals who carry babies in pouches. Some key details are: kangaroos carry baby joeys in pouches; koala babies live in their mother's pouch for five to seven months.) *What special feature does the author use to tell you a fun fact on page 7?* (The author uses a box with text next to the photo.)

## Go Digital

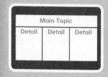

**Leveled Readers**

**Graphic Organizer**

**Pages 10–11** *What key detail do you learn about how father penguins protect eggs on page 10?* (The father penguin's stomach hangs over the egg at his feet to keep it warm.)

**Pages 12–14** *How will rereading page 13 help you understand what you read about the size of alligators on page 14?* (I can reread page 13 to remember that baby alligators are only six inches long. This will help me picture how big an alligator grows each year.) *What are two meanings for* foot *on page 14?* (the end of a leg; a unit of length)

## After Reading

### Respond to Reading

Have children complete Respond to Reading on page 15 after reading.

### Retell

Have children take turns retelling what they learned. Have children make a personal connection by writing about other animal parents. Say: *Write about another animal family. How do the parents care for the babies? Are the parents and babies alike?*

**PAIRED READ ...**

## "Tadpoles into Frogs"

### Make Connections: Write About It  *Analytical Writing*

**Leveled Reader**

Before reading, have children preview the title page and identify the genre. Then discuss the Compare Texts statement. After reading, have partners discuss what they read in "Tadpoles into Frogs" and *Animal Families*. Ask children to make connections by comparing and contrasting the parents and babies in each selection. Prompt children to discuss what they learned about animal families.

 **FOCUS ON SCIENCE**

Children can extend their knowledge of how baby animals and their parents are alike by completing the science activity on page 20. **STEM**

 **Literature Circles**

Lead children in conducting a literature circle using the Thinkmark questions to guide the discussion. You may wish to discuss what children have learned about baby animals and their parents from both selections in the leveled reader.

## Gifted and Talented

**SYNTHESIZE** Challenge students to compare and contrast how animal parents care for their young. Have them write about similarities and differences in how the parents look, feed, raise, and protect their babies.

**EXTEND** Have them use facts they learned from the week or do additional research to find out which living things would be most affected.

# Beyond Level

## Vocabulary

### REVIEW DOMAIN-SPECIFIC WORDS

**OBJECTIVES**

Use words and phrases acquired through conversations, reading and being read to, and responding to texts, including using adjectives and adverbs to describe (e.g., *When other kids are happy that makes me happy*).
**L.2.6**

 **Model** Use the Visual Vocabulary Cards to review the meaning of the words *mammal* and *offspring*. Write science-related sentences on the board using the words.

Write the words *groom* and *adult* on the board and discuss the meanings with children. Then help children write sentences using these words.

 **Apply** Have children work in pairs to review the meanings of the words *habitat* and *nature*. Then have partners write sentences using the words.

### MULTIPLE-MEANING WORDS

**OBJECTIVES**

Determine or clarify the meaning of unknown and multiple-meaning words and phrases based on *grade 2 reading and content,* choosing flexibly from an array of strategies.
**L.2.4**

 Use sentence-level context as a clue to the meaning of a word or phrase. **L.2.4a**

 **Model** Read aloud the first two paragraphs of the Comprehension and Fluency passage on Beyond Level Practice Book pages 83–84.

**Think Aloud** When I read these paragraphs, I'm not sure what the word *pass* means. It could mean "to take place" or "a ticket." I'll use other words in the sentence to see which meaning makes sense. Two clues help me: "after" and "two months." I think the first meaning makes sense here.

With children, continue reading the second paragraph. Help them figure out the meaning of *back*.

 **Apply** Have pairs of children read the rest of the passage. Ask them to use context clues to determine the meaning of the following words: *own, pointed,* and *foot.*

 **Shades of Meaning** Using their definition of *pass*, have partners write an explanation of the difference between *passage* and *movement*. Encourage them to also use artwork to depict the two words.

# Comprehension

## REVIEW MAIN TOPIC AND KEY DETAILS

**OBJECTIVES**

 Ask and answer such questions as *who, what, where, when, why,* and *how* to demonstrate understanding of key details in a text. **RI.2.1**

Identify the main topic of a multi-paragraph text as well as the focus of specific paragraphs within the text. **RI.2.2**

 **Model**
Remind children that the main topic of a passage is what the passage is mostly about. Explain that key details give information about the main topic. Point out that each paragraph has its own topic that is part of the main focus of the passage.

Have children read the first paragraph of the Comprehension and Fluency passage of Beyond Level Practice Book pages 83–84. Ask open-ended questions to facilitate discussion, such as *What is this paragraph mostly about? What key details give us information about the main topic?* Children should support their responses with examples and details from the text.

 **Apply**
Have children identify the main topic and the key details in the rest of the passage. Have them independently record this information in a Main Topic and Key Details chart. Then have partners use their work to summarize the whole passage.

## SELF-SELECTED READING

**OBJECTIVES**

 Ask and answer such questions as *who, what, where, when, why,* and *how* to demonstrate understanding of key details in a text. **RI.2.1**

Identify the main topic of a multi-paragraph text as well as the focus of specific paragraphs within the text. **RI.2.2**

### Read Independently

Have children choose an informational book for sustained silent reading.

→ As children read, have them fill in a Main Topic and Key Details chart.

→ Remind them to reread difficult sections of the text.

### Read Purposefully

Encourage children to keep a reading journal. Ask them to read different books in order to learn about a variety of subjects.

→ Children can write summaries of the books in their journals.

→ Ask children to share their reactions to the books with classmates.

 **Independent Study** Challenge children to discuss how their books relate to the weekly theme of adult and baby animals. What features do many baby animals share? How are the ways that parents care for their babies alike and different?

# English Language Learners

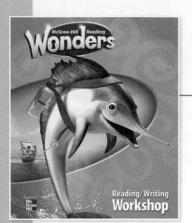

**Reading/Writing Workshop**

**ACADEMIC LANGUAGE**

*reread, main topic, key details*

## Shared Read
### *Eagles and Eaglets*

### Before Reading

#### Build Background

Read the Essential Question: *How are offspring like their parents?*

→ Explain the meaning of the Essential Question: *Parents are the mom and the dad. The offspring are the young. You are the offspring of your mom and dad.*

→ **Model an answer:** *Puppies are the offspring of dogs. Puppies are smaller than their parents, but they have fur. Mothers take care of young puppies. They feed them and keep them safe.*

→ Ask children a question that ties the Essential Question to their own background knowledge: *Turn to a partner and tell about a baby animal. What is the baby like? How do the parents help it?* Call on several pairs.

### During Reading

#### Interactive Question Response

→ Ask questions that help children understand the meaning of the text after each paragraph.

→ Reinforce the meanings of key vocabulary providing meanings embedded in the questions.

→ Ask children questions that require them to use key vocabulary.

→ Reinforce strategies and skills of the week by modeling.

**Go Digital**

**Eagles and Eaglets**

**Graphic Organizer**

## "Eagles and Eaglets"

### Pages 150–151

Point to the title on page 150. *Listen as I read the title of the selection.* Point to each word as you read it. What is the title? (Eagles and Eaglets)

*An eagle is a kind of bird. Its babies are called eaglets. Find the eaglets in the picture. The eaglets are the baby eagles. Now find the parent. The parent is the grown eagle.*

*What does the parent eagle look like? What do the eaglets look like?* (The parent is big. It is brown and white and has a sharp beak. The babies are small. They are white and fluffy.)

*The eagles build a nest for their eggs and babies. Listen as I read about the eagle's nest:* Their nests are built of sticks and grass. *Find the nest in the picture. What is the nest made of?* (sticks and grass)

*The eagles make their nests bigger. They can be nine feet across. Show students how big nine feet is. Do the eagles make big nests or small nests?* (big nests)

### Page 152

*Let's read this page together. Let's think about what eaglets are like. They are helpless at first. They cannot walk. They cannot fly. They cannot see very well. They cannot catch their own food.*

**Explain and Model the Phonics Skill** *Repeat the sentence:* They also use their claws and beak to catch fish. *Listen carefully. Raise your hand when you hear a word that has the /sh/ sound.* (fish) *Let's practice saying the word together:* fish. *Repeat with* /tch/ (catch) *and* /th/ (they, their).

### Page 153

*Let's look at the diagram on this page. The diagram shows a bald eagle. Is this a parent eagle or an eaglet?* (parent eagle) *Let's look at the labels on this diagram. Find the beak. The beak is hooked and*

yellow. Hooked means curved. *Now find the claws. Where are the claws? What do they look like?* (on the feet; they are long and sharp)

**Explain and Model the Strategy** *We can reread parts of the text when we don't understand something. Let's reread to make sure we understand how birds are different from mammals. It says here that birds have feathers. Mammals don't have feathers. Mammals have fur.*

### Page 154

*An eaglet learns to do the things its parents do. Then it is an adult.*

*Let's look at the photo and the caption on this page. Let's read the caption together:* When the bald eagle soars, the feathers on its huge wings spread out like fingers. *Let's pretend we are bald eagles soaring. Now stretch out your huge wings.*

*When does an eaglet become an adult? How long does it take?* (It becomes an adult when it learns to do the things its parents do. This can take five years.)

### Page 155

*Let's read this page together. Let's think about what the eaglet was like and what it is like when it grows up. The grown eagle can soar for hours. It can fly for a long time.*

*How is the adult eagle different from the eaglet?* (The adult can fly for hours. The baby is helpless.)

### After Reading

**Make Connections**

→ Review the Essential Question.

# English Language Learners

**Lexile** 390
*TextEvaluator* 4

## OBJECTIVES

Ask and answer such questions as *who, what, where, when, why,* and *how* to demonstrate understanding of key details in a text. **RI.2.1**

Identify the main topic of a multi-paragraph text as well as the focus of specific paragraphs within the text. **RI.2.2**

## ACADEMIC LANGUAGE

*reread, retell*

## Leveled Reader:
## *Animal Families*

### Before Reading

**Preview**

Read the title. Ask: *What is the title? Say it again.* Repeat with the author's name. Preview the selection's photos. Have children describe the images. Use simple language to tell about each page. Follow with questions, such as *What animal is this? Do the baby and its parents look alike?*

**ESSENTIAL QUESTION**

Remind children of the Essential Question. Say: *Let's read to find out about animal babies and their parents.* Encourage children to seek clarification when they encounter a confusing word or phrase.

### During Reading

**Interactive Question Response**

**Pages 2–3** Point to the photo of the fawn on page 2. *Look at the baby deer. A baby deer is called a fawn. What does a fawn look like? Why does it have spots? Let's reread the sentence that tells us. Say the words with me:* The spots help them hide in the leaves. *Tell your partner what you learned so far.* (Deer are mammals. Their spots help them hide.)

**Pages 4–5** *What do bucks grow?* (antlers) *Where are the antlers? Let's look at the photo. Find the label that points to antlers. Say the word with me:* antlers. *Let's use our hands to show where antlers grow on a buck. Read the caption on page 5. Tell your partner what antlers are made of.*

**Pages 6–7** *Let's read the chapter title together. Say it with me: Babies in Pouches. A pouch is like a pocket. Where can some baby animals live?* (pouch) *Talk to your partner about a baby that lives in a pouch.*

**Pages 8–9** *The baby kangaroo comes out of the pouch. Let's read the sentence that tells us what it does:* It begins to hop. *Tell your partner why. What other kind of baby animal lives in a pouch?* (a koala)

**Pages 10–11** *Penguins are birds. They are not mammals. The mother penguin lays an egg. What happens next?* (She leaves to find food.)

**Pages 12–13** *An alligator mother lays eggs, too. What does the alligator baby look like? Look at the picture.* (An alligator baby is smaller.)

**Go Digital**

**Leveled Readers**

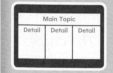

**Graphic Organizer**

**Retelling Cards**

**Page 14** *Look at page 14. How long does the alligator mother care for her babies? Let's read the sentence that tells us. Say it with me.* Alligator mothers take care of the babies for about two years. *How are animal families like human families? Share ideas with your partner.*

## After Reading

### Respond to Reading

Have partners answer the questions. Pair children with peers of varying language abilities.

### Retell

Model retelling using the Retelling Card prompts. Then guide children to retell the selection to a partner.

### Fluency: Intonation

Read the sentences in the book, one at a time. Help children echo-read the pages expressively and with appropriate intonation. Remind them to read exclamations in a way that shows excitement.

**Apply** Partners practice reading. Pair children with peers of varying language abilities.

## PAIRED READ ...

### "Tadpoles into Frogs"

### Make Connections: Write About It ✏ *Analytical Writing*

Before reading, tell children that this text is expository text. Then discuss the Compare Texts statement.

After reading, ask children to make connections between what they read in "Tadpoles into Frogs" and *Animal Families*. Prompt children by providing sentence frames: _____ *watch their eggs.* _____ *do not watch their eggs.*

**Leveled Reader**

 **FOCUS ON SCIENCE**

Children can extend their knowledge of the different features of animal habitats by completing the science activity on page 20.

**STEM**

---

### Literature Circles

Lead children in conducting a literature circle using the Thinkmark questions to guide the discussion. You may wish to discuss what children have learned about animal parents and their offspring from both selections in the leveled reader.

### Level Up

*Level-up lessons available online.*

**IF** children read the **ELL Level** fluently and answered the questions

**THEN** pair them with children who have proficiently read the **On Level** and have children

• echo-read the **On Level** main selection with their partners.

• list difficult words and phrases and discuss them with their partners.

### A C T **Access Complex Text**

The **On Level** challenges children by including more **specific vocabulary** and **complex sentence structures**.

# English Language Learners
## Vocabulary

## PRETEACH VOCABULARY

### OBJECTIVES

Use words and phrases acquired through conversations, reading and being read to, and responding to texts, including using adjectives and adverbs to describe (e.g., *When other kids are happy that makes me happy*). **L.2.6**

### LANGUAGE OBJECTIVE

Use vocabulary words.

**I Do** Preteach vocabulary from "Eagles and Eaglets," following the Vocabulary Routine found on the Visual Vocabulary Cards for words *adult, alive, covered, fur, giant, groom, mammal,* and *offspring.*

**We Do** After completing the Vocabulary Routine for each word, point to the word on the Visual Vocabulary Card and read the word with children. Ask children to repeat the word.

**You Do** Have partners give clues about two or more of the vocabulary words. Then have each pair read their clues and ask the class to guess the word.

| Beginning | Intermediate | Advanced/High |
|---|---|---|
| Help children write clues correctly and read aloud. | Ask children to write two clues. | Challenge children to write one clue for each. |

## REVIEW VOCABULARY

### OBJECTIVES

Use words and phrases acquired through conversations, reading and being read to, and responding to texts, including using adjectives and adverbs to describe (e.g., *When other kids are happy that makes me happy*). **L.2.6**

### LANGUAGE OBJECTIVE

Use vocabulary words.

**I Do** Review the previous week's vocabulary words over a few days. Read each word aloud pointing to the word on the Visual Vocabulary Card. Have children repeat after you. Then follow the Vocabulary Routine on the back.

**We Do** Ask children to guess the word you describe. Provide clues, such as synonyms. Have children name the word and use it in a sentence.

**You Do** In pairs, have children make a list of clues for two or more words. Ask them to read them aloud for the class to guess the word.

| Beginning | Intermediate | Advanced/High |
|---|---|---|
| Help children list clue words and read aloud. | Have children write clues as sentences. | Ask children to use antonyms in their clues. |

# MULTIPLE-MEANING WORDS

**OBJECTIVES**

CCSS Determine or clarify the meaning of unknown and multiple-meaning words and phrases based on *grade 2 reading and content*, choosing flexibly from an array of strategies. **L.2.4**

CCSS Use sentence-level context as a clue to the meaning of a word or phrase. **L.2.4a**

**LANGUAGE OBJECTIVE**

Use multiple-meaning words.

**I Do** Read aloud the first paragraph of "Eagles and Eaglets" on page 151, while children follow along. Summarize the paragraph. Point to the word *safe*. Explain that sometimes a word can have more than one meaning. We can try reading the other word in the sentence to see which makes sense.

**Think Aloud** When I read this paragraph, I'm not sure what the word *safe* means. This word could mean "free from harm" or "a strong box." I'll use the other words in the sentence to see which meaning makes sense. A clue helps me: "eggs will be." I think the first meaning makes sense here.

**We Do** Have children point to the word *watch* on page 151. Help children use context clues to determine the meaning of this multiple-meaning word. Write the meaning on the board.

**You Do** In pairs, have children write a definition for *own* on page 152, using context clues to determine its meaning.

| Beginning | Intermediate | Advanced/High |
|---|---|---|
| Help children complete the activity. | Help children complete the activity. | Ask children to explain how they applied the skill. |

# ADDITIONAL VOCABULARY

**OBJECTIVES**

CCSS Use knowledge of language and its conventions when writing, speaking, reading, or listening. **L.2.3**

CCSS Compare formal and informal uses of English. **L.2.3a**

**LANGUAGE OBJECTIVE**

Use transition words.

**I Do** List academic language and additional vocabulary from "Eagles and Eaglets": *soar, young, mammal, offspring;* and *Animal Families: hatches, protects, enemies, human.* Define each word for children: *When you soar, you fly high in the air.*

**We Do** Model using the words for children in a sentence: *An eagle can soar for hours. The player hit the ball and it soared up high.* Then provide sentence frames and complete them with children: *If I could fly, I would soar _____.*

**You Do** Have pairs make up their own sentences for the class to complete.

| Beginning | Intermediate | Advanced/High |
|---|---|---|
| Help children complete the activity. | Provide support to help children use the words. | Ask children to define the words. |

# English Language Learners
## Writing/Spelling

### WRITING TRAIT: WORD CHOICE

**OBJECTIVES**

 With guidance and support from adults and peers, focus on a topic and strengthen writing as needed by revising and editing. **W.2.5**

 Demonstrate command of the conventions of standard English grammar and usage when writing or speaking. **L.2.1**

**LANGUAGE OBJECTIVE**

Use linking words.

**I Do** Explain that writers use linking words such as *and, but, so, also,* and *because* to show how words and ideas are connected. Write and read the sentence: *Many bears live in the forest, but some bears live on mountains.* Point out the linking word *but.* Explain that it shows that the second idea is different from the first.

**We Do** Read the section "Proud Parents" on page 152. Emphasize the word *also* in the fourth sentence. Explain that *also* shows that the sentence tells another reason that eaglets are helpless. It links this sentence to the main idea. Repeat the exercise with the third sentence in "Eaglets Grow Up."

**You Do** Have children write two sentences about an animal they read about this week. Have them use a linking word to show how the ideas are connected.

| Beginning | Intermediate | Advanced/High |
|---|---|---|
| Help children describe the animal. Provide simple sentence frames with linking words. | Ask children to describe two things about the animal. Give sentence frames. | Ask children to describe an animal. Ask questions to elicit information about how the facts are related. |

### WORDS WITH CONSONANT DIGRAPHS *ch, tch, sh, ph, th, ng, wh*

**OBJECTIVES**

 Demonstrate command of the conventions of standard English grammar and usage when writing or speaking. **L.2.1**

**LANGUAGE OBJECTIVE**

Spell words with consonant digraphs.

**I Do** Read aloud the Spelling Words on page T290. Segment the word *chop* into sounds and attach a spelling to each sound. Read aloud, segment, and spell the remaining words. Point out the spelling of consonant digraphs.

**We Do** Read the first sentence from the Dictation Routine on page T290. Read the consonant digraph *ch* word. Ask children to repeat and write the word.

**You Do** Display the words. Have partners work to check their spelling lists.

| Beginning | Intermediate | Advanced/High |
|---|---|---|
| Help children copy the words with correct spelling and say the word. | After children have corrected their words, have pairs quiz each other. | Challenge children to think of other words with these consonant digraphs. |

# Grammar

## MORE PLURAL NOUNS

### OBJECTIVES

CCSS Demonstrate command of the conventions of standard English grammar and usage when writing or speaking. **L.2.1**

CCSS Form and use frequently occurring irregular plural nouns (e.g., *feet, children, teeth, mice, fish*). **L.2.1b**

---

### LANGUAGE OBJECTIVE

Recognize irregular plural nouns.

**ELL Language Transfers**

Reinforce for English language learners that the plurals of some nouns are irregular and can't be formed with the -s or -es ending. To help children learn irregular nouns, sort the nouns into categories, such as body parts (feet, teeth); people (man, woman, child, person); and animals (fish, mouse, goose, deer, sheep).

 **I Do**  Remind children that to form the plural of most nouns they add the letters -s or -es to the end. Explain that for some irregular plural nouns the whole word changes. Other irregular plurals use the same spelling as the singular form of the noun. Write these sentences on the board and point out the singular and plural irregular nouns:

> The child saw a mouse and a fish at the pet store.
> The children saw seven mice and eight fish at the pet store.

**We Do**  Write the sentences on the board and underline the irregular nouns. Have children name the plural of each underlined noun. Have them say: *I see one _____. I see two _____* for each irregular noun.

> That animal has a sharp <u>tooth</u> for eating a <u>fish</u>.
> The <u>child</u> read that a baby <u>deer</u> has spots.
> The <u>man</u> and <u>woman</u> saw a baby <u>sheep</u>.

 **You Do**  Write the following sentence frames on the board.

> We read about baby _____. They have _____.

Pair children and have them complete each sentence frame. Circulate, listen in, and take note of each child's language use and proficiency.

| **Beginning** | **Intermediate** | **Advanced/High** |
|---|---|---|
| Describe the photos in *Animal Families.* Ask: *What are these animals?* Model a response by providing a sentence frame: *They are _____.* Help children identify the plural nouns, pointing out any irregular plurals. | Ask children to describe the same photos and then identify the plural nouns they used. Encourage children to use complete sentences. | Ask children to look at the photos, name the animals, and describe their features. Prompt children to use irregular plurals by asking questions such as *How many feet does this animal have? Does it have teeth?* |

# PROGRESS MONITORING

## Weekly Assessment

**CCSS TESTED SKILLS**

| ✓ **COMPREHENSION:** | ✓ **VOCABULARY:** | ✓ **WRITING:** |
|---|---|---|
| Main Idea and Key Details **RI.2.1, RI.2.2** | Multiple-Meaning Words **L.2.4c** | Writing About Text **RI.2.1, RI.2.2** |

### Assessment Includes

→ Pencil-and-Paper administration

→ Online administration

→ Approaching Level Weekly Assessment also available

 FLUENCY

**Fluency Goal** 41 to 61 words correct per minute (WCPM)

**Accuracy Rate Goal** 95% or higher

Administer oral reading fluency assessments using the following schedule:

→ **Weeks 1, 3, 5** Provide Approaching Level children at least three oral reading fluency assessments during the unit.

→ **Weeks 2 and 4** Provide On Level children at least two oral reading fluency assessments during the unit.

→ **Week 6** If necessary, provide Beyond Level children an oral reading fluency assessment at this time.

**Also Available: Selection Tests online PDFs**

*Go Digital!* http://connected.mcgraw-hill.com

# Using Assessment Results

| TESTED SKILLS | If ... | Then ... |
|---|---|---|
| **COMPREHENSION** | Children answer 0–6 multiple-choice items correctly ... | ... assign Lessons 85–87 on Main Idea and Key Details from the ***Tier 2 Comprehension Intervention online PDFs.*** |
| **VOCABULARY** | Children answer 0–6 multiple-choice items correctly ... | ... assign Lesson 92 on Multiple-Meaning Words from the ***Tier 2 Vocabulary Intervention online PDFs.*** |
| **WRITING** | Children score less than "3" on the Constructed response ... | ... assign Lessons 85–87 and/or Write About Reading Lessons from Section 13 of the ***Tier 2 Comprehension Intervention online PDFs.*** |
| **FLUENCY** | Children have a WCPM score of 36–40 ... | ... assign a lesson from Section 1, 9, or 10 of the ***Tier 2 Fluency Intervention online PDFs.*** |
| | Children have a WCPM score of 0–35 ... | ... assign a lesson from Sections 2–8 of the ***Tier 2 Fluency Intervention online PDFs.*** |

## Response to Intervention

Use the appropriate sections of the ***Placement and Diagnostic Assessment*** as well as students' assessment results to designate students requiring:

 **Intervention Online PDFs**

 **WonderWorks Intervention Program**

# WEEKLY OVERVIEW

**Reading/Writing Workshop**

# TEACH AND MODEL

**CCSS** Shared Read · Genre · Poetry

## Cats and Kittens

Cats and kittens **express** their views
With hisses, purrs, and little mews.

Instead of taking baths like me,
They use their tongues quite handily.

I wonder what my mom would say
If I tried cleaning up that way.

They stay as still as still can be,
Until a mouse they chance to see.

And then in one great flash of fur
They pounce on a toy with a PURRRR.

— by Constance Keremes

**? Essential Question**
**What do we love about animals?**
Read how poets describe animals they love.

166     167

## ✔ Vocabulary

behave

express

feathers

flapping

## 🔍 Close Reading of Complex Text

**Shared Read** "Cats and Kittens," "Desert Camels," "A Bat Is Not a Bird," 166–169
**Genre** Poetry

**Lexile** N/A
**ETS** *TextEvaluator*™ N/A

## Minilessons        ✔ Tested Skills **CCSS**

| | |
|---|---|
| ✔ **Comprehension Strategy** | Reread, T398–T399 |
| ✔ **Comprehension Skill** | Key Details, T400–T401 |
| ✔ **Genre** | Poetry, T410–T411 |
| ✔ **Vocabulary Strategy** | Multiple-Meaning Words, T412–T413 |
| ✔ **Writing Traits** | Word Choice, T388–T389 |
| ✔ **Grammar** | Possessive Nouns, T390–T391 |

☞ **Go** Digital

http://connected.mcgraw-hill.com

ANIMAL DISCOVERIES
**Essential Question**
What do we love about animals?

WEEK 5

# APPLY WITH CLOSE READING

## Complex Text

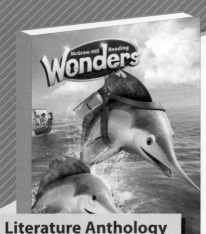

**Literature Anthology**

**PAIRED READ**

"Beetles" and "The Little Turtle", 206–209
**Genre** Poetry
**Lexile** N/A
ETS *TextEvaluator* N/A

"Gray Goose," 210–211
**Genre** Poetry
**Lexile** N/A
ETS *TextEvaluator* N/A

## Differentiated Text

**Leveled Readers** *Including Paired Reads*

APPROACHING
**Lexile** 250
ETS *TextEvaluator* 5

ON LEVEL
**Lexile** 470
ETS *TextEvaluator* 13

BEYOND
**Lexile** 570
ETS *TextEvaluator* 24

ELL
**Lexile** 350
ETS *TextEvaluator* 5

## Extended Complex Text

Nate the Great on the Owl Express
**Genre** Fiction
**Lexile** 280L
ETS *TextEvaluator* 16

Cam Jansen: The Mystery at the Monkey House #10
**Genre** Fiction
**Lexile** 530L
ETS *TextEvaluator* 9

**Classroom Library**

Classroom Library lessons available online.

# TEACH AND MANAGE

## How You Teach

### INTRODUCE

**Weekly Concept**
Animals in Poems

Reading/Writing Workshop
162–163

### TEACH

**Close Reading**
"Cats and Kittens", "Desert Camels",
"A Bat Is Not a Bird"

**Minilessons**
Reread, Key Details, Poetry, Multiple-
Meaning Words, Writing Traits

Reading/Writing
Workshop
166–169

### APPLY

**Close Reading**
*Beetles* and *The Little Turtle*
*Gray Goose*

Student
Anthology
206–211

 **Go Digital**

Interactive Whiteboard

Interactive Whiteboard

Mobile

## How Students Practice

### Weekly contract

**PDF Online**

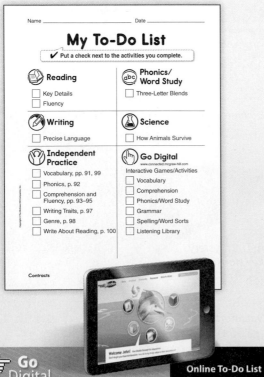

Name _____ Date _____

**My To-Do List**

✔ Put a check next to the activities you complete.

**Reading**
☐ Key Details
☐ Fluency

**Phonics/Word Study**
☐ Three-Letter Blends

**Writing**
☐ Precise Language

**Science**
☐ How Animals Survive

**Independent Practice**
☐ Vocabulary, pp. 91, 99
☐ Phonics, p. 92
☐ Comprehension and Fluency, pp. 93–95
☐ Writing Traits, p. 97
☐ Genre, p. 98
☐ Write About Reading, p. 100

**Go Digital**
www.connected.mcgraw-hill.com
Interactive Games/Activities
☐ Vocabulary
☐ Comprehension
☐ Phonics/Word Study
☐ Grammar
☐ Spelling/Word Sorts
☐ Listening Library

Contracts

### Leveled practice and online activities

**Your Turn Practice Book**
**91–100**

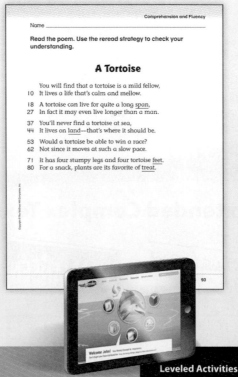

Comprehension and Fluency

Name _____

Read the poem. Use the reread strategy to check your
understanding.

**A Tortoise**

You will find that a tortoise is a mild fellow,
10  It lives a life that's calm and mellow.

18  A tortoise can live for quite a long span,
27  In fact it may even live longer than a man.

37  You'll never find a tortoise at sea,
44  It lives on land—that's where it should be.

53  Would a tortoise be able to win a race?
62  Not since it moves at such a slow pace.

71  It has four stumpy legs and four tortoise feet.
80  For a snack, plants are its favorite of treat.

93

**Leveled Readers**

 **Go Digital**

Online To-Do List

Leveled Activities

Writer's Workspace

## DIFFERENTIATE

**SMALL GROUP INSTRUCTION**

**Leveled Readers**

Mobile

## INTEGRATE

**Research and Inquiry**
Create Animal Anthology,
T422–423

**Text Connections**
Compare Animal Poems, T424

*Analytical Writing* **Write About Reading**
Write an Analysis, T425

Online Research
and Writing

## ASSESS

Wonders
Grade 2
**Weekly
Assessment**

Assessing the Common Core
State Standards

**Weekly Assessment
109–120**

Online
Assessment

# Leveled workstation cards

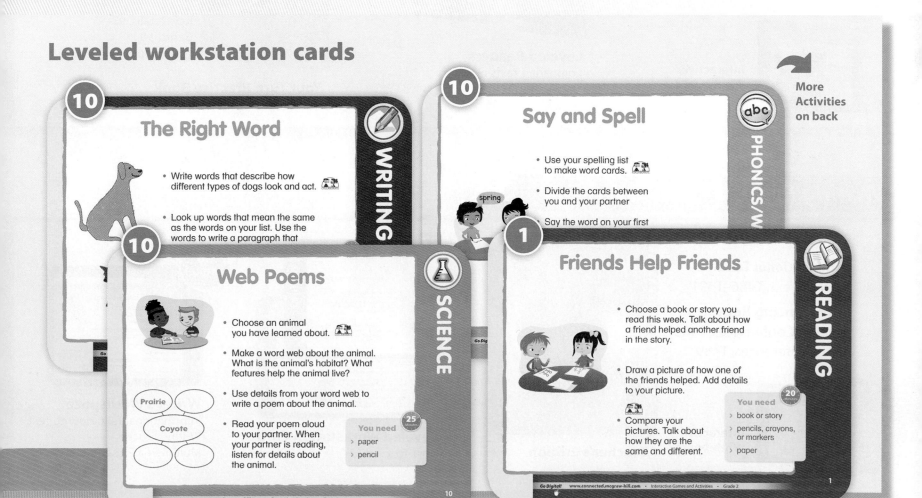

More
Activities
on back

**10**

## The Right Word

- Write words that describe how
  different types of dogs look and act.

- Look up words that mean the same
  as the words on your list. Use the
  words to write a paragraph that

WRITING

**10**

## Say and Spell

- Use your spelling list
  to make word cards.

- Divide the cards between
  you and your partner

- Say the word on your first

spring

PHONICS/W

**10**

## Web Poems

- Choose an animal
  you have learned about.

- Make a word web about the animal.
  What is the animal's habitat? What
  features help the animal live?

- Use details from your word web to
  write a poem about the animal.

- Read your poem aloud
  to your partner. When
  your partner is reading,
  listen for details about
  the animal.

Prairie

Coyote

You need
> paper
> pencil

25

SCIENCE

**1**

## Friends Help Friends

- Choose a book or story you
  read this week. Talk about how
  a friend helped another friend
  in the story.

- Draw a picture of how one of
  the friends helped. Add details
  to your picture.

- Compare your
  pictures. Talk about
  how they are the
  same and different.

You need
> book or story
> pencils, crayons,
  or markers
> paper

20

READING

Go Digital! www.connected.mcgraw-hill.com • Research and Inquiry • Grade 2

10

Go Digital! www.connected.mcgraw-hill.com • Interactive Games and Activities • Grade 2

1

# DEVELOPING READERS AND WRITERS

## Write to Sources and Research

Key Details, T400–T401, T404, T413D

Note Taking, T413A, T419A

Make Connections: Essential Question, T413D, T419B, T424

Research and Inquiry, T422–T423

Analyze to Inform/Explain, T425

Comparing Texts, T431, T441, T445, T451

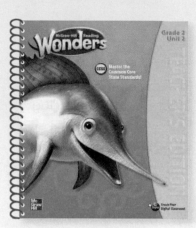

**Teacher's Edition**

Key Details, 209

**Literature Anthology**

**Interactive Whiteboard**

**Leveled Readers**
Comparing Texts
Key Details

Key Details, 93–95
Genre, 98
Write About Reading, 100

**Your Turn Practice Book**

**Informational Text**
How-to Text, T486–T491

**Conferencing Routines**
Teacher Conferences, T488
Peer Conferences, T489

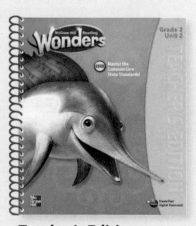

**Interactive Whiteboard**

**Teacher's Edition**

**Leveled Workstation Card**
How-To, Card 23

**Writer's Workspace**
Informational Text: How-to Text
Writing Process
Multimedia Presentations

## *Writing Traits* • **Write Every Day**

**Writing Trait: Word Choice**
Precise Words, T388–T389

**Conferencing Routines**
Teacher Conferences, T420
Peer Conferences, T421

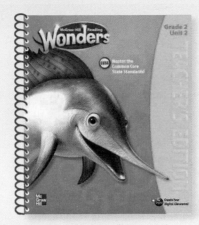

**Teacher's Edition**

Word Choice: Precise
Words, 174–175

**Reading/Writing Workshop**

**Go Digital**

**Interactive Whiteboard**

Word Choice:
Precise Words,
Card 10

**Leveled Workstation Card**

Word Choice: Precise
Words, 97

**Your Turn Practice Book**

## *Grammar and Spelling*

**Grammar**
Possessive Nouns, T390, T403,
T415, T421, T429

**Spelling**
Three-Letter Blends, T382,
T396, T407, T418, T427

**Go Digital**

**Interactive Whiteboard**

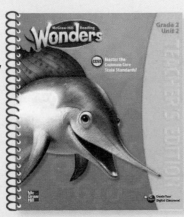

**Teacher's Edition**

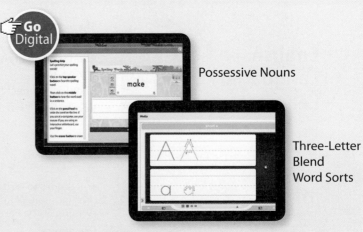

**Go Digital**

Possessive Nouns

Three-Letter
Blend
Word Sorts

**Online Spelling and Grammar Games**

# SUGGESTED LESSON PLAN

## READING

### Teach, Model, and Apply
*Whole Group*

**Reading/Writing Workshop**
Wonders

**DAY 1**

**Build Background** Animals in Poems, T376–T377

**Oral Vocabulary Words** *alarm, howling, knobby, munch, problem;* T378

**Listening Comprehension** Strategy: Reread, T379

**Interactive Read-Aloud Cards** "The Furry Alarm Clock" and "Little Crocodile," T379

**Word Work**
Phonemic Awareness: Identify and Generate Rhymes, T380
Phonics/Spelling: Introduce Three-Letter Blends, T380–T382
High-Frequency Words: *bird, far, field, flower, grow, leaves, light, orange, ready, until;* T383

✓**Vocabulary** Words in Context: *behave, flapping, express, feathers;* T384–T385

**Close Reading of Complex Text** "Cats and Kittens," "Desert Camels," "A Bat is Not a Bird," 166–169

**Practice** *Your Turn* 91–92

**DAY 2**

**Oral Language** Animals in Poems, T392

**Review Oral Vocabulary Words,** T392

**Listening Comprehension** Strategy: Reread, T393

**Interactive Read-Aloud Cards** "The Furry Alarm Clock" and "Little Crocodile," T393

**Word Work**
Phonemic Awareness: Phoneme Substitution, T394
Phonics/Spelling: Words with Three-Letter Blends, T394–T396
Structural Analysis: Compound Words, T395
High-Frequency Words, T396

**Vocabulary** Expand Vocabulary, T397

✓**Comprehension**
• Genre: Poetry, T398–T399
• Skill: Key Details, T400–T401

**Practice** *Your Turn* 92–97

## DIFFERENTIATED INSTRUCTION   Choose across the week to meet your student's needs.

*Small Group*

### Approaching Level

**Leveled Reader** *Amira's Petting Zoo,* T430–T431
**Phonemic Awareness** Identify and Generate Rhyme, T432 **2**
**Phonics** Connect to Three-Letter Blends, T434 **2**
**High-Frequency Words** Review Words, T437 **2**
**Vocabulary** Review Words, T437

**Leveled Reader** *Amira's Petting Zoo,* T430–T431
**Phonemic Awareness** Phoneme Substitution, T433
**Phonics** Blend Words with Three-Letter Blends, T434 **2**
**Comprehension** Identify Key Details, T438 **2**

### On Level

**Leveled Reader** *Alice's New Pet,* T440–T441
**Phonics** Build Words with Three-Letter Blends, T442

**Leveled Reader** *Alice's New Pet,* T440–T441
**Comprehension** Review Key Details, T443

### Beyond Level

**Leveled Reader** *Ava's Animals,* T444–T445
**Vocabulary** Review Domain-Specific Words, T446

**Leveled Reader** *Ava's Animals,* T444–T445
**Comprehension** Review Key Details, T447

### English Language Learners

**Shared Read** "Cats and Kittens," "Desert Camels," "A Bat Is Not a Bird," T448–T449
**Phonemic Awareness** Identify and Generate Rhyme, T432
**Phonics** Connect to Three-Letter Blends, T434
**Vocabulary** Preteach Vocabulary, T452

**Leveled Reader** *Alice's New Pet,* T450–T451
**Phonemic Awareness** Phoneme Substitution, T433
**Phonics** Blend Words with Three-Letter Blends, T434
**Vocabulary** Review Vocabulary, T452
**Writing** Writing Trait: Word Choice, T454

## LANGUAGE ARTS   Writing Process: How-To T486–T491

Use with Weeks 4–6

*Whole Group*

### Writing
### Grammar

**DAY 1**

✓**Readers to Writers**
• Writing Trait: Word Choice, T388–T389
• Writing Entry: Prewrite and Draft, T388

**Grammar**
• Possessive Nouns, T390
• Mechanics: Apostrophes, T391

**DAY 2**

✓**Readers to Writers**
• Writing Trait: Word Choice, T402
• Writing Entry: Revise, T402

**Grammar**
• Possessive Nouns, T403
• Mechanics: Apostrophes, T403

Go
Digital

CUSTOMIZE YOUR OWN
LESSON PLANS

http://connected.mcgraw-hill.com

# WEEK 5 →

| DAY 3 | DAY 4 | DAY 5  Review and Assess |

## READING

**DAY 3**

**Interactive Read-Aloud Cards** "The Furry Alarm Clock" and "Little Crocodile," T404

**Review Oral Vocabulary Words,** T404

**Comprehension** Maintain Skill: Key Details, T405

**Word Work**
Phonemic Awareness: Phoneme Blending, T406
Phonics/Spelling: Words with Three-Letter Blends, T406–T407
Structural Analysis: Compound Words, T407

**Fluency** Phrasing, T408

**Vocabulary** Reinforce Vocabulary, T409

✓ **Literary Element** Rhythm, T410–T411

✓ **Vocabulary Strategy**
Multiple-Meaning Words, T412–T413

**Close Reading** "Beetles" and "The Little Turtle", 206–209  *Analytical Writing*

**Practice** *Your Turn* 98–99

**Literature Anthology**

**DAY 4**

**Oral Language** Animals in Poems, T416

**Word Work**
Phonemic Awareness: Phoneme Substitution, T417
Phonics/Spelling: Words with Three-Letter Blends, T417–T418
Structural Analysis: Compound Words, T417
High-Frequency Words, T418

**Fluency** Phrasing, T419

**Vocabulary Strategy** Review: Root Words, T419

**Close Reading** "Gray Goose," 210–211 *Analytical Writing*

**Integrate Ideas** Research and Inquiry, T422–T423 *Analytical Writing*

**Practice** *Your Turn* 93–95

**DAY 5**

**Integrate Ideas** *Analytical Writing*
• Text Connections, T424
• Write About Reading, T425
• Research and Inquiry, T425

**Word Work**
Phonemic Awareness: Phoneme Blending, T426
Phonics/Spelling: Words with Three-Letter Blends, T426–T427
Structural Analysis: Compound Words, T426
High-Frequency Words, T427

**Vocabulary** Review Words, T427

**Practice** *Your Turn* 100

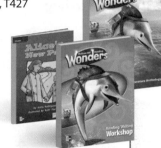

## DIFFERENTIATED INSTRUCTION

**Leveled Reader** *Amira's Petting Zoo*, T430–T431
**Phonemic Awareness** Phoneme Blending, T432 ②
**Phonics** Build Words with Three-Letter Blends, T435
**Structural Analysis** Review Compound Words, T436 ②
**Comprehension** Review Key Details, T439

**Leveled Reader** Paired Read: "Sheep Season," T431 *Analytical Writing*
**Phonemic Awareness** Phoneme Substitution, T433
**Phonics** Blend Words with Three-Letter Blends, T435
**Structural Analysis** Reteach Compound Words, T436
**Comprehension** Read for Fluency, T438 ②

**Leveled Reader** Literature Circle, T431
**Phonemic Awareness** Phoneme Blending, T432 ②
**Phonics** Blend Words with Three-Letter Blends, T435
**Comprehension** Self-Selected Reading, T439

---

**Leveled Reader** *Alice's New Pet*, T440–T441
**Vocabulary** Review Words, T442

**Leveled Reader** Paired Read: "Baby Joey," T441 *Analytical Writing*

**Leveled Reader** Literature Circle, T441
**Comprehension** Self-Selected Reading, T443

---

**Leveled Reader** *Ava's Animals*, T444–T445
**Vocabulary**
• Multiple-Meaning Words, T446
• Independent Study, T446
*Gifted and Talented*

**Leveled Reader** Paired Read: "Nanook," T445 *Analytical Writing*

**Leveled Reader** Literature Circle, T445
**Comprehension**
• Self-Selected Reading, T447
• Independent Study:
  Animals in Poetry, T447
*Gifted and Talented*

---

**Leveled Reader** *Alice's New Pet*, T450–T451
**Phonemic Awareness** Phoneme Blending, T432
**Phonics** Build Words with Three-Letter Blends, T435
**Structural Analysis** Review Compound Words, T436
**Vocabulary Strategy** Multiple-Meaning Words, T453
**Grammar** Possessive Nouns, T455

**Leveled Reader** Paired Read: "Four Little Ducklings," T451 *Analytical Writing*
**Phonemic Awareness** Phoneme Substitution, T433
**Phonics** Blend Words with Three-Letter Blends, T435
**Structural Analysis** Reteach Compound Words, T436
**Vocabulary** Additional Vocabulary, T453

**Leveled Reader** Literature Circle, T451
**Phonemic Awareness** Phoneme Blending, T432
**Phonics** Blend Words with Three-Letter Blends, T435
**Spelling** Words with Three-Letter Blends, T454

## LANGUAGE ARTS

✓ **Readers to Writers**
• Writing Trait: Word Choice, T414
• Writing Entry: Prewrite and Draft, T414

**Grammar**
• Possessive Nouns, T415
• Mechanics: Apostrophes, T415

✓ **Readers to Writers**
• Writing Trait: Word Choice, T420
• Writing Entry: Revise, T420

**Grammar**
• Possessive Nouns, T421
• Mechanics: Apostrophes, T421

✓ **Readers to Writers**
• Writing Trait: Word Choice, T428
• Writing Entry: Share and Reflect, T428

**Grammar**
• Possessive Nouns, T429
• Mechanics: Apostrophes, T429

# DIFFERENTIATE TO ACCELERATE

**IF** the text complexity of a particular selection is too difficult for children

**THEN** use the Access Complex Text prompts to scaffold instruction.

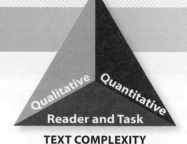

Qualitative / Quantitative
**Reader and Task**
**TEXT COMPLEXITY**

| Reading/Writing Workshop | Literature Anthology | Leveled Readers | Classroom Library |
|---|---|---|---|

## Quantitative

**Reading/Writing Workshop**

"Cats and Kittens"
**Lexile** N/A
*TextEvaluator*™ N/A

**Literature Anthology**

"Beetles"
**Lexile** N/A
*TextEvaluator*™ N/A

"Gray Goose"
**Lexile** N/A
*TextEvaluator*™ N/A

**Leveled Readers**

**Approaching Level**
**Lexile** 250
*TextEvaluator*™ 5

**Beyond Level**
**Lexile** 570
*TextEvaluator*™ 24

**On Level**
**Lexile** 470
*TextEvaluator*™ 13

**ELL**
**Lexile** 350
*TextEvaluator*™ 5

**Classroom Library**

*Nate the Great on the Owl Express*
**Lexile** 280
*TextEvaluator*™ 16

*Cam Jansen: The Mystery at the Monkey House #10*
**Lexile** 530
*TextEvaluator*™ 9

## Qualitative

**What Makes the Text Complex?**

- **Organization** Poetry Structure, T387
- **Sentence Structure** Line and Stanza Breaks, T401

**A C T** *See Scaffolded Instruction in Teacher's Edition T387 and T401.*

**What Makes the Text Complex?**

- **Purpose** Entertain, T413C
- **Specific Vocabulary** Context Clues, T419B

**A C T** *See Scaffolded Instruction in Teacher's Edition T413C, T419B.*

**What Makes the Text Complex?**

- **Specific Vocabulary**
- **Sentence Structure**
- **Connection of Ideas**
- **Genre**

**A C T** *See Level Up lessons online for Leveled Readers.*

**What Makes the Text Complex?**

- **Genre**
- **Specific Vocabulary**
- **Prior Knowledge**
- **Sentence Structure**
- **Organization**
- **Purpose**
- **Connection of Ideas**

**A C T** *See Scaffolded Instruction in Teacher's Edition T496–T497.*

## Reader and Task

The Introduce the Concept lesson on pages T376–T377 will help determine the reader's knowledge and engagement in the weekly concept. See pages T386–T387, T398–T401, T410–T413, and T422–T425 for questions and tasks for this text.

The Introduce the Concept lesson on pages T376–T377 will help determine the reader's knowledge and engagement in the weekly concept. See pages T413A–T413D, T419A–T419B, and T422–T425 for questions and tasks for this text.

The Introduce the Concept lesson on pages T376–T377 will help determine the reader's knowledge and engagement in the weekly concept. See pages T430–T431, T440–T441, T444–T445, T450–T451, and T422–T425 for questions and tasks for this text.

The Introduce the Concept lesson on pages T376–T377 will help determine the reader's knowledge and engagement in the weekly concept. See pages T496–T497 for questions and tasks for this text.

## Monitor and *Differentiate*

**IF** If you need to differentiate instruction

**THEN** use the Quick Check to assess children's needs and select the appropriate small group instruction focus.

### Quick Check

**Comprehension Strategy** Reread, T399

**Comprehension Skills** Key Details, T401

**Genre** Poetry, T411

**Vocabulary Strategy** Multiple-Meaning Words, T413

**Phonics/Fluency** Three-Letter Blends; Phrasing, T407, T419

| If No → | Approaching Level | Reteach T430–T439 |
| | ELL | Develop T448–T455 |
| If Yes → | On Level | Review T440–T443 |
| | Beyond Level | Extend T444–T447 |

## Level Up with Leveled Readers

**IF** children can read their leveled text fluently and answer comprehension questions

**THEN** assign the next level up to accelerate children reading with more complex text.

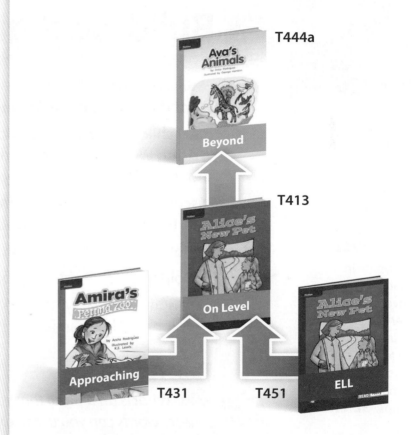

T444a

T413

T431    T451

## ENGLISH LANGUAGE LEARNERS
### SCAFFOLD

**IF** ELL students need additional support.  **THEN** scaffold instruction using the small group suggestions.

| Reading/Writing Workshop "Cats and Kittens," "Desert Camels," "A Bat Is Not a Bird," T448–T449 | Leveled Reader *Alice's New Pet,* T450–T451 "Four Little Ducklings," T451 | Additional Vocabulary T453 behave    explain express    imagine | Multiple-Meaning Words T453 | Writing Word Choice, T454 | Spelling Three-Letter Blends, T454 | Grammar Possessive Nouns, T455 |
|---|---|---|---|---|---|---|

Note: Include ELL Students in all small groups based on their needs.

## Materials

**Reading/Writing Workshop**

**Visual Vocabulary Cards**

behave    feathers
express    flapping

**Word-Building Cards**

**Interactive Read-Aloud Cards**

**Think Aloud Cloud**

orange

**High-Frequency Word Cards**

**Reading/Writing Workshop**

---

### OBJECTIVES

**CCSS** Participate in collaborative conversations with diverse partners about *grade 2 topics and texts* with peers and adults in small and larger groups. **SL.2.1**

Build background knowledge.

---

### ACADEMIC LANGUAGE

• *express*
• cognate: *expresar*

---

# → Introduce the Concept

### MINILESSON
**5** Mins

# Build Background

**ESSENTIAL QUESTION**

***What do we love about animals?***

Have children read the Essential Question on page 162 of the **Reading/Writing Workshop**. Explain that when you **express** something, you show how you feel or what you think.

Discuss the photo with children. Focus on how the dolphin **behaves**, or acts, toward the boy, and what feelings the boy and dolphin express.

→ Dolphins are a kind of mammal that lives in the water.

→ Dolphins make whistling sounds to communicate or talk to one another.

→ At some special water parks, people can touch and swim with tame dolphins. They can feel the dolphins' smooth skin.

## Talk About It

**Ask:** *What is an animal that you like? How does that animal **behave**? What sensory words can you use to **express** your ideas?* Have children discuss.

Model using the Concept Web to generate words and phrases.

### Collaborative Conversations

**Be Open to All Ideas** As children engage in partner, small-group, and whole-group discussions, remind them

that all ideas are important and should be heard.

to respect the opinions of others.

to ask questions if something is unclear.

to offer opinions, even if they're different from others' opinions.

---

## Go Digital

**Animal In Poems**

**Video**

**Photos**

**Graphic Organizer**

peered

**Visual Glossary**

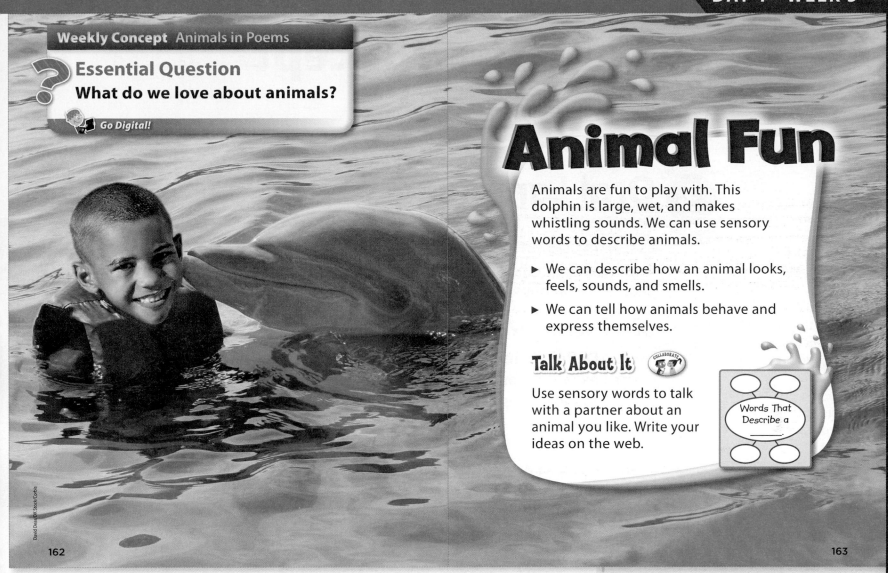

**Weekly Concept** Animals in Poems

## Essential Question
**What do we love about animals?**

Go Digital!

# Animal Fun

Animals are fun to play with. This dolphin is large, wet, and makes whistling sounds. We can use sensory words to describe animals.

▶ We can describe how an animal looks, feels, sounds, and smells.

▶ We can tell how animals behave and express themselves.

## Talk About It

Use sensory words to talk with a partner about an animal you like. Write your ideas on the web.

Words That Describe a

162

163

David Dovl/DK Stock/Corbis

**READING/WRITING WORKSHOP,** pp. 162–163

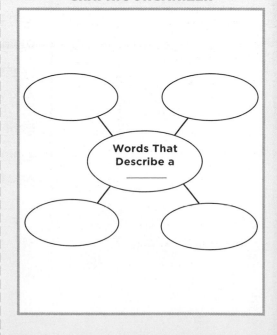

## ENGLISH LANGUAGE LEARNERS
## SCAFFOLD

| Beginning | Intermediate | Advanced/High |
|---|---|---|
| **Use Visuals** Point to the photograph and say: *The boy swims with a dolphin.* Pantomime swimming. Say: *The boy likes the dolphin. He has fun.* Point to the boy's smile. *He expresses his feelings. He is happy.* Have children describe the photo in their own words. Model correct pronunciation as needed. | **Describe** Have children discuss the photograph. Lead them to use concept words in their responses. Ask: *How does the boy feel? What feelings does he express? How does the dolphin behave?* Repeat children's responses, correcting for grammar and pronunciation as necessary. | **Discuss** Ask children to explain what the boy is doing and how he feels about swimming with the dolphin. Ask questions to help them elaborate, such as, *Why is the boy smiling? What does he love about the dolphin? How does the dolphin behave?* Elicit information that supports children's responses. |

**GRAPHIC ORGANIZER**

Words That Describe a ____

**Build the Concept**

**MINILESSON**
**5 Mins**

# Oral Language

**OBJECTIVES**

Ask and answer questions about what a speaker says in order to clarify comprehension, gather additional information, or deepen understanding of a topic or issue.

**SL.2.3**

- Develop oral language.
- Discuss the Essential Question.

**ACADEMIC LANGUAGE**

*poem, solution, reread*

**ESSENTIAL QUESTION**

Remind children that this week you'll be talking and reading about what people love about animals.

## Oral Vocabulary Words

Use the **Define/Example/Ask** routine to introduce the Oral Vocabulary words below. Prompt children to use the words as they discuss the animals in the poems.

### Oral Vocabulary Routine

**Define:** An **alarm** is a bell, a buzzer, or some other thing that makes a loud noise.

**Example:** The school alarm rings when we have a fire safety drill.

**Ask:** Tell about an alarm you have heard.

**Define:** **Howling** is a loud wailing or crying.

**Example:** We heard the howling of a lonely wolf in the darkness.

**Ask:** Describe how howling might sound.

**Define:** **Knobby** things are covered with lumps or bumps.

**Example:** The bullfrog's back felt knobby when I touched it.

**Ask:** Tell about something you have touched that felt knobby.

**Define:** **Munch** means to chew something in a noisy way.

**Example:** My rabbit likes to munch carrots.

**Ask:** What foods do you like to munch?

**Define:** A **problem** is a question that needs to be thought about and answered.

**Example:** I solved the math problem by adding up all the numbers.

**Ask:** Tell about a time when you found the answer to a problem.

**Go Digital**

**The Furry Alarm Clock and Little Crocodile**

When I read _____, I had to reread…

**Reread**

# Listening Comprehension

## Interactive Read Aloud

### Read "The Furry Alarm Clock" and "Little Crocodile"

Tell children that you will be reading two poems about animals. Display the Interactive Read-Aloud Cards.

**Interactive Read-Aloud Cards**

### Strategy: Reread

**1 Model** Explain to children that when they are not sure about the meaning of a word or what is happening in a poem, they can go back and reread the poem. This can help them understand the meaning.

**Think Aloud** When you aren't sure what a poem is about or what a word means as you are reading, you can reread part or all of it. Today, as we read the poems, we'll go back and reread any parts that are unclear or confusing.

**2 Apply** As you read, use Think Aloud Cloud to model applying the strategy. Have children indicate what was unclear to them, and reread to help clarify their understanding.

**Think Aloud** Remember that you can reread when you don't understand something. When I read the first part of "The Furry Alarm Clock," I wasn't sure what the words *break of day* meant. Then I reread the first part of the poem. The girl in the poem says she doesn't need an alarm clock because her dog starts howling. *Break of day* must mean "early morning," when it first becomes light outside.

### Make Connections

After reading, have children share what they learned about why people love the animals in the poems. Then have them discuss words or ideas in the poems that were unclear to them and how rereading helped them understand these parts.

**ENGLISH LANGUAGE LEARNERS**

**Non-Verbal Cues** Remind children that they can use non-verbal cues to share information when they are not able to do so verbally. Encourage children to use pantomime or draw. Elaborate on the information to model fluent speaking and grammatical patterns.

 **Word Work**

## Phonological Awareness

**OBJECTIVES**

**CCSS** Know and apply grade-level phonics and word analysis skills in decoding words. **RF.2.3**

- Apply phonics when decoding words with 3-letter blends.
- Identify and generate rhymes.

**ACADEMIC LANGUAGE**
*rhyme, blend*

### Identify and Generate Rhymes

**❶ Model** Model how to identify and then generate rhyming words. *I am going to say two words: scrap, strap. The words* scrap *and* strap *rhyme because they both end in the same sounds, /ap/. Listen: /skr/ /ap/, scrap; /str/ /ap/, strap. Rhyming words end in the same sounds. Now I will say another word that rhymes with* scrap *and* strap. *Listen: /m/ /ap/, map. The word* map *also ends with /ap/, so* map *rhymes with* scrap *and* strap.

**❷ Guided Practice/Practice** *Listen to each pair of words. If the words rhyme, repeat the words. If the words do not rhyme, remain silent.* Do the first one with children.

| | | |
|---|---|---|
| throw, show | screw, threw | throat, throne |
| strip, flip | scratch, match | shrug, rag |

*Listen as I say the rhyming words again. Let's think of other words that rhyme with each rhyming pair.*

**Go Digital**

**Phonological Awareness**

straw

**Phonics**

## Phonics

### Introduce Three-Letter Blends *scr, spr, str, thr, spl, shr*

**SKILLS TRACE**

**Three-Letter Blends**

**INTRODUCE** Unit 2 Week 5 Day 1

**REVIEW** Unit 2 Week 5 Day 2, day 3, Day 4, Day 5

**ASSESS** Unit 2

**❶ Model** Use Word-Building Cards to display the word *spring*. *This is the word* spring. *When the consonants* s, p, r *come together in a word, their sounds blend together.* Write the blends *scr, spr, str, thr, spl, shr.* Point to each three-letter blend and blend the sounds: /skr/, /spr/, /str/, /thr/, /spl/, /shr/. Write these words on the board: *scrap, spring, stripe, throne, splash, shrink.* Model by slowly blending the first three letters of each word and then reading the whole word.

**❷ Guided Practice/Practice** Have children practice blending *scr*. Say: *Do it with me. Say /skr/ as I write the letters* s, c, *and* r. *This time, write the letters* scr *five times as you say the sounds /skr/.* Repeat with *spr, str, thr, spl, shr.*

# Blend Words with Three-Letter Blends
## scr, spr, str, thr, spl, shr

**①Model** Display **Word-Building Cards** *s, t, r, i, p. Model how to blend the sounds. This is the letter* s. *It stands for /s/. This is the letter* t. *It stands for /t/. This is the letter* r. *It stands for /r/. The letter* i *stands for /i/, and the letter* p *stands for /p/. Listen as I blend these sounds together: /strip/.*

Continue by modeling the words *scram, sprint, thrill, split,* and *shrug.*

**②Guided Practice/Practice** Display the Day 1 Phonics Practice Activity. Read each word in the first row, blending the sounds, for example, /spring/. *The word is* spring. Have children blend each word with you. Prompt children to read the connected text, sounding out the decodable words.

| | | | | |
|---|---|---|---|---|
| spring | strong | scratch | shrug | strict |
| thrill | split | strip | scrap | shrink |
| throb | shred | splash | stress | sprint |
| stretch | sprung | scrape | throne | stripe |

The shrub got big in the spring.

The cat stretches and then chases a scrap of string.

It is a thrill to splash in the lake.

**Also online**

**Phonics Practice**

### Corrective Feedback

**Sound Error** Model the sounds that children missed, then have them repeat the sounds. Say: *My turn. Tap under the three letters and blend them together. What are the sounds?* Return to the beginning of the word. Say: *Let's start over.* Blend the word with children again.

## ENGLISH LANGUAGE LEARNERS

**Phonemic Awareness: Minimal Contrasts** Focus on articulation. Say /str/ and note your mouth position. Have children repeat. Use the articulation photos. Repeat for /st/. Have children say both sounds and notice the differences. Continue with: *string/sting, shred/shed, spice/splice, spring/ring.*

**Phonics: Variations in Language** In some languages, such as Cantonese, Hmong, Korean, and Khmer, there is no direct sound transfer for the /th/ in the blend *thr.* Emphasize the sound /th/ and show correct mouth position. Practice with Approaching Level phonics lessons.

### ON-LEVEL PRACTICE BOOK p. 92

Three letters can be blended together. Listen to the beginning sounds in *scrap* and *split.*

**A. Look at the picture. Write the missing blend for each word on the blank line.**

1. thr___ one    2. spl___ ash

3. scr___ ub    4. spr___ ing

5. str___ ap    6. shr___ ub

A **compound word** is made up of two smaller words.

**B. Circle each compound word. Write the two smaller words that make it up.**

7. beaches (bedspread) ___ bed ___ spread
8. (wishbone) wonder ___ wish ___ bone
9. (springtime) spotted ___ spring ___ time

| APPROACHING p. 92 | BEYOND p. 92 | ELL p. 92 |
|---|---|---|

→ # Word Work

### MINILESSON 5 Mins

## Spelling

### OBJECTIVES

**CCSS** Demonstrate command of the conventions of standard English capitalization, punctuation, and spelling when writing. **L.2.2**

**CCSS** Generalize learned spelling patterns when writing words (e.g., cage → badge; boy → boil). **L.2.2d**

**CCSS** Know and apply grade-level phonics and word analysis skills in decoding words. **RF.2.3**

**CCSS** Recognize and read grade-appropriate irregularly spelled words. **RF.2.3f**

### Words with Three-Letter Blends *scr, spr, str, thr, spl, shr*

**Dictation** Use the spelling dictation routine to help children transfer their growing knowledge of sound-spellings to writing. Follow the **Dictation Routine**.

**Pretest** After dictation, pronounce each spelling word. Read the sentence and pronounce the word again. Ask children to say each word softly, stretching the sounds, before writing it. After the pretest, display the spelling words and write each word as you say the letter names. Have children check their words.

| | |
|---|---|
| **scratch** | Our dogs **scratch** at the door to go out. |
| **scrape** | How did Mike **scrape** his knee? |
| **spring** | The flowers bloom in the **spring**. |
| **throne** | The queen sits on her **throne**. |
| **stripe** | My dog has a white **stripe** on his back. |
| **strange** | We heard a **strange** noise outside. |
| **shred** | Dad uses a machine to **shred** paper into bits. |
| **shrub** | There is a big **shrub** growing near the mailbox. |
| **splash** | Connie jumped in the pool and made a big **splash**. |
| **split** | We **split** the apple into two halves. |
| **catch** | Who will **catch** the ball? |
| **sting** | Did that bee **sting** you? |
| **far** | The Moon is **far** from Earth. |
| **flower** | I picked a pretty **flower** for my mom. |
| **until** | We will not go **until** the game ends. |

For Approaching Level and Beyond Level children, refer to the Differentiated Spelling Lists for modified word lists.

### Go Digital

**Spelling Word Routine**

| they | together |
|---|---|
| how | eat |

**High-Frequency Word Routine**

### ELL

#### ENGLISH LANGUAGE LEARNERS

**Spelling** Review the meaning of these words by using pictures, pantomime, or gestures when possible. Have children repeat or act out the definition as they repeat the word.

**MINILESSON 5 Mins**

# High-Frequency Words

## *bird, far, field, flower, grow, leaves, light, orange, ready, until*

**❶ Model** Display the **High-Frequency Word Cards** *bird, far, field, flower, grow, leaves, light, orange, ready,* and *until*. Use the Read/Spell/Write routine to teach each word.

→ **Read** Point to and say the word *orange. This is the word* orange. *Say it with me:* orange. *We peeled the juicy orange.*

→ **Spell** *The word* orange *is spelled* o-r-a-n-g-e. *Spell it with me.*

→ **Write** *Let's write the word in the air as we say each letter:* o-r-a-n-g-e.

→ Follow the same steps to introduce *bird, far, field, flower, grow, leaves, light, ready,* and *until*.

→ As children spell each word with you, point out the irregularities in sound/spellings, such as the /e/ sound spelled *ea* in the word *ready*.

**COLLABORATE**

→ Have partners create sentences using each word.

**❷ Guided Reading** Have children read the sentences. Prompt them to identify the high-frequency words in connected text and to blend the decodable words.

1. Tim has on an **orange** top and black pants.
2. Can I smell the **flower**?
3. We do not have **far** to walk.
4. In the fall, the **leaves** are orange and yellow.
5. Open the shades to let in the **light**.
6. The kitten will **grow** into a cat.
7. We are **ready** for school!
8. Can we play ball on that **field**?
9. I see a **bird** in the sky.
10. We can play **until** it is time to go in.

---

## Monitor and Differentiate

 **Quick Check**

Can children read and decode words with Three-letter blends? Can children recognize and read high-frequency words?

⬇

### Small Group Instruction

| | | |
|---|---|---|
| If No → | **Approaching** | Reteach pp. T432–T437 |
| | **ELL** | Develop pp. T448–T455 |
| If Yes → | **On Level** | Review pp. T442–T443 |
| | **Beyond Level** | Extend pp. T446–T447 |

→ # Vocabulary

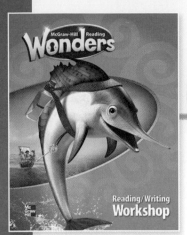

**Reading/Writing Workshop**

**Reading/Writing Workshop**

## OBJECTIVES

**CCSS** Determine the meaning of words and phrases in a text relevant to a *grade 2 topic or subject area.* **RI.2.4**

**CCSS** Demonstrate understanding of word relationships and nuances in word meanings. **L.2.5**

**CCSS** Identify real-life connections between words and their use (e.g., describe foods that are *spicy* or *juicy*). **L.2.5a**

## ACADEMIC LANGUAGE

• *express, poem, rhyme, rhythm, word choice*

• cognates: *expresar, poema, rimar, ritmo*

---

**MINILESSON 10 Mins**

## Words in Context

### Model the Routine

**Visual Vocabulary Cards**

Introduce each vocabulary word using the Vocabulary Routine found on the Visual Vocabulary Cards.

> **Vocabulary Routine**
>
> **Define:** When you **behave**, you act in a way that is good or correct.
>
> **Example:** The boy is teaching the dog to behave.
>
> **Ask:** How do you *behave* when you are in the library?

**Vocabu**
**Define:**
**Example**
**Ask:**

### Definitions and Poetry Words

→ **express**     When you **express** your feelings, you tell or show how you feel about something. **Cognate:** *expresar*

→ **feathers**   **Feathers** are the soft things that cover a bird's body.

→ **flapping**   If something is **flapping**, it is moving up and down.

Introduce each poetry term on **Reading/Writing Workshop** page 165. Present the definitions below. Explain that children will find examples of these words in the selections they read this week.

→ **poem**     A **poem** is a form of writing that expresses imagination or feelings. **Cognate:** *poema*

→ **rhyme**    When two words **rhyme**, they have the same ending sounds. **Cognate:** *rimar*

→ **rhythm**   **Rhythm** is the repeating accents, or beats, in a poem. **Cognate:** *ritmo*

→ **word choice**  **Word choice** is the use of rich, colorful, exact words.

### Talk About It

Have partners look at each picture and explain what each vocabulary word means. Tell each partner to pick three vocabulary words and write three questions for their partner to answer.

**Go Digital**

**peered**

**Visual Glossary**

# Vocabulary

**Use the picture and sentence to learn each word.**

**behave**

The boy is teaching the dog to **behave**.

*How do you behave when you are in the library?*

**flapping**

The bird was **flapping** its wings quickly.

*Describe what flapping is.*

**express**

This baby is smiling to **express** how he feels.

*How do you express your feelings?*

**feathers**

A peacock is covered in colorful **feathers**.

*Where else have you seen feathers?*

(t) Shalom Ormsby/Blend Images/Getty Images; (tc) Ingram Publishing; (bc) Marc Debnam/Digital Vision/Getty Images; (b) Sara Venter/Alamy

164

# Poetry Words

**poem**

A **poem** is a form of writing that expresses imagination or feelings.

*How is a poem different from a story?*

**rhyme**

When two words **rhyme**, they have the same ending sounds.

*What words could a poet use to rhyme with cat?*

**rhythm**

**Rhythm** is the repeating accents, or beats, in a poem.

*Why would a poet want a poem to have rhythm?*

**word choice**

**Word choice** is the use of rich, colorful, exact words.

*What exact word could you use to describe how you feel right now?*

**Your Turn**  COLLABORATE

Pick three words and write a question about each for your partner to answer.

*Go Digital!* *Use the online visual glossary*

165

---

**READING/WRITING WORKSHOP, pp. 164–165**

## ELL ENGLISH LANGUAGE LEARNERS SCAFFOLD

| Beginning | Intermediate | Advanced/High |
|---|---|---|
| **Use Visuals** Say: *Let's look at the picture for the word* flapping. Point to the hummingbird. *This tiny bird is flapping its wings.* Demonstrate flapping your arms. Elicit from children that *flapping* means moving back and forth or up and down. Ask: *What things can you see flapping on a windy day?* Repeat correct answers slowly and clearly to the class. | **Describe** Have children talk about the picture for *flapping.* Ask: *What body parts is this bird flapping? Who can show me what* flapping *looks like?* Then have children turn to a partner and talk about other things that flap. Ask children to share their responses. Model correct pronunciation as needed. | **Discuss** Ask partners to describe the picture and then define the word *flapping.* Have children share their responses. Elicit more details to support children's answers. |

VOCABULARY **T385**

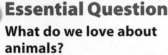

CCSS **Shared Read** | Genre · Poetry

# Cats and Kittens

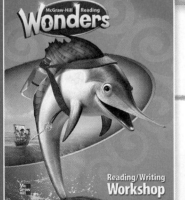

**? Essential Question**

**What do we love about animals?**

Read how poets describe animals they love.

Cats and kittens **express** their views
With hisses, purrs, and little mews.

Instead of taking baths like me,
They use their tongues quite handily.

I wonder what my mom would say
If I tried cleaning up that way.

They stay as still as still can be,
Until a mouse they chance to see.

And then in one great flash of fur
They pounce on a toy with a PURRRR.

— **by Constance Keremes**

166 / 167

**Reading/Writing Workshop**

**READING/WRITING WORKSHOP, pp. 166–167**

# Shared Read CLOSE READING

## Connect to Concept
### Animals in Poems

Explain that children will read three poems about animals. Read each poem with children. Note that the vocabulary words previously taught are highlighted in the text.

## Close Reading

**Reread "Cats and Kittens":** Reread the poem together. Say: *Think about the words the poet uses. How do the words help us understand what cats are like?* Model how to cite evidence to answer.

*At the beginning of the poem, the poet uses words such as* hisses, purrs, *and* mews *to help us hear and understand the sounds cats and kittens make. At the end, she uses the words* one great flash of fur *to help us picture how a cat jumps on a toy.*

**Reread "Desert Camels":** Model how to paraphrase the ideas in "Desert Camels." Remind children that retelling ideas in your own words helps you understand what you are reading. *The author tells about what makes camels special. Camels have a hump that people can ride on. Camels are very strong and don't mind the sun. They do not need to drink that much, even when they are walking in the hot sun.*

## Desert Camels

Camels have a hump on their backs
To carry people and their sacks.

They're very strong, don't mind the Sun,
Won't stop for drinks until they're done.

They give people a bouncy ride.
They sway and move from side to side.

I'd like a camel for a pet,
But haven't asked my mother yet!

— by Martine Wren

168

## A Bat Is Not a Bird

A bat has neither **feathers** nor beak.
He does not chirp, just gives a shriek.

He flies by hearing sounds like pings,
**Flapping**, flapping his leathery wings.

At night when I'm asleep in my bed,
He gets to fly around instead!

— by Trevor Reynolds

### Make Connections

Talk about what the poet loves about the animal in each poem.
ESSENTIAL QUESTION

Describe how your favorite animal **behaves**. TEXT TO SELF

169

**READING/WRITING WORKSHOP, pp. 168–169**

## Make Connections

**ESSENTIAL QUESTION**
Encourage children to go back into the poems for evidence as they explain what each poet loves about the animal in the poem.

## Continue Close Reading

Use the following lessons for focused rereadings.
→ Genre, T398–399
→ Key Details, T400–401
→ Rhythm, T410–411
→ Multiple-Meaning Words, T412–413

## A C T Access Complex Text

▶ **Organization**

Children may need support in understanding the organization and structure of a poem and how the three poems in this selection differ from fiction and nonfiction text.

→ Explain that the words in a poem are organized by lines. Each line is a row of words. Have children count the number of lines in "A Bat is Not a Bird."

→ In all three poems, each line begins with a capital letter, even if the words in the line are not a complete sentence.

**WHOLE GROUP**
# DAY 1

 Language Arts

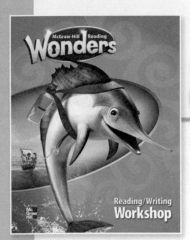

**Reading/Writing Workshop**

## OBJECTIVES

**CCSS** With guidance and support from adults and peers, focus on a topic and strengthen writing as needed by revising and editing. **W.2.5**

**CCSS** Demonstrate command of the conventions of standard English grammar and usage when writing or speaking. **L.2.1**

**CCSS** Demonstrate command of the conventions of standard English capitalization, punctuation, and spelling when writing. **L.2.2**

**CCSS** Demonstrate understanding of word relationships and nuances in word meanings. **L.2.5**

**MINILESSON**
**10 Mins**

# Writing Traits: Word Choice

## Discuss the Expert Model

**Explain** Tell children that writers use precise words to help readers picture and understand their topic. Precise words

→ help readers form a clear picture in their mind.

→ tell readers exactly what the writer means.

→ name exact things rather than general things.

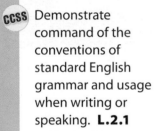 Read aloud the expert model from "Cats and Kittens." Ask children to listen for precise words that help them understand exactly why cats and kittens are like. Have children work with partners to identify these precise words.

## Discuss the Student Model

Remind children that precise words help readers understand the writer's message. Read aloud the student draft of a poem. As children follow along, have them listen for precise words in the writer's draft.

 Invite partners to talk about the draft and the precise words Teresa added. Ask them to suggest other places Teresa could include precise words.

### WRITING ENTRY: PRECISE WORDS

**❶ Prewrite** Provide children with the prompt below:

*Write a poem about an animal you like. Include precise words in your poem.*

**❷ Draft** Have children choose a topic and use their notes to write a draft. Remind children to use precise words as they write.

**Go Digital**

**Present the Lesson**

**Writing**

**Editing Marks**

(SP) Check spelling.

∧ Add.

ℐ Take out.

**Grammar Handbook**

**Possessive Nouns**
See page 9.

**CCSS** **Writing Traits**   **Word Choice**

# Readers to ...

Writers use precise words to tell exactly what they mean so readers form a clear picture in their minds. Reread "Cats and Kittens" below.

**Word Choice**
Identify a **precise word** the writer uses. How does this word help you understand how cats act?

**Expert Model**

Cats and kittens express their views
With hisses, purrs, and little mews.
Instead of taking baths like me,
They use their tongues quite handily.

# Writers

Teresa wrote a poem. Read Teresa's revisions.

**Student Model**

## A Turtle

A turtle has a hard shell.

It fits him very very well.

The turtle's shell can be very gray.

It's a ~~nice~~ ^safe^ place to stay.

When danger is very neer, (SP)

The shy turtle doesn't fear.

He pulls in his head and feet

And he's gone. How very neat!

**Your Turn**  COLLABORATE

☑ Identify the precise words Teresa used.
☑ Identify the possessive nouns.
☑ Tell how revisions improved her writing.

*Go Digital!*
*Write online in Writer's Workspace*

174   175

**READING/WRITING WORKSHOP,** pp. 174–175

![ELL] **ENGLISH LANGUAGE LEARNERS SCAFFOLD**

| **Beginning** | **Intermediate** | **Advanced/High** |
|---|---|---|
| **Generate Ideas** Provide model sentences based on the prompt: *An animal I like is _____. It has _____.* Help children complete the sentence frames with precise words. Clarify children's responses as needed by providing vocabulary. | **Replace Words** Ask children to write two lines of their poem. Provide sentence frames as needed. Help them identify places where they can replace general words with precise ones. Prompt them with questions, such as: *What is another word that means the same thing? What exact word can you use here?* | **Respond** Ask children to respond to the prompt. Before writing, have partners help one another generate a list of precise words that will help readers create a picture in their mind. |

**Genre Writing**

**Informative/Explanatory Text**
For full writing process lessons and rubrics, see:

→ How-to, pp. T480–485

→ How-to, pp. T486–491

Susanne Danegger/PhotoLibrary; (mouse) D. Hurst/Alamy

→ # Language Arts

MINILESSON
**10** Mins

# Grammar

## Possessive Nouns

**OBJECTIVES**

**CCSS** Demonstrate command of the conventions of standard English grammar and usage when writing or speaking. **L.2.1**

**CCSS** Demonstrate command of the conventions of standard English capitalization, punctuation, and spelling when writing. **L.2.2**

**CCSS** Use an apostrophe to form contractions and frequently occurring possessives. **L.2.2c**

**ACADEMIC LANGUAGE**
*noun, possessive, apostrophe*

❶ **Explain/Model** Remind children that a noun names a person, place, or thing. A **possessive noun** is a noun that shows who or what owns something. Display the following sentences:

The <u>dog of Jackie</u> knows many tricks.

<u>Jackie's dog</u> knows many tricks.

Point out how the underlined words in the two sentences say the same thing in different ways. Model identifying the possessive noun in the second sentence.

**Think Aloud** Who owns something? Jackie owns something. *Jackie's* in the second sentence is a possessive noun. It shows that Jackie owns the dog. It is Jackie's dog.

Explain that to make a singular noun possessive, we add an apostrophe and an -s to the end of the noun. Point out that the apostrophe and -s make the noun *Jackie's* possessive.

❷ **Guided Practice/Practice** Display the sentences below and read them aloud together. Ask children to rewrite the underlined parts with a possessive noun. Prompt children by asking, *Who or what owns something? What does it own?*

The <u>stripes of the zebra</u> are black and white. (zebra's stripes)

Matt touched the <u>skin of the pig</u>. (pig's skin)

<u>The pets of Lily</u> are friendly. (Lily's pets)

## Talk About It

**Tell About an Animal** Have one partner name a kind of animal. The other partner should make the animal name possessive by naming a feature of the animal. For example, one partner says, *lizard*. The other partner says *lizard's rough skin*. Partners then reverse roles.

# Mechanics: Apostrophes with Possessive Nouns

**① Explain/Model** Remind children that we add an apostrophe and an -*s* to the end of a noun to show possession, or who or what owns something. Show students these examples:

> a bat's wings
>
> a turtle's shell

Point out that the apostrophe and -s at the end of *bat's* and *turtle's* show that these are possessive nouns.

**② Guided Practice/Practice** Write the following phrases on the board and read them aloud. Ask children what should be added to the underlined nouns to make them possessive. (an apostrophe and an -*s*) Have partners rewrite each phrase to make the underlined noun possessive.

> a <u>camel</u> hump (camel's)
>
> my <u>cat</u> whiskers (cat's)
>
> the <u>kitten</u> toy (kitten's)

---

**GRAMMAR PRACTICE BOOK** p. 46

- A **possessive noun** shows who or what owns something.
- Add an **apostrophe** (') and **-s** to a singular noun to make it possessive.

  I walk the <u>dog of my friend</u>.  I walk my <u>friend's</u> dog.

  The <u>bowl of the fish</u> is round.  The <u>fish's</u> bowl is round.

Rewrite the underlined parts with a possessive noun. Write it on the line.

1. The <u>bowl of the cat</u> is empty.   cat's bowl
2. The <u>fur of a camel</u> is brown.   camel's fur
3. The <u>dog of Mia</u> likes to run.   Mia's dog
4. That cave might be the <u>home of a bear</u>.   bear's home
5. The <u>skin of a snake</u> is very slimy.   snake's skin
6. The <u>tongue of a cat</u> is very rough.   cat's tongue
7. The <u>goldfish of Alicia</u> is a very quiet pet!   Alicia's goldfish

---

# Daily Wrap Up

→ Review the Essential Question and encourage children to discuss using the new concept and oral vocabulary words. Ask: *What kinds of animals did you read about today? What do people love about these animals?*

→ Prompt children to share what skills they learned. How might they use those skills?

## Materials

**Reading/Writing Workshop**

behave

**Visual Vocabulary Cards**
behave express
feathers flapping

a b c

**Word-Building Cards**

**Interactive Read-Aloud Cards**

orange

**High-Frequency Word Cards**

scratch

**Spelling Word Cards**

# → Build the Concept

MINILESSON
**5** Mins

## Oral Language

### OBJECTIVE

**CCSS**
Recount or describe key ideas or details from a text read aloud or information presented orally or through other media. **SL.2.2**

- Develop oral language.
- Discuss the Essential Question.
- Retell ideas in poems.

### ACADEMIC LANGUAGE
*reread*

**ESSENTIAL QUESTION**

**COLLABORATE**

Remind children that this week you are talking and reading about what people love about animals. Remind them of the animals they read about in "The Furry Alarm Clock," "Little Crocodile," "Cats and Kittens," "Desert Camels," and "A Bat Is Not a Bird." Guide children to talk about the Essential Question using information from what they read and talked about on Day 1.

### Review Oral Vocabulary

Review the oral vocabulary words *alarm, howling, knobby, munch, and problem* using the Define/Example/Ask routine. Encourage children to discuss animals they have read about when coming up with examples for each word.

# Listening Comprehension

**MINILESSON 5 Mins**

## Interactive Read Aloud

### Reread "The Furry Alarm Clock" and "Little Crocodile"

Tell children that you will reread "The Furry Alarm Clock" and "Little Crocodile." Display the Interactive Read-Aloud Cards.

**Interactive Read-Aloud Cards**

### Strategy: Reread

Remind children that they can reread part or all of a poem if they do not understand a word or idea. This can help them figure out what the poem describes. *As we reread "The Furry Alarm Clock," we may find words or ideas that are not familiar. For example, when I read the poem, I wasn't sure why the author was telling about a rooster. When I reread that part of the poem, I understood that a rooster also makes a lot of noise early in the morning. The author likes the dog better, though, because a dog is devoted.*

Read aloud "Little Crocodile." Pause to model using the strategy. Prompt children to indicate words or ideas that are unclear. Demonstrate how rereading those parts of the text can help them understand words and ideas in the poem.

### Model Retelling

Pause to retell parts of "The Furry Alarm Clock." *I will put the ideas from the poem in my own words. The speaker in the poem has a Great Dane. The dog is like an alarm clock because he wakes the speaker each day.*

Explain that when children retell a poem, they should tell the important ideas.

### Retell the Selection

After reading, guide children to retell each poem. Remind them to tell the important ideas and details about each animal. You may wish to let children use the pictures on the Interactive Read-Aloud Cards to help them retell the poems.

 **Word Work**

## Quick Review
**Build Fluency: Sound-Spellings**
Display the **Word-Building Cards** *scr, spr, str, thr, spl, shr, ch, th, sh, wh, tch, ph, ng, o_e, o, u_e, u, i_e, i, a_e, a.* Have children say each sound.

## Phonemic Awareness

### Phoneme Substitution

**①  Model**  Demonstrate that you can change, or substitute, the last sound in a word to form a new word. *Listen for the last sound in the word* strain. *The last sound is /n/. I'll change the /n/ in* strain *to /t/ and make a new word. The new word is* straight.

Continue modeling phoneme substitution with the last sound in *scream/screen, street/streak, throat/thrown.*

**②  Guided Practice/Practice**  Have children practice substituting phonemes. Do the first one together. *The word is* strike. *The last sound in* strike *is /k/. I'll change the last sound /k/ to /p/ to make a new word. The new word is* stripe.

Have children substitute the last phoneme to form new words.

three/through        struck/strut        splat/splash

## Phonics

### Review Three-Letter Blends: *scr, spr, str, thr, spl, shr*

**①  Model**  Display the Word-Building Cards *s, t, r, a, p.* Review the three-letter blend *str* using the word *strap.* Repeat for *scr, spr, thr, spl,* and *shr* using *scrap, sprint, thrill, splash,* and *shrug.*

**②  Guided Practice/Practice**  Point to each blend and blend the sounds: /skr/, /spr/, /str/, /thr/, /spl/, and /shr/. Have children connect the letters and the sounds. Point to the letters in each blend and say: *What are these letters? Together what sounds do they stand for?* Remind children that the letters *th* in the blend *thr* and *sh* in the blend *shr* stand for one sound.

## Go Digital

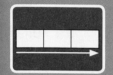
**Phonemic Awareness**

**Phonics**

**Structural Analysis**

### OBJECTIVES

**CCSS** Know and apply grade-level phonics and word analysis skills in decoding words. **RF.2.3**

**CCSS** Determine or clarify the meaning of unknown and multiple-meaning words and phrases based on *grade 2 reading and content,* choosing flexibly from an array of strategies. **L.2.4**

**CCSS** Use knowledge of the meaning of individual words to predict the meaning of compound words (e.g., *birdhouse, lighthouse, housefly; bookshelf, notebook, bookmark*). **L.2.4.d**

Substitute phonemes to form new words.

### ACADEMIC LANGUAGE
*blend, substitute*

# Blend Words with Three-Letter Blends

**1 Model** Display Word-Building Cards *s, c, r, a, p*. Model how to generate and blend the sounds to say the word. *This is the letter* s. *It stands for /s/. This is the letter* c. *It stands for /k/. This is the letter* r. *It stands for /r/. Together, these letters stand for /skr/. This is the letter a. It stands for /a/. This is the letter p. It stands for /p/. Listen as I blend these sounds together: /skrap/. Say it with me:* scrap.

→ Continue by modeling the words *sprint, struck, throb, splint,* and *shred.*

**2 Guided Practice/Practice** Repeat the routine with children with *scram, sprung, string, thrash, split, shrug.*

# Build Words with Three-Letter Blends

**1 Model** Display Word-Building Cards *s, t, r, i, k, e*. Blend: /s/ /t/ /r/, /ī/, /k/, *strike*.

→ Replace *k* with *d* and repeat with *stride*.

→ Change *d* to *p* and repeat with *stripe*.

**2 Guided Practice/Practice** Continue with *strip, strap, scrap, scrape; sprung, spring, sprint; shrug, shrub, scrub*. Guide children to build and blend each word.

## ENGLISH LANGUAGE LEARNERS

**Phonics: Build Vocabulary**
Review the meanings of example words that can be explained or demonstrated in a concrete way. For example, point to a striped shirt and a scrap of paper. Demonstrate the actions for *shrug, scratch,* and *shred*. Have children repeat the actions and say the words with you. Provide sentence starters such as *I can scrub the _____. The _____ has a strap* for children to complete. Correct grammar and pronunciation as needed.

---

**MINILESSON 5 Mins**

# Structural Analysis

## Compound Words

**1 Model** Write the word *springtime* and read it aloud. Tell children that *springtime* is a compound word. Explain that a compound word is made of two shorter words. Say: *To read a compound word we look for the two smaller words and then blend them together: /spring/ /time/, springtime.*

Explain that identifying the smaller words in a compound word can also help them figure out the word's meaning. Springtime *is the time of year when it is spring.*

**2 Guided Practice/Practice** Write the following compound words on the board: *backpack, pancake, racetrack, sunshine*. Ask children to identify the two shorter words in each compound word and blend them to read the word. Then have them tell what each word means and use it in a sentence.

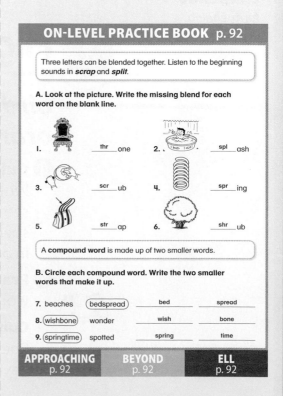

**ON-LEVEL PRACTICE BOOK** p. 92

Three letters can be blended together. Listen to the beginning sounds in *scrap* and *split*.

**A. Look at the picture. Write the missing blend for each word on the blank line.**

1. thr one
2. spl ash
3. scr ub
4. spr ing
5. str ap
6. shr ub

A **compound word** is made up of two smaller words.

**B. Circle each compound word. Write the two smaller words that make it up.**

7. beaches (bedspread) — bed — spread
8. (wishbone) wonder — wish — bone
9. (springtime) spotted — spring — time

| APPROACHING p. 92 | BEYOND p. 92 | ELL p. 92 |
|---|---|---|

**Word Work**

### MINILESSON 5 Mins
## Spelling

### Word Sort with Three-Letter Blends

**①  Model**  Display the **Spelling Word Cards** one at a time. Have children read each word, listening for the three-letter blend at the beginning of each. Use cards for *scratch, spring, throne, stripe, shred,* and *splash* to create a six-column chart. Say each word and pronounce the blend. Say each word again. Ask children to chorally spell each word.

**②  Guided Practice/Practice**  Have children place each remaining Spelling Word Card in the column with the same three-letter blend (*scr, spr, str, thr, spl, shr*).

When completed, have children chorally read the words in each column. Have them identify the three-letter blend and its sounds.

**③  Build Fluency: Word Automaticity**  Have children chorally read words to build fluency. Conclude by asking children to orally generate additional words with that blend. List them in the correct columns.

### MINILESSON 5 Mins
## High-Frequency Words

*bird, far, field, flower, grow, leaves, light, orange, ready, until*

**①  Guided Practice**  Say each word and have children Read/Spell/Write it. Ask children to picture the word and write it the way they see it. Display the word for children to self-correct. Point out sound spellings that may be unfamiliar, such as the short *i* sound spelled *a* in *orange.*

**②  Practice**  Add this week's high-frequency words to the cumulative word bank. Have partners create sentences using the words.

**Cumulative Review**  Review last week's words using the Read/Spell/Write routine. Repeat the above routine, mixing the words and having children say each one.

**Go Digital**

**Spelling Word Sort**

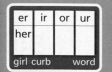

**High-Frequency Word Routine**

**Visual Glossary**

# → Vocabulary

## Expand Vocabulary

**5 Mins**

Have children use the **Visual Vocabulary Cards** to review this week's vocabulary words: *behave, express, feathers, flapping.*

**❶ Explain** Tell children that words can have different forms. Help them generate different forms of this week's words by using the inflectional endings *-ing, -ed,* and *-s/-es.* Review when each ending is used.

**❷ Model** Draw a four-column T-chart on the board. Write the vocabulary word *express* in the first column. Model how to add endings to the word *express.* Then write *expressing, expressed,* and *expresses* in the next three columns. Point out that because *express* ends in *-ss,* it takes the ending *-es.* Read aloud the words with children.

Point out how the different endings change the meaning of *express.* Discuss each form of the word and its meaning.

Have children share aloud sentences using *express, expressing, expressed,* and *expresses.*

**❸ Guided Practice** Have children work in pairs to fill in charts for *behave* and *flapping.* Remind children to drop the silent *e* on *behave* when adding the *-ing* ending. Point out that *flapping* already has the *-ing* ending. Ask children to use each form of the words in sentences.

## ENGLISH LANGUAGE LEARNERS

**More Practice** Practice spelling by helping children generate more words with three-letter blends *scr, spr, str, thr, spl, shr.* Use prompts such as: *When I change the blend* spr *in* spring *to* str, *I get the new word _____.* Write the word (*string*) and have children practice reading it. Correct pronunciation as needed.

## Monitor and *Differentiate*

### ✓ Quick Check

Can children read and spell words with three-letter blends *scr, spr, str, thr, spl, shr?*

⬇

### Small Group Instruction

If No → | Approaching | Reteach pp. T432–T437
| ELL | Develop pp. T448–T455
If Yes → | On Level | Review pp. T442–T443
| Beyond Level | Extend pp. T446–T447

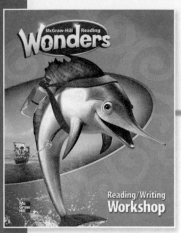

# Genre: Poetry

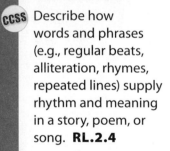

**Reading/Writing Workshop**

---

## OBJECTIVES

**CCSS** Describe how words and phrases (e.g., regular beats, alliteration, rhymes, repeated lines) supply rhythm and meaning in a story, poem, or song. **RL.2.4**

Recognize the characterstics of rhyming poetry.

---

## ACADEMIC LANGUAGE

*rhyming, poem, poet, line*

---

**MINILESSON**
**10 Mins**

# Rhyming Poem

### ❶ Explain

Share with children the following key characteristics of **rhyming poetry**.

→ A rhyming poem expresses a poet's thoughts and feelings. It often includes images and uses sensory details to describe something.

→ A rhyming poem is written in lines rather than paragraphs.

→ Rhyming poems have words that rhyme, or end with the same sounds. The rhyming words are usually at the end of lines of the poem.

### ❷ Model Close Reading: Text Evidence

Model identifying the genre of "Cats and Kittens" on page 167. Say: *I can tell that this selection is a poem. It is written in lines, not paragraphs. It tells the author's thoughts and feelings about cats and kittens. It includes sensory details that help me picture what a cat looks and sounds like and how it acts. It also has words that rhyme. So it is a rhyming poem.*

**Rhyme** Remind children that a rhyming poem has words that rhyme. Rhyming words end with the same sounds. Read aloud lines 1 and 2. Say: *The last words in these lines of the poem are* views *and* mews. Views *and* mews *rhyme because they end in the same sound. What other words in this poem rhyme?* (say, way; me, handily; be, see; fur, purrrr)

### ❸ Guided Practice of Close Reading

Have children work with partners to reread "Desert Camels" and "A Bat Is Not a Bird." Have children identify lines of the poems that rhyme and name the rhyming words.

**Go Digital**

**Cats and Kittens**

**Present the Lesson**

 **Genre** Poetry

# Rhyming Poem

A **rhyming poem**:
- has words that end with the same sounds.
- tells a poet's thoughts or feelings.

 **Find Text Evidence**

I can tell that "Cats and Kittens" is a rhyming poem. The author tells her thoughts about cats. Also, the last words in lines one and two rhyme.

**page 167**

Cats and kittens express their views
With hisses, purrs, and little mews.

Instead of taking baths like me,
They use their tongues quite handily.

I wonder what my mom would say
If I tried cleaning up that way.

They stay as still as still can be,
Until a mouse they chance to see.

And then in one great flash of fur
They pounce on a toy with a PURRRR.

— by Constance Keremes

Sometimes pairs of lines **rhyme** in a rhyming poem.

**Your Turn**  COLLABORATE

Read the poems "Desert Camels" and "A Bat Is Not a Bird." Tell which lines rhyme.

170

**READING/WRITING WORKSHOP,** p. 170

---

## ON-LEVEL PRACTICE BOOK p. 93-95

Read the poem. Use the reread strategy to check your understanding.

### A Tortoise

|    | |
|---|---|
|    | You will find that a tortoise is a mild fellow, |
| 10 | It lives a life that's calm and mellow. |
| 18 | A tortoise can live for quite a long span, |
| 27 | In fact it may even live longer than a man. |
| 37 | You'll never find a tortoise at sea, |
| 44 | It lives on land—that's where it should be. |
| 53 | Would a tortoise be able to win a race? |
| 62 | Not since it moves at such a slow pace. |
| 71 | It has four stumpy legs and four tortoise feet, |
| 80 | For a snack, plants are its favorite of treat. |

| APPROACHING p. 93-95 | BEYOND p. 93-95 | ELL p. 93-95 |
|---|---|---|

---

## ELL ENGLISH LANGUAGE LEARNERS SCAFFOLD

| Beginning | Intermediate | Advanced/High |
|---|---|---|
| Reread lines 1 and 2 of "Cats and Kittens." Use the lines to point out characteristics of a rhyming poem. *What kind of animal is this poem about?* (cats and kittens) *The poet wants us to picture what a cat is like. What words in line 2 tell the sounds a cat makes?* (hisses, purrs, mews) *Listen to these words:* views, mews. *Do* views *and* mews *rhyme?* | Reread lines 1 and 2 of "Cats and Kittens." Prompt children to identify the genre. Ask: *Which words in lines 1 and 2 rhyme? How do you know those words rhyme?* (views, mews; they end with the same sound. Have children offer rhyming words for *cat* and *fur.* (cat, bat, hat, mat; fur, purr) Allow children ample time to respond. | Reread lines 1 and 2 of "Cats and Kittens." Have children explain how they know the selection is a poem. Ask: *Is the selection written in paragraphs or in lines? Why does the poet use the words* hisses, purrs, *and* mews? *What examples of rhyming words can you find in the poem?* Repeat correct answers slowly and clearly to the class. |

---

## Monitor and *Differentiate*

 **Quick Check**

Can children identify rhyming words? Can children tell which lines of a poem rhyme?

**Small Group Instruction**

If No → | **Approaching** | Reteach pp. T430–T431 |
| **ELL** | Develop pp. T448–T449 |
If Yes → | **On Level** | Review pp. T440–T441 |
| **Beyond Level** | Extend pp. T444–T445 |

GENRE **T399**

# Comprehension Skill

CLOSE READING

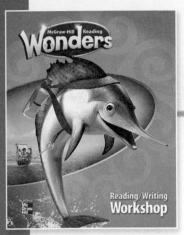

**Reading/Writing Workshop**

**OBJECTIVE**

CCSS Ask and answer such questions as *who, what, where, when, why,* and *how* to demonstrate understanding of key details in a text. **RL.2.1**

**ACADEMIC LANGUAGE**
*key details*

MINILESSON
**10** Mins

## Key Details

### ❶ Explain

Explain to children that in a poem, key details give important pieces of information that help them understand the poem.

→ Children can find key details in a poem's words and in the pictures or photos that go with a poem.

→ As they read, children can ask themselves whether a fact or idea helps them understand what the poem is about, or how the poet feels about the topic. This will help them decide if a detail is a key detail.

### ❷ Model Close Reading: Text Evidence

Model identifying a key detail about camels from the first two lines of the poem "Desert Camels" on page 168. Record it in the graphic organizer.

 **Write About Reading: Summary** Model for children how to use a detail from the graphic organizer to write a summary of what they learned about camels at the beginning of the poem.

### ❸ Guided Practice of Close Reading

 Have children work in pairs to complete the graphic organizer with two more key details from the poem "Desert Camels." Remind children that key details are important ideas or facts in the poem.

**Write About Reading: Summary** Have pairs use their completed graphic organizer for "Desert Camels" to write a summary of what they learned about camels and the author's feelings about camels. Select pairs of children to share their summaries with the class.

## Go Digital

**Cats and Kittens**

**Present the Lesson**

**Graphic Organizer**

**SKILLS TRACE**

**Key Details**

**INTRODUCE** Unit 1 Week 1

**REVIEW** Unit 1 Weeks 2, 4, 5, Unit 2 Weeks 1, 2, 3, 4, 5; Unit 4 Week 5

**ASSESS** Units 1, 2

## Comprehension Skill CCSS

# Key Details

Key details give important information about a poem. You can find important information in the words, pictures, or photos.

### Find Text Evidence

*As I read "Desert Camels," I understand that camels are very strong. I read that they can carry people and their sacks.*

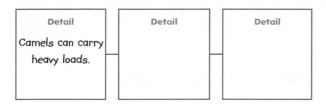

| Detail | Detail | Detail |
|---|---|---|
| Camels can carry heavy loads. | | |

### Your Turn

Reread "Desert Camels." Find the key details and list them in the graphic organizer.

*Go Digital!*
*Use the interactive graphic organizer*

171

**READING/WRITING WORKSHOP, p. 171**

## A C T Access Complex Text

### ▶ Sentence Structures

Line and stanza breaks may make it difficult for children to identify the beginning and end of ideas, as well as what words refer to.

→ Ask: *What words does the contraction* They're *at the beginning of line 3 stand for?* (They are) *Who are "they"?* (camels)

→ Say: *Lines 3 and 4 form a sentence. The subject of this sentence is* They, *or the camels. The sentence has three parts that tell what camels do. Use the commas to break the sentence into three parts.*

→ Ask: *What three details do lines 3 and 4 tell about camels?* (They're strong. They don't mind the Sun. They won't stop for drinks or can go for a long time without water.)

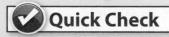
### ON-LEVEL PRACTICE BOOK pp. 93–95

A. Reread the passage and answer the questions.

1. How long can a tortoise live?

   A tortoise can live longer than a man.

2. Where does a tortoise live?

   A tortoise lives on land.

3. How does a tortoise use its shell?

   A tortoise hides inside its shell to stay safe.

B. Work with a partner. Read the passage aloud. Pay attention to how you pause and group words together. Stop after one minute. Fill out the chart.

|  | Words Read | − | Number of Errors | = | Words Correct Score |
|---|---|---|---|---|---|
| First Read | | − | | = | |
| Second Read | | − | | = | |

| APPROACHING pp. 93–95 | BEYOND pp. 93–95 | ELL pp. 93–95 |
|---|---|---|

## Monitor and *Differentiate*

### ✓ Quick Check

As children complete the graphic organizer, do they find the key details in the poem?

⬇

### Small Group Instruction

If No → **Approaching** Reteach pp. T438–T439

**ELL** Develop pp. T448–T451

If Yes → **On Level** Review pp. T442–T443

**Beyond Level** Extend pp. T446–T447

→ # Language Arts

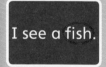

# Writing Traits: Word Choice

### OBJECTIVES

**CCSS** With guidance and support from adults and peers, focus on a topic and strengthen writing as needed by revising and editing. **W.2.5**

**CCSS** Use an apostrophe to form contractions and frequently occurring possessives. **L.2.2c**

**1 Explain** Remind children that writers use precise words to help readers create a picture in their mind. Writers revise their writing by replacing general words with more descriptive and precise words.

**2 Model** Read aloud the model from Your Turn Practice Book page 97. Then think aloud to model revising to add precise words.

I went outside one night.

Something moved, so I turned on the light.

It was a little toad,

Hopping across the road.

**Think Aloud** I can help readers create a clearer picture of the toad in this poem by adding precise words. For example, in the third line, I can replace *little toad* with the more precise and descriptive words *tiny brown toad*.

**3 Guided Practice** Invite partners to add precise words or replace general words with more precise details in the draft. Use the prompts on Your Turn Practice Book page 97 as a guide.

### Conferencing Routines

**Teacher Conference**

**STEP 1** Talk about the strengths of the writing.

**STEP 2** Focus on the target trait.

**STEP 3** Make concrete suggestions for revisions.

**Peer Conferences**

Provide these questions to guide peers as they review a partner's draft.

☑ Is the writing clear and easy to understand?

☑ Does the poem help you picture an animal in your mind?

☑ Which words can be more precise?

## WRITING ENTRY: PRECISE DETAILS

**1 Revise** Have children review their poems from Day 1. Ask them to revise by finding general words they can replace with more precise words that help create a picture in the reader's mind.

Use the **Conferencing** Routines to help children revise. Circulate among children and stop briefly to talk to individuals. Provide opportunities for partners to work together using the **Peer Conferences** routine.

**2 Edit** Ask children to review the rules on Grammar Handbook page 9. Have them check that they have used possessive nouns correctly and placed apostrophes in the correct place. Have children use a dictionary to check their spelling.

**Go Digital**

**Writing Model**

**Writing**

I see a fish.

**Grammar**

## Grammar

### Possessive Nouns

**① Review** Remind children that a **plural noun** names more than one person, place, or thing and usually ends in -*s* or -*es*. Explain that plural nouns can also be **possessive**, or show who or what owns something. We add an apostrophe after the final *s* to make a plural noun possessive. Display the following sentence:

> The girls' pets marched in the parade.

Point out that *girls'* is a plural possessive. It shows that more than one girl owned the pets.

**② Guided Practice/Practice** Have partners rewrite the underlined plural nouns to make them possessive.

> The two <u>dogs</u> toys are all over the floor. (dogs')
>
> The <u>birds</u> cages are large and clean. (birds')
>
> The <u>foxes</u> paws left prints in the snowy field. (foxes')

### Mechanics: Apostrophes with Possessive Nouns

**① Review** Remind children that to make a plural noun possessive, we add an apostrophe after the *s*. Display this example:

> On my street, all the houses' yards have fences.

Point out that *houses'* is a plural possessive noun. The apostrophe after the *s* shows that the yards belong to more than one house.

**② Practice** Write the following phrases on the board. Have volunteers rewrite each plural possessive noun with an apostrophe in the correct position.

> kittens fur (kittens' fur)
>
> animals sounds (animals' sounds)
>
> bats cave (bats' cave)

## Daily Wrap Up

Review with children the skills they learned today:

→ Discuss the Essential Question and encourage children to use the oral vocabulary words.

→ Prompt children to review and discuss the skills they used today. How do those skills help them?

## Materials

**Reading/Writing Workshop**

**Literature Anthology "Beetles" and "The Little Turtle"**

**behave**

**Visual Vocabulary Cards**

behave  feathers
express  flapping

a b c

**Word-Building Cards**

**Interactive Read-Aloud Cards**

**orange**

**High-Frequency Word Cards**

**scratch**

**Spelling Word Cards**

→ # Build the Concept

**MINILESSON**
**5 Mins**

## Interactive Read Aloud

### OBJECTIVES

Ask and answer such questions as *who, what, where, when, why,* and *how* to demonstrate understanding of key details in a text. **RL.2.1**

- Develop oral language.
- Discuss the Essential Question.

### ACADEMIC LANGUAGE
*key details*

**ESSENTIAL QUESTION**

Remind children that this week they are talking and reading about what people love about animals. Remind them of the different animals they have read about in poems so far this week: a Great Dane, a crocodile, cats and kittens, camels, and bats. Guide children to discuss the Essential Question using information from what they have read and discussed throughout the week.

### Review Oral Vocabulary

Review the oral vocabulary words *alarm, howling, knobby, munch,* and *problem* using the Define/Example/Ask routine. Encourage children to discuss what people love about animals and what animals are like when coming up with examples for each word.

### Reread "The Furry Alarm Clock" and "Little Crocodile"

Tell children that you will reread "The Furry Alarm Clock" and "Little Crocodile." Model how to reread difficult parts of the poems to better understand the poets' words and ideas. Prompt children to identify the key details about each animal.

**Interactive Read-Aloud Cards**

### *Analytical Writing* Write About Reading

Have children write about details that show what each poet loves about the animal in their poem.

## Go Digital

**The Furry Alarm Clock and Little Crocodile**

**Cats and Kittens**

# Comprehension

 ## Key Details

**① Explain** Remind children that this week and last week they have been finding the key details in a text.

Review the definition of the term *key details*.

→ Key details are the important ideas and pieces of information in a text.

→ Key details help us understand the topic of a text.

→ Key details can be found in the text and the pictures and photos that go with it.

**② Model** Display "Cats and Kittens" on pages 166–167. *"Cats and Kittens" tells what cats are like. As I reread the poem, I see details about what cats do and how they behave. Cats make different noises like hisses, purrs, and mews. They use their tongues to clean themselves. They move quickly and pounce on toys.*

**③ Guided Practice** Reread "A Bat Is Not a Bird" on page 169. Model how rereading can help you understand the ideas in the poem and find key details. Prompt children to identify key details about bats.

→ Guide children to understand that lines 1 and 2 explain how a bat is not like a bird. *How are bats different from birds? What key details do you learn about bats in these lines? (A bat doesn't have feathers or a beak. A bat also doesn't chirp, but just gives a shriek.)*

→ Prompt children to find key details in lines 3 and 4. *How does a bat fly? What are a bat's wings like? (A bat flies by hearing sounds. A bat's wings aren't feathery, but leathery.)*

→ Ask children to reread lines 5 and 6. Have them identify the key detail about bats in these lines. *(Bats fly at night.)*

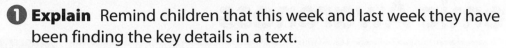

**ENGLISH LANGUAGE LEARNERS**

**Use Visuals** Have children use the photograph of a bat on page 169 to describe and identify key details about bats. Ask children to describe the bat's body. How is its body different from a bird's? What key details can they get from the picture? (The bat has ears on top of its head. It has a nose and mouth instead of a beak, and it's covered in fur instead of feathers. Its wings also don't have feathers.)

 → # Word Work

### Quick Review

**Build Fluency: Sound-Spellings** Display the **Word-Building Cards** *scr, spr, str, thr, spl, shr, ch, th, sh, wh, tch, ph, ng, o_e, o, u_e, u, i_e, i, a_e, a.* Have children say each sound. For fluency in connected text, see the Decodable Reader lesson in Small Group.

## Phonemic Awareness

### Phoneme Blending

**OBJECTIVES**

**CCSS** Know and apply grade-level phonics and word analysis skills in decoding words. **RF.2.3**

**CCSS** Generalize learned spelling patterns when writing words (e.g., cage → badge; boy → boil). **L.2.2d**

**CCSS** Use knowledge of the meaning of individual words to predict the meaning of compound words (e.g., *birdhouse, lighthouse, housefly; bookshelf, notebook, bookmark*). **L.2.4.d**

- Blend phonemes to form words.
- Decode words with three-letter consonant blends.
- Identify and read compound words.

**ACADEMIC LANGUAGE**
*blend, compound word*

❶ **Model** Place markers in the Response Boards to represent sounds. Show children how to orally blend phonemes. *I'm going to put one marker in each box as I say each sound. Then I will blend the sounds to form a word.* Place a marker for each sound you say. */s/ /t/ /r/ /i/ /p/. This word has five sounds: /s/ /t/ /r/ /i/ /p/. Listen as I blend these sounds to form a word: /striiip/,* strip. *The word is* strip.

❷ **Guided Practice/Practice** *Let's do some together. Using your own boards, place a marker for each sound you hear. I will say one sound at a time. Then we will blend the sounds to say the word.* Do the first one with children.

| | | |
|---|---|---|
| scram | spread | strange |
| throat | splash | shriek |
| street | thrill | scrape |

## Phonics

### Blend Words with Three-Letter Blends
### *scr, spr, str, thr, spl, shr*

❶ **Model** Display **Word-Building Cards** *sh, r, u, g.* Model how to blend the sounds. *These are the letters s and h. Together they stand for /sh/. This is the letter r. It stands for /r/. This is the letter u. It stands for /u/. This is the letter g. It stands for /g/. Let's blend all four sounds: /shruuug/. The word is* shrug.

Continue by modeling the words *split, throb, strike, sprung,* and *scrub.*

❷ **Guided Practice/Practice** Repeat the routine with *scrap, spring, string, stress, throne, splint, shrimp, shrink.*

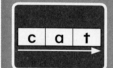

**Go Digital**

**Phonemic Awareness**

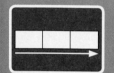

**Phonics**

**Structural Analysis**

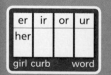

**Spelling Word Sort**

# Structural Analysis

## Compound Words

**❶ Model** Write the word *backbone* and read it aloud. Tell children that *backbone* is a compound word. Remind children that compound words are made of two shorter words. Draw a line between *back* and *bone*. Have children read the two shorter words and then put the words together to say *backbone*. Explain that children can read and figure out the meaning of a compound word by identifying each smaller word.

**❷ Guided Practice/Practice** Write the words *sandbox*, *bathtub*, and *cupcake*. Have children identify the smaller words in each compound. Then help children blend the words. Have children use the smaller words to figure out the meaning of the compound words.

# Spelling

## Word Sort with Three-Letter Blends

**❶ Model** Make index cards for *scr*, *spr*, *str*, *thr*, *spl*, and *shr* and place them in columns in a pocket chart. Blend the sounds with children.

Hold up the Spelling Word Card *scratch*. Say and spell it. Pronounce each sound clearly: /s/ /k/ /r/ /a/ /ch/. Blend the sounds. Repeat this step with *scrape*. Place both words in the *scr* column. Read and spell both spelling words together with children. Ask: *What do you notice about these spelling words?* Guide them to see that both words have the /skr/ sounds at the beginning and begin with the three-letter blend *scr*.

**❷ Guided Practice/Practice** Display the remaining Spelling Word Cards. Read and spell the words with children. Have children decide how to sort each word.

Display the words *catch*, *sting*, *far*, *flower*, and *until* in a separate column. Read and spell the words together with children. Point out that these spelling words do not start with three-letter blends.

Conclude by asking children to orally generate additional words for each three-letter blend. Write the additional words in the correct column. Underline the three-letter blends in the additional words.

---

**PHONICS/SPELLING PRACTICE BOOK** p. 48

| scratch | scrape | spring | throne | stripe |
|---------|--------|--------|--------|--------|
| strange | shred  | shrub  | splash | split  |

**A. Word Sort**
Match the spelling words above with the three-letter blend.

| *scr* | *str* | *spl* |
|-------|-------|-------|
| 1. scratch | 3. stripe | 5. splash |
| 2. scrape | 4. strange | 6. split |

| *shr* | *spr* | *thr* |
|-------|-------|-------|
| 7. shred | 9. spring | 10. throne |
| 8. shrub | | |

**B. Pattern Smart**
Write the spelling words with the same three-letter blend pattern as *string*.

11. stripe  12. strange

Write the spelling words with the same three-letter blend pattern as *shrink*.

13. shred  14. shrub

Write the spelling word with the same three-letter blend pattern as *sprig*.

15. spring

---

**Monitor and *Differentiate***

 **Quick Check**

Can children blend words with three-letter blends *scr, spr, str, thr, spl, shr?*

⬇

**Small Group Instruction**

| If No → | **Approaching** | Reteach pp. T432–T437 |
|---------|-----------------|----------------------|
| | **ELL** | Develop pp. T448–T455 |
| If Yes → | **On Level** | Review pp. T442–T443 |
| | **Beyond Level** | Extend pp. T446–T447 |

 **Fluency**

## Quick Review

**High-Frequency Words** Read, Spell, and Write to review this week's high-frequency words *bird, far, field, flower, grow, leaves, light, orange, ready, until.*

MINILESSON
**5** Mins

# Phrasing

### OBJECTIVES

**CCSS** Read with sufficient accuracy and fluency to support comprehension. **RF.2.4**

**CCSS** Read on-level text orally with accuracy, appropriate rate, and expression on successive readings. **RF.2.4b**

**CCSS** Demonstrate understanding of word relationships and nuances in word meanings. **L.2.5**

**CCSS** Identify real-life connections between words and their use (e.g., describe foods that are *spicy* or *juicy*). **L.2.5a**

---

### ACADEMIC LANGUAGE
*phrasing, punctuation*

**❶ Explain** Tell children that using correct phrasing means grouping words together in a natural way. Tell children that they should pay attention to punctuation marks like commas and periods for clues about where to pause and how to group words into phrases. Explain that children can also use the lines of a poem to group words together.

**❷ Model** Model prosody by reading "Cats and Kittens" on page 167 aloud. Point out how you paused at the end of each line of the poem. Explain that you also paused at the commas and periods and used these punctuation marks to help you group words into phrases. Model reading at an appropriate rate and with accuracy.

**❸ Guided Practice** Have children read the poem on page 167 aloud to a partner. Observe children's ability to read the poem with accuracy and with appropriate phrasing. Offer corrective feedback as needed.

## Fluency Practice

Children can practice fluency using Practice Book passages.

**Go Digital**

peered

**Visual Glossary**

# → Vocabulary

**MINILESSON**
**5 Mins**

## Reinforce Vocabulary

**❶ Guided Practice** Use the Visual Vocabulary Cards to review this week's and last week's vocabulary words. Work together with children to generate a new context sentence for each word.

**❷ Practice** Have children work with a partner to orally complete each sentence stem using this week's and last week's vocabulary words.

1. Lisa writes songs that ____ her feelings. (express)
2. Our dogs ____ very well when friends visit. (behave)
3. The ducks were ____ their wings and quacking. (flapping)
4. The birds at our feeder have colorful ____. (feathers)
5. A dolphin is a kind of ____ that lives in the sea. (mammal)
6. Many ____ look just like their parents. (offspring)
7. Cats ____ themselves to stay clean. (groom)
8. The tree stayed ____ even though it was burned by fire. (alive)
9. We saw an ____ bear and three bear cubs. (adult)
10. The tree was ____ with flowers in the spring. (covered)
11. Jim's puppy has soft and fluffy ____. (fur)
12. There is a ____ shopping mall with lots of stores in the city. (giant)

# Literary Elements

CLOSE READING

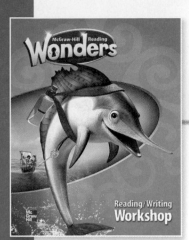

**Reading/Writing Workshop**

 **MINILESSON**

**10 Mins**

# Rhythm

## ① Explain

Explain that when children read poems, they can listen for the rhythm of the words.

→ The rhythm is the pattern of repeating accents in a poem.

→ Children can clap the beats in a poem to identify the rhythm.

→ Finding the rhythm can help readers better understand the ideas in a poem. A poet may use different rhythms in a poem to point out certain words and ideas. The rhythm may also help readers "feel" what is going on in the poem.

## ② Model Close Reading: Text Evidence

Model identifying a poem's rhythm. Reread "Desert Camels," emphasizing the beats in each line. Discuss how the rhythm in this poem can help readers "feel" a camel's bouncy ride. Clap out the beats in lines 1 and 2 to help children identify the rhythm.

## ③ Guided Practice of Close Reading

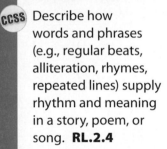

**COLLABORATE**

Have children work in pairs to read aloud and listen for the rhythm in lines 1 and 2 of "Cats and Kittens" on page 167. Have children clap the beats and discuss the rhythm. Compare its rhythm to that of "Desert Camels." Ask: *Is the rhythm the same or different in the two poems? Explain.*

**OBJECTIVES**

**CCSS** Describe how words and phrases (e.g., regular beats, alliteration, rhymes, repeated lines) supply rhythm and meaning in a story, poem, or song. **RL.2.4**

Identify rhythm in poems.

**ACADEMIC LANGUAGE**
*rhythm*

# Go Digital

**Present the Lesson**

**Literary Elements**

# Rhythm

Poems have rhythm. Rhythm is the repeating accents in a poem. You can clap the rhythm, or beats, in a poem.

### Find Text Evidence

*Reread "Desert Camels," and listen to the rhythm. Listen to the beats in each line. Think about why the poet uses rhythm.*

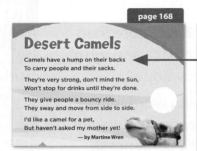

page 168

**Desert Camels**

Camels have a hump on their backs
To carry people and their sacks.

They're very strong, don't mind the Sun,
Won't stop for drinks until they're done.

They give people a bouncy ride.
They sway and move from side to side.

I'd like a camel for a pet,
But haven't asked my mother yet!
— by Martine Wren

*I clap the beats in the first line. There are eight beats. There are also eight beats in the second line. The beats make the poem fun to read.*

**Your Turn**  COLLABORATE

Clap the first two lines of "Cats and Kittens." Tell if the rhythm is the same as "Desert Camels" or different.

172

Tom Schwabel/Flickr/Getty Images

**READING/WRITING WORKSHOP, p. 172**

## A C T Access Complex Text

▶ **Genre**

If children have trouble understanding rhythm, use simple rhyming poems to point out the pattern of beats. Use simple rhymes, such as "One, two/Buckle my shoe/Three, four/Shut the door. Then clap out the rhythm of lines 1 and 2 of "Cats and Kittens." Ask: *How many beats did you hear in each line? Why do you think the poet uses this rhythm?* (There are eight beats in each line. The poet uses rhythm to make the poem fun to read. The poet may also be trying to imitate the way that cats or kittens move.)

---

**ON-LEVEL PRACTICE BOOK** p. 98

**The Robin**

A robin gathers twigs and fluff,
And sticks and string and other stuff.
She chooses things she likes the best,
And weaves them in to build her nest.

**Answer the questions about the text.**

1. How do you know this text is a poem?
   It has rhythm and rhyming words.

2. How many beats do you hear in each line?
   I hear eight beats in each line.

3. Why do you think the poet uses rhythm?
   Possible response: to emphasize the things the robin uses to build
   her nest.

| APPROACHING p. 98 | BEYOND p. 98 | ELL p. 98 |
|---|---|---|

## Monitor and *Differentiate*

### ✓ Quick Check

**Can children identify rhythm in a poem? Can they clap the beats in a line of poetry?**

⬇

### Small Group Instruction

| If No → | **Approaching** | Reteach pp. T430–T431 |
|---|---|---|
| | **ELL** | Develop pp. T448–T451 |
| If Yes → | **On Level** | Review pp. T440–T441 |
| | **Beyond Level** | Extend pp. T444–T445 |

# Vocabulary Strategy

CLOSE READING

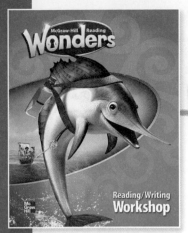
---

**MINILESSON 10 Mins**

## Multiple-Meaning Words

**OBJECTIVES**

CCSS Use sentence-level context as a clue to the meaning of a word or phrase. **L.2.4a**

CCSS Use glossaries and beginning dictionaries, both print and digital, to determine or clarify the meaning of words and phrases. **L.2.4e**

**ACADEMIC LANGUAGE**
*multiple-meaning word, context clues*

### ❶ Explain

Explain that some words are spelled the same but have more than one meaning. For example, *flap* can mean "to shake back and forth" or "piece of paper that covers the opening on an envelope."

→ To find out which meaning of a multiple-meaning word is in a sentence, children should read the whole sentence and look for **context clues**, or clues in the sentence or nearby sentences.

→ Children can also think about how the word is used. For example, is the multiple-meaning word used as a verb or a noun?

→ Children should think about which meaning makes sense in the sentence.

### ❷ Model Close Reading: Text Evidence

Model using context clues to find the meaning of *bat* in the first line of "A Bat Is Not a Bird" on page 169. Have children confirm that the meaning makes sense in the sentence.

### ❸ Guided Practice of Close Reading

COLLABORATE

Have children work in pairs to use context clues to figure out the correct meanings of the multiple-meaning word *flies* in "A Bat Is Not a Bird" and *pet* in "Desert Camels."

---

**Use Reference Sources**

**Dictionary** Explain that children can use a dictionary to help them find the meaning of a multiple-meaning word. Children can look up the word in the dictionary, read each definition, and decide which meaning best fits the sentence.

Review how to use alphabetical order to find words, and how to read a dictionary entry. Then have children use the dictionary to find the meaning of *express* in the first line of "Cats and Kittens."

---

# Go Digital

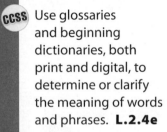

**Present the Lesson**

---

**SKILLS TRACE**

**Multiple-Meaning Words**

**INTRODUCE** Unit 2 Week 4

**REVIEW** Unit 2 Week 5; Unit 4 Weeks 3, 5; Unit 5 Week 5

**ASSESS** Units 2, 5

---

## Vocabulary Strategy CCSS

# Multiple-Meaning Words

Multiple-meaning words are words that are spelled the same but have more than one meaning. You can use context clues to help you understand the correct meaning.

 **Find Text Evidence**

In "A Bat Is Not a Bird," I see the word bat. I know a bat is an animal and also something you use to play baseball. The words "feathers" and "beak" tell me the author is talking about an animal.

 page 169

A **bat** has neither feathers nor beak.

 **Your Turn** COLLABORATE

Reread the poems "A Bat Is Not a Bird" and "Desert Camels." Use context clues to decide on the meaning of these words:

**flies,** *"A Bat Is Not a Bird"*
**pet,** *"Desert Camels"*

173

Photri Images/Alamy

**READING/WRITING WORKSHOP, p. 173**

**Multiple-meaning words** have more than one meaning. Use other words in the sentence to figure out which meaning is being used.

**Read the lines from the poem. Circle the meaning of the word in bold print.**

1. You'll never find a tortoise at sea,
   It lives on **land**—that's where it should be.
   (the ground)      to come down from above

2. A tortoise wears a hard outer shell,
   That always works to serve it **well**.
   (in a good way)      a hole in the ground that stores water

3. It has four stumpy legs and four tortoise **feet**.
   measurements of 12 inches      (parts of the body)

4. When a tortoise doesn't know where to hide,
   It just pulls its head and four **limbs** inside.
   tree branches      (legs)

5. For a tortoise is a marvel of the animal **pack**,
   It carries its home right on its back.
   to put things in a suitcase      (a group of animals)

| APPROACHING p. 99 | BEYOND p. 99 | ELL p. 99 |
|---|---|---|

## ENGLISH LANGUAGE LEARNERS
**ELL SCAFFOLD**

| **Beginning** | **Intermediate** | **Advanced/High** |
|---|---|---|
| Read aloud this line in "Desert Camels": *I'd like a camel for a pet.* Say: *The word* pet *can mean "animal friend." It can also mean "to pat an animal." Which meaning makes sense in the poem?* Repeat this process for *flies* in "A Bat Is Not a Bird." Use illustrations and pantomime petting and flying to support children's understanding. | Have children find the word *pet* in "Desert Camels" and *flies* in "A Bat Is Not a Bird." Ask partners to write two meanings for each word. Use illustrations or gestures for support if necessary. Have partners decide which meaning makes sense in each poem. Elicit from children what context clues helped them figure out the correct meaning. | Have children find the word *pet* in "Desert Camels" and *flies* in "A Bat Is Not a Bird." Ask partners to discuss the different meanings of each word. Then have them explain which meaning makes sense in the poems. Have students explain how they know which meaning is correct and identify the context clues they used. |

## Monitor and *Differentiate*

 **Quick Check**

Can children identify the correct meanings of the multiple-meaning words *pet* and *flies*?

### Small Group Instruction

| | | |
|---|---|---|
| If No → | **Approaching** | Reteach pp. T430–T439 |
| | **ELL** | Develop pp. T452–T453 |
| If Yes → | **On Level** | Review pp. T442–T443 |
| | **Beyond Level** | Extend pp. T446–T447 |

CCSS **Genre · Poetry**

# Beetles
by Monica Shannon

**1** Beetles must use polish,
They look so new and shiny,
Just like a freshly painted car,
Except for being tiny. **2**

**3**

207

**LITERATURE ANTHOLOGY, pp. 206–207**

**Essential Question**
**What do we love about animals?**
Read poems that **express** what
we love about animals.

**Go Digital!**

# Develop Comprehension · CLOSE READING

## Read Literature Anthology

**Literature Anthology**

**Review Genre: Poetry** Review with children the key characteristics of rhyming poems:

→ Include words that rhyme, or end with the same sounds.

→ Tell the poet's thoughts or feelings.

→ May have rhythm and include images.

### ESSENTIAL QUESTION

Read the Essential Question: *What do we love about animals?* Tell children that as they read they should think about what each poet expresses about animals.

*Analytical Writing* **Note Taking: Graphic Organizer**
As children read the selection, guide them to fill in **Your Turn Practice Book page 96.**

### ❶ Skill: Key Details

Let's read "Beetles" and look at the illustrations on pages 206–207. What key details do we learn about beetles from the poem and illustrations? Let's write this information in a Key Details graphic organizer.

### ❷ Genre: Rhyming Poem

A rhyming poem uses words that rhyme. Words that rhyme end with the same sounds. Which two words in this poem rhyme? *(shiny, tiny)*

**T413A** UNIT 2 WEEK 5

## The Little Turtle
### by Vachel Lindsay

**4** There was a little turtle.
He lived in a box.
He swam in a puddle.
He climbed on the rocks.

**5** He snapped at a mosquito.
He snapped at a flea.
He snapped at a minnow.
And he snapped at me.

He caught the mosquito.
He caught the flea.
He caught the minnow.
But he didn't catch me.

208

**LITERATURE ANTHOLOGY, p. 208**

---

### ❸ Author's Craft: Word Choice

Poets choose their words carefully to help readers create pictures in their minds. Even though this poem is short, we can form a clear picture of what a beetle is like. Why does the poet say that beetles must use polish? *(because they look so shiny and new)* What does the poet compare a beetle to? *(a car)* How are a freshly painted car and a beetle alike? *(Both are bright and shiny.)*

### ❹ Strategy: Reread

Remind children to reread when they come across unfamiliar words, such as *puddle* or *climbed*.

### ❺ Literary Element: Rhythm

Remind children that rhythm is the pattern of repeating accents or beats in a poem. Reread lines 5 through 8 aloud with a partner. Then read the lines again and clap the beats. Ask: *How many beats do you hear in each line?* (7, 5, 6, 5) Say: *The poet repeats some words in each of these lines to help create rhythm. With your partner, find the words that repeat.* (He snapped.)

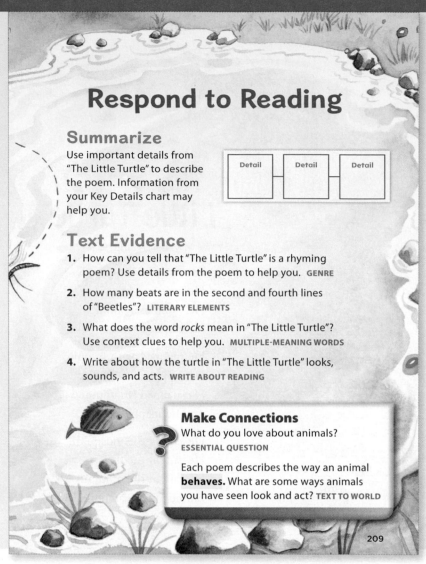

# Respond to Reading

## Summarize

Use important details from "The Little Turtle" to describe the poem. Information from your Key Details chart may help you.

| Detail | Detail | Detail |
|--------|--------|--------|
|        |        |        |

## Text Evidence

1. How can you tell that "The Little Turtle" is a rhyming poem? Use details from the poem to help you. GENRE

2. How many beats are in the second and fourth lines of "Beetles"? LITERARY ELEMENTS

3. What does the word *rocks* mean in "The Little Turtle"? Use context clues to help you. MULTIPLE-MEANING WORDS

4. Write about how the turtle in "The Little Turtle" looks, sounds, and acts. WRITE ABOUT READING

**Make Connections**
What do you love about animals?
ESSENTIAL QUESTION

Each poem describes the way an animal **behaves.** What are some ways animals you have seen look and act? TEXT TO WORLD

209

**LITERATURE ANTHOLOGY, p. 209**

# Develop Comprehension CLOSE READING

## A C T  Access Complex Text

### ▶ Purpose of the Text

The purpose of these poems is to entertain while presenting ideas and images that describe animals. Children may need help finding the playfulness and humor in "The Little Turtle." Guide them to identify the repeating words and ideas in lines 5 through 8 and lines 9 through 12. Ask them what happens in line 12 and how it is different from what happens to the mosquito, flea, and minnow.

## Skill: Key Details

Ask, *What key details did you read about the turtle?* Work with children to complete a Key Details graphic organizer for the poem.

| Detail | Detail | Detail |
|--------|--------|--------|
| The little turtle lives in a box. | The turtle swims in a puddle and climbs on rocks. | The turtle snaps at and eats a mosquito, flea, and minnow. |

# Respond to Reading

## Summarize

Guide children through steps to summarize. Explain that summarizing the ideas in the poem can help children better understand it.

→ First, think about the important parts of the poem.

→ Next, find the key details you read about the turtle.

→ Then, use your own words to retell the most important parts.

## Text Evidence

Guide children to use text evidence to answer the Text Evidence questions on Literature Anthology page 209. Model answering the questions as needed.

1. **Genre** This question asks how we know that the selection is a rhyming poem. The text is written in lines. Some of the words at the end of the lines rhyme, or end with the same sound. For example, *box* and *rocks* rhyme. So do *flea* and *me*. The text also uses rhythm to tell the writer's thoughts about a turtle. All these things are clues that "The Little Turtle" is a rhyming poem.

2. **Literary Elements** Rhythm is the pattern of beats in a poem. Read aloud lines 2 and 4 and clap out the number of beats you hear. There are seven beats in lines 2 and 4.

3. **Multiple-Meaning Words** To figure out the meaning of *rocks* on page 208, we can look for context clues. I know that *rocks* can mean "stones that make up Earth's surface" or "to move gently from side to side." The poem says the turtle climbed on rocks, so I can tell that *rocks* means "stones" here.

4. **Write About Reading** Remind children to look for key details about what the turtle does in the poem. The turtle makes a snapping sound when it snaps at a mosquito, flea, and minnow. Although the turtle is little, it is brave to snap at "me."

## Make Connections

**ESSENTIAL QUESTION**

Have partners discuss an animal they love and list reasons why they love it. Invite pairs to share their ideas with the class.

**Text-to-World** Have children choose an animal they have seen and explain how it looks and acts.

# → Language Arts

**MINILESSON**
**5 Mins**

# Writing Traits: Word Choice

## Discuss Precise Words

**Review** Invite children to recall that writers use precise words to tell exactly what they mean and to form a clear picture in readers' minds.

**Share** Ask a volunteer to share his or her revised writing from Day 2. Have the class listen for precise words in the volunteer's poem. Invite the volunteer to identify his or her favorite precise word and explain why he or she chose it.

### WRITING ENTRY: PRECISE WORDS

❶ **Prewrite** Ask children to choose a new topic for writing by searching their Writer's Notebook for ideas for a poem. Or, provide a prompt such as the following one:
Write a poem about an animal that you think is funny. Tell how the animal looks and acts. Use precise words in your poem.

❷ **Draft** Once children have chosen their topic, ask them to use a word web to generate details and precise words to describe the animal in their poems. Encourage children to refer to their webs as they write their drafts.

## OBJECTIVES

**CCSS** Demonstrate understanding of word relationships and nuances in word meanings. **L.2.5**

**CCSS** Demonstrate command of the conventions of standard English grammar and usage when writing or speaking. **L.2.1**

**CCSS** Demonstrate command of the conventions of standard English capitalization, punctuation, and spelling when writing. **L.2.2**

**CCSS** Use an apostrophe to form contractions and frequently occurring possessives. **L.2.2c**

## ACADEMIC LANGUAGE

*apostrophe, possessive noun*

## Go Digital

**Present the Lesson**

**Writing**

**Graphic Organizer**

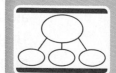

I see a fish.

**Grammar**

# Grammar

## Possessive Nouns

**Review** Remind children that a possessive noun shows who or what owns something. To make a singular noun possessive, we add an apostrophe and an -s to the end of the noun. To make a plural noun possessive, we add an apostrophe after the final s. To make a plural noun that does not end in -s possessive, we add an apostrophe and an -s at the end. Write these examples on the board and review the rules for forming the possessive nouns.

*Grace's goat      ducks' feathers      children's pets*

**Practice** Display the following sentences. Have partners write the correct possessive form of the noun in parentheses.

The cat played with my (sister) ball. (sister's)

The two (boys) dogs chased each other. (boys')

We cleaned the (mice) cages. (mice's)

## Mechanics: Apostrophes with Possessive Nouns

**Review** Remind children that a singular possessive noun has an apostrophe and an -s at the end. A plural possessive noun has an apostrophe after the final s. A plural possessive noun that does not end in -s has an apostrophe and an -s at the end.

**Practice** Write the following sentences on the board. Have children circle the correct form of the possessive noun in parentheses.

A (cat's / cats') whiskers help it feel its way around. (cat's)

The (cubs / cubs') mother watched them closely. (cubs')

The (women / women's) cats jumped up on the sofa. (women's)

## Talk About It

**Share and Compare** Have children create sentences with possessive nouns that tell something about the animals they read about this week. Have children then share their sentences with a partner. Partners point out the possessive nouns in the sentences.

## ELL

### ENGLISH LANGUAGE LEARNERS

**Possessive Nouns** Display pages 166–167 of the Reading/ Writing Workshop. Point to the gray cat and say: *The cat's toy is a mouse.* Write the sentence on the board. *How many cats have the toy?* Underline *cat's* and explain that it is a singular possessive noun. The apostrophe and *s* at the end mean that one cat has the toy.

Gesture to both cats in the picture and say: *Both cats' fur is soft.* Write the sentence on the board. Ask: *How many cats have soft fur?* Underline *cats'* and explain that it is a plural possessive noun. The apostrophe at the end means that more than one cat has fur that is soft.

# Daily Wrap Up

→ Review the Essential Question and encourage children to discuss it using the oral vocabulary words.

→ Prompt children to review and discuss the skills they used today. Help them give examples of how they used each skill.

## Materials

**Literature Anthology**

a b c
**Word-Building Cards**

orange
**High-Frequency Word Cards**

scratch
**Spelling Word Cards**

Dinah Zike's
**FOLDABLES**
rhyme, rhythm | images, rhymes
**Dinah Zike's Foldables**

→ # Extend the Concept

MINILESSON
**5** Mins

# Oral Language

## OBJECTIVES

**CCSS** Participate in collaborative conversations with diverse partners about *grade 2 topics and texts* with peers and adults in small and larger groups. **SL.2.1**

**CCSS** Know and apply grade-level phonics and word analysis skills in decoding words. **RF.2.3**

**CCSS** Use knowledge of the meaning of individual words to predict the meaning of compound words (e.g., *birdhouse, lighthouse, housefly; bookshelf, notebook, bookmark*). **L.2.4.d**

**ESSENTIAL QUESTION**

Remind children that this week they have been reading poems that describe what people love about animals. Guide children to discuss the question using information from what they have read and discussed.

Use the Define/Example/Ask routine to review the oral vocabulary words *alarm, howling, problem, knobby,* and *munch.*

**Talk About Animal Poems** Have partners discuss the animal poems they have read this week. Ask: *Which poem did you enjoy the most? What did you enjoy about it? What do you like about the animal in the poem?*

Review last week's oral vocabulary words *provide, protect, guide, separate* and *leader* using the Define/Example/Ask routine.

## Go Digital

**Phonemic Awareness**

m a
n t p
**Phonics**

I __ the jar.
fill | fills | filling
**Structural Analysis**

# → Word Work

**MINILESSON 5 Mins**

# Phonemic Awareness

## Phoneme Substitution

**1 Model** Say: *Listen as I say a word:* stretch. *Now listen as I change the last sound in* stretch, /ch/, *to* /s/. *The new word is* stress.

**2 Guided Practice/Practice** Have children practice substituting final phonemes in these words. Do the first one together.

| | |
|---|---|
| scrap/scratch | shrub/shrug |
| strung/struck | thread/threat |

**MINILESSON 5 Mins**

# Phonics

## Build Words with Three-Letter Blends

**Review** Review that the letters *s, p, l* can be blended together and stand for the sounds /spl/. Repeat for *scr, spr, str, thr,* and *shr.*

Use Word-Building Cards *s p l, a, s, h. Let's blend the sounds and read the word:* /splaaash/, splash. *Now change the* sh *to* t. *Blend the sounds and read the word.*

Continue with *split, splint, sprint, spring, string, strike, shrink, shrill, thrill, throne, throb.*

**MINILESSON 5 Mins**

# Structural Analysis

## Compound Words

**Review** Write *sunshine* on the board and read it aloud. Point out that the compound word *sunshine* is made of the smaller words *sun* and *shine.* Explain that children can use what they know about the smaller words to read and figure out the meaning of the compound word.

**Practice** Write the following words: *sunglasses, pigpen, flagpole.* Have children work in pairs to identify the two shorter words in each compound. Then have them write sentences with each word.

## Quick Review

**Build Fluency: Sound-Spellings** Display the **Word-Building Cards** *scr, spr, str, thr, spl, shr, ch, th, sh, wh, tch, ph, ng, o_e, o, u_e, u, i_e, i, a_e, a.* Have children say each sound. Repeat, and vary the pace. For fluency in connected text, see the Decodable Reader lesson in Small Group.

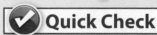

## Monitor and *Differentiate*

### ✓ Quick Check

**Can children read and decode words with three-letter blends** *scr, spr, str, thr, spl, shr*?

⬇

### Small Group Instruction

If No → **Approaching** Reteach pp. T432–T437

**ELL** Develop pp. T448–T455

If Yes → **On Level** Review pp. T442–T443

**Beyond Level** Extend pp. T446–T447

 → **Word Work**

### Quick Review

**High-Frequency Words:** Read, Spell, and Write to review this week's high-frequency words: *bird, far, field, flower, grow, leaves, light, orange, ready, until.*

---

**MINILESSON 5 Mins**

# Spelling

### Word Sort with Three-Letter Blends *scr, spr, str, thr, spl, shr*

**Review** Provide pairs of children with copies of the Spelling Word Cards. As one partner reads the words one word at a time, the other partner should orally segment the word and then write the word. After reading all the words, partners should switch roles.

**Practice** Have children correct their own papers. Then have them sort the words by initial three-letter blends *scr, spr, str, thr, spl, shr*, and words without these blends.

**MINILESSON 5 Mins**

# High-Frequency Words

### *bird, far, field, flower, grow, leaves, light, orange, ready, until*

**Review** Display High-Frequency Word Cards *bird, far, field, flower, grow, leaves, light, orange, ready,* and *until.* Have children Read/Spell/Write each word.

→ Point to a word and call on a child to use it in a sentence.

→ Review last week's words using the same procedure.

## OBJECTIVES

**CCSS** Know and apply grade-level phonics and word analysis skills in decoding words. **RF.2.3**

**CCSS** Recognize and read grade-appropriate irregularly spelled words. **RF.2.3f**

**CCSS** Read with sufficient accuracy and fluency to support comprehension. **RF.2.4**

**CCSS** Determine or clarify the meaning of unknown and multiple-meaning words and phrases based on *grade 2 reading and content,* choosing flexibly from an array of strategies. **L.2.4**

**CCSS** Use a known root word as a clue to the meaning of an unknown word with the same root (e.g., *addition, additional*). **L.2.4c**

## ACADEMIC LANGUAGE
*phrasing, root word*

### Go Digital

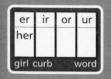

**Spelling Word Sort**

**High-Frequency Word Routine**

# Fluency/Vocabulary Strategy

## Phrasing

**Review** Remind children that correct phrasing means grouping words together naturally as they read. Explain that children can use punctuation to help them read with correct phrasing. Point out that commas tell readers where to make a short pause. Periods, question marks, and exclamation points can be used to group the words in a sentence. Explain that correct phrasing can help children understand words and ideas that go together.

**Practice** Have children read one of the poems from the Shared Read aloud to a partner. Remind them to pause at the end of each line and to use punctuation to group words together. Observe their ability to read with appropriate phrasing. Offer corrective feedback as needed.

### Fluency Practice

Children can practice fluency using Practice Book passages.

## Root Words

❶ **Explain/Model** Remind children that a root word is the basic form of a word to which a prefix, suffix, or ending has been added. Explain that when children see an unfamiliar word, they can figure out the meaning by looking for a root word that they know.

Write these examples on the board: *thankful, flapping, unlock*. Model separating the root from the ending, suffix, or prefix. Underline the root of each word and explain how children can use the root to figure out the meaning of the longer word.

❷ **Guided Practice** Write lines three and four of "Beetles" on the board: "Just like a freshly painted car, / Except for being tiny." Have children work with a partner to identify the root words in *freshly*, *painted*, and *being*. Ask children to explain the words' meanings by using what they know about the root words.

## Monitor and *Differentiate*

### ✔ Quick Check

Can children recognize and read high-frequency words?

Can children read fluently with proper phrasing?

### Small Group Instruction

If No → **Approaching** Reteach pp. T430–T439

**ELL** Develop pp. T448–T455

If Yes → **On Level** Review pp. T440–T443

**Beyond Level** Extend pp. T444–T447

# Develop Comprehension

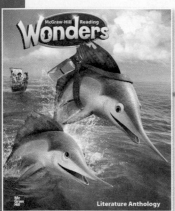

**Literature Anthology**

MINILESSON
**5** Mins

## Read Literature Anthology

### Compare Texts

*Analytical Writing*

Review with children what they read about the animals in "Beetles" and "The Little Turtle." Guide them to describe what the animals were like. Explain that now they will read a poem about another animal, a mother goose. Tell children that as they read they should think about how the poems and the animals they describe are alike and different. Have them **take notes**.

### ❶ Ask and Answer Questions

This is a rhyming poem. Reread the first three lines. What words rhyme? (tizzy, dizzy) Find another example of words that rhyme in the poem. (Possible responses: muddle/puddles; slapping/flapping/napping)

### ❷ Ask and Answer Questions

A poem's rhythm is the pattern of accented beats. This poet uses rhythm to help you understand how worried the mother goose is and how she rushes around looking for her baby gosling. Let's clap the beats in lines 5, 6, and 7. How many beats do you hear? (6, 4, 4)

## AUTHOR'S CRAFT

**Sound Words**

Authors choose words to help readers create a clear picture in their minds.

→ In "Gray Goose," the author chooses words that evoke sounds and help capture the feeling of the poem. Point out how the repeated words *honk-honk-honking* capture the sound of a goose and help readers understand the goose's frantic behavior.

→ Have children find other words that help them hear and imagine what's happening in the poem, such as *webbed feet slapping, splashing through puddles, wings flapping,* and *Ah.*

## OBJECTIVES

**CCSS** Ask and answer such questions as *who, what, where, when, why,* and *how* to demonstrate understanding of key details in a text. **RL.2.1**

**CCSS** Describe how words and phrases (e.g., regular beats, alliteration, rhymes, repeated lines) supply rhythm and meaning in a story, poem, or song. **RL.2.4**

## ACADEMIC LANGUAGE
*rhyme, rhythm*

## Go Digital

**Beetles and The Little Turtle**

# Gray Goose

### by Julie Larios

Gray mama goose
in a tizzy,
**1** honk-honk-honking herself dizzy,
can't find her gosling,
she's honking and running,
**2** webbed feet slapping,
all wild waddle,
her **feathers** a muddle,
splashing through puddles,
wings **flapping**. . . .

Ah,
there's her gold baby,
**3** all fuzz,
napping.

**Make Connections**
What do you love about this goose and her baby? ESSENTIAL QUESTION

What did the poems you have read this week **express** about how animals **behave**? TEXT TO TEXT

210

211

**LITERATURE ANTHOLOGY, pp. 210–211**

## ❸ Ask and Answer Questions

The first part of the poem tells about what the mother goose is like when she is trying to find her gosling. Let's reread the last four lines of the poem to find out what happens. What is the baby like? (gold and fuzzy) How is the gosling acting differently from its mother? (It's napping while its mother is running around in a tizzy.)

## Make Connections • *Analytical Writing*

COLLABORATE Have partners make connections between how animals act in "Beetles," "The Little Turtle," and "Gray Goose."

### **A C T** **A**ccess **C**omplex **T**ext

#### ▶ Specific Vocabulary

Authors of poems use language evoke a feeling or even an action in a poem. Tell children that this poem contains words that may be new to them. Talk about the words *tizzy, waddle, muddle.* Tell children that they can use context clues to figure out the meanings of these words.

# Language Arts

### MINILESSON 5 Mins

# Writing Traits: Word Choice

## OBJECTIVES

**CCSS** With guidance and support from adults and peers, focus on a topic and strengthen writing as needed by revising and editing. **W.2.5**

**CCSS** With guidance and support from adults, use a variety of digital tools to produce and publish writing, including in collaboration with peers. **W.2.6**

**CCSS** Demonstrate command of the conventions of standard English grammar and usage when writing or speaking. **L.2.1**

**CCSS** Demonstrate command of the conventions of standard English capitalization, punctuation, and spelling when writing. **L.2.2**

**CCSS** Use an apostrophe to form contractions and frequently occurring possessives. **L.2.2c**

**Revise** Have children revise their draft from Day 3 by replacing general words with more precise ones or by adding precise words. Provide help with using digital resources.

As children revise their drafts, hold teacher conferences with individuals. You may also want to have partners conduct peer conferences.

**Edit** Model using proofreading marks to edit. Then have children use proofreading marks to correct errors in their writing.

Invite children to review Grammar Handbook page 480 and check that they have used possessive nouns correctly.

Encourage children to proofread for other errors, including correct placement of apostrophes with possessive nouns and spelling.

## Conference Routines

### Teacher Conference

**Step 1:** Talk about the strengths of the writing. *I like how you've used your voice in the poem. I can understand how you feel about this animal.*

**Step 2:** Focus on the target trait. *This is a precise word that helps me understand exactly how this animal acts.*

**Step 3:** Make concrete suggestions for revisions, such as those below, and then meet again to review progress.

## Suggested Revisions

**Focus on a Sentence** Read the draft and target one sentence or line of the poem for revision. *This word is very general. Rewrite this line of your poem to replace _____ with a precise word.*

**Focus on a Section** Underline a section that needs revision. Provide specific suggestions. *It's hard to picture what you mean in this part. Add precise words to help readers understand _____.*

**Focus on a Revision Strategy** Underline a section of the writing and ask children to use a specific revision strategy, such as substituting. *Your poem has good ideas about _____, but you can improve it by replacing general words with precise ones that create a clearer picture.*

## Go Digital

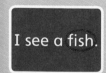

**Writing**

🔳 Make a capital letter.
⋀ Add.
✐ Take out.

**Proofreader's Marks**

I see a fish.

**Grammar**

## Peer Conference

Provide these questions to guide peers as they review a partner's draft.

→ Is the writing clear and easy to understand?

→ Which words create a picture in your mind?

→ What precise words could be added to improve the writing?

# Grammar

MINILESSON
5 Mins

## Possessive Nouns

**Review** Review that a possessive noun shows who or what owns something. To make a singular noun possessive, we add an apostrophe and an *s* to the end of the noun. To make a plural noun possessive, we add an apostrophe and an *-s* after the final *s*. To make a plural noun that does not end in *-s* possessive, we add an apostrophe and an *-s* at the end of the noun.

**Practice** Have partners write sentences with possessive nouns to tell about animals they like. Have children check that they have added an apostrophe and an *s* to the end of singular nouns, an apostrophe to the end of plural nouns ending in *s*, and an apostrophe and an *s* to the end of plural nouns that do not end in *s*.

## Mechanics: Apostrophes with Possessive Nouns

**Review** Remind children how apostrophes are used in possessive nouns: A singular noun ends in an apostrophe and an *s*. A plural noun has an apostrophe after the final *s*. A plural noun that does not end in *s* has an apostrophe and an *s* at the end.

**Practice** Write the following sentences on the board. Have children change the underlined noun in each to a possessive noun.

The two <u>beetles</u> colors were different. (beetles')

A <u>bat</u> wings are leathery. (bat's)

We saw many <u>children</u> pets at the show. (children's)

### Talk about It

**In Your Own Words** Have partners describe features of an animal they've read about in this week's poems, using possessive nouns in their descriptions. Partners should identify the possessive nouns in the descriptions.

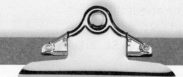

## Daily Wrap Up

→ Review the Essential Question and encourage children to discuss it using the oral vocabulary words.

→ Prompt children to discuss the skills they practiced and learned today. Guide them to share examples of how they used each skill.

→ **Wrap Up the Week**
# Integrate Ideas

☞ **Go** Digital

**www.connected.mcgraw-hill.com**
RESOURCES
Research and Inquiry

## RESEARCH AND INQUIRY

**Animals in Poems**

### OBJECTIVES

 Participate in shared research and writing projects (e.g., read a number of books on a single topic to produce a report; record science observations). **W.2.7**

 Participate in collaborative conversations with diverse partners about *grade 2 topics and texts* with peers and adults in small and larger groups. **SL.2.1**

 Follow agreed-upon rules for discussions (e.g., gaining the floor in respectful ways, listening to others with care, speaking one at a time about the topics and texts under discussion). **SL.2.1a**

## Make a Poetry Anthology

 Tell children that today they will work with a small group to create an anthology, or collection, of their favorite animal poems. They will include facts about each animal.

**STEP 1 Choose a Topic**

Have groups think about animals they would like to find poems about.

**STEP 2 Find Resources**

Guide groups to find poems about animals using the selections, collections of poems, and online poetry resources. They can find facts about animals in books and online. Children can use the Research Process Checklist online.

**STEP 3 Keep Track of Ideas**

Have children make a Three-Pocket Foldable® to store poems and facts about animals.

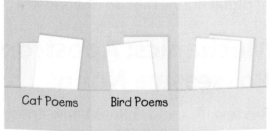

Cat Poems    Bird Poems

Dinah Zike's

### Collaborative Conversations

**Be Open to All Ideas** As children engage in partner, small-group, and whole-group discussions, remind them

→ that all ideas are important and should be heard.

→ to respect the opinions of others.

→ not to be afraid to offer opinions, even if they're different from others' opinions.

**Beetle**

**STEP 4** **Create the Project: Poetry Anthology**

Tell children that they will collect their poems in an anthology. Explain the features of their anthology.

→ The anthology will include poems about animals from different authors. Poems may be photocopies, printouts, or hand-written versions.

→ The poems will have illustrations or photographs showing the animals.

Have group members work together to create their poetry anthology.

→ Guide children to include the title and author's name along with text of the poems.

→ Prompt children to illustrate each poem or to include a photograph of the animal.

→ Guide children to write facts about the animals in each poem and include this information in the anthology.

## ELL ENGLISH LANGUAGE LEARNERS
### SCAFFOLD

| Beginning | Intermediate | Advanced/High |
|---|---|---|
| **Use Sentence Frames** Use sentence frames to help children discuss their poems. For example: *This poem is about _____. The _____ is _____. In the poem, the words _____ and _____ rhyme.* | **Discuss** Guide children to discuss the poems they selected for their anthology. Ask: *What do you like about this poem? How does the poet help you understand the animal? Which words help you picture the animal?* | **Describe** Prompt children to describe why they selected the poems they did. Elicit information about how the poet used rhyme, rhythm, and word choices to make the poem interesting and to help readers imagine the animal. |

## Materials

**Reading/Writing Workshop**

**Literature Anthology**

**Word-Building Cards**

**High-Frequency Word Cards**

Desert Camels | Gray Goose

backs, sacks

Dinah Zike's **FOLDABLES**

## → Integrate Ideas

# TEXT CONNECTIONS  *Analytical Writing*

**Connect to Essential Question**

### OBJECTIVES

 **CCSS** Ask and answer such questions as *who, what, where, when, why,* and *how* to demonstrate understanding of key details in a text. **RL.2.1**

- Develop answers to the Essential Question.
- Make text connections to the world.

### ACADEMIC LANGUAGE

- *compare, evidence, present*
- Cognates: *comparar, presentar*

## Text to Text

**Cite Evidence** Remind children that this week they have been reading poems about animals. Tell them that now they will compare these texts. Model comparing texts using "Desert Camels," **Reading/Writing Workshop** page 168, and "Gray Goose," **Literature Anthology** page 210. Use a Shutter Foldable® to record comparisons.

**Think Aloud** "Desert Camels" and "Gray Goose" are both poems that tell things people love about animals. In "Desert Camels," the poet uses rhythm to help me understand how camels move. In "Gray Goose," the rhythm helps me understand how the mother goose runs around, frantically looking for her baby.

 **Complete the Organizer** Have children use a Shutter Foldable® to record comparisons. Guide them to discuss and write about how the poems show what people love about the animals.

**Present Information** Ask children to present their information to the class. Have children compare information from different groups.

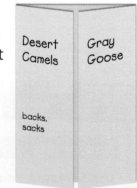

Desert Camels | Gray Goose

backs, sacks

Dinah Zike's **FOLDABLES**

## Text to Self

**Discuss** Have children discuss a pet. Ask: *What do people love about that pet?*

## Text to World

**Discuss** Have children discuss what they have learned about animals. Ask: *What kinds of things do people love most about animals?*

# WRITE ABOUT READING  *Analytical Writing*

### OBJECTIVES

 **CCSS** Draw evidence from literary or informational texts to support analysis, reflection, and research. **W.4.9**

**CCSS** Describe how words and phrases (e.g., regular beats, alliteration, rhymes, repeated lines) supply rhythm and meaning in a story, poem, or song. **RL.2.4**

## Write an Analysis

**Cite Evidence** Using text evidence, children will analyze how the author (or poet) of a poem they have read this week used word choice. Guide children to analyze text evidence in "Cats and Kittens" by asking "how" and "why" questions about word choice, and ask how these word choices help readers understand how the animal looks, sounds, and acts.

→ Why do you think the poet chose the words *hisses*, *purrs*, and *mews* to describe cats and kittens?

→ Which words rhyme in the poem? Why do you think the poet used rhyming words?

→ How does the poet help you understand how cats move in the last two lines of the poem?

> The poet uses the word _____ to show _____.
>
> The words _____ and _____ rhyme. The poet uses rhyme to _____.
>
> The poet helps me understand _____ by using the words _____.

Work with children to complete the sentence frames using evidence from "Cats and Kittens."

Then have children select another poem they have read this week. Have children use the sentence frames to write about how the poet's word choices help them understand the animal in the poem.

**Present Your Ideas** Ask partners to share their paragraphs and discuss how the evidence they cited supports their ideas. Partners may suggest additional text evidence if necessary.

# RESEARCH AND INQUIRY

### OBJECTIVES

 **CCSS** Participate in shared research and writing projects (e.g., read a number of books on a single topic to produce a report; record science observations). **W.2.7**

## Wrap Up the Project

Guide children to share the poems and animal facts they included in their anthologies. Prior to the presentations, review the Presenting and Listening checklists online with children.

 → **Word Work**

## Phonemic Awareness

**OBJECTIVES**

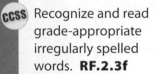 Know and apply
grade-level phonics
and word analysis
skills in decoding
words. **RF.2.3**

 Recognize and read
grade-appropriate
irregularly spelled
words. **RF.2.3f**

**CCSS** Use knowledge
of the meaning of
individual words to
predict the meaning
of compound words
(e.g., *birdhouse,
lighthouse, housefly;
bookshelf, notebook,
bookmark*). **L.2.4.d**

• Blend phonemes to
form new words.

• Decode words
with three-letter
consonant blends.

### Phoneme Blending

**Review** Guide children to blend phonemes to form words. *Listen as I
say a group of sounds. Then blend those sounds to form a word.*

/th/ /r/ /e/ /d/      /s/ /p/ /r/ /ou/ /t/      /s/ /t/ /r/ /ē/ /k/

/s/ /k/ /r/ /ē/ /m/      /s/ /p/ /l/ /i/ /t/      /sh/ /r/ /i/ /n/ /k/

## Phonics

### Blend and Build with Three-Letter Blends *scr, spr, str, thr, spl, shr*

**Review** Have children read and say the words *scrape, stripe, thrill,
splash, shred,* and *sprint.* Then have them follow the word building
routine with Word-Building Cards to build *spring, string, shrink, shrunk,
shrug, shrub, scrub, scrap, scratch, stretch, stress.*

**Word Automaticity** Help children practice word automaticity. Display
decodable words and point to each word as children chorally read it.
Test how many words children can read in one minute. Model blending
words children miss.

## Structural Analysis

### Compound Words

**Review** Have children explain what a compound word is. Then have
children practice reading and figuring out the meaning of compound
words such as *notepad, rosebud, hatbox, suntan, padlock,* and *bedtime.*

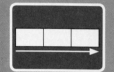

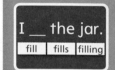

# Spelling

## Word Sort with Three-Letter Blends *scr, spr, str, thr, spl, shr*

**Review** Have children use the Spelling Word Cards to sort the weekly words by three-letter blend. Remind children that five of the words do not begin with a three-letter blend.

**Assess** Assess children on their ability to spell words with three-letter blends *scr, spr, str, thr, spl,* and *shr*. Say each word and provide a sentence so that children can hear the words used in a correct context. Then allow them time to write the words. In order to challenge children, you may wish to provide an additional word for each three-letter blend in order to assess whether they understand the concept.

# High-Frequency Words

## *orange, flower, far, leaves, light, grow, ready, field, bird, until*

**Review** Display High-Frequency Word Cards *orange, flower, far, leaves, light, grow, ready, field, bird, until*. Have children Read/Spell/Write each word. Have them write a sentence with each word.

# Vocabulary Words

## *behave, express, feathers, flapping*

**Review** Display Visual Vocabulary Cards for *behave, express, feathers, flapping*. Provide a clue for each word and have children name it.

---

## Monitor and *Differentiate*

 **Quick Check**

Can children read and decode words with 3-letter blends *scr, spr, str, thr, spl,* and *shr*?

Can children recognize and read high-frequency words?

### Small Group Instruction

If No → **Approaching** Reteach pp. T434–T437

**ELL** Develop pp. T448–T455

If Yes → **On Level** Review pp. T442–T443

**Beyond Level** Extend pp. T446–T447

→ # Language Arts

**MINILESSON 5 Mins**

# Writing Traits: Word Choice

## Share and Reflect

**Discuss** Discuss with the class what they learned about using precise words in their writing. Guide them to recall that precise words are exact, rather than general, and help readers form clear pictures in their mind.

**Present** Invite volunteers to choose a writing entry from the week to share with the class. Compare the volunteer's draft with his or her revised poem. Encourage the group to identify precise words the volunteer added. Have children discuss the poem by focusing on how precise words helped them understand exactly what the writer meant and created a clear picture in their mind.

**Reflect** Have children use their Writer's Notebook to reflect on their progress as writers. Invite them to consider the following prompts as they write:

*How did using precise words improve your writing this week?*

*What other topics would you like to write about? What precise words could you use in your writing? Why would you use them?*

**Publish** After children finish presenting their poems, discuss how the class will make a bulletin board of all their poems. Have children suggest how to prepare the bulletin board. Guide them to use digital tools to create the bulletin board. Have them make decisions about the placement and assembly.

### OBJECTIVES

**CCSS** With guidance and support from adults, use a variety of digital tools to produce and publish writing, including in collaboration with peers. **W.2.6**

**CCSS** Demonstrate command of the conventions of standard English grammar and usage when writing or speaking. **L.2.1**

**CCSS** Demonstrate command of the conventions of standard English capitalization, punctuation, and spelling when writing. **L.2.2**

**CCSS** Use an apostrophe to form contractions and frequently occurring possessives. **L.2.2c**

**CCSS** Demonstrate understanding of word relationships and nuances in word meanings. **L.2.5**

### ACADEMIC LANGUAGE

*apostrophe, possessive noun, singular, plural*

**Writing**

**Checklists**

I see a fish.

**Grammar**

# Grammar

## Possessive Nouns

**Review** Review with children that a possessive noun shows who or what owns something. To make a singular noun possessive, we add an apostrophe and an -s to the end of the noun. To make a plural noun possessive, we add an apostrophe after the final s. To make a plural noun that does not end in -s possessive, we add an apostrophe and an -s at the end.

**Practice** Display the following sentences. Have children complete each sentence with a singular or plural possessive noun.

A ____ feathers are colorful. (Possible response: parrot's)

____ ears twitch when they eat. (Possible response: Rabbits')

____ tails are long and thin. (Possible response: Mice's)

## Mechanics: Apostrophes with Possessive Nouns

**Review** Review with children that we add an apostrophe and an s to make a singular noun possessive. We add an apostrophe after the final s to make a plural noun possessive. We add an apostrophe and an s to make a plural noun that does not end in s possessive.

**Practice** Display the following phrases. Have partners read each phrase and then change the underlined noun into a possessive noun. Last, have partners use each phrase in a sentence.

| | |
|---|---|
| a _turtle_ shell | that _bird_ wing |
| those _kittens_ toys | both children pets |

(turtle's; kittens'; bird's; deer's) (Sentences will vary.)

## Reteach

If children have difficulty forming possessive nouns or using apostrophes in possessive nouns, review the use of each. Provide opportunities for children to practice the skills in a small group, with a partner, or independently.

## Talk About It

**Sentence Starters** Have one partner say a singular or plural possessive noun in a phrase. The other partner thinks of a sentence with the possessive noun and says the sentence aloud. Partners then reverse roles.

# Wrap Up the Week

→ Review the Essential Question and encourage children to discuss using the oral vocabulary words.

→ Review the comprehension skill and literary element.

→ Review words with 3-letter blends _scr, spr, str, thr, spl, shr_.

→ Use the High-Frequency Word Cards to review the Words to Know.

→ Review the purposes for writing poetry.

# → Approaching Level

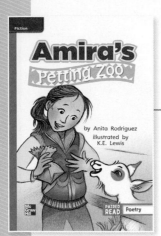

**Lexile** 250
*TextEvaluator* 5

## OBJECTIVES

Describe how words and phrases (e.g., regular beats, alliteration, rhymes, repeated lines) supply rhythm and meaning in a story, poem, or song. **RL.2.4**

Read with sufficient accuracy and fluency to support comprehension. **RF.2.4**

Use context to confirm or self-correct word recognition and understanding, rereading as necessary. **RF.4.4c**

## MATERIALS

Leveled Reader
*Amira's Petting Zoo*

## Leveled Reader:
## *Amira's Petting Zoo*

### Before Reading

#### Preview and Predict

Have children turn to the title page. Read the title and author name and have children repeat. Preview the selection's images. Prompt children to predict what the selection might be about.

#### Review Genre: Fiction

Have children recall that fiction is a made-up story with characters, a setting, and plot. A fiction story has a beginning, middle, and end. A fiction story usually has a problem at the beginning that is resolved by the end of the story.

#### ESSENTIAL QUESTION

Remind children of the Essential Question: *What do we love about animals?* Set a purpose for reading: *Let's read to find out if Amira will have a chance to pet the animals.*

Remind children that as they read a selection, they can ask questions about what they do not understand or want to know more about.

### During Reading

#### Guided Comprehension

As children whisper read *Amira's Petting Zoo*, monitor and provide guidance, correcting blending and modeling the key strategies and skills.

#### Strategy: Reread

Remind children that they can reread details in fiction they did not understand the first time they read. Say: *Rereading can help us learn important details about the characters and plot in a story.* Model using the text on page 5. Say: *What does Amira want to do at the petting zoo? Why is she unable to pet the piglets?*

#### Skill: Key Details

Remind children that key details support the theme or topic of a story. After reading, ask: *What key details helped you understand the problem in the story?* Display a Key Details chart for children to copy.

**Go Digital**

**Leveled Readers**

**Graphic Organizer**

**Retelling Cards**

Model recording children's answers in the clue boxes. Have children record the answers in their own charts.

**Think Aloud** Amira is worried when the line to see the bunnies is too long. She is excited to see the piglets but then learns the pen is closed. These are key details about the topic. Let's add this to the Key Details chart.

Guide children to identify additional key details as they read.

## After Reading

### Respond to Reading

Have children complete Respond to Reading on page 16.

### Retell

Have children take turns retelling the selection using the retelling cards as a guide. Help children make a personal connection by asking: *How would you feel if you couldn't pet animals at the zoo?*

### Model Fluency

Read the sentences one at a time. Have children chorally repeat. Point out how you read with phrasing. Model reading the dialogue on pages 8 and 9 using phrasing.

**Apply** Have children practice reading with partners. Provide feedback as needed.

## PAIRED READ ...

### "Sheep Season"

#### Make Connections:
#### Write About It ✏ *Analytical Writing*

Before reading, ask children to note that the genre of this text is poetry. Then discuss the Compare Texts statement. After reading, ask children to make connections between the animals they read about from "Sheep Season" and *Amira's Petting Zoo.*

**Leveled Reader**

---

### FOCUS ON LITERARY ELEMENTS

Children can extend their knowledge of poetry by completing the literary elements activity on page 20.

---

## Literature Circles

Lead children in conducting a literature circle using the Thinkmark questions to guide the discussion. You may wish to discuss what children have learned about animals from both selections in the leveled reader.

## Level Up

Level-up lessons available online.

**IF** children read the **Approaching Level** fluently and answered the questions

**THEN** pair them with children who have proficiently read the **On Level** and have approaching children

• echo-read the **On Level** main selection.

• identify key details they would like to discuss.

### A C T Access Complex Text

The **On Level** challenges children by including more **specific vocabulary** and **complex sentence structures**.

# → Approaching Level
## Phonemic Awareness

## IDENTIFY AND GENERATE RHYME

**OBJECTIVES**

Demonstrate understanding of spoken words, syllables, and sounds (phonemes). **RF.1.2**

Identify and generate rhyming words.

 **I Do** Explain to children that they will be identifying and producing rhyming words. Say: *Listen as I say two words:* scrap, strap. *The words* scrap *and* strap *end with the same sounds,* /ap/. Scrap *and* strap *rhyme. The word* map *also rhymes with* scrap *and* strap.

 **We Do** Say: *Listen as I say:* thread, spread. *Say them with me.* Thread *and* spread *rhyme. What other word rhymes? Yes,* bread *and* read *rhyme. Listen:* thread, spread, bread, read *all rhyme. Repeat this routine by having children think of words that rhyme with:*

scream, stream      scratch, batch      stretch, fetch      scrunch, lunch

 **You Do** *It's your turn. Repeat the words if they rhyme. Tell another word that rhymes.*

splash, trash      straw, claw      through, change      spring, string

**Repeat** the rhyming routine with additional words.

## PHONEME BLENDING

**OBJECTIVES**

Orally produce single-syllable words by blending sounds (phonemes), including consonant blends. **RF.1.2b**

 **I Do** Say: *Listen as I say five sounds:* /s/ /t/ /r/ /a/ /p/. *Say them with me:* /ssss/ /t/ /rrr/ /aaa/ /p/. *Blend the sounds with me:* /ssstrrraaap/, strap. *The word is* strap.

 **We Do** *Listen as I say four sounds:* /sh/ /rrr/ /eee/ /d/. *Repeat them:* /sh/ /rrr/ /eee/ /d/. *Let's blend the sounds:* /shred/, shred. Repeat the routine with:

stroke      spruce      scrape      shrub      splint      throb

 **You Do** *It's your turn. I want you to blend the sounds I say to form words.*

spring      shrimp      split      scrap      thrill      string

**Repeat** the blending routine with additional words with triple blends.

You may wish to review Phonemic Awareness with **ELL** using this section.

# PHONEME SUBSTITUTION

**OBJECTIVES**

 **CCSS** Demonstrate understanding of spoken words, syllables, and sounds (phonemes). **RF.1.2**

Substitute phonemes to form a new word.

 **I Do** Explain to children that they will be substituting phonemes. Say: *When you substitute a phoneme, you trade one sound for another sound to form a new word.*

*Listen as I say a word:* thread. *What sound do you hear at the beginning of the word* thread? *I hear the sound /th/. If I replace the sound /th/ with /b/ I get the word* bread.

 **We Do** Say: *Listen as I say* chose. *Say it with me:* chose. *The beginning sound in* chose *is /ch/. Let's replace /ch/ in* chose *with /th/. We change the word* chose *to* those.

Repeat this routine with the following pairs of words:

cape, shape    grow, throw    drink, shrink    nerve, serve

**You Do** Say: *It's your turn. Replace the sound at the beginning of each word with a new sound.*

limp, chimp    blame, flame    vine, shine    zone, shone

 **ENGLISH LANGUAGE LEARNERS**

For the ELLs who need **phonics, decoding,** and **fluency** practice, use scaffolding methods as necessary to ensure children understand the meaning of the words. Refer to the Language Transfer Handbook for phonics elements that may not transfer in children's native languages.

# → Approaching Level

## Phonics

**TIER 2**

### CONNECT 3-LETTER BLENDS TO *scr, spr, str, thr, spl, shr*

**OBJECTIVES**

Know and apply grade-level phonics and word analysis skills in decoding words. **RF.2.3**

Recognize words with *scr, spr, str, thr, spl, shr.*

 **I Do**
Display the **Word Building Cards** s, c, r. Say: *These letters are lowercase* s, c, r. *I am going to trace the letters* s, c, r *while I say the sound these letters stand for.* Trace the letters *s, c, r* while saying /skr/ five times. Repeat with *spr, str, thr, spl, shr.*

 **We Do**
Say: *Now do it with me.* Have children trace lowercase *s, c, r* on the Word Building Cards while saying /skr/ with children. Repeat the process with *spr, str, thr, spl, shr.*

 **You Do**
Have children connect the letters *s, c, r* to the sounds /skr/ by tracing a lowercase *s, c, r* with their finger, while saying /skr/ five to ten times. Then have them write the letters *scr* five to ten times. Repeat with *spr, str, thr, spl, shr.*

**Repeat,** identifying words with 3-letter blends throughout the week.

**Sound/Spellings Fluency** Display the following Word-Building Cards: *scr, spr, str, thr, spl, shr, ch, th, sh, wh, tch, ph, ng, o_e, o, u_e, u, i_e, i, a_e, a.* Have children chorally say each sound. Repeat and vary the pace.

**TIER 2**

### BLEND WORDS WITH 3-LETTER BLENDS *scr, spr, str, thr, spl, shr*

**OBJECTIVES**

Know and apply grade-level phonics and word analysis skills in decoding words. **RF.2.3**

Decode words with with *scr, spr, str, thr, spl, shr.*

 **I Do**
Display Word-Building Cards s, t, r, i, n, g. Say: *The letter s stands for /s/. Let's say it: /s/. Letter* t *stands for /t/. The letter* i *stands for /i/. The letters* ng *stand for /ng/. I'll blend the sounds: /ssstrrriiing/,* string.

 **We Do**
Guide children to blend sounds and read *spring, split, shred, thresh, scrap, sprint.*

 **You Do**
Have children blend and decode *scrape, spruce, stroke, throne, splint, shrink.*

**Repeat,** blending additional words with *scr, spr, str, thr, spl, shr.*

You may wish to review Phonics with **ELL** using this section.

## BUILD WORDS WITH 3-LETTER BLENDS *scr, spr, str, thr, spl, shr.*

**OBJECTIVES**

 Know and apply grade-level phonics and word analysis skills in decoding words. **RF.2.3**

Build and decode words with *scr, spr, str, thr, spl, shr.*

 Display Word-Building Cards *t, r, a, p.* Say: *The letters* t, r, a, *and* p *stand for /t/, /r/, /a/, /p/. I will blend the four sounds: /trrraaap/,* trap.

 Say: *Now, let's do one together. Make* trap *using Word-Building Cards. Place the letter* s *in front of it. Let's blend: /s/ /t/ /r/ /a/ /p/: /ssstrrraaap/,* strap. *Change the letter* t *to* c. Say: *I am going to change the* t *in* strap *to* c. *Let's blend and read: /sss/ /k/ /rrr/ /aaa/ /p/: /skrap/,* scrap.

 Have children build the words: *scrub, strip, thrill, thrift, splash, splint.*

**Decodable Reader** Introduce the Decodable Reader, *Mrs. Sprig's Spring Flowers*. Point to the title. Have children sound out each word. Discuss the illustrations.

**First Read** Turn to the inside back cover. Have children point to each word, sounding out decodable words and saying the high-frequency words quickly. Children should chorally read the story the first time through.

## BLEND WORDS WITH 3-LETTER BLENDS *scr, spr, str, thr, spl, shr*

**OBJECTIVES**

 Know and apply grade-level phonics and word analysis skills in decoding words. **RF.2.3**

 Display Word-Building Cards *s, c, r, u, b.* Say: *This is letter* s. *It stands for /s/. The letter* c *stands for /k/. The letter* r *stands for /r/. This is* u. *It stands for /u/. The letter* b *stands for /b/. Listen as I blend these sounds: /ssskrrruuub/,* scrub.

 Say: *Let's do some together.* Blend and read the words *shrink, strong, spruce.*

 Display the following words: *scrunch, sprang, strike, throb, splint, shrug.* Have children blend and read the words.

**Decodable Reader** Have children reread the Decodable Reader selection.

**Check Comprehension** As children read, monitor their comprehension. Ask the following: *Who helps Mrs. Sprig plant her garden? What can Thad do to help?*

## BLEND WORDS WITH 3-LETTER BLENDS *scr, spr, str, thr, spl, shr*

**Fluency in Connected Text**

Have children review the **Decodable Reader** selection. Identify words with 3-letter blends, blending as needed. Have children reread the selection on their own or with a partner.

**Approaching Level**

## Structural Analysis

### REVIEW COMPOUND WORDS

 **TIER 2**

**OBJECTIVES**

 **CCSS** Use knowledge of the meaning of individual words to predict the meaning of compound words (e.g., *birdhouse, lighthouse, housefly; bookshelf, notebook, bookmark*). **L.2.4.d**

**I Do** Remind children that compound words are two words joined together to make one longer word. Write *backpack*. Read the word: *backpack*. Say: *I look at this word and see two smaller words I know:* back *and* pack. *When I put the words together, they form the compound word* backpack, *a pack or bag that is carried on the back.*

**We Do** Write *sandbox*. Say: *Let's read: /sandboks/. I see the smaller words* sand *and* box. *A* sandbox *is a box made to hold* sand. Write sentences with the word. Remind children to look at the smaller words to figure out the meaning.

Repeat this routine with the following words: *wishbone, spaceship, sunshine.*

**You Do** Have children work with partners. Give them several compound words to read and define. Use: *cupcake, windmill, inland.*

**Repeat** Have children form other compound words.

### RETEACH COMPOUND WORDS

**OBJECTIVES**

 **CCSS** Use knowledge of the meaning of individual words to predict the meaning of compound words (e.g., *birdhouse, lighthouse, housefly; bookshelf, notebook, bookmark*). **L.2.4.d**

**I Do** Write *bedroom*. Say: *A compound word is two smaller words joined to make a longer word.* Bedroom *contains the words* bed *and* room.

**We Do** Say: *To understand the meaning of a compound word, look at the smaller words it contains.* Write and say: *backbone*. Say: *I see the words* back *and* bone. *A* backbone *is a bone in your back. Use it in a sentence.* Form sentences with the compound words:

homemade     rosebud     suntan     pigpen     drumstick

**You Do** Have partners read other compound words and use them in sentences.

**Repeat** Have children identify compound words and their meanings.

You may wish to review Phonics with **ELL** using this section.

# High-Frequency Words/ Vocabulary

TIER 2

## REVIEW HIGH-FREQUENCY WORDS

**OBJECTIVES**

 CCSS Read with sufficient accuracy and fluency to support comprehension. **RF.2.4**

Review high-frequency words.

 **I Do** Use Word Cards 91–100. Display one word at a time, following the routine:

Display the word. Read the word. Then spell the word.

**We Do** Ask children to state the word and spell the word with you. Model using the word in a sentence and have children repeat after you.

**You Do** Display the word. Ask children to say the word and then spell it. When completed, quickly flip through the word card set as children chorally read the words. Provide opportunities for children to use the words in speaking and writing. For example, provide sentence starters, such as *The flower in the field looked _____*. Ask children to write each word in their Writer's Notebook.

## REVIEW VOCABULARY WORDS

**OBJECTIVES**

CCSS Use words and phrases acquired through conversations, reading and being read to, and responding to texts, including using adjectives and adverbs to describe (e.g., *When other kids are happy, that makes me happy*). **L.2.6**

 **I Do** Display each Visual Vocabulary Card and state the word. Explain how the photograph illustrates the word. State the example sentence and repeat the word.

 **We Do** Point to the word on the card and read the word with children. Ask them to repeat the word. Engage children in structured partner talk about the image as prompted on the back of the vocabulary card.

 **You Do** Display each visual in random order, hiding the word. Have children match the definitions and context sentences of the words to the visuals displayed. Then ask children to complete Approaching Level Practice Book page 91.

# → Approaching Level

## Comprehension

### READ FOR FLUENCY

**OBJECTIVES**

 Read with sufficient accuracy and fluency to support comprehension. **RF.2.4**

 Read on-level text with purpose and understanding. **RF.2.4a**

 Read on-level text orally with accuracy, appropriate rate, and expression on successive readings. **RF.2.4b**

 **I Do** Read the first paragraph of the Practice Book selection. Model using appropriate phrasing as you read. Pause for commas and end punctuation.

 **We Do** Read the next paragraph and have children repeat each sentence after you. Point out how you pause slightly for commas and pause for end punctuation.

 **You Do** Have children read the rest of the selection aloud. Remind them to use proper phrasing and to pause for punctuation.

### IDENTIFY DETAILS

**OBJECTIVES**

 Ask and answer such questions as *who, what, where, when, why,* and *how* to demonstrate understanding of key details in a text. **RL.2.1**

 Read on-level text with purpose and understanding. **RF.2.4a**

 **I Do** Remind children that they have been reading fiction and poetry. Tell them that they can find details in the words and the pictures. Say: *When we read fiction and poetry, we look for details in the words and illustrations.*

**We Do** Read the first two stanzas of the Practice Book selection aloud. Pause to identify details in the selection. Say: *We read that a tortoise can live for a very long time. Tortoises can live longer than people.*

 **You Do** Guide children to read the rest of the Practice Book selection. As they read, prompt them to look for details. Have them explain why the details in the words and illustrations are important.

## REVIEW KEY DETAILS

**OBJECTIVES**

 Ask and answer such questions as *who, what, where, when, why,* and *how* to demonstrate understanding of key details in a text. **RL.2.1**

 Read with sufficient accuracy and fluency to support comprehension. **RF.2.4**

 Read on-level text with purpose and understanding. **RF.2.4a**

Apply skill to identify key details.

 Remind children that key details are important pieces of information in a poem. Readers can find key details in the words and the illustrations. These key details help the reader understand the topic of the poem.

 Read the first page of the Practice Book selection together. Pause to point out a key detail. *We read that a tortoise lives on land, not in the sea.*

**You Do** After reading, say: *Let's think about the key details. The details tell us many things about tortoises. The poem includes key details about what tortoises look like, what they eat, and when they live. I will use these details to help me determine the theme.* Record each clue on a Key Details chart. Then guide children to use the key details to talk about the topic and how the author feels about that topic.

## SELF-SELECTED READING

**OBJECTIVES**

 Read with sufficient accuracy and fluency to support comprehension. **RF.2.4**

 Read on-level text with purpose and understanding. **RF.2.4a**

Apply the strategy and skill to summarize text.

### Read Independently

Have children pick a story or poem that they have read for sustained silent reading. Remind them that:

→ they should identify key details in the words and images to determine the topic.

→ they can reread text to better understand the story or poem.

### Read Purposefully

Have children record key details on a Key Details chart. After reading, guide them to participate in a discussion about the text. Guide them to:

→ share the information they recorded on their Key Details chart.

→ tell what interesting pictures they imagined as they read.

→ share what parts they reread and how rereading helped them.

# → On Level

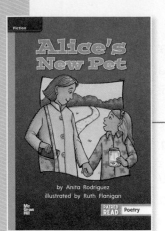

by Anita Rodriguez
illustrated by Ruth Flanigan

**Lexile** 470
*TextEvaluator™* 13

## OBJECTIVES

 Describe how words and phrases (e.g., regular beats, alliteration, rhymes, repeated lines) supply rhythm and meaning in a story, poem, or song. **RL.2.4**

 Read with sufficient accuracy and fluency to support comprehension. **RF.2.4**

 Use context to confirm or self-correct word recognition and understanding, rereading as necessary. **RF.2.4c**

## MATERIALS

Leveled Reader
*Alice's New Pet*

## Leveled Reader:
### *Alice's New Pet*

### Before Reading

#### Preview and Predict

Have children turn to the title page. Read the title and author name and have children repeat. Preview the selection's illustrations. Prompt children to predict what the selection might be about.

#### Review Genre: Fiction

Have children recall that fiction is a made-up story with characters, a setting, and plot. A fiction story has a beginning, middle, and end. A fiction story usually has a problem at the beginning that is resolved by the end of the story.

#### ESSENTIAL QUESTION

Remind children of the Essential Question: *What do we love about animals?* Set a purpose for reading: *Let's read to find out if Alice will get a new pet so she can do her homework.*

Remind children that as they read a selection, they can ask questions about what they do not understand or want to know more about.

### During Reading

#### Close Reading

**Note taking** Ask students to use their graphic organizer while they read.

**Pages 2–4** *Turn to a partner and discuss details you did not understand the first time you read these pages. Which part can you reread to help you?* (Possible response: I didn't understand why Alice needs a pet to do her homework. I can reread the last paragraph on page 3 to help me better understand this part of the plot.)

**Pages 5–9** *Paraphrase how the key details help you understand the problem in the story.* (Alice tries to write about a robin but it flies away. She begs for a kitten, but Mom says her brother gets sick around cats. Alice still has no animal to help her do her homework.)

**Leveled Readers**

**Graphic Organizer**

**Retelling Cards**

Go
Digital

**Pages 10–13** *What is the meaning of* express *on page 11?* (to show your thoughts) *What is another meaning of* express? (having to do with fast transportation or delivery) *What words on page 13 help you know that Alice doesn't think the bug is that interesting at first?* (plain, old)

**Pages 14–15** *What is the meaning of* back *on page 14?* (the part of the body with the spine) *What part can you reread if you don't understand why Alice carries a glass jar in the picture?* (I can reread the first paragraph on page 15.)

## After Reading

### Respond to Reading

Have children complete Respond to Reading on page 16 after reading.

### Retell

Have children take turns retelling the selection. Help children make a personal connection by asking: *Have you ever wanted something very much? What did you say to convince your family to get it?*

### Model Fluency

Read the sentences one at a time. Have children chorally repeat. Point out how you read with phrasing. Model reading the dialogue on pages 2 and 3 using phrasing.

**Apply** Have partners practice repeated reading. Provide feedback.

## PAIRED READ ...

**Leveled Reader**

## "Baby Joey"

### Make Connections: Write About It *Analytical Writing*

Before reading, ask children to note that the genre of this text is poetry. Then discuss the Compare Texts statement. After reading, ask children to make connections between the animals in "Baby Joey" and *Alice's New Pet*.

> **FOCUS ON LITERARY ELEMENTS**
>
> Children can extend their knowledge of literary elements by completing the activity on page 20.

## Literature Circles

Lead children in conducting a literature circle using the Thinkmark questions to guide the discussion. You may wish to discuss what children have learned about animals from both selections in the leveled reader.

## Level Up

Level-up lessons available online.

**IF** children read the **On Level** fluently and answered the questions

**THEN** pair them with children who have proficiently read the **Beyond Level** and have on-level children

• partner-read the **Beyond Level** main selection.

• Identify key details they would like to learn more about.

## A C T Access Complex Text

The **Beyond Level** challenges children by including more **specific vocabulary** and **complex sentence structures**.

# On Level

## Phonics

### BUILD WORDS WITH 3-LETTER BLENDS *scr, spr, str, thr, spl, shr*

**OBJECTIVES**

 Know and apply grade-level phonics and word analysis skills in decoding words. **RF.2.3**

 Identify words with inconsistent but common spelling-sound correspondences. **RF2.3e**

 **I Do**

Display **Word-Building Cards** s, t, r, i, p. Say: *This is letter* s. *It stands for /sss/. This is letter* t. *It stands for /t/. Letter* r *stands for /r/. This is letter* i. *It stands for the sound /i/. Letter* p *stands for /p/. I'll blend these sounds: /ssstrrriiip/,* strip.

 **We Do**

Say: *Now, let's do one together.* Make the word *strip* using Word-Building Cards. *Change the* i *to* a. *Let's blend: /s / /t/, /r/ /a/ /p/,* strap. Change the *str* to *scr. I am going to change the letters* str *to the letters* scr. *Let's blend and read: /sss/ /k/ /rrr/ /aaa/ /p/, /ssskrrraaap/,* scrap.

 **You Do**

Have children build and blend these words: *shrank, shrink, shrine.*

**Repeat** with additional words with three-letter blends *scr, spr, str, thr, spl, shr.*

**Read for Fluency**  Have children read this week's Decodable Reader, *Mrs. Sprig's Spring Flowers.* Work with them to read with appropriate expression.

## Vocabulary

### REVIEW WORDS

**OBJECTIVES**

 Use words and phrases acquired through conversations, reading and being read to, and responding to texts, including using adjectives and adverbs to describe (e.g., *When other kids are happy that makes me happy*). **L.2.6**

 **I Do**

Use the **Visual Vocabulary Cards** to review each vocabulary word. Point to each word, read it aloud, and have children chorally repeat it.

 **We Do**

Guide children to use the **Define/Example/Ask** routine for a few Vocabulary words using their **Response Boards**. Ask sample questions to help students respond and explain their answers.

 **You Do**

Have children work with a partner to do the **Define/Example/Ask** routine on their own for the remaining vocabulary words. Then have children write sentences about this week's selections. Each sentence must contain at least one vocabulary word.

# Comprehension

## REVIEW KEY DETAILS

### OBJECTIVES

Ask and answer questions such as *who, what, where, when, why,* and *how* to demonstrate understanding of key details in a text.
**RL.2.1**

Identify the theme in a poem.

**I Do** Remind children that when they read fiction and poetry, they can look for key details. Say: *When we read fiction, we pay attention to the words and illustrations. These clues help us identify key details. We can look for important details in the words and illustrations.*

**We Do** Read the first few stanzas of the Practice Book selection together. Pause to point out key details that tell about the topic or theme. *We read a tortoise lives on land. It moves at a slow pace, and has four legs and four feet.*

**You Do** Guide children to read the rest of the Practice Book selection. Remind them to look for key details that tell about the topic. Have them explain why the words and illustration are important.

## SELF-SELECTED READING

### OBJECTIVES

Read with sufficient accuracy and fluency to support comprehension.
**RF.2.4**

Read on-level text with purpose and understanding.
**RF.2.4a**

Apply the strategy and skill to reread text.

### Read Independently

Have children pick a story or poem that they have read for sustained silent reading. Remind them that:

→ they should determine the topic and read to understand what the poet is writing about.

→ they should identify key details in the words and images to determine the topic of the poem.

→ they can reread text to better understand the message of the poem.

### Read Purposefully

Have children record the clues and theme on their Theme chart. After reading, guide partners to:

→ share what they recorded on the Key Details chart.

→ tell what the selection was mostly about.

→ share what they reread and how it helped them better understand the theme.

**Beyond Level**

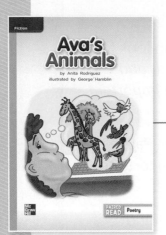

**Lexile** 570
*TextEvaluator*™ 24

---

## OBJECTIVES

 Describe how words and phrases (e.g., regular beats, alliteration, rhymes, repeated lines) supply rhythm and meaning in a story, poem, or song. **RL.2.4**

 Read with sufficient accuracy and fluency to support comprehension. **RF.2.4**

 Use context to confirm or self-correct word recognition and understanding, rereading as necessary. **RF.2.4c**

---

## MATERIALS

Leveled Reader
*Ava's Animals*

# Leveled Reader:
# *Ava's Animals*

### Before Reading

#### Preview and Predict

Read the title and author name. Have children preview the title page and the images. Ask: *What do you think this book will be about?*

#### Review Genre: Fiction

Have children recall that fiction is a made-up story with characters, a setting, and plot. A fiction story has a beginning, middle, and end. A fiction story usually has a problem at the beginning that is resolved by the end of the story.

#### ESSENTIAL QUESTION

Remind children of the Essential Question: *What do we love about animals?* Set a purpose for reading: *Let's read to find out why Ava has a difficult time choosing an animal to use for her assignment.*

### During Reading

#### Close Reading

**Note taking** Ask students to use their graphic organizer while they read.

**Pages 2–6** *Turn to a partner and discuss details you did not understand the first time you read these pages. Which part can you reread to help you?* (Possible response: I didn't understand why Ruth chose beavers. I can reread the last paragraph on page 5 to help me understand that Ruth chose beavers because of their behavior, and how they use their body parts like tools to build dams.) *What does the word* bark *mean on page 4?* (the outer layer of a tree) *What is another meaning of* bark? (the yap or woof sound a dog makes)

**Pages 7–9** *Paraphrase how the key details help you understand the problem in the story.* (Ava only has ten minutes at the computer to choose her animal, but her mind is swirling with too many choices. Mr. Edson reminds her she has a time limit.)

**Go
Digital**

**Leveled
Readers**

**Graphic
Organizer**

**Pages 10–13** *What phrases on page 12 help you picture Ava daydreaming?* (swaying in her chair; dreamy smile on her face) *What part can you reread if you forgot who Mr. Edson is and what he wants Ava to do?* (I can turn back and reread page 2 and page 9.)

**Pages 14–15** *Paraphrase how the key details help you understand how Ava solves her problem.* (Ava realizes that she is being slow and steady, like a turtle. This makes her choose a turtle as her animal.)

## After Reading

### Respond to Reading

Have children complete the Respond to Reading on page 16 after reading.

### Retell

Have children take turns retelling the selection. Help children make a personal connection by writing about animals. Say: *What animals are your favorites? Why do you like them?*

## Literature Circles

Lead children in conducting a literature circle using the Thinkmark questions to guide the discussion. You may wish to discuss what children have learned about animals from both selections in the leveled reader.

## PAIRED READ ...

**Leveled Reader**

## "Nanook"

### Make Connections: Write About It ✏ *Analytical Writing*

Before reading "Nanook," have children preview the title page and prompt them to identify the genre. Then discuss the Compare Texts statement. After reading, have children work with a partner to discuss what they read in "Nanook" and *Ava's Animals*. Ask children to make connections by comparing and contrasting the similarities and differences between dolphins and polar bears. Prompt children to discuss what they learned about the different animals.

## Gifted and Talented

### INDEPENDENT STUDY

Challenge children to research their favorite land or water animal. Guide them to include this animal's natural habitat and what it eats to survive. Have them include a drawing of their favorite animal in its habitat. Permit them to use the library or online resources.

**EXTEND** Have the children use information they learned from the week and do additional research.

## FOCUS ON LITERARY ELEMENT

Children can extend their knowledge of poetry by completing the literary elements activity on page 20.

# Beyond Level

## Vocabulary

### REVIEW DOMAIN-SPECIFIC WORDS

**OBJECTIVES**

 Use words and phrases acquired through conversations, reading and being read to, and responding to texts, including using adjectives and adverbs to describe (e.g., *When other kids are happy, that makes me happy*). **L.2.6**

 **Model** Use the Visual Vocabulary Cards to review the meaning of the words *express* and *behave*. Have children tell how they behave when they are expressing different emotions, such as anger and sadness.

Write the words *herd* and *observe* on the board and discuss the meanings with children. Then help children write sentences using these words.

 **Apply** Have children work in pairs to discuss the meanings of the words *splashing* and *playful*. Then have partners take turns describing their favorite animal. The other partner should guess the animal and describe its behavior.

### MULTIPLE-MEANING WORDS

**OBJECTIVES**

 Determine or clarify the meaning of unknown and multiple-meaning words and phrases based on *grade 2 reading and content*, choosing flexibly from an array of strategies. **L.2.4**

 Use sentence-level context as a clue to the meaning of a word or phrase. **L.2.4a**

Use knowledge of multiple-meaning words to determine the meaning of a word.

 **Model** Read aloud the first three stanzas of the Comprehension and Fluency passage on Beyond Level Practice Book pages 93–94.

**Think Aloud** When I read the poem, I want to understand the word *land*. I know the word can mean "the part of Earth that isn't underwater" or "to come to rest." I think about the context. Since it says you won't find tortoises in the sea, I think the first meaning makes sense in this sentence.

With children, read the fourth and fifth stanzas. Help them figure out the meaning of *feet* and *treat*.

 **Apply** Have pairs of children read the rest of the passage. Ask them to use paragraph clues to determine the meaning of the following words: *shell, well, head, limbs, pack, right*, and *back*.

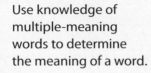  **Independent Study** Have children think of their favorite animal and list descriptive words to tell about it. Children can conduct research to learn additional facts about the animal. Ask children to draw a picture of the animal and write related words around the border.

# Comprehension

## REVIEW KEY DETAILS

**OBJECTIVES**

Ask and answer such questions as *who, what, where, when, why,* and *how* to demonstrate understanding of key details in a text. **RL.2.1**

Identify key details.

 **Model**

Remind children that key details are the most important ideas or facts in a story or poem. The key details may be in the words or in illustrations. Explain that the key details help you understand the main topic, message, or theme.

Have children read the first page of the Comprehension and Fluency passage of Beyond Level Practice Book pages 93–94. Ask open-ended questions to facilitate discussion of the key details and how they tell about the topic. For example, *What does a tortoise do when it doesn't know where to hide?* Children should support their responses with examples.

 **Apply**

Have children identify the key details as they independently fill in a Key Details chart. Then have partners use the key details to discuss the poem's theme or message.

## SELF-SELECTED READING

**OBJECTIVES**

Read with sufficient accuracy and fluency to support comprehension **RF.2.4**

Read on-level text with purpose and understanding. **RF.2.4a**

Reread difficult sections in a text to increase understanding.

### Read Independently

Have children choose a poetry selection for sustained silent reading.

→ As children read, have them fill in a Key Details chart.

→ Remind them to reread to better understand the message of the poem.

### Read Purposefully

Encourage children to keep a reading journal. Ask them to read different books in order to learn about a variety of subjects.

→ Children can write summaries of the books in their journals.

→ Ask children to share their reactions to the books with classmates.

 **Independent Study** Challenge children to discuss how their books relate to the weekly theme of animals in poetry. Have partners compare different poems featuring animals. Are all the poems favorable? Are some "unlovable" animals given likable characteristics in poems? What makes the animals lovable?

# → English Language Learners

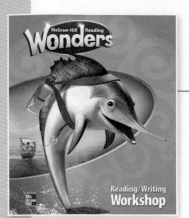

**Reading/Writing
Workshop**

## Shared Read
### *Cats and Kittens*

**Go
Digital**

**Cats and
Kittens**

### Before Reading

#### Build Background

Read the Essential Question: *What do we love about animals?*

→ Explain the Essential Question: *You can see animals in nature, at the zoo, or maybe you have a pet at home. Animals need care, but they bring joy to many people. Animals can be fun to watch. They make many people happy.*

→ **Model an answer:** *In the poem, "Cats and Kittens," we will read a poem that tells why this author loves kittens. Let's see why kittens make interesting pets.*

→ Ask children a question that ties the Essential Question to their own background knowledge: *Turn to a partner and talk about the different things kittens can do. What words would you use to describe an animal you love?* Call on several pairs. Encourage them to use sentences in responses.

**Graphic
Organizer**

### During Reading

#### Interactive Question Response

→ Ask questions that help children understand the meaning of the text after each verse.

→ Reinforce the meanings of key vocabulary providing meanings embedded in the questions.

→ Ask children questions that require them to use key vocabulary.

→ Reinforce strategies and skills of the week by modeling.

## OBJECTIVES

 Describe how words and phrases (e.g., regular beats, alliteration, rhymes, repeated lines) supply rhythm and meaning in a story, poem, or song. **RL.2.4**

 Read with sufficient accuracy and fluency to support comprehension. **RF.2.4**

 Use context to confirm or self-correct word recognition and understanding, rereading as necessary. **RF.2.4c**

## Page 166

### Cats and Kittens

Point to each word as you read the title. Ask: *What is the title of this poem?* (Cats and Kittens) Point to the kittens and say: *These are kittens. Say kittens:* kittens. Write the words *hisses, purrs,* and *mews.* Demonstrate these sounds. Say: *Cats hiss when they are scared and purr when they are happy. Mews are how cats talk.*

Ask: *What words would you use to describe kittens?* (possible responses: cute, playful, curious, funny, soft, furry)

## Page 167

### Cats and Kittens

Say: *Listen as I read this poem. I see rhyming words. Rhyming words end with the same sounds. This is a rhyming poem.*

Reread the first verse: <u>Cats and kittens express their views with hisses, purrs, and little mews.</u> Explain the meaning of the word *views* and say: *The words* views *and* mews *rhyme. What is a rhyming word?* (Words that end with the same sounds.)

Say: *Poets can make sound patterns with rhyme. A pattern is something that is repeated. It can be copied again and again. In the poem, "Cats and Kittens," there are pairs of rhyming lines. In the first two lines of this poem, what words rhyme?* (views, mews)

Say: *Talk about the rhyming words with your partner.* (views, mews; me, handily; say, way; be, see; fur, PURRRR)

## Page 168

### Desert Camels

Say: *This poem tells about a* camel. *Look at the photo. A camel is a large animal with a long neck,* long legs, and a hump on its back. A hump is a big bump. Some camels have two humps. Camels live in the hot, dry desert. They can go for a long time without water. Read the poem, emphasizing the rhyming words.

**Explain and Model the Strategy** Reread to help children understand why camels are suited to a desert habitat. Say: *I didn't understand why camels do well in the desert. Let's reread this poem.* Reread the poem slowly, emphasizing key details. *Now I see. They don't mind the Sun and they don't need to stop for drinks of water.*

*What does a camel's ride feel like? Find the words and show your partner.* Guide children to demonstrate these movements. (bouncy, swaying)

## Pages 169

### A Bat Is Not a Bird

Say: *Let's read this poem about bats. A bat is a small mammal. It looks like a mouse with wings. It is not a bird. Let's reread this poem to learn how bats and birds are the same and different.* (Bats and birds fly. Bats don't have feathers or a beak. Their wings look like leathery skin. They shriek instead of chirp.)

**Explain and Model Phonics** Write the word *shriek* on the board. Say: *Listen as I read the word and then say each sound: /sh/ /rrrr/ /ēēē/ /k/, /shrrrēēēk/. The word is* shriek. *Let's say it:* shriek. Point out the three-letter blend at the beginning of *shriek, shr.*

*Tell which animal is your favorite. What do you love about this animal?* (Responses will vary.)

### After Reading

**Make Connections**

→ Review the Essential Question.

# English Language Learners

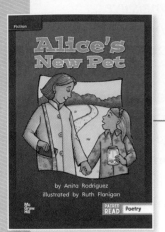

**Lexile** 350
*TextEvaluator™* 5

## OBJECTIVES

 Describe how words and phrases (e.g., regular beats, alliteration, rhymes, repeated lines) supply rhythm and meaning in a story, poem, or song. **RL.2.4**

 Read with sufficient accuracy and fluency to support comprehension. **RF.2.4**

 Use context to confirm or self-correct word recognition and understanding, rereading as necessary. **RF.2.4c**

## MATERIALS

Leveled Reader
*Alice's New Pet*

## Leveled Reader:
### *Alice's New Pet*

### Before Reading

#### Preview

Read the title. Ask: *What is the title? Say it again.* Repeat with the author's name. Preview the selection's illustrations. Have children describe the images. Use simple language to tell about each page. Follow with questions, such as *What is Alice doing?*

#### ESSENTIAL QUESTION

Remind children of the Essential Question. Say: *Let's read to find out about animals.* Encourage children to seek clarification when they encounter a confusing word or phrase.

### During Reading

#### Interactive Question Response

**Pages 2–3** Point to Alice on page 2. Say: *This is Alice. She is the main character in the story. What do you think Alice is doing?* (She is working on her homework assignment.) Point to Alice's mother. Say: *This is Alice's mother. She is reading a book. When Alice tells her mom she needs a pet so she can do a homework assignment, why does her mom ask if a pet can do math?* (Her mom is joking. She doesn't understand why Alice needs a pet for homework.)

**Pages 4–5** Ask: *What is the problem? How does Alice's mom suggest she solve the problem?* (Alice wants a kitten, so she can write a poem about it. Her mom suggests Alice can write a poem about a bird.)

**Pages 6–7** Ask: *Why can't Alice write a poem about the robin?* (It flies away.)

**Pages 8–9** Say: *Alice is upset and gives more reasons to get a kitten. What does her mom do to solve the problem?* (She suggests that they take a walk to watch other animals in nature.) *What animals do you think they'll see?* (Accept reasonable responses.)

**Pages 10–11** Say: *Do they see any animals on the walk?* (No.) *What does Alice suggest?* (They could go to the zoo.)

**Pages 12–13** Say: *Why couldn't Alice write about the rabbit they saw on the walk?* (It hopped away.)

## Go Digital

**Leveled Readers**

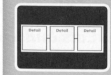

**Graphic Organizer**

**Retelling Cards**

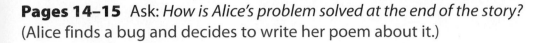

**Pages 14–15** Ask: *How is Alice's problem solved at the end of the story?* (Alice finds a bug and decides to write her poem about it.)

## After Reading

### Respond to Reading

Ask children to work with partners to answer the Respond to Reading questions. Pair children with peers of varying language abilities.

### Retell

Model retelling using the Retelling Card prompts. Then guide children to retell the selection to a partner.

### Fluency: Phrasing

Read the sentences in the book, one at a time. Help children echo-read the pages expressively and with appropriate phrasing. Remind them to read the way they think each character would sound.

### Apply

Have children practice reading with a partner. Pair children with peers of varying language abilities.

---

## PAIRED READ ...

## "Four Little Ducklings"

### Make Connections:
### Write About It · *Analytical Writing*

Before reading, tell children that this selection is a poem. Then discuss the Compare Texts statement. After reading, ask children to make connections between what they read in "Four Little Ducklings" and *Alice's New Pet*. Prompt children by providing sentence frames, such as *The ducklings are like a _____ because they are both _____. The ducklings are not like a _____ because _____.*

**Leveled Reader**

---

### FOCUS ON LITERARY ELEMENTS

Children can extend their knowledge of poetry by completing the literary elements activity on page 20.

---

### Literature Circles

Lead children in conducting a literature circle using the Thinkmark questions to guide the discussion. You may wish to discuss what children have learned about animals from both selections in the leveled reader.

## Level Up

Level-up lessons available online.

**IF** children read the **ELL Level** fluently and answered the questions

**THEN** pair them with children who have proficiently read the **On Level** and have children

- echo-read the **On Level** main selection with their partners.

- list difficult words and phrases and discuss them with their partners.

### **A C T** **A**ccess **C**omplex **T**ext

The **On Level** challenges children by including more **specific vocabulary** and **complex sentence structures.**

# English Language Learners
## Vocabulary

### PRETEACH VOCABULARY

**OBJECTIVES**

CCSS Use words and phrases acquired through conversations, reading and being read to, and responding to texts, including using adjectives and adverbs to describe (e.g., *When other kids are happy, that makes me happy*). **L.2.6**

**LANGUAGE OBJECTIVE**

Use vocabulary words.

**I Do** Preteach vocabulary from "Cats and Kittens," "Desert Camels," and "A Bat Is Not a Bird," following the Vocabulary Routine found on the Visual Vocabulary Cards for words *behave, express, feathers,* and *flapping.*

**We Do** After completing the Vocabulary Routine for each, point to the word on the Visual Vocabulary Card and read it with children. Ask them to repeat.

**You Do** Have partners write vocabulary words correctly on small cards. Have them take turns picking a word, pronouncing it, and using it in an oral sentence.

| Beginning | Intermediate | Advanced/High |
|---|---|---|
| Help children write two or three words correctly and read them aloud. | Ask children to write the words, select two words, and write one sentence and one question. | Challenge children to write one sentence and one question for each word. |

### REVIEW VOCABULARY

**OBJECTIVES**

CCSS Demonstrate understanding of word relationships and nuances in word meanings. **L.2.5**

CCSS Determine the meaning of words and phrases in a text relevant to a *grade 2 topic or subject area.* **RI.2.4**

**I Do** Review the previous week's vocabulary words over a few days. Read each aloud pointing to the word on the Visual Vocabulary Card. Have children repeat after you. Then follow the Vocabulary Routine on the back of each.

**We Do** Show children one of the Vocabulary words. Have children read the word. Then have them either give the definition or use the word in a sentence.

**You Do** Have one partner show the card. The other says the meaning. Switch roles.

| Beginning | Intermediate | Advanced/High |
|---|---|---|
| Prompt children in stating the definition. Provide sentence frames. | Help children provide a definition in their own words. | Have children provide both a definition and an example sentence. |

# MULTIPLE-MEANING WORDS

### OBJECTIVES

**CCSS** Determine or clarify the meaning of unknown and multiple-meaning words and phrases based on *grade 2 reading and content*, choosing flexibly from an array of strategies. **L.2.4**

**CCSS** Use sentence-level context as a clue to the meaning of a word or phrase. **L.2.4a**

### LANGUAGE OBJECTIVE

Use multiple-meaning words.

**I Do** Read the first and second stanza on page 167 of "Cats and Kittens," while children follow along. Summarize the stanzas. Point to the word *like*. Explain that you can use what you know about multiple-meaning words and context to determine the meaning of the word.

**Think Aloud** I know that *like* can mean "to be pleased with" or "similar to." Here the word *like* compares the speaker and cats. This helps me know it means "similar to." Cats are not similar to the speaker.

**We Do** Have children point to *can* in the fourth stanza on page 167. Use knowledge of multiple-meaning words to identify and write the meaning.

**You Do** Write these sentences on the board: *I sleep when it is dark. My kitten likes to sleep when it is light!* In pairs, have children work with a partner to use context clues to write the meaning of *light*.

| Beginning | Intermediate | Advanced/High |
|---|---|---|
| Help children locate the word *light*. Guide them to identify the meanings of *light* and choose one. | Ask children to locate the word *light*. Guide them to identify the correct meaning. | Have children explain how they determined the meaning of the word. |

# ADDITIONAL VOCABULARY

### OBJECTIVES

**CCSS** Use knowledge of language and its conventions when writing, speaking, reading, or listening. **L.2.3**

**CCSS** Compare formal and informal uses of English. **L.2.3a**

**I Do** Use academic language and additional vocabulary from "Cats and Kittens," "Desert Camels," and "A Bat Is Not a Bird": *behave, express;* and "Alice's New Pet:" *explain, imagine*. Define each word for children.

**We Do** Model using the words for children in a sentence: *The teacher will explain the difference between a bat and a bird*. Then provide sentence frames and complete them with children: *Please explain how a bird _____*.

**You Do** Have pairs use the images in the selections to make up their own sentences with the words and share them with the class to complete.

| Beginning | Intermediate | Advanced/High |
|---|---|---|
| Help children copy the sentence frames correctly and read them aloud. | Provide support to help children use the words in the activity. | Lead children to define the words they used. |

# English Language Learners
## Writing/Spelling

## WRITING TRAIT: WORD CHOICE

**OBJECTIVES**

 With guidance and support from adults and peers, focus on a topic and strengthen writing as needed by revising and editing. **W.2.5**

 Demonstrate understanding of word relationships and nuances in word meanings. **L.2.5**

**LANGUAGE OBJECTIVE**

Use precise words.

 **I Do** Explain that writers use precise words to help readers form a picture in their minds. Write and read: *The bird made a loud sound. The bird with a bright orange beak made a loud squawk.* Help children compare them and identify the precise words.

**We Do** Read the second and third stanzas on page 168 of "Desert Camels." Explain that the writer uses precise words. Help children identify precise words, including *strong, drinks, bouncy, sway.* Talk about how the words help readers know exactly what the writer means.

**You Do** Have partners write a sentence describing something an animal does. Remind children to use precise words to describe the animal and action.

| Beginning | Intermediate | Advanced/High |
|---|---|---|
| Help children write a sentence. Provide a sentence frame. | Ask children to describe the animal. Repeat their responses. Give frames. | Elicit descriptive details. *What sound does the animal make?* |

## WORDS WITH 3-LETTER BLENDS TO *scr, spr, str, thr, spl, shr*

**OBJECTIVES**

 Know and apply grade-level phonics and word analysis skills in decoding words. **RF.2.3**

**LANGUAGE OBJECTIVE**

 Spell words with *scr, spr, str, thr, spl, shr.*

 **I Do** Read aloud the Spelling Words on T382. Segment *scratch* into sounds and attach a spelling to each sound. Point out the three-letter blend *scr.* Read aloud, segment, and spell the remaining words, and have children repeat.

 **We Do** Read the first sentence from the Dictation Routine on page T382 aloud. Read the word with the three-letter blend and ask children to repeat. Have them write it. Repeat the process for the remaining sentences.

**You Do** Display the words. Have partners check and correct their spelling lists.

| Beginning | Intermediate | Advanced/High |
|---|---|---|
| Help children copy the words with correct spelling and say the word. | After children have corrected their words, have pairs quiz each other. | Challenge children to think of other words with three-letter blends. |

# Grammar

## POSSESSIVE NOUNS

### OBJECTIVES

 Demonstrate command of the conventions of standard English grammar and usage when writing or speaking. **L.2.1**

 Demonstrate command of the conventions of standard English capitalization, punctuation, and spelling when writing. **L.2.2**

---

### LANGUAGE OBJECTIVE

Use possessive nouns.

**ELL Language Transfers**

Spanish, Hmong, and Khmer avoid the use of apostrophe-*s* (*my sister's arm*) to show possession. Instead, speakers of these languages will exclusively or more commonly use a prepositional phrase (*the arm of my sister*) to show possession. Model correct usage and have children repeat. Point out the use of apostrophe-*s* and *s*-apostrophe in text whenever opportunities present themselves.

**I Do**  Review that a possessive noun shows who or what has something. To make a singular possessive noun, add an apostrophe and an *s* to the end of a noun. To make a plural possessive, add an apostrophe after the final *s*.

**We Do**  Write the sentences on the board. Help children read the sentence and name the possessive noun. Have them say: *The possessive noun is _____. It shows that _____ belongs to _____.*

*Kim's cats are black.*

*The two cats' beds are soft.*

*My friend's pet is a horse.*

**You Do**  Write the following sentences on the board.

*A _____ 's tongue helps it stay clean.*

*The _____ 's back has a hump.*

*A _____ 's wings flap.*

Pair children and have them complete the sentence frames by providing details from this week's readings. Circulate, listen in, and take note of each child's language use and proficiency.

| Beginning | Intermediate | Advanced/High |
|---|---|---|
| Review photos and illustrations in "Cats and Kittens," "Desert Camels," and "A Bat is Not a Bird," and *Alice's New Pet.* Ask: *What is a kitten like?* Model a response by providing a sentence frame, such as *A _____ 's body has fur.* Help children identify nouns and possessive nouns. | Ask children to describe the same photographs and illustrations and then identify the nouns and possessive nouns. Encourage children to use complete sentences. | Ask children to look at the photographs and illustrations and describe what is happening using possessive nouns as appropriate. |

# PROGRESS MONITORING

## Weekly Assessment

| ✔**COMPREHENSION:** Key Details **RL.2.1** | ✔**VOCABULARY:** Multiple-Meaning Words **L.2.4b** | ✔**WRITING:** Writing About Text **RL.2.1** |
|---|---|---|

### Assessment Includes

→ Pencil-and-Paper administration

→ Online administration

→ Approaching Level Weekly Assessment also available

FLUENCY

**Fluency Goal** 41 to 61 words correct per minute (WCPM)

**Accuracy Rate Goal** 95% or higher

Administer oral reading fluency assessments using the following schedule:

→ **Weeks 1, 3, 5** Provide Approaching Level children at least three oral reading fluency assessments during the unit.

→ **Weeks 2 and 4** Provide On Level children at least two oral reading fluency assessments during the unit.

→ **Week 6** If necessary, provide Beyond Level children an oral reading fluency assessment at this time.

**Also Available: Selection Tests online PDFs**

*Go Digital!* http://connected.mcgraw-hill.com

# Using Assessment Results

| TESTED SKILLS | If ... | Then ... |
|---|---|---|
| **COMPREHENSION** | Children answer 0–6 multiple-choice items correctly ... | ... assign Lessons 10–12 on Key Details from the *Tier 2 Comprehension Intervention online PDFs.* |
| **VOCABULARY** | Children answer 0–6 multiple-choice items correctly ... | ... assign Lesson 92 on Multiple-Meaning Words from the *Tier 2 Vocabulary Intervention online PDFs.* |
| **WRITING** | Children score less than "3" on the Constructed response ... | ... assign Lessons 10–12 and/or Write About Reading Lessons from Section 13 of the *Tier 2 Comprehension Intervention online PDFs*. |
| 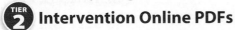 | Children have a WCPM score of 36–40 ... | ... assign a lesson from Section 1, 9, or 10 of the *Tier 2 Fluency Intervention online PDFs.* |
| | Children have a WCPM score of 0–35 ... | ... assign a lesson from Sections 2–8 of the *Tier 2 Fluency Intervention online PDFs.* |

## Response to Intervention

Use the appropriate sections of the *Placement and Diagnostic Assessment* as well as students' assessment results to designate students requiring:

**2** TIER **Intervention Online PDFs**

**3** TIER **WonderWorks Intervention Program**

# WEEKLY OVERVIEW

**The Big Idea:** *How do animals play a part in the world around us?*

## REVIEW AND EXTEND

### Reader's Theater

*The Secret Song*

**Genre** Choral Read

**Fluency** Accuracy, Rate, and Prosody

### Reading Digitally

TIME FOR KIDS "Under the Sea"

**Comprehension** Close Reading

**Study Skills** Using Online Resources

**Research** Navigate Links to Information

*Go Digital!*

## Level Up Accelerating Progress

| From **APPROACHING** To **ON LEVEL** | From **ON LEVEL** To **BEYOND LEVEL** | From **ENGLISH LANGUAGE LEARNERS** To **ON LEVEL** | From **BEYOND LEVEL** To **SELF-SELECTED TRADE BOOK** |
|---|---|---|---|

Advanced Level **Trade Book**

# ASSESS

## Presentations

### Research and Inquiry
Project Presentations
Project Rubric

### Writing
Informational Text Presentations
Writing Rubric

## Unit Assessments

**UNIT 2 TEST**

**FLUENCY**

## Evaluate Student Progress

Use the McGraw-Hill Reading Wonder eAssessment reports to evaluate children's progress and help you make decisions about small group instruction and assignments.

→ Student and Class Assessment Report

→ Student and Class Standards Proficiency Report

→ Student Profile Summary Report

# SUGGESTED LESSON PLAN

| | | DAY 1 | DAY 2 |
|---|---|---|---|
| **READING** | | | |
| **Whole Group** | Reader's Theater "The Secret Song" "Under the Sea" | **Reader's Theater,** T462 "The Secret Song" Assign Roles Model Fluency: Accuracy, Rate, and Prosody **Research and Inquiry,** T466–T469 Gathering Information from Multiple Sources Group Project | **Reader's Theater,** T462 "The Secret Song" Model Fluency: Accuracy, Rate, and Prosody **Research and Inquiry Projects** |
| **DIFFERENTIATED INSTRUCTION** Level up to Accelerate | | | |
| **Small Group** | **Approaching Level** | **Level Up to On Level** *A Tree Full of Life,* T472 | **Level Up to On Level** *A Tree Full of Life,* T472 |
| | **On Level** | **Level Up to Beyond Level** *A Tree Full of Life,* T473 | **Level Up to Beyond Level** *A Tree Full of Life,* T473 |
| | **Beyond Level** | **Level Up to Self-Selected Trade Book,** T475 | **Level Up to Self-Selected Trade Book,** T475 |
| | **English Language Learners** | **Level Up to On Level** *A Tree Full of Life,* T474 | **Level Up to On Level** *A Tree Full of Life,* T474 |
| **LANGUAGE ARTS** | | | |
| **Whole Group** | **Writing** | **Informative/Explanatory Writing** Prepare to Present Your Writing, T470 | **Informative/Explanatory Writing** Discuss Peer Feedback, T470 |

Writing Process

|  | DAY 3 | DAY 4 | DAY 5 |
|---|---|---|---|
|  | **Reading Digitally,** T464 | **Reading Digitally,** T464 | **Research and Inquiry,** T468–T469 |
|  | **TIME** **FOR KIDS** "Under the Sea" | **TIME** **FOR KIDS** "Under the Sea" | Presentation |
|  | Close Reading | Write About Reading *Analytical Writing* | ✓ **Unit Assessment,** T476–T477 |
|  |  | **Reader's Theater,** T462 |  |
|  |  | Performance |  |
|  | **Research and Inquiry Projects** | **Research and Inquiry Projects** |  |
|  | **Level Up to On Level** | **Level Up to On Level** | **Level Up to On Level** |
|  | *A Tree Full of Life,* T472 | "Life in a Termite Mound," T472 | Literature Circle, T472 |
|  | **Level Up to Beyond Level** | **Level Up to Beyond Level** | **Level Up to Beyond Level** |
|  | *A Tree Full of Life,* T473 | "Life in a Termite Mound," T473 | Literature Circle, T473 |
|  | **Level Up to Self-Selected** | **Level Up to Self-Selected** | **Level Up to Self-Selected** |
|  | **Trade Book,** T475 | **Trade Book,** T475 | **Trade Book,** T475 |
|  | **Level Up to On Level** | **Level Up to On Level** | **Level Up to On Level** |
|  | *A Tree Full of Life,* T474 | "Life in a Termite Mound," T474 | Literature Circle, T474 |
|  | **Informative/Explanatory Writing** | **Informative/Explanatory Writing** | **Informative/Explanatory Writing** |
|  | Rehearse Your Presentation, T470 | Present Your Writing, T471 | Portfolio Choice, T471 |
|  |  | Evaluate Your Presentation, T471 |  |

# Reader's Theater

*The Secret Song*

by Margaret Wise Brown

Group 1: Who saw the petals drop from the rose?
Group 2: I, said the spider, But nobody knows.
Group 1: Who saw the sunset flash on the bird?
Group 2: I, said the fish, But nobody heard.
Group 1: Who saw the fog come over the sea?
Group 2: I, said the pigeon, Only me.
Group 1: Who saw the first green light of the sun?
Group 2: I, said the night owl, The only one.
Group 1: Who saw the moss creep over the stone?
Group 2: I, said the grey fox, All alone.

*The Secret Song* 47

**Go Digital!**

Teacher's Resource PDF Online, p. 11

### OBJECTIVES

**CCSS** Read with sufficient accuracy and fluency to support comprehension. **RF.2.4**

**CCSS** Read on-level text with purpose and understanding. **RF.2.4a**

**CCSS** Read on-level text orally with accuracy, appropriate rate, and expression on successive readings. **RF.2.4b**

**CCSS** Use context to confirm or self-correct word recognition and understanding, rereading as necessary. **RF.2.4c**

## The Secret Song

### Introduce

Explain that *The Secret Song* is a poem for groups to read (choral read). Distribute scripts from the Online **Teacher's Resource PDF Online, 11.**

→ Explain that this play only has two parts: Group 1 and Group 2.

→ Build background on things animals might see in nature.

### Shared Reading

Model reading the play as the children follow along in their scripts.

**Focus on Vocabulary** Stop and discuss any vocabulary words that children may not know. You may wish to teach:

→ petals          → flash

→ nobody          → creep

**Model Fluency** Explain that this play has only two parts. The goal is for children to read as a group (chorally). Then model fluent reading of the play, and read each part emphasizing the appropriate phrasing and expression.

### Discuss Each Role

→ Tell children that each group must practice reading each part together paying attention to expression and pace . They need to work together so that as they read, as a group they communicate the correct tone and feeling the writer intended.

### Assign Roles

You may wish to pair children to perform read together. Depending on the number of children, you may wish to split the class into an even number of groups and have children perform each part as Group 1 or Group 2.

### Practice the Play

Each day, allow children time to practice their parts. Pair fluent readers with less fluent readers. Pairs can echo-read or choral-read their parts. As needed, work with less fluent reader to mark pauses in their script using one slash for a short pause and two slashes for longer pauses.

Throughout the week have children work on the Reader's Theater **Workstation Activity Card 26.**

Once children have practice reading their parts several times, allow them time to practice performing the script.

### Perform

→ Lead a class discussion about ways each group could make their performances more enjoyable to the audience.

→ If children need to work in groups, remind children to listen for other members of their group when its time to read their parts. All group members should do their best to read together.

# ACTIVITIES

## WHO'S SPEAKING?

Have children recall the two parts that were read. Explain that there are no character names but groups that read the two parts. Reread *The Secret Song*. Then discuss the following questions with children:

1. What animal do you read about first? Why might this animal be near a flower?

2. What animals make up Group 2?

3. Who might be speaking in Group 1?

4. What words do the animals use to answer Group 1's questions? What do these words tell you about the animals?

## ANIMAL VOICES

Ask children to identify the animals in the poem Then have them share what they think each animal might sound like. Ask questions to help guide children, such as: *Would a spider sound the same as a fish? What do a pigeon and an owl have in common? Would they sound the same?* Have children work in groups to generate animal voices and then reread the poem aloud.

## ELL ENGLISH LANGUAGE LEARNERS

→ Review the definitions of difficult words including: *sunset, fog, first green light of the sun, moss*.

→ Team an ELL child with a fluent reader who is also reading the same character parts. Have each reader take turns reading the lines. Determine which reader will read which lines at the performance.

# Reading Digitally

## OBJECTIVES

 **CCSS** Know and use various text features (e.g., captions, bold print, subheadings, glossaries, indexes, electronic menus, icons) to locate key facts or information in a text efficiently. **RI.2.5**

**CCSS** Participate in shared research and writing projects (e.g., read a number of books on a single topic to produce a report; record science observations). **W.2.7**

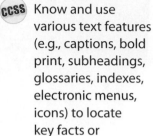

**TIME FOR KIDS®**

# Under the Sea

## Before Reading

**Preview**  Scroll through the online article "Under the Sea" at **connected.mcgraw-hill.com** and have children identify text features. Clarify how to navigate through the article. Point out the interactive features, such as a **hyperlink, map,** and **pop-up.** Explain that you will read the article together first, and then access these features.

## Close Reading Online

**Take Notes**  Scroll back to the top and read the article aloud. As you read, ask questions to draw children's attention to how certain events in the text caused others. Have children take notes using **Graphic Organizer 13**. After each section, have partners paraphrase the main ideas, giving text evidence. Make sure children understand domain-specific terms, such as *species*.

**Access Interactive Features**  Help children access the interactive features by clicking or rolling over each feature. Discuss what information these elements add to the text.

Tell children they will reread parts of the article to help them answer a specific question: *What kinds of animals live in the deep sea?* Point out they need not read every word. Have children skim the article to find details that tell about some new species that scientists found in the deep sea. Have partners share what they find.

**Navigate Links to Information**  Point out that online texts may include **hyperlinks**. Hyperlinks provide a connection from the Web page you are on to another Web page with related information.

Model how to use a hyperlink to jump to another Web page. Discuss any information on the new Web page related to the question *What kinds of animals live in the deep sea?* Model evaluating the Web page as a source for information for children. Find the author or organization that published the site. Show any dates that tell when the information was last updated. Tell children that the best Web sites to use for research are usually written by educational organizations or government sources.

## WRITE ABOUT READING  *Analytical Writing*

**Summarize** Review children's graphic organizers. Model using the information to summarize "Under the Sea."

Ask children to write a brief summary of the article, telling some different events and ideas that caused scientists to learn more about deep-sea animals. Partners should discuss their summaries.

**Make Connections** Have children compare what they learned about deep sea animals with what they have learned about animals and their habitats. Have children use texts they have read this unit.

## SCIENCE CONNECT TO CONTENT

**Habitats** Remind children that animals live all over the planet, including on land, in the air, and deep in the sea. Discuss with children how these different habitats help animals meet their basic needs for food, water, and air.

Help children identify information in this article about what deep sea habitats and the animals that live there are like.

→ The deep sea is more than three miles from the surface of the ocean, so it receives very little light.

→ Tiny sea creatures live buried in the thick mud of the ocean floor.

## RESEARCH ONLINE

**Key Words** Tell children that picking good key words will help them conduct online research. Explain that they should use a few key words that show the most important ideas to their topics. Tell them that using more words will give them fewer, narrower results.

**Choosing Reliable Sources** Tell children that they can use the endings of Web addresses to help find out who publishes a certain Web site. The ending *.com* means that a commercial organization publishes a Web page, and that *.edu*, *.gov*, and *.org* show education, government, and non-profit organizations.

## INDEPENDENT STUDY

**Investigate**

**Choose a Topic** Children should brainstorm questions related to the article. For example, they might ask: *How do animals live deep in the sea?* Then have children choose a question to research. Help them narrow it.

**Conduct Internet Research** Help children select a few key words to begin their online research. After they enter the key words into a search engine, work with children to choose a reliable *.edu* or *.gov* Web page to begin their research.

**Present** Have groups present a round-table discussion on the topic of deep sea animals.

# RESEARCH AND INQUIRY

**The Big Idea:** *How do animals play a part in the world around us?*

**Assign the Projects** Have children work in five groups. Assign each group one of the five Projects that follow or let groups self-select their project. Before children begin researching, present these minilessons.

## Research Skill: Gathering Information from Multiple Sources

### OBJECTIVES

**CCSS** With guidance and support from adults, use a variety of digital tools to produce and publish writing, including in collaboration with peers. **W.2.6**

**CCSS** Participate in shared research and writing projects (e.g., read a number of books on a single topic to produce a report; record science observations). **W.2.7**

**CCSS** Ask and answer questions about what a speaker says in order to clarify comprehension, gather additional information, or deepen understanding of a topic or issue. **SL.2.3**

**CCSS** Create audio recordings of stories or poems; add drawings or other visual displays to stories or recounts of experiences when appropriate to clarify ideas, thoughts, and feelings. **SL.2.5**

### Selecting Appropriate Sources

→ Children may gather information from a variety of print and digital resources. In print resources, they may look at text features such as tables of contents, headings and subheadings, indices, and boldface words to help them research. In digital resources, they may investigate features such as hyperlinks, pop-ups, roll-over features, and interactive charts.

→ Both primary and secondary sources may be helpful for children's research. Appropriate primary sources may include video footage and photographs. Appropriate secondary sources may include reference work or informative Web pages.

→ Children should evaluate print and digital sources for relevance and reliability. The best and most trustworthy Web resources are educational and government Web sites ending in *.edu* or *.gov*.

### Alphabetical Order

→ Remind children that organizing a list into alphabetical order means ordering it according to the first letter of the first word, beginning with *A* and working through to *Z*. Explain that entries beginning with numerals are usually listed separately at the beginning of an alphabetical list.

→ Suggest that children write their notes from various sources on individual note cards. Then, children may organize their note cards in alphabetical order according to the first letter of the author's last name.

→ Tell children that a bibliography, or a listing of all sources cited, is usually added to a research project. Explain that bibliographies are normally organized alphabetically by the author's last name. Then model alphabetizing sources in a bibliography.

 Go Digital

 **COLLABORATE**
Manage and assign Projects online. Children can also work with their group online.

# Choose a Project!

## Compare and Contrast Animals

**1**

**ESSENTIAL QUESTION**
*How do animals survive?*

**Goal**
Research groups will use the list of facts from the weekly research to determine the main features and characteristics of animals that live in cold and hot environments.

STEM

## Review of Two Fables

**2**

**ESSENTIAL QUESTION**
*What can animals in stories teach us?*

**Goal**
Group members will research to find two versions of the same fable. Then they will write a review comparing how each version communicates the lesson.

## Shared Habitat Posters

**3**

**ESSENTIAL QUESTION**
*What are features of different animal habitats?*

**Goal**
Group members will explore which animals share habitats and group them to create posters showing the variety of animals living in one environment.

STEM

## Life Cycle Booklet

**4**

**ESSENTIAL QUESTION**
*How are offspring like their parents?*

**Goal**
Research groups will select one of the animals from the weekly project and create a life cycle booklet that shows in words and pictures how their animal grows.

STEM

## Animal Poems

**5**

**ESSENTIAL QUESTION**
*What do we love about animals?*

**Goal**
Group members will do research on an animal they find funny or interesting and collaborate to write a poem.

STEM

# RESEARCH AND INQUIRY

Distribute the Research Roadmap found online. Have children use the roadmap to complete the project.

## Conducting the Research

**STEP 1** **Set Research Goals**

Discuss with children the Essential Question and the research project. As appropriate, have them look at the Shared Research Board for information they have already gathered. Each group should

→ make sure they are clear on their research focus and end product.

→ decide on each member's role. *Who will do the primary research? Who will gather the information? Who will be in charge of technology? Who will provide art or music? Who will speak during the presentation?*

**STEP 2** **Identify Sources**

Have the group brainstorm where they can find the information. Sources might include

→ print works, such as informational texts and reference books

→ digital media, such as online newspapers, videos, maps, and community Web sites

→ interviews with experts

Remind children that using a variety of sources will ensure a more complete and accurate presentation.

**STEP 3** **Find and Record Information**

Have children review the research strategies presented on page T466. Then have them do the research. Remind them to list their sources carefully.

**STEP 4** **Organize**

After team members have completed the research, they can review and analyze all the information they collected. First they should classify and categorize their notes in order to determine the most useful information. Then they can create a rough version of their end product as a way to clarify categories of information.

**STEP 5** **Synthesize and Present**

Have team members synthesize their research and decide on their final message.

→ Encourage children to use all available technologies, such as audio recordings and visual displays, to enhance their presentations.

→ Children shoud make sure research relates to the Big Idea.

### Audience Participation

→ Encourage the audience to make comments and ask clarifying questions.

→ Have children respond to others' audio or visual presentations by suggesting a topic for another verse or visual to add.

# Review and Evaluate

Distribute the **online PDF** of the checklists and rubric. Use the following **Teacher Checklist** and rubric to evaluate children's research and presentations.

## Student Checklist

### Research Process

- ☑ Did you create a research topic?
- ☑ Did you work with your teammates?
- ☑ Did you gather information from print and digital sources?
- ☑ Did you take notes and organize your information?

### Presenting

- ☑ Did you practice your presentation?
- ☑ Did you express your ideas clearly?
- ☑ Did you support your topic with appropriate facts and details?
- ☑ Did you speak clearly at an understandable pace?
- ☑ Did you make eye contact with your audience?
- ☑ Did you use appropriate drawings or visual displays in your presentation?

## Teacher Checklist

### Assess the Research Process

- ☑ Selected a research topic.
- ☑ Worked well with teammates.
- ☑ Used information from multiple sources.
- ☑ Used important facts and details.

### Assess the Presentation

- ☑ Expressed ideas clearly.
- ☑ Supported the topic with facts and details.
- ☑ Spoke clearly and at an appropriate pace.
- ☑ Maintained eye contact.
- ☑ Used appropriate audio or visual displays.
- ☑ Shared responsibility among members.

### Assess the Listener

- ☑ Listened quietly and attentively.
- ☑ Asked questions to understand.
- ☑ Contributed to the discussion by linking his or her comments with others.
- ☑ Contributed to the discussion by describing the key details of the presentation.

# Project Rubric

| **4** Excellent | **3** Good | **2** Fair | **1** Unsatisfactory |
|---|---|---|---|
| → Presents the information clearly. <br> → Includes information from many sources. <br> → May include sophisticated observations. | → Presents the information adequately. <br> → Provides adequate information from adequate sources. <br> → Includes relevant observations. | → Attempts to present information. <br> → Relied on few sources. <br> → May include few or irrelevant observations. | → May show little grasp of the task. <br> → May rely on no sources. <br> → May reflect extreme difficulty with research or presentation. |

# Celebrate Share Your Writing

## Publishing Celebrations

### Giving Presentations

Now is the time for children to share one of their pieces of informative writing and how-to writing they have worked on through the unit.

You may wish to invite parents or students from other classes to the Publishing Celebrations.

### Preparing for Presentations

Tell children that they will present their writing. Remind them that preparing for their presentation will help them best share their information with listeners.

Allow children time to rehearse their presentation. Encourage them to reread their writing a few times. Point out that children may wish to demonstrate the how-to process told about in their writing to help listeners understand.

Children should consider any visuals or digital elements that they may want to use to present their information. Discuss a few possible options with children.

→ Do they wish to have illustrations or posters to show how to do the tasks and steps told about in their writing?

→ Are there props or objects that will show the end products for how-to pieces?

→ Is there a Web site or slideshow related to their writing that they can project?

Children can practice presenting to a partner in the classroom. They can also practice with family members at home or in front of a mirror. Share the following checklist with children to help them focus on important parts of their presentation as they rehearse. Discuss each point on the checklist.

### Speaking Checklist

Review the Speaking Checklist with children as they practice.

- ☑ Have all your notes, visuals, and props ready.
- ☑ Take a few breaths.
- ☑ Stand up straight.
- ☑ Make eye contact with listeners in the audience.
- ☑ Speak clearly and slowly.
- ☑ Speak loud enough so everyone can hear.
- ☑ Use appropriate gestures and props to show key steps.
- ☑ Remember to show your drawings or visuals.
- ☑ Be sure to include all the relevant facts and details.
- ☑ Remember to smile!

# Listening to Presentations

Remind children that they not only will take on the role of a presenter, but also the audience. As a listener, children have an important role.

## Listening Checklist

### During the Presentation

☑ Watch the speaker carefully.

☑ Take notes on one or two things you liked about the presentation.

☑ Write one question about something you would like to know more about.

☑ Listen quietly and respectfully.

☑ Wait for the speaker to finish presenting before asking questions.

### After the Presentation

☑ Be sure that your comments relate to the presentation.

☑ Tell why you liked the presentation.

☑ If someone else makes the same comment first, tell why you agree.

☑ Explain something you would like to know more about.

☑ Ask your question.

## Portfolio Choice

Ask children to select one finished piece of writing, as well as two revisions, to include in their writing portfolio.

### Published Writing

Does your writing

→ include a clear sequence?

→ give enough details to explain your ideas?

→ use good transitions?

→ have few or no spelling errors?

→ have a neat and clear final draft?

### Sample Revisions

Did you choose a revised entry that shows

→ a better sequence of steps?

→ good linking words to connect your ideas?

→ key details to help the reader understand?

**GO DIGITAL**
Children can submit their writing to be considered for inclusion in their digital portfolio. Children's portfolios can be shared with parents.

# Level Up Accelerating Progress

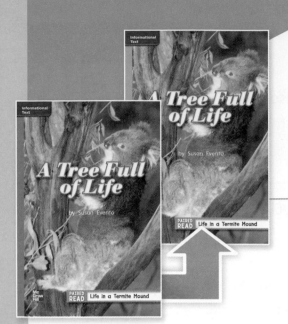

**Leveled Reader**

### OBJECTIVES

**CCSS** By the end of the year, read and comprehend informational texts, including history/ social studies, science, and technical texts, in the grades 2–3 text complexity band proficiently, with scaffolding as needed at the high end of the range. **RI.2.10**

## Approaching Level to On Level

### *A Tree Full of Life*

Level Up Lessons **also available online**

### Before Reading

**Preview** Discuss what children remember about eucalyptus trees. Tell them they will be reading a more challenging version of *A Tree Full of Life*.

**Vocabulary** Use the Visual Vocabulary Cards and routine.

### A C T Access Complex Text During Reading

▶ **Genre** Tell children that writers of informational texts may tell a story to help readers understand a complex idea. Read about the koala on pages 4–6 with children. Help them understand that this text tells a story about a koala. It follows a sequence, or order, of events in the day of a life of a koala. Be sure that children understand the difference between a fictional story about an animal and a story like this one.

▶ **Sentence Structures** Children may need help understanding the use of introductory phrases. Read the first sentence on page 8 with children. Point out the phrase *Like the koala*. Explain that this phrase shows that the author is comparing the koalas to the termites. Tell children that the subject of the sentence is *the termites*.

▶ **Lack of Prior Knowledge** Draw children's attention to the map on page 2. Tell them that they will be reading about Australia. Explain that Australia is a continent located far to the southwest of North America. Point out that Australia is also an island. Tell children that many plants and animals live on Australia that do not live elsewhere on Earth.

### After Reading

Have children complete the Respond to Reading on page 15. Have students complete the Paired Read and hold Literature Circles.

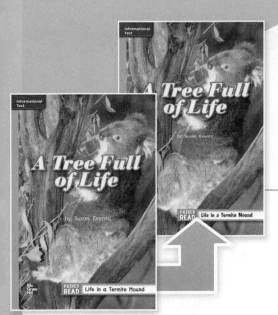

**Leveled Reader**

---

**OBJECTIVES**

CCSS By the end of the year, read and comprehend informational texts, including history/ social studies, science, and technical texts, in the grades 2–3 text complexity band proficiently, with scaffolding as needed at the high end of the range. **RI.2.10**

# On Level to Beyond Level

## *A Tree Full of Life*

**Level Up Lessons** also available online

### Before Reading

**Preview**  Discuss what children remember about eucalyptus trees. Tell them they will be reading a more challenging version of *A Tree Full of Life.*

**Vocabulary**  Use the Visual Vocabulary Cards and routine.

### A C T  Access Complex Text During Reading

▶ **Specific Vocabulary**  Review with children the following science words that are new to this title. Model how to use sentence clues or the glossary to determine their meaning. *marsupial     shelter*

▶ **Purpose**  Explain that authors of informative texts sometimes subtly present ideas and opinions along with facts. They may use different tones to encourage the reader to think a certain way. After children finish reading, ask them to share what they think the author's opinion of the eucalyptus might be. Ask: *Does the author think the eucalyptus tree is good or bad?* (Good.) *How do you know?* (The author provides facts and details about how the eucalyptus tree helps animals survive. This shows that the tree is good.)

▶ **Organization**  Remind children that informational texts rely on a text structure. Read pages 6–7 with children. Point out the features of the compare/contrast text structure. Work with children to find one way that both koalas and termites are alike. Then help them find one way that koalas and termites are different.

### After Reading

Have children complete the Respond to Reading on page 15. Have students complete the Paired Read and hold Literature Circles.

# Level Up Accelerating Progress

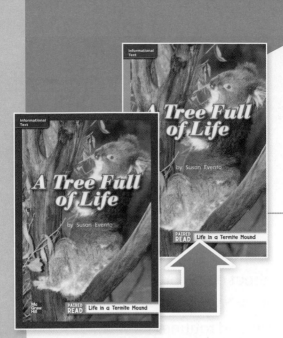

**Leveled Reader**

**OBJECTIVES**

By the end of the year, read and comprehend informational texts, including history/ social studies, science, and technical texts, in the grades 2–3 text complexity band proficiently, with scaffolding as needed at the high end of the range. **RI.2.10**

# English Language Learners to On Level

## A Tree Full of Life

**Level Up Lessons** also available online

### Before Reading

**Preview** Remind children that informational text gives facts about a topic. Point out the map on page 2. Discuss what children remember about eucalyptus trees. Tell them they will be reading a more challenging version of *A Tree Full of Life*.

**Vocabulary** Use the Visual Vocabulary Cards and routine. Point out the cognates: *pasta, vitaminas.*

### A C T Access Complex Text During Reading

▶ **Lack of Prior Knowledge** Draw children's attention to the map on page 2. Tell them that they will be reading about Australia. Explain that Australia is a continent located far to the southwest of North America. Point out that Australia is also an island. Tell children that many plants and animals live on Australia that do not live elsewhere on Earth.

▶ **Specific Vocabulary** Children may need help understanding and using unfamiliar names of animals such as *koala, termite,* and *kookaburra*. Point out the photographs on pages 4, 7, and 9. Invite children to share the name for each animal in their home language.

▶ **Connection of Ideas** Children may need help connecting and synthesizing ideas from page to page and section to section. After completing each paragraph, model for children how to make connections from the information in the paragraph they just read to the information from the previous paragraph.

### After Reading

Have children complete the Respond to Reading on page 15. Have students complete the Paired Read and hold Literature Circles.

## Listening to Presentations

Remind children that they not only will take on the role of a presenter, but also the audience. As a listener, children have an important role.

### Listening Checklist

**During the Presentation**

- ☑ Watch the speaker carefully.
- ☑ Take notes on one or two things you liked about the presentation.
- ☑ Write one question about something you would like to know more about.
- ☑ Listen quietly and respectfully.
- ☑ Wait for the speaker to finish presenting before asking questions.

**After the Presentation**

- ☑ Be sure that your comments relate to the presentation.
- ☑ Tell why you liked the presentation.
- ☑ If someone else makes the same comment first, tell why you agree.
- ☑ Explain something you would like to know more about.
- ☑ Ask your question.

## Portfolio Choice

Ask children to select one finished piece of writing, as well as two revisions, to include in their writing portfolio.

**Published Writing**

Does your writing

→ include a clear sequence?

→ give enough details to explain your ideas?

→ use good transitions?

→ have few or no spelling errors?

→ have a neat and clear final draft?

**Sample Revisions**

Did you choose a revised entry that shows

→ a better sequence of steps?

→ good linking words to connect your ideas?

→ key details to help the reader understand?

**GO DIGITAL**

Children can submit their writing to be considered for inclusion in their digital portfolio. Children's portfolios can be shared with parents.

# Level Up Accelerating Progress

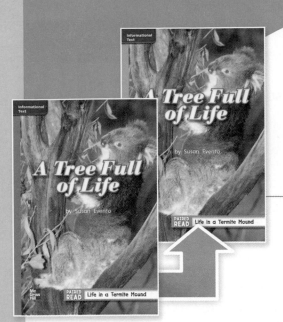

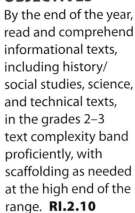

**Leveled Reader**

 **OBJECTIVES**
By the end of the year, read and comprehend informational texts, including history/ social studies, science, and technical texts, in the grades 2–3 text complexity band proficiently, with scaffolding as needed at the high end of the range. **RI.2.10**

## Approaching Level to On Level

### *A Tree Full of Life*

**Level Up Lessons** also available online

### Before Reading

**Preview**  Discuss what children remember about eucalyptus trees. Tell them they will be reading a more challenging version of *A Tree Full of Life*.

**Vocabulary**  Use the Visual Vocabulary Cards and routine.

### A C T  Access Complex Text During Reading

▶ **Genre**  Tell children that writers of informational texts may tell a story to help readers understand a complex idea. Read about the koala on pages 4–6 with children. Help them understand that this text tells a story about a koala. It follows a sequence, or order, of events in the day of a life of a koala. Be sure that children understand the difference between a fictional story about an animal and a story like this one.

▶ **Sentence Structures**  Children may need help understanding the use of introductory phrases. Read the first sentence on page 8 with children. Point out the phrase *Like the koala*. Explain that this phrase shows that the author is comparing the koalas to the termites. Tell children that the subject of the sentence is *the termites*.

▶ **Lack of Prior Knowledge**  Draw children's attention to the map on page 2. Tell them that they will be reading about Australia. Explain that Australia is a continent located far to the southwest of North America. Point out that Australia is also an island. Tell children that many plants and animals live on Australia that do not live elsewhere on Earth.

### After Reading

Have children complete the Respond to Reading on page 15. Have students complete the Paired Read and hold Literature Circles.

**Leveled Reader**

---

**OBJECTIVES**

By the end of the year, read and comprehend literature/informational text in the grades 2–3 text complexity band proficiently, with scaffolding as needed at the high end of the range. **RL/RI.2.10**

**Advanced Level Trade Book**

# Beyond Level
# to Self-Selected Trade Book

## Independent Reading

**Level Up Lessons also available online**

### Before Reading

Together with children, identify the particular focus of their reading, based on the text they choose. Children who have chosen the same title will work in groups to closely read the selection throughout the week.

### Close Reading

**Taking Notes** Assign a graphic organizer for children to use to take notes as they read. Reinforce a specific comprehension focus from the unit by choosing one of the graphic organizers that best fits the book.

**Examples:**

| Fiction Titles | Informational Text |
|---|---|
| Character, Setting, Plot | Main Topic and Key Details |
| Graphic Organizer 43 | Graphic Organizer 42 |

**Ask and Answer Questions** Remind children to ask questions as they read. As children meet, have them discuss the section that they have read. They can share the questions they noted and work together to find text evidence to support their answers.

You may wish to have children write their responses to their questions.

### After Reading

**Write About Text**

Have children work together to respond to the text using text evidence to support their writing.

**Examples:**

| Fiction | Informational Text |
|---|---|
| How do the characters in this story work to solve the main problem? | What is the main idea of this text, and what important details support the main idea? |

# SUMMATIVE ASSESSMENT

# Unit Assessment

**✓ COMPREHENSION:**
- Character, Setting, Plot **RL.2.3**
- Plot: Problem and Solution **RL.2.5**
- Main Topic and Key Details **RI.2.1, RI.2.2**
- Key Details **RL.2.1**

**✓ VOCABULARY:**
- Prefixes **L.2.4b**
- Suffixes **L.1.4b**
- Multiple-Meaning Words **L.2.4a**

**✓ PHONICS:**
- Short *o*, Long *o*: *o_e* **RF.2.3a**
- Short *u*, Long *u*: *u_e* **RF.2.3a**
- Soft *c* and *g* **RF.2.3**
- Consonant Digraphs **RF.2.3**
- Three-Letter Blends **RF.2.3**

**✓ ENGLISH LANGUAGE CONVENTIONS:**
- Nouns **L.2.1**
- Singular and Plural Nouns **L.2.1**
- Kinds of Nouns **L.2.1**
- Plural Nouns **L.2.1b**
- Possessive Nouns **L.2.2c**

**✓ WRITING:**
- Writing About Text **RI.2.1, RI.2.2, RL.2.**
- Informative Writing Prompt **W.2.2**

## Assessment Includes

→ Pencil-and-Paper administration

→ Online administration

→ Performance Tasks

→ Writing Prompt

## Additional Assessment Options

Conduct assessments individually using the differentiated passages in **Fluency Assessment**. Children's expected fluency goal for this Unit is **41–61 WCPM** with an accuracy rate of 95% or higher.

### Running Records

Use the instructional reading level determined by the Running Record calculations for regrouping decisions. Children at Level 13 or below should be provided with reteaching on specific Comprehension Skills.

# Using Assessment Results

| TESTED SKILLS | If ... | Then ... |
|---|---|---|
| **COMPREHENSION** | Children answer 0–9 items correctly ... | ... reteach tested skills using the *Tier 2 Comprehension Intervention online PDFs.* |
| **VOCABULARY** | Children answer 0–7 items correctly ... | ... reteach tested skills using the *Tier 2 Vocabulary Intervention online PDFs.* |
| **PHONICS** | Children answer 0–3 items correctly ... | ... reteach tested skills using the *Tier 2 Phonics and Word Study Intervention online PDFs.* |
| **ENGLISH LANGUAGE CONVENTIONS** | Children answer 0–4 items correctly ... | ... reteach tested skills using the *Grammar online PDFs.* |
| **WRITING** | Children score less than "2" on short-response items and less than "3" on extended constructed response items ... | ... reteach tested skills using the appropriate lessons from the Strategies and Skills and/or Write About Reading sections in the *Tier 2 Comprehension Intervention online PDFs.* |
| | Children score less than "3" on the Writing Prompt ... | ... reteach tested skills using the *Writing Process* lessons on pages T480–T491, as needed. |
| **FLUENCY** | Children have a WCPM score of 0–40 ... | ... reteach tested skills using the *Tier 2 Fluency Intervention online PDFs.* |

# Response to Intervention

Use the appropriate sections of the *Placement and Diagnostic Assessment* as well as students' assessment results to designate students requiring:

 **Intervention Online PDFs**

 **WonderWorks Intervention Program**

### Reevaluate Student Grouping

View the *McGraw-Hill Reading Wonders e-Assessment* reports available for this Unit Assessment. Note children who are below the overall proficiency level for the assessment, and use the report to assign small group instruction for students with similar needs.

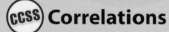

www.connected.mcgraw-hill.com

# INFORMATIONAL TEXT: How-to Text

**Expert Model PDF Online**

### OBJECTIVES

**CCSS** Write informative/explanatory texts in which they introduce a topic, use facts and definitions to develop points, and provide a concluding statement or section. **W.2.2**

**CCSS** Recall information from experiences or gather information from provided sources to answer a question. **W.2.8**

### ACADEMIC LANGUAGE

*explain, time-order words, step, details, concluding statement, purpose, audience, topic, brainstorm, prewrite, draft*

### Read Like a Writer

Point out that when you want to know how to do something, such as making a robot, you might ask someone who knows about robots to explain how to do it. When writers explain how to do something, they use a form of writing known as a how-to text. Read and discuss the features of a how-to text.

Provide copies of the Expert Model "Make a Puppy Sock Puppet" and the features of a How-To Text found online in Writer's Workspace.

**Go Digital**

**Writer's Workspace**

#### Features of a How-to Text

→ It explains how something works or how to do something.

→ It lists numbered steps in an order that makes sense.

→ It uses time-order words.

→ It gives clear details to support each step.

→ It ends with a concluding statement.

### Discuss the Expert Model

**COLLABORATE**

Use the questions below to prompt discussion of the features of how-to texts.

→ When would you write a how-to text? (when you want to tell someone how to do something or explain how something works)

→ Why is it important that the steps be done in a certain order? (It won't turn out right if done in the wrong order.)

→ What words help us know when to do something? (the time-order words *first, next, then,* and *last*)

→ What details does the writer give us? (Draw ovals on the felt for a mouth, a nose, and two ears; the ears can be short and pointy or long and u-shaped; the middle of the bottom of the sock; onto the top of the sock; in front of the ears; below the eyes)

→ What does the concluding statement tell us? (what to do with your puppet)

# PREWRITE

## Discuss and Plan

**Purpose** Discuss with children the purpose for writing a how-to text: to explain how to do something. Invite them to share things they know how to do and that they could explain to someone else. Write their ideas on the board.

**Audience** Have children think about who will be reading their how-to texts, such as classmates, friends, family members, and teachers. Ask: *What information do you think your readers will want to know?*

## Teach the Minilesson

**Order Ideas** Explain that writers must give the steps for a how-to text in the right order. That will help readers understand the steps and when to do them. Time-order words such as *first, next,* and *last* help readers follow the correct order of steps.

Distribute copies of Model Graphic Organizer 23 found online in the Writer's Workspace. Point out that the steps in Jennie's how-to are numbered and given in an order that makes sense. Draw attention to the writer's use of words such as *first* and *then* that help the reader follow from one step to the next.

## Your Turn

**Choose Your Topic** Have partners brainstorm simple things they know how to do well that they could easily explain in 3 or 4 steps, such as how to make a paper airplane, how to make a favorite snack, how to set the table for dinner, how to make a mobile, and so on. Then ask them to focus in on the topics that interest them the most. Ask questions to prompt thinking. Have children record their topics in their Writer's Notebooks.

→ What topic interests you the most?

→ What materials are needed?

→ How many steps are needed?

→ What would you do first? Next? Last?

**Plan** Provide copies of Graphic Organizer 24 found online in Writer's Workspace. Ask children to list the materials at the top of the page and record the main steps in the chart. Remind children to write their steps in the right order.

### ENGLISH LANGUAGE LEARNERS

**Beginning**

**Demonstrate Comprehension** Have children draw pictures of what their how-to will be about. Alternatively, partners can use pantomime to show their how-to.

**Intermediate**

**Explain** Have partners work together to identify and record their materials and steps, using simple words and phrases.

**Advanced/High**

**Expand** Have partners write answers to the Your Turn questions, using simple sentences.

**MODEL GRAPHIC ORGANIZER 23**

1. Draw a mouth, nose, and two eyes on the felt.

2. Cut out the mouth. Glue it onto the bottom of the sock. Let dry.

3. Cut out the ears and nose. Glue the ears onto the top of the sock.

4. Glue the button eyes onto the sock. Glue the nose below the eyes. Let dry.

5. Tell a story using your puppet.

# INFORMATIONAL TEXT: How-to Text

## DRAFT

**OBJECTIVES**

CCSS Write informative/ explanatory texts in which they introduce a topic, use facts and definitions to develop points, and provide a concluding statement or section. **W.2.2**

CCSS Recall information from experiences or gather information from provided sources to answer a question. **W.2.8**

**ACADEMIC LANGUAGE**

*draft, explain, logical order, supporting details, facts, definitions, time-order words, step, materials, revise, conference, peer review*

### Discuss the Student Model

Review the features of how-to texts. Provide copies of the Student Model found online in Writer's Workspace.

### Teach the Minilesson

**Time-Order Words** Explain that writers use time-order words to help their readers follow the sequence of steps.

Read the following steps aloud, leaving out the time-order words at the beginning. Then reread the steps, adding in the time-order words.

1. (First,) get out of bed and go to the kitchen.
2. (Next,) eat your breakfast.
3. (Then) brush your teeth and get dressed for school.
4. (Last,) grab your jacket and school things and head out the door.

Ask children what might happen if the above steps were done out of order.

### Your Turn

**Write a Draft** Have children review the materials lists and numbered steps lists they prepared in Prewrite. Remind them to use time-order words as they draft their how-to text.

**Go Digital**

Writer's Workspace

# Conferencing Routines

## Teacher Conferences

**STEP 1**

Talk about the strengths of the writing.

*The time-order words really help to make the sequence of your steps clear.*

**STEP 2**

Focus on how a writer uses a writing trait.

*Your materials are organized in a logical order that makes it easy to understand when they are used.*

**STEP 3**

Make concrete suggestions for revision.

*Your steps would be clearer if you added a little more detail to them, so that readers knew exactly what to do at each step.*

# REVISE

## Discuss the Revised Model

Distribute copies of the Revised Student Model found online in Writer's Workspace. Read aloud the model, and have children point out the revisions that Max made. Use the specific revisions to show how adding time-order words and details make the how-to text clearer and make the length of the sentences vary, which is more interesting for readers.

## Teach the Minilesson

**Supporting Details** Remind children that writers use details to support and explain a main idea. Supporting details include specific details, facts, and definitions that help readers understand a topic. Point out that Max added the factual detail "such as carrots, lettuce, or sunflower seeds" to his first step so that it would be clear what types of treats a hamster eats. Explain that details change the length of some sentences. Have children find another example of a revision in the Revised Student Model where Max added a supporting detail.

## Your Turn

COLLABORATE

**Revise** Have children to use the peer review routine and questions to review their partner's drafts. Then have children select suggestions from the peer review to incorporate in their revisions. Provide the Revise and Edit Checklist from Writer's Workspace. Suggest they consider adding supporting details to make the steps in their how-to texts clearer.

### REVISED STUDENT MODEL

Revised Student Model • How-to Text • 26

**Caring for Your Hamster**
by Max D.

**What You Need**

cage

hay or shreded paper

plane tissues

hamster food

water bottle

excercise wheel and toys

1. First, feed your hamster some hamster food
   once a day. Give fresh treats two days a week.
   *such as carrots, lettuce, or sunflower seeds*

2. Next, put fresh water in your hamster's water
   bottle. *every day*

3. Then, Remove dirty beding and food from the
   day before.

4. Last, clean your hamster's cage and give it fresh
   beding. *once a week*

   *Most of all,* Play with your hamster every day.

Unit 2 • How-to Text

## Peer Conferences

Review with children the routine for peer review of writing. They should listen carefully as the writer reads his or her work aloud. They should begin by telling what they like about the writing. Then they should ask a question that will help the writer think more about the writing. Finally, they should make a suggestion that will make the writing stronger.

Use these questions for peer review.

- ☑ Does the writing list all the materials in order?
- ☑ Are steps complete and in order?
- ☑ Are supporting details included to make text clearer?
- ☑ Is there a sentence at the end that concludes the how-to text?

# INFORMATIONAL TEXT: How-to Text

## PROOFREAD/EDIT AND PUBLISH

**OBJECTIVES**

**CCSS** With guidance and support from adults and peers, focus on a topic and strengthen writing as needed by revising and editing. **W.2.5**

**CCSS** With guidance and support from adults, use a variety of digital tools to produce and publish writing, including in collaboration with peers. **W.2.6**

**ACADEMIC LANGUAGE**

*proofread, edit, publish, diagrams, video, audio, format, visual, multimedia, evaluate, self-evaluation, rubric*

### Discuss the Edited Model

Provide copies of the Edited Student Model found online in the Writer's Workspace. Read aloud the model and invite children to point out the editing changes that Max made. Use the specific edits to show how editing for complete sentences, spelling, capitalization, and punctuation improves the how-to text.

### Your Turn

**Edit** Have children use the edit questions from the Revise and Edit Checklist to guide them as they independently review and edit their drafts. Remind them that they should look for one type of error at a time.

### Publish

For the final presentation of their how-to texts, have children choose a format for publishing. Children may want to consider:

| Print Publishing | Digital Publishing |
|---|---|
| How-To Index Cards | Writer's Workspace |
| Collaborative Class Book | Class CD of How-To's |
| Collaborative Class Magazine | Class How-To Video |

Whether children handwrite or use a computer, remind them to use standard margins and to format their final drafts so that readers can easily follow their how-to texts.

Point out that visual and multimedia elements can help readers understand informational text. Encourage children to add such elements. Provide time for children to design and include diagrams, photos, illustrations, videos, audio, and other visual or multimedia elements in their writing and presentation.

**Go Digital**

**Writer's Workspace**

**EDITED STUDENT MODEL**

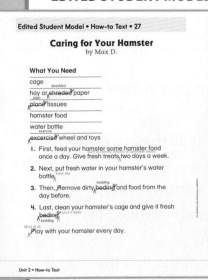

# EVALUATE

## Discuss Rubrics

Guide children in using the Student Rubric found online in Writer's Workspace. Point out that using a rubric helps them identify and focus on areas that might need further work. Work with the class to review the bulleted points on the rubric.

→ **Focus and Coherence** Does the how-to text clearly explain how to do or make something?

→ **Organization** Are all the materials and steps needed on the list? Are they in an order that makes sense?

→ **Ideas and Support** Are enough supporting details provided to help readers understand exactly what to do?

→ **Word Choice** Are time-order words used to show when certain steps are to be done?

→ **Voice/Sentence Fluency** Are the audience and purpose obvious in the writing? Does the writing include a variety of sentence types?

→ **Conventions** Have errors in grammar, spelling, punctuation, and capitalization been corrected?

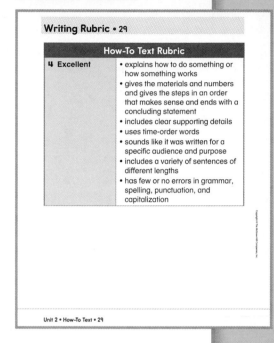

Writing Rubric • 29

| How-To Text Rubric | |
|---|---|
| **4 Excellent** | • explains how to do something or how something works<br>• gives the materials and numbers and gives the steps in an order that makes sense and ends with a concluding statement<br>• includes clear supporting details<br>• uses time-order words<br>• sounds like it was written for a specific audience and purpose<br>• includes a variety of sentences of different lengths<br>• has few or no errors in grammar, spelling, punctuation, and capitalization |

Unit 2 • How-To Text • 29

## Your Turn

**Reflect and Set Goals** After children have evaluated their own how-to texts, ask them to reflect on their progress as writers. Encourage them to think about specific ways in which they have improved as writers and areas in which they need further work. Have them set writing goals to prepare for their conference with you.

### Conference with Students

Use the Rubric and the Anchor Papers provided online in Writer's Workspace to help you evaluate children's work. The anchor papers provide samples of papers with scores from 4 to 1. These papers reflect the criteria described in the Rubric. Anchor papers offer a standard against which to judge children's writing.

Review with individual children the writing goals they have set. Discuss ways to achieve these goals and suggest any further areas of improvement children may need to target.

# INFORMATIONAL TEXT: How-To

**Writing Process Lesson 2**

**Go Digital**

**Writer's Workspace**

### Read Like a Writer

Tell children that everyone needs to know how to get to places they've never been before. Explain that to find out how get to such a place, people can ask for directions. When writers explain how to get from one place to another, they use a form of writing known as how-to directions. Read and discuss the features of how-to directions.

Provide copies of the Expert Model "How to Find the Pet Food" and the features of How-To Directions found online in Writer's Workspace.

**Expert Model PDF Online**

---

**OBJECTIVES**

**CCSS** Write informative/explanatory texts in which they introduce a topic, use facts and definitions to develop points, and provide a concluding statement or section. **W.2.2**

**CCSS** Recall information from experiences or gather information from provided sources to answer a question. **W.2.8**

---

**ACADEMIC LANGUAGE**
*explain, directions, direction words, left, right, step, order, ideas, graphic organizer, purpose, audience*

### Features of How-To Directions

→ They explain how to go from one place to another.

→ They give steps in an order that makes sense.

→ They use direction words, such as *right, left,* and *just before.*

→ They give clear details to support each step.

→ They end with a concluding statement.

### Discuss the Expert Model

**COLLABORATE**

Use the questions below to prompt discussion of the features of how-to directions.

→ Why did the writer write his how-to directions? (to tell someone how to find the pet food)

→ Would it make a difference if the steps were in a different order? (Yes, it would confuse readers and would not get them where they wanted to go.)

→ What words help us know which way to go? (the direction words *straight ahead, right,* and *left*)

→ What details help us picture what we should do? (go in the main doors, walk straight ahead, turn right, go past the check-out lines, look up, turn left when you see the sign for Pets )

→ How does the writer conclude the directions? (He says "It's easy to find pet food at the food store.")

# PREWRITE

## Discuss and Plan

**Purpose** Discuss with children the purpose for writing how-to directions: to explain how to get from one place to another. Invite them to share familiar places at school to which they think they could give directions. Write their ideas on the board.

**Audience** Ask children to tell who their audience, or readers, of their how-to directions will be. If needed, suggest classmates, friends, family members, or teachers. Ask: *What information do you think your readers will need to know?* Record reasonable ideas on the board.

## Teach the Minilesson

**Order Ideas** Explain that for how-to directions writers must give the steps in the right order. This helps readers "see" the steps in their mind and understand what to do. Direction words such as *left, right, after,* and *just before* give readers important details about where and when to do something.

Distribute copies of the Model Graphic Organizer 33 found online in the Writer's Workspace. Point out that Carlos numbered his how-to directions steps in a clear, logical order. Draw attention to the direction words *straight ahead, right, past,* and *left* that give readers clear information about where to go. Point out the conclusion that Carlos gives at the end to sum up his how-to directions.

## ENGLISH LANGUAGE LEARNERS

### Beginning

**Demonstrate Comprehension** Have children partner with a child advanced in the same language and draw a map of their directions.

### Intermediate

**Explain** Have partners work together to create maps and label them with short phrases and sentences for directions.

### Advanced/High

**Expand** Using simple sentences, have partners write and discuss their answers to the Your Turn questions.

## Your Turn

**Choose Your Topic** Have partners or small groups brainstorm places they could give directions to in 3 or 4 steps. Then ask them to think about the topics and choose the most interesting one. Ask questions to prompt thinking. Have children record their topics in their Writer's Notebooks.

→ What topic seems most interesting to you? Why?

→ Who would be interested in reading your directions?

→ What direction would you give first? Next? Then? Last?

**Plan** Provide copies of the Graphic Organizer 34 found online in Writer's Workspace. Ask children to record ideas for their how-to directions and conclusion on the graphic organizer. Remind children to use direction words and to list their steps in the right order.

**MODEL GRAPHIC ORGANIZER 33**

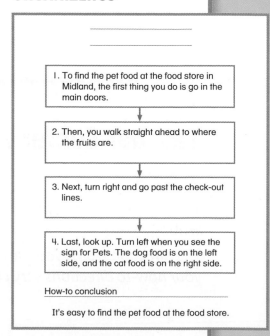

1. To find the pet food at the food store in Midland, the first thing you do is go in the main doors.

2. Then, you walk straight ahead to where the fruits are.

3. Next, turn right and go past the check-out lines.

4. Last, look up. Turn left when you see the sign for Pets. The dog food is on the left side, and the cat food is on the right side.

How-to conclusion

It's easy to find the pet food at the food store.

# INFORMATIONAL TEXT: How-To

## DRAFT

### OBJECTIVES

 **CCSS** Write informative/ explanatory texts in which they introduce a topic, use facts and definitions to develop points, and provide a concluding statement or section. **W.2.2**

**CCSS** With guidance and support from adults and peers, focus on a topic and strengthen writing as needed by revising and editing. **W.2.5**

### ACADEMIC LANGUAGE

*explain, draft, revise, audience, purpose, voice, formal, informal, graphic organizer, precise, language*

## Discuss the Student Model

Review the features of how-to directions. Provide copies of the Student Model found online in Writer's Workspace.

## Teach the Minilesson

**Audience and Purpose** Remind children that whenever writers write, they think about their audience and purpose for writing. Point out that for adult audiences, writers often use formal language; for an audience of children, informal language. Give some examples of each for children to discuss. Read the following directions aloud. Work with children to determine the audience and purpose. (adults/formal language; explain how to get to a vet's office)

> To get to the vet's office, turn right onto Park Ave. Drive 5 miles.
>
> Just past the Kleen Car Wash, turn left onto First St.
>
> After passing the middle school, look for #200 on the right. Park in the parking lot across the street.

## Your Turn

**Write a Draft** Have children review the ideas they wrote in their numbered steps graphic organizer. Remind them to keep their audience and purpose in mind as they draft their how-to directions.

# Conferencing Routines

## Teacher Conferences

**STEP 1**

Talk about the strengths of the writing.

*The direction words you use make your how-to directions very clear.*

**STEP 2**

Focus on how a writer uses a writing trait.

*Your writing shows a clear purpose—to explain how to get to the park ranger's office.*

**STEP 3**

Make concrete suggestions for revision.

*Your audience would be clearer if you used a more formal voice for adults or a more informal voice for classmates.*

# REVISE

## Discuss the Revised Model

Distribute copies of the Revised Student Model found online in Writer's Workspace. Read aloud the model, and have children point out the revisions that Peter made. Use the specific revisions to show how adding direction words and details make the how-to directions clearer and more specific and how varying the sentence length makes the directions easier to read and more natural sounding.

## Teach the Minilesson

**Precise Language** Remind children that writers use details to support and explain a main idea. Point out that precise words also help give readers a clear and accurate understanding of directions. Draw attention to Peter's revisions in the first sentence: he added the direction word *left* and the detail *from my home*. Explain that such details make his how-to directions clear and accurate.

Have children find another example in the Revised Student Model where the writer added precise language. Discuss how this revision makes the step clearer for readers.

## Your Turn

COLLABORATE

**Revise** Have children use the peer review routine and questions to review their partner's draft. Then have children select suggestions from the peer review to incorporate in their revisions.

**REVISED STUDENT MODEL**

Revised Student Model • How-To Directions • 36

### How to Get to School
by Peter J.

left from my home
1. First, go on Elm st. Go one block to Pine St.

2. Then, at Pine St, go left.

four
3. Next, go blocks on pine St.

left
4. Last, turn wen you get to #320.

way
That is the fastest to get to School.

Unit 2 • How-To Directions

## Peer Conferences

Review with children the routine for peer review of writing. They should listen carefully as the writer reads his or her work aloud. They should begin by telling what they like about the writing. Then they should ask a question that will help the writer think more about the writing. Finally, they should make a suggestion that will make the writing stronger.

Use these questions for peer review.

☑ Does the writing explain how to get somewhere?

☑ Are the steps complete and in order?

☑ Are direction words and details used to make the steps clear?

☑ Is there a concluding statement at the end?

# INFORMATIONAL TEXT: How-To

## PROOFREAD/EDIT AND PUBLISH

**ACADEMIC LANGUAGE**

*proofread, edit, capitalization, abbreviations, punctuation, proper nouns, publish, margins, formats, map, audio, visual, multimedia, evaluate, self-evaluation, rubric*

**EDITED STUDENT MODEL**

Edited Student Model • How-To Directions • 37

**How to Get to School**
by Peter J.

left from my home
1. First, go on Elm st. Go one block to Pine St.

2. Then, at Pine St. go left.

four
3. Next, go blocks on pine St.

 turn when
4. Last, turn left you get to #320.

 way
That is the fastest, to get to School.

Unit 2 • How-To Directions

### Discuss the Edited Model

Provide copies of the Edited Student Model found online in the Writer's Workspace. Read aloud the model and invite children to point out the edits that Peter made. Use the specific edits to show how editing for spelling, capitalization, and punctuation improves the how-to directions.

### Your Turn

**Edit** Have children use the edit questions on the Revise and Edit Checklist as a guide as they individually review and edit their drafts. Remind them to look for one type of error at a time.

### Publish

For the final presentation of their how-to directions, have children choose a format for publishing. Children may want to consider:

| Print Publishing | Digital Publishing |
|---|---|
| Handwritten Directions and Map | Writer's Workspace |
| Computer-created Directions and Map | E-mail |
| Poster of Directions and Map | PDF or Audio Recording |

Regardless of the mode children use to create their final presentation, remind them to use standard margins and formats so that readers can easily read their how-to directions.

Point out that visual and multimedia elements, such as a map or images of landmarks, can add helpful details for readers. Encourage children to add such elements. Provide time for children to design and include maps, photos, audio, and other visual or multimedia elements in their writing and presentation.

**Go Digital**

**Writer's Workspace**

# EVALUATE

## Discuss Rubrics

Draw attention to the Student Rubric found online in Writer's Workspace. Explain that using a rubric can help them identify and focus on areas needing more work. Review the bulleted points on the rubric with children.

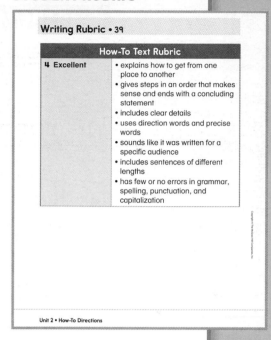

→ **Focus and Coherence** Does the how-to directions clearly explain how to go from one place to another place?

→ **Organization** Are the steps given in an order that makes sense? Do the directions end with a concluding statement?

→ **Ideas and Support** Are the ideas developed so that readers can easily and clearly understand what to do?

→ **Word Choice** Are direction words used to help readers understand the directions? Are precise words used to help readers "see" and follow the directions?

→ **Voice/Sentence Fluency** Does the writing sound as if it was written for a specific audience? Does it include a variety of sentence lengths?

→ **Conventions** Have errors in grammar, spelling, punctuation, and capitalization been corrected?

## Your Turn

**Reflect and Set Goals** After children have evaluated their own how-to directions, ask them to reflect on their progress as writers. Encourage them to think about how they have improved as writers and how they could improve more. Have them record personal writing goals that can be shared during their conference with you.

### Conference with Students

Use the Rubric and the Anchor Papers provided online in Writer's Workspace to help you assess children's work. The Anchor Papers provide sample papers with scores from 4 to 1. These papers reflect the criteria described in the Rubric. Anchor Papers offer a standard against which to evaluate children's writing.

Review with individuals the writing goals they have set. Discuss ways to achieve these goals and suggest additional areas of improvement children may need to target.

### Read the Text  *What does the author tell us?*

**Assign the Reading**

Depending upon the needs of your children, you can

→ ask children to read the text silently

→ read the text together with children

→ read the text aloud.

**Take Notes**

Children generate questions and take notes about aspects of the text that might be confusing for them. Encourage children to note

→ difficult vocabulary words or phrases

→ details that are not clear

→ information that they do not understand

Children complete a graphic organizer to take notes on important information from the text.

### Reread the Text  *What does the text mean?*

**Ask Text Dependent Questions/Generate Questions**

Children reread and discuss and take notes on important shorter passages from the text. Children should

→ generate questions about the text

→ work with partners or small groups to answer questions using text evidence.

### Write About the Text  *Think about what the author wrote.*

Children write a response to the text, using evidence from the text to support their ideas or arguments.

# Use the Literature Anthology

**Getting Ready**

Close Reading of *Turtle, Turtle, Watch Out!*,
pages 164–181

Use the suggestions in the chart to assign reading of the text and to chunk the text into shorter passages for rereading.

**ESSENTIAL QUESTION**  *What are features of different animal habitats?*

 Ask children to discuss the different features of animal habitats that they have learned about.

**Suggested Pacing**

| | | |
|---|---|---|
| Days 1–3 | **Read** | |
| | pp. 164–171 | |
| | pp. 172–177 | |
| | pp. 178–181 | |
| Days 4–9 | **Reread** | |
| | pp. 164–169 | |
| | pp. 170–171 | |
| | pp. 172–175 | |
| | pp. 176–177 | |
| | pp. 178–179 | |
| | pp. 180–181 | |
| Days 10–11 | **Write** | |
| | **About Text** | |

---

**Read the Text**  *What does the author tell us?*

**Assign the Reading** Ask children to read the text independently. You may wish to read together pages 164–171 due to the difficult domain-specific vocabulary in the text.

**Take Notes** As children read, ask them to generate questions and other notes on features in the text they find difficult to understand. For this selection, children may note:

→ uncertainty about the author's purpose

→ lack of prior knowledge about the science content

→ words they do not know

→ difficulty making connections between text sections

Model for children how to take notes.

**Think Aloud** I do not know what some of the words mean, such as *yolk sac* and *hatchlings*. The picture shows baby turtles, but I'm not sure how that idea connects to what the author is trying to tell me.

p. 170
Yolk sac?
Hatchlings?

Assign **Graphic Organizer 42** to help children take notes on the main topic and key supporting details in the text.

As children share their questions and notes, use the Access Complex Text suggestions on pages T231A–T231I to help address features about the text that children found difficult.

### Reread the Text   *What does the text mean?*

### Ask Text Dependent Questions/Generate Questions

Ask children to reread the shorter passages from the text, focusing on **how** the author provides information about how the turtle survives in its habitat.

→ **Author's Purpose, pp. 164–169**

→ What does the author want the reader to learn about in this text?

→ How does the information show this purpose?

→ **Word Choice, pp. 170–171, 172–175**

→ How does the author use science words to give important details in this text?

→ **Text Structure, pp. 178–179**

→ How does the author use repetition in this text?

→ Why does the author include this repeated text throughout the story?

→ **Connections within Text, pp. 164–169, 170–171, 178–179**

→ How does the author show how the turtle grows and changes throughout the story?

→ What evidence connects the beginning of the story to the end of the story?

Use the prompts on Teacher Edition pages T231A–T231I for suggested text dependent questions. Remind children that they are to look back into the text to cite evidence to support their answers.

Model citing text evidence as needed.

Why does the author use repetition throughout this text?

**Think Aloud**  I see that the author says "Turtle, turtle, watch out!" on page 167. As I read the text, I see that the author includes this sentence several times. The story and illustrations give evidence that the author says this when the turtle faces a problem or danger. This evidence tells me that the author uses repetition to draw my attention to important dangers the turtle faces in the text.

As they reread each section, children should continue to generate their own questions about the text. As each child shares a question, ask all children to go back into the text to find text evidence to answer the question. Encourage children to

→ point out the exact place within the text they found the evidence

→ reread and paraphrase the section of the text that they think supports their answer

→ discuss how strong the evidence cited is in answering the question

→ identify when an answer to a question cannot be found in the text.

## Write About the Text  *Think about what the author wrote.*

### Essential Question

Have children response in writing to the Essential Question using evidence from the text.

What are features of different animal habitats?

Children should use their notes and graphic organizers to cite evidence from the text to support their answer.

Model how to use notes to response to the Essential Question.

**Think Aloud**  My notes tell me how the turtle lives and survives in different habitats. My notes on page 166 tell about the turtle's beach habitat. I can use this information in part of my answer. I will read through the rest of my notes to look for more evidence about the turtle's habitats to support my answer.

Children can work with a partner and use their notes and graphic organizer to locate evidence that can be used to answer the question. Encourage children to discuss the strength of the evidence cited and give arguments about what may be strong or weak about a particular citation.

## Use Your Own Text

### Classroom Library

Classroom Library lessons available online.

or **Choose from your own Trade Books**

*Let's Look at Monarch Butterflies*
**Genre** Nonfiction

**Lexile** 510
*TextEvaluator™* 6

*Cam Jansen: The Mystery at the Monkey House #10*
**Genre** Fiction

**Lexile** 530
*TextEvaluator™* 9

*Nate the Great on the Owl Express*
**Genre** Fiction

**Lexile** 280
*TextEvaluator™* 16

*Life in an Ocean*
**Genre** Narrative Nonfiction

**Lexile** 290
*TextEvaluator™* 6

- → Use this model with a text of your choice. Go online for title-specific Classroom Library book lessons.
- → Assign reading of the text. You may wish to do this by section or chapters.
- → Chunk the text into shorter important passages for rereading.
- → Present an Essential Question. You may want to use the Unit Big Idea.

### Read the Text   *What does the author tell us?*

#### Assign the Reading

Ask children to read the assigned sections of the text independently. For sections that are more difficult for children, you may wish to read the text aloud or ask children to read with a partner.

#### Take Notes

As children read, ask them to take notes on difficult parts of the text. Model how to take notes on

- → identifying details or parts that are unclear
- → words they do not know
- → information they feel is important
- → ways in which information or events are connected
- → the genre of the text

You may wish to have children complete a graphic organizer, chosen from within the unit, to take notes on important information as they read. The graphic organizer can help them summarize the text.

Help children access the complex features of the text. Scaffold instruction on the following features as necessary:

- → Purpose
- → Genre
- → Organization
- → Specific Vocabulary

- → Sentence Structure
- → Connections of Ideas
- → Prior Knowledge

## Reread the Text *What does the text mean?*

### Ask Text-Dependent Questions/Generate Questions

 Ask children to reread the shorter passages from the text, focusing on how the author provides information or develops the characters, setting, and plot. Focus questions on the following:

**Literature Selections**

Character, Setting,
Plot: Problem/Solution

Word Choice

Genre

**Informational Text**

Main Topic and Key Details

Word Choice

Text Structure

Text Features

Genre

Have children discuss questions they generated. As each child shares a question, ask all children to go back into the text to find text evidence to answer the question. Encourage children to

- → point out the exact place within the text they found the evidence.
- → reread and paraphrase the section of the text that they think supports their answer.
- → discuss how strong the evidence cited is in answering the question.
- → identify when an answer to a question cannot be found in the text.

## Write About the Text *Think about what the author wrote.*

### Essential Question

Have children respond in writing to the Essential Question, considering the complete text. Children can work with a partner and use their notes and graphic organizer to locate evidence that can be used to answer the question.

# SCOPE & SEQUENCE

| | K | 1 | 2 | 3 | 4 | 5 | 6 |
|---|---|---|---|---|---|---|---|
| **READING PROCESS** | | | | | | | |
| **Concepts About Print/Print Awareness** | | | | | | | |
| Recognize own name | | | | | | | |
| Understand directionality (top to bottom; tracking print from left to right; return sweep, page by page) | ✔ | | | | | | |
| Locate printed word on page | ✔ | | | | | | |
| Develop print awareness (concept of letter, word, sentence) | ✔ | | | | | | |
| Identify separate sounds in a spoken sentence | ✔ | | | | | | |
| Understand that written words are represented in written language by a specific sequence of letters | ✔ | | | | | | |
| Distinguish between letters, words, and sentences | ✔ | | | | | | |
| Identify and distinguish paragraphs | | | | | | | |
| Match print to speech (one-to-one correspondence) | ✔ | | | | | | |
| Name uppercase and lowercase letters | ✔ | | | | | | |
| Understand book handling (holding a book right-side-up, turning its pages) | ✔ | | | | | | |
| Identify parts of a book (front cover, back cover, title page, table of contents); recognize that parts of a book contain information | ✔ | | | | | | |
| **Phonological Awareness** | | | | | | | |
| Recognize and understand alliteration | | | | | | | |
| Segment sentences into correct number of words | | | | | | | |
| Identify, blend, segment syllables in words | | ✔ | | | | | |
| Recognize and generate rhyming words | ✔ | ✔ | | | | | |
| Identify, blend, segment onset and rime | ✔ | ✔ | | | | | |
| **Phonemic Awareness** | | | | | | | |
| Count phonemes | ✔ | ✔ | | | | | |
| Isolate initial, medial, and final sounds | ✔ | ✔ | | | | | |
| Blend spoken phonemes to form words | ✔ | ✔ | | | | | |
| Segment spoken words into phonemes | ✔ | ✔ | | | | | |
| Distinguish between long- and short-vowel sounds | ✔ | ✔ | | | | | |
| Manipulate phonemes (addition, deletion, substitution) | ✔ | ✔ | | | | | |
| **Phonics and Decoding /Word Recognition** | | | | | | | |
| Understand the alphabetic principle | ✔ | ✔ | | | | | |
| Sound/letter correspondence | ✔ | ✔ | ✔ | ✔ | | | |
| Blend sounds into words, including VC, CVC, CVCe, CVVC words | ✔ | ✔ | ✔ | ✔ | | | |
| Blend common word families | ✔ | ✔ | ✔ | ✔ | | | |

| KEY | ✔ = Assessed Skill<br>Tinted panels show skills, strategies, and other teaching opportunities. |
|---|---|

| | K | 1 | 2 | 3 | 4 | 5 | 6 |
|---|---|---|---|---|---|---|---|
| Initial consonant blends | | ✔ | ✔ | ✔ | | | |
| Final consonant blends | | ✔ | ✔ | ✔ | | | |
| Initial and medial short vowels | ✔ | ✔ | ✔ | ✔ | ✔ | ✔ | ✔ |
| Decode one-syllable words in isolation and in context | ✔ | ✔ | ✔ | ✔ | | | |
| Decode multisyllabic words in isolation and in context using common syllabication patterns | | ✔ | ✔ | ✔ | ✔ | ✔ | ✔ |
| Distinguish between similarly spelled words | ✔ | ✔ | ✔ | ✔ | ✔ | ✔ | ✔ |
| Monitor accuracy of decoding | | | | | | | |
| Identify and read common high-frequency words, irregularly spelled words | ✔ | ✔ | ✔ | ✔ | | | |
| Identify and read compound words, contractions | | ✔ | ✔ | ✔ | ✔ | ✔ | ✔ |
| Use knowledge of spelling patterns to identify syllables | | ✔ | ✔ | ✔ | ✔ | ✔ | ✔ |
| Regular and irregular plurals | ✔ | ✔ | ✔ | ✔ | ✔ | ✔ | ✔ |
| Long vowels (silent *e*, vowel teams) | ✔ | ✔ | ✔ | ✔ | ✔ | ✔ | ✔ |
| Vowel digraphs (variant vowels) | | ✔ | ✔ | ✔ | ✔ | ✔ | ✔ |
| *r*-Controlled vowels | | ✔ | ✔ | ✔ | ✔ | ✔ | ✔ |
| Hard/soft consonants | | ✔ | ✔ | ✔ | ✔ | ✔ | |
| Initial consonant digraphs | | ✔ | ✔ | ✔ | ✔ | ✔ | |
| Medial and final consonant digraphs | | ✔ | ✔ | ✔ | ✔ | | |
| Vowel diphthongs | | ✔ | ✔ | ✔ | ✔ | ✔ | ✔ |
| Identify and distinguish letter-sounds (initial, medial, final) | ✔ | ✔ | ✔ | | | | |
| Silent letters | | ✔ | ✔ | ✔ | ✔ | ✔ | ✔ |
| Schwa words | | | | ✔ | ✔ | ✔ | ✔ |
| Inflectional endings | | ✔ | ✔ | ✔ | ✔ | ✔ | ✔ |
| Triple-consonant clusters | | ✔ | ✔ | ✔ | ✔ | | |
| Unfamiliar and complex word families | | | | ✔ | ✔ | ✔ | ✔ |

**Structural Analysis/Word Analysis**

| | K | 1 | 2 | 3 | 4 | 5 | 6 |
|---|---|---|---|---|---|---|---|
| Common spelling patterns (word families) | | ✔ | ✔ | ✔ | ✔ | ✔ | ✔ |
| Common syllable patterns | | ✔ | ✔ | ✔ | ✔ | ✔ | ✔ |
| Inflectional endings | | ✔ | ✔ | ✔ | ✔ | ✔ | ✔ |
| Contractions | | ✔ | ✔ | ✔ | ✔ | ✔ | ✔ |
| Compound words | | ✔ | ✔ | ✔ | ✔ | ✔ | ✔ |
| Prefixes and suffixes | | ✔ | ✔ | ✔ | ✔ | ✔ | ✔ |
| Root or base words | | | ✔ | ✔ | ✔ | ✔ | ✔ |
| Comparatives and superlatives | | | ✔ | ✔ | ✔ | ✔ | ✔ |
| Greek and Latin roots | | | ✔ | ✔ | ✔ | ✔ | ✔ |

**Fluency**

| | K | 1 | 2 | 3 | 4 | 5 | 6 |
|---|---|---|---|---|---|---|---|
| Apply letter/sound knowledge to decode phonetically regular words accurately | ✔ | ✔ | ✔ | ✔ | ✔ | ✔ | ✔ |
| Recognize high-frequency and familiar words | ✔ | ✔ | ✔ | ✔ | ✔ | ✔ | ✔ |
| Read regularly on independent and instructional levels | | | | | | | |
| Read orally with fluency from familiar texts (choral, echo, partner, Reader's Theater) | | | | | | | |
| Use appropriate rate, expression, intonation, and phrasing | | ✔ | ✔ | ✔ | ✔ | ✔ | ✔ |
| Read with automaticity (accurately and effortlessly) | | ✔ | ✔ | ✔ | ✔ | ✔ | ✔ |
| Use punctuation cues in reading | | ✔ | ✔ | ✔ | ✔ | ✔ | ✔ |

| | K | 1 | 2 | 3 | 4 | 5 | 6 |
|---|---|---|---|---|---|---|---|
| Adjust reading rate to purpose, text difficulty, form, and style | | | | | | | |
| Repeated readings | | | | | | | |
| Timed readings | | ✔ | ✔ | ✔ | ✔ | ✔ | ✔ |
| Read with purpose and understanding | | ✔ | ✔ | ✔ | ✔ | ✔ | ✔ |
| Read orally with accuracy | | ✔ | ✔ | ✔ | ✔ | ✔ | ✔ |
| Use context to confirm or self-correct word recognition | | ✔ | ✔ | ✔ | ✔ | ✔ | ✔ |

## READING LITERATURE

### Comprehension Strategies and Skills

| | K | 1 | 2 | 3 | 4 | 5 | 6 |
|---|---|---|---|---|---|---|---|
| Read literature from a broad range of genres, cultures, and periods | | ✔ | ✔ | ✔ | ✔ | ✔ | ✔ |
| Access complex text | | ✔ | ✔ | ✔ | ✔ | ✔ | ✔ |
| Build background | | | | | | | |
| Preview and predict | | | | | | | |
| Establish and adjust purpose for reading | | | | | | | |
| Evaluate citing evidence from the text | | | | | | | |
| Ask and answer questions | ✔ | ✔ | ✔ | ✔ | ✔ | ✔ | ✔ |
| Inferences and conclusions, citing evidence from the text | ✔ | ✔ | ✔ | ✔ | ✔ | ✔ | ✔ |
| Monitor/adjust comprehension including reread, reading rate, paraphrase | | | | | | | |
| Recount/Retell | ✔ | ✔ | | | | | |
| Summarize | | | ✔ | ✔ | ✔ | ✔ | ✔ |
| Story structure (beginning, middle, end) | ✔ | ✔ | ✔ | ✔ | ✔ | ✔ | ✔ |
| Visualize | | | | | | | |
| Make connections between and across texts | | ✔ | ✔ | ✔ | ✔ | ✔ | ✔ |
| Point of view | | ✔ | ✔ | ✔ | ✔ | ✔ | ✔ |
| Author's purpose | | | | | | | |
| Cause and effect | ✔ | ✔ | ✔ | ✔ | ✔ | ✔ | ✔ |
| Compare and contrast (including character, setting, plot, topics) | ✔ | ✔ | ✔ | ✔ | ✔ | ✔ | ✔ |
| Classify and categorize | | ✔ | ✔ | | | | |
| Literature vs informational text | ✔ | ✔ | ✔ | | | | |
| Illustrations, using | ✔ | ✔ | ✔ | ✔ | | | |
| Theme, central message, moral, lesson | | ✔ | ✔ | ✔ | ✔ | ✔ | ✔ |
| Predictions, making/confirming | ✔ | ✔ | ✔ | | | | |
| Problem and solution (problem/resolution) | | ✔ | ✔ | ✔ | ✔ | ✔ | ✔ |
| Sequence of events | ✔ | ✔ | ✔ | ✔ | ✔ | ✔ | ✔ |

### Literary Elements

| | K | 1 | 2 | 3 | 4 | 5 | 6 |
|---|---|---|---|---|---|---|---|
| Character | ✔ | ✔ | ✔ | ✔ | ✔ | ✔ | ✔ |
| Plot development/Events | ✔ | ✔ | ✔ | ✔ | ✔ | ✔ | ✔ |
| Setting | ✔ | ✔ | ✔ | ✔ | ✔ | ✔ | ✔ |
| Stanza | | | | ✔ | ✔ | ✔ | ✔ |
| Alliteration | | | | | | ✔ | ✔ |
| Assonance | | | | | | ✔ | ✔ |
| Dialogue | | | | | | | |
| Foreshadowing | | | | | | ✔ | ✔ |

| KEY | ✔ = Assessed Skill |
|---|---|
| | Tinted panels show skills, strategies, and other teaching opportunities. |

| | K | 1 | 2 | 3 | 4 | 5 | 6 |
|---|---|---|---|---|---|---|---|
| Flashback | | | | | | ✔ | ✔ |
| Descriptive and figurative language | | ✔ | ✔ | ✔ | ✔ | ✔ | ✔ |
| Imagery | | | | | ✔ | ✔ | ✔ |
| Meter | | | | | ✔ | ✔ | ✔ |
| Onomatopoeia | | | | | | | |
| Repetition | | ✔ | ✔ | ✔ | ✔ | ✔ | ✔ |
| Rhyme/rhyme schemes | | ✔ | ✔ | ✔ | ✔ | ✔ | ✔ |
| Rhythm | | ✔ | ✔ | | | | |
| Sensory language | | | | | | | |
| Symbolism | | | | | | | |
| **Write About Reading/Literary Response Discussions** | | | | | | | |
| Reflect and respond to text citing text evidence | | ✔ | ✔ | ✔ | ✔ | ✔ | ✔ |
| Connect and compare text characters, events, ideas to self, to other texts, to world | | | | | | | |
| Connect literary texts to other curriculum areas | | | | | | | |
| Identify cultural and historical elements of text | | | | | | | |
| Evaluate author's techniques, craft | | | | | | | |
| Analytical writing | | | | | | | |
| Interpret text ideas through writing, discussion, media, research | | | | | | | |
| Book report or review | | | | | | | |
| Locate, use, explain information from text features | | ✔ | ✔ | ✔ | ✔ | ✔ | ✔ |
| Organize information to show understanding of main idea through charts, mapping | | | | | | | |
| Cite text evidence | ✔ | ✔ | ✔ | ✔ | ✔ | ✔ | ✔ |
| Author's purpose/ Illustrator's purpose | | | | | | | |

## READING INFORMATIONAL TEXT

### Comprehension Strategies and Skills

| | K | 1 | 2 | 3 | 4 | 5 | 6 |
|---|---|---|---|---|---|---|---|
| Read informational text from a broad range of topics and cultures | ✔ | ✔ | ✔ | ✔ | ✔ | ✔ | ✔ |
| Access complex text | | ✔ | ✔ | ✔ | ✔ | ✔ | ✔ |
| Build background | | | | | | | |
| Preview and predict | ✔ | ✔ | ✔ | | | | |
| Establish and adjust purpose for reading | | | | | | | |
| Evaluate citing evidence from the text | | | | | | | |
| Ask and answer questions | ✔ | ✔ | ✔ | ✔ | ✔ | ✔ | ✔ |
| Inferences and conclusions, citing evidence from the text | ✔ | ✔ | ✔ | ✔ | ✔ | ✔ | ✔ |
| Monitor and adjust comprehension including reread, adjust reading rate, paraphrase | | | | | | | |
| Recount/Retell | ✔ | ✔ | | | | | |
| Summarize | | | ✔ | ✔ | ✔ | ✔ | ✔ |
| Text structure | ✔ | ✔ | ✔ | ✔ | ✔ | ✔ | ✔ |
| Identify text features | | ✔ | ✔ | ✔ | ✔ | ✔ | ✔ |
| Make connections between and across texts | ✔ | ✔ | ✔ | ✔ | ✔ | ✔ | ✔ |
| Author's point of view | | | | | ✔ | ✔ | ✔ | ✔ |
| Author's purpose | | ✔ | ✔ | | | | |
| Cause and effect | ✔ | ✔ | ✔ | ✔ | ✔ | ✔ | ✔ |

| | K | 1 | 2 | 3 | 4 | 5 | 6 |
|---|---|---|---|---|---|---|---|
| Compare and contrast | ✔ | ✔ | ✔ | ✔ | ✔ | ✔ | ✔ |
| Classify and categorize | | ✔ | ✔ | | | | |
| Illustrations and photographs, using | ✔ | ✔ | ✔ | ✔ | | | |
| Instructions/directions (written and oral) | | ✔ | ✔ | ✔ | ✔ | ✔ | ✔ |
| Main idea and key details | ✔ | ✔ | ✔ | ✔ | ✔ | ✔ | ✔ |
| Persuasion, reasons and evidence to support points/persuasive techniques | | | | | | ✔ | ✔ |
| Predictions, making/confirming | ✔ | ✔ | | | | | |
| Problem and solution | | ✔ | ✔ | ✔ | ✔ | ✔ | ✔ |
| Sequence, chronological order of events, time order, steps in a process | ✔ | ✔ | ✔ | ✔ | ✔ | ✔ | ✔ |

**Writing About Reading/Expository Critique Discussions**

| | K | 1 | 2 | 3 | 4 | 5 | 6 |
|---|---|---|---|---|---|---|---|
| Reflect and respond to text citing text evidence | | ✔ | ✔ | ✔ | ✔ | ✔ | ✔ |
| Connect and compare text characters, events, ideas to self, to other texts, to world | | | | | | | |
| Connect texts to other curriculum areas | | | | | | | |
| Identify cultural and historical elements of text | | | | | | | |
| Evaluate author's techniques, craft | | | | | | | |
| Analytical writing | | | | | | | |
| Read to understand and perform tasks and activities | | | | | | | |
| Interpret text ideas through writing, discussion, media, research | | | | | | | |
| Locate, use, explain information from text features | | ✔ | ✔ | ✔ | ✔ | ✔ | ✔ |
| Organize information to show understanding of main idea through charts, mapping | | | | | | | |
| Cite text evidence | | ✔ | ✔ | ✔ | ✔ | ✔ | ✔ |
| Author's purpose/Illustrator's purpose | | | | | | | |

**Text Features**

| | K | 1 | 2 | 3 | 4 | 5 | 6 |
|---|---|---|---|---|---|---|---|
| Recognize and identify text and organizational features of nonfiction texts | | ✔ | ✔ | ✔ | ✔ | ✔ | ✔ |
| Captions and labels, headings, subheadings, endnotes, key words, bold print | ✔ | ✔ | ✔ | ✔ | ✔ | ✔ | ✔ |
| Graphics, including photographs, illustrations, maps, charts, diagrams, graphs, time lines | ✔ | ✔ | ✔ | ✔ | ✔ | ✔ | ✔ |

**Self-Selected Reading/Independent Reading**

| | K | 1 | 2 | 3 | 4 | 5 | 6 |
|---|---|---|---|---|---|---|---|
| Use personal criteria to choose own reading including favorite authors, genres, recommendations from others; set up a reading log | | | | | | | |
| Read a range of literature and informational text for tasks as well as for enjoyment; participate in literature circles | | | | | | | |
| Produce evidence of reading by retelling, summarizing, or paraphrasing | | | | | | | |

**Media Literacy**

| | K | 1 | 2 | 3 | 4 | 5 | 6 |
|---|---|---|---|---|---|---|---|
| Summarize the message or content from media message, citing text evidence | | | | | | | |
| Use graphics, illustrations to analyze and interpret information | ✔ | ✔ | ✔ | ✔ | ✔ | ✔ | ✔ |
| Identify structural features of popular media and use the features to obtain information, including digital sources | | | | ✔ | ✔ | ✔ | ✔ |
| Identify reasons and evidence in visuals and media message | | | | | | | |
| Analyze media source: recognize effects of media in one's mood and emotion | | | | | | | |
| Make informed judgments about print and digital media | | | | | | | |
| Critique persuasive techniques | | | | | | | |

**KEY** ✔ = Assessed Skill
Tinted panels show skills, strategies, and other teaching opportunities.

## WRITING

| | K | 1 | 2 | 3 | 4 | 5 | 6 |
|---|---|---|---|---|---|---|---|
| **Writing Process** | | | | | | | |
| Plan/prewrite | | | | | | | |
| Draft | | | | | | | |
| Revise | | | | | | | |
| Edit/proofread | | | | | | | |
| Publish and present including using technology | | | | | | | |
| Teacher and peer feedback | | | | | | | |
| **Writing Traits** | | | | | | | |
| Conventions | | ✔ | ✔ | ✔ | ✔ | ✔ | ✔ |
| Ideas | | ✔ | ✔ | ✔ | ✔ | ✔ | ✔ |
| Organization | | ✔ | ✔ | ✔ | ✔ | ✔ | ✔ |
| Sentence fluency | | ✔ | ✔ | ✔ | ✔ | ✔ | ✔ |
| Voice | | ✔ | ✔ | ✔ | ✔ | ✔ | ✔ |
| Word choice | | ✔ | ✔ | ✔ | ✔ | ✔ | ✔ |
| **Writer's Craft** | | | | | | | |
| Good topic, focus on and develop topic, topic sentence | | | ✔ | ✔ | ✔ | ✔ | ✔ |
| Paragraph(s); sentence structure | | | ✔ | ✔ | ✔ | ✔ | ✔ |
| Main idea and supporting key details | | | ✔ | ✔ | ✔ | ✔ | ✔ |
| Unimportant details | | | | | | | |
| Relevant supporting evidence | | | ✔ | ✔ | ✔ | ✔ | ✔ |
| Strong opening, strong conclusion | | | ✔ | ✔ | ✔ | ✔ | ✔ |
| Beginning, middle, end; sequence | ✔ | ✔ | ✔ | ✔ | ✔ | ✔ | ✔ |
| Precise words, strong words, vary words | | | ✔ | ✔ | ✔ | ✔ | ✔ |
| Figurative and sensory language, descriptive details | | | | | | | |
| Informal/formal language | | | | | | | |
| Mood/style/tone | | | | | | | |
| Dialogue | | | | ✔ | ✔ | ✔ | ✔ |
| Transition words, transitions to multiple paragraphs | | | | ✔ | ✔ | ✔ | ✔ |
| Select focus and organization | | | ✔ | ✔ | ✔ | ✔ | ✔ |
| Points and counterpoints/Opposing claims and counterarguments | | | | | | | |
| Use reference materials (online and print dictionary, thesaurus, encyclopedia) | | | | | | | |
| **Writing Applications** | | | | | | | |
| Writing about text | ✔ | ✔ | ✔ | ✔ | ✔ | ✔ | ✔ |
| Personal and fictional narrative (also biographical and autobiographical) | ✔ | ✔ | ✔ | ✔ | ✔ | ✔ | ✔ |
| Variety of expressive forms including poetry | ✔ | ✔ | ✔ | ✔ | ✔ | ✔ | ✔ |
| Informative/explanatory texts | ✔ | ✔ | ✔ | ✔ | ✔ | ✔ | ✔ |
| Description | ✔ | ✔ | ✔ | ✔ | | | |
| Procedural texts | | ✔ | ✔ | ✔ | ✔ | ✔ | ✔ |
| Opinion pieces or arguments | ✔ | ✔ | ✔ | ✔ | ✔ | ✔ | ✔ |
| Communications including technical documents | | ✔ | ✔ | ✔ | ✔ | ✔ | ✔ |
| Research report | ✔ | ✔ | ✔ | ✔ | ✔ | ✔ | ✔ |
| Responses to literature/reflection | | | | ✔ | ✔ | ✔ | ✔ |

| | K | 1 | 2 | 3 | 4 | 5 | 6 |
|---|---|---|---|---|---|---|---|
| Analytical writing | | | | | | | |
| Letters | | ✔ | ✔ | ✔ | ✔ | ✔ | ✔ |
| Write daily and over short and extended time frames; set up writer's notebooks | | | | | | | |

## Penmanship/Handwriting

| | K | 1 | 2 | 3 | 4 | 5 | 6 |
|---|---|---|---|---|---|---|---|
| Write legibly in manuscript using correct formation, directionality, and spacing | | | | | | | |
| Write legibly in cursive using correct formation, directionality, and spacing | | | | | | | |

# SPEAKING AND LISTENING

## Speaking

| | K | 1 | 2 | 3 | 4 | 5 | 6 |
|---|---|---|---|---|---|---|---|
| Use repetition, rhyme, and rhythm in oral texts | | | | | | | |
| Participate in classroom activities and discussions | | | | | | | |
| Collaborative conversation with peers and adults in small and large groups using formal English when appropriate | | | | | | | |
| Differentiate between formal and informal English | | | | | | | |
| Follow agreed upon rules for discussion | | | | | | | |
| Build on others' talk in conversation, adding new ideas | | | | | | | |
| Come to discussion prepared | | | | | | | |
| Describe familiar people, places, and things and add drawings as desired | | | | | | | |
| Paraphrase portions of text read alone or information presented | | | | | | | |
| Apply comprehension strategies and skills in speaking activities | | | | | | | |
| Use literal and nonliteral meanings | | | | | | | |
| Ask and answer questions about text read aloud and about media | | | | | | | |
| Stay on topic when speaking | | | | | | | |
| Use language appropriate to situation, purpose, and audience | | | | | | | |
| Use nonverbal communications such as eye contact, gestures, and props | | | | | | | |
| Use verbal communication in effective ways and improve expression in conventional language | | | | | | | |
| Retell a story, presentation, or spoken message by summarizing | | | | | | | |
| Oral presentations: focus, organizational structure, audience, purpose | | | | | | | |
| Give and follow directions | | | | | | | |
| Consider audience when speaking or preparing a presentation | | | | | | | |
| Recite poems, rhymes, songs | | | | | | | |
| Use complete, coherent sentences | | | | | | | |
| Organize presentations | | | | | | | |
| Deliver presentations (narrative, summaries, research, persuasive); add visuals | | | | | | | |
| Speak audibly (accuracy, expression, volume, pitch, rate, phrasing, modulation, enunciation) | | | | | | | |
| Create audio recordings of poems, stories, presentations | | | | | | | |

## Listening

| | K | 1 | 2 | 3 | 4 | 5 | 6 |
|---|---|---|---|---|---|---|---|
| Identify musical elements in language | | | | | | | |
| Determine the purpose for listening | | | | | | | |
| Understand, follow, restate, and give oral directions | | | | | | | |
| Develop oral language and concepts | | | | | | | |
| Listen openly, responsively, attentively, and critically | | | | | | | |

| KEY | ✔ = Assessed Skill |
|---|---|
| | Tinted panels show skills, strategies, and other teaching opportunities. |

| | K | 1 | 2 | 3 | 4 | 5 | 6 |
|---|---|---|---|---|---|---|---|
| Listen to identify the points a speaker makes | | | | | | | |
| Listen responsively to oral presentations (determine main idea and key details) | | | | | | | |
| Ask and answer relevant questions (for clarification to follow-up on ideas) | | | | | | | |
| Identify reasons and evidence presented by speaker | | | | | | | |
| Recall and interpret speakers' verbal/nonverbal messages, purposes, perspectives | | | | | | | |

## LANGUAGE

### Vocabulary Acquisition and Use

| | K | 1 | 2 | 3 | 4 | 5 | 6 |
|---|---|---|---|---|---|---|---|
| Develop oral vocabulary and choose words for effect | | | | | | | |
| Use academic language | | ✔ | ✔ | ✔ | ✔ | ✔ | ✔ |
| Identify persons, places, things, actions | | ✔ | ✔ | ✔ | | | |
| Classify, sort, and categorize words | ✔ | ✔ | ✔ | ✔ | ✔ | ✔ | ✔ |
| Determine or clarify the meaning of unknown words; use word walls | | ✔ | ✔ | ✔ | ✔ | ✔ | ✔ |
| Synonyms, antonyms, and opposites | | ✔ | ✔ | ✔ | ✔ | ✔ | ✔ |
| Use context clues such as word, sentence, paragraph, definition, example, restatement, description, comparison, cause and effect | | ✔ | ✔ | ✔ | ✔ | ✔ | ✔ |
| Use word identification strategies | | ✔ | ✔ | ✔ | ✔ | ✔ | ✔ |
| Unfamiliar words | | ✔ | ✔ | ✔ | ✔ | ✔ | ✔ |
| Multiple-meaning words | | ✔ | ✔ | ✔ | ✔ | ✔ | ✔ |
| Use print and online dictionary to locate meanings, pronunciation, derivatives, parts of speech | | ✔ | ✔ | ✔ | ✔ | ✔ | ✔ |
| Compound words | | ✔ | ✔ | ✔ | ✔ | ✔ | ✔ |
| Words ending in -er and -est | | ✔ | ✔ | ✔ | ✔ | | |
| Root words (base words) | | ✔ | ✔ | ✔ | ✔ | ✔ | ✔ |
| Prefixes and suffixes | | ✔ | ✔ | ✔ | ✔ | ✔ | |
| Greek and Latin affixes and roots | | | ✔ | ✔ | ✔ | ✔ | ✔ |
| Denotation and connotation | | | | | ✔ | ✔ | ✔ |
| Word families | | ✔ | ✔ | ✔ | ✔ | ✔ | ✔ |
| Inflectional endings | | ✔ | ✔ | ✔ | ✔ | ✔ | ✔ |
| Use a print and online thesaurus | | | ✔ | ✔ | ✔ | ✔ | ✔ |
| Use print and online reference sources for word meaning (dictionary, glossaries) | | ✔ | ✔ | ✔ | ✔ | ✔ | ✔ |
| Homographs | | | | ✔ | ✔ | ✔ | ✔ |
| Homophones | | | ✔ | ✔ | ✔ | ✔ | ✔ |
| Contractions | | ✔ | ✔ | ✔ | | | |
| Figurative language such as metaphors, similes, personification | | | | ✔ | ✔ | ✔ | ✔ |
| Idioms, adages, proverbs, literal and nonliteral language | | | ✔ | ✔ | ✔ | ✔ | ✔ |
| Analogies | | | | | | | |
| Listen to, read, discuss familiar and unfamiliar challenging text | | | | | | | |
| Identify real-life connections between words and their use | | | | | | | |
| Use acquired words and phrases to convey precise ideas | | | | | | | |
| Use vocabulary to express spatial and temporal relationships | | | | | | | |
| Identify shades of meaning in related words | ✔ | ✔ | ✔ | ✔ | ✔ | ✔ | ✔ |
| Word origins | | | | ✔ | ✔ | ✔ | ✔ |
| Morphology | | | | ✔ | ✔ | ✔ | ✔ |

| | K | 1 | 2 | 3 | 4 | 5 | 6 |
|---|---|---|---|---|---|---|---|
| **Knowledge of Language** | | | | | | | |
| Choose words, phrases, and sentences for effect | | | | | | | |
| Choose punctuation effectively | | | | | | | |
| Formal and informal language for style and tone including dialects | | | | | | | |
| **Conventions of Standard English/Grammar, Mechanics, and Usage** | | | | | | | |
| Sentence concepts: statements, questions, exclamations, commands | | ✔ | ✔ | ✔ | ✔ | ✔ | ✔ |
| Complete and incomplete sentences; sentence fragments; word order | | ✔ | ✔ | ✔ | ✔ | ✔ | ✔ |
| Compound sentences, complex sentences | | | | ✔ | ✔ | ✔ | ✔ |
| Combining sentences | | ✔ | ✔ | ✔ | ✔ | ✔ | ✔ |
| Nouns including common, proper, singular, plural, irregular plurals, possessives, abstract, concrete, collective | | ✔ | ✔ | ✔ | ✔ | ✔ | ✔ |
| Verbs including action, helping, linking, irregular | | ✔ | ✔ | ✔ | ✔ | ✔ | ✔ |
| Verb tenses including past, present, future, perfect, and progressive | | ✔ | ✔ | ✔ | ✔ | ✔ | ✔ |
| Pronouns including possessive, subject and object, pronoun-verb agreement, indefinite, intensive, reciprocal; correct unclear pronouns | | ✔ | ✔ | ✔ | ✔ | ✔ | ✔ |
| Adjectives including articles, demonstrative, proper adjectives that compare | | ✔ | ✔ | ✔ | ✔ | ✔ | ✔ |
| Adverbs including telling how, when, where, comparative, superlative, irregular | | ✔ | ✔ | ✔ | ✔ | ✔ | ✔ |
| Subject, predicate; subject-verb agreement | | ✔ | ✔ | ✔ | ✔ | ✔ | ✔ |
| Contractions | | ✔ | ✔ | ✔ | ✔ | ✔ | ✔ |
| Conjunctions | | | | ✔ | ✔ | ✔ | ✔ |
| Commas | | | ✔ | ✔ | ✔ | ✔ | ✔ |
| Colons, semicolons, dashes, hyphens | | | | | | ✔ | ✔ |
| Question words | | | | | | | |
| Quotation marks | | | ✔ | ✔ | ✔ | ✔ | ✔ |
| Prepositions and prepositional phrases, appositives | | ✔ | ✔ | ✔ | ✔ | ✔ | ✔ |
| Independent and dependent clauses | | | | | | ✔ | ✔ |
| Italics/underlining for emphasis and titles | | | | | | | |
| Negatives, correcting double negatives | | | | | | ✔ | ✔ | ✔ |
| Abbreviations | | | ✔ | ✔ | ✔ | ✔ | ✔ |
| Use correct capitalization in sentences, proper nouns, titles, abbreviations | | ✔ | ✔ | ✔ | ✔ | ✔ | ✔ |
| Use correct punctuation | | ✔ | ✔ | ✔ | ✔ | ✔ | ✔ |
| Antecedents | | | | ✔ | ✔ | ✔ | ✔ |
| Homophones and words often confused | | | ✔ | ✔ | ✔ | ✔ | ✔ |
| Apostrophes | | | | ✔ | ✔ | ✔ | ✔ |
| **Spelling** | | | | | | | |
| Write irregular, high-frequency words | ✔ | ✔ | ✔ | | | | |
| ABC order | ✔ | ✔ | | | | | |
| Write letters | ✔ | ✔ | | | | | |
| Words with short vowels | ✔ | ✔ | ✔ | ✔ | ✔ | ✔ | ✔ |
| Words with long vowels | ✔ | ✔ | ✔ | ✔ | ✔ | ✔ | ✔ |
| Words with digraphs, blends, consonant clusters, double consonants | | ✔ | ✔ | ✔ | ✔ | ✔ | ✔ |
| Words with vowel digraphs and ambiguous vowels | | ✔ | ✔ | ✔ | ✔ | ✔ | ✔ |
| Words with diphthongs | | ✔ | ✔ | ✔ | ✔ | ✔ | ✔ |

KEY  ✔ = Assessed Skill
Tinted panels show skills, strategies, and other teaching opportunities.

| | K | 1 | 2 | 3 | 4 | 5 | 6 |
|---|---|---|---|---|---|---|---|
| Words with r-controlled vowels | | ✔ | ✔ | ✔ | ✔ | ✔ | ✔ |
| Use conventional spelling | | ✔ | ✔ | ✔ | ✔ | ✔ | ✔ |
| Schwa words | | | | ✔ | ✔ | ✔ | ✔ |
| Words with silent letters | | | ✔ | ✔ | ✔ | ✔ | ✔ |
| Words with hard and soft letters | | | ✔ | ✔ | ✔ | ✔ | ✔ |
| Inflectional endings including plural, past tense, drop final e and double consonant when adding -ed and -ing, changing y to i | | ✔ | ✔ | ✔ | ✔ | ✔ | ✔ |
| Compound words | | ✔ | ✔ | ✔ | ✔ | ✔ | ✔ |
| Homonyms/homophones | | | ✔ | ✔ | ✔ | ✔ | ✔ |
| Prefixes and suffixes | | ✔ | ✔ | ✔ | ✔ | ✔ | ✔ |
| Root and base words (also spell derivatives) | | | | ✔ | ✔ | ✔ | ✔ |
| Syllables: patterns, rules, accented, stressed, closed, open | | | | ✔ | ✔ | ✔ | ✔ |
| Words with Greek and Latin roots | | | | | | ✔ | ✔ |
| Words from mythology | | | | | | ✔ | ✔ |
| Words with spelling patterns, word families | | ✔ | ✔ | ✔ | ✔ | ✔ | ✔ |

## RESEARCH AND INQUIRY

### Study Skills

| | K | 1 | 2 | 3 | 4 | 5 | 6 |
|---|---|---|---|---|---|---|---|
| Directions: read, write, give, follow (includes technical directions) | | ✔ | ✔ | ✔ | ✔ | ✔ | ✔ |
| Evaluate directions for sequence and completeness | | | | ✔ | ✔ | ✔ | ✔ |
| Use library/media center | | | | | | | |
| Use parts of a book to locate information | | | | | | | |
| Interpret information from graphic aids | | ✔ | ✔ | ✔ | ✔ | ✔ | ✔ |
| Use graphic organizers to organize information and comprehend text | | ✔ | ✔ | ✔ | ✔ | ✔ | ✔ |
| Use functional, everyday documents | | | | ✔ | ✔ | ✔ | ✔ |
| Apply study strategies: skimming and scanning, note-taking, outlining | | | | | | | |

### Research Process

| | K | 1 | 2 | 3 | 4 | 5 | 6 |
|---|---|---|---|---|---|---|---|
| Generate and revise topics and questions for research | | | | ✔ | ✔ | ✔ | ✔ |
| Narrow focus of research, set research goals | | | | ✔ | ✔ | ✔ | ✔ |
| Find and locate information using print and digital resources | | ✔ | ✔ | ✔ | ✔ | ✔ | ✔ |
| Record information systematically (note-taking, outlining, using technology) | | | | ✔ | ✔ | ✔ | ✔ |
| Develop a systematic research plan | | | | ✔ | ✔ | ✔ | ✔ |
| Evaluate reliability, credibility, usefulness of sources and information | | | | | | ✔ | ✔ |
| Use primary sources to obtain information | | | | | ✔ | ✔ | ✔ |
| Organize, synthesize, evaluate, and draw conclusions from information | | | | | | | |
| Cite and list sources of information (record basic bibliographic data) | | | | | ✔ | ✔ | ✔ |
| Demonstrate basic keyboarding skills | | | | | | | |
| Participate in and present shared research | | | | | | | |

### Technology

| | K | 1 | 2 | 3 | 4 | 5 | 6 |
|---|---|---|---|---|---|---|---|
| Use computer, Internet, and other technology resources to access information | | | | | | | |
| Use text and organizational features of electronic resources such as search engines, keywords, e-mail, hyperlinks, URLs, Web pages, databases, graphics | | | | | | | |
| Use digital tools to present and publish in a variety of media formats | | | | | | | |

# INDEX

## A

**Abbreviations**, **2**:T209, T221, T233, T239, T247, T301, T313, T325, T331, T339, **3**:T25, T37, T49, T55, T63, **4**:T297, T309, T319, T328, T338

**Academic language**, **1**:T8, T10, T16, T18, T22, T24, T26, T28, T32, T34, T38, T40, T44, T46, T48, T50, T53A, T54, T56, T62, T82, T100, T102, T108, T110, T114, T116, T118, T120, T124, T126, T130, T132, T136, T138, T140, T142, T146, T148, T150, T154, T174, T192, T194, T196, T200, T206, T208, T210, T216, T218, T222, T224, T228, T230, T232, T237A, T238, T240, T242, T246, T266, T284, T286, T292, T298, T300, T302, T304, T308, T310, T314, T320, T322, T324, T329A, T330, T332, T334, T338, T358, T376, T378, T380, T384, T390, T392, T394, T396, T398, T400, T404, T406, T408, T410, T412, T414, T418, T419A, T420, T428, T480, T482, T484, T486, T488, T490, **2**:T8, T10, T12, T14, T16, T22, T24, T26, T28, T30, T32, T34, T38, T40, T42, T44, T46, T48, T50, T52, T54, T58, T60, T62, T82, T100, T102, T108, T110, T114, T116, T118, T120, T124, T126, T130, T132, T136, T138, T140, T142, T146, T148, T154, T174, T192, T194, T200, T206, T210, T212, T216, T218, T222, T224, T228, T230, T234, T238, T242, T246, T266, T268, T284, T286, T292, T298, T300, T302, T304, T308, T310, T314, T320, T322, T329A, T330, T332, T334, T338, T358, T360, T376, T378, T380, T384, T390, T392, T394, T396, T398, T400, T404, T408, T410, T412, T414, T418, T419A, T424, T428, T480, T486, T488, T490, **3**:T8, T10, T16, T22, T24, T26, T28, T32, T34, T38, T44, T46, T48, T50, T53A, T54, T58, T62, T82, T100, T102, T108, T110, T114, T118, T120, T126, T130, T132, T136, T138, T142, T154, T174, T192, T194, T200, T206, T208, T210, T212, T218, T228, T230, T234, T237A, T240, T242, T246, T266, T284, T286, T288, T292, T298, T300, T302, T304, T306, T308, T310, T314, T316, T320, T322, T324, T326, T329A, T330, T338, T358, T376, T378, T384, T390, T392, T398, T400, T404, T406, T410, T412, T416, T419A, T420, T424, T480, T482, T484, T486, T488, T490, **4**:T8, T10, T12, T16, T20, T22, T24, T28, T30, T32, T36, T38, T40, T42, T44, T46, T50, T51A, T52, T56, T58, T60, T80, T98, T100, T102, T106, T110, T112, T114, T116, T120, T122, T126, T128, T132,
T134, T136, T138, 141A, T142, T150, T188, T190, T196, T200, T202, T204, T206, T210, T212, T216, T218, T222, T228, T236, T240, T278, T280, T286, T290, T292, T294, T296, T300, T302, T306, T312, T318, T322, T330, T350, T370, T372, T376, T380, T382, T390, T392, T396, T398, T400, T402, T404, T411A, T412, T416, T420, T472, T474, T476, T478, T480, **5**:T8, T10, T12, T16, T20, T22, T24, T26, T28, T30, T32, T36, T38, T40, T42, T44, T46, T52, T56, T60, T80, T82, T98, T100, T106, T110, T112, T114, T116, T120, T122, T126, T132, T138, T141A, T142, T146, T150, T170, T188, T190, T196, T202, T204, T206, T210, T212, T231A, T234, T236, T278, T280, T282, T286, T290, T292, T294, T296, T300, T302, T308, T312, T314, T316, T318, T322, T330, T350, T372, T376, T382, T390, T392, T398, T400, T402, T404, T406, T412, T417, T472, T474, T476, T478, T480, T482, **6**:T8, T10, T12, T16, T20, T22, T24, T26, T30, T32, T36, T40, T44, T48, T56, T60, T98, T100, T106, T110, T112, T114, T116, T120, T122, T126, T128, T132, T134, T136, T142, T144, T146, T150, T188, T190, T192, T196, T200, T202, T204, T206, T208, T210, T212, T216, T218, T220, T222, T226, T230, T231A, T232, T240, T278, T280, T282, T286, T290, T292, T294, T296, T300, T302, T306, T314, T316, T318, T324, T326, T370, T382, T384, T386, T390, T392, T396, T398, T400, T402, T406, T410, T411A, T412, T416, T420, T472, T474, T476, T478, T480, T482

**Access complex text**

connection of ideas, **1**:T47B, T47D, T47H, T137, T139B, T139F, T472, T474, **2**:T45, T111, T203, T231B, T231H, T474, **3**:T47B, T47D, T139B, T139D, T203, T323D, T473, **4**:T403, T466, **5**:T45B, T45H, T109, T135B, T135E, T135H, T135J, T315D, T315F, T465, **6**:T135B, T135H, T223, T379, T465, T466

genre, **1**:T19, T45, T47B, T229, T231B, T231D, T295, T472, T473, **2**:T139B, T229, T295, T323B, T411, T472, **3**:T19, T137, T219, T472, T474, **4**:T19, T45B, T45C, T289, T315B, T379, T464, T466, **5**:T133, T199, T223, T464, T465, T466, **6**:T19, T43, T45B, T135B, T135D, T313, T315G, T464, T466

lack of prior knowledge, **1**:S5, T111, T139B, T139H, T323B, **2**:T323B, T472, T474, **4**:T109, T135B, T199, **5**:T45B, T45G, T289, T379, **6**:T199, T403, T405C, T464, T465, T466

organization, **1**:T203, T387, T473, T474, **2**:T47B, T47D, T47H, T127, T387, T473, **3**:T47B, T139B, T139C, T309, T387, T473, T474, **4**:T123, T225B, T225F, T465, **5**:T19, T135B, T135F, T464, T466, **6**:T289, T315C, T464

purpose, **1**:T139B, T139J, T311, T401, T413C, **2**:T19, T231B, T413C, T473, **3**:T111, T231B, T295, T413C, **4**:T313, T315B, T464, T465, **5**:T393, T405C, **6**:T225B, T465

sentence structures, **1**:T473, **2**:T309, T401, T472, **3**:T45, T231B, T231I, T399, T472, T474, **4**:T225H, T465, **5**:T33, T465, **6**:T109, T225B, T225C

specific vocabulary, **1**:T53B, T145B, T237B, T323B, T323G, T329B, T419B, T472, T474, **2**:T47B, T47E, T53B, T139B, T139E, T139J, T145B, T237B, T323B, T329B, T419B, T473, T474, **3**:T53B, T145B, T231B, T231C, T237B, T329B, T419B, T472, T473, **4**:T31, T45B, T45E, T45H, T51B, T135B, T141B, T225, T225B, T225K, T231B, T321B, T405B, T411B, T464, T466, **5**:T45B, T45D, T51B, T141B, T225D, T231B, T321B, T411B, T464, T466, **6**:T45B, T45G, T51B, T141B, T225B, T231B, T315F, T321B, T405B, T411B

**Adjectives**. *See* **Grammar: adjectives.**

**Adverbs**. *See* **Grammar: adverbs.**

**Alliteration**, **3**:T394, T432, **4**:T376

**Alphabetical order, using**, **2**:T466, **3**:T466, **5**:T387, T399, T409, T418, T428, T458

**Analytical writing**, **1**: T65, T75, T79, T85, T249, T259, T263, T269, **2**: T65, T75, T79, T85, T157, T167, T171, T177, **3**: T157, T167, T171, T177, **4**: T243, T253, T257, T263, T333, T343, T347, T353, **6**: T63, T73, T77, T83, T423, T433, T437, T443

*See also* **Write About Reading.**

**Antonyms**. *See* **Vocabulary skills and strategies**.

**Approaching level options**

comprehension, **1**:T72–T73, T164–T165, T256–T257, T348–T349, T438–T439, **2**:T72–T73, T164–T165, T256–T257, T348–T349, T438–T439, **3**:T72–T73, T164–T165, T256–T257, T348–T349, T438–T439, **4**:T70–T71, T160–T161, T250–T251, T340–T341, T430–T431, **5**:T70–T71, T160–T161, T250–T251,

Kalman, Bobbie, **2**:T323A–T323H

Keller, Holly, **1**:T47A–T47K

Khan, Rukhsana, **1**:T139A–T139K

Levinson, Nancy Smiler, **4**:T45A–T45J

Lindsay, Vachel, **2**:T413B–T413C

London, Jonathan, **2**:T47A–T47J

Markle, Sandra, **4**:T135A–T135F

McCarthy, Meghan, **6**:T225A–T225I

Moore, Helen H., **1**:T53A–T53B

Rocco, John, **2**:T139A–T139K

Ruiz-Flores, Lupe, **5**:T315A–T315I

Rylant, Cynthia, **3**:T139A–T139J

Sayre, April Pulley, **2**:T231A–T231J

Shannon, Monica, **2**:T413A

Simon, Seymour, **3**:T323A–T323F

Sullivan, Sarah, **5**:T135A–T135N

Tonatiuh, Duncan, **4**:T225A–T225O

Velasquez, Eric, **5**:T225A–T225F

Winter, Jeanette, **3**:T231A–T231J

**Author's craft**

characters, **4**:T321A

descriptive details, **6**:T231A

descriptive language, **5**:T45K, T225F

details and facts, **2**:T323G

dialogue, **1**:T139K, **2**:T139L, **4**:T315E, **5**:T135J

examples, **4**:T135F

figurative language, **4**:T51A, T405C

giving information, **4**:141A

idioms, **6**:T225G

imagery, **2**:T47K

informal language, **6**:T315J

interview format, **1**:T329A

metaphors, **2**:T47H

onomatopoeia, **2**:T47E, **5**:T231A, **6**:T135H

organization, **3**:T323F, **4**:T45J

paragraphs, **5**:T141A

photographs and charts, **3**:T53A

photographs and diagrams, **2**:T323H

point of view, **6**:T315B

repetition, **1**:T231J, **2**:T231J, **3**:T329A, **6**:T45C, T135C

rhyming poems, **1**:T237A

rhyming words, **1**:T53A

sensory images, **4**: 411A, **6**:T45K

similes, **3**:T419A, **6**:T135J

sound words, **2**:T419A

story structure, **5**:T45H

strong verbs, **6**:T411A

style, **5**:T135D

supporting details, **1**:T419A, **5**:T51A, T411A

text features, **2**:T139G, T231G, T329A

text size, **3**:T47I

theme, **3**:T139J

tone, **6**:T225I

vivid verbs, **1**:T47K, **2**:T237A

vivid words, **6**:T321A

word choice, **1**:T47E, T139C, T231C, T323E, T323J, **2**:T47K, T139D, T413B, **3**:T231C, T231K, T237A, **4**:T45H, T225D, **5**:T45C, T135N, T315G

**Author's purpose**, **1**:T47K, T231J, T323J, T494, **2**:T47K, T231J, T323I, T494, **3**:T34–T35, T47B, T47C, T47E, T47H, T47I, T47J, T64, T72, T73, T74, T77, T79, T81, T139J, T218–T219, T231B, T231D, T231F, T231G, T231J, T231L, T248, T256, T257, T258, T261, T263, T265, T315, T323C, T323F, T405, **4**:T45J, T135F, T225O, T315E, **5**:T45K, T135N, T217, T225D, T225F, T315J, T486, **6**:T45K, T122–T123, T135C, T135E, T135F, T135H, T135I, T135J, T135L, T152–T153, T160, T161, T162–T163, T165, T167, T169, T225I, T315J

**Author's use of language**, **2**:T494

**Automatic recognition of words.** *See* **Fluency.**

# B

**Base words.** *See* **Vocabulary skills and strategies: root words.**

**Beyond level options**

comprehension, **1**:T81, T173, T265, T357, T447, **2**:T81, T173, T265, T357, T447, **3**:T81, T173, T265, T357, T447, **4**:T79, T169, T259, T349, T439, **5**:T79, T169, T259, T349, T439, **6**:T79, T169, T259, T349, T439

leveled reader lessons, **1**:T78–T79, T170–T171, T262–T263, T354–T355, T444–T445, **2**:T78–T79, T170–T171, T262–T263, T354–T355, T444–T445, **3**:T78–T79, T170–T171, T262–T263, T354–T355, T444–T445, **4**:T76–T77, T166–T167, T256–T257, T346–T347, T436–T437, **5**:T76–T77, T166–T167, T256–T257, T346–T347, T436–T437, **6**:T76–T77, T166–T167, T256–T257, T346–T347, T436–T437

level up, **1**:T475, **2**:T475, **3**:T475, **4**:T467, **5**:T467, **6**:T467

self-selected reading, **1**:T81, T173, T265, T357, T447, T475, **2**:T81, T173, T265, T357, T447, **3**:T81, T173, T265, T357, T447, **4**:T79, T169, T259, T349, T439, **5**:T79, T169, T259, T349, T439, **6**:T79, T169, T259, T349, T439

vocabulary, **1**:T80, T172, T264, T356, T446, **2**:T80, T172, T264, T356, T446, **3**:T80, T172, T264, T356, T446, **4**:T78, T168, T258, T348, T438, **5**:T78, T168, T258, T348, T438, **6**:T78, T168, T258, T348, T438

**Big idea, big question**, **1**:xii, T1, T92, T184, T276, T368, T458, T466–T467, **2**:xii, T1, T92, T184, T264, T276, T368, T458, T466–T467, **3**:xii, xiii, T1, T92, T184, T276, T368, T458, T466–T467, **4**:xii, T1, T90, T180, T270, T360, T450, T458, **5**:xii, T1, T90, T180, T270, T360, T450, T458–T459, **6**:xii, T1, T90, T180, T270, T360, T450, T458–T459

**Biography**, **5**:T222–T223, T225A, T225H, T242–T243, T252–T253, T256–T257

**Brainstorming**, **1**:T57, T140, T241, T299, T333, T465, T466, T468, **2**:T115, T241, T465, **3**:T87, T149, T241, T363, T465, **4**:T235, T457, T460, **5**:T135A, T144, T457, T460, **6**:T111, T457, T460

**Build background**, **1**:T8, T82, T100, T174, T192, T266, T284, T358, T376, T448, **2**:T8, T82, T100, T174, T192, T266, T284, T358, T376, T448, **3**:T8, T82, T100, T174, T192, T266, T284, T358, T376, T448, **4**:T8, T80, T98, T170, T188, T260, T278, T350, T368, T440, **5**:T8, T80, T98, T170, T188, T260, T278, T350, T368, T440, **6**:T8, T80, T98, T170, T188, T260, T278, T350, T368, T440

# C

**Capitalization.** *See* **Grammar.**

**Cause and effect, identifying.** *See* **Comprehension skills.**

**Character.** *See* **Comprehension skills.**

**Classroom library**, **1**:T492–T497, **2**:T492–T497, **3**:T492–T497, **4**:T484–T489, **5**:T484–T489, **6**:T484–T489

**Close reading**

informational text, **1**:T145A–T145B, T294–T297, T308–T311, T320–T323I, T329A–T329B, T386–T387, T398–T401, T410–T413C, T419A–T419B, T464–T465, T475, **2**:T53A–T53B, T202–T205, T216–T219, T228–T231I, T237A–T237B, T294–T297, T308–T311, T320–T323H, T329A–T329B, T464–T465, T475, **3**:T18–T21, T32–T35, T44–T45, T44–T47I, T53A–T53B, T145A–T145B, T202–T205, T216–T219, T228–T231J, T294–T297, T308–T311, T320–T323E, T329A–T329B, T386–T387, T398–T401, T410–T413D, T475, **4**:T18–T19, T30–T33, T42–T45I,

**Formal and informal English, 2:**T488, **4:**T200, T214, T226, T232, T240, T266, **5:**T380, T394, T406, T412, T420, T446, **6:**T315J

**Foundational Skills.** *See* **Fluency; Phonemic awareness; Phonics.**

# G

**Generate questions.** *See* **Comprehension strategies: ask and answer questions.**

**Genre**

 reading informational text

  biography, **5:**T222–T223, T225A, T225H, T242–T243, T252–T253, T256–T257

  expository text, **1:**S16, S22, T340, T341, T350, T354, T410–T411, T413A, T413B, T413D, T430, T440, T444, **2:**T320–T321, T323A–T323H, T323J, T340–T341, T350–T351, T354–T355, **3:**T44–T45, T47A–T47I, T47J, T64–T65, T74–T75, T78–T79, T320–T321, T323A–T323E, T323H, T340–T341, T350–T351, T354–T355, T410–T411, T413A–T413D, T430, T440, T444, T472, **4:**T42–T43, T45A–T45I, T45L, T72–T73, T76–T77, T132–T133, T135A–T135F, T135H, T152–T153, T162–T163, T166–T167, **5:**T402–T403, T405A–T405D, T422, T432, T436, **6:**T132–T133, T135A–T135I, T135L, T152–T153, T162–T163, T166–T167, T222–T223, T225A–T225H, T225J, T242–T243, T252–T253, T256–T257, T312–T313, T315A–T315I, T315L, T332, T342, T346

  narrative nonfiction, **1:**T295, T320, T323A, T323E, T323L, **2:**T228, T231A–231I, T231L, T248, T258, T262, **3:**T228, T231A–T231J, T231L, T248–T249, T258–T259, T262–T263

  quotations, **5:** xii

 reading literature

  drama, **2:**T462–T463, **3:**T462–T463, **4:**T312–T313, T315A–T315D, T315F, T332–T333, T342–T343, T346–T347

  fable, **1:**S4, S10, **2:**T136, T139A, T139K, T139N, T156, T166, T170

  fantasy, **1:**T19, T44, T47A, T47L, T64, T74, T75, T78, T79, T85

 fiction, **1:**T228, T231A, T231L, T248, T258, T262, **2:**T430, T440, T444, **3:**T136–T137, T139A–T139I, T139L, T156–T157, T166–T167, T170–T171, **4:**T422, T432, T436, **5:**T76, T132–T133, T135A–T135M, T135P, T152–T153, T162–T163, T166–T167, T312–T313, T315A–T315I, T315L, T332–T333, T342–T343, T346–T347, **6:**T422, T432, T436

 folktale, **4:**T288–T289, T312–T313, T315A–T315D, T315F, T332–T333, T342–T343, T346–T347, **5:**T454–T455

 myth, **6:**T42–T43, T45A–T45J, T45L, T62–T63, T72–T73, T76–T77, T83

 play, **2:**T462–T463, **6:**T454

 poetry, **1:**xii, **2:**T379, T386–T387, T393, T398–T399, T404, T445, **4:**T390, T405A, T405D, T423, T433, T437, T443, **6:**T390–T391, T405A–T405C, T405D, T423, T433, T437, T443

 realistic fiction, **1:**T136, T139A, T139C, T139L, T156, T166, T170, **2:**T44, T47A–T47I, T47L, T64, T74, T78, **4:**T222–T223, T225A–T225O, T242–T243, T252–T253, T256–T257, **5:**T42–T43, T45A–T45J, T45L, T62–T63, T72–T73

 *See also* **Writing text types/purpose.**

**Gifted and Talented, 1:**T79, T80, T81, T171, T172, T173, T263, T264, T265, T355, T356, T357, T445, T446, T447, **2:**T79, T80, T81, T171, T172, T173, T263, T264, T265, T355, T356, T357, T445, T446, T447, **3:**T79, T80, T81, T171, T172, T173, T263, T264, T265, T355, T356, T357, T445, T446, T447, **4:**T77, T78, T79, T167, T168, T169, T257, T258, T259, T347, T348, T349, T437, T438, T439, **5:**T77, T78, T79, T167, T168, T169, T257, T258, T259, T347, T348, T349, T437, T438, T439, **6:**T77, T78, T79, T167, T168, T169, T257, T258, T259, T347, T348, T349, T437, T438, T439

**Glossary, 6:**T466

**Grammar**

 adjectives, **6:**T413, T421

  that compare, **6:**T202, T215, T227, T233, T241, T267

  that tell how close, **6:**T112, T125, T137, T143, T151, T177

  that tell how many, **6:**T35, T47, T53, T87, T112, T125, T137, T143, T151, T177

  that tell what kind, **6:**T22, T47, T53, T61, T87, T407

 adverbs, **6:**T292, T305, T317, T323, T331, T357, T407, T413, T421

 articles, **6:**T112, T125, T137, T143, T151, T177

 capitalization

  abbreviations, **2:**T209, T221, T233, T239, T247, T301, T313, T325, T331, T339, **3:**T25, T37, T49, T55, T63

  book titles, **3:**T301, T313, T325, T331, T339, **4:**T202, T215, T227, T233, T241, **5:**T383, T395, T407, T413, T421

  letters, **4:**T305, T317

  months, days of the week, **2:**T209, T233, T239, T247

  pronoun *I*, **5:**T113, T125, T137, T143, T151, **6:**T293, T305, T317, T323, T331

  proper nouns, **2:**T209, T221, T233, T239, T247, **4:**T23, T35, T47, T53, T60, **5:**T203, T215, T227, T233, T241, **6:**T113, T125, T137, T143, T151, T293, T305, T317, T323, T331

  sentences, **1:**T24, T25, T37, T49, T55, T63, T116, T129, T141, T147, T155

  titles of people, **2:**T209, **6:**T113, T125, T137, T143, T151

 contractions, **4:**T382, T395, T407, T413, T421, T447, **5:**T292, T293, T305, T317, T323, T331, T357

 nouns

  kinds of, **2:**T208, T221, T233, T239, T247, T273

  name of person, place, thing, **2:**T24, T37, T49, T55, T63, T89

  plural, **2:**T116, T129, T141, T147, T155, T181, T300, T313, T325, T331, T339, T365

   *See also* **Vocabulary skills and strategies: inflectional endings.**

  possessive, **2:**T390, T403, T415, T421, T429, T455, **5:**T293, **6:**T203, T215, T227, T233, T241

  proper, **2:**T209, T221, T233, T239, T247, **4:**T23, T35, T47, T53, T60, **5:**T202, T215, T227, T233, T241, **6:**T137, T143, T151, T293, T305, T317, T323, T331

  singular, **2:**T116, T129, T141, T147, T155, T181

 predicates, **1:**T300, T313, T325, T331, T339, T365

 prepositions and prepositional phrases, **6:**T292, T305, T317, T323, T331, T357

 pronouns

  *I, me, we, us*, **5:**T112, T137, T143, T151, T177

# H

# M

# N

# O

# Q

# R

prefixes, **2**:T46–T47, T47F, T47L, T80, T87, T145, **3**:T412–T413, T413D, T446, T453, **4**:T51

root words, **1**:T138, T139H, T139L, T172, T179, T322, T356, T363, T418, **2**:T53, T237, T419, **3**:T53, **4**:T314–T315, T315F, T348, T355

shades of meaning, **1**:T264, **2**:T80, **3**:T80, T172, T264, T356, T446, **4**:T348, **5**:T258, T438, **6**:T78, T258

similes, **3**:T46–T47, T80, T87, T145, **4**:T224–T225, T225B, T225C, T225P, T258, T265, T438, **6**:T51

suffixes, **2**:T138–T139, T139G, T139N, T172, T179, T230–T231, T231F, T231L, T264, T271, **4**:T321, **5**:T44–T45, T45F, T45H, T45L, T78, T85, T141

synonyms, **3**:T230–T231, T231E, T231L, T264, T271, T329, **5**:T224–T225, T225H, T258, T265, **6**:T141, T231

use reference sources, **2**:T412–T413

word automaticity, **1**:T30, T122, T214, T306, T396, **2**:T30, T122, T214, T306, T396, **3**:T30, T122, T214, T306, T396, **4**:T28, T118, T208, T298, T388, **5**:T28, T118, T208, T298, T388, **6**:T28, T118, T208, T298, T388

word parts. *See* **Vocabulary skills and strategies: inflectional endings; Vocabulary skills and strategies: prefixes; Vocabulary skills and strategies: suffixes; Vocabulary skills and strategies: Greek and Latin roots.**

*See also* **Phonics: structural analysis.**

**Vowels.** *See* **Phonics.**

# W

**Weekly contract**, **1**:T2, T94, T186, T278, T370, **2**:T2, T94, T186, T278, T370, **3**:T2, T94, T186, T278, T370, **4**:T2, T92, T182, T272, T362, **5**:T2, T92, T182, T272, T362, **6**:T2, T92, T182, T272, T362

**Word analysis/Vocabulary.** *See* **Phonics; Vocabulary development; Vocabulary skills and strategies.**

**Word Automaticity.** *See* **Fluency: word automaticity.**

**Word Bank**, **1**:S8, S14, S20, S26, S31

**Word parts.** *See* **Phonics; Vocabulary skills and strategies.**

**Word Work**, **1**:T12–T15, T104–T107, T196–T199, T288–T291, T380–T383, **2**:T12–T15, T104–T107, T196–T199, T288–T291, T380–T383, **3**:T12–T15, T104–107, T196–T199, T288–T291, T380–T383, **4**:T12–T15, T102–T105, T192–T195, T282–T285, T372–T375,

**5**:T12–T15, T102–T105, T192–T195, T282–T285, T372–T375, **6**:T12–T15, T102–T105, T192–T195, T282–T285, T372–T375

**Workstation activities**

reading, **1**:T3, T95, T186, T279, T371, **2**:T3, T95, T187, T279, T371, **3**:T3, T95, T187, T279, T371, **4**:T3, T93, T183, T273, T363, T454, **5**:T3, T93, T183, T273, T363, T454, **6**:T3, T93, T183, T273, T363, T454

science, **1**:T3, T95, T186, T279, T371, **2**:T3, T95, T187, T279, T371, **3**:T3, T95, T187, T279, T371, **4**:T3, T93, T183, T273, T363, **5**:T3, T93, T183, T273, T363, **6**:T3, T93, T183, T273, T363

social studies, **1**:T3, T95, T186, T279, T371, **2**:T3, T95, T187, T279, T371, **3**:T3, T95, T187, T279, T371, **4**:T3, T93, T183, T273, T363, **5**:T3, T93, T183, T273, T363, **6**:T3, T93, T183, T273, T363

word study/phonics, **1**:T3, T95, T186, T279, T371, **2**:T3, T95, T187, T279, T371, **3**:T3, T95, T187, T279, T371, **4**:T3, T93, T183, T273, T363, **5**:T3, T93, T183, T273, T363, **6**:T3, T93, T183, T273, T363

writing, **1**:T3, T95, T186, T279, T371, **2**:T3, T95, T187, T279, T371, **3**:T3, T95, T187, T279, T371, **4**:T3, T93, T183, T273, T363, T454, **5**:T3, T93, T183, T273, T363, T454, **6**:T3, T93, T183, T273, T363, T454

**Write about it**. *See* **Journal writing**.

**Write about reading**, **1**:T34, T38, T47L, T48, T59, T126, T130, T139L, T151, T218, T222, T231L, T243, T310, T314, T323L, T335, T400, T404, T425, T465, T475, T495, T497, **2**:T34, T38, T47L, T59, T126, T130, T139N, T151, T218, T222, T231L, T243, T310, T314, T323J, T335, T404, T413D, T425, T465, T475, T495, T497, **3**:T34, T38, T47J, T59, T126, T130, T139L, T222, T231L, T310, T314, T323H, T335, T404, T413D, T425, T465, T475, T495, T497, **4**:T32, T36, T45L, T57, T122, T126, T135H, T147, T212, T216, T225P, T237, T302, T306, T315F, T392, T396, T405D, T417, T457, T467, T487, T489, **5**:T32, T36, T45L, T56, T126, T135P, T147, T216, T225H, T237, T302, T306, T315L, T327, T392, T396, T417, T457, T467, T487, T489, **6**:T32, T36, T45L, T57, T126, T135L, T147, T212, T216, T225J, T237, T302, T306, T315L, T327, T396, T405D, T417, T457, T467, T487, T489

**Writer's Checklist**, **1**:T62, T154, T246, T338, T428, **2**:T62, T154, T246, T338, T428, T469, T481, T487, T488, T490, **3**:T62, T154, T246, T338, T428, **4**:T60,

T150, T240, T330, T420, **5**:T60, T150, T240, T330, T420, **6**:T60, T142, T150, T240, T330, T420, T479

**Writer's Notebook**, **1**:T48, T62, T140, T154, T232, T246, T324, T338, T414, T428, **2**:T48, T62, T140, T154, T232, T246, T324, T338, T414, T428, **3**:T62, T154, T246, T338, T414, T428, **4**:T46, T60, T136, T150, T226, T240, T316, T330, T406, T420, **5**:T46, T60, T136, T142, T150, T226, T240, T316, T330, 406, T420, **6**:T46, T60, T136, T150, T479

**Write to a prompt**, **1**:T22, T48, T114, T140, T206, T232, T298, T324, **2**:T22, T48, T114, T140, T206, T232, T298, T324, **3**:T22, T48, T114, T140, T206, T232, T298, T324, T388, T414, **4**:T20, T46, T110, T136, T150, T200, T226, T290, T316, T380, T406, **5**:T20, T46, T110, T124, T136, T200, T226, T290, T316, T380, T381, T406, **6**:T20, T46, T110, T136, T200, T226, T316, T380, T406

*See also* **Writing process: edit/ proofread; Writing process: revise.**

**Write to sources.** *See* **Write about reading.**

**Writing**

analytical writing. *See* **Write about reading.**

analyze writing models, **1**:S9, S15, S21, S27, T22, T114, T128, T206, T220, T298, T312, T324, T388, T480, T482, T483, T484, T486, T488, T489, T490, **2**:T22, T36, T114, T128, T206, T298, T312, T388, T402, T480, T482, T483, T486, T488, T489, T490, **3**:T22–T23, T114, T206, T298, T324, T388, T480, T482, T483, T486, T488, T489, **4**:T20, T110, T200, T290, T380, T472, T474, T475, T478, T480, T481, **5**:T20, T46, T110, T136, T200, T290, T380, T472, T474, T475, T478, T480, T481, **6**:T20, T110, T200, T290, T380, T472, T474, T475, T478, T480, T481

audience and purpose for, **1**:T481, T487, **2**:T468, T481, T487, T488, **3**:T468, T481, T487, **4**:T473, T479, **5**:T460, T473, T479, **6**:T460, T473, T479

concluding sentence, **6**:T474

conclusions, **3**:T482, T488

content words, **6**:T110, T124, T136

daily writing. *See* **Journal writing**.

descriptive details, **2**:T22, T48, **5**:T20, T34, T475

details, **4**:T474, T475, **5**:T474

development of characters, **4**:T290, T304, T316

development of ideas, **5**:T479

events, **1**:T22

fact opposed to opinions, **5**:T473

**Common Core State Standards Correlations**

**English Language Arts**

# College and Career Readiness Anchor Standards for READING

The K–5 standards on the following pages define what students should understand and be able to do by the end of each grade. They correspond to the College and Career Readiness (CCR) anchor standards below by number. The CCR and grade–specific standards are necessary complements—the former providing broad standards, the latter providing additional specificity—that together define the skills and understandings that all students must demonstrate.

## Key Ideas and Details

1. Read closely to determine what the text says explicitly and to make logical inferences from it; cite specific textual evidence when writing or speaking to support conclusions drawn from the text.

2. Determine central ideas or themes of a text and analyze their development; summarize the key supporting details and ideas.

3. Analyze how and why individuals, events, and ideas develop and interact over the course of a text.

## Craft and Structure

4. Interpret words and phrases as they are used in a text, including determining technical, connotative, and figurative meanings, and analyze how specific word choices shape meaning or tone.

5. Analyze the structure of texts, including how specific sentences, paragraphs, and larger portions of the text (e.g., a section, chapter, scene, or stanza) relate to each other and the whole.

6. Assess how point of view or purpose shapes the content and style of a text.

## Integration of Knowledge and Ideas

7. Integrate and evaluate content presented in diverse media and formats, including visually and quantitatively, as well as in words.

8. Delineate and evaluate the argument and specific claims in a text, including the validity of the reasoning as well as the relevance and sufficiency of the evidence.

9. Analyze how two or more texts address similar themes or topics in order to build knowledge or to compare the approaches the authors take.

## Range of Reading and Level of Text Complexity

10. Read and comprehend complex literary and informational texts independently and proficiently.

# CCSS Common Core State Standards
# English Language Arts

## Grade 2

Each standard is coded in the following manner:

| Strand | Grade Level | Standard |
|:---:|:---:|:---:|
| RL | 2 | 1 |

## Reading Standards for Literature

| Key Ideas and Details | | McGraw–Hill Reading Wonders |
|---|---|---|
| **RL.2.1** | Ask and answer such questions as *who, what, where, when, why,* and *how* to demonstrate understanding of key details in a text. | **READING/WRITING WORKSHOP: Unit 1:** 29, 60 **Unit 2:** 171 **Unit 3:** 204, **Unit 6:** 410 <br> **LITERATURE ANTHOLOGY: Unit 1:** 31, 71 **Unit 2:** 131, 159, 209 **Unit 3:** 251 **Unit 4:** 365, 385 **Unit 5:** 409, 439, 475 **Unit 6:** 507 <br> **LEVELED READERS: Unit 1, Week 1:** *Cat and Dog* (A), *The Quest* (O), *Class Pets* (B); **Unit 1, Week 3:** *Too Many Pets?* (A), *A New Home for Henry* (O), *Hello, Koko!* (B); **Unit 2, Week 5:** *Amira's Petting Zoo* (A), *Alice's New Pet* (O), *Ava's Animals* (B); **Unit 3, Week 2:** *A Special Sunset* (A); *A Different Set of Stars* (O); *Shadows in the Sky* (B); **Unit 3, Week 3:** *City Communities* (A, O, B) <br> **YOUR TURN PRACTICE BOOK:** 3, 5, 93–95, 138 <br> **READING WORKSTATION ACTIVITY CARDS:** 1 <br> **TEACHER'S EDITION: Unit 1:** T34, T39, T47A–T47L, T58, T64, T72, T73, T74, T77, T131, T139C, T150, T195, T211, T216–T217, T231A–T231L, T237A, T242, T248, T258, T262, T266 **Unit 2:** T145A–T145B, T148, T400–T401, T404–T405, T443, T447 **Unit 3:** T124–T125, T145A–T145B, T156–T157, T166–T167, T174–T175, T237A–T237B **Unit 4:** T315C, T321A–T321B, T397, T411A–T411B, T422, T432, T436, T439, T440, T442 **Unit 5:** T30–T31, T56–T57, T120–T121, T147, T326 **Unit 6:** T30–T31, T321A–T321B, T397, T411A–T411B |
| **RL.2.2** | Recount stories, including fables and folktales from diverse cultures, and determine their central message, lesson, or moral. | **READING/WRITING WORKSHOP: Unit 2:** 126 **Unit 4:** 309, 310 **Unit 5:** 338 **Unit 6:** 411, 412 <br> **LITERATURE ANTHOLOGY: Unit 2:** 159 **Unit 3:** 278–279 **Unit 4:** 379, 385 **Unit 5:** 409, 475 **Unit 6:** 507, 576–577 <br> **LEVELED READERS: Unit 2, Week 2:** *The Cat and the Mice* (A), *The Dog and the Bone* (O), *The Spider and the Honey Tree* (B); **Unit 3, Week 3:** *City Communities,* pp. 17–18 (A) *City Communities,* pp. 16–18 (O, B); **Unit 4, Week 4:** *Why Turtles Live in Water* (A), *How Butterflies Came to Be* (O), *Why Spider Has 8 Thin Legs* (B); **Unit 4, Week 5:** *A Hike in the Woods* (A), *A Little World* (O), *Star Party* (B); **Unit 6, Week 1:** *The Apples of Idun* (A), *Hercules and the Golden Apples* (O), *Demeter and Persephone* (B) <br> **YOUR TURN PRACTICE BOOK:** 183–185, 203–204, 253–254, 293–294 <br> **READING WORKSTATION ACTIVITY CARDS:** 14, 27 <br> **TEACHER'S EDITION: Unit 2:** T103, T110–T113, T118–T119, T136–T137, T139M–T139N, T145A–T145B, T150, T156–T157, T166–T167, T170–T171 **Unit 3:** T237A–T237B **Unit 4:** T295, T302–T303, T306, T312–T313, T315A–T315F, T321A–T321B, T327, T332, T340–T341, T342, T346, T350–T351, T352, T378, T392–T393, T405A, T430, T432, T436, T439, T440, T442 **Unit 5:** T30–T31, T37, T45I, T315K–T315L **Unit 6:** T32–T33, T42–T43, T45A–T45L, T62–T63, T70, T71, T72–T73, T80–T81, T82, T321A–T321B, T396–T397, T423, T435 |

# Reading Standards for Literature

| Key Ideas and Details | McGraw–Hill Reading Wonders |
|---|---|
| **RL.2.3**    Describe how characters in a story respond to major events and challenges. | **READING/WRITING WORKSHOP: Unit 1:** 45, 61,   **Unit 2:** 109, 125   **Unit 4:** 295   **Unit 5:** 339, 381   **Unit 6:** 411 <br> **LITERATURE ANTHOLOGY: Unit 1:** 55, 79   **Unit 2:** 131, 159   **Unit 3:** 251   **Unit 4:** 365   **Unit 5:** 409, 475   **Unit 6:** 507 <br> **LEVELED READERS: Unit 1, Week 2:** *Music in My Family* (A), *Happy New Year!* (O), *I'm Down Under* (B);   **Unit 1, Week 3:** *Too Many Pets?* (A), *A New Home For Henry* (O), *Hello, Koko!* (B); **Unit 2, Week 1:** *Hippos at the Zoo* (A), *Where Are They Going?* (O), *An Arctic Life for Us* (B); **Unit 2, Week 2:** *The Cat and the Mice* (A), *The Dog and the Bone* (O), *The Spider and the Honey Tree* (B);   **Unit 3, Week 2:** *A Special Sunset* (A), *A Different Set of Stars* (O), *Shadows in the Sky* (B); **Unit 4, Week 3:** *Sharing Cultures* (A), *A New Life in India* (O), *Akita and Carlo* (B);   **Unit 5, Week 1:** *Fixing the Playground* (A), *The Food Crew* (O), *How Many Greats?* (B); **Unit 5, Week 4:** *Let's Carpool* (A), *Our Beautiful Tree* (O), *Family Night Unplugged* (B); **Unit 6, Week 1:** *The Apples of Idun* (A), *Hercules and the Golden Apples* (O), *Demeter and Persephone* (B) <br> **YOUR TURN PRACTICE BOOK:** 23–24, 63–64, 173–174, 183–184, 253–254, 283–284 <br> **READING WORKSTATION ACTIVITY CARDS:** 2, 3, 5, 6, 13 <br> **TEACHER'S EDITION: Unit 1:** S4, S10, T126–T127, T139A–T139L, T156–T157, T165, T166–T167, T169, T170–T171, T173, T174–T175, T218–T219, T231A–T231L, T248–T249, T256–T257, T258–T259   **Unit 2:** T34–T35, T47A–T47L, T64–T65, T72–T73, T74–T75, T77, T78–T79, T80, T82–T83, T126, T139A–T139L, T156–T157, T164–T165, T166, T169, T170–T171, T173, T174–T177, T443   **Unit 3:** T131, T139A–T139L   **Unit 4:** T212–T213, T216, T225A–T225P, T237, T242–T243, T250–T251, T252–T253, T255, T295, T302–T303, T306, T315A–T315F, T345, T349   **Unit 5:** T32–T33, T45A–45L, T302–T303, T315A–T315L, T327, T332, T340–T341, T345, T346, T352   **Unit 6:** T32–T33, T62–T63, T70–T71; T72–T73, T75, T76–T77, T79 |

| Craft and Structure | McGraw–Hill Reading Wonders |
|---|---|
| **RL.2.4**    Describe how words and phrases (e.g., regular beats, alliteration, rhymes, repeated lines) supply rhythm and meaning in a story, poem, or song. | **READING/WRITING WORKSHOP: Unit 2:** 165, 170, 172   **Unit 4:** 317, 324, 325   **Unit 6:** 461 466, 468 <br> **LITERATURE ANTHOLOGY: Unit 2:** 209   **Unit 4:** 385   **Unit 6:** 581 <br> **LEVELED READERS: Unit 2, Week 5:** *Amira's Petting Zoo,* pp. 17–20(A), *Alice's New Pet,* pp. 17–20(O), *Ava's Animals,* pp. 17–20(B);   **Unit 4, Week 5:** *A Hike in the Woods,* pp. 17–20 (A), *A Little World* pp. 17–20(O), *Star Party,* pp. 17–20(B);   **Unit 6, Week 5:** *Matt's Journey,* pp. 17–19(A), *A Fantastic Day!,* pp. 17–19(O), *A Day in Ancient Rome,* pp. 17–19(B) <br> **YOUR TURN PRACTICE BOOK:** 98, 293–294, 298 <br> **READING WORKSTATION ACTIVITY CARDS:** 24 <br> **TEACHER'S EDITION: Unit 1:** T53A–T53B, T231J, T237A–T237B   **Unit 2:** T386–T387, T398–T399, T410–T411, T413A–T413D, T419A–T419B, T425, T440–T441, T444, T449, T450–T451 **Unit 4:** T378–379, T390–T391, T396, T402–T403, T405A–T405D, T411A–T411B, T417, T433, T437   **Unit 6:** T45C, T376, T379, T390–T391, T402–T403, T405A–T405D, T411A–T411B, T423, T433, T437, T440–T441, T442 |
| **RL.2.5**    Describe the overall structure of a story, including describing how the beginning introduces the story and the ending concludes the action. | **READING/WRITING WORKSHOP: Unit 1:** 46, 62   **Unit 2:** 109, 126   **Unit 3:** 205   **Unit 4:** 295   **Unit 5:** 354, 382   **Unit 6:** 405 <br> **LITERATURE ANTHOLOGY: Unit 2:** 131, 159   **Unit 3:** 251   **Unit 5:** 475 <br> **LEVELED READERS: Unit 3, Week 2:** *A Special Sunset* (A), *A Different Set of Stars* (O, ELL), *Shadows in the Sky* (B);   **Unit 2, Week 1** (A), (O), (B):   **Unit 5, Week 2** (A) (O), (B) <br> **YOUR TURN PRACTICE BOOK:** 18, 28, 183–184, 253–254, 293–294 <br> **READING WORKSTATION ACTIVITY CARDS:** 6, 9, 13 <br> **TEACHER'S EDITION: Unit 1:** S4, S10, T136–T137, T139A–T139L, T151, T228, T243   **Unit 2:** T34–T35, T47A–T47L, T126–T127, T136–T137, T139A–T139N,   **Unit 3:** T126–T127, T130–131, T136–T137, T139A–T139L, T151, T156–T157, T164–T165, T166–T167, T169, T170–T171, T173, T174–T175, T176–T177   **Unit 4:** T212, T216–T217, T237   **Unit 5:** T18–T19, T132–T133, T312–T313, T315B–T315E, T315H   **Unit 6:** T42–T43 |

## Reading Standards for Literature

| RL.2.6 | Acknowledge differences in the points of view of characters, including by speaking in a different voice for each character when reading dialogue aloud. | **READING/WRITING WORKSHOP:** Unit 4: 296, 304–307, 310  **Unit 5:** 339, 340, 353, 382  **Unit 6:** 467<br>**LITERATURE ANTHOLOGY:** Unit 4: 370–377  **Unit 5:** 409, 439  **Unit 6:** 581<br>**LEVELED READERS:** Unit 4, Week 4: *Why Turtles Live in Water* (A), *How Butterflies Came to Be* (O), *Why a Spider Has 8 Thin Legs* (B);  **Unit 5, Week 1:** *Fixing the Playground* (A), *The Food Crew* (O), *How Many Greats?* (B);  **Unit 5, Week 2:** *Rainy Day* (A), *Thirteen Is a Crowd* (O), *Partners* (B);  **Unit 6, Week 5:** *Matt's Journey* (A), *A Fantastic Day!* (O), *A Day in Ancient Rome* (B)<br>**YOUR TURN PRACTICE BOOK:** 178, 205, 293–294<br>**TEACHER'S EDITION:** Unit 2: T139G, T139L  Unit 3: T139C, T237A,  **Unit 4:** T222–T223, T225A–T225P, T228–T229, T312–T313, T315A–T315F  **Unit 5:** T18–T19, T32–T33, T42–T43, T45A–T45L, T56–T57, T62–T63, T71–T72, T75, T76–T77, T79, T80–T83, T147, T307, T315C, T315G  **Unit 6:** T45E, T392–T393, T405A–T405C, T411A, T417, T422, T430–T431, T432, T436, T439, T440–T441, T442 |
|---|---|---|
| **Integration of Knowledge and Ideas** | | *McGraw–Hill Reading Wonders* |
| RL.2.7 | Use information gained from the illustrations and words in a print or digital text to demonstrate understanding of its characters, setting, or plot. | **READING/WRITING WORKSHOP:** Unit 1: 28, 29, 30, 44, 45, 61  **Unit 2:** 110, 171  **Unit 4:** 294, 308<br>**LITERATURE ANTHOLOGY:** Unit 1: 55, 79  **Unit 2:** 131<br>**YOUR TURN PRACTICE BOOK:** 3–4, 5, 8, 13–14, 15, 25, 58, 173–174<br>**READING WORKSTATION ACTIVITY CARDS:** 3<br>**LEVELED READERS:** Unit 1, Week 1: *Cat and Dog* (A), *The Quest* (O), *Class Pets* (B);  **Unit 1, Week 2:** *Music in My Family* (A), *Happy New Year!* (O), *I'm Down Under* (B);  **Unit 1, Week 3:** *Too Many Pets?* (A), *A New Home for Henry* (O), *Hello, Koko!* (B);  **Unit 4, Week 3:** *Sharing Cultures* (A), *A New Life in India* (O, ELL), *Akita and Carlo* (B);  **Unit 4, Week 4:** *Why Turtles Live in Water* (A), *How Butterflies Came to Be* (O), *Why Spider Has 8 Thin Legs* (B)<br>**TEACHER'S EDITION:** Unit 1: S4, S10, T32–T33, T34–T35, T38–T39, T44–T45, T47A–T47L, T53A–T53B, T64, T74, T82, T84, T124, T126, T130, T139A–T139L, T156, T166, T170, T174, T218, T223, T231A–T231L, T248, T258, T261, T262, T265, T266  Unit 2: T34–T35, T38–T39, T44–T45, T47A–T47L, T59, T131, T139A–T139N, T223  Unit 3: T124–T125, 139A–T139L,  **Unit 4:** T210–T211, T215–T216, T225A–T225L, T242, T252, T256, T260–T261, T262, T300–T301, T315A–T315F, T321A–T321B, T332, T342, T346, T350–T351, T352  **Unit 6:** T321A |
| RL.2.8 | (Not applicable to literature.) | |
| RL.2.9 | Compare and contrast two or more versions of the same story (e.g., Cinderella stories) by different authors or from different cultures. | **READING/WRITING WORKSHOP:** Unit 2: 118–123<br>**LITERATURE ANTHOLOGY:** Unit 2: 136–159, 160–163<br>**READING WORKSTATION ACTIVITY CARDS:** 23<br>**TEACHER'S EDITION:** Unit 2: T139B, 145A–T145B, T150–T151, T95, T467 |
| **Range of Reading and Level of Text Complexity** | | *McGraw–Hill Reading Wonders* |
| RL.2.10 | By the end of the year, read and comprehend literature, including stories and poetry, in the grades 2–3 text complexity band proficiently, with scaffolding as needed at the high end of the range. | **READING/WRITING WORKSHOP:** These units reflect the range of text complexity found throughout the book. Unit 1: 54–59  **Unit 2:** 118–123  **Unit 3:** 198–203  **Unit 4:** 318–321  **Unit 5:** 376–379  **Unit 6:** 406–409<br>**LITERATURE ANTHOLOGY:** These units reflect the range of text complexity found throughout the book.  Unit 1: 34–55  **Unit 2:** 206–208,  **Unit 3:** 232–249  **Unit 4:** 336–363  **Unit 5:** 456–473  **Unit 6:** 486–506<br>**LEVELED READERS:** Unit 1, Week 2: *Music in My Family* (A), *Happy New Year!* (O), *I'm Down Under* (B);  **Unit 2, Week 5:** *Amira's Petting Zoo* (A), *Alice's New Pet* (O, ELL), *Ava's Animals* (B);  **Unit 3, Week 2:** *A Special Sunset* (A), *A Different Set of Stars* (O), *Shadows in the Sky* (B);  **Unit 4, Week 3:** *Sharing Cultures* (A), *A New Life in India* (O), *Akita and Carlo* (B);  **Unit 5, Week 1:** *Fixing the Playground* (A), *The Food Crew* (O), *How Many Greats?* (B);  **Unit 6, Week 5:** *Matt's Journey* (A), *A Fantastic Day!* (O), *A Day in Ancient Rome* (B)<br>**TEACHER'S EDITION:** Unit 1: T53A–T53B, T472–T475  **Unit 2:** T472–T475  **Unit 3:** T472–T475,  **Unit 4:** T464–T467  **Unit 5:** T464–T467  **Unit 6:** T390, T464–T467 |

CORRELATIONS

# Reading Standards for Informational Text

| Key Ideas and Details | | McGraw–Hill Reading Wonders |
|---|---|---|
| **RI.2.1** | Ask and answer such questions as *who, what, where, when, why,* and *how* to demonstrate understanding of key details in a text. | **READING/WRITING WORKSHOP: Unit 1:** 76, 77, 90, 91 **Unit 2:** 141, 156, 157 **Unit 3:** 188, 220, 236, 237, 246–249, 250, 251 **Unit 4:** 265, 266 **Unit 6:** 409, 410, 423, 424 **LITERATURE ANTHOLOGY: Unit 1:** 90, 99, 101, 105, 107 **Unit 2:** 183, 203 **Unit 3:** 263, 285, 286, 291, 293, 295, 297 **Unit 4:** 316, 319 **Unit 6:** 553, 575 **LEVELED READERS: Unit 1, Week 4:** *People Helping Whales* (A, O, B); **Unit 1, Week 5:** *Families at Work* (A, O, B); **Unit 2, Week 3:** *A Tree Full of Life* (A, O, B); **Unit 2, Week 4:** *Animal Families* (A, O, B); **Unit 3, Week 1:** *Forces at Work* (A, O, B); **Unit 3, Week 3:** *City Communities* (A, O, B); **Unit 3, Week 4:** *Weather All Around* (A, O, B); **Unit 3, Week 5:** *The Sounds of Trash* (A, O, B); **Unit 4, Week 1:** *Rocky Mountain National Park* (A, O, B); **Unit 6, Week 2:** *Wind Power* (A, O, B) **YOUR TURN PRACTICE BOOK:** 33, 35, 43, 45, 73–74, 83–85, 103–104, 113–114, 123–124, 133–134, 143–144, 153–154, 253–254, 263–264 **READING WORKSTATION ACTIVITY CARDS:** 7, 10 **TEACHER'S EDITION: Unit 1:** T308–T309, T310–T311, T321A–T321I, T334–T335, T398–399, T400–T401, T413A–T413I, T430, T438, T440, T448, T450 **Unit 2:** T218–T219, T231A–T231L, T308–T309, T310–T311, T323A–T323I, T340–T341, T350–T351, T358–T359, T360–T361, T419A **Unit 3:** T32–T33, T47A–T47J, T53A–T53B, T145A–T145B, T216–T217, T237A–T237B, T308–T309, T310–T311, D43, T398–T399, T400–T401, T413A–T413D, T419A, T424–T425 **Unit 4:** T30–T31, T45F, T45G, T51A, T135E, T146, T231A–T231B **Unit 5:** T51A–T51B, T141A–T141B, T321A–T321B, T411A–T411B **Unit 6:** T120–T121, T141A–T141B, T152, T164, T166, T170–T171, T231A |
| **RI.2.2** | Identify the main topic of a multiparagraph text as well as the focus of specific paragraphs within the text. | **READING/WRITING WORKSHOP: Unit 2:** 141, 157 **Unit 3:** 230–235, 237, 246–249, 251 **Unit 4:** 265, 279 **Unit 6:** 439 **LITERATURE ANTHOLOGY: Unit 2:** 183, 203 **Unit 3:** 291, 297 **Unit 6:** 553 **LEVELED READERS: Unit 2, Week 3:** *A Tree Full of Life* (A, O, B); **Unit 2, Week 4:** *Animal Families* (A, O, B); **Unit 3, Week 4:** *Weather All Around* (A, O, B); **Unit 3, Week 5:** *The Sounds of Trash* (A, O, B); **Unit 6, Week 3:** *Digging for Sue* (A, O, B) **YOUR TURN PRACTICE BOOK:** 73–75, 83–85, 113–114, 133–134, 143–145, 273–275 **READING WORKSTATION ACTIVITY CARDS:** 7, 10 **TEACHER'S EDITION: Unit 2:** T218–T219, T231A–T231K, T248–T249, T256–T257, T258–T259, T262–T263, T265, T266–T267, T310–T311, T321A–T321J, T335 **Unit 3:** T39, T47D, T310–T311, T323A–T323J, T400–T401, T413A–T413D, T430–T431, T44–T441, T442–T443, T444–T445 **Unit 4:** T36–T37, T45D, T127–T128, T135D **Unit 6:** T212–T213, T225A–T225J, T242–T243, T250–T251, T252–253, T256–T257, T258–T259, T306–T307 |
| **RI.2.3** | Describe the connection between a series of historical events, scientific ideas or concepts, or steps in technical procedures in a text. | **READING/WRITING WORKSHOP: Unit 4:** 262–265, 267, 276–279, 280, 281 **Unit 5:** 362–365, 367, 390–393, 395 **Unit 6:** 448–451, 453 **LITERATURE ANTHOLOGY: Unit 4:** 319, 333 **Unit 5:** 453, 481, 483 **Unit 6:** 575 **LEVELED READERS: Unit 4, Week 1:** *Rocky Mountain National Park* (A, O, B); **Unit 4, Week 2:** *Earthquakes* (A, O, B); **Unit 5, Week 3:** *Rudy Garcia–Tolson* (A, O, B); **Unit 5, Week 5:** *Government Rules* (A, O, B), **Unit 6, Week 4:** *How to Be a Smart Shopper* (A, O, B) **YOUR TURN PRACTICE BOOK:** 153–155, 163–165, 173–175, 243–245, 283–285 **READING WORKSTATION ACTIVITY CARDS:** 11, 12, 16, 17 **TEACHER'S EDITION: Unit 4:** T32–T33, 45A–T45L, T62–T63, T70–T71, T72–T73, T74–T75, T79, T122–T123, T135A–T135H **Unit 5:** T212–T213, T225A–T225H, T242–T243, T250–T251, T252–T253, T256–T257, T258–T259 **Unit 6:** T127, T217, T302–T203, T315A–T315L, T332–T33, T340–T241, T342–T343, T344–T345, T346–T347, T 348–T349 |

| Craft and Structure | | McGraw–Hill Reading Wonders |
|---|---|---|
| **RI.2.4** | Determine the meaning of words and phrases in a text relevant to a *grade 2 topic or subject area.* | **READING/WRITING WORKSHOP: Unit 1:** 68–69, 70–75, 79, 84–85, 86–89, 93 **Unit 2:** 132–133; 134–139, 143, 148–149, 150–155, 159 **Unit 3:** 180–181,182–187,191, 212–213, 214–219, 223, 228–229, 230–235, 239, 244–245, 246–249, 253 **Unit 4:** 260–261, 262–265, 269, 274–275, 276–279, 283 **Unit 5:** 360–361, 362–365, 369, 388–389, 390–393, 397 **Unit 6:** 418–419, 420–423, 427, 432–433, 434–437, 441, 446–447, 448–451, 455 **LITERATURE ANTHOLOGY: Unit 1:** 101, 107 **Unit 2:** 183, 203 **Unit 3:** 229, 277, 291, 297 **Unit 4:** 319, 333 **Unit 5:** 453, 483 **Unit 6:** 531, 553, 575 **LEVELED READERS: Unit 1, Week 4:** *People Helping Whales* 0 (A, O, B); **Unit 1, Week 5:** *Families at Work* (A, O, B); **Unit 2, Week 3:** *A Tree Full of Life* (A, O, B); **Unit 2, Week 4:** *Animal Families* (A, O, B); **Unit 3, Week 1:** *Forces at Work* (A, O, B); **Unit 3, Week 3:** *City Communities* (A, O, B); **Unit 3, Week 4:** *Weather All Around* (A, O, B); **Unit 3, Week 5:** *The Sounds of Trash* (A, O, B); **Unit 4, Week 1:** *Rocky Mountain National Park* (A, O, B); **Unit 4, Week 2:** *Earthquakes* (A, O, B); **Unit 5, Week 3:** *Rudy Garcia–Tolson* (A, O, B); **Unit 5, Week 5:** *Government Rules* (A, O, B); **Unit 6, Week 2:** *Wind Power* (A, O, B); **Unit 6, Week 3:** *Digging For Sue* (A, O, B); **Unit 6, Week 4:** *How to Be a Smart Shopper* (A, O, B) **YOUR TURN PRACTICE BOOK:** 31, 41, 71, 81, 101, 121, 131, 141, 151, 161, 221, 231, 241, 261, 271, 281 **TEACHER'S EDITION: Unit 1:** T292–T293, T322–T323, T347, T 362, T384–T385, T396–T397, T437, T452 **Unit 2:** T200–T201, T230–T231, T255, T270, T292–T293 T322–T323, T347, T362 **Unit 3:** T16–T17, T71, T86, T200–T201, T255, T270, T292–T293, T347, T362, T384–T385, T437, T452 **Unit 4:** T16–T17, T69, T84, T106–T107, T159, T174 **Unit 5:** T196–T197, T249, T264; T286–T287, T339, T355, T376–377, T429, T445 **Unit 6:** T106–T107, T159, T174, T196–T197, T249, T265, T286–T287, T339, T354 |
| **RI.2.5** | Know and use various text features (e.g., captions, bold print, subheadings, glossaries, indexes, electronic menus, icons) to locate key facts or information in a text efficiently. | **READING/WRITING WORKSHOP: Unit 1:** 70–75, 77, 78, 86–89, 91, 92 **Unit 2:** 102–107, 110, 136–139, 142, 158 **Unit 3:** 182–187, 190, 230–235, 238, 248, 252 **Unit 4:** 262–265, 268, 276–279, 282 **Unit 5:** 362–365, 368, 390–393, 396 **Unit 6:** 420–423, 426, 434–437, 440, 448–451, 454 **LITERATURE ANTHOLOGY: Unit 1:** 56–59, 82–89, 90, 102–103, 104–109 **Unit 2:** 132–135, 164–181, 184–185, 186–201, 204–205 **Unit 3:** 212–227, 230–231, 252–255, 280–291, 292–293, 294–297, 298–299 **Unit 4:** 300–317, 320–321, 322–333, 334–335, 366–369 **Unit 5:** 410–411, 440–441, 443–453, 454, 476–479, 480–483, 484–485 **Unit 6:** 508–511, 512–529, 533, 536–551, 556–573 **LEVELED READERS: Unit 1, Week 4:** *People Helping Whales* (A, O, B); **Unit 2, Week 3:** *A Tree Full of Life* (A, O, B); **Unit 3, Week 1:** *Forces at Work* (A, O, B); **Unit 4, Week 1:** *Rocky Mountain National Park* (A, O, B); **Unit 5, Week 5:** *Government Rules* (A, O, B); **Unit 6, Week 2:** *Wind Power* (A, O, B) **YOUR TURN PRACTICE BOOK:** 38, 48, 78, 108, 169, 225, 243–244, 247 **TEACHER'S EDITION: Unit 1:** T310–T311, T320–T321, T323A_T323J, T329A, T340, T350, T354, T358, T360, T405, T410, T413A–T413D, T419A, T464 **Unit 2:** T228–T229, T320–T321,T323AT323J, T464–T465 **Unit 3:** T53A–T53B, T228–T229, T320, T329B, T410––T411, T419A, T464–T465 **Unit 4:** T42–T43, T51A–T51B, T132–T133, T141A–T141B, T222–T223, T225A–T225N, T231A–T231B **Unit 5:** T222–T223, T402–T403, T411A–T411B, T456–T457 **Unit 6:** T132–T133, T141A–T141B, T222–T223, T231A–T231B, T237, T312–T313, T456–T457 |
| **RI.2.6** | Identify the main purpose of a text, including what the author wants to answer, explain, or describe. | **READING/WRITING WORKSHOP: Unit 3:** 189, 221 **Unit 6:** 425, 439 **LITERATURE ANTHOLOGY: Unit 3:** 229 **Unit 5:** 452 **Unit 6:** 531, 553 **LEVELED READERS: Unit 3, Week 1:** *Forces at Work* (A, O, B); **Unit 3, Week 3:** *City Communities* (A, O, B); **Unit 6, Week 2:** *Wind Power* (A, O, B); **Unit 6, Week 3:** *Digging for Sue* (A, O, B, ELL); **Unit 6, Week 4:** *How To Be a Smart Shopper* (A, O, B) **YOUR TURN PRACTICE BOOK:** 105, 115, 123–125, 263–264, 273–274 **READING WORKSTATION ACTIVITY CARDS:** 8, 20 **TEACHER'S EDITION: Unit 3:** T33–T34, T47A–T47J, T218–T219, T231A–T231J, T256–T257, T258–T259, T261, T262–T263, T265, T266–T267, T322C, T405, T413B **Unit 5:** T216–T217, T225D **Unit 6:** T122–T123, T135A–T135L, T152, T160, T161, T162, T165, T166, T169, T170–T171, T172, T212–T213, T225A–T225J, T242, T250, T251, T253, T255, T256, T259, T262, T332, T342, T346, T349, T350–T351, T352 |

# Reading Standards for Informational Text

| Integration of Knowledge and Ideas | *McGraw–Hill Reading Wonders* |
|---|---|
| **RI.2.7** Explain how specific images (e.g., a diagram showing how a machine works) contribute to and clarify a text. | **READING/WRITING WORKSHOP: Unit 2:** 150–155, 158 **Unit 3:** 182–187, 190, 246–249, 252 **Unit 4:** 262–265, 268 **Unit 5:** 390–393, 396 **Unit 6:** 420–423, 426, 434–437, 440, 448–451, 454<br>**LITERATURE ANTHOLOGY: Unit 1:** 56–59, 106–107, 109 **Unit 2:** 133–135, 184–185, 186–201, 204–205 **Unit 3:** 212–227, 230–231, 252–255, 280–291, 292–293, 294–297, 298–299 **Unit 4:** 300–317, 320–321, 322–333, 335, 366–369 **Unit 5:** 410–411, 443–451, 454, 476–479, 480–483, 484–485 **Unit 6:** 508–511, 512–529, 533, 546, 547, 556–573<br>**TEACHER'S EDITION: Unit 2:** T320–T321, T323A–T323H, T329A–T329B **Unit 3:** T44–T45, T335, T410, T419A **Unit 4:** T42–T43, T51A–T51B **Unit 5:** T222–T223, T402–T403, T411B **Unit 6:** T132–T133, T141A–141B , T222–T223, T225F, T312–T313, T315A–T315I |
| **RI.2.8** Describe how reasons support specific points the author makes in a text. | **READING/WRITING WORKSHOP: Unit 3:** 189, 221 **Unit 6:** 425, 439<br>**LITERATURE ANTHOLOGY: Unit 3:** 229, 277 **Unit 6:** 531<br>**LEVELED READERS: Unit 3, Week 3:** *City Communities* (A, O, B); **Unit 6, Week 2:** *Wind Power* (A, O, B); **Unit 6, Week 3:** *Digging for Sue* (A, O, B)<br>**YOUR TURN PRACTICE BOOK:** 105, 125, 263–265, 275, 283–284<br>**TEACHER'S EDITION: Unit 1:** T335 **Unit 3:** T33–T34, T72–T73, T77, T82–T83, T218–T219, T243, T256–T257, T258–T259, T261, T262, T413B–T413C **Unit 5:** T216–T217 **Unit 6:** T122–T123, T152, T161, T162, T165, T166, T169, T170–T171, T172, T212–T213, T225B, T250, T251, T255, T288–T289, T315A–T315I, T349 |
| **RI.2.9** Compare and contrast the most important points presented by two texts on the same topic. | **READING/WRITING WORKSHOP: Unit 4:** 262–265<br>**LITERATURE ANTHOLOGY: Unit 1:** 103, 109 **Unit 2:** 185, 205 **Unit 3:** 231, 293, 299 **Unit 4:** 321, 355 **Unit 5:** 455, 485 **Unit 6:** 535, 555<br>**LEVELED READERS: Unit 4, Week 1:** *Rocky Mountain National Park* (A, O, B)<br>**READING WORKSTATION ACTIVITY CARDS:** 22<br>**TEACHER'S EDITION: Unit 1:** T334, T424 **Unit 2:** T242, T334 **Unit 3:** T58, T329A–T329B, T334, T424 **Unit 4:** T51A–T51B, T56–T57, T62–T63, T72–T73, T76–T77 **Unit 5:** T236, T416 **Unit 6:** T146, T236 |

| Range of Reading and Level of Text Complexity | *McGraw–Hill Reading Wonders* |
|---|---|
| **RI.2.10** By the end of year, read and comprehend informational texts, including history/social studies, science, and technical texts, in the grades 2–3 text complexity band proficiently, with scaffolding as needed at the high end of the range. | **READING/WRITING WORKSHOP:** These units reflect the range of text complexity found throughout the book.<br>**Unit 1:** 70–75 **Unit 2:** 134–139 **Unit 3:** T182–T187 **Unit 4:** T262–T265 **Unit 5:** 362–365 **Unit 6:** 434–437<br>**LITERATURE ANTHOLOGY:** These units reflect the range of text complexity found throughout the book.<br>**Unit 1:** 82–99 **Unit 2:** 186–201 **Unit 3:** 294–297 **Unit 4:** 322–331 **Unit 5:** 442–451 **Unit 6:** 536–551<br>**LEVELED READERS: Unit 1, Week 4:** *People Helping Whales* (A, O, B, ); **Unit 2, Week 4:** *Animal Families* (A, O, B); **Unit 3, Week 3:** *City Communities* (A, O, B,); **Unit 4, Week 2:** *Earthquakes* (A, O, B,); **Unit 5, Week 3:** *Rudy Garcia–Tolson* (A, O, B); **Unit 6, Week 4:** *How To Be a Smart Shopper* (A, O, B)<br>**TEACHER'S EDITION: Unit 1:** T472–T475 **Unit 2:** T472–T475 **Unit 3:** T472–T475, **Unit 4:** T464–T467 **Unit 5:** T464–T467 **Unit 6:** T464–T467 |

# Reading Standards: Foundational Skills

| Phonics and Word Recognition | | McGraw–Hill Reading Wonders |
|---|---|---|
| **RF.2.3** | Know and apply grade–level phonics and word analysis skills in decoding words. | |
| **RF.2.3a** | Distinguish long and short vowels when reading regularly spelled one–syllable words. | **YOUR TURN PRACTICE BOOK:** 32, 42, 52, 62, 72, 82, 92 102, 112, 122, 132, 142<br>**PHONICS/WORD STUDY WORKSTATION ACTIVITY CARDS:** 1, 2, 4, 5, 6, 7, 11, 12, 13, 14, 15<br>**TEACHER'S EDITION: Unit 1:** S24, S25, S30, T288, T289, T304, T305, T306, T316, T327, T336, T344, T352, T380, T381, T394, T395, T396, T406, T417, T426, T434, T435, T442, T454 **Unit 2:** T12, T13, T128, T29, T30, T40, T41, T51, T60, T68, T69, T76, T88, T104, T105, T120, T121, T122, T132, T133, T143, T144, T153, T160, T161, T168, T180, T199, T212, T214, T224, T288, T289, T304, T305, T306 **Unit 3:** T12, T13, T28, T29, T40, T41, T51, T60, T104, T105, T120, T121, T132, T143, T196, T197, T212, T213, T253, T272, T288, T289, T302, T380 T382, T394, T396, T406, T417, T426, T434, T435, T442, T454 **Unit 5:** T372, T373, T386, T387, T398, T409, T418<br>**DECODABLE READERS: Unit 1, Week 4:** *You Can Bake a Cake!;* **Unit 1, Week 5:** *Mike's Big Bike;* **Unit 2, Week 1:** *At Home in Nome;* **Unit 2, Week 2:** *Duke and Bud's Run;* **Unit 3, Week 2:** *High in the Sky;* **Unit 3, Week 3:** *Three Goats and a Troll;* **Unit 3, Week 5:** *Luke's Tune*<br>www.connected.mcgraw–hill.com**: RESOURCES**<br>**Phonics/Spelling PRACTICE BOOK:** 17, 18, 22, 23, 27, 28, 32, 33 |
| **RF.2.3b** | Know spelling–sound correspondences for additional common vowel teams. | **YOUR TURN PRACTICE BOOK:** 102, 112, 122, 132, 202, 232<br>**TEACHER'S EDITION: Unit 3:** T12, T13, T14, T28, T29, T40, T41, T68, T69, T76, T152, T153, T160, T161, T168, T196, T197, T198, T213, T214, T224, T225, T244, T253, T260, T288, T289, T304, T305, T306, T316, T317, T336, T344, T345, T352 **Unit 4:** T282, T283, T284, T296, T297, T298, T372, T373, T374, T386, T387, T388 **Unit 5:** T12, T13, T14, T26, T27, T28, T38, T39, T49, T50, T58, T59, T102, T103, T104, T116, T117, T118, T148, T149, T192, T193, T194, T206, T207, T208, T218, T219, T229, T246, T247, T254, T282, T283, T284, T296, T297, T298, T308, T309, T336, T344, T388 **Unit 6:** T282, T283, T284, T296, T297, T298, T308, T309, T319, T328, T336, T337, T344<br>**DECODABLE READERS: Unit 3, Week 1:** *Ray Saves the Play;* **Unit 3, Week 2:** *High in the Sky;* **Unit 3, Week 3:** *Three Goats and a Troll;* **Unit 3, Week 4:** *It Won't Be Easy;* **Unit 4, Week 2:** *Shirl and Her Tern;* **Unit 4, Week 3:** *More Fun Than a Hat!;* **Unit 5, Week 4:** *Paul Saw Arctic Foxes;* **Unit 6, Week 4:** *The Rainy Day*<br>www.connected.mcgraw–hill.com**: RESOURCES**<br>**Phonics/Spelling PRACTICE BOOK:** 52, 53, 57, 58, 62, 63, 67, 68, 72, 73, 87, 88, 92, 93, 97, 98, 102, 103, 107, 108 |
| **RF.2.3c** | Decode regularly spelled two–syllable words with long vowels. | **YOUR TURN PRACTICE BOOK:** 272<br>**PHONICS/WORD STUDY WORKSTATION ACTIVITY CARDS:** 11, 12, 13, 14, 15, 16, 26<br>**TEACHER'S EDITION: Unit 2:** T121, T133, T143, T152, T162 **Unit 3:** T121, T133, T143, T152, T162, T396, T406, T417, T426, T434–T435, T442 **Unit 5:** T129, T139, T297, T309, T328 **Unit 6:** T12, T13, T26, T27, T28, T38, T39, T49, T102, T103, T116, T117, T118, T128, T139, T148, T156, T157, T164, T192, T193, T206, T218, T238, T246, T254, T282, T283, T296, T298, T308, T319, T328, T336, T337, T338, T340, T344, T356<br>**DECODABLE READERS: Unit 3, Week 5:** *Luke's Tune;* **Unit 6, Week 1:** *Clever Doggie;* **Unit 6, Week 2:** *Tadpole Decides;* **Unit 6, Week 3:** *Jamal and Rachel's Camping Trip;* **Unit 6, Week 4:** *The Rainy Day*<br>www.connected.mcgraw–hill.com**: RESOURCES**<br>**Phonics/Spelling PRACTICE BOOK:** 127, 128, 132, 133, 137, 138, 142, 143 |

# Reading Standards: Foundational Skills

| Phonics and Word Recognition | | McGraw–Hill Reading Wonders |
|---|---|---|
| **RF.2.3d** | Decode words with common prefixes and suffixes. | **READING/WRITING WORKSHOP:** Unit 2: 111  Unit 3: 253<br>**LITERATURE ANTHOLOGY: Unit 2:** 131  **Unit 3:** 297<br>**YOUR TURN PRACTICE BOOK:** 2, 12, 63–65, 82<br>**TEACHER'S EDITION: Unit 1:** T51, T53, T120, T133, T143, T152, T346  **Unit 2:** T46–T47, T138–T139, T145, T172, T213, T219, T225, T230–T231, T235, T244, T254, T305, T317, T327, T336, T346  **Unit 3:** T412–T413  **Unit 4:** T27, T38–T39, T49, T51, T58, T68, T321  **Unit 5:** T44–T45  **Unit 6:** T117, T129, T139, T148, T158, T266, T321<br>**DECODABLE READERS: Unit 2, Week 3:** *Animal Places and Spaces;*  **Unit 4, Week 1:** *The Thumbs–Up Rain Forest;*  **Unit 6, Week 2:** *Tadpole Decides* |
| **RF.2.3e** | Identify words with inconsistent but common spelling–sound correspondences. | **YOUR TURN PRACTICE BOOK:** 152, 162, 172, 182<br>**PHONICS/WORD STUDY WORKSTATION ACTIVITY CARDS:** 16, 17, 18, 19, 20, 21, 22, 23, 24, 25<br>**TEACHER'S EDITION: Unit 1:** T305, T317, T327, T336  **Unit 2:** T29, T41, 51, T60, T288, T289, T304, T305, T316  **Unit 3:** T12, T30, T122, T290  **Unit 4:** T12–T13, T14, T27, T28, T38–T39, T48, T59, T74, T86, T156, T176, T192–T193, T206–T207, T238, T254, T282, T296, T308, T336–T337, T338, T344, T356, T386, T426–T427, T446  **Unit 5:** T372, T386, T398, T409, T418, T426–T427, T434  **Unit 6:** T74, T372, T386<br>**DECODABLE READERS: Unit 2, Week 5:** *Mrs. Sprig's Spring Flowers;*  **Unit 4, Week 2:** *Shirl and Her Tern;*  **Unit 4, Week 3:** *More Fun Than a Hat!;*  **Unit 4, Week 4:** *Cheer Up, Dot;*  **Unit 4, Week 5:** *The Caring King's Fair Wish;*  **Unit 6, Week 1:** *Clever Doggie* |
| **RF.2.3f** | Recognize and read grade–appropriate irregularly spelled words. | **YOUR TURN PRACTICE BOOK:** 3,152<br>**TEACHER'S EDITION: Unit 1:** S8, S14, S20, S26, S31, T107, T199, T291, T306, T383, **Unit 2:** T15, T69, T69 (Decodable Reader), T76, T76 (Deocable Reader), T107, T199, T396 **Unit 3:** T15, T107, T199, T291, T383  **Unit 4:** T28, T105, T118, T195, T208, T285, T375  **Unit 5:** T15, T28, T105, T118, T195, T285, T298, T375  **Unit 6:** T15, T67, T67 (Decodable Reader), T74, T74 (Decodable Reader), T105, T195, T208, T285, T375<br>**DECODABLE READERS:** *Start Smart: I Can Plant;*  **Unit 1, Week 1:** *Pat and Tim;*  **Unit 1, Week 2:** *Len and Gus;*  **Unit 2, Week 3:** *Animal Places and Spaces;*  **Unit 2, Week 5:** *Mrs. Sprig's Spring Flower;*  **Unit 4, Week 1:** *The Thumb's–Up Rain Forest;*  **Unit 6, Week 5:** *How Bird Was Lured Away from Fire* |

# Reading Standards: Foundational Skills

| Fluency | | McGraw–Hill Reading Wonders |
|---|---|---|
| **RF.2.4** | Read with sufficient accuracy and fluency to support comprehension. | |
| **RF.2.4a** | Read on–level text with purpose and understanding. | **READING/WRITING WORKSHOP:** Unit 1: 22, 38, 54, 70  Unit 2: 102–107, 118–123, 134–139, 150–155  Unit 3: 182–187, 198–203, 214–219, 230–235  Unit 4: 262–265, 276–279  Unit 5: 334–337, 362–365  Unit 6: 406–409, 420–423 <br> **LEVELED READERS: Unit 1, Week 1:** *Cat and Dog* (A), *The Quest* (O), *Class Pets* (B); **Unit 1, Week 3:** *Too Many Pets?* (A), *A New Home for Henry* (O), *Hello, Koko!* (B);  **Unit 1, Week 4:** *People Helping Whales* (A);  **Unit 1, Week 5:** *Families at Work* (A, O, B); **Unit 2, Week 1:** *An Arctic Life for Us* (B);  **Unit 2, Week 2:** *The Dog and the Bone* (O); **Unit 2, Week 3:** *A Tree Full of Life,* (A, O, B );  **Unit 2, Week 4:** *Animal Families* (A, O, B); **Unit 3, Week 1:** *Forces at Work* (A, O, B);  **Unit 3, Week 2:** *A Special Sunset* (A), *A Different Set of Stars* (OL), *Shadows in the Sky* (B);  **Unit 3, Week 3:** *City Communities* (A, O, B);  **Unit 3, Week 5:** *The Sounds of Trash* (A, O, B); **Unit 4, Week 2:** *Earthquakes* (A, O, B);  **Unit 4, Week 4:** *Why Turtles Live in Water* (A), *How Butterflies Came to Be* (O), *Why Spider Has 8 Thin Legs* (B);  **Unit 5, Week 4:** *Let's Carpool!* (A), *Our Beautiful Tree* (O), *Family Night Unplugged!* (B);  **Unit 5, Week 5:** *Government Rules* (A, O, B); **Unit 6, Week 1:** *The Apples of Idun* (A), *Hercules and the Golden Apples* (O), *Demeter and Persephone* (B) <br> **YOUR TURN PRACTICE BOOK:** 3, 13, 33, 73, 103, 113, 123, 133, 143, 153, 163, 173, 183, 203, 253, 263 <br> **TEACHER'S EDITION: Unit 1:** T18, T124, T165, T353, T398, T438, T462  **Unit 2:** T18–T21, T164–T165, T340–T341, T438–T439,  **Unit 3:** T18, T42, T64–T65, T164–T165, T294–T297, T438–T439  **Unit 4:** T30, T170–T171, T251, T350–T351  **Unit 5:** T230–T231, T249, T250–T251, T340–T341, T342, T345, T346, T350–T351, T442, T454  **Unit 6:** T30, T165, T169, T249, T250–T251, T349, T454, T435, T439 |
| **RF.2.4b** | Read on–level text orally with accuracy, appropriate rate, and expression on successive readings. | **LEVELED READERS: Unit 1, Week 1:** *Cat and Dog* (A), *The Quest* (O), *Class Pets* (B); **Unit 2, Week 3:** *A Tree Full of Life,* (A, O, B);  **Unit 2, Week 4:** *Animal Families* (A, O, B);  **Unit 3, Week 2:** *A Special Sunset* (A), *A Different Set of Stars* (O), *Shadows in the Sky* (B);  **Unit 3, Week 3:** *City Communities* (A, O, B);  **Unit 4, Week 2:** *Earthquakes* (A, O, B);  **Unit 4, Week 4:** *Why Turtles Live in Water* (A), *How Butterflies Came to Be* (O), *Why Spider Has 8 Thin Legs* (B) <br> **YOUR TURN PRACTICE BOOK:** 14, 103–104, 113–114, 123–124, 133–134, 143–144, 163–164, 173–174, 183–184, 253–254, 293–294 <br> **TEACHER'S EDITION: Unit 1:** S32, T42, T53, T134, T145, T226, T237, T318, T329, T408, T438, T462  **Unit 2:** T42, T53, T71, T134, T145, T167, T226, T248, T258, T262, T340–T341, T408, T438–T439, T462  **Unit 3:** T30, T42, T53, T72, T78–T79, T134, T145, T164, T170–T171, T226, T237, T248, T256, T318, T348, T408, T437, T439, T462–T463  **Unit 4:** T40, T140, T152, T160–T161, T220, T230, T249, T250, T321, T332, T339, T340, T346, T400, T411, T430–T431, T454  **Unit 5:** T40, T51, T250, T340, T400, T430, T454  **Unit 6:** T40, T51, T69, T70, T141, T160, T144, T221, T250, T321, T340, T400, T411, T430, T454 |
| **RF.2.4c** | Use context to confirm or self–correct word recognition and understanding, rereading as necessary. | **READING/WRITING WORKSHOP: Unit 2:** 155;  **Unit 3:** 188, 204;  **Unit 4:** 266, 280  **Unit 6:** 410, 424; <br> **LEVELED READERS: Unit 2, Week 5:** *Amira's Petting Zoo* (A), *Alice's New Pet* (O, ELL), *Ava's Animals* (B) <br> **YOUR TURN PRACTICE BOOK:** 83–85, 103–105, 153–155, 163–165, 263–265 <br> **TEACHER'S EDITION: Unit 1:** T237, T408, T462  **Unit 2:** T318, T430–T431, T440–T441, T448–T449, T450–T451, T462–T463  **Unit 3:** T408, T462–T463  **Unit 4:** T18, T130, T454  **Unit 5:** T400, T454  **Unit 6:** T62, T72, T76, T315, T355, T454 |

# College and Career Readiness Anchor Standards for WRITING

The K–5 standards on the following pages define what students should understand and be able to do by the end of each grade. They correspond to the College and Career Readiness (CCR) anchor standards below by number. The CCR and grade-specific standards are necessary complements—the former providing broad standards, the latter providing additional specificity—that together define the skills and understandings that all students must demonstrate.

| Text Types and Purposes |
|---|
| **1.** Write arguments to support claims in an analysis of substantive topics or texts, using valid reasoning and relevant and sufficient evidence. |
| **2.** Write informative/explanatory texts to examine and convey complex ideas and information clearly and accurately through the effective selection, organization, and analysis of content. |
| **3.** Write narratives to develop real or imagined experiences or events using effective technique, well-chosen details, and well-structured event sequences. |

| Production and Distribution of Writing |
|---|
| **4.** Produce clear and coherent writing in which the development, organization, and style are appropriate to task, purpose, and audience. |
| **5.** Develop and strengthen writing as needed by planning, revising, editing, rewriting, or trying a new approach. |
| **6.** Use technology, including the Internet, to produce and publish writing and to interact and collaborate with others. |

| Research to Build and Present Knowledge |
|---|
| **7.** Conduct short as well as more sustained research projects based on focused questions, demonstrating understanding of the subject under investigation. |
| **8.** Gather relevant information from multiple print and digital sources, assess the credibility and accuracy of each source, and integrate the information while avoiding plagiarism. |
| **9.** Draw evidence from literary or informational texts to support analysis, reflection, and research. |

| Range of Writing |
|---|
| **10.** Write routinely over extended time frames (time for research, reflection, and revision) and shorter time frames (a single sitting or a day or two) for a range of tasks, purposes, and audiences. |

# CCSS Common Core State Standards
# English Language Arts

## Grade 2

Each standard is coded in the following manner:

| Strand | Grade Level | Standard |
|--------|-------------|----------|
| W | 2 | 1 |

## Writing Standards

| Text Types and Purposes | McGraw–Hill Reading Wonders |
|-------------------------|------------------------------|
| **W.2.1** | Write opinion pieces in which they introduce the topic or book they are writing about, state an opinion, supply reasons that support the opinion, use linking words (e.g., *because, and, also*) to connect opinion and reasons, and provide a concluding statement or section. | **READING/WRITING WORKSHOP:** Unit 3: 225<br>**WRITING WORKSTATION ACTIVITY CARDS:** 11, 18, 24, 25<br>**TEACHER'S EDITION:** Unit 3: T220, T388, T414, T480–T485, T486–491 |
| **W.2.2** | Write informative/explanatory texts in which they introduce a topic, use facts and definitions to develop points, and provide a concluding statement or section. | **READING/WRITING WORKSHOP:** Unit 1: 80–81, 94–95  Unit 2: 144–145, 160–161  Unit 3: 192–193, 224–225, 240–241  Unit 4: 270–271, 284–285  Unit 5: 370–371, 398–399  Unit 6: 428–429, 442–443, 456–457<br>**YOUR TURN PRACTICE BOOK:** 137, 277<br>**WRITING WORKSTATION ACTIVITY CARDS:** 14, 27<br>**TEACHER'S EDITION:** Unit 1: T298, T324, T388, T414  Unit 2: T206, T220, T298, T324, T330  Unit 3: T22–T23, T48, T298, T312, T324, T338  Unit 4: T20, T46, T110, T136  Unit 5: T200–T201, T214, T226 T232, T472–T477, T478–T483  Unit 6: T110, T136, T200, T214, T226, T290, T304, T316, T330, T472–T477, T478–T483 |
| **W.2.3** | Write narratives in which they recount a well–elaborated event or short sequence of events, include details to describe actions, thoughts, and feelings, use temporal words to signal event order, and provide a sense of closure. | **READING/WRITING WORKSHOP:** Unit 1: 32–33, 48–49  Unit 2: 112–113, 128–129  Unit 3: 208–209  Unit 4: 298–299, 312–313, 326–327  Unit 5: 342–343, 356–357, 384–385  Unit 6: 414–415<br>**WRITING WORKSTATION ACTIVITY CARDS:** 1, 2, 12<br>**TEACHER'S EDITION:** Unit 1: S9, T22, T114, T480–T482, T486–T491  Unit 2: T22, T36, T48, T114–T115  Unit 3: T114, T128, T140, T146–T147  Unit 4: T200, T226, T291, T316, T472–T477  Unit 5: T20–T21, T46–T47, T316  Unit 6: T20–T21, T46 |

# Writing Standards

| Production and Distribution of Writing | | McGraw–Hill Reading Wonders |
|---|---|---|
| **W.2.4** | (Begins in grade 3.) | |
| **W.2.5** | With guidance and support from adults and peers, focus on a topic and strengthen writing as needed by revising and editing. | **READING/WRITING WORKSHOP: Unit 1:** 32–33, 80–81, 94–95 **Unit 2:** 112–113, 160–161 **Unit 3:** 192–193, 208–209, 224–225 **Unit 4:** 270–271, 298–299, 312–313, 326–327 **Unit 5:** 342–343, 356–357, 370–371, 384–385 **Unit 6:** 414–415, 428–429, 442–443, 456–457 <br> **YOUR TURN PRACTICE BOOK:** 7, 17, 27, 37, 47, 87, 157, 167, 177, 187, 257, 267, 297 <br> **TEACHER'S EDITION: Unit 1:** T36, T54, T128, T146, T220, T312, T330, T338, T364, T402, T420, T484–T485, T490–T491 **Unit 2:** T36, T53, T128, T140, T146–T147, T220, T298, T312, T324, T364, T388, T402–T403, T420, T454 **Unit 3:** T36, T54–T55, T107, T128, T146–T147, T220, T238, T246, T330–T331, T338 **Unit 4:** T34, T52, T124, T142–T143, T214, T232–T233, T291, T304, T316, T322–T323, T330, T394, T406, T412–T413, T446 **Unit 5:** T34, T52–T53, T60, T124, T142, T150–T151, T232–T233, T304, T394, T406, T412 **Unit 6:** T34, T52–T53, T124, T142, T149, T232–T233, T322–T323, T394, T406, T412–T413 |
| **W.2.6** | With guidance and support from adults, use a variety of digital tools to produce and publish writing, including in collaboration with peers. | **TEACHER'S EDITION: Unit 1:** T148, T240, T332, T420, T422, T428, T484, T490 **Unit 2:** T56, T148, T240, T332, T420, T422, T428, T466–T469, T471, T484, T490 **Unit 3:** T54, T56, T148, T240, T332. T420–T421, T422, T466, T484, T490 **Unit 4:** T54, T144, T234, T324, T414, T420, T458, T476, T482 **Unit 5:** T54, T144, T234, T324, T414, T420, T458, T476, T482 **Unit 6:** T54, T144, T234, T240, T324, T326, T414, T420, T458, T476, T482 <br> www.connected.mcgraw–hill.com**: DIGITAL RESOURCES AND TOOLS: WRITER'S WORKSPACE; GRAPHIC ORGANIZERS; MY BINDER (My Work, My Portfolio); COLLABORATE (PROJECTS)** |

## Writing Standards

| Research to Build and Present Knowledge | | McGraw–Hill Reading Wonders |
|---|---|---|
| W.2.7 | Participate in shared research and writing projects (e.g., read a number of books on a single topic to produce a report; record science observations). | **TEACHER'S EDITION: Unit 1:** T56–T57, T58–T59, T148–T149, T150–T151, T240–T241, T242–T243, T332, T335, T422, T425, T466  **Unit 2:** T56–T57, T58–T59, T148–T149, T150–T151, T240–T241, T242–T243, T232–T233, T335, T422, T425, T464–T465, T466–T469  **Unit 3:** T56–T57, T58–T59, T148–T149, T150–T151, T240–T241, T242–T243, T335, T422, T425, T466  **Unit 4:** T54–T55, T56–T56, T144–T145, T146–T147, T234–T235, T236–T237, T237, T414–T415, T417, T456, T458  **Unit 5:** T54–T55, T56–T56, T144–T145, T146–T147, T234–T235, T236–T237, T237, T414–T415, T417, T456, T458  **Unit 6:** T54–T55, T56–T56, T144–T145, T146–T147, T234–T235, T236–T237, T237, T414–T415, T417, T456, T458 |
| W.2.8 | Recall information from experiences or gather information from provided sources to answer a question. | **TEACHER'S EDITION: Unit 1:** T59, T243, T422, T466–T468, T480–T485, T486–T491  **Unit 2:** T422, T425, T466–T468, T480–T485, T486–T491  **Unit 3:** T298, T422, T467–T468, T480–T485, T486–T491  **Unit 4:** T110, T136, T200, T226, T417  **Unit 5:** T20, T54, T56, T144, T147, T226, T413, T458  **Unit 6:** T54, T147, T200, T234–T235, T414–T415, T417, T458–T461, T472–T483 |
| W.2.9 | (Begins in grade 4.) | |
| **Range of Writing** | | *McGraw–Hill Reading Wonders* |
| W.2.10 | (Begins in grade 3.) | |

# College and Career Readiness Anchor Standards for
# SPEAKING AND LISTENING

The K–5 standards on the following pages define what students should understand and be able to do by the end of each grade. They correspond to the College and Career Readiness (CCR) anchor standards below by number. The CCR and grade–specific standards are necessary complements—the former providing broad standards, the latter providing additional specificity—that together define the skills and understandings that all students must demonstrate.

### Comprehension and Collaboration

1. Prepare for and participate effectively in a range of conversations and collaborations with diverse partners, building on others' ideas and expressing their own clearly and persuasively.

2. Integrate and evaluate information presented in diverse media and formats, including visually, quantitatively, and orally.

3. Evaluate a speaker's point of view, reasoning, and use of evidence and rhetoric.

### Presentation of Knowledge and Ideas

4. Present information, findings, and supporting evidence such that listeners can follow the line of reasoning and the organization, development, and style are appropriate to task, purpose, and audience.

5. Make strategic use of digital media and visual displays of data to express information and enhance understanding of presentations.

6. Adapt speech to a variety of contexts and communicative tasks, demonstrating command of formal English when indicated or appropriate.

# CCSS Common Core State Standards
# English Language Arts

## Grade 2

### Each standard is coded in the following manner:

| Strand | Grade Level | Standard |
|--------|-------------|----------|
| SL | 2 | 1 |

## Speaking and Listening Standards

| Comprehension and Collaboration | | McGraw–Hill Reading Wonders |
|---|---|---|
| **SL.2.1** | Participate in collaborative conversations with diverse partners about *grade 2 topics and texts* with peers and adults in small and larger groups. | |
| **SL.2.1a** | Follow agreed–upon rules for discussions (e.g., gaining the floor in respectful ways, listening to others with care, speaking one at a time about the topics and texts under discussion). | **READING/WRITING WORKSHOP: Unit 1:** 18, 34, 50, 82 **Unit 2:** 146–147 **Unit 3:** 194–195, 242–243 **Unit 4:** 314–315 **Unit 5:** 330–331<br>**TEACHER'S EDITION: Unit 1:** T8, T118, T148, T192, T234, T240, T376, T416, T422 **Unit 2:** T8, T26, T142, T284, T332, T422 **Unit 3:** T8, T118, T148, T234, T284, T326, T332, T376, T422, T466 **Unit 4:** T48, T98, T100, T368, T414, T460 **Unit 5:** T8, T24, T36, T48, T54, T98, T100, T114, T126, T145 **Unit 6:** T8, T24, T36, T48, T54, T414, T460 |
| **SL.2.1b** | Build on others' talk in conversations by linking their comments to the remarks of others. | **READING/WRITING WORKSHOP: Unit 1:** 50, 66 **Unit 3:** 210–211 **Unit 4:** 272–273, 300–301, 304–307 **Unit 5:** 386–387 **Unit 6:** 402–403, 430–431, 462–465<br>**TEACHER'S EDITION: Unit 1:** T50, T56, T192, T284, T334 **Unit 2:** T100, T148, T416 **Unit 3:** T142, T192, T240, T416, T468 **Unit 4:** T98, T144, T188, T228, T234, T278, T324–T325, T326, T458 **Unit 5:** T8, T188, T228, T368, T414 **Unit 6:** T8, T188, T228, T234, T408, T416, T458 |
| **SL.2.1c** | Ask for clarification and further explanation as needed about the topics and texts under discussion. | **READING/WRITING WORKSHOP: Unit 2:** 162–163 **Unit 5:** 372–373 **Unit 6:** 444–445, 458–459<br>**TEACHER'S EDITION: Unit 1:** S29, T332, T468 **Unit 2:** T192, T376, T468 **Unit 3:** T56, T466 **Unit 4:** T8, T54, T278–T279 **Unit 5:** T278, T324, T460 **Unit 6:** T98, T278, T324 |

# Speaking and Listening Standards

| Comprehension and Collaboration | | McGraw–Hill Reading Wonders |
|---|---|---|
| **SL.2.2** | Recount or describe key ideas or details from a text read aloud or information presented orally or through other media. | **TEACHER'S EDITION: Unit 1:** T27, T59, T119, T211, T303, T393, **Unit 2:** T27, T50, T59, T119, T211, T303, T393 **Unit 3:** T27, T119, T211, T303, T326, T393 **Unit 4:** T25, T115, T205, T295, T385 **Unit 5:** T25, T115, T205, T295, T385, T416, T458 **Unit 6:** T25, T115, T138, T205, T228, T281, T295, T385 <br><br> **INTERACTIVE READ–ALOUD CARDS: Unit 1, Week 4:** "All Kinds of Vets"; **Unit 2, Week 2:** "The Fox and the Crane"; **Unit 3, Week 3:** "Color Your Community"; **Unit 3, Week 4:** "Clouds All Around"; **Unit 3, Week 5:** "Why People Drum"; **Unit 4, Week 1:** "Where Do You Live?"; **Unit 4, Week 2:** "Earth Changes"; **Unit 4, Week 3:** "My New School"; **Unit 4, Week 4:** "How Thunder and Lightning Came to Be"; **Unit 4, Week 5:** "Redwood National Forest," "The Amazing Meadow," and "The Sahara Desert"; **Unit 5, Week 4:** "Clean Water"; **Unit 5, Week 5:** "Town Rules"; **Unit 6, Week 1:** "The Bluebell"; **Unit 6, Week 2:** "How Does Energy Make Your Hair Stand Up?" |
| **SL.2.3** | Ask and answer questions about what a speaker says in order to clarify comprehension, gather additional information, or deepen understanding of a topic or issue. | **TEACHER'S EDITION: Unit 1:** S29, T11, T103, T195, T287, T379, T468 **Unit 2:** T11, T103, T195, T287, T379, T468 **Unit 3:** T11, T103, T195, T287, T379, T468 **Unit 4:** T11, T101, T 191, T281, T371 **Unit 5:** T11, T24–T25, T101, T191, T281, T371, T458 **Unit 6:** T11, T101, T191, T281, T371 <br><br> **INTERACTIVE READ–ALOUD CARDS: Unit 1, Week 4:** "All Kinds of Vets"; **Unit 2, Week 2:** "The Fox and the Crane"; **Unit 3, Week 2:** "The Hidden Sun"; **Unit 3, Week 5:** "Why People Drum"; **Unit 4, Week 2:** "Earth Changes"; **Unit 4, Week 3:** "My New School"; **Unit 4, Week 4:** "How Thunder and Lightning Came to Be"; **Unit 4, Week 5:** "Redwood National Forest," "The Amazing Meadow," and "The Sahara Desert"; **Unit 5, Week 4:** "Clean Water"; **Unit 6, Week 2:** "How Does Energy Make Your Hair Stand Up?"; **Unit 6, Week 5:** "Give Me a Brown Box" and "Music Sends Me" |

## Speaking and Listening Standards

| Presentation of Knowledge and Ideas | | McGraw–Hill Reading Wonders |
|---|---|---|
| **SL.2.4** | Tell a story or recount an experience with appropriate facts and relevant, descriptive details, speaking audibly in coherent sentences. | **WRITING WORKSTATION ACTIVITY CARDS:** 1, 22, 26 <br> **TEACHER'S EDITION: Unit 1:** T424–T425, T466, T470–T471 **Unit 2:** T424–T425, T470–T471 **Unit 3:** T424–T425, T470–T471 **Unit 4:** T416–T417, T462–T463 **Unit 5:** T416–T417, T462–T463 **Unit 6:** T416–T417, T462–T463 |
| **SL.2.5** | Create audio recordings of stories or poems; add drawings or other visual displays to stories or recounts of experiences when appropriate to clarify ideas, thoughts, and feelings. | **TEACHER'S EDITION: Unit 1:** T466–T469, T470–T471 **Unit 2:** T466–T469, T470–T471 **Unit 3:** T422–T423, T424–T425, T470–T471 **Unit 4:** T414–T415, 416–T417, T462–T463 **Unit 5:** T414–T415, T416–T417, T462–T463 **Unit 6:** T414–T415, T416–T417, T462–T463 |
| **SL.2.6** | Produce complete sentences when appropriate to task and situation in order to provide requested detail or clarification. | **TEACHER'S EDITION: Unit 1:** T59, T151, T243, T335, T425, T468 **Unit 2:** T24, T59, T151, T243, T335, T425, T468 **Unit 3:** T59, T151, T243, T335, T425 **Unit 4:** T8, T57, T147, T237, T327, T417 T460 **Unit 5:** T57, T147, T237, T278, T327, T417 **Unit 6:** T57, T147, T237, T278, T327, T417 |

CORRELATIONS

# College and Career Readiness Anchor Standards for
# LANGUAGE

The K–5 standards on the following pages define what students should understand and be able to do by the end of each grade. They correspond to the College and Career Readiness (CCR) anchor standards below by number. The CCR and grade–specific standards are necessary complements—the former providing broad standards, the latter providing additional specificity—that together define the skills and understandings that all students must demonstrate.

## Conventions of Standard English

1. Demonstrate command of the conventions of standard English grammar and usage when writing or speaking.

2. Demonstrate command of the conventions of standard English capitalization, punctuation, and spelling when writing.

## Knowledge of Language

3. Apply knowledge of language to understand how language functions in different contexts, to make effective choices for meaning or style, and to comprehend more fully when reading or listening.

## Vocabulary Acquisition and Use

4. Determine or clarify the meaning of unknown and multiple–meaning words and phrases by using context clues, analyzing meaningful word parts, and consulting general and specialized reference materials, as appropriate.

5. Demonstrate understanding of figurative language, word relationships, and nuances in word meanings.

6. Acquire and use accurately a range of general academic and domain–specific words and phrases sufficient for reading, writing, speaking, and listening at the college and career readiness level; demonstrate independence in gathering vocabulary knowledge when encountering an unknown term important to comprehension or expression.

# CCSS Common Core State Standards
# English Language Arts

## Grade 2

### Each standard is coded in the following manner:

| Strand | Grade Level | Standard |
|--------|-------------|----------|
| L | 2 | 1 |

## Language Standards

| Conventions of Standard English | *McGraw–Hill Reading Wonders* |
|---------------------------------|-------------------------------|
| **L.2.1** | Demonstrate command of the conventions of standard English grammar and usage when writing or speaking. |
| **L.2.1a** | Use collective nouns (e.g., *group*). | **READING/WRITING WORKSHOP:** Grammar Handbook: 480 <br> **TEACHER'S EDITION: Unit 2:** T T221, T232, T233, T238 T239, T247 <br> **www.connected.mcgraw–hill.com: RESOURCES** <br> **Grammar PRACTICE BOOK:** 37, 40 |
| **L.2.1b** | Form and use frequently occurring irregular plural nouns (e.g., *feet, children, teeth, mice, fish*). | **READING/WRITING WORKSHOP: Unit 2:** 161, Grammar Handbook: 479 <br> **YOUR TURN PRACTICE BOOK:** 172, 202 <br> **TEACHER'S EDITION: Unit 2:** T300, T313, T325, T339  **Unit 4:** T207, T219, T229, T238, T248  **Unit 5:** T27, T39, T49, T58 <br> **www.connected.mcgraw–hill.com: RESOURCES** <br> **Phonics/Spelling PRACTICE BOOK:** 202, 203 <br> **Grammar PRACTICE BOOK:** 41, 42, 45 |
| **L.2.1c** | Use reflexive pronouns (e.g., *myself, ourselves*). | **READING/WRITING WORKSHOP:** Grammar Handbook: 489 <br> **TEACHER'S EDITION: Unit 5:** T125, T137, T142, T150, T151 <br> **www.connected.mcgraw–hill.com: RESOURCES** <br> **Grammar PRACTICE BOOK:** 107, 109, 110 |
| **L.2.1d** | Form and use the past tense of frequently occurring irregular verbs (e.g., *sat, hid, told*). | **READING/WRITING WORKSHOP: Unit 4:** 299, 313 Grammar Handbook: 486 <br> **TEACHER'S EDITION: Unit 4:** T202, T215, T227, T233, T241, T292, T305, T317, T323, T331 <br> **www.connected.mcgraw–hill.com: RESOURCES** <br> **Grammar PRACTICE BOOK:** 66, 68, 70 |
| **L.2.1e** | Use adjectives and adverbs, and choose between them depending on what is to be modified. | **READING/WRITING WORKSHOP: Unit 6:** 415, 443, 457, 471 Grammar Handbook: 492, 494 <br> **TEACHER'S EDITION: Unit 3:** T395, T407, T417, T426  **Unit 6:** T22, T35, T47, T53, T61, T202, T215, T227, T233, T241, T292, T297, T305, T309, T317, T319, T323, T328, T331, T380, T382, T394, T395, T406, T407, T413, T421 <br> **www.connected.mcgraw–hill.com: RESOURCES** <br> **Grammar PRACTICE BOOK:** 146, 147, 150 |
| **L.2.1f** | Produce, expand, and rearrange complete simple and compound sentences (e.g., *The boy watched the movie; The little boy watched the movie; The action movie was watched by the little boy*). | **READING/WRITING WORKSHOP: Unit 1:** 94–95  **Unit 3:** 254–255 Grammar Handbook: 476 <br> **YOUR TURN PRACTICE BOOK:** 147 <br> **WRITING WORKSTATION ACTIVITY CARDS:** 16, 17 <br> **TEACHER'S EDITION: Unit 1:** T388, T389, T390, T403, T415, T421, T429  **Unit 3:** T388, T389, T390, T402, T403, T414, T415, T421, T428, T429 <br> **www.connected.mcgraw–hill.com: RESOURCES** <br> **Grammar PRACTICE BOOK:** 21–22, 24–25, 71–2, 74–75 |

# Language Standards

| Conventions of Standard English | | McGraw–Hill Reading Wonders |
|---|---|---|
| **L.2.2** | Demonstrate command of the conventions of standard English capitalization, punctuation, and spelling when writing. | |
| **L.2.2a** | Capitalize holidays, product names, and geographic names. | **READING/WRITING WORKSHOP: Unit 2:** 144–145<br>**TEACHER'S EDITION: Unit 2:** T208, T209, T221, T233, T239, T247  **Unit 4:** T23, T35, T47, T53, T61  **Unit 5:** T203, T215, T227, T233, T241  **Unit 6:** T113, T125, T137, T143, T151, T293, T305, T317, T331<br>**www.connected.mcgraw–hill.com: RESOURCES**<br>**Grammar PRACTICE BOOK:** 38, 40, 78 |
| **L.2.2b** | Use commas in greetings and closings of letters. | **READING/WRITING WORKSHOP: Unit 1:** 64–65<br>**YOUR TURN PRACTICE BOOK:** 61<br>**TEACHER'S EDITION: Unit 1:** T209, T221, T233, T239, T247, T480  **Unit 3:** T209, T221, T233, T239, T247  **Unit 4:** T292, T305, T317, T323, T331<br>**www.connected.mcgraw–hill.com: RESOURCES**<br>**Grammar PRACTICE BOOK:** 13–14, 63–64, 93–94 |
| **L.2.2c** | Use an apostrophe to form contractions and frequently occurring possessives. | **READING/WRITING WORKSHOP: Unit 4:** 327  **Unit 5:** 385 Grammar Handbook: 480, 485, 491<br>**YOUR TURN PRACTICE BOOK:** 42, 102, 122, 222, 272<br>**TEACHER'S EDITION: Unit 1:** T395, T407, T417, T426, T436  **Unit 2:** T390, T391, T402, T403, T420, T421, T429  **Unit 3:** T29, T41, T51, T60, T213, T225, T244  **Unit 4:** T382, T383, T394, T395, T407, T413, T421  **Unit 5:** T292, T293, T305, T317, T331  **Unit 6:** T203, T207, T215, T219, T227, T229, T233, T238, T241<br>**www.connected.mcgraw–hill.com: RESOURCES:**<br>**Grammar PRACTICE BOOK:** 46, 47, 48, 49, 50, 96, 97, 98, 99, 100, 116, 117, 118, 119, 120 |
| **L.2.2d** | Generalize learned spelling patterns when writing words (e.g., cage → badge; boy → boil). | **TEACHER'S EDITION: Unit 1:** T14, T41, T52, T61, T106, T133, T144, T153, T198, T225, T244, T290, T382  **Unit 2:** T14, T61, T106, T133, T153, T198, T225, T236, T245, T290, T306, T317, T336, T380, T407, T427  **Unit 3:** T14, T41, T106, T198, T236, T290, T306, T317, T337, T382, T396, T407, T416, T427, T436  **Unit 4:** T104, T129, T140, T149, T194, T208, T219, T230, T284, T298, T309, T328, T374, T388, T399, T410, T428, T434  **Unit 5:** T14, T28, T29, T50, T59, T104, T129, T140, T149, T208, T219, T230, T284, T309, T374, T398, T410  **Unit 6:** T14, T39, T50, T59, T129, T140, T149, T194, T219, T239, T309, T321, T328, T374, T386, T388, T399, T410, T428 |
| **L.2.2e** | Consult reference materials, including beginning dictionaries, as needed to check and correct spellings. | **TEACHER'S EDITION: Unit 1:** T16, T36, T54, T108, T128, T146, T200, T220, T238, T292, T312, T330, T384, T402, T420, T484, T490  **Unit 2:** T16, T36, T54, T108, T128, T146, T200, T220, T238, T292, T312, T330, T384, T402, T420, T484, T490  **Unit 3:** T16, T36, T54, T108, T128, T146, T200, T220, T238, T292, T312, T330, T384, T402, T420, T484, T490  **Unit 4:** T16, T34, T52, T106, T124, T142, T196, T214, T232, T286, T304, T322, T376, T394, T412, T476, T482  **Unit 5:** T16, T34, T52, T106, T124, T142, T196, T214, T232, T286, T304, T322, T376, T394, T412, T476, T482  **Unit 6:** T16, T34, T52, T106, T124, T142, T196, T214, T232, T286, T304, T322, T376, T394, T412, T476, T482<br>**www.connected.mcgraw–hill.com: RESOURCES**<br>**Visual Glossary:** Units 1–6 |

## Language Standards

| Knowledge of Language | McGraw–Hill Reading Wonders |
|---|---|
| **L.2.3** | Use knowledge of language and its conventions when writing, speaking, reading, or listening. |
| **L.2.3a** | Compare formal and informal uses of English. |

**L.2.3a** (continued):
**READING/WRITING WORKSHOP:** Unit 4: 298, 299 **Unit 5:** 398, 399
**YOUR TURN PRACTICE BOOK:** 247
**WRITING WORKSTATION ACTIVITY CARD:** 20
**TEACHER'S EDITION:** Unit 4: T200, T201, T214, T226, T232, T240, T363 (Writing Workstation Activity Cards) **Unit 5:** T200, T201, T214, T226, T232, T240

| Vocabulary Acquisition and Use | McGraw–Hill Reading Wonders |
|---|---|
| **L.2.4** | Determine or clarify the meaning of unknown and multiple–meaning words and phrases based on grade 2 reading and content, choosing flexibly from an array of strategies. |

**L.2.4a** Use sentence–level context as a clue to the meaning of a word or phrase.

**READING/WRITING WORKSHOP:** Unit 1: 63 **Unit 2:** 143, 159 **Unit 4:** 283 **Unit 5:** 369, 383 **Unit 6:** 413, 427, 455
**LITERATURE ANTHOLOGY:** Unit 1: 79 **Unit 2:** 203, 209 **Unit 4:** 333 **Unit 5:** 439, 483 **Unit 6:** 507
**LEVELED READERS:** Unit 6, Week 1: *The Apples of Idun* (A), *Hercules and the Golden Apples* (O), *Demeter and Persephone* (B)
**YOUR TURN PRACTICE BOOK:** 29, 63–65, 89, 93–94, 99, 103–104, 113–114,123–124, 133–134, 163–164, 169, 229, 239, 249, 253–254, 263–264, 283–284
**TEACHER'S EDITION:** Unit 1: T230, T231, T231G, T231L, T329 **Unit 2:** T322, T323, T323F, T323J, T412, T413 **Unit 3:** T135, T227, T319, T409, T419 **Unit 4:** T134, T135D, T135H, T231, T411 **Unit 5:** T134, T135, T135F, T135P, T224, T225, T231, T314, T315, T315F, T321, T404, T411, T438 **Unit 6:** T44, T45, T45G, T45L

**L.2.4b** Determine the meaning of the new word formed when a known prefix is added to a known word (e.g., *happy/unhappy, tell/retell*).

**READING/WRITING WORKSHOP:** Unit 2: 111 **Unit 3:** 253
**LITERATURE ANTHOLOGY:** Unit 2: 131 **Unit 3:** 297
**YOUR TURN PRACTICE BOOK:** 59, 69, 149
**TEACHER'S EDITION:** Unit 2: T46, T47, T47F, T53, T145, T213, T225, T235, T244 **Unit 3:** T412, T413 **Unit 4:** T27, T39, T49, T51, T58 **Unit 6:** T27, T39, T49, T58

**L.2.4c** Use a known root word as a clue to the meaning of an unknown word with the same root (e.g., *addition, additional*).

**READING/WRITING WORKSHOP:** Unit 1: 31, 47, 79, 93 **Unit 4:** 311 **Unit 6:** 441
**LITERATURE ANTHOLOGY:** Unit 1: 55, 101 **Unit 4:** 379
**YOUR TURN PRACTICE BOOK:** 9, 19, 39, 49, 73–74, 93–95, 183–184, 189, 209, 273–274, 279
**TEACHER'S EDITION:** Unit 1: T46, T47, T138, T139, T145, T215, T322, T323, T412, T419, T446, T453 **Unit 2:** T53, T123, T145, T237, T419 **Unit 3:** T53 **Unit 4:** T314, T315, T389 **Unit 5:** T44–T45, T389 **Unit 6:** T119, T209, T224, T225, T225D, T321, T389

**L.2.4d** Use knowledge of the meaning of individual words to predict the meaning of compound words (e.g., *birdhouse, lighthouse, housefly; bookshelf, notebook, bookmark*).

**READING/WRITING WORKSHOP:** Unit 3: 207 **Unit 4:** 269
**LITERATURE ANTHOLOGY:** Unit 3: 251 **Unit 4:** 319
**YOUR TURN PRACTICE BOOK:** 92, 113–114, 119, 153–154, 159
**TEACHER'S EDITION:** Unit 2: T395, T407, T417, T426, T436 **Unit 3:** T138, T172, T179, T235 **Unit 4:** T44, T45D, T45G, T78, T85, T141 **Unit 6:** T27, T38, T49, T58, T68

# Language Standards

| Vocabulary Acquisition and Use | | McGraw–Hill Reading Wonders |
|---|---|---|
| **L.2.4e** | Use glossaries and beginning dictionaries, both print and digital, to determine or clarify the meaning of words and phrases. | **LITERATURE ANTHOLOGY:** Glossary: 584–599<br>**TEACHER'S EDITION: Unit 1:** T16, T36, T54, T108, T128, T146, T200, T220, T238, T292, T312, T330, T384, T402, T420, T484, T490 **Unit 2:** T16, T36, T54, T108, T128, T146, T200, T220, T238, T292, T312, T330, T384, T402, T412, T420, T484, T490 **Unit 3:** T16, T36, T54, T108, T128, T146, T200, T220, T238, T292, T312, T330, T384, T402, T412, T420, T484, T490 **Unit 4:** T16, T34, T52, T106, T124, T142, T196, T214, T232, T286, T304, T322, T376, T394, T412, T476, T482 **Unit 5:** T16, T34, T52, T106, T124, T142, T196, T214, T224, T232, T286, T304, T322, T376, T394, T412, T476, T482 **Unit 6:** T16, T34, T52, T106, T124, T142, T196, T214, T224, T232, T286, T304, T322, T376, T394, T412, T476, T482<br>**www.connected.mcgraw–hill.com: RESOURCES**<br>**Visual Glossary:** Units 1–6 |
| **L.2.5** | Demonstrate understanding of word relationships and nuances in word meanings. | |
| **L.2.5a** | Identify real–life connections between words and their use (e.g., describe foods that are *spicy* or *juicy*). | **READING/WRITING WORKSHOP: Unit 1:** 20–21, 36–37, 52–53, 68–69, 84–85 **Unit 2:** 109, 132–133, 148–149, 164–165 **Unit 3:** 160–161, 196–197, 212–213, 244–245 **Unit 4:** 260–261, 274–275, 276–279, 288–289, 302–303, 316–317, 318–321, 325 **Unit 5:** 332–333, 346–347, 360–361, 374–375, 388–389 **Unit 6:** 418–419, 432–433, 446–447, 460–461<br>**YOUR TURN PRACTICE BOOK:** 1, 11, 21, 31, 41, 61, 71, 101, 111, 121, 129, 131, 139, 141, 151, 171, 179, 181, 191, 199, 201, 211, 219, 221, 229, 281, 291, 293–294, 299<br>**PHONICS/WORD STUDY WORKSTATION ACTIVITY CARDS:** 11, 13, 14, 22<br>**TEACHER'S EDITION: Unit 1:** T16, T86, T108, T200, T292, T384, T409, T452, T453 **Unit 2:** T16, T43, T108, T109, T200, T227, T292, T384, T408, T454 **Unit 3:** T16, T42, T86, T106, T135, T178, T200, T227, T270, T292, T319, T362, T384, T452–T453 **Unit 4:** T12, T16. T40, T84, T106, T130, T174 T196, T264, T265, T286, T310, T354, T376, T400, T404, T410–T411, T411A, T444 **Unit 5:** T16–T17, T50, T106–T107, T196–T197, T286, T311, T354, T376, T400, T444 **Unit 6:** T16, T40, T84, T106, T196, T221, T264, T287, T354, T376, T400, T404, T411, T438, T444–T445 |
| **L.2.5b** | Distinguish shades of meaning among closely related verbs (e.g., *toss, throw, hurl*) and closely related adjectives (e.g., *thin, slender, skinny, scrawny*). | **READING/WRITING WORKSHOP: Unit 2:** 174–175 **Unit 3:** 223<br>**YOUR TURN PRACTICE BOOK:** 26, 67, 97, 129, 139, 197, 297<br>**TEACHER'S EDITION: Unit 1:** T206, T220, T232, T238 **Unit 2:** T22, T36, T48, T54, T178, T388, T402, T414, T420, T429 **Unit 3:** T230, T231E, T322, T329 **Unit 4:** T380, T394, T406, T412 **Unit 6:** T141, T380, T394, T406, T412 |
| **L.2.6** | Use words and phrases acquired through conversations, reading and being read to, and responding to texts, including using adjectives and adverbs to describe (e.g., *When other kids are happy that makes me happy*). | **READING/WRITING WORKSHOP: Unit 3:** 223, 239 **Unit 4:** 290–293, 297 **Unit 6:** 462–465, 469<br>**LITERATURE ANTHOLOGY: Unit 3:** 229 **Unit 4:** 385 **Unit 6:** 581<br>**YOUR TURN PRACTICE BOOK:** 1, 11, 21, 27, 57, 91, 97, 129, 139, 141, 161, 177, 179, 181, 197, 207, 251, 261, 267, 291, 297<br>**WRITING WORKSTATION ACTIVITY CARDS:** 2, 10, 13, 14, 15<br>**TEACHER'S EDITION: Unit 1:** T71, T76, T80, T86, T168, T172, T178, T255, T260, T264, T270, T347, T352, T356, T362, T437, T442, T446 **Unit 2:** T71, T76, T80, T86, T153, T168, T172, T178, T255, T260, T264, T270, T342, T352, T356, T362, T437, T442, T446, T452 **Unit 3:** T230, T231E, T322, T329 **Unit 4:** T69, T74, T78, T159, T164, T168, T224, T225B, T225C, T249, T254, T258, T339, T344, T348, T429, T434, T438 **Unit 5:** T249, T254, T344, T429, T434, T438 **Unit 6:** T69, T74, T78, T159, T164, T168, T249, T254, T258, T328, T339, T344, T348, T404, T429, T434, T438, T444–T445<br>**www.connected.mcgraw–hill.com: RESOURCES:**<br>**Visual Glossary:** Units 1–6 |